MARY ELLEN'S CLEAN HOUSE!

MARY ELLEN'S CLEAN HOUSE!

THE

ALL-IN-ONE-PLACE

ENCYCLOPEDIA OF

CONTEMPORARY HOUSEKEEPING

MARY ELLEN PINKHAM

with Dale Burg

Crown Publishers, Inc.
New York

**To our sons, Andrew and Alden,
who have brought so much to our lives—
including many opportunities to learn more
about cleaning!**

Published by Crown Publishers, Inc., 201 East 50th Street, New York, New York 10022. Member of the Crown Publishing Group.

Random House, Inc. New York, Toronto, London, Sydney, Auckland

CROWN is a trademark of Crown Publishers, Inc.

Manufactured in the United States of America

Library of Congress Cataloging-in-Publication Data
Pinkham, Mary Ellen.
    [Clean house]
    Mary Ellen's clean house! : the all-in-one-place encyclopedia of contemporary housekeeping / by Mary Ellen Pinkham, with Dale Burg.—1st ed.
       p. cm.
    Includes index.
    1. Home economics. 2. Cleaning. I. Burg, Dale. II. Title. III. Title: Clean house.
    TX158.P58 1993
    640—dc20   92-41105
                     CIP

ISBN 0-517-58823-4
10 9 8 7 6 5 4 3 2 1
First Edition

CONTENTS

WHAT THIS BOOK IS ABOUT AND HOW TO USE IT—

BY MARY ELLEN PINKHAM

IT'S EVERY AUTHOR'S GOAL to write a book the whole world needs. With this one, I actually think I've done it.

This book is for people who live in apartments, houses, co-ops, condominiums, and trailer parks. It's also for people who are hoping to find, moving out of, or trying to sell an apartment, house, co-op, condo, or trailer.

This book is for anybody who has ever had (or will have) to buy a rug, clean a sink, do a wash, turn on the heat, hang a picture, or zap a roach. It's even for people who plan to hire someone else to do any or all of these jobs, just in case you can't find them, don't know how to judge their work, or decide they're charging too much.

It is for men and women, for the newly wed

Do you know...
- How to get raspberries off your shirt, wax off your carpet, water stains off your furniture?
- Why it's dangerous if the gas flame is yellow?
- What clauses should be in a renovation contract?
- Which noises *don't* mean trouble in the dishwasher?
- Why it's pointless to add the bleach at the wrong time?
- When plugging in a hair dryer will cause a power failure?
- Which plaster crack means your foundation is in trouble?
- What candy store item will keep the weevils off your pantry shelves?
- What simple check may prevent your whole drainage system from backing up?

If you own this book, you will.

---

and the newly unwed, for college students who are about to enroll in Life 101, and even for experienced homemakers like me who know a lot of the answers but can't remember where we filed them.

Here's why I wrote this book.

Years ago, I published a collection of household hints that launched my career as an expert in housekeeping. Since then, I've been a regular columnist for two of the nation's leading women's magazines, and my columns have appeared weekly in a newspaper with a readership of more than 20 million people. I invite questions about household care, and I get thousands of them. The questions run the gamut: How to buy a new home. How to pack up an old one. How to care for every surface of the house. How to clean everything inside it and a lot of things—such as the decking, the patio chairs, and the whitewall tires—outside of it.

The number and variety of these questions convinced me that what used to be considered "common knowledge" is increasingly uncommon.

The world is more electronic and more chemical than it used to be. There are new brands, new fibers, new things to buy and clean and maintain.

And while there's more to know, many of us know less of it. In the past, Mom took care of the white appliances and Dad took care of the others. That's changed, too. There's no such thing as "woman's work" in a home headed by a divorced dad, and a lot of my friends are as comfortable with a tool kit as with a makeup kit. Even in traditional families the work is being split up in untraditional ways. It seems that into any life may come a pot that's dirty, a carpet that's stained, or a toilet that's backing up.

Here are some of the times you'll need this book:

• When you'll be hiring a professional to do anything connected with your home—from inspecting it to painting it to renovating it—so you'll know what to expect.

• When you'll be making any major household purchase, from appliances to burglar alarms. Styles and fashion may change but not the standards of this book: Is whatever you're buying durable, practical, and easy to care for?

• When you have to clean anything at all—from your rug to your ceiling, from your baby's bronzed shoes to your computer keyboard. I'll tell you what to use and how to use it. How often you do it, with a few exceptons, is your business. In writing about cleaning products, I've mentioned brand names, not necessarily because a product is the best one, although sometimes it is the only one, but to help you understand what I am talking about. Saying "Jet Dry" is probably a lot clearer than saying "dishwashing rinse-aid product." (As you may know, I manufacture some cleaning products of my own, and I think it would be unduly modest of me not to mention them when I think they're appropriate.)

• When there's a home repair or maintenance or sprucing up job to be done. The book will help you decide which you can do and should do, and tell you how to do them. It will also make it clear when you're better off leaving it to a pro. Sometimes knowing *Whether To* is as important as knowing *How To*.

Here's why I think you'll like this book:

• *It's realistic.* I know you're not going to sort your wash six different ways or vacuum your rug from corner to corner once a week. In my opinion, being taught this sort of stuff in home ec class is what drove millions of women out of the house and into the work force. I've suggested shortcuts that make sense and get the job done well enough.

• *It's to the point.* Let's face it. Information about how to check your oil heating system or how to calculate how many rolls of wallpaper you'll need or the best way to get a burn mark off the coffee table, though important, isn't stuff you're dying to hear anyone go on and on about. Rather than show off how much I know, I've tried to include only what you need to know to get the job done right.

• *It's comprehensive.* If there was a home-related topic that I thought you'd ever wonder about, I included it. That's why you'll find information about what food to toss when the freezer fails, or how to buy a smoke detector, or the best way to clean a floor that's turning yellow—the kind of information you clip out of magazines and newspapers and then can't find when you need it. Now it's all in one place.

I won't claim that this book includes the last word on every home-related subject, but I can tell you one thing proudly—it sure has the first. There is no book on the market like it.

PART I
FINDING

CHOOSING YOUR HOME

My heart beats so fast when I make an expensive purchase that I consider shopping aerobic exercise. When I bought my first house, my heart was pumping overtime for weeks on end, a workout that may have added at least three to four months to my life. That worked out nicely because it just about balanced the three to four months that my life was probably shortened by the accompanying emotional stress.

Whether you plan to buy or rent, are considering a co-op or a condo, or choose to live in a house, an apartment, or a town house—or, for that matter, a teepee or a trailer—finding a home is always a Very Big Deal. There are books that deal with buying a house in great detail, and you probably have family members, friends, and a lawyer or accountant or two who are all available to give you their opinions and advice, free and otherwise.

Still, I'm about to add some opinions and advice of my own, since I couldn't imagine writing a book about caring for a home without first making a few suggestions about how to find it. I'm hoping they will help make the process a little easier and help keep you out of trouble.

● ●

RENTING

The least you need to know about renting:
- How to choose the rental
- Your rights and responsibilities

Where to Start

The easiest way to find a place to live is to move in with someone who already happens to be living there, which of course may turn out to be a mixed blessing.

If you don't have such an opportunity, and none of your friends knows of an available apartment—maybe you're new in town or living where the rental market is tight—you'll no doubt wind up looking through the classified ads. As you will quickly learn, classified writing is a form of fiction writing, and when you show up to inspect the place, what you see is often not at all what you hoped to get. Still and all, people do find apartments through the newspapers and save themselves a brokerage fee.

But you may wind up going through a broker because you do not have a lot of time, because you want someone to separate the apartments that are unacceptable from those that are just unaffordable, or because you discover that the most desirable apartments are generally represented by brokers. The broker's fee will probably be the equivalent of one month's to three month's rent, payable once you sign the lease. (While most rentals are apartments, obviously houses can also be rented. In most cases, the same information—about fees, leases, etc.—applies.)

You'll save a lot of time if you trust your instincts when you meet the broker. Don't hook up with someone you don't like. The whole experience will certainly become more irritating and probably more fruitless as well.

Everyone who has dealt with brokers, especially in a market where rentals are scarce, seems to have horror stories to tell about them. Novelist and playwright Bruce Jay Friedman once wrote a hilarious article about apartment hunting in New York City. Standing in the cell-like kitchen, he asked where the stove was. "In that drawer," said the broker, pointing. And the refrigerator? "The drawer above it." Friedman suggested it might not be a good idea to have the refrigerator directly over the stove. "Are you a thermal engineer?" asked the broker.

There are also referral services that promise to send you out on leads. Unfortunately some of these people get their "leads" from the same place you do—the classifieds—but charge you a lot more than the price of a newspaper. Call the local Better Business Bureau to get a report on the service before you sign up.

A building superintendent who lets you know that an apartment has become available or renters who are about to vacate a very desirable apartment may ask you for "key money" to ensure that you're next in line for it. (The landlord may or may not be part of the deal, actively or passively.) This is a fancy way of asking for a bribe, which happens to be illegal in the many towns where you need to be licensed to share a commission. But if the apartment looks like a great deal, you can serve your own interests best by paying up, moving in, and then contacting the D.A.'s office. Similarly, if you're having a legitimate problem with the broker about the fee but you want the apartment, pay the fee and then seek action with the state department of licensing.

As you probably know, there are laws about discriminating against tenants, but if a landlord lives on the property and there are fewer than four units the rules don't apply. Whether a landlord can refuse to rent to people with children or to unmarried couples depends on local laws. If you're single when you move in, try to have a clause included in the lease that will let you share with anyone not a member of your immediate family. Who knows? Your luck may change. Also be sure to find out the policy about pets if you have one or may some day want one. If you plan to run a business out of your home, find out if that's acceptable.

If there is an application fee, ask if it will be given back if you're rejected or applied toward the rent if you do move in.

INSPECTING THE RENTAL

Test whatever you can. Don't be shy. Flush the toilet, run the water to see if the sink drains, check that the stove burners work, flick on light switches, look for telephone jacks, flip on the exhaust fans, and check if the air conditioner (if it exists) is in working order. One thing you can't check in advance is the sound-proofing, unless you happen to arrive when the rock band next door is having a practice session. One positive feature is a bedroom where there is no shared wall.

If you love the apartment, you'll probably take it, but if you're undecided, check out the common areas to see if they help bend your opinion in one direction or another. Are the incinerator room or garbage area and laundry room clean and well lit? Do you see several machines, a sink, a work space in the laundry? Is there a storage area for residents somewhere in the building or complex? Is the building wired for cable TV? What's the deal on parking?

Is someone on the premises to help in case of an emergency? Who does repairs? What appliances are you responsible for and which will be maintained by the landlord (dishwasher, refrigerator, air conditioner)? What's the policy (or local regulation) regarding repainting? (In certain New York City apartments, for example, the landlord has to repaint when you sign a three-year lease.)

Make a checklist of things you want corrected and note any flaws (burns in the counter, holes in the floor, etc.) Write a letter mentioning every one of these things and send it to the landlord certified mail, return receipt requested. If you have lived with the hole in the floor and burn in the counter, you don't want to be charged for them when you move out. Ask the landlord to respond to your letter and let you know what will be corrected. At least have the landlord sign a copy of your original letter. Attach it to your lease along with a copy of the check you give for your security deposit, and put them where you can find them when you move out.

Your Rights and Obligations

In addition to the broker's fee, you will probably have to pay a month's rent in advance plus a security deposit that is held by the landlord in case there are any repairs to be made after you move out. Normal wear and tear can't be deducted, but holes in the wall and burns on the floor can. Very cautious (or should I say very *experienced*) landlords may ask also for a "cleaning deposit" to pay for a cleanup before the next tenant moves in and a "damage deposit" besides. Local laws may require that the landlord put these payments into an interest-bearing bank account and refund them

within a certain period of time after you leave.

THE LEASE

A prospective landlord may give you an agreement or a lease. An agreement is shorter and more informal than a lease, and usually commits you to only a month-to-month arrangement (which means you haven't locked in the amount of the rent). An apartment lease usually runs for one to two years, sometimes three, and officially guarantees you some rights and imposes some obligations. Get one or the other of these in writing. Don't rely only on a verbal agreement. It's amazing how fuzzy the memories of verbal deals can become.

Landlords are not allowed to write leases that allow them to keep your property if you don't pay the rent or retain your security if you haven't created any damage or moved out during the term of the lease. They must be responsible for negligence that causes you any harm, and they can't make you waive your rights to a legal hearing in case of a dispute.

But landlords still have plenty of leeway to write a lease that favors their side over yours. In this case, and whenever you have to sign a contract, particularly one drawn by the other party, have a lawyer review it. Points that should be covered:

• **Upkeep, repairs, and maintenance.** In a rented house, you may pay for these, but in a rental apartment the landlord usually covers the costs of major repairs—plumbing, electric, structural.

• **Utilities, garage, and other services.** Are they included in the rental charge or not?

• **Termination or renewal.** Do you have to give notice if you plan to move out? How much notice does the landlord have to give you if he plans to change the terms? Is the lease automatically renewed?

• **Charges.** Is the rent fixed for the term of the lease? Do you have to pay an extra fee if your rent is late?

SUBLETTING

If the lease says nothing whatsoever about subletting, I would assume it is permissible within the municipality (which may regulate the length of the sublease and the amount you are allowed to charge). Check with a lawyer about your rights to sublet and have him draw up a sublet lease. This is important because if the sublessee doesn't fulfill the obligations of the lease (paying the rent, for one thing), the responsibility is back in your lap.

Though you usually need the landlord's permission to sublet, it can't be unreasonably withheld. On the other hand, the landlord is entitled to make a financial check on the candidate, so don't bother to present someone who doesn't have a bank account—for your own protection as well.

If you plan to sublet, notify the landlord of your plans in writing. If he doesn't respond within a certain period—either with an approval or disapproval—you may be allowed by law to go right ahead with your plans.

If you decide to move out without providing your own subtenant candidate, the landlord can sue you for whatever rent is due for the remainder of the lease. However, he must make a reasonable attempt to find another tenant.

THE LANDLORD'S RIGHTS AND OBLIGATIONS

Your landlord probably will be allowed to have "reasonable" access to your apartment, but this doesn't mean strolling in at will. He or she has the right to inspect the property but you have a right to set reasonable conditions—receiving notice of such plans in advance and withholding blanket permission to enter your premises.

Certain obligations of the landlord—such as painting, repairing an air conditioner or dishwasher, keeping the halls clean—are different in different states. If the landlord agrees to put in a new piece of equipment or make any repairs, your lawyer should get the details in writing.

If you have a question, contact the local district attorney's office or housing authority.

PROBLEMS WITH THE LANDLORD

If the landlord has refused to make necessary repairs and you've paid for them yourself, local laws may allow you to deduct the expenses from your rent or withhold part of the rent until the landlord corrects the problem. If you and other tenants are having an argument with the landlord over the same issue, the best way to get action is to organize a tenants' group. A friend of mine didn't know how to go about this and finally just put up an unsigned notice saying, "Tenants Association organization meeting in lobby at 6:00" and planned to arrive at 6:30. She counted on the fact that a few people would show up on time and mill around until some take-charge type started to run the meeting, and that's exactly what happened.

As a tenant, your job is to keep the place from being destroyed and to pay the rent on time. If you violate these or any other of the terms of the agreement, a landlord can evict you. This can't happen as fast as the landlord would like you to believe. First you must get a "Notice to quit," then a summons must be delivered. Only then does a hearing take place.

You can also be evicted if your lease has a cancellation clause and the owner has decided to convert the property to a co-op or condo rather than maintain it as a rental. To stay, you may need to buy your home. However, in a conversion, tenants usually hire a lawyer and work together in negotiating the terms in accordance with local laws. The deal may include a "non-evict" clause allowing tenants who want to remain as renters to stay until a specified date or for an unlimited time.

• •

BUYING

The least you need to know about buying your home:
- Facts involved in buying
- Evaluating the purchase
- Weighing alternatives: new home or old, co-op apartment or condo

Where to Start

A good rule of thumb is never to buy anything that you can't afford to ruin or lose. Though like most of the rules you set for yourself, this one may occasionally be broken, on the whole it does tend to keep you out of jewelry stores and yacht showrooms and frees you to concentrate your anxieties on other areas.

Eventually, in the course of your life, you will have to cope with one or more major purchases—things like carpeting (big), a car (bigger), and a house (biggest).

Understanding the financial consequences of home-buying is one major concern. Educating yourself will be an experience similar to having a first child: While you'll be full of hard-earned information it seems a waste not to put to future use, you'll be extremely cautious about taking on the project a second time.

Your other concern is learning the "rules" of home-buying. After years of shopping for clothing, you are experienced in spotting potential problems—anything white, canvas shoes, gauzy clothing bought at street fairs—but this is a whole new area for making judgments.

As a first-time home buyer you'll have to rely on professional help and the opinions of people you trust, but the best thing you can do is educate yourself as well as you can. If someone experienced can go home-shopping with you, at least at the beginning, that would be a tremendous help.

How Much Can You Pay?

Your essential concern in buying is the same whether you are buying a house, a town house, an apartment—or even a mobile home: Is the property sound and worth the money you have to pay for it? Obviously, the first decisions you make are where you want to live and how much you can afford to pay. Once you've decided to buy, make an appointment with a bank loan officer or a mortgage counselor to find out what monthly payment you're qualified to carry. Budget for the down payment, local taxes, insurance, and closing costs—and moving costs—when you make your plans.

The Role of the Broker

When it comes to real estate brokers, what many people feel recalls Henry Kissinger's comment about politicians—"Ninety percent of them give the other ten percent a bad reputation"—but that is probably unfair. However, it is true that the broker is not there to be your friend but to close a deal and so should be approached with goodwill and the normal healthy skepticism you would feel toward anyone whose main purpose is to sell you something. (In some states, the law now obliges the broker to remind you that he or she is working for the seller and not for you.)

Brokers are licensed. Many belong to the National Association of Realtors, which has certain professional standards, but as with so-called experts in every field, some will be terrific and helpful and others will be peculiar if not out-and-out scam artists. (In Canada, the Canadian Real Estate Association—CREA—sets the standards.)

If you believe a broker is not just pushy but actually unethical, you may decide to file charges through the local board of realtors or the state real estate board. A broker who is found guilty may be penalized or even lose his or her license.

The broker's fee, a percentage of the cost, is charged to the seller. In a direct sale, which happens about a quarter of the time, the price is obviously lower because the seller doesn't have to factor in the broker's fee. Working without a broker is probably more of a disadvantage if you're moving to a community that is not well known to you, in which case the broker may be able to help you make some decision about what part of town would best suit you, give you some information about the community, and so forth. A broker may also be able to help you secure financing.

Judging Value

On a first visit to a home or apartment that's for sale, you'll be getting an overall impression. Obviously, you'll have to know something about the asking price (and what maintenance fees are involved if it's a co-op and condominium), but you can also get an idea of the general condition of the place.

If it's unoccupied, turn on the heating and (if the temperature is over 60° F.) the cooling system. See how fast each goes on. If it's an air-conditioned apartment building, are there individual units or is the building centrally air-conditioned? (If the latter, you control the degree of heat or coldness electrically with fan units in each room; fuel costs aren't paid by you but are part of the common charges.)

Open and close a few windows and doors and see how well they work. This gives you a clue to how well the house has been maintained and whether you may have to replace the windows.

Turn on the faucets and flush the toilet to check out the water power and see how fast the water drains.

Open the kitchen cabinet doors and drawers to see if they work properly and if the interiors are in good condition.

If it's a house, check the exterior basement area for stains. You may not be able to tell which come from water seepage. Mortar splotches at 18-inch intervals are a sign of termite treatment.

After you've seen several possibilities, additional questions will occur to you. Bring a notebook; carry a Polaroid camera; use any method that will help you remember details, because after a while they all start to blur together.

Once you are seriously considering purchasing a place, I assume you will pay it a second visit. As you zero in on your choice, you may want to investigate the home more thoroughly before you call in the experts.

MAKING YOUR OWN INSPECTION

Obviously, most sellers have the sense to make a house look good cosmetically. If you find the place charmless, you won't be interested even if the price is good and the structure sound, while if you're won over, you may be willing to overlook some problems. But don't get so distracted by a pretty window box that you don't notice the pile of termite wings underneath.

How many of the items I've listed below you will be able to investigate will depend, in part, on your own personality and how aggressively you are prepared to investigate. Some items may matter more to you than others (and many will be inapplicable if you're buying an apartment rather than a town house or house). In any event, you will be able to rely on the professional inspection to cover any ground you may have missed.

There is no way an inspection by you can substitute for a professional inspection, but the professional report will make a lot more sense to you if you've taken a look at the key checkpoints yourself. In fact, if you notice problems that are potentially very costly or that show the house or apartment wasn't very well maintained, you might decide to pull out of the deal before you spend the money on an inspection.

POINTS TO COVER

Water supply. You either get city water or water from a well. If the house uses well water, you should ask the rate of flow (it should be at least 6 gallons a minute) and establish the purity of the water. If you need help in locating a tester, call the local Department of Health.

Electricity. What is the capacity of the house? If the house or apartment has a dryer, hot water heater, and air conditioner, you can assume it has the capacity to run all that equipment. If you do not see air conditioners, you should ask whether they can be installed or whether you will need rewiring.

Heating. The heater should be less than 10 years old and for a family of four should have a capacity of at least 40 gallons. Check the pipes. Iron pipes last only about 5 years. If they're older, you may wind up having to replace them. Copper pipes last 25 years or more.

Insulation. R-ratings are the amount of insulating value of a material. You should have at least 6 inches of insulation with R-19 rating in the attic or roof and 4 inches with R-16 rating underneath floors that are above unheated space. Outside walls should have $3^1/_2$ inches of insulation.

Septic system. Is there a city sewer line or does the house depend on an independent septic system? Does the system conform to local codes? Was tank pumped within the last 4 to 5 years? If not, drains may be clogged and need expensive cleaning.

Foundation. Probably made of concrete or poured masonry. Hairline cracks may indicate problems. Cracks are perfect entry points for termites and for water that could cause basement leaks. But if they're small, fixing them is just a matter of filling small cracks with caulking compound or larger ones (over $1/_4$ inch) with cement mortar, preferably waterproof.

There should be openings in foundation walls—ideally, one in each wall—so air can circulate. The openings should be screened so bugs won't come in.

Is there any sign of termites? (Some mortgage lenders insist on a separate, professional termite inspection.) Look for swarms in spring or early fall; for piles of discarded wings; or $1/_4$-inch-wide tunnels along foundation walls, along posts set into the ground, and along water pipes. (Also see Termites, p. 315.) The best way to size up the situation is to ask for the exterminator's bill.

Sills, wood planks fastened to the foundation, form the edges to which other wood elements are fastened. Cracks or large spaces between the top of the foundation wall and the sill will need caulking compound or insulating strips to prevent cold air and moisture from coming in.

Boards or other evidence of the foundation being shored up is a sign that an adobe house may be sinking.

Roof. Since replacing a roof is one of your biggest home repair costs, you ought to know what you're in for. Roofs have three layers. The bottom layer consists of rafters, 2×6s, spaced 16 inches apart, which frame the roof. Sheafing made of plywood or boards covers the rafters, and roofing material covers the sheafing.

Most roofs are good for 15 to 25 years, but even a casual look can tell you if you're in for problems soon. The south roof, because it gets the most sun, is usually the first to go.

• **Asphalt shingle roof construction** is probably the most common. Roofing felt covers the sheafing, and shingle strips are nailed on top of it. Asphalt shingles are flexible and easier to repair than wood. As they get old, they dry out and become brittle. If there is any section of the roof you can reach, bend the corner of a shingle. If it breaks, the shingles are old. They also may leak or tear, or corner tabs may be turned up, allowing water to come in. Cement and roofing nails will repair small problems, or you can replace a strip of shingle. But if the granules have worn off and the black felt roof base is exposed, you know the roof may soon need replacing. A lumpy roof is a sign that there are wood shingles under the asphalt and reroofing will be a more expensive process. While you can put a whole new asphalt shingle roof over an old one, you're advised never to cover two layers with a third; if there's a problem, the second layer should be removed and a new roof installed over the original.

• **Wood shingle roofs** last about 25 years. They are similar to asphalt but the shingles come in individual pieces rather than strips so they're easier to repair. Moss growing on top of the shingles may have caused rotting. Individual shingles that have pulled loose or curled up at the edges need to be replaced or can, in some cases, be nailed down. Roofing paper can be slipped under some shingles to stop leaking, too.

• **Slate roofs,** which were installed on many older houses because of their durability, are too expensive for most new home construction. To make them waterproof, alternate rows of slates are staggered. Each one overlaps the one below it by half. If there are missing or broken slates, you can buy new (or secondhand) ones, or you can get imitation asbestos-based slates.

• **Copper, painted tin, and galvanized iron roofs** are also long-lasting, but if there are signs of rust you may have problems.

Look up at the **flashing,** the strips of metal that make a watertight joint where two different planes of the roof meet or roofing material meets another surface or material such as a chimney. Flashing can be made of aluminum, sheet lead, zinc, or galvanized iron, but copper is best. If the flashing is pulling away from the surface, it needs to be repaired or you'll have leaks. Galvanized iron, which rusts, should be painted, but badly corroded flashing can be replaced with a self-adhesive.

Look up also at the **gutters and leaders,** the drain-off ditches that carry melted snow and rain off the roof and into an outlet. Gutters run parallel with the roof, and leaders, or downspouts, run down. They may be made of aluminum, galvanized steel, plastic, vinyl, copper, and wood (in which case they need to be treated with preservative). They should be large enough for a heavy rainfall, and the downspout should have a small extension to carry water away from the house. Otherwise, moisture problems, like mildew and rotting, can affect the foundation.

In the winter, snow and ice may pull gutters away from the house. In the spring, if you see leaves or seedlings growing in the gutters, you know they haven't been properly cleaned out. That kind of debris—or ice dams from melting snow—can cause water to overflow and create water damage (peeling paint, cracks in plaster) inside the house.

Siding. Siding is the generic term for the exterior covering of the house.

• If the siding is **wood,** ask when the exterior was last painted. The job usually needs to be redone every 5 to 6 years. Moisture can cause some decay in the wood, but this can be minimized if the plants and shrubs are at least 18 inches from the house. Check the seams between wood and masonry (such as the chimney) to see if they have cracks. The cracks aren't a great cause for concern, since they can be patched easily with caulking, but their presence will give you some idea of how well the house has been taken care of. Weathered wood (shakes) need regular treatment, and natural wood needs a lot of recoating—about once every three years—but almost no preparation.

• Buckling in **aluminum or vinyl siding,** which is a result of improper installation, may require professional repair. Vinyl made to look like wood stands up very well, which is fortunate because it's hard to repair. Aluminum siding is very susceptible to scratches, and paint may eventually fade. While the heaviest grade aluminum is very durable, it is as expensive as steel, which is also used as siding because it can last up to 30 years.

• White crust on **bricks,** called efflorescence, is a sign of too much moisture, which can cause interior leaking. (It may also be a normal process of brick or plaster drying out, in which case you just brush it off—if you wash it, it'll be reabsorbed—and use a primer if you'll be painting over it.) Sometimes this is solved cheaply by painting a waterproofing compound right over the mortar between the bricks, but the moisture then may enter through the bricks and the whole wall will fall apart. Since the wall must breathe, the proper solution is to "point" the brick—chip out the mortar wherever it's loose or crumbling and replace it. A good pointing job should last 15 to 20 years. If buying an apartment, you may want to ask if the building was recently pointed as it may become an expense apartment owners may have to face. Since pointing is the only maintenance necessary, brick is an excellent siding choice. So is **stone.** And so is **masonry,** but you may not want a house that looks as if it belongs in a mall.

• **Stucco** needs painting every 5 to 6 years and it also is susceptible to moisture problems. If the stucco was applied to masonry blocks, it's very durable stuff, but if the stucco finish was applied to metal lathe (which is like chicken wire) over wood framing, it may crack and require patching with cement mortar or patching compound.

If the foundation is exposed, you may be tempted to make it look prettier by painting it, but you'll have to do the job repeatedly. If it's cracking, it may need an asphalt coating, which involves digging up the surrounding earth.

Basement. Flooding is a possibility just about everywhere and a chronic, occasionally major problem in some low-lying and coastal areas.

Is the basement dry? Take a look at the windows for signs of decay or rust. If they're in bad shape, they'll leak and allow insects to enter. If scraping and repainting won't help, you may need to replace them.

Waterproofing the walls is expensive, so people sometimes make do by installing a sump pump to handle excess moisture or flooding. If there's chronic moisture in the area where the house is located, you may never be able to finish the basement as a rec room.

WET ROT/DRY ROT

Ordinary mold leaves white furry deposits or black spots, but wet and dry rot, caused by dampness, looks different and is much more serious.

The first signs of **wet rot** may be around doors and windows or under peeling paint. Wood affected by wet rot is spongy when damp, brown and crumbly when dry. To eliminate the problem, first eliminate the cause of the dampness, then cut away and replace affected wood, and treat the area by applying fungicidal wood preservative.

Dry rot thrives in closed-in, poorly ventilated indoor spots, first appearing as fine, pale gray tubes and white cottonlike growths. It eventually develops wrinkled round growths with rust-colored spores. The infested wood is brown and brittle and the area smells musty. If you suspect this problem, call in a specialist and make sure that the specialist checks thoroughly, because this problem spreads fast and widely. Dry rot can even affect masonry, causing the affected surface to disintegrate.

You definitely need a functioning floor drain, especially if there is a hot water heater or laundry setup. If the room seems smelly, the drain probably hasn't been used in a while. Pouring fresh water down the drain should solve the problem unless there's no trap or a damaged trap, which calls for a visit from the plumber.

If there is no basement, take a look at the crawl space (so called because there isn't enough room to stand in it). Ask the agent or the seller if the undersides of the floors are insulated. If the crawl space is not properly sealed, cold air will be coming into the house. If the earth underneath is bare, you may need to have it covered with sheeting.

Attic. Attic louvers, vents that allow warm moist air to escape in cold weather, should be covered with screens to prevent animals from coming inside. Exhaust fans are helpful to eliminate heat and moisture.

If you plan to use the attic, you'll need a sealed subfloor of 3/4" plywood. Even if it's primarily used for storage, you should have some light in the attic—not just one little bulb.

Floors. Bringing children along for the house tour is a big plus, because they can do a couple of informal "tests" less awkwardly than a grownup. For example: Tell one to roll a marble across the floor. If the marble goes very fast, the floor is uneven and there may be construction problems. When the kids jump (and they probably will), see if there are any vibrations. If so, the construction or bracing is inadequate.

Under the base of the floor are joists, horizontal wood planks, that rest on the sill, the wood planks that form the basic frame. (Very long planks are also supported by heavy wood or steel girders and in some cases additional wood or metal posts.)

Since wood shrinks over time, open spaces are created and joists may not be properly supported. The solution is to have thin wood

IS A PLASTER CRACK SERIOUS?

You can't make a wall out of plaster alone: It has to hang on something, called the lath. Houses built before 1935 used wood lath, slats of wood nailed horizontally onto studs topped with several layers of plaster which made a very heavy, rigid surface.

Rock lath houses, built after 1935, used perforated gypsum instead of wood lath with thinner coats of plaster. Plaster on rock lath cracks less often than plaster over wood lath.

Houses built after 1950 are usually covered with gypsum drywall, which cracks even less because it is lighter and more flexible than plaster. *The pattern of the crack shows how serious it is.* Foundation cracks, caused by settling, are the worst. They generally run along the ceiling, spring out from the doorways and windows, then continue down a wall, accompanied by some floor sagging or sloping; in a masonry wall, there are also some cracking sounds along the outside wall as if someone is hammering on the outside bricks.

Other cracks should be repaired but aren't cause for great concern. Typically, these include cracks in a wood lath ceiling where different surfaces meet (walls come together, or ceiling meets wall). In a rock lath house, you may see one or two long parallel cracks lengthwise in ceilings, cracks starting at doorway corners and reaching the ceilings, cracks from corners of windows, cracks at stairway openings. In drywall houses, you see cracks above doorways and at ceiling wall joints on the second floor. Usually these start near end walls and open wider toward the middle of the house. They are caused mainly by changing humidity conditions.

wedges inserted between the top of the post and girder, the top of the girder and joist, or the top of the joists and rough flooring.

If the floor is covered by carpeting, ask what's underneath. Better yet, take a look. You may find rough flooring, boards, plywood, or cement. Or you may discover a nice wooden floor that can be cleaned and resurfaced.

Walls. Water stains or bulging or chipping plaster may indicate leaks. Cracks may also be a sign of water damage or just a result of natural settling. The pattern of the crack gives you a clue as to how big a concern it is. (See box, preceding page.)

Windows. See if they open. Check the sashes for damage. Are there leaks underneath? Does the house have storm windows/screens? What sort of material are the windows made of? Glass lasts about 50 years, acrylic 25, polycarbonates 10 to 15 years. Double-glazed windows (with double panes) are much better insulators than single pane. Old-fashioned single pane windows may need replacing—particularly if the frames aren't in good shape. Wood frames are better insulators than aluminum, but they need regular sealing and painting. If they're starting to peel they may have been neglected.

If the windows look bad, get an estimate of the replacement costs. If you're looking at an apartment, find out if there are any plans to upgrade the entire building (and how this will be shared); or will you be on your own if new windows must be installed?

Heating. If the boiler or furnace is 25 years old or more, it may soon need replacing. Ask to see the heating bills and other utility bills from last season. Ask if the flues are open and whether they draw.

In an apartment, the fuel costs will be part of your common charges.

Appliances. Ask if they come with the house. Find out the age of each and whether they're covered by warranty or service contract.

WHEN YOU'RE READY TO BUY

Once you've made a decision to buy a house or an apartment, you need an appraisal, a financial assessment of its worth, so you will know whether the asking price is realistic or wishful thinking on the part of the seller. Your lender may recommend an appraiser. Or get a recommendation from a lawyer, the local building inspector, or a local bank officer; or look in the Yellow Pages under Real Estate Appraisers (choose someone who is a member of Society of Real Estate Appraisers or some other professional organization).

The appraisal evaluates the site, neighborhood, extra features (such as recreational facilities in a town house development, pools), and the house or apartment in detail (type of floors, windows, appliances); judges the overall condition; and analyzes the market to take into account what other similar properties in the area have sold for and other factors that together help calculate a fair price.

Either before or after the appraisal, you'll also need to have a building inspection or survey to get specific information about the physical condition of your prospective home. An inspection is required of both a house and an apartment.

INSPECTING THE INSPECTOR

A home that's in bad shape can wind up costing you thousands of dollars more than the purchase price. That's why an accurate inspection is so important and can save you so much money—by helping you negotiate a reasonable price that takes into account how much more money is needed to fix up the place or by convincing you to back out of the deal before it's too late.

Though most purchase contracts are subject to professional inspection, that's not so with an auction or tax sale. In such a case, have the inspection done before you bid so you don't wind up overpaying for a lemon.

Since it is clearly in the agent's interest to let you believe the house is perfect so he can close the deal, I wouldn't rely on him to recommend an inspector. Your lender will probably refer you to a home inspector. You can also get a name from an attorney or from the Yellow Pages (under Building Inspection).

Inspectors are not necessarily engineers or building contractors. Some people say that they can't understand a thing an engineer tells them, but I assume that depends on the individual engineer. Others feel an engineer's report is more professional. It's a matter of personal preference. What you do want is someone who is thorough, leaning toward the obsessive-compulsive side.

A couple I know chose an inspector without any references only because he charged a couple of hundred dollars less than one who was recommended. They bought the house, and within three months of moving in, had to replace the water pipes, discovered a termite problem, and coped with a toilet backing up because the septic tank hadn't been maintained. A good inspector would have warned them about all of these problems.

There is no licensing requirement for an inspector except in the state of Texas. If your inspector is a member of one of the professional societies (such as the American Society of Home Inspectors), you may have some reassurance that he or she has met certain stan-

dards, but as I've said before, you have no guarantees.

With a new home, you may get a one-year **builder-backed warranty** or an **insured 10-year warranty** from an independent company that screens builders before they grant coverage. Ask the builder about the availability of such coverage.

A PROFESSIONAL INSPECTION

Even if you've done some preliminary legwork, tell the inspector that you want to know everything possible about the house: how to anticipate problems, how to solve them, what it will cost to fix them, how long the house should last.

To completely answer all your questions, the inspector should do the following (with some modifications, obviously, if it is an apartment building rather than a house that is being inspected):

• Walk the roof and attic crawl space
• Open electricity distribution panels
• Check the furnace, heat exchangers, and heating pump elements
• Operate all installed appliances and equipment
• Report visual evidence of basement or crawl space water problems

Afterward, the inspector should prepare a written report including these items:

• Projected systems and components budget (to let you know what you will have to replace or repair over the next few years)
• Identification of any remodeling problems (such as asbestos-containing material, an electrical or plumbing system without the capability of being upgraded)
• Information about any substandard work
• Notification of any potential dangers: aluminum wiring instead of copper (a 40% greater fire risk), inadequate electric systems, lighting fixtures buried in attic insulation;

PLANS FOR THE FUTURE

Before you and the seller of the house part ways, make sure you have obtained a copy of the house plans. When you need a major repair or if you decide to do a renovation, they'll be required.

unlined fireplaces and unvented space heaters, inadequate air combustion supplies, cracks and holes in heat exchanges, untempered glass in shower doors; inadequate venting in attics and crawl spaces, potential rot and/or termite damage; lead plumbing material

• Disclosures about radon, lead, asbestos, and other safety issues are now required by some states. If you are particularly concerned, you can hire a specialist to do an environmental assessment (check the Yellow Pages under Environmental and Ecological Services) or check with your local Department of Health. Check Environmental Hazards, on p. 283 for more details.

You may find the inspection report overwhelming because of the amount of information it contains. That's why it generally includes a summary of the main points as well as some help in putting everything in perspective. For example, if you're buying an older house—as two out of three home buyers do—you probably expect some maintenance problems, but what's really helpful is knowing how the condition of this house compares to others of its age and type.

A good report may even suggest how to relieve the problem, with notes such as "Kitchen: Rear window—does not open. Ease this by using a painter's putty knife between sash and sash stops and insill, then wax."

Bottom line: The report is supposed to help you make a decision about whether the house is a good investment, not send you into a panic.

No matter what help you get and no matter how much you educate yourself, once you buy you will run into some problems you hadn't foreseen and deficiencies you hadn't anticipated. The situation is a lot like marriage in that respect. And in both cases, having enough money will often solve some of the problems. What's different about solving a house problem is that it requires the full cooperation of only one person.

Housing Alternatives

BUYING FROM A MODEL HOUSE OR APARTMENT

Although a model home has obvious advantages—newer equipment, energy-conserving windows and other features, the possibility of customizing many details according to your own wishes—you're the guinea pig. And if you're living far away, it's hard to coordinate all the details involved.

In a new neighborhood, you may have to kick in some costs for street paving, sidewalks, water and sewage lines. And the model house may have a lot of extras that aren't part of your package unless you pay for them. Make sure you know what you're getting and what you're not.

Before you buy, if it is possible check the reputation of the builder. Go to other communities he's built and find the courage to knock on the door and ask people what they think of the builder. People are usually glad to talk about their experiences with a house—particularly bad experiences.

The builder may just hand over the property and make it clear that at that point, his obligations to you have ended; or he may be very pleasant and promise to make repairs over the first year or two and then disappear from the country. As protection, you may be able to get an insured warranty that is covered in the purchase price: The builder warrants the home to be free from major structural problems and various system problems for the first year; against some of the problems in the second year; and against fewer still of the problems in the third year. If the builder doesn't fix them, you are covered for repair costs over a certain deductible.

It may be easier to get financing for a new home than for an older one.

HOME-BUYING VOCABULARY

Binder. Commitment to buy at a given price and under certain terms. Deposit paid at this point should be held (usually by an attorney) in interest-bearing escrow account and is usually applied to down payment unless sale falls through. Then deposit reverts to you or goes to seller, depending on terms of purchase contract.

Purchase contract. Signed agreement that accompanies deposit, which includes amount of deposit; purchase price, down payment, and type of financing; provisions for getting your down payment back (usually your failure to sell current house or to get financing, failure of sellers to prove title or house passing inspection); description of property (house and any items inside it); description of type of deed you will get including any "encumbrances" or restrictions on the property (such as liens, rights of utility company to run wires through, etc.). Contract may be refused by seller if price isn't right, and then you renegotiate. *Do not sign anything until you have some preliminary financing information.*

Title. Assurance that owner has a legal right to sell the property; search is usually done by a specialized title company to make sure no one has liens on the property—such as a bank that holds a mortgage that seller may not have told you about.

Deed. *General warranty deed* guarantees the property is free of any major encumbrances and obliges the seller to defend you against future claims; *special warranty deed* offers you more limited protection, but a *quit-claim deed* gives you the property without assuring you title to it.

Rights of ownership. *Fee simple estate* or *fee simple absolute ownership* gives you all rights to your property; *life estate* gives you rights only during your lifetime; *concurrent estate* means that spouses are co-owners.

Mortgage. Financing plan. Giving advice about money is completely out of my league. Check with the bank.

Closing costs. These can be a killer if you're not prepared, because they can run as much as 5% or more of the total price of the house. The Department of Housing and Urban Development or your lender should be able to give you full information. The total includes costs of getting a loan (called "points," each equal to 1% of the total amount), appraisal fee, title search, legal fee, and so on.

Tranquilizers. What you may need during one or more steps of the process.

CONDOMINIUMS AND CO-OPERATIVES

In a **condo**, you own your own living unit and share an interest with the other residents in common areas (such as hall and basement in an apartment and heating, plumbing, and electric systems). In town house communities, residents own their home and may own the front and back yard. The rest of the land is usually "common area," jointly owned by the homeowners' association, representing all the residents. An elected board of managers runs the property according to legal bylaws established when it is built but hires a manager for the hands-on work. Condominums are usually less expensive to buy and maintain than single-family housing—in town houses, for example, land, windows, etc., cost less than in detached housing—but may be harder to finance, and you may not always like being bound by the decisions of a board.

In a **co-op**, you own nothing directly, just shares of stock in a corporation that holds the title to the whole property and has a board of directors (who usually hire a managing agent to take charge of day-to-day affairs). The tenants who are elected to the board of directors, like the managing board of a condo, hire managers to do the hands-on work. The board has rather broad powers.

If you want to sell your apartment, they must approve the buyers, and approval is not always forthcoming. For example, celebrities who try to buy into co-ops in New York City are often refused because the privacy of the other owners might be jeopardized. The board can also restrict your right to sublet and rent (to restrict "absentee" landlords who may rent to "undesirable" tenants) and may even impose restrictions about your house interior (some percentage of the floor may have to be carpeted as a soundproofing measure) and determine hours and days when workmen can come. This may either protect your property or restrict your rights—depending on your point of view. When the board decides to redecorate the lobby (and can impose its taste), the fur has been known to fly. There are many fewer co-ops than condominiums.

New **condominium town house communities** are often attractively built and offer a lot of recreational facilities. On the plus side, you are freed of many maintenance problems (dealing with garbage collection, landscaping, etc.) but have all the rights of any homeowner to change the interior of your house and to rent or sell as you wish. But the common area isn't all that's communal—many of your homeowner's responsibilities will probably be shared, and your independence will also be somewhat limited.

Get a copy of the association rules if you're planning to buy. The sight of the huge document may discourage you, but it's worth your while to go through it. Your lawyer should review it, too; make sure yours knows the ins and outs of town houses and condos, because there are a few special areas of concern. For example:

Who's responsible for taking care of the roads, curbs, driveways, gardening, and land-scaping? The town house association may or may not maintain your individual plot of land and some of the exterior features, like decks, doors, roofs, and gutters.

When the association is responsible for your yard, you may not be able to put up a swing set or even a bush where you'd like one. And though you may think of yourself as a red front-door type, you may have to have a front door just the same color as everyone else's. Some rules are even more stringent: no kids, no pets, not even a cat.

Before you buy, check the structure of a town house as you would any other house. If it's still under construction, you can get a good look at it. Are there firewalls separating each unit? Could you add extra soundproofing between your home and your neighbor's? Would there be any problem with local building codes if you wanted to refinish the basement?

If the property is just converting to a co-op or condo, get a copy of the engineer's report, which will assess the condition of everything.

What is the maintenance or common charge? How often can it be increased? And what does it cover? Are there any extra costs? If the assessment at the time of conversion seems incredibly low, there probably is a catch; the developer is covering some of the costs but they'll eventually be turned over to the homeowners and the maintenance may zoom upward.

See if there's a "reserve fund" for upcoming repairs and find out whether the maintenance includes regular contributions to it. Otherwise, you may be hit with a special assessment if there is an unexpected expense, such as roofing repair. In many town houses, there have been problems with a kind of roofing plywood used during the 1980s. It was fire-resistant but liable to disintegrate. Would such a problem be handled and paid for communally?

There should be a master hazard insurance policy and liability insurance coverage for every unit owner.

And make sure your down payment is held in escrow. If the developer isn't properly financed, the developer might be planning to use would-be homeowners' money to finish the project, though this is probably prohibited by law. The contract should guarantee that your deposit will be returned if a certain number of units aren't sold by a certain date.

Many town house developments have swimming pools and other such facilities. If these are only promised, and not built, see if you can get the promise written into your contract. Find out how large these will be. Will the pool be capable of handling the needs of the whole community? May you bring guests? How often, and for how much?

Knock on doors or wander around the area and try to find out what the current owners' feelings are about the community. Ask them how the houses are holding up, how well common maintenance is being performed, whether they're satisfied with the facilities. Are there many nonresident owners who rent to transients?

Are the association rules burdensome? Someone I know didn't like the adjoining decks in her development but bought anyway, figuring she'd add a trellis for privacy. "Uh-uh," said the management. The trellis was a "permanent structure." The homeowner wasn't. She decided condo living wasn't for her and moved out not long afterward.

Some friendly private investigating can tell you a lot. Your best bet is to attend a meeting of the residents' organization, which will give you a really uncensored view of how satisfied people are.

BUILDING YOUR OWN HOUSE

If you're buying property to build your own home, you have three major concerns.

One is that the property is suitable for building. A surveyor can warn you if the dream house you're planning will be built on solid hunk of granite or a swamp. ("I had great news from Florida," Milton Berle used to say. "They found property on my property.")

The second is that your title to the property is clear, which you should find out in the course of the title search that is routine in the buying process.

Finally, you need to make sure that what you build conforms to zoning laws, which should be part of your contract with your architect.

Choosing the right architect is the key to the process. Obviously, the best way to get a contractor is through personal references, which I've advised you to do in other circumstances. Unfortunately, references are not always 100% reliable. (Remember all those blind dates you went out on?)

While most professionals are members of the American Association of Architects, your primary guide in choosing an architect should be your gut feeling. Meet with a few people and immediately rule out anyone who is intimidating or unresponsive. This person is going to be your new best friend, in charge of a lot of your money and involved in a long and tension-provoking process, so don't make it any more difficult by choosing someone who's going to struggle with you from the start.

Make sure you understand exactly what your obligation is at every stage of the process. If the architect proposes to draw up some plans, don't agree until you've asked what the cost can be.

Dealing with architects is like dealing with doctors and lawyers. You'll have a lot of tense moments and will resent paying for their mistakes. But if you love the end results, you'll feel they were the greatest.

PART 2

$\mathscr{E}$QUIPPING

SMART BUYING FOR YOUR HOME

GENERAL HOME FURNISHING

For a lot of people, the words *shopping* and *entertainment* are directly connected—except when it comes to things like buying a major appliance, selecting a rug, and other major purchases.

A lot of these things come with features that you don't understand—not just a few features, but a whole lot of them. My new refrigerator came with more options than my new husband.

What's more, these things cost a lot of money. If you make the wrong choice—which you generally don't discover until you've thrown away the packing carton or the day after the return option has expired—you'll be living with it for a long, long time.

On the other hand, the right choices are a pleasure to use, and they're less trouble to care for. This section is dedicated to helping you make the right choices.

The least you need to know about shopping for your home:
- How to proceed
- Anticipating and avoiding problems
- Getting repair service

Keeping Mistakes to a Minimum

Although you have the leisure in outfitting a new home to plan most of your purchases, you often find yourself in an appliance store without warning. The refrigerator conks out at 9 P.M. and the next morning you're surrounded by display models and writing out a check.

When you can, obviously, it's a good idea to plan for a purchase. If the refrigerator repairman warns that the compressor is going, start then to ask opinions from your friends, write for booklets, keep a folder of ads, and browse in stores.

Before you go shopping for a new appliance, make a list of everything you want it to do, and when you're ready to buy, ask about the features one by one. Not too long ago, I didn't follow my own advice when I went out to buy a telephone/answering machine combination. I was sure it could do everything that my old machine could and more, assuming that manufacturers just kept adding more features to the ones already available. Which is why I came home with a machine with no HOLD button and no way to change the message from outside—

a fact I discovered two weeks after I'd thrown away the box.

One way to decide among a group of similar appliances is to find out the frequency with which each brand needs repairs. No matter what you're buying, always think about maintenance. Talk to the serviceman at a shop that handles all brands and check out *Consumer Reports* (subscribe to it, or check the library) for the lowdown. The magazine will also give you an exhaustive list of features.

Obviously, you won't always make choices that are based on what's practical—if people did that, no one would ever manufacture a white rug—but knowing that a medium color rug is easier to keep clean than either a very light or very dark one still gives you a lot of colors from which to choose. And knowing that textured linoleum or countertops trap dirt, or that high-gloss paint stands up to washing and is better for high-traffic areas, might be the factor that helps you decide between two choices that you find equally attractive. That's the kind of advice I've tried to include here. Before you leave the house with your wallet, I suggest you read it.

WHAT WARRANTIES WARRANT

Any major purchase—goods or services—should come with a warranty. Whether or not the warranty is worth anything is another matter. Remember, this warranty was written by the other side, so it is often full of exclusions. But it can't hurt and may help to fill out and send in the registration that puts your warranty in effect, if this is required.

A 30- or 60-day warranty in my opinion is fairly meaningless. Most things don't break down that soon unless they're completely defective to start with, in which case you can return them immediately. A lot of people are under the assumption that a warranty is based on use, but in fact it is based on time. The company doesn't care that you barely used the refrigerator in your vacation home. If the compressor goes during the second year, and you have a one-year warranty, you have a problem.

If you do have a problem that you think is covered by a warranty, contact the manufacturer before the term expires; the only thing more frustrating than having the rug stained in the last month of the fifth year of the five-year warranty is waiting to report the problem until the second month of the sixth year and being told the warranty has expired.

Know your rights. In the case of appliances, a full warranty means any problem must be remedied within a reasonable time and without charge (though limitations—such as food loss or floor damage—may be spelled out). If reasonable attempts to correct a problem fail, you may have your choice of a refund or replacement. A partial or limited warranty may guarantee parts but not labor. Since the labor is the bulk of any cost, that is where the warranty counts the most. The warranty from the manufacturer of roof shingles is worth a great deal less to you than the warranty of the roofer who installs them.

Even if a warranty has expired, if you have a problem call the company number or hot-line listed on it. Often you can find a technician who will give you some assistance.

If you don't send in the registration card you won't invalidate the warranty (see box, next page), but if you do send it in, the manufacturer will be able to notify you if there is any kind of defect or recall.

SERVICE CONTRACTS

You are usually offered a service contract when you buy any kind of appliance or electronic equipment. It's a kind of repair insurance that (unlike the warranty) costs extra. I feel it's less expensive to pay for service on an as-needed basis than to pay for a lot of service contracts. If you own a lot of appliances, as most people do, you may wind up paying service contracts on a dozen or more. The total cost is probably much more than a service call or two, and the odds are that not all of them are going to break down in the same year. My own rule of thumb is not to buy service contracts on items I think are less likely to need repair (like a refrigerator) but to purchase them for items with a shorter lifespan or more complex parts (like a video camera). What to do depends on how much of a gambler (or optimist) you are.

Like any contract written by the other party, the service contract may have one or more "buts" in it. It will pay but—only for labor, only for parts, only for selected parts, only for a certain number of repairs, only for repairs that are done on the premises, only with the addition of a service call charge. It also may overlap with certain guarantees on your warranty, so unless you can limit what it covers, you may be paying extra.

On the other hand, your warranty may be only short-lived, so the service contract is a necessary backup. Some contracts offer good deals, covering even routine maintenance, like cleaning the VCR heads. Ask how long you have to decide whether to take the contract, and take it home, if necessary, to read it. If it's no good but you've signed on the dotted line, you're stuck with it.

Also check out who you're buying the contract from. The store may be selling it to you, but it may be the manufacturer or a separate service operation that will be giving you the service. To find out if the manufacturer offers a service contract (one may be offered to you automatically when the warranty expires), look for the telephone number on the instruction booklet; if it's a big company, try 800 information (1-800-555-1212) to see if there's a toll-free line.

If you want some information about the separate service operation, you can check with the Better Business Bureau, to see if the company is stable—whether it is likely to be around for the term of your contract.

See if the contract is renewable and for how much, since the service will mean more to you as what you buy gets older. Finally, find out whether the contract is valid if you move or can be transferred if you sell the item to someone else.

DELIVERY

Along with death and taxes, the other thing you know for certain is that there will be delays and problems with anything that you spend a lot of money on. It definitely is to your advantage to make every effort humanly possible to be home when the purchases arrive or the work is done. Leave the house for a few minutes and you may come back to find a wall installed where it shouldn't be or the refrigerator door hanging the wrong way. (It's happened to me.) If you don't know what to do with yourself while hanging around and killing time, I have a suggestion: Read any instructions or warranties that may come with your purchase and ask questions of servicemen or installers if there's anything you don't understand.

Do not let the workmen or deliverymen leave the house without looking over the work or testing what they have delivered. (One way to keep them on the premises is to stall on signing the bill until this is done.) If it's totally unsatisfactory but the person who delivered it won't take it back, don't sign the receipt without noting the problem right on it. If the item is boxed and the delivery man can't hang around until you get it out, write on the slip that the approval is subject to inspection.

Why Read the Manual?

Read the manual. This is a piece of advice often given and seldom taken (including by myself). Although manuals often seem to be written by people for whom English is a second language (the English-speaking people, I figure, write the manuals for people in foreign countries), if you actually try to read them you may occasionally pick up a bit of information. Some people feel they understand intuitively how machinery works and refuse to read the manuals on principle. You frequently meet very nice people like this on line at the appliance repair center.

Even if you don't read the manual at first, at least take it out and look at it when you have a problem. Many manuals include troubleshooting suggestions that will save you a lot of time and money. Often the manual has advised that you perform some routine maintenance, such as vacuuming your refrigerator coils, and warned that if you do not, accumulated dust may cause the refrigerator to break down. Reading the manual might inspire you to get

out the vacuum before you request an unnecessary service call. A friend of mine called for help because of a mysterious odor, then found a drain button at the bottom of the refrigerator. She later discovered that the manual had said to remove and clean it regularly to prevent mildew.

TESTING THE NEW PURCHASE

Even though you may find this an awesome task, try every feature and control on your new appliance as soon as possible. Find a gadget-loving friend to do it if you can't face it yourself. Otherwise, you may be in the unpleasant situation of having the warranty expire before you discover that your self-cleaning oven doesn't clean. If something isn't working, tell the warrantor right away.

Pay attention to problems that are just starting. Chances are they will not cure themselves. If the motor on the refrigerator runs more often than it should or the water from your pipes is running a little rusty, something is wrong and it will need attention. Handling the problem early may prevent it from turning into an even bigger problem.

When You Need Service

Gas, electric, and/or oil suppliers generally have service departments that are quite helpful because one of their main functions is to generate goodwill among customers. But in most cases, you're on your own in locating good help.

If you buy a house, ask the previous owners to supply you with the names of recommended service people. If they forget, you may be able to get such a list from the real estate broker who sold you the house.

The instruction manual on appliances and electronics or your service warranty probably tells you to send the item for repair directly to the manufacturer and/or lists a manufacturer-owned product repair center or an authorized repair shop. If you have a service contract, you void the contract unless you have the item repaired at one of the authorized shops. If a personal visit to one of these repair centers isn't convenient and shipping it would be difficult, contact the shop where you bought the item to see if it will handle the shipping. I'm a big booster of local retailers. Even if they charge a little more than a large discount store, they'll often go out of the way to provide you with extra help, advice, and service.

The surest way to get a broken appliance to work is to show it to a repairman.

(One way to get around this: Make a video or tape recording of the problem.)

Otherwise, check the Yellow Pages to find authorized or independent repair shops. The mention of the manufacturer's name in an ad doesn't mean the service center is authorized. On the other hand, an unauthorized service center isn't necessarily unqualified. It may just not have applied for authorization.

ANTICIPATING REPAIR COSTS

When you call regarding a repair, here's what to ask:
- If the shop can repair your particular brand
- If there are charges for a diagnosis, an estimate, and/or a house call
- If the labor charge is by the hour or a flat rate
- If you will get an estimate of the total cost before the work begins
- If the repair is under warranty (for what and how long)

When you need something repaired always get an estimate. In fact, if possible get estimates from a couple of suppliers for both parts and labor. Get them in writing, together with a signed statement saying that if it appears that the job will exceed the estimate, you'll be notified in time to decide whether or not to go ahead with the work. If the work is free because the service center is making good on the warranty, have them write "no charge" on your receipt.

Get a receipt with the date and description of your product and a description of what will be done—in plain language and in handwriting you can read—along with the clerk's signature. You may have insurance (for, say, a broken car window) or a warrantee that will reimburse you for the work done, but if the receipt is illegible or incomprehensible, your claim may be jeopardized.

"Get it in writing" is a phrase you should take very seriously in all your dealings with both repairmen and contractors. And be specific. When I had some extensive carpentry work done, I discovered (much too late) that what I had in mind and what the contractor had in mind weren't the same. A wall cabinet that I thought would go clear up to the ceiling turned out to be quite a bit shorter. And while I thought I was getting a laminate covering on both counters and shelves below, he claimed that the word *laminate* on the order form referred to the countertops only.

WHEN THE SERVICEMAN COMES TO YOU

Check your manual, call the company hot line (often a technician can help you make a minor repair), and refer to the Fixing section about appliances troubleshooting —in other words, do everything you can before you pick up the phone to order a service call. If it appears to be inevitable, find out in advance what it will cost you.

A "diagnostic" or "trip" charge, which may seem to you the size of the down payment on a really nice weekend vacation, is only the beginning. It generally covers just the cost of the serviceperson's arrival at your home and a set amount of time—perhaps a half an hour—to diagnose the problem. It is especially painful to fork over money when the serviceperson spends only a minute determining that the reason your washing machine isn't working is that it isn't plugged in.

Correcting a real problem may jack up the cost considerably. Extra time charges are usually billed in 15-minute increments, though if the serviceperson is missing a part required for the repair and has to make a second trip to bring it, you may not be charged for the follow-up time.

Be there when the serviceperson arrives. If the folks in your house concentrate only on what's in the refrigerator and not what's wrong with it, don't count on them to describe the problem to the serviceperson.

This is also a valuable time for you to clarify anything that might not be clear to you about the operation and maintenance of your appliance or system. If you don't know where the shut-off valves are, or how to deal with a pilot light, now's the time to ask.

You can also deal with other minor problems that aren't worth a call by themselves. When the man came to check my refrigerator, I also asked him to see if he could figure out why the grill had fallen off (Was a part missing? and if so, could he replace it?) and to order a new shelf to replace one that had been damaged. Sometimes the serviceperson may even have the spare part with him.

REPAIR OR REPLACE?

Many household appliances are meant to last a long time and are worth the relatively small investment in repair. A new compressor for a refrigerator might cost $200. Replacing the whole refrigerator would cost at least three times that. But if the refrigerator is getting

close to retirement (it lasts about 16 years), it may not be worth fixing. Of course, some workhorse appliances, like some people, chug along way past retirement age.

ESTIMATED LIFE SPAN OF VARIOUS APPLIANCES	
Dryer	14
Washer	11
Freezer	15
Dishwasher	11
Hot water heater	10
Range	16
Refrigerator/Freezer	16
Sewing Machine	14
Toaster	15
Vacuum Cleaner	15

CHECKING THE WORK

Before you leave the shop or before the service person leaves your home, check that the appliance, or whatever was fixed, is working. I can pretty much guarantee that you will occasionally find that either the wrong thing was fixed or the thing was fixed wrong. Make sure the receipt describes what was done (in language you can read and understand) and gives the terms of the warranty or service contract.

● ●

BUYING APPLIANCES

The most important thing to keep in mind when buying an appliance is to make sure that whatever you get fits the space you are going to put it in. This seems obvious, but the smartest couple I know bought a refrigerator that had to be returned because it was one foot too big all around.

Measure all dimensions—width, height, and depth—and, if applicable, make a note of which way the door opens. (Some appliances have doors that can be reversed). Also, check your door and hallway clearances to make sure you can get the thing into the house. You can often find dimensions on the label, but it's a good idea to bring along a tape measure (as well as the room dimensions) when you go shopping. If you're replacing an older with a newer model, you also need to know if you have enough current for the appliance and an adequately grounded three-hole outlet.

You can get specification sheets from several manufacturers of models you are considering, or you can write to the Association of Home Appliance Manufacturers, 20 North Wacker Drive, Chicago, Illinois 60606, to get a listing of all available models of current appliances such as air conditioners, refrigerators, etc., together with size and energy cost.

Reading a use and care manual before you purchase an appliance gives you a lot of insight into what the equipment offers and how much trouble it will be to maintain. For the models on display, a dealer should have extra manuals.

To ensure that it is made safely, any electric appliance you buy should be Underwriters Laboratories (UL) listed. Gas appliances should be design-certified by the American Gas Association (AGA) and have a Blue Star Certified Seal on the rating plate.

HOT WATER HEATERS

The chart above gives guidelines only. If the family includes teenaged daughters, your shower needs will be greater than average, and if you have teenaged daughters with long hair, you'll be off the scale.

To calculate your needs, list each use that occurs during the hour of the day when your family uses the most hot water. The total is the capacity your hot water heater should supply. If you have a heater that's too small, you'll run short of hot water. One that's too large wastes fuel and will raise your costs unnecessarily. In

ESTIMATING YOUR HOT WATER NEEDS

Major Use of Hot Water	Estimated Gallons of Hot Water Per Use
Clothes washer (warm/cold rinse)	10–12
Shower	10–15
Bath	15–20
Automatic dishwasher	12–15
Hand dishwashing	4
Shaving	2
Hair shampoo	4
Food preparation	5
Hand and face washing	2

SOURCE: AMERICAN GAS ASSOCIATION

any case, a separate hot water heater makes more economic sense than a system that heats both hot water and the house.

Most hot water heaters hold between 20 and 50 gallons, but you can also get a small 30-gallon "low boy," which can be installed neatly into cabinets, or tankless/instantaneous heaters that come in different sizes—from models that are small enough for one sink tap to larger ones that replace conventional heaters.

In most systems, vents carry gases from the water heater up and outside through flues in the roof or chimney. New water heaters can vent directly through the wall from the heater so the installation can be a lot more flexible.

REFRIGERATORS

The most important consideration in buying a refrigerator is storage capacity. Although you may be of the too-much-is-never-enough school, powering a large refrigerator is a fuel- and money-waster if all that's inside are a couple of ice cube trays and cartons of leftover takeout. On the other hand, if your refrigerator is always packed full, it should be big enough to provide enough air circulation or it will drive up your operating costs unnecessarily. The size is measured in cubic feet. As a rule of thumb, some people figure on 12 cubic feet (cf) for the first two people in the family plus 2 cf for each additional family member. I can warn you that the manufacturer's estimates of usable space that you see on the tag tend to be overly optimistic, so buy accordingly.

Install the refrigerator so that the door opens in such a way that it allows access to the counter. You need at least 18 inches of counter space for loading and unloading. If you ever plan to move, look for a refrigerator with interchangeable door hinges (in the next house, the fridge might open from a different side) and/or interchangeable door panels so you can change colors.

Years ago, all refrigerators had to be manually defrosted. This involves turning the refrigerator to "Off" or "Defrost" and waiting for accumulated ice to melt, all the while forcing yourself to resist the urge to chip away at it with a knife, icepick, or other tool that may result in serious damage either to what is being defrosted (the refrigerator) or the defroster (you). (Less dangerous ways to speed things up are described in the part of this book that covers cleaning the kitchen.)

Today, some models are partially automatic—which means that the refrigerator defrosts automatically but the freezer section does not—but most refrigerator-freezers are completely automatic.

Although manual defrost is an inconvenience, it is also a terrific energy saver, as you will note if you compare the yellow Energy Guide labels on the doors of the display models. (The label gives you an approximate idea of the electric costs of running the unit for a year.) On the other hand, if ice accumulates to more than $1/4$ inch on a manual defrost, the unit uses extra energy because it must work harder.

Most of the smaller single-door refrigera-tors, which range from 1.6 cf for table models to 17.5 cf at the larger end, are manual defrost. They often have what is referred to as a "freezer section" or "freezer compartment." Those words are a tipoff that the refrigerator will keep ice cubes frozen and may store frozen vegetables (which freeze at 29° to 31° F.) and meat (25° to 29° F.) but does not have a cold enough temperature (8° F. or lower) to keep ice cream or frozen juice concentrate hard. For that you need a "food freezer" or "frozen food storage compartment" that is found in many combination refrigerator-freezers, with the freezer section on top of, under, or alongside the refrigerator.

I personally hate the freezer on the bottom. You lose a lot of energy each time you open it, but more important to me, everything seems to get jumbled up. Some people prefer it because putting the freezer at the bottom means that more fresh food is at eye level.

Never assume that the freezer door is as cold as the interior. Many freezers don't keep temperatures uniform.

If you need the food storage space, and have the room and budget, side-by-side models (freezer on one side, refrigerator on the other, storage capacity of 19.0 to 28.8 cf) are most convenient.

Other options include automatic ice makers (very useful, especially if you entertain a lot), an exterior ice and/or water dispenser (somewhat useful), and special storage area with adjustable controls (don't you have enough controls in your life already?).

With refrigerators, as with everything else you buy, consider the amount of cleaning required. Darker appliances and dark glass doors show more dirt and fingerprints, and textured finishes collect grime and are harder to clean. Glass shelves need more wiping than wire racks. Features that speed up cleanup include removable shelves and drawers—you can take them out to clean them when there's a spill— and casters so you can move the whole unit out to clean behind it. Coils at the back are easier to clean than coils underneath.

Door shelves should be deep enough to hold large containers, and the retainer bars should be sturdy. In some cases, refrigerators are almost all badly designed: Though egg storage is usually on the door, eggs should be held at a higher temperature. And while the crisper should be near-freezing temperature, in most refrigerators it isn't.

Combination refrigerator-freezers should not be in unheated areas or near a heat source (heat vent, oven, even direct sun). The unit should have enough room around it so that the heat it produces can escape and opening the doors or cleaning behind it is no problem.

The whole unit should be level (or it will make a lot of noise) and on a floor that can support it, for obvious reasons.

FREEZERS

A separate freezer is very convenient if you can't shop often, entertain a lot, and grow a lot of zucchini, but it's a big energy eater. One way to cut energy costs is to keep it full. If you don't have a lot of food stored in it, fill large containers with water and put them inside. Though manual defrost freezers may be operated in unheated areas with no problem (check the manual to be sure), like combination refrigerator-freezers, separate freezers with automatic defrost systems are sensitive to the temperature around them. If you plan to keep one in an unheated garage or other unheated space where the temperature will fall below 55° or 60° F., buy a model specifically designed for operation in low temperatures. Otherwise, the compressor activity decreases. Below 42° F., it may shut down completely and the food may defrost and spoil.

Almost all chest-style freezers have to be manually defrosted, but upright freezers may do the job automatically. Three popular freezer sizes are 5, 12, and 15 cubic feet. There's a rule of thumb about 3 to 4 cf of freezer room per person, but obviously this varies depending on how often you get to the market and the size of your family's appetites.

Look for adjustable shelves, casters, a drain for easier manual defrosting, and a safety light that warns of a power failure.

RANGES AND OVENS

Drop-in or slide-in ranges aren't finished on the sides. Freestanding ranges are. Built-ins have a separate cooktop or oven.

CAUTION: Freestanding kitchen ranges or improperly installed built-ins can tip over if someone puts too much pressure on an open door. They should be fitted with anti-tip devices.

There are those who swear by gas stoves and those who wouldn't be without an electric stove. Gas stove fans say they give you heat immediately and you can control it more subtly. Electric stove people like the absence of carbon pollution. If you compare pots from a gas stove house and from an electric stove house, you'll find that the latter look a lot cleaner. But electric ranges cost more to operate and to buy.

To ignite the gas for old-style ranges and ovens, appliances had pilot lights—eternal flames that ensured that even if the power went out, your stove was still working. But to conserve fuel, new stoves use electronic ignition. A minispark created by electricity ignites the gas and makes the clicking sound that you hear when you turn the stove on and continue to hear until you set the flame to the proper intensity. Gas stoves come with either conventional burners or, in newer models, with sealed-up designs that are easier to clean.

Electric units come in a variety of models. The advantages of solid **discs of cast iron** sealed to the cooktop are very even heat and the fact that boil-overs can't flow into them. **Glass ceramic tops** have a nice-looking surface but take a little longer to heat, cool slowly, and stain fairly easily. Some models can hold more than four pots at a time. On these newer range tops, since there are no flames or standard burners, a heat-warning feature should let you know when it's safe to touch the surface.

Induction cooktops (also **glasstops**) get their heat from magnetic energy. They offer instant heating and cool-down, stay cool except directly under the heating utensil, are stain-resistant, and have no burners to clean. However, they're not good for fast, very hot cooking, and you can use only stainless steel, carbon steel, or cast-iron cookware.

Halogen cooktops, which cook with light, are brand-new and seem to cook very cleanly.

A **range hood** and **fan filter** over the stove prevent greasy walls and curtains, and the time saved in cleanup justifies the expense of this feature.

New **down-draft gas cooktop units** eliminate the need for a vent and are designed for a stove that's in a kitchen island. But they're noisy and not always effective. The large fans can also create a vacuum-type situation that could cause non-vented chimneys to reverse direction, which could be dangerous.

If your stove comes with removable burners, check that they lift out for easy cleaning. Pull-off knobs are easier to keep clean than buttons. Knobs on top rather than on front are safer if there are children in the house.

Top-of-the-line gas or electric ranges may come with permanent or modular grills, griddles, and other special cooking surfaces. Check how easy these are to clean and how easy they are to change—and be realistic about whether you'll actually bother to use them before you buy.

If you do a lot of complicated cooking or large-scale entertaining, you may want a restaurant-type, six-burner 40-inch range.

Some ranges are manufactured to use either natural or LP (liquid propane, or bottled) gas, but most are adjusted for natural gas when they leave the factory. Every gas range has a nameplate that indicates the type of gas to use and the type for which it was adjusted for initial use. To find the nameplate, you either lift the top, remove an accessory panel, or open a door or drawer. Have the salesperson find the nameplate or tell you what type of gas to use if you are not sure.

The oven may or may not be attached to the cooktop. I like wall ovens separate from cooktops myself, since they allow you to bake and broil at a far more comfortable height than a regular range.

Modern **self-cleaning** ovens have a separate cleaning cycle that burns up spills and grease splatters at high temperatures, but you may have to sacrifice cooking space for this feature. A **continuous cleaning oven** has a special coating that works as it goes—when you've got something baking in the oven, the cleaning process is working. This system keeps the dirt to a minimum, though spills should be wiped up. But—and this is a big but—the wall coating of continuous cleaning ovens may dissipate or not do as good a job as promised. Also, the broilers may be less conveniently located beneath the oven. New glass-ceramic walls now in the works should make oven cleaning even easier.

The major disadvantage of self-cleaning ovens is that they're expensive to operate and may produce pollutants. If you buy one, get a model that's vented.

An **electric oven** is preferable to a **gas oven** because it holds an even temperature and doesn't dry out food. Also, the broiler is inside the oven, not underneath it.

A **convection oven**, which cooks foods faster and at lower temperatures—heat is continually recirculated through the oven by a power-driven fan—saves both time and energy. You'll have to adjust your recipes to make them come out right and learn some of the special tricks of working with this kind of heat, such as putting a bowl of water in the oven so some baked goods don't dry out.

There are two schools of thought about the optional glass window in the oven door. On the one hand, it gets dirty immediately and is a pain to clean. On the other hand, if it keeps you from continually checking the oven, which loses as much as 50 degrees each time you open it, it's a big energy saver.

Having a pair of ovens—side by side or one on top of the other—is extremely handy, but if you haven't got the room, see if you can get an extra-wide oven. With even an inch or two more than the usual 19 to 20 you may be able to squeeze some of your pans in side by side.

MICROWAVE OVENS

Most people do not cook in microwaves. They use them to make popcorn, heat coffee, and bake potatoes. If that's what you have in mind, maybe you should save your money.

But if you've got a family where everyone is on different schedules, a microwave is an unbeatable way to serve everyone a hot meal in a hurry.

A microwave oven is powered by household electricity. Inside is a vacuum tube that converts electric energy into the form of microwaves. They bounce off the interior metal surface and pass through most plastics, glass, or paper, which stay cool. But they make the molecules in food vibrate and rub against each other. The friction causes heat, which cooks the food.

Since microwaves penetrate only from $1/4$ inch to 2 inches into the food, the center of food doesn't cook until the heat from outside is conducted inward, mainly during standing time. (Which is why, no matter how rushed, you shouldn't eliminate the standing time.) Generally, a cookbook comes with the microwave that tells you how to gauge cooking time and position the food so it is cooked properly.

Microwave cooking doesn't heat the room because outside the container, microwaves spread out and their energy diminishes, like heat leaving a match. Microwaves one inch from an energy source have 100 times the power that they have at 10 inches.

People who don't absolutely love them tend to mistrust microwaves, but manufacturers insist that they are safe, that ordinary X-rays have more than a million times as much energy as microwaves. Take care to follow instructions, have it repaired if there is any problem, and clean it as the manufacturer recommends (especially the door seal).

I made the mistake of buying a microwave that was supposed to microwave and also toast, broil, and bake. It did all of them equally badly—even the microwaving, since it turned out to be a low-wattage oven. The whole point of a microwave is speed, so I'd recommend buying the highest-powered (highest-wattage) one you can find. Also make sure it's big enough to hold any casserole dish you'll be using routinely.

A turntable inside the microwave takes up valuable room, but since rotating the dish while it cooks is a good way to ensure even cooking, it's worth the sacrifice.

There are microwaves designed to fit over a gas range, under a cabinet, or on the counter. If you have children, they're going to want to use it, so put it wherever it's most accessible and safest—or they may tip it over or fall trying to reach it over the stove—and make sure they know the dangers. (For example, the jelly inside jelly doughnuts can become scalding hot while the pastry around it is just warm.)

DISHWASHERS

Portable dishwashers that hook up to the faucet might be worth considering if you move around a lot, but built-ins are conveniently out of the way. There are very compact models that can be built in even under the sink.

Most machines use between 9 and 13 gallons of water per cycle, but the more washing levels (water sources) and spray holes in the machine, the better the cleaning job. Also, look for models with a lot of storage room. The machine should ideally hold a service for twelve. Some models have a fold-down rack for extra glassware.

A stainless steel interior lasts longest, and solid plastic is second best. Porcelain is not very durable.

By law, new dishwashers have a power saver option to let you dry dishes without heat (though sometimes a fan is involved). While it's a slower process, if you're doing only one load a day, it makes sense.

A delay start option allows you to set the machine to operate when hot water or energy is more plentiful and cheaper. However, manufacturers advise you not to turn on the dishwasher and then go to sleep or leave the house. People tend to ignore the advice until after the first flood.

In the summer, when you're using a lot of cups and glasses, a rapid cycle option can be helpful. A pre-rinse setting prevents food from caking: everything is rinsed, then held for a later, large wash. But a two-cycle machine (normal and heavy) is sufficient. Incidentally, a heavy cycle doesn't wash dishes more thoroughly. It just washes them longer. The same is true of a pot-scrubber cycle, which promises more than it delivers. If badly soiled, pots will need hand washing.

All machines require that you scrape away large particles, and your care manual will probably warn you about certain foods that may cause problems, but as a general rule, little rinsing and no washing is required before you put dishes in the dishwasher. I would like to go down in history as the person who breaks the national habit of pre-washing. It wastes water and your time.

If your water heater is heating all the house water to 140° F. for the sake of the dishwasher—nowhere else in the house do you need water this hot—check out the new models that have internal hot water heaters. You can set the house water to 120° F., and the heater boosts the water supply for the dishwasher up to 140° F.

Putting the dishwasher next to the refrigerator strains the refrigerator, since the dishwasher gives off so much heat. Install insulation with at least an R-12 rating between the two appliances.

I don't mind getting into a little hot water now and then. At least it gets you clean.

GARBAGE DISPOSALS

Banana peels, corn hulks or silks, and celery give a garbage disposal indigestion, but it can handle most other foods.

There are three parts to a garbage disposal system: the grinding chamber into which you pour the food, a shredder plate with an attached motor at the bottom, and a grinder ring around the edge. Water carries the food particles to the sewer or to the septic system. (Yes, you can use a garbage disposal with a septic system. About 20% of users do.)

In a batch feed system, the motor doesn't start until a stopper is placed in the opening, so it's the safest. But machines of this type are hard to find and cost more than continuous feed machines that operate with running water at the flick of a wall switch.

Horsepower is the best gauge of durability. A top-quality machine is rated 1 hp, a low-quality $1/3$ hp. Most are in the $1/2$ to $3/4$ hp range. A larger motor isn't necessarily faster, it just doesn't work as hard—so a $3/4$ hp model may last as much as 3 to 4 times longer than a $1/2$ hp model.

Other features that help prolong the life of the machine are an automatic reverse motor, an anti-jam mechanism, an overload protector, and a detergent shield that protects the motor from caustic cleaners.

Machines with stainless steel parts will last longer than machines made of carbon steel or aluminum, which may rust or corrode.

A quieter machine is probably better balanced, which means less wear on the motor. But none is noiseless. Have the disposal installed with a cushioned mounting bracket to reduce the noise a little.

Some disposals have a do-it-yourself repair feature—a wrench that you can use under the sink to turn the shaft when something has jammed it. This helps keep the service calls down.

TRASH COMPACTORS

Some people install a trash compactor in the kitchen, but if you use it for everything including wet garbage and aren't careful about washing out cans and bottles, it doesn't smell so great. I think a better place is the garage.

I wish I had something that would work on my body as efficiently as these things can work on trash. However, though I like the concept I have mixed feelings about these machines. Since they interfere with the natural breakdown of waste, compactors can add to the global waste disposal problem.

AUTOMATIC WASHING MACHINES

Though there are a number of different brands, there are only about a half-dozen companies that actually manufacture washing machines so, as you might guess, the differences among them don't mean much. Most are 27 inches wide (though some special models are stackable, together with a dryer, and some hook up to your sink).

If you're buying stackable machines, or all-in-one washer-dryers for a small apartment, check the power needs. Some operate on 120 volts, but some need 220, and running a line where there is none can cost thousands. (One alternative is a gas-powered unit). You also need outside venting unless you buy a European machine with a condenser dryer.

Small machine stackables with an 8-pound capacity may take a long time to dry clothes.

Some machines claim to have "extra large" capacity, but the people who gauge this seem to be the same people who think one size fits all. To really qualify as extra large, the washer should hold $12^1/_2$ pounds. The typical machine holds 8 to 10 pounds.

While front-loaders use only half the water, they're more expensive and don't hold as much as the more common top loaders. For a few extra dollars, you can get a two-speed model. The extra speed is slower, for washing delicates.

There are other options (including different finishes) on more expensive models, but with the exception of water levels that help you conserve water for smaller loads, you can do without them and without the electronic settings. Extra temperature setting options let you choose a warm rinse, which is unnecessary because all fabrics should be rinsed in cold water. (See washing temperatures in the Washing and Wearing section.) And while a fancy machine lets you dial a prewash or soak setting, setting the dial appropriately on any machine can give you the same results. Cold and warm water settings vary, depending on how your water heater is set, so some fancier washing machines have sensors that ensure the water is at about 80° F. for cold washes and 110° F. for warm, but I don't think this is particularly useful. Do check how much detergent and water the machine uses, especially if you're in a metered area.

Obviously, the more you wash, the sooner your machine—and possibly you as well—will break down. Machines that do eight or more loads a week need repairs about 25% of the time, and those that do four or less need repairs about 14% of the time, according to a recent *Consumer Reports* survey. I think we all do too much wash.

AUTOMATIC DRYERS

A dryer is usually twinned in size to the washing machine, anywhere from 27 to 31 inches wide and 43 inches high.

Electric dryers generally require a 240-volt circuit. The 120-volt models take much longer to dry the same load.

Most people have gas dryers. These don't have Energy Guide labels to show you how much it costs to run them, but there are four features that can keep energy costs down.

One is **pilotless ignition**, which means the dryer ignites electronically rather than having a pilot light burning all the time. To get the

initial spark, you must have the dryer plugged into an electric outlet. The other energy-saving features are optional: **electronic sensors** in the dryer drum that "feel" the moisture and stop the dryer when garments are at the selected level of dryness; a **diagonal airflow** pattern that allows faster drying at lower temperatures; and a polymer-coated **drum seal** made of 100% wool that keeps hot air inside the drum.

Other features are a matter of convenience:

Temperature control: All machines give you some choice of temperature settings, from "High" (for towels and heavy clothes), to "Medium" (for permanent press), to "Low" (for sheers and heat-sensitive fabrics), plus "Air Only," which dries without heat. This feature is useful with a lot of the newer fabrics, which are easily scorched, and to dust certain items like drapes and children's stuffed animals, which I often suggest in the Cleaning section of this book.

Temperature auto-dry: You choose the fabric setting and degree of dryness. When the thermostat in the exhaust senses the proper temperature, the dryer stops. If the load is made of similar items, this works perfectly, but if you've got a heavy terrycloth robe in there with a polyester nightgown, you may wind up with a nightgown that's ready to wear and a robe that could damp-mop the floor.

Moisture-sensing automatic control: Very sophisticated. Machine "feels" the clothes for moisture and automatically shuts off when they're properly dry. When the load is mixed, this may not always work perfectly.

Since one of the biggest problems with machine-dried clothes is when they get "overdried" and wrinkle, a machine with an **end-of-cycle signal** so you can remove items promptly makes sense to me. So does a **cool-down option** that tumbles clothes without heat at the end of the cycle.

If the inside of the drum rusts, you will have problems with the dryer. See if the finish is

---

WHEN YOU HAVE YOUR WASHER-DRYER INSTALLED

If the washer's on the right the dryer door should open to the left (and vice versa). Some doors open a full 180 degrees so they are accessible from either direction.

The straighter and shorter the venting duct the better, since it's less likely to clog up with lint. Check outside from time to time to make sure the vent lid opens and closes easily. If the lid remains open, it will let drafts in and heat out.

The dryer should be perfectly level or the movement of the drum may make the dryer move and stress the gas connections.

Keep the dryer in a warm area, since drying time is longer in unheated garages or utility rooms.

Install it on a foot-high platform and you won't have to bend to lift the clothes out. Use the space underneath to store cleaning supplies, etc.

under warranty. Also check whether both the cabinet and legs have been rust-proofed.

WATER SOFTENERS

If you have hard water (explained in the section Washing and Wearing), you'll have a variety of problems—soap deposits on your appliances, dull laundry, spots on dishes, and scale on your pipes and fixtures. To eliminate the calcium and magnesium, you'll need a water softener: water flows through a tank filled with synthetic resins that attract the "hard" components. Periodically the resins have to be regenerated by a flow of salt water (which is later flushed down the drain).

The first thing to check is how easy the softener is to refill. And if you're in a metered water situation (or you're simply concerned about wasting water), find out how much water the softener uses in regenerating the resin.

The simplest, cheapest timer-only units work on a fixed schedule but are less efficient than demand-control units. Pick one with the fewest dials!

IRONS

New irons come with a dry heat setting, a steam setting, and (in most cases) a steam-spray, to shoot out a jet of steam to dampen clothes like linens that wrinkle a lot and are hard to iron. My ideal iron would also be able to steam milk for cappuccino, but so far I haven't come across it.

Because sometimes you are offered what is called "gray market goods," which are items made in other countries that don't meet U.S. standards in one way or another, check to see that the iron, like all other appliances you buy, has an UL (Underwriters Laboratories, Inc.) seal to guarantee its safety.

Pick up the iron to see if it is comfortable to hold. I bought a cordless model that seemed practical but turned out to be so awkward to

handle that I eventually returned it.

The best steam irons have the most holes to let the steam through. Older models would clog unless you filled them with distilled water, but new ones can be filled right from the tap, although they may still clog unless they are emptied after each use. Always unplug the iron before you fill it and before you empty it.

If there is a cord on the iron, it should be out of the way, and the heel rest should be stable so that the iron is less likely to tip over. Other safety features include warning bells and other devices that alert you to the fact that you've left the iron plate-side down for too long and automatic shutoffs that turn off the power, which are great if you forget to turn off the iron before leaving the house.

If you iron only in the most extreme circumstances (pressing clothes for a job interview, for example), a relatively inexpensive and compact travel iron may be all that you need. Look for the largest one you can find, to make the work go faster. Because they're lightweight, you'll have to press down harder than with a conventional iron, but I think it's unlikely that anyone will wind up with tennis elbow from this chore.

IRONING BOARDS

I have an immaculate friend who leaves her ironing board permanently ready in her bedroom; I suggested she either have it upholstered in a fabric that blends with her decor or buy one of the fold-out boards that hangs over a door or stows away in its own closet, which I think is the ideal solution. These used to be expensive but I now see low-priced knockoffs in the hardware store. If you do little ironing, this is a perfect solution.

If for some reason you own or are buying a conventional board, hang it conveniently on one of the over-the-door holder caddies which also holds the iron and has room for a can of spray starch.

The difference between an expensive and inexpensive ironing board is just a matter of balance, although you can buy very high-priced boards with optional features such as a collapsible hanging rack.

You will also need an ironing board cover (of silicone fabric, usually) and clips that fit underneath the board to hold the ironing board cover in place. Without them, it keeps sliding around. Regular fabric covers scorch, but I know some home sewers who use checkerboard or gingham-patterned fabric so they can measure or iron a straight line. They just replace the fabric when it's burned or torn.

Foam pads that you put over your ironing board cover speed up ironing tremendously, but I've never seen them on sale anywhere but at state fairs and home shows.

If you iron very infrequently, you can rig up an arrangement on the dining room table. (Use padding, such as a mattress pad or blanket, and top it with a sheet; otherwise, you may scorch the garment as well as the surface of the table below.) There is something called a sleeve board, which perfectionists use to avoid making crease marks when they iron sleeves.

AIR CONDITIONERS

Here is one case where size really counts. Buy an air conditioner that's too small and you'll still have the hots. Buy one that's too big and you'll think you've got a fever because the room will be humid, the air chilly and clammy. Measurements of air conditioning capacity are in BTUs. If you want to gauge how much you need extremely scientifically, send $2 to the Home Appliance Manufacturers, 20 North Wacker Drive, Chicago, Illinois 60606, and ask for the current AHAM Consumer Selection Guide for Room Air Conditioners. You will get a very long form that the scientifically inclined will no doubt find fascinating.

Personally, I collect the following information: room dimensions; number of outside walls and direction in which they face; number, size, and type of windows; type of room (bedroom, kitchen)—then I bring it to two different stores. I let them both calculate the size conditioner they feel I need, and if they come up with the same number, I figure it's okay.

The Energy Guide label on an air conditioner helps you estimate the running cost based on an EER (Energy Efficiency Rating). The higher it is, the more energy-efficient the machine. On the label, you'll also see the unit's cooling capacity and how it compares in cooling efficiency to models of a similar size. There is also a cost grid on the label that will help you estimate the annual cost of running the air conditioner.

Some run on 115 volts but need their own circuit and others require their own 230 volt circuit. If you're not sure what you've got, check with a licensed electrician and have the necessary work done.

The filter should be changed as recommended or cleaned every two to four weeks, especially if you live in a dirty city or have a lot of allergies, so make sure it's easily accessible.

DEHUMIDIFIERS

Dehumidifiers take in and cool air so the moisture "rains" out. They collect from 10 to 40 pints a day. The rule of thumb is that the capacity should be about 10 pints per 100 square feet.

Some machines turn themselves off when the water collection unit is removed. (Otherwise, you have to remember to do this job.) Some can be drained directly into a sink or floor drain.

VACUUM CLEANERS

If you have a lot of carpeting, you need an upright vacuum cleaner with a revolving brush, beater bar, and strong suction. You may need a shag adjustment (or attachment) and a special shag rake to stir the pile up again. Since uprights depend on the beater brush to clean the rug rather than on strong suction, they're not always suitable for bare floor cleaning.

It's useful for an upright to have a height adjustment setting for different carpet piles and a caddy that holds additional tools like an upholstery brush, a small round brush, and a crevice tool, a long and flat piece meant to get into corners. If you can adjust the brush for the pile (so there's no drag) and the wheels are powered, an upright is easier to push.

If you have mostly bare floors, choose a round or tank-shaped canister vacuum, which usually has superior suction power.

A canister should be compact, have swivel canisters and large wheels that make it easy to roll, and should come with attachments for both floor and rugs, crevices, and fabrics. It also should have an easy locking system to put the pieces together—the kind that clicks when the pieces are in place—rather than a system that depends on friction. Those sometimes get stuck, and I know you have better things to do than stand around trying to separate your vacuum cleaner parts.

If you have both carpeting and bare floors, you need a good all-purpose machine—a canister with a power nozzle attachment that has an agitator that beats the deep dirt and dust out of the carpeting. Some power nozzles can alternate between cleaning a carpet (with a brush) and a hard floor (no brush) with a flip of the switch.

A canister with a power nozzle should have all the features of a regular canister plus a rotating brush and bar (for rugs and even upholstery), and a two-speed motor (one for rugs).

In all models, look for a dustbag that's big (so it won't need frequent changing) and easy to remove and replace, a rubber bumper to protect furniture, and a quiet motor. A well-designed model will get close to the wall and will be low enough to go under the lowest furniture.

Variable suction is a good optional feature. Otherwise, when you're trying to dust lightweight items like sheer curtains, they get pulled into the machine. You usually just open a vent to vary the suction, although some models have variable speed motors.

Another good option in a vacuum is the capacity to blow out as well as sucking in. This comes in handy for cleaning in narrow areas and for unblocking the hose. Some have a lip with a metal piece designed to pick up metal items without sucking them into the bag.

Mistakes to avoid: I bought a brand once that wasn't widely available. It was a good machine, but I had trouble getting service and supplies. Also: Remember that a spacecraft-sized vacuum cleaner is not necessary in a small apartment.

The ideal, of course, is a central (built-in) system: quiet, with no equipment to carry. Tubing runs from the motor and dust receptacle (which may be in the garage, basement, etc.) to outlets all over the house, and you connect a light hose wherever you want to work. You can easily put central vacuuming in a house you're building from scratch, but it may not be possible to install in an existing home. It usually comes with an accessory package that includes tools for cleaning the floor and other surfaces plus a power nozzle for deep carpet cleaning. Be sure to get one with a powerful motor so the suction is strong enough.

An indoor-outdoor vacuum (or a wet-dry vacuum) can suck up spills, dirty rinse water, accidents, floods, plugged drains. If you buy a wet-dry vacuum, get a 5-gallon capacity stainless steel or plastic tank.

In 1992 Bissell came out with a home steam extraction machine called the Big Green Machine that has all the features of a wet-dry vac and can also spot-clean as well as deep-clean your upholstery, mattress, and stuffed animals. Not only were these people clever enough to have produced a unique product, they also had the good judgment to ask me to promote it.

Since it's the only one of its type and I thought it was revolutionary, I agreed.

The cleaning solution, which is in one compartment, is injected under pressure. Then dirty water containing the excess solution and loosened soil is extracted into another compartment so the item is thoroughly cleaned but won't be mildewed or soggy. If you've run into the problem of having a stain reappear no matter how many times you clean it, it's because it's soaked down in the bottom of the fiber and only an extraction machine can take it out. Professionals use a similar process, but (a) I think you'll probably do a more careful and thorough job yourself; and (b) most important, you wouldn't call them in to handle just one or two spots. If you have carpet or upholstery in the house, I really believe this machine is a great help.

FLOOR MACHINES
(POLISHER-BUFFER/SCRUBBER/SHAMPOOER)

A floor machine is a one-man band. It can shampoo rugs, scrub, spread wax on, and buff (polish) hard floors. Polishers can be rented if you're doing your floors only once a year, but if you have a lot of hardwood and resilient floors, this machine might be worth investing in. Though a sealed-surface (polyurethane-type) floor usually needs only a damp mopping, if it's very dirty a floor machine can be used on it as well.

As shampooers, these sometimes can be a little hard on the rug, so if possible rent a model to see if it causes pilling.

Find out how hard or easy it is to convert the machine from shampooer to polisher before you buy. If the process is complicated, you won't want to do it.

I don't think a floor machine is a good substitute for a wax applicator, even if it has a dispenser for both sudsy water and wax. Solvent-based waxes, which you need on wood and other types of floors, tend to clog up the works. Use a manual wax applicator for applying wax and reserve this machine for buffing.

HAND-HELD VACUUMS

One of the greatest gadgets invented in recent years, these are wonderful for small pickup jobs.

Compared to the cordless models, plug-in minivacuums have the edge. They are more powerful (particularly if they come with revolving brushes), don't run out of power in ten minutes, sometimes come with extender wands, and are much better for cleaning the car. However, the cordless models can fit into tight spaces, and because they store neatly on the wall, they're handy to use.

Wet-dry minivacs can handle spills (though you need to wipe dry the remaining moisture), but they aren't as effective as vacuums.

Make sure to mount the cordless models in a safe, convenient place. It shouldn't be near water or near heat (as I found out when one of mine melted away).

TELEPHONES

I didn't want to get into electronics here—the whole CD/stereo/VCR/TV thing is much too complicated—but I thought it might be helpful to list optional features on telephones for you to mull over. They include:

• Automatic redial that redials the last number. Teenagers attempting to buy tickets to rock concerts or phone radio disc jockeys love this one.

• Memory or speed dialing that lets you program frequently used numbers so they can be dialed with one key. While this feature is helpful for very young children (you can use picture symbols as a key to help them dial), I think as soon as they are able, and as a safety precaution, they should be encouraged to memorize useful numbers rather than rely on memory. They won't always be calling from home.

• "Speakers," that allow you to talk into the phone without lifting the handpiece. You always sound as if you're calling from the bottom of a well. Nice, however, if the whole family wants to sing "Happy Birthday" to Grandma across the continent.

• Amplifiers, to increase volume. Good for the elderly.

• Home security system. Ties into alarm system.

• Hold button, that allows you to put the handpiece back in the cradle and pick up the call from another extension.

An answering machine, which can be built into the phone unit or function separately, also has many options, of which these tend to be most useful:

• Double microcassette. Lets you record incoming messages on one, outgoing on the other. Retrieving messages is faster. Some have a chip system for outgoing messages, a cassette for incoming. Serves the same purpose.

• Remote operation. Pick up calls from outside by just dialing your home number and punching in a code. Ideally, this includes the full range of features, such as retrieving your messages, fast forwarding, rewind, and changing your message from outside (very useful when you're trying to meet someone for an appointment outside the house).

• Disconnect from another extension. So that when you pick up the phone the machine doesn't continue to play your message and then go on to record the conversation.

• Remote "On" operation. If you forgot to turn the machine on before you left the house, you can dial in and activate it.

You can lease a phone, but over the long run, you'll be paying much more. Sometimes the place where you buy the phone will give you a loaner while yours is being repaired.

WHAT'S UNDERFOOT: CARPETS AND FLOORING

If you move into a rental apartment that comes carpeted, it will generally be covered in a neutral shade. You can make the place reflect your taste by putting area rugs on top. They won't need any padding, and they'll also protect the carpeting from damage that you might otherwise pay for at the end of your lease.

But if you own your home or apartment, carpeting and/or flooring is your responsibility. Floor coverings are the biggest purchase you will make, both in terms of size and cost.

So it's pretty depressing to consider the fact that it's also the purchase most subject to stains and other damage. The history of many families can be written in the carpeting—different spots representing the year Fido was a pup, the summer Junior was learning to drink from a glass, the New Year's Eve of the Great Sangria Party.

Wood and other floor surfaces can also show signs of stains and wear after years of spills, drips, scuffs, and the occasional skateboard run.

Though I'm going to tell you how to cope with most of these disasters in the Cleaning section of the book—or how to protect the floor so they will do as little damage as possible—you'll have fewer problems if you buy the most maintenance-free carpeting and flooring that suits your taste.

The least you need to know about rugs and carpeting:

• Types of soft carpeting, judging quality, and cutting costs

• Rug and mat alternatives to broadloom carpeting

Broadloom Carpeting

I always used the words *rug* and *carpet* interchangeably, but my friend Harold the carpet expert set me straight. Carpeting is wall-to-wall coverage. Rugs are not. They are either pieces of carpet that have been cut and bound along the edges or made individually in a variety of shapes, sizes, and designs. (The so-called "flying carpet" should, technically speaking, be called a "flying rug.")

The obvious advantage of soft flooring—which includes both carpets and rugs—is that it feels good. It also keeps the room warm, absorbs sound, and cushions the blow when you drop a vase or someone trips.

The main disadvantage of carpeting compared to other floor coverings used to be that it was not only expensive but also easily destroyed. In recent years, both those problems have been minimized.

Carpeting is woven on looms 9, 12, or 15 feet wide (which is why it is sometimes called broadloom). Thanks to a post–World War II invention called tufting (which is now used in about 85% of manufacturing), carpet makers can produce 6 to 8 thousand square yards a day, compared to about two hundred square yards the old-fashioned way. While manufacturers aren't giving carpeting away, the prices have come way down relative to the price of other goods.

And within the past few years, stain-protecting techniques have been enormously improved. Spills that once meant curtains for carpets can now often be wiped away.

On the other hand, carpeting is still a major expense and far from indestructible, so get a good night's sleep before you go shopping for it and stay off any medications that may affect your judgment in the carpet showroom. Otherwise you may wind up like my cousin, who bought pale rose carpeting for the family room. She must somehow have forgotten that her family room also happens to be the only passageway between her outdoor pool and the bathroom. The carpeting looked lovely at the beginning of the summer, but by Labor Day, there was a bleached pathway worn into it that was nice for anyone who needed directions to the bathroom but not terrific as a decorative touch. Since chlorine would be a chronic problem, I'm not sure carpeting made any sense in this room at all.

If you plan to carpet a room that will get heavy wear, think resilience and camouflage. For example, if you're carpeting a room that is entered directly from the outside and you live in a sandy area, a light-colored carpet makes sense, but if people are going to be tracking in dark soil, forget beige. (And by all means get a doormat. Using doormats at every entrance cuts your cleaning problems tremendously.)

One possibility for temporary or inexpensive carpeting is to make a "crazy quilt" out of carpeting samples if the dealer will sell them to you.

CARPETING STYLES

In loop carpeting, the yarn on the top (or face) side of the carpet forms a loop. Both ends are anchored in the back. When all the loops are the same size, they make a smooth, level, long-wearing surface. Multilevel carpeting, with loops of different heights, is considered sculptured or carved. A level carpet is easier to clean, but a multilevel carpet hides the footsteps better.

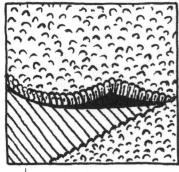

Loop Pile

One variation on loop carpeting is shag carpeting, which is made up of extra-long loops, either level or multilevel. It not only hides dirt and footsteps but also small change, paper clips, and the cat's toys. (A woman I know actually went over her shag rug each year with a metal detector.) Berber is another, bulkier type of loop carpeting, with colored flecks scattered at random over the background color.

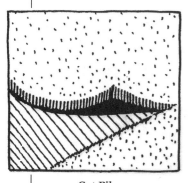

Cut Pile

The most common type of carpeting is cut pile, which is made by shearing off the tops of the loops. (Think crewcut.) There are many types of cut pile, depending on the thickness and the shine of the yarn. All of them have different names. Velvet cut pile has densely packed yarns; plush cut pile is packed more loosely; Saxonies are a variation of plush with a deep pile. What's important in terms of maintenance is that because it's fairly smooth, cut pile, like level loops, shows footprints.

The best carpets to hide both soil and footprints are a combination cut and loop pile. These will be described by salesmen in various ways. In one showroom you may see a

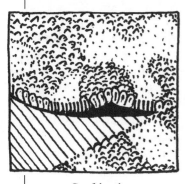

Combination

rough-textured carpeting that hides footprints and wears well described as a twist; in a more expensive shop, the salesman might describe it as a frieze and give it the French pronunciation: free-ZAY.

Any time the carpet surface is broken (with a cut pile or a combined cut and loop, or a multilevel loop), light is reflected at different angles. Dirt, lint, footprints, cat hairs, and other signs of life will not be as noticeable as they would be on a smooth surface.

CARPETING FIBERS

There are only five basic carpet fibers. The most expensive and therefore the least common is wool. Only about 3 % of carpets in the United States are made of wool. As for the others, although manufacturers advertise dozens of carpets by different brand names, which may lead you to believe these are all different fibers, they aren't. There are only four generic synthetics: **nylon, polypropylene, polyester,** and **acrylic.**

Check the label to find out exactly what you're getting. By law, rug and carpet samples have to be labeled with the generic names of the fiber contents and percentage of each.

About 80 % of the synthetic carpeting sold in the United States is made of **nylon.** It's the number one choice because it's very long-wearing, it's easy to clean, and it's unaffected by mildew. Many of the brands, like Antron, Enkalon with Scotchgard, and Wear-Dated Ultron with Scotchgard, conceal and resist soil and have built-in static control.

Polypropylene (examples: Olefin, Herculon), also called **industrial** or **indoor-outdoor** carpeting, is often used in kitchens and basements because it's very resistant to moisture and mildew. It's strong, it wears well, and because it's cheaper than nylon, it's becoming increasingly popular.

Polyester carpeting feels luxurious and is relatively inexpensive, but since it's not very durable or soil-resistant, it's impractical for high-traffic areas.

Acrylic, which looks a lot like wool but costs a lot less, is well suited to velvet and level-loop constructions. But since it creates a lot of ecological problems in the manufacture, it's on the decline.

Though some rugs have a jute or foam cushion backing, most rugs are backed with polypropylene. It's strong, it's inexpensive, and because it's also mildew-resistant, it's a must for carpets in damp areas such as the kitchen or basement.

LAYING ON OF HANDS

To get a sense of how carpet will wear, run the palm of your hand over the surface of the carpet. If the fibers are flexible and bend easily, the carpet will wear out quickly. But if they resist the pressure from your hand, the carpet should wear well.

"HELP! MY CARPET'S LOSING ITS HAIR!"

Don't be concerned when a new carpet sheds after being vacuumed. All new carpets, especially cut piles, have a lot of loose fibers left in them. This is a natural result of the manufacturing process.

The shedding will taper off. Vacuuming an older carpet may cause some fuzzing or pilling that is also natural, a result of wear. Over time the fiber ends separate and the extra yarn will loosen. If the pilling seems excessive, or if it's happening on a fairly new rug, contact the manufacturer.

DURABILITY

To make carpeting durable, the yarn should be, and usually is, heat-set (like hair that is permanented). Three other characteristics also help determine durability: **density, pile,** and **twist**.

The closer the tufts, the higher the **density**. High-density rugs wear best because when the yarn is packed tightly, the tufts won't—can't!—collapse.

Pile refers to the upright yarns that form the surface. In terms of durability, loops wear better than cut pile, multilevel pile wears bet-

ter than single-level pile, and deep pile wears better than short pile.

Twist describes the winding of the yarn around itself. The ends of the individual yarns should be neat and compact and not blossom open.

Having said this, I can assure you that if you're buying a nylon rug—and the overwhelming odds are that you are—you don't have to worry. Nylon is virtually indestructible. This is not to say that the carpeting won't get grungy or dirty or tired-looking, of course. But chances are that the nylon carpeting will wear out its welcome long before it wears out.

STAIN RESISTANCE

There is no such thing as a stain-proof carpet, but today's carpet resists stains if the yarn has been treated with a sealer such as Scotchgard that keeps them from soaking in. However, if a spill is unnoticed and left to set, it still may cause permanent staining.

Certain stains recolor the yarn so quickly that there's no remedy. If you read the fine print on even the best stain-resistant carpeting, you will no doubt find that the warranty excludes: (a) stains that aren't made by foods and beverages; (b) stains from foods and beverages that contain strongly colored dye, such as mustard or tea; and (c) stains from substances that destroy or change the color of the carpet, such as bleaches, acne medications, drain cleaners, plant food, and vomit.

In high-traffic areas, such as stairs, carpets also lose some stain resistance.

PADDING

Padding makes a carpet (or rug) more comfortable by acting as a shock absorber. It also prolongs the life of the carpet.

There are three types of padding.

Rubberized hair and jute felting is the most popular for all the right reasons: It offers the best cushioning for the least cost. Use it for stairs because it "bounces" less than other choices.

Urethane is another option. It comes in two categories, virgin or bonded, which sound like categories for adult films but aren't. Virgin urethane has been manufactured from scratch. Bonded urethane, a better product, is made of by-products from furniture manufacture. If the furniture manufacturers are having a slow season, it may not be available.

"Bubble gum" **rubber**, once the most common padding choice, is now outmoded.

However, rubber or urethane are preferred if you have an allergy problem.

KEEPING THE COSTS DOWN

You can get a one-color look throughout the house without paying the price for top-grade carpeting in rooms that get little wear. Choose the highest-graded carpet (with the greatest density, the tightest twist, and the best fiber) for areas that get the most traffic. Match the color and texture in a less expensive grade for rooms like the den or bedrooms.

To save money, also check out the remnants. Remnants in unusual colors—ones you might not have chosen if they weren't bargain-priced—can sometimes be a pleasant decorating surprise. (Or a surprise, anyway.) If you have a small room, you can get low-cost wall-to-wall carpeting by buying a large remnant that the installer can cut to size. For a small

cost, you can also have the dealer bind and trim a remnant and deliver it finished for use as an area rug. Be careful. Some remnants are flawed. Though they should be so identified on the tag, make sure to have the remnant unrolled so you can inspect it before you purchase it. If the flaw winds up under your bed, it won't matter. If it's the centerpiece of your living room, it will.

When you're getting an estimate of the rug, be sure to ask if the price includes pad and installation. (It usually doesn't.) Ask also if the installation price includes moving the furniture and removing the old carpet. Get a guarantee for installation because you may notice wrinkling months later. And save bits and pieces of carpeting in case you need a patch in the future.

You may be tempted to save a few dollars by having the installer do some cutting and piecing rather than buying several extra yards of carpet. If the seams are in high-traffic areas, this is a mistake because they won't wear well.

Don't overeconomize. Poor quality rugs shed, fray, and fade while good ones last for years. On the other hand, my friend Harold the carpet salesman says $25 a yard is the most you have to pay for durability. What you're paying for beyond that point is style. Personally, I believe in investing in great-looking carpeting. After all, the kids will leave home some day!

THE BEST-LAID CARPET

Carpet stretches and wrinkles because of climate changes, not because of poor installation. Today, air-conditioning keeps these extreme changes to a minimum, but you still may notice some wrinkling. The only solution is for the installer to come in and "kick it out." Usually the installer's warranty will include one free restretching, which is a lot better deal than you get from a plastic surgeon.

Area Rugs

My Scandinavian ancestors invented the word *rugge* (meaning tough, or coarse). When they invaded the British Isles in the Bronze Age, they brought their woven clothing and bedcovers with them. You may not admire their aggressiveness, but you do have to respect their practicality.

Rugs today run the gamut from tiny rag ovals to long, two-to-three-feet-wide hall runners to huge, room-sized Orientals. And they aren't just for floors. Flat-weave rugs can be tossed on a bed, draped on the sofa, and made into pillows. Some are beautiful enough to use as wall art and are priced accordingly. But 80 % of rugs available are in the $100 to $2,000 range—even less in the spring, the traditional time for rug sales.

Standard area rug sizes are 3×5, 4×6, 5×7, 6×9, 8×11, 9×12, 12×18, and up. Runners come in a variety of lengths. And in addition to specially designed modern area rugs, you can buy area rugs in solid colors, florals, geometrics, and other patterns and distinctive designs from countries around the world.

SPOTTING A REAL ANTIQUE

A rug is considered semi-antique if it's 50 to 100 years old, antique if it's older. A rare antique rug can be worth several hundred thousand dollars.

Real antiques are dyed differently than modern rugs. Though low-cost, quick-working chemical (aniline) dyes were introduced as early as 1870, vegetable dyes were standard until around World War I. Collectors prefer vegetable dyes since the colors tend to mellow rather than fade with age. Sometimes new chemically dyed rugs are artificially aged in a chemical bath that strips some color. When you examine the threads, you'll see a gradation of color from dark (the root) to light (the tip). Vegetable dyes age in the same way, but if the bands of gradation are uniform throughout the rug, chances are it's been chemically aged. If they vary, the rug has probably aged naturally.

Fringes of antique rugs are different also. In a handmade rug, it extends naturally from the foundation threads of the rug. In a machine-made rug, it's sewn on.

The value of an antique rug is also dependent on whether (and where) the rug has been repaired, and whether it is complete, with no borders or edging missing.

Antique or semi-antiques are all hand-knotted. The more knots per square inch, the finer the weave.

"ORIENTALS" FROM THE MIDDLE EAST

I happen to like the look of light-colored Oriental rugs contrasted against dark furniture, but their major benefit is how they hide dirt. I think Orientals were made for stairways, hallways, and entryways; you can go without vacuuming these rugs for a year. (People who put light-colored carpeting in entryways are in another dimension.) Every couple of years, you just roll them up and send them for professional cleaning.

Authentic Orientals—made in Iran (Persia), Turkey, and India and at least 100 years old—are the finest of all rugs. And of this group, the craftsmanship in Persian rugs makes them the Rolls-Royces of floor coverings. They also have a natural luster despite their age—supposedly because the yarn came from the breast wool of sheep.

Particular designs distinguish one type of rug from another. Kermans, with a long pile and velvety feel, usually have a tree of life, animals, and birds in the border. A Sarouk has a large central circular design on an open contrasting field. Tabriz rugs usually show a hunting scene, and Isfahans usually have an ivory background and large center medallion of multicolored floral and vine designs. Rugs from Muslim regions are primarily geometric; they rarely show human or animal forms.

The Kermans and Sarouks have about 140 or so knots per square inch. The more expensive Tabriz and Isfahans have between 400 and 500 per inch. Hand-knotted rugs are each unique and the sizes are not uniform.

Machine-made reproductions of classic Persian designs, called "rack rugs," come in standard sizes and duplicate nearly every handmade style, coloring, weave type, or pile height. They are made in countries like Belgium and India, where manufacturers can produce in a single day a rug that would have taken ten months to make by hand, knot by knot, on a loom. Reproductions may have many knots—perhaps 210 to 280 per inch—but you can actually feel the difference between them and the top-of-the-line originals, which are thicker and more luxurious. Still, machine-made rugs

can look just as good as the really great handmade rugs. They also cost less, but of course, unlike antiques, they will not increase in value as they age.

If you have your heart set on an antique, go to a dealer who will guarantee its authenticity, since it will be an expensive purchase. A fine quality hand-knotted 9 × 12 rug may cost $7,000 and more, while a mid-range rug may cost between $2,000 and $7,000. You may find a smaller hand-knotted rug in fairly good condition for anywhere from $500 up.

FLAT-WEAVE KILIMS

Flat weaves—called kilims or dhurries or Navajo-style rugs—are made in India, Pakistan, Turkey, Morocco, the U.S. southwest, and many other countries. These very popular, drapeable, and tightly woven reversible rugs are known for their patterns and distinctive colors. They have a nice informal look, like folk art, and are very inexpensive. You may be able to get a rug as large as 6 × 9 for as little as $100, while semi-antique or antique kilims cost thousands, depending on how rare they are and what condition they're in.

CHINESE RUGS

Many Chinese rugs imitate the delicately designed, needlepoint Aubusson rugs that decorate the most expensive homes. Thick, handmade, and densely piled, they usually have a pastel-colored, floral central design and wide borders that may also feature dragons, flying cranes, entwined leaves, and elephants. (I say if you're paying $20,000 and up for a rug, you're entitled to all the elephants you want.) Though the knockoffs look hand-knotted, the threads are looped and glued in place.

But Chinese rugs come in all styles, including carved: The rug is sheared in spots to make it look three-dimensional. They vary in cost depending on age and size and pattern.

Hooked and Braided Rugs

Rag rugs are made with fabric strips pulled through burlap; punch needle rugs are made of uniformly sized loops that are cut to make a surface pile; and a latch-hook rug is made with yarn to produce a deep pile. Though they tend to feature folk patterns, flower gardens, portraits of the family dog, and "Bless Our Home" designs, today most are made in India.

Another type of handmade rug that's fairly common (and fairly inexpensive) is made of wool and other fabric scraps usually braided into a large oval, often in shades of red, blue, or brown.

Padding for an Area Rug

You can use the same kind of padding for an area rug as for wall-to-wall carpeting. If the area rug is to be anchored by furniture, just lay the padding down and put the rug and furniture on top of it. If the rug slips around, you may also need a two-faced, nonslip pad, usually a synthetic with a gripping surface, to hold it firmly in place. Also see "Slipping" in the box on p. 114.

Discoloration

Be warned that when you put an area rug on top of a carpet (or on top of any other kind of flooring), the spots that are hidden from light will not fade to match the area surrounding it. There's nothing you can do about this.

Mats and Mat-type Flooring

"Walk-off mats"—what we usually call "welcome mats"—are made of coconut or its relative, coir.

In recent years, trendy people—people who spend unnatural amounts of money to get a "natural" look—have popularized mat-type flooring, both coir and its sophisticated cousin sisal as well as split cane and rush matting, which come in tile form. These are all excellent choices if you're in training to walk on coals. They are uncomfortable, easily stained and damaged by water, likely to collect dust, and costlier to install than $100-a-yard carpeting. The reason for this is unclear to me, but it may be the installers' way of imposing a luxury tax.

This flooring is strictly for people who have enough money to do everything over again next year.

The least you need to know about buying hard surface flooring:
- Advantages and disadvantages of wood floors
- Advantages and disadvantages of resilient and nonresilient flooring.

Wood Floors

Wood floors have good acoustic and insulating properties, they're durable, and they're easy to maintain. Most of them require very little care beyond a weekly vacuuming or dust mopping. Because water harms wood, in the past wood was rarely used in the kitchen, but modern sealing products make it a possibility today.

Most wood floors are hardwoods. Open-grained hardwoods include oak—used in 95 % of all floors—as well as northern walnut, pecan, ash, elm, and chestnut. Close-grained hardwoods include maple, birch, beech, Douglas fir, and yellow pine.

The flooring usually comes as planks that can be laid in a variety of designs—on the diagonal, in a herringbone pattern, with nails at the end and so forth. Parquet floors, which are intricately patterned in one or more kinds and colors of wood, come in ready-to-install tiles.

If you buy a house with dark wood floors but want a modern look, you may have the floors stripped and then bleached to a lighter color or painted and/or pickled (a light wash of white is painted across the floor), then coated with polyurethane. (The process is very similar to stripping furniture, which I explain in the section on Fixing.) The disadvantage is that the lighter the floor, the more clearly dirt shows up. Also, during periods when the humidity is low, all flooring will contract; when the floors are light, the natural separations between the boards will be noticeably darker than the floor boards. This is not a big deal, but it may bother you if you are a perfectionist.

Two main types of finishes are used on wood floors:

Penetrating seals actually soak into the wood and dye it all the way through but must be waxed and require a lot of upkeep.

Surface finishes, like polyurethane, seal the surface and make it stain-resistant and water-resistant. These surfaces can be spot refinished. Choose a matte finish if the floor below isn't in great shape.

Other surface finishes include varnish, which darkens with age but can also be spot refinished; shellac, easy to apply but needs waxing, gets dirty fast, and can't be spot finished; lacquer, which dulls quickly, shows scuffs, and can't be spot-finished, and Swedish systems, which need professional application but are the strongest and easiest to maintain.

If you are going to have your floors refinished, it's important to get a recommendation from someone whose opinion you trust. This is an expensive job and the quality of the work varies a lot. When you interview the finisher, ask a lot of questions, including—very specifically—what color the floor will be when the floor is finished. A friend of mine thought her floor would be bleached and coated to a light oak color but came home to discover the finisher had painted the floor to match the walls. This particular story had a happy ending, but it's best to make sure everyone knows exactly what to expect.

Be prepared for an incredible amount of mess. To refinish a floor, the worker has to sand down the current surface and remove prior coats of wax, grime, and irregularities in the surface. The sandstorm that is raised would make Lawrence nostalgic for Arabia and will send you into total depression if you have not prepared for it. The fine particles get in everywhere, including inside closed kitchen cupboards and into every cup and onto every plate. Use drop cloths everywhere.

Resilient Flooring

No-wax resilient flooring is a good choice wherever wood flooring would be too expensive or impractical or to cover an existing floor that has worn out. It comes in a wide variety of patterns, colors, and grades, either as tiles or as sheet flooring. (It has completely replaced linoleum, which hasn't been manufactured in this country since 1974.) It is relatively inexpensive, water-resistant, and easy to clean. Because it is cushioned, it's more comfortable to stand on and causes less breakage than hard flooring.

But despite the "no-wax" name, this type of flooring is not completely maintenance-free. Its clear-gloss top layer does stay in good condition somewhat longer than ordinary vinyl but not forever. It's also easily damaged by sharp or hard objects and won't stand up to major wear and tear like a wood floor does.

RESILIENT TILE FLOORING

It seems practical to buy tile flooring in hope that you could easily replace any damaged section if necessary in the future. But over time tiles fade, and the replacement section usually

COMPARING RESILIENT TILE FLOORINGS

Type	Characteristics	Advantages	Disadvantages
Solid vinyl (Tiles are 12 × 12 or 12 × 18 inches)	Bright patterns print all the way through tile. (Compare to printed vinyl and vinyl asbestos, which look worn when pattern wears off.)	Easier to lay than sheet flooring.	May be slippery when wet. Wasteful for unusual shaped rooms.
Embossed vinyl and vinyl asbestos	Uneven surface.	Gives visual interest to room.	Uneven surface traps dirt and wears unevenly.
Cushioned tile	May be backed with felt, felt and foam, or asbestos with foam.		Expensive. Furniture may make permanent indents. Don't use felt below ground in cellar (may mildew).
Rubber		Very pleasant to stand on; durable.	Limited color range.
Cork		Pleasant to stand on.	Hard to clean; not so durable.

RESILIENT SHEET FLOORING

Vinyl and rubber flooring comes in sheets. It can be laid flat or stuck to subflooring around the edges only with double-sided tapes or staples. While sheet flooring is harder to install than tiles, it makes more sense in heavy traffic areas. On tiled surfaces, there are many edges for water and soil to seep under, creating the possibility of water damage and mildew growth.

Non-Resilient Flooring

Hard floorings, such as ceramic and quarry tiles, concrete, brick, and stone, are often used in high-traffic areas. Stone and tile floors are not inexpensive—the lowest-priced unglazed quarry tile costs about the same as vinyl flooring, but the others all cost more. But though tiles crack and there are some maintenance problems with grouting, they're generally easy to maintain, durable, and beautiful.

stands out. (If there is a suitable place in the house—a mudroom or section of the basement—you can leave out a few tiles to "age." When the time comes to install them, they may not be exactly the same color as those in the kitchen, but they probably won't be quite as obvious as tiles that are fresh from the carton.)

Asphalt and vinyl asbestos are used primarily in institutions because they are very cheap. Asphalt is easily pitted and doesn't wear well.

COMPARING RESILIENT SHEET FLOORINGS

Type	Characteristics	Advantages	Disadvantages
Sheet vinyl	Wide variety of designs and textures; better grades are often cushioned so they are quiet and comfortable.	Impervious to water, oil, fat, and most household chemicals.	Cigarette burns can harm.
Rubber flooring		Durable, quiet, waterproof. Many modern designs have ribs and studs that make floor non-slip. Easy cleaning with soapy water and rinse.	Expensive.

Ceramic and quarry tiles are available unglazed and glazed. Glazed tile has a glass-like surface that may be shiny, matte (flat), or textured. You can also purchase tiles made of granite (the hardest), slate, marble, onyx, and flagstone (the softest). Sometimes quarry and ceramic tiles are combined.

Tiles are laid in a base made of grout, a sticky mortar of matching or contrasting color that holds them in place and defines the pattern. The patterns range from very simple arrangements of rectangles and squares to very complicated diamond/hexagon patterns.

Although colored grouting doesn't get dirty as fast as white grouting, at least you can find a white grout cleaner or touchup; cleaners for

COMPARING NON-RESILIENT (HARD) FLOORINGS

Type	Characteristics	Advantages	Disadvantages
Ceramic tiles (Square and oblong shapes, usually 4 × 5 inches, though they can be in interlocking circular and "Provencale" shapes	Almost unbreakable— fired at such high temperatures that the particles fuse. Unglazed tiles in earth tones must be sealed before use.	Hard-wearing, waterproof, stain-resistant; great for kitchens, baths, halls, indoor-outdoor rooms. Many effects available through use of contrasting borders, etc.	Expensive. Glazed tiles may be slippery (but you can buy slip-resistant ones), scratch easily, can be uncomfortably cold underfoot.
Quarry Tiles	Unglazed, rough, in earth tones. Must be laid in a mortar bed, then sealed and polished.	Durable, suitable for indoor or outdoor use. Develops a natural gloss as it ages.	
Brick		Durable; good for paths and hallways.	Porous (absorbs stains) and rough (hard to clean).
Stone	Variety of types are quarried (see above).	Very long wearing, waterproof, good in kitchens and bath.	Needs finishing. Softer onyx and flagstone need sealing.
Aggregates	Combine pieces of stone in a solid base to make new pattern— terrazzo is one type.	Very durable.	Expensive.

purple and other colors of grout do not exist.

Before the 1950s, all tiles were individually mounted. In order to save time, manufacturers began to mount tiles to backings like paper, jute, nylon, mesh, and other surfaces. These backings sometimes fall off. Before buying mounted tiles to use in bathrooms or other wet areas, always make sure they are suitable for that purpose.

When you've picked the tile you think you want, buy several to bring home. If after you've looked at them for a few days, you decide you'd prefer another pattern, you can always use them for hot pads. Sometimes you can select every single tile you want, one at a time (though obviously this is more likely when you are using a few tiles decoratively than a whole floor's worth). If so, be choosy. Imperfect tiles and tiles of varying thickness may crack.

COVERING THE WALLS

In a really extravagant mood, I hired a muralist to cover one of my walls with flowers and vines. But the rest of my home is covered more conventionally with paint and wallpaper. Together with paneling (which today is no longer limited to finished-basement-walnut), they are available in an almost endless variety of choices.

Paint

The least you need to know about having your home painted:
- The importance of preparation
- Choosing type, quality, and color of the paint

Do not assume that anyone can paint. Being able to hold a brush doesn't make you into a Michelangelo. It doesn't even make you a competent wall painter. I wouldn't hire a painter who wasn't referred by a friend (or who didn't come with excellent references), nor should you.

THREE TIPS FOR HIRING A PAINTER (OR ANY OTHER WORKMAN)

- Check the truck. A worker with a clean truck will probably do a clean job.
- Avoid smokers. They take a lot of breaks.
- Don't hire anyone who can't wear a belt. They spend a large part of the day hitching up their pants.

Based on these standards, of course, there were many times in my life when I wouldn't have hired myself.

WHAT IT WILL COST

Painting can be staggeringly expensive, especially if your walls are in bad shape. Ask at least two painting contractors for estimates to compare prices before you sign the contract.

If your walls need a lot of plastering and/or stripping, prepping—making sure the wall is smooth and sealed—may represent the major cost in a professional paint job. The prepping is what separates a great paint job from an inferior one. If it's not done right, the paint may begin to peel, the color may not look right, and you'll be unhappy with the job from the minute the drop cloths are rolled up.

PREPARING THE SURFACE

Even if you're doing the actual painting yourself (in which case look in the Fixing section for more information), if there are big holes or cracks, you'll need a professional plastering job.

Different problems cause different kinds of cracks, as I discuss in Making Your Own Inspection. Whatever caused a wall crack (generally a leak) should be repaired before the plastering is done or the crack will come right back. If the crack is a foundation problem and is not attended to, you might as well not bother to paint at all, since the house may fall down.

(Plaster in rooms that are very humid or which are subject to frequent temperature changes—for example, rooms with fireplaces—may crack chronically. A friend of mine experienced this problem until one craftsman mixed the plaster with sand and that job lasted for years.)

Once a repair is made, the loose plaster must be chipped away and the area coated with a substance that helps the plaster adhere. Then the plastering can be completed.

Before it is painted, plaster should be allowed to cure, or come to full strength, for at least a couple of weeks. This will come as startling news to those of you who have seen the plasterer finish up moments before the painter starts, but some people recommend leaving plaster to cure for as long as three months! You may have a hard time persuading most painting contractors to have your plastering done weeks before a paint job, but you can try.

A careful craftsman should sand the plastered area until it is absolutely smooth. Bulges or dimples will show up if covered by a semigloss or glossy paint.

A wall that's badly pitted can be covered with white lining paper to create a smooth surface before it's painted. The lining is pasted on like wallpaper. Though it's a lot of work, it may be worth the bother.

The next step is to apply a prime coat, primarily to lay down a uniform surface for the top coat, but also to cover up colors that may otherwise bleed through and/or seal the underlying surface.

The primer is chosen based on whether the paint job is indoors or out, what kind of surface you're painting (floor, wall, or ceiling), what's underneath it (wood, plaster, paneling, wallpaper), and what condition the surface is in (never painted, peeling, etc.). Wood is so porous that unless it is primed, it will soak up the top coat of paint. Some professional painters recommend that the wood primer always be oil-based because it's better at sealing the pores.

Some new paints combine the primer and top coat all in one, so you can skip this step.

CHOOSING THE TYPE OF PAINT

Oil-based paint colors are very intense, with a glossy, durable finish. These paints have good "hiding power" (they easily cover the colors below), are easy to apply, adhere to smooth surfaces better than latex paints, and weather and age well. Since oil-based paints repel moisture, they can be washed repeatedly without wearing away, so they're the best choice for kitchens and bathrooms, ceilings, walls, the basement, and kids' rooms.

Oil paints used to contain lead, which if ingested or absorbed into the body can cause serious damage to the neurological system, especially in children. Because the chips were sweet, small children would sometimes eat them, but lead can also be taken in passively, since it is absorbed through the skin and mucous membranes. (If you're remodeling, you should be aware of lead paint hazards. Check the information on lead paint in the section Securing.) In addition to the lead problem, certain solvents in the oil-based paints combined with sunlight and oxygen as the paint dried to form ground-level ozone, a component of smog.

Newer paint substitutes **alkyd** for lead. Oil/alkyds dry faster than the originals, smell less, and are easier to work with. However, you still need thinner or turpentine to clean the brushes and wipe up spills, and the odor of these as well as of the alkyds is unpleasant. Worse, the main ingredients of alkyds are petrochemical solvents that are harmful to breathe and contribute to air pollution. Use alkyd paint only to cover surfaces already coated with three or

PAINT AND THE ENVIRONMENT

- Since the U.S. Environmental Protection Agency doesn't yet regulate the composition of paint, there is no control over the fact that as alkyd paint dries, some of its components evaporate and pollute the air. Some states have passed laws to limit these compounds, which are the very substances that make the paint easy to apply, quick-drying, and long-lasting. Let's hope the chemists come up with something as good as alkyd without its drawbacks.

- In 1990 the Environmental Protection Agency banned the use of mercury (which helps fight mildew) in latex paint composition. Vapors escaped as paints dried, building up to toxic levels in poorly ventilated rooms. External latex paints still contain some mercury, but the fumes are less risky outdoors.

more layers of paint or to cover another coat of alkyd paint that you don't want to strip.

Latex paints offer protection against mildew and hold their color better than alkyds as they weather. More important, latex paints are easier to handle (when you make a mistake, the brush strokes don't show), don't smell, dry quickly, and clean up easily. And they're nontoxic.

Among the few drawbacks: latex paint wears thin, tends to soil faster, and is more likely to peel after a couple of coats. (Any paint, latex or alkyd, will peel after four coats and should be stripped to the bare wood). Since bedrooms, living rooms, and entrance halls don't usually need scrubbing, you won't have any problems with latex.

One hundred percent acrylic latex is the best quality; vinyl acrylic is second. The paint store manager can give you advice about which to choose.

CHOOSING THE FINISH

In paint, the opposite of flat is shiny. At one end of the range is a matte finish, and then—in order of increasing shine—you can find eggshell, satin, semi-gloss, and glossy finishes. But a glossy latex isn't anywhere near as shiny as a shiny enamel.

High-gloss paints are durable, washable, and a little like certain entertainment figures: There's nothing subtle about them, and they reveal everything. Every brush and roller stroke is permanently on display; every spot where the wall isn't perfectly even is highlighted. To complete a high-gloss enamel room requires a lot of expensive paint and labor.

Semi-gloss is a good compromise. It's durable and moisture-proof, so it holds up well to washing, and it's not as shiny as high-gloss. It's also good for dens or kids' rooms, and especially for window sills.

The only reason to choose the hint of shine in a **satin** or **eggshell** finish is if you prefer the texture to a **matte** look.

THE QUALITY OF THE PAINT

You'll need about one gallon of paint for every 400 square feet, or 250 for a porous or unsealed wall (see box, Calculating Your Paint Needs, p. 51.). Even so, the cost of the paint compared to the cost of labor is a drop in the bucket, so to speak. I can never understand how people who are paying thousands for the painters try to save a few dollars on the paint itself.

FOR THE RECORD

When buying anything for the house—from shelf liner to drapes, carpeting to paint—make a 3 × 5 card noting how much you needed as well as the name and ID number of the product so you know where to buy extras or replacements.

Cheap paints are no bargain. Manufacturers of cheap paint save on paint solids and instead use fillers or pigment extenders (such as finely ground talc, refined minerals, clays, etc.) to thicken the paint and improve the flow. As a result, you'll need more coats to cover the surface or the paint won't hold up to washings.

The first time a painter recommended a more expensive paint, I was a little skeptical. But I saw the results. While paint jobs I'd paid for in the past lasted no more than three years, this one is still looking good after five.

CHOOSING THE COLOR

Always give yourself plenty of time to change your mind about the color before the painter has covered the whole room with it. What looked like a vibrant pink on the color sample may turn out to be operating room magenta when it's covering the four walls and the ceiling of your living room.

The best approach is to buy a small amount of the paint you're considering, brush it on a wall—not just a dab, but a great big patch of it—and live with it for a couple of days. Colors in the light of your living room will always look different than they did in the paint store. When you're testing, check the effect of different types of lighting—such as an overhead light or a lamp—which can radically change how the color looks. Natural light has an effect on colors, too. Windows that look north get a cooler light than those that face south.

Paint always looks much darker on the wall than on the paint chip card and will also darken with age. When you use it on a ceiling as well as the walls—and they're all reflecting off each other—it gets even more intense. That is why many people recommend that you use white paint on the ceilings and why there is even a paint color called ceiling white (though any shade of white will be okay next to a colored wall). White ceilings also make a room seem

---

COLOR SCHEMING

If you're ready to paint and you're tired of the same old colors and combinations, get some inspiration by going to the men's department of a retail clothier and checking out the ties. You'll get some jazzy new ideas.

---

higher, and of course you cannot be too thin or too rich or have ceilings that are too high.

There are plenty of books telling you that cool colors make you feel calm and warm colors make you feel cheerful and that black is not a great color for a bedroom, but I think all that is nonsense. Do what you want. Wallpaper the ceilings. Use checks with stripes. Have fun with what you're doing.

Pigment, or color, is what makes paint expensive, so the darker colors will cost more and white ceiling paint is the cheapest paint you can buy—but if you have your heart set on dark green walls, I doubt the price difference is going to make you choose lime.

If you can't find the color you want, bring in a swatch of fabric or a picture from a magazine—or one of your child's crayons—and have it mixed to order in a good paint store. Color-matching computers can duplicate just about any shade and one batch should be virtually identical to the next, so if you need an extra gallon halfway through the job, it's not a problem.

If you don't think color means a lot, how come it takes you so long to figure out which toothbrush to buy?

HOW MUCH TO BUY

If a professional is doing your painting, generally you'll pick the color at the paint store and the pro, who often gets a professional discount, will make the actual purchase. However, if you're buying the paint yourself or simply want to know how much the paint will cost, go to a specialty paint store with your room measurements and the salesman can help you estimate the amount of paint you need. If you'd like to do it yourself, check the box below.

CALCULATING YOUR PAINT NEEDS

Add the length and width of the room, multiply by two (because you're painting all four walls), then multiply that sum by the room height to get the square footage.

Take a typical room of 16 feet × 20 feet, with 9-foot ceiling:
Add 16 + 20 multiply by 2 = 72
Multiply 72 × 9 = 648 square feet

If you're painting the ceiling, multiply the length times the width to get the square footage:
Multiply 16 × 20 = 320 square feet
Sum of totals = 968 square feet

Subtract the following:

Each door (if a different color):
subtract 21 square feet
Each window: subtract 15 square feet

The label on the paint will tell you how many square feet of paint one can will yield for one coat of coverage. Buy a little extra. You don't want to have the painter hanging around while someone goes out for another can of paint.

BEFORE THE PAINTER COMES

Ask the painter exactly what you can do to get ready and what steps he will assist with (moving furniture, supplying drop cloths). In my experience, workers who are very particular about how they will cover the floors and furniture and windows are usually particular about every detail of the job. A painter who is giving you a bargain price may not be as careful about masking all the windowpanes, etc., so it's in your best interest if you deal with it yourself.

Wallpaper and Other Wall Coverings

The least you need to know about buying wallcoverings:
- What to consider when buying wallpaper
- Nonpaper options

Wallpaper lasts nine or ten years, while a paint job usually lasts no more than five, so it's a durable alternative. It's also a great coverup for joints, cracks, etc. And if it's not peeling, wallpaper that's in place can be covered by another paper (or by paint) with no problem. Since top-quality wallpaper makes even inexpensive furnishings look good, I think it's worth the cost.

PAPER CONTENT

Standard wallpaper is just paper with a pattern printed on it. More expensive papers may be hand-printed; textured to resemble stucco, plaster, or other surfaces; or flocked, with a raised pile surface, for some reason a favorite of steakhouse restaurant decorators.

Be cautious about very expensive hand-painted silk-screened papers. They're difficult to work with and very fragile. Using the wrong adhesive may cause the colors to run.

Vinyl makes wall coverings stain-resistant and—depending on the percentage of the vinyl content—either washable or scrubbable.

Nearly three-fourths of all wall coverings are now all or part vinyl. Others are vinyl-coated paper or paper-backed vinyl. There's even a foamed vinyl paper with a raised pattern (created by heat) that you're supposed to paint.

You can see sample books with large swatches in home decorating centers; specialty, paint, furniture, or department stores; or through decorators. They're usually organized by type and texture so you can look at only solids, vinyls, vinyl patterns, florals, or whatever. Each pattern or texture is shown in its range of color choices. Some manufacturers print a matching or closely related design on fabric so you can coordinate your upholstery or have a bedspread or curtains made to match the paper.

Some products are guaranteed against fading.

As with paint, check the wall covering sample at home. Showrooms tend to be lit with fluorescents and your home—with the exception of the bath and/or kitchen—probably is not. If you can't take home a sample, at least carry the book to a window where you can look at it in natural light.

MAKING PAPER MORE DURABLE

If your wallpaper doesn't have the stain resistance of vinyl, apply satin finish polyurethane with a sponge brush over wallpaper. This waterproofs the paper so that fingerprints and marks come right off. This may affect the color of some papers, so try it on a sample before you put it on the wall, or check with your dealer.

Matching Paper to Wall

Wallpaper can create optical illusions. For example, long, narrow, bowling alley–type rooms will look wider and warmer if you use lighter, textured wall coverings. You can "open up" small rooms with bright patterns, like a trellis, or small, widely spaced flowers on a light background.

If walls are bumpy or the ceiling line uneven, or there are other architectural or structural faults (the door lintel slants, the moldings are crooked), avoid stripes and untextured light-colored or shiny covering.

If wall surfaces are flawed, hide them with embossed or textured surfaces.

Basically, the same rules apply as with clothes: light makes things look larger, dark makes them look smaller, vertical stripes give height and horizontal ones give width. These are rules that every fat person knows. When I was doing a TV tour for my first book, I always made a point of wearing a dress the same color as the sofa I would be interviewed on, hoping no one would be able to make out exactly where the sofa left off and I began.

Ease of Hanging and Stripping

I've explained the technique of hanging wallpaper in the Fixing section of this book, but at this point I want to point out potential problems that—if you plan to do it yourself—may affect your choice.

Check the manufacturer's recommendations for installation and for the type of adhesive to use. Some are premixed; others are dry and have to be mixed with water.

Prepasted wallpaper is the greatest. After it's cut in the right size strips, it just needs moistening.

Patterns with a random match—which means there's no exact pattern to be matched from strip to strip—are, obviously, easiest to hang. But if you've chosen a wallpaper with a complicated pattern, you'll have to allow for the pattern "repeat." The repeat is the vertical distance between two points where the pattern is identical. This measurement is shown on the label. Hanging a paper with a big repeat is hard

Random Match

Drop Match

Straight Match

(because the pattern must line up perfectly) and expensive (because you may need more rolls to get the strip just perfect).

A drop match means the pattern at one side edge is half a repeat lower than the other edge. A straight match means the design along the top edge of a strip starts and ends at the same vertical point.

Expensive hand-painted wallpapers and high-gloss metal-look (silver, gold, bronze) wall coverings should be applied by an expert; the surface underneath metal-look papers must be perfect. Bumps and lumps and irregularities in the walls are accented by the shine; smudges, dirt, and especially grease, even crayon marks left on the walls, can leak through to the surface and ruin the paper.

If you anticipate removing this paper, choose one that is peelable (it leaves behind both adhesive and backing, which comes off with hot soapy water and a scraper) or strippable (which leaves only adhesive). European papers are easier to remove than U.S. papers, and I'm sure there's some hidden meaning in that, but I can't figure it out.

THE COST OF WALLPAPER

The most economical choice is a wallpaper with a small pattern that repeats every 6 to 8 inches. If you have large geometric or floral, the pattern repeats only every 24 inches or so and you'll waste a lot when you match the strips.

Cheap papers may fade, not hold up to scrubbing, or shrink after being applied, but good papers that are closed out or marked down can be great bargains. You can pay $40 to $200 a roll (and more) for good foil and hand-printed papers, and the rule of thumb is that the more it costs, the harder it is to hang.

Sometimes you can pick up an odd roll or two of wall covering very inexpensively. These are great for a small space (as in the bathroom, where you may want to cover only the upper part of one half-tiled wall) but can also be used to spruce up an old file cabinet or to cover an inexpensive Parsons table to use in the office or living room. (Cover the table with a glass top and it can be a very decorative piece.)

You can use an odd bit of wall covering to cover a plywood cornice over windows, to customize a three-panel folding screen with "scenic" or outdoor mural prints, or to cover a small bathroom window shade.

If you happen to spot a wallpaper sample book destined for the garbage—not unlikely, since stores discard their sample books at least twice a year—retrieve it to use as wrapping paper for small gifts, clothes for paper dolls, and other craft projects.

HOW MUCH TO BUY

Bring accurate measurements to the dealer.

Measure as if you were measuring a carton. Get the overall height and width of each wall to be covered. Do not subtract the dimensions of windows, fireplace, doors, etc. (The extra few feet of paper may come in handy.)

If your room is 12 feet by 18 feet, and the walls are 9 feet high, first add two widths

(12 + 12) and two lengths (18 + 18). The result is 60 feet. Multiply this by the height and you get 540 square feet.

If a roll contains 36 feet, the dealer may advise you to leave as much as 6 feet allowance for trimming and matching patterns, so you'll get about 30 feet out of a roll. Divide 540 by 30 and the total purchase should be 18 rolls.

Border strips are sold by the yard, not the roll, so measure the perimeter of the room to fit.

Most wall coverings are priced by the single roll, even though they come packed in double or triple roll bolts. The square footage of the rolls will vary (lengths can run up to 72 square feet or so), and the width of the paper can range from 20 to 28 inches. The packages are labeled with square footage information.

European bolts, which are measured in meters, have less paper than American rolls.

Always buy at least one roll more than you need to cover the space, since manufacturers change dye lots or discontinue patterns.

WOOD PANELING

You can get paneling at different price points, but panels that sell for less than $12 may be of questionable quality. Neither vinyl printed to look like wood or sheetrock with a glued-on vinyl finish is as durable as plywood covered with a wood veneer or solid wood. Knot-free oak is the best-quality solid wood.

All surfaces should be sealed with a matte finish polyurethane so you can wipe them easily.

TILEBOARD

Tileboard, available in 4 × 8 and 5 × 5 sheets, is hardboard-based material with special surface coatings that are similar to ceramic tile in durability. Some resemble ceramic tile, with hard, glossy squares surrounded by recessed "grouting," but a variety of other styles are available, from simulated stone to florals.

Tileboard is usually treated with melamine, a baked-on finish, or VPC, a polyester-epoxy coating. Both are durable, mildew-, stain-, scratch-, and mar-resistant. VPC finishes are also flexible and crack-resistant. Tileboard is lightweight and easy to install, usually onto wallboard (but not to studs, concrete, furring, brick, cinderblock, or plaster). Some brands can be applied to plywood and existing ceramic tile.

OTHER OPTIONS

Vinyl flooring and carpeting are also good wall covering choices. They're low-maintenance and good insulators. The person who installs your tile or carpet on the floors can do it on the walls, or you can do it yourself.

Stone and brick are very durable, but cleaning the grouting may be a problem.

Brick veneer over wood or concrete is not expensive and can be wiped clean.

Ceilings

Both painted and wood ceilings are low-maintenance, but an acoustical tile ceiling tends to stain. If you paint it, you may reduce sound absorption, though there are special paints for this purpose. (In any case, to quiet sound that is coming through the floor, sound proofing the ceiling is less effective than putting down carpeting. If you live in an apartment and your downstairs neighbor complains of noise, that's exactly what you may be asked to do.)

● ●

CLEAR ADVANTAGES: WINDOWS AND WINDOW COVERINGS

The point of replacing windows is to improve insulation, and new windows are increasingly more effective at doing this job. If you replace old-fashioned windows, you probably will see significant fuel savings.

In a private home, this decision is yours. If you own an apartment, you may be permitted to replace your windows on your own or obliged to share in the costs of a window replacement for the entire building.

Window coverings, for privacy and/or decoration, run the gamut from shades to blinds to curtains to drapes. Years ago, you got the works (blinds or shades plus curtains plus drapes) and after that you got the work—of cleaning all this stuff. Today, many people use miniblinds or curtains alone. And some people (say my friends the apartment dwellers with binoculars) use nothing at all.

The least you need to know about buying windows and window coverings:
- Insulating qualities of windows
- Checking frames and screens
- Window styles
- Varieties of window coverings

Windows and Heat Loss

The most attractive feature of a house—the windows—is also the most expensive because they're such bad insulators. You spend a lot of money generating heat or cooling your home, then the window lets the hot air out and the cold air in, or vice versa, which is probably where the expression "throwing money out the window" got its start.

Here's how bad it is: The insulation value of any surface is measured in terms of R value (which stands for resistance to heat transfer). A roof, for example, should have an R rating of at least 19 and, according to some experts, as much as 30. An ordinary single-glaze window (that is, a window with a single pane) has an R rating of 1.

The area around a standard single-pane window can lose up to 15 times more heat than a comparable area of wall space. The more windows you have, the more you're heating the outdoors. (Sliding glass patio doors, as you may have guessed, are a complete heating/cooling disaster.)

Most manufacturers today are making only double- or triple-glaze windows for new houses or as replacement units. It's not the additional pane or two that makes the difference but the space between them. The trapped air cuts down on the amount of heat going in or out. The space between the panes should be no less than $1/2$" and no more than $5/8$". Double-glaze windows have an approximate R value of 1.5 to 1.8, triple-glaze between 1.8 and 2.

To add even more insulating value, windows can have a low-E (low emissivity) feature, an invisible metallic coating on the surface of the glass that reduces the transfer of heat by another 35%. In a cold climate they put the low-E coating on the outside of the inside pane to keep heat in; in warm states, low-E coatings are inside the outer pane, to reflect heat out.

Even though low-E windows are a bit more expensive to install and cost from 10% to 25% more than regular insulated glass, over the long run they mean great savings in heating costs in winter and air-conditioning bills during the summer. As a side benefit, they screen out UV (ultraviolet light) rays, so they keep drapes and upholstery from fading and wood floors from yellowing.

Double-glazed, low-E windows have about the same R values as triple-glazed uncoated windows (2.5–3.2) at less cost and with more protection. Triple-glazed coated windows can have R values as high as 4.

Even better insulating windows have been introduced. One double-glaze window has an R value of 4 because it uses argon gas, a poor heat conductor, instead of air between the panes. (A possible drawback: Eventually the argon leaks and needs replacing.) A low-E, quadruple-glaze window with an extremely high R value of 8 uses a combination of specially tinted film and a well-sealed, environmentally friendly gas.

Superwindows now being developed may approach the R value of walls. These include windows that have a vacuum between the panes, others that use krypton gas (yes, from Superman's home planet); and still others that use holographic optical film that bounces sunlight to any spot in the room. Since this cuts down the need for artificial lighting, the windows may revolutionize both lighting and heating/cooling in homes. You'll be able to have more and more windows (including skylights) without higher heating and cooling bills.

If you're buying new double-paned windows, you should have two major concerns, seal and fit. If the seal isn't good, moisture appears between the two panes and the only solution is replacement. (The Sealed Insulated Glass Manufacturers' Association says its members must issue a minimum five-year warranty on glazed pieces.) If the window is loose, it won't insulate properly.

GLASS ACT

Window glass has various ratings—AA is the best but A is satisfactory for most needs—and various thicknesses, which determine its strength:

- Single-strength glass (less than $1/8"$ thick) is okay for small windows. But if you have "lights," small windows around an old-fashioned door, you should have them replaced with stronger glass for your safety and security. Building codes have required nonbreakable glass in doors and in windows next to doors or near the floor since 1979.
- Double-strength glass (at least $1/8"$ thick) is necessary for windows up to 3' × 4'.
- Plate glass (over $1/4"$) is necessary for picture windows.
- Safety glass (needed in skylights, shower doors, patio doors) comes as tempered glass (which disintegrates into beads instead of large shards), safety plate, or wire-reinforced glass.

SPECIAL WINDOW FINISHES

Windows may be treated to allow light to pass through but block heat, a useful feature in warm climates. You can also buy sheets of polyester window tints that reduce ultraviolet rays and heat. You just wet the window, press on the precut sheets, and smooth them with a squeegee. Static electricity holds them in place. When the weather cools, you can pull the sheets off, then store them. They're reusable and inexpensive. Some people love them and others complain that they peel when they shouldn't and don't come off easily when they should.

Plexiglas is fine for some purposes, but I'm not crazy about it for windows and doors. It's strong and shatter-resistant but much harder to keep clean and more likely to scratch than glass.

CHECKING THE FRAMES

You lose heat through the frame around the window as well as through the windows if the frames aren't well maintained or if the windows aren't hung straight.

In the winter, put your hand near the window frame and feel the temperature of the nearby wall. If it's cold, the frame hasn't been set in properly. There's not much that you can do about this after the fact. But when and if you replace windows, do your best to get an installer who knows what he's doing so the new ones are put in correctly. Have your contractor check that everything is level, or plumb.

You should also keep the frame in good condition. Wood has a pretty good R rating, but over the years it will shrink if it hasn't been maintained with regular painting, and air will seep in along the crack line. If you don't want to bother with maintenance, you can use aluminum frames. They don't have as good an R value, but they don't need painting or scraping. The best is anodized aluminum, which oxidizes more slowly than mill-finished. Vinyl, which is also easy to maintain and a good insulator, is not as strong as wood or metal. The top-of-the-line choice is a wood frame with metal or vinyl covering since it combines good insulation and low maintenance. Before you buy, check the corners of the frames. If all angles don't meet properly and you can see light through them, they'll admit air.

REPLACING WINDOWS

Wooden windows with frames in decent condition can be repaired and covered with storm windows, but if the frames are going, the entire window should be replaced. Single-pane steel and aluminum windows, since they are poor insulators, should probably also be replaced.

Putting a new window in an old steel casement frame is easier for the contractor but not helpful to you, since the insulation will be inferior. The old frame as well as the old window should be removed and insulated, especially in cold climates.

When you get a new window estimate, make sure you clarify whether the entire frame is being replaced, if weatherproofing around the frame is included, and if the price is inclusive of shipping costs.

If you can't afford new windows or have some other reason not to replace the frame, buy replacement windows that are slightly smaller than the originals, as they are easier to fit.

Preassembled and oversize windows will cost extra to install.

STORM WINDOWS

If they fit tightly, storm windows can cut air leakage by 50%. There should be weatherstripping around each frame, sealant on both sides of the glass, pins to keep frames pressed into the tracks, no cracks at the joints. The frame should be heavy, have weep holes, which allow moisture to drain, and be well caulked around the glass.

WINDOW STYLES

Which window you select will ultimately be a matter of taste, but there are some cleaning and maintenance considerations you should know about.

Though windows come in standard sizes, manufacturers are used to customizing windows (for a price, of course) in odd sizes and shapes.

Double-hung windows (independent upper and lower units, with multiple panes, in a single frame) are the most common of all. You can tip or flip the units in some of the newer models in order to make cleaning easier. These are awkward to reach over sinks.

Casement windows have a hinge on the vertical side, come with single or multiple panes, and are cranked open. **Rotary or pivot windows** are also cranked, but they are hinged in the middle and rock back and forth. **Awning-type windows,** which open like flaps (often paired and set in place below a nonopening window) are cranked open, too. Though all of these provide nice ventilation and are easy to clean, the cranks tend to break. They may also block traffic if installed over decks.

Double-Hung

Casement

Rotary

Awning

Sliding

Sliding windows open like sliding doors. They're easy to operate and inexpensive. Both sliding and awning windows are often used in clerestory windows—a horizontal strip of windows set high in a wall.

French windows, with their multiple panes, are difficult to clean. But two smooth panes of glass with the lattice sandwiched in between, a recent innovation, give you the look of French windows without the work.

Bow and bay windows project outward from an outside wall, bow in a rounded shape, bay at angles. At floor level, you can use them to create a little alcove in the kitchen for a breakfast nook. Installed 18" to 24" high, they can be fitted as a window seat—a great way to lighten and take advantage of the space in a dark stair landing. With multipaned panels, they have a more old-fashioned look, but with five solid verticals, they appear modern. They come prefabricated and ready to install.

Bay

Multiform windows, or dormers, add extra light and a decorative effect but can't be opened and closed. Many window manufacturers make standardized shapes that you can order from a lumberyard or contractor. They usually come double-glaze, with vinyl-clad or aluminum exteriors and ready-to-finish interior wood surfaces.

Skylights can be set into a

French

flat or sloping roof. The glass may open for ventilation but is usually fixed. It should be carefully installed to avoid problems due to leaks of snow or rain. Bronze-tinted glass can cut down the intensity if the room is already bright. For safety, most skylights come with tempered glass layered over laminated glass (or with embedded wires) and are low-E, some argon-filled.

Your local building code may require a basement escape window, depending on which of the three national building codes (the Basic Building Code, the Uniform Building Code, and the Standard Building Code) applies in your part of the country. Check with your local building inspector. The window should be no more than 44" from the floor. All three codes require a minimum width of 20" and minimum height of 20"–24."

WINDOW SCREENS

Nylon is superior to metal: It doesn't rust, is easier to repair, and doesn't lose its shape as fast. Some screens fit into their frame with clips and can be removed easily for cleaning.

Curtains, Drapes, and Other Window Coverings

Fabrics used on windows include polyester, cotton, rayon, and blends. Unless you've got maid service, I'd go with the polyester. It can't fade, it's easy to wash, and it doesn't need ironing. The only reason to choose a heavier fabric is for insulation purposes, but some heavy curtains won't pull open easily.

If you look through the curtain catalogs, you may be somewhat confused by the possibilities, but in fact there are just four basic types of curtains.

Dormer

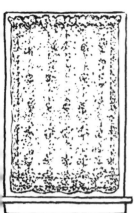

Panel

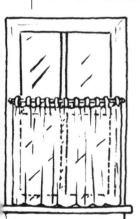

Sash

Panel or glass curtains hang in place next to the glass.

Draw curtains are on pulleys. Priscilla curtains (sheer, or nearly sheer) have ruffles across the top, sides, and bottom and are hung in two panels to meet at the middle or crisscross on two separate rods.

Sash curtains, of thin fabrics, cover the lower half of the window. On many-paned French doors, there are rods that hold them in place both at the top and at the bottom.

Café curtains (or tier curtains) are a two-tier variation of sash curtains—one tier is on the lower half of the window, one tier is on top—but aren't necessarily made of sheer fabrics.

A **valence** is a short, decorative piece of fabric that covers the tops of curtains or drapes. It can be pleated or it can hang in folds if it has a channel for the curtain rod to go through.

Curtains can be made to measure (in which case you provide measurements), custom-made (the manufacturer takes measurements), or ready-made. Getting the measurements exactly right may be tricky, which is why there is sometimes a charge for this service.

Ready-made panels come in standard widths, such as 25, 48, 72, 96, 120, or 144 inches, and

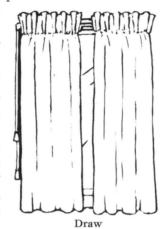

Draw

Café

standard lengths, 36, 45, 54, 63, 84, or 90 inches. Measure across the *inside* of the frame.

Hang curtains lower than the windowsill or they'll attract dirt from it like a magnet.

The simplest kind of curtain rod is just that—a rod—that passes through the top curtain hem. Sometimes rings are slipped over the rod to attach to the curtain, as with café curtains.

If you are planning to use curtains that draw open and closed, you need a rod with pulleys, and if you'll use curtains plus drapes, you need a double rod with pulleys, one for the curtains and one for the drapes.

DRAPES

Drapes are just draw curtains that are opaque and usually lined for insulation purposes. Hooks attached to the rear of the drape are slipped over pulley rods, and cords from the rods pull the drapes across the window.

Drape fabrics may be stain-resistant or stain-retardant. They also should be preshrunk. Moisture from rain, humidity, or radiator steam or pet stains may leave water spots that can't be safely removed.

Often fabrics that claim to be dry-cleanable aren't. The best thing you can do is to avoid surface prints (which often bleed), screen prints (which fade), and chintz (which loses its luster.)

Custom-made drapes have a measurement tag sewn inside the top. If you use these measurements to guide you when buying new drapes from a reputable store, you can hang them yourself and they'll fit perfectly.

The Fair Claims guide, nationally recognized by dry cleaners, estimates that lined drapes last 4 years, fiberglass and unlined drapes last 3, and sheer curtains last 2. However, these estimates are for reimbursement or replacement costs if the drapes are destroyed in cleaning; you may keep your window coverings around much longer than this.

BLINDS

The advantage of blinds over curtains is that they can be washed less often. They are a big nuisance to clean, however, with the possible exception of the rollup wooden shades. But these don't last very long and are a real attractor of grease and dust.

When you buy blinds, especially from a mail order catalog, make sure you measure correctly. The right place to measure is from side to side inside the frame.

If you're buying custom-made miniblinds you may be able to supply your own measurements or be charged for someone to come and do them for you. Since you're stuck if you've supplied the measurements and the blinds don't fit, I think it's worth having the measurements made professionally.

Get miniblinds that match the color of the walls or in a neutral shade. If you change the decor, you don't want to have to buy new blinds.

The best miniblinds are the ones that are sandwiched between two pieces of glass. You have the flexibility of the shades combined with the easy cleanup of the glass.

SHADES

Shades are a more effective room darkener than miniblinds and are less expensive than drapes.

For non-standard windows, custom-made shades are cheaper than custom-made miniblinds. They're also available in standard sizes.

They can be ordered in fabrics that match your room or you can glue your own fabric to a standard shade to customize it.

SHUTTERS

Shutters are a low-maintenance, durable window covering. Custom-made, custom-finished shutters may be costly, but you can buy unfinished ones and paint or stain them yourself. Use the same ones that you would use outside for the most inexpensive but good-looking window treatment you can buy.

● ●

LIGHTING UP

The least you need to know about buying lighting:
- General, task, and accent lighting and how to plan it
- Which bulbs to use where

General Lighting

You're the character *in* the room. The general lighting is the character *of* the room—the amount and kind of light that fills the room when you flip on the switch or throw open the curtains. Obviously, it shouldn't be too glaring or too dim.

In a kitchen the general lighting often comes from track lighting or recessed or surface-mounted overhead fixtures. In a dining room, it may come from a chandelier.

In a living room or family room, the table and standing lamps—and maybe a couple of wall fixtures, called sconces—provide the general lighting. Or it may come from indirect lighting hidden behind a structure that's built high along the walls:

Behind a **cornice,** the bulbs all point downward.

Behind a **valence** (hung slightly lower than a cornice), the bulbs point up and down.

Behind a **cove**, the bulbs all point upwards.

One nice thing about this kind of lighting is that there are no lamps to clean.

Task Lighting

If you cast a shadow over the cutting board when you're working in the kitchen or the table lamp bulb blinds you when you sit on the living room couch, your task lighting—which is defined as the light you work by—needs to be redesigned. Task lights can be over, on, or even underneath a surface, like the lights hung under kitchen cabinets. The goal is soft, even illumination without glare or shadows. Children seem to be able to read in the dark, but this ability disappears with age. As a matter of fact, it is one of the great ironies of life that the older you grow and the more dim light becomes you, the brighter the light you need in order to see.

Table lamps, lamps that clamp onto shelves, swing-arm or fixed wall sconces, and under-cabinet lights fitted with either incandescent or halogen lights can all serve as task lights.

Buying a task lamp is rarely a problem. Finding a place to plug it in may be. The invention I'm waiting for is the cordless lamp! I always remind people who are building or remodeling a house to include plenty of outlets so they can plug in lamps (radios, electric clocks, VCRs, hair dryers, and so on) without trails of extension cords. (If you're short on outlets, see the information about raceways in the Maintaining section of the book.)

Also, when installing built-in furniture, make sure that any outlets that will be hidden are repositioned somewhere accessible. They can be put flush into a countertop, for example. You would think this is the kind of thing that a contractor should be thinking about. If you find one who does, please send me his name.

When buying lamps, always be sure to get one that has been UL safety-tested. To avoid the danger of shocks, never use a lamp outdoors, around pools or hot tubs, or in bathrooms next to sinks, tubs, or showers. And halogen lamps, which give a very high-intensity light, are not recommended for children's rooms. They get too hot.

Be very careful never to place a lamp near fabric. The first time my friend Maureen's son brought home a date, Maureen made a special effort to clean up the family room, newly decorated with floor-level spots that cast interesting shadows on the ceiling. After dinner the two kids went in to watch TV. It turned out to be a truly memorable evening, when the drapes caught fire. One of the spotlights knocked aside during vacuuming had heated them up.

Accent Lighting

Accent lights are what I call the beauty marks of home decorating. They can call attention to

---

CUTTING THE CORD

If you have a floor or table lamp placed near an outlet, you probably have a lot of excess cord hanging around. If you don't expect to be moving the lamp, you can shorten the cord permanently and easily in less time than it would take to make a three-minute egg. You just cut the lamp cord and push the cut portion into a slot in a replacement flat-wire plug made for this purpose (instructions are on the package). When you press a lever or push two parts together, tiny internal prongs penetrate the insulation and complete the circuit.

whatever they're near. For example, painting lights are made to fit over the top center of the picture frame.

To be effective, accent lighting requires at least three times as much light on the object as the general lighting around it.

The most interesting new development in accent lighting consists of low-voltage strip lights. These are tiny incandescent or halogen bulbs, as small as $1^{1}/_{2}$ watts, spaced $1^{1}/_{2}$" to 2" apart on an adhesive backing.

When you put a number of strips side by side, you get a low general glow. If you space them, you see overlapping "scallops" of light. A single strip can light up each shelf of your collection of old bottles or other castoffs that in your opinion are worthy of display. Or use them by the yard under the "toe space" in kitchen cabinets, living room, or den wall units or along the top moldings of furniture or the wall.

If you buy any of these light strips, make sure the bulbs are replaceable. You don't want one of those Christmas-light situations where when one bulb goes, the whole thing is shot. On the other hand, good quality Christmas light strings can be used as accent lights.

Decorating with Light

If you've noticed how the lighting can transform a stage, you know that it has tremendous potential to change the look of any area. Spots and "wall washers" directed around the edges of a room can make it appear larger. Up-lights that direct light from the floor toward the ceiling can give it a dramatic look. Place a floor spot so it casts the shadow of a huge potted palm, and all of a sudden you're in a night club in the Caribbean. Well, almost—you may need a few of those drinks with the umbrellas first.

If you've darkened the walls or the room just seems dim, you can brighten it without spending much money. Just adding higher-watt bulbs to the lamps (if you've checked to make sure the lamp can accept them) can make a difference. And/or replace the shades with others that are more translucent. Replacing old, yellow shades with new ones can make a striking difference. Or add more track lights. Or use a larger overhead fixture, or one that can accommodate more or higher wattage bulbs. If you're buying a new fixture, I should point out that globes collect less dust than the platter types.

If you need professional help with your lighting, a local lamp showroom may be able to suggest someone. You may get better value from a consultation on lighting than on interior decorating. Changing the lighting can completely transform a room for relatively little money but unless you have a real knack for this sort of thing you need expert help.

TRACK AND RECESSED LIGHTS

Whether you choose track or recessed lighting depends on how much ceiling room is available to "bury" fixtures, whether you want the softer look of recessed lighting, and of course whether you want to go for the cost of recessed lights (and professional installation).

Track lighting, also called "canned" or "can" light, is easy to install. The track, usually screwed to the ceiling but sometimes mounted on walls, can be as short as one foot, as long as 100 feet or more. The newest invention is minitracks a few inches long—"monopoints" —that hold a single can.

The center of the first track or recessed light should be about $2^{1}/_{2}$ to 3 feet from the wall. Because the track is wired along the length, fixtures can be moved, swiveled, rotated, and aimed in different directions. If you get an urge to move the furniture around, resetting the lights in the room is just a matter of getting out the ladder. With special attachments, you can even position a chandelier or a pendant light along the track. "Pendants" are technically any hanging light, including a chandelier, but the word usually refers to a smaller fixture without arms. Compact low-voltage halogen models cost a little more than standard track lights.

Recessed fixtures are either down-lights, which fit the hole snugly in a fixed position, or "eyeballs," which rotate. You can use eyeballs to aim light anywhere from straight downward to a 45° angle. They're easier to clean than lights in cans.

If you insulate your ceilings after recessed lighting is installed, make sure that the contractor installs the insulation far enough from the housing of the fixture to avoid a fire risk. The lights blinking on and off can be a sign that you have this problem, but it can just be a sign that the bulbs aren't the right wattage. Before you panic, try changing the bulb.

KEEPING ON THE TRACK

If the beams of light cast by your track lighting don't overlap, the cans aren't spaced closely enough. You need more.

Lamps and Shades

Using lamps instead of overhead lights as general lighting makes your choices slightly more confusing since you've got even more options than with overhead lighting. A shaded lamp gives a very different kind of light from a paper-covered lamp or halogen lamp. Most lamp showrooms are so crammed that it's very hard to tell which effect you get from any single one. The best way to figure out what kind of lamps you like, and what kind of illumination they provide, is to check out the lamps in other people's homes or to look at department store display rooms.

When you buy a lamp, leave on the tags until you've tried it out at home. See how it looks and

see how it lights. You may find that a "pharmacy" lamp, whose bulb hangs below the shade, may glare uncomfortably when you're seated on your sofa. Other lamps may be the wrong proportion—if the lamp is too low, the top of the room will remain dark, and if the shade is too narrow, the light from the lamp may not cover a big enough area for your needs.

Standing lamps that throw light up are excellent for general illumination. With bright halogen bulbs, a single lamp can light an entire small room. Floor lamp cords should be out of the way, preferably tacked along the baseboard or molding with special two-prong insulated staples.

Wall lamps help with general illumination, too, but they aren't much use as task lights. One exception is the swing-arm lamp (generally wall-mounted but also comes in standing versions), which can be swung into place right over your book or your work and is excellent for either living room or on either side of the bed. Swing-arm lamps are also low maintenance (no base to clean) and efficient (they take up no table space). Mount wall lamps about 42" from the floor, and if you don't like the look of the cord hanging down the wall, buy and mount a cord cover.

Hanging fixtures should be positioned so that the bottom of the shade is at eye level when a person is seated, about 40" to 42" above the floor or 30" to 36" above a table.

Table lamps should be placed so the bottom of the shade is just below eye level.

Shades range in color from white to cream, which means that the light they emit ranges from very white to yellowish. Personally, I think the room looks better if you have the same "color" of light coming from each lamp. Some shades darken as they age; sometimes, simply replacing shades can make the room seem much brighter. Pink shades cast a flattering warm light. Dark, opaque shades can only be used for accent lighting.

Japanese rice paper ("washi") around a wire

frame is used for table lamps, standing lamps, and even a 6-to-8-foot tube lamp hung from the ceiling. It can't be washed or cleaned, but you can replace a torn shade with sheets of washi paper from an art store or upscale stationery store.

If you've ever had the experience of trying to decide whether a shade is or is not washable, you'll understand why I recommend checking the tag for this information when the lamp or shade is new and filing the information in your memory (or someplace more reliable).

If you're thinking of buying a lamp because you like the base but the shade is too wide or tall, you can always replace it, but inquire how much a new shade will cost before you make the purchase. It may be considerably less expensive just to look for another lamp with a shade you like better.

When you shop for a replacement, bring along the measurements. Shades are measured by height and diagonally across the bottom. If you want to change the shape or size of the shade, choose one 2 to 3 inches longer than the width at the top. If the shade's not in the right proportion to the base, it will look strange, like a hat that's too big or too small. Shades that are too long or too wide may wobble, and if they're too short, they won't cover the bulb properly. Your best bet is to bring the lamp base to the store and try on shades.

If you lose, don't like, or damage the **finial**—the screw-on piece that holds the shade to the lamp—it can be replaced. In fact, finials are often used as decorative accents.

A sticker on every new lamp or hanging fixture gives you recommended maximum **wattage.** If you want the lamp for reading or detail work, choose one that accepts 75 to 150 watts. For bedside lamps, 75 to 100 watts will do. Never exceed the recommended wattage. The bulbs will burn out faster and the heat from a too-hot bulb may even cause a glass fixture to break. Also, a bulb that's too high in wattage may be a fire hazard anywhere.

DIMMERS

Dimmers that reduce general lighting at the touch of the switch are installed at the outlet. Once the power is turned off, it's a matter of putting in a couple of screws and connecting a couple of wires. With older systems, when you moved the dimmer tab up and down (or twisted the knob), every light would dim uniformly. New, digitally controlled dimming systems—all in one spot—can turn the lights down 50% in most of the room, 80% near the TV, and keep them on high in a reading corner. Some systems control the light switches in a room. Others work the whole house and some can be preset to operate when you're not at home.

Dimmers are sold in different wattages. To calculate what you need, if most of your lights in the room are controlled by a single switch, just add up the bulb wattage of the lamps—100 watts for the table lamp, 300 for the wall sconces, etc. The total wattage that the dimmer can control is indicated on its housing. Don't overload the dimmer beyond these limits. Halogens and fluorescents require a more expensive low-voltage dimmer than incandescent bulbs.

Lighting Specific Rooms

Kitchen. You can light an average kitchen with overhead fixtures that take 75-watt reflector flood bulbs or compact fluorescents totaling 60 watts, either recessed, mounted on the surface, or mounted behind a "faceboard" that covers the whole ceiling. At the sink and range, you can add down-lights to illuminate the work area.

Bedroom. Over the headboard, you can use a track of lights the width of the mattress with 20- to 50-watt reflector bulbs or a bracket to hold one of the new fluorescents, which give off a warmer light. The lower edge should be 30" above the mattress.

Dining Room. Along with a chandelier,

you'll probably also need additional lights, either recessed fixtures over each corner of the table or wall sconces on either side of the buffet mounted 60" above the floor. Halogens will give you a good, white light for this purpose.

Bathroom. One of the trickiest task lighting jobs. If the light above the mirror or ceiling is too bright, it casts shadows down; you look as if you've come out of a police lineup. The ideal is recessed lighting or a globe ceiling fixture plus lighting on the sides of the mirror that will help block the glare. But if the only light in the room is around the mirror, make sure the fixture is at least 22" wide with three or four 60-watt bulbs. Fluorescent tubes in "natural color" are available for some fixtures. They're more expensive but give a better light.

Never put up any lights around tubs or showers unless the fixture specifies that it's okay for this use.

WHEN THE (FLUORESCENT) LIGHTS GO DOWN LOW

New lights may flicker when they're cold and old ones blink before they're about to die. Otherwise, blinking may be a signal that the bulbs are not seated properly; take them out and put them back into place.

Old bulbs usually dim and blacken at the ends before they go out. But if they go out abruptly, hum, or smell funny, there's a problem in the fixture. Call the electrician.

Lightbulbs

The lumen is the measure of light a bulb gives off: A typical 100-watt bulb produces about 1,750 lumens.

Most household, car headlight, and flashlight bulbs are incandescent, with a life of about 750 to 1000 hours—because that's what suits manufacturers. They have the capability to make bulbs that last longer. For example, a traffic light, which is a standard incandescent, is designed to last 8,000 hours. If you need a cause to demonstrate about, here's a good one.

An **incandescent** bulb contains argon and nitrogen gas. When electricity passes through it, the thin wire inside heats up, producing heat (99% of the energy) and light (only 1%). When the bulb burns out, it's because the filament has broken. That's why you can shake a bulb to tell whether it's good or not: You can hear the broken filament.

Some bulbs have two filaments to create a higher wattage. For example, a 50-watt and 100-watt filament together make up a 150-watt bulb.

Fluorescent light once had a glaring, bluish glow that made it the "bus station" of lighting. Under this lighting your makeup would appear normal in the bathroom mirror or cosmetic department, but in incandescent or natural light you'd look like Morticia Addams.

Nowadays fluorescents come in pink and yellow tones and in classic lightbulb shapes. Fluorescent warm-toned tubing around a bathroom mirror has none of the drawbacks and all of the advantages of traditional fluorescents. It casts light evenly, gives off little if any glare, and saves money and energy. To produce the same amount of light as incandescents, fluorescents use about a fifth the electricity and give off a fifth the heat. Sylvania claims that its Soft White Compact 6" fluorescent tube bulb, for example, costs several times as much as a comparable incandescent but lasts 13 times as long as a comparable incandescent bulb and can save $57 in electricity costs over its 10,000-hour life span.

The **halogen** bulb emits light that is closest to the natural white light of the sun; in this light the human eye can see (and distinguish) the broadest range of colors. The major drawback is that halogen bulbs get very hot (so they are not recommended for children's rooms) and require delicate handling. The oil from your skin when you touch the bulb may cause it to

65

explode. Halogen bulbs cost about three times as much as incandescent bulbs but last about 2,000–3,000 hours, or three times as long.

A long-lasting bulb that operates on radio waves may be the bulb of the future.

LONG-LASTING LIGHT FOR INACCESSIBLE PLACES

High-efficiency, low-voltage bulbs use transformers that reduce the amount of current so they produce less light but last longer. Use them in a fixture that's very hard to get at, like the entrance foyer light that's two stories high. Ask for low-voltage bulbs at an electrical supply house or lighting store. When you buy, check the package to make sure that they can be used in the temperature or humidity situation in your house.

FURNITURE

The least you need to know about buying furniture:
- Judging wood furniture
- How to look at upholstered pieces
- Other furniture options: unfinished, used, custom-made, non-wood

Where to Start

You will probably have some general idea about the kind of furniture you want—period or antique, traditional, modern, or we'll-take-whatever-we-can-get. Unless you have a big budget for antique furniture or plan to spend your weekends at flea markets, you'll probably be shopping in stores that specialize in either reproduction, traditional, or modern furniture.

In buying furniture, you're really flying blind. There are few brand names, there is little warranty coverage, and price is not always a guarantee of quality.

On top of that, you've got a lot of options on even a single sofa—size, style, color, with or without wood, and so on. A sectional couch that's in one store may come with slightly different proportions, different arms, and different fabrics in another. If you've got a whole room (or rooms) to furnish you have to make a lot of decisions and then do a lot of trekking around to find just what you want and at the right price.

If you are shopping with a partner you may also have to factor in arguing time and prepare for the fact that you may have many second thoughts about whether you will wish to spend your lifetime with a person who has such strange ideas about sofas.

If the time and the choices involved become overwhelming, consider hiring an interior decorator. They buy at a discount, you pay the regular price, and the difference is their fee, so it doesn't cost you a lot extra to get some help. On the other hand, decorators take you to showrooms where the furniture is not exactly bargain-priced. It isn't worth their while to guide you around the local Cheap Sofas 'R' Us. If you're looking to save as much as you can, you're on your own. Very much on your own, for as a general rule, people who sell furniture in department stores are not going to spend a lot of time helping you with matters of taste.

While they should be civil and will answer your questions, furniture salesmen I have encountered are there just to take your order. I have a friend who didn't understand this and plagued these people with questions like, "Do you feel this is a vibrant color?" until I became too embarrassed to shop with him.

Take home upholstery samples to see how they look in your house and measure the prospective purchases carefully. Don't forget to measure the doors to make sure the furniture you're buying can fit through them. In apartment buildings, check the height of the elevator. If you've measured wrong, your only solution may be the rather expensive one of hiring a hauling company to bring it through the window (if in fact that's possible) or having the piece cut into parts that can then be pushed, nailed, or glued back together.

If you haven't bought furniture before, let me warn you about delivery. A piece of upholstered furniture in a fabric the store is featuring may arrive quickly, but if you want something different, and quite often you will, you may wait weeks or even months—and there may be no laws holding the manufacturer to a specific date. The sales contract, which should include a description of the furniture in detail (and usually has a five-year warranty for construction and a one-year warranty for fabric), should also indicate the delivery date and give you the option to cancel, though there may be some charge for cancellation. In some states, if the furniture doesn't arrive within a certain time after it's promised, you can cancel without penalty. (And then you get to start all over again.)

Check the section Delivery on p. 19 so you will know what you should do when the piece finally arrives, assuming you're still at the same address and still young enough to remember buying it.

Wood and Wood Veneers

Household furnishings are divided into case goods—pieces that have no upholstered parts— and upholstered furniture.

The majority of furniture is made of wood. In the past, all furniture was made of solid wood. Today only the structural framework of case goods is solid hardwood. While you would think a product made of solid wood would be preferable, in fact, it's hard to care for (it's more likely to warp and swell) and it's heavy, and so is the price tag. As a result, the top, sides, front, and back panels of 75% of furniture made today, at all price levels, is veneered.

Veneer used to be regarded as a second-class finish, but new methods of cutting veneer

sheets, better construction, and a better selection have given it a little more class. A face veneer is a thin sheet of wood of a type that may be too expensive, too heavy, or too light for furniture construction. A veneer or laminate panel is actually a strong wood "sandwich"— from three to seven layers including the face veneer and a plywood core—bonded together with adhesives.

Don't confuse veneer, which is real wood, with plastic laminates that just resemble wood. The plastic—unlike wood—is resistent to heat and water staining. But it doesn't have the same shine and finish as wood.

WHY YOU SHOULD READ THE LABEL CAREFULLY

"Solid oak" means all the exposed parts must be made of a solid piece of oak.

"Genuine oak" means the piece is made entirely of oak, but it may be a combination of veneer and solid wood. It may also be described as "oak veneer."

"Oak finish" means that the wood has been finished to look like oak through a printing or engraving process.

The most common furniture hardwoods today, grouped roughly from lightest to darkest, are maple and beech; oak and pecan; teak (out of favor because it's from the rain forests), mahogany, and cherry; rosewood and walnut. Softwoods, like redwood, fir, cypress, cedar, and spruce are used primarily for outdoor or rec room furniture rather than living room furniture, though pine, a softwood, is used for both.

CHARACTERISTICS OF WOOD

Hardwood and softwood refers to the type of tree wood comes from, not to the quality of the wood. Hardwoods are leaf-shedding trees like maple and oak. Softwoods have needles or cones, like fir and redwood.

Color comes from the heartwood, or inner portion of the tree. Sapwood, which contains the living cells, is almost always white.

Figure describes the wood surface—texture, knots, and whether it has distinctive growth rings. Most woods are fine-grained (or closed-grained), not porous, with subtle growth rings. But a few hardwoods are open-grained (or coarse-grained), with distinctive growth rings, and the kind of pores Clearasil got rich on. Figure depends on the natural growth pattern of the wood and how and from where on the tree it is cut.

Wood Product Furniture

Three major types of wood products are used in furniture construction.

Laminated wood consists of sheets of wood placed in one direction, as in a bentwood chair.

Hardboard is a bonded mix of tiny wood fibers that looks like cork, tile, or hardwood. You often see it on the back panels of bookcases and as drawer dividers.

Particle board consists of wood particles and adhesives bonded together. It's very versatile; it can be veneered, stained, and painted.

FINISHES

To let the natural color show through, wood may be finished with transparent stain or varnish. Light "washes" of color—whitewashing, pickling, or country finishes—also let the wood grain show through. But sometimes the wood is covered with an opaque finish such as paint or lacquer.

No matter what the look, while expensive furniture may be given as much as twenty-five coats, inexpensive furniture is usually finished in a one-process dip, spray, or coating and generally given a second protective finish with polyurethane, acrylic lacquers, polyesters, var-

COMMON WOODS AND THEIR COLORS

Hardwoods	Color
White ash	Brown to grayish brown; sometimes cream or off white; bleaches well
Beech	Reddish white to reddish brown; takes water-based stain
Black cherry	Light to dark reddish brown; takes stain well, doesn't bleach
Mahogany	Various shades of red to a rich dark brown; can be painted or stained
Maple	Light reddish brown; takes stain and wax well
Oak	"White" oak is grayish brown; red oak has a reddish tinge; English oak is deeper brown
Teak	Yellowish brown

Softwoods	Color
Cedars	Various types, including Eastern red (which must be sealed) and Western red (lightweight)
Pine	Ranges from light brown Eastern white pine to yellow (which may be yellow, orange, or light brown)
Redwood	Deep reddish brown

nish, or shellac. Sometimes vinyl surfaces are built right into the furniture. They look like wood but don't need any waxing, staining, or varnish. They're also stain-resistant and easy to maintain.

JUDGING QUALITY

If the quality of the finish is good, it will be hard and smooth with no drips, cracks, or bubbles. The grain should match and the color should be uniform where it's supposed to be. In good furniture, even the parts that don't show—the underside of the table, the inside of drawers, and the backs of the panels—are sanded smooth and stained to match the rest. The leaves of a table should be grained and colored to blend with the others.

Check that the furniture is not so lightweight that it wobbles. The framework and seat base should be heavy. Good pieces of furniture sometimes have levelers—devices screwed into the bottom of the legs that can raise or lower them fractionally—to compensate for uneven floors. The legs should stand squarely and have metal tips that protect the floor. Casters—metal, rubber, or plastic balls at the end of the leg—are helpful on pieces like a heavy sofa, so you can move it to clean behind it.

Joints are what make furniture strong. If the furniture is good, the pieces fit tightly. Today, most joints are sealed with epoxy adhesives. Well-made furniture will not have excess glue around the joints. Larger joints should have extra reinforcement, with blocks of wood that are screwed as well as glued into place.

Pull out the extensions to a desk or a table. They shouldn't sag, and the piece they're connected to shouldn't tip.

In a dresser or end table, pull out one of the drawers. It should fit flush in front and glide out without wobbling. The sides and back should be at least $1/2$" thick and rigid. There should be center or side glides to guide the drawer, stops that keep the drawer from going

SAVING THE SURFACE

Having a glass top cut to fit tables, low bookcases, or end tables is a wonderful way to protect the finish at very little cost. Bring a paper pattern for the glass cutter (generally, any mirror place will cut glass for you). The thinnest weight should do. Under the glass, put a felt circle in each corner or at intervals to keep the glass from slipping. (You can buy these at a department or chain store.)

too far back, and reinforcement blocks for it to rest on. The hardware should be screwed firmly into place. Unfortunately, you probably won't know whether a handle will snap or break until after the piece has been in use for a while.

Check out doors. They should meet exactly, open and close easily, and have magnetic catches to hold them shut.

Some inexpensive furniture will generally hold up with no problems—for example, bookcases, small tables, things that don't get much wear. But anything that is subject to stress, such as dressers and end tables with drawers, may fall apart fairly quickly.

FURNISHING THE DINING ROOM

If you rarely have more than four or six people to dinner, you can manage with a small table or one that can be expanded. For small apartments or dining areas, the tables with the self-storing leaves are the most practical choice. If the table comes with separate leaves, you may

WHICH COMES FIRST, THE CARPET OR THE SOFA?

It makes sense to find the carpet color you like first and then the sofa to match it. Chances are you'll be replacing the upholstery before you replace the carpeting, so it's the carpeting that ought to guide your choice.

be able to store them right underneath using a few L-shaped brackets.

Even a table without leaves, like a glass table, can be made larger with a specially made top. You can buy them or have one made. For big family gatherings, my friend Miriam makes do with a plywood table cover that expands her table by one foot all around. It was made in two parts for easy storing. Hinging the pieces would have been costly, so she uses a metal hook and eye to fasten them together, lays a cloth over the plywood, then puts her fancy cloth over that. Since the table surface is generally covered with linen when people entertain, I never much saw the point of an expensive dining table anyway.

The most practical and adaptable table I ever saw starts as a 48" round, which can seat 4 to 6; adds one leaf to get a 68" table, seating 6 to 8; two leaves for dinner-party size, 88", seating 8 to 10; three for large dinner party, 108", seating 10 to 12; and four for "Thanksgiving or Christmas size," 128", seating 12 to 14.

If you can't find this kind of table to buy, maybe you can use an expandable arrangement a friend of mine set up. She had two identical rectangular tables, one of which was in the center of the dining room and one of which she used as a sideboard. If she needed a bigger table, she pushed them together.

Upholstered chairs are most comfortable, but don't select a fragile fabric. Food will be dropped on these chairs, particularly if there are any children in the family or if you have exuberant guests. One solution, of course, is to serve only food that matches your upholstery.

Upholstered Furniture

It's particularly hard to judge the quality of upholstered furniture because so much is hidden. The price usually depends not on the quality of the furniture construction but on the covering fabric, which is the most variable—and most expensive—element.

But you can make some superficial checks.

The guidelines for checking furniture quality, mentioned a few pages back, obviously apply. And while less expensive seats can be supported by fabric or steel webbing or wooden slats, good quality furniture has springs. In zigzag construction, which is less expensive, flat zigzag or S-type springs are nailed to the frame and linked by other tiny springs. In coil construction, which is costlier, hand-tied deep cone-shaped springs, 8 or 12 to a seat, are attached to webbing or steel bands. (Springs are tied eight times in good quality pieces, only four in others, which may not be enough to keep them from poking up and tearing.) In both cases, the spring is covered by some type of padding.

Cushions can be made of urethane foam or natural latex foam, often covered by softer layers of foam and a wrap of polyester fiberfill. Decorative buttons should be hand-sewn through the filling. When you see zippers around the cushions, do not jump to the conclusion that the covers can be removed or cleaned, since they may shrink. The zippers are there only to improve the fit.

Removable (and reversible) cushions will help your couch last twice as long. But be careful. If there are buttons on one side only, the cushion isn't reversible.

Under the cushions, the deck, or platform, should be covered with a color-coordinated fabric. Run your hands around the frame. It should be well enough padded so that you don't feel the wood or any lumps.

Sit in the couch to see if it feels too high or too low (or just right). Is the cushion deep (wide) enough, or too wide? If you like to curl up in the corner, try it and see if you feel comfortable.

Your biggest decision is the covering. It is often (though not always) much cheaper to order the couch in the fabric in which it is shown. Selecting a fabric from the swatch book may drive the price up to many times what you see on the hang tag. Before you fall in love with a particular fabric, think about how it will wear. And check it out.

- Test the fabric with your fingernail to see if it will pill or shred.
- Look at the reverse side of the fabric. Cheaper fabrics are surface-printed; in good quality fabric, the pattern comes right through.
- Hold the swatch up to the light: You shouldn't be able to see any light between the threads.
- Pull at it. A good weave won't separate. I thought the heavily textured fabrics would be more durable, but actually, because they're easily rubbed, they wear down faster. They are also major dust and hair catchers. Slightly textured fabrics, however, have the advantage of hiding dirt and wrinkles.
- Does the fabric scratch or feel sticky? Might it feel that way in warm weather?

Dark fabrics show lint and light ones get dirty. I assume this information doesn't come as a revelation, yet I often see people buying light-colored expensive sofas even though they have a child or pet in the house. I assume these people are trying to make the point that their children/pets are so well trained they won't jump or lie on the sofa and are putting money on this. Bad idea. If you're in the kid/pet category, you can also forget rayon, silk, cotton, or tapestry, which need professional cleaning, or velours or velvets, which spot, shrink, and discolor from even a water stain.

Soil, friction, and sunlight all reduce the life of fabric.

On the label, upholstered furniture now has a cleanability code. The fabric is rated W, S, W-S, or X to show how it must be cleaned. W means clean with a water-based cleaner; S means use a dry-cleaning solvent; W-S means use either; and X means no liquids, just brush or vacuum it. Obviously an X rating in furniture is like an X rating in the movies—not for kids. W-rated fabrics are the easiest to clean.

The dealer will probably offer to spray on a stain-repellent finish—for a fee, of course—but look at the information on the swatch in the sample book. You may discover that the finish was already applied at the factory. In other words, you'll be paying for the same process twice. Covering it with a protective coating like Scotchgard increases the cleanability but not, unfortunately, how it wears. Nor does it mean you'll never have to clean it at all. And whether the protecting finish is even effective on your particular fabric is questionable, since this depends on the fiber content and texture of the yarn. Even if you get a stain-repelling "guarantee," read the fine print. If there is a stain, you may only be able to collect for the cost of the finishing.

The only absolute sure protection is a plastic covering. I personally don't like furniture that people can stick to. But one of my readers suggested an interesting compromise. She had one side only of the cushions covered with plastic, then flipped them when company came.

When the fabric gets too worn or shabby, you can make do by throwing a serape or a bedspread over it for a little while, but eventually you'll have to decide whether to reupholster, slipcover, or leave it on the curb for the Sanitation Department. If the springs are good and you paid a lot of money for it—and most of all, if you love it—it may be worth reupholstering. This involves removing the fabric and may involve repairing the springs and repadding.

Slipcovering simply means making a new cover, like a pillowcase on a pillow. I have found that slipcovering is often as costly (or nearly so) as reupholstering without looking nearly as good, but this is a matter of taste.

With inexpensive furniture such as an old sofa bed or couch, there is no point to slipcovering or reupholstering. Once the furniture looks worn, the frame is probably about to go as well. Just replace it.

If you need an extra sofa or sofa bed for a guest room or den, check the sale areas that are in most stores. In the sea of beige furniture that's usually there, occasionally you find an unusual piece at a great price, from an order that's been canceled or a floor sample that was deliberately offbeat. What may be too eccentric for a living room might be just the thing to make a small guest room or den livelier.

Unfinished Furniture

New unpainted or unstained ready-made furniture—the kind you may get in a paint store or a place like Home Depot—is a lot less expensive than finished. The cost is low because it's mass-produced and because this furniture is made of the most inexpensive wood. As a result, it's very likely to contain surface imperfections like knotholes.

You can cover the wood entirely, with an opaque finish, such as paint, or you may decide to make it look like another (more expensive) kind of wood by applying a stain—a painted-on coating that changes the color of wood to a shade that's more red, brown, or yellowish while allowing the grain to show through. The newest stains are pastels, like pale white, gray, and blue, that give you a muted or "pickled" effect with just one coat. If you want something different from a wood tone, just wipe on fabric dye with a soft cloth. Water it down if you want to lighten the color.

Custom-made unfinished furniture is generally made from fine hardwoods. Because it has fewer imperfections, it may be more suitable for a clear finish. Buy it from a cabinet maker, or if you like this sort of thing, assemble it yourself from a kit (there are mail order houses that sell not only kits and furniture plans but woods and veneers plus legs and other accessories).

"Antique" or Secondhand Furniture

Buying used furniture, other than genuine antiques, is probably the least expensive—and certainly the most distinctive—way to furnish.

Though you will have to put in a fair amount of time and energy to find it and then may have to strip it and refinish it to suit your purposes, your efforts will be worth it, since used furniture is more likely to be better made and of better quality wood than new furniture that costs just as much.

Even if you like very plain, modern styles, an unusual traditional piece—such as a beautiful, old carved rocking chair—can sometimes make a great addition to your room. If your spouse's family has an old piece that you're going to inherit whether you like it or not, you may find it much more acceptable once you've cleaned it up and refinished it or stripped it and bleached it. (See the Fixing section for more information on furniture refinishing.)

In buying used furniture, remember that though the sign outside the dealer's shop may refer to all the stuff on sale as "antiques," in most cases the dealer is stretching a point. He has decided that "antique" sounds nicer and more valuable than "old." Unless you are an expert, it's unlikely you're going to stumble across a genuine antique as you pick your way through flea markets and secondhand shops. The dealer has already gone through the stock for anything of value and sent it for professional refinishing himself.

Not only are genuine antiques scarce, but it would be difficult for someone who is not knowledgeable to know whether an "antique" is the real thing or an imitation, assess whether the piece has already been partially restored, which makes it less valuable, or judge its value. If you see something you like and are willing to pay the price for it, buy it, but don't count on it to help put your child through college. Even if it has no value in monetary terms, it may be a comfortable piece of furniture that you will enjoy having, and that's good enough.

Some people think that finishing furniture is a lot of fun, and a lot of people would rather be out playing golf. My feeling is that you ought to start small until you know this is the kind of thing you enjoy. I would certainly consider tackling a bookcase. Even if you do a less-than-perfect job, you know that the mistake will be hidden by books. Or perhaps you can work on a single chair. But buying a whole dining room set that needs refinishing is overreaching unless you've had a lot of experience.

Custom-made Furniture

PRO: YOU CAN GET EXACTLY WHAT YOU WANT.

A custom-made headboard can have built-in lighting, extra storage, and just the sort of shelves you need to hold the magazines and books you read.

A custom unit for your entertainment center can have just the right amount of space to accommodate your particular turntable, VCR, and TV needs. But be careful if you're having something custom-made; keep in mind that your next TV may be bigger and your next sound system may have a different kind of speaker. Or upgrade now, and build around the newer equipment. Still, no electronic equipment lasts forever.

One thing that adds a lot of cost is building drawers. When I have had things custom-built, I have found it makes a lot of sense to order shelves rather than drawers and buy dividers, boxes, etc., that fit into the unit instead.

If furniture is to be built-in, consider what's behind it. It is amazing how many carpenters will not consider that the desktop they build is just low enough to prevent a serviceman from getting to the radiator behind it. And if electrical outlets are to be covered, have an electrician move them elsewhere—into the top of a headboard, into the top of a cabinet, into a hidden but accessible wall of a bookcase. Finally, make sure the telephone outlet is also placed so that you can get to it.

CON: YOU MAY GET EXACTLY WHAT THE CABINETMAKER WANTS.

As in every other transaction involving two people, there is likely to be a communication problem between you and your cabinetmaker. Be as clear as possible about exactly what you expect: type of finish, how many shelves, whether the bookcase will reach clear to the ceiling or not. You will be surprised at how many things you thought were understood were not (though perhaps you have already learned this from other life experiences).

If the cabinetmaker takes the wrong measurements, the problem is his to correct, but if you haven't been clear about your specifications, the chances are you will just have to learn to live with the problem. So bring drawings, lists, etc., to the meetings and have the bill of sale made out with as many details as possible.

If the prospect of painting or staining custom-made furniture makes you feel overwhelmed, the cabinetmaker will probably be able to recommend someone to do it (for a sum many times what Michelangelo was paid to do the entire Sistene Chapel). Or you can choose to have him cover everything in laminate, such as Formica. It may not be as elegant, but it's very low-maintenance. If you want elegance, spend a night in a fancy hotel where the maids do the cleaning.

Non-Wood Furniture

Molded plastic furniture should be thick, edges smooth, surfaces free of flaws, and completely finished. It may get dented and scratched, but it's easy to care for.

Metal furniture—such as aluminum, wrought iron, and chrome- or brass-finished steel—is generally very strong. Make sure that the connecting points are securely riveted or bolted, and ask if the finish is rustproof. If the metal holds a glass tabletop, there should be a groove or rubber pads to keep the glass firmly in place. Glass for tabletops should be no less than $1/2$" thick.

Wicker, rattan, and bamboo are sealed with the same materials as used on wood. They're easy to maintain but can be damaged if kept outside. Not good in homes with kids or pets.

Leather furniture lasts but needs some conditioning; **naugahyde** is also durable but uncomfortably sticky in hot weather. The top of the line is full-grain (natural grain) leather that has been aniline-dyed (that is, the dye actually permeated the hide). It gets even softer with use, but it fades and stains. Full-grain "aniline-plus" is much more durable. It has been sprayed to resist liquids and grease. White leather may yellow with age.

CHECKING LEATHER QUALITY

Unzip a chair, or look at the bottom of a chair or sofa, to see the edge of the leather. If it shows color on the outside and white in the middle, like a sandwich, the pigment was only sprayed on and white may show through as it wears. Heavily sprayed pigment may also peel.

• •

BEDS AND BED COVERINGS

The least you should know about buying beds and bed linens:
- How to buy a conventional mattress-box spring combination
- Alternative possibilities: waterbed, foam mattress, convertible sofa
- What to look for when buying bedtables, sheets, blankets

You spend a third of your life sleeping, and unless you live like certain movie stars and others in the fast lane, you spent most of it in your own bed (typically 350 out of 365 days).

But even though you're predictable, you're not inert. The average person turns forty to sixty times a night, and probably more after eating chili. It's worth investing in a bed that gives you comfort and support.

Conventional Mattresses

THE RIGHT SIZE

It's recommended that you buy a bed 6" longer than your standing height, but the width is optional. Standard sizes include:
- Youth bed (30" × 75").
- Single or twin-size mattresses (39" × 75") fit the standard bunk bed, or high-riser, which is a pair of beds in which one fits under the other, but you can find twins in extra-long (39" × 80").
- Full or double beds (54" × 75") allow the two people sleeping in it only 27" apiece—the width of a standard crib.
- Queen size (60" × 80") has replaced the double as the most popular bed size for sleeping two.
- King size (72" × 80") or California king (72" × 84"!) is the most luxurious and wonderful for Sunday mornings when the whole family crawls into bed. Assuming you have room for it, the only drawback is that sheets, pillows, and blankets tend to be quite a bit more expensive than those for smaller sizes.

A MATTRESS-BOX SPRING COMBINATION

The bed setup that 80% of people choose consists of a mattress-box spring combination (supported by a bed frame).

The box spring, or foundation, is more than just a platform for holding the mattress. It's the shock absorber that reduces wear and tear on the mattress, and the right one can extend the life of the mattress by 50%. If you've got a built-in platform bed, or if you keep your mattress directly on the floor, you could add a buffer of a layer of foam rubber to cushion the mattress. (Some mattresses, however, are made to be used on either a box spring or a platform. If you have a platform bed, ask the salesman for a mattress recommendation.)

The bed frame is a set of four-sided L-shaped iron bars on casters (rolling wheels) that hold the box spring and mattress in place, and off the floor. Many box spring and mattress sets come with the price of a bed frame included or add it for a nominal charge. A queen- or king-size bed frame should come with a center support rail.

Ask if the bed will be assembled for you. Otherwise, what will be delivered to your home are the mattress, box spring, and disassembled bars: two rigid ones (the length) and two that have been collapsed (the width). Open the frame, adjusting the width bars to fit the mattress, and tighten the screw, which is provided, to hold them in place. Place the box spring in the frame, then the mattress. Place rubber cups under casters if they're on carpeting to help prevent caster "pitting"—the dents casters make in a carpet. The rubber cups will also keep the casters from rolling around on a wood floor. A friend puts an outgrown sneaker under each bed leg in her son's room for the same purpose and for decorative effect.

SELECTING A MATTRESS

What distinguishes one mattress from another is the ticking (covering), the filling, and the construction.

There is no reason to buy a mattress based on the beauty of the ticking. Once it's in your home, it will be covered, preferably with a mattress pad and certainly with a sheet. You will never see it again except on the rare occasions you turn the mattress to give it even wear. Some people recommend spending a little extra money for an all-cotton ticking rather than the shiny fabric most mattresses come with, which has a tendency to slide around

on the box spring. A heavy mattress probably won't slide. (If it does, just slip a blanket between mattress and box spring or buy rubber padding meant to keep an area rug from slipping around.)

As for the filling, your personal ecology may be comforted or offended by the amount of chemistry found in your new mattress. Many or all commercially made mattresses are treated with biocides to prevent mold and mildew, flame retardants, and stain guards; the inner batting or foam and the upholstery is treated with formaldehyde. Read the tag carefully if you have any special concerns, such as allergy to formaldehyde.

The biggest issue is the support and comfort you get from the mattress. Some people like more give, and others prefer mattresses that feel like a marble slab. But how do you know if one brand's "maxipedic" is firmer than another's "orthotonic" or "deluxe firm"? It seems a little confusing because it is.

For one thing, price isn't always a good gauge of what you're getting. Department stores and bedding retailers may work with manufacturers to create "exclusives," which are simply standard models with minor alterations. A nationally known brand name's "superfirm posture deluxe" can be identical to a department store's "super firm posturelux," except for the model name, the specially ordered ticking, and the cost. "Exclusives" will cost about $80 to $100 more than manufacturer's brand-name models.

In general, I think you're better off buying a mattress from a store that sells only mattresses than from a department store, because as a rule the salesmen are more knowledgeable in the mattress store. In either case, you may have a difficult time resisting the sales pitch of an eager commission salesman trying to sell you a mattress if you don't have some idea of what you're looking for. Read the information that follows, and ask around to see what brands have served your friends well.

The objective considerations are the padding material and upholstery as well as the number and thickness of the coils and how they work together. These are points to check.

Height. A good mattress is no less than 7" thick. Most are between 9" and 12". Deluxe new models from 14" to 16" high are for customers who equate size with luxury and comfort even though that is not the case. It also will be a problem to find fitted sheets for these monsters.

Coils. Find out the number of coils, either by examining the tag or asking the salesman. For adequate support, a twin should have at least 275 coils; a full size, 300; a queen, 375; and a king, 450. Coils range up to 15 gauge wire but the usual advice is to get nothing larger than $13\frac{1}{2}$ gauge. Firmer beds use heavier wire—which has a smaller gauge number—and fewer layers of cushioning. Compare mattresses by the number of coils, not by the manufacturer's description: If a "firm" in one brand has more coils and padding than a "superfirm" in another, stick with the former.

Feel. Most important, judge the mattress yourself by trying it on. (Yes, just as you would try on a suit or a pair of boots). You may feel a little uncomfortable about the idea, but bed shops are used to people slipping off their shoes and rolling around on their mattresses, alone or in pairs. Once you get over your self-consciousness, concentrate on the following:

Does the mattress distribute your weight evenly?

Is it firm enough—or too firm? If it feels as if it's giving under your lower back, it's too soft and may cause back problems. If you feel too much pressure around hips, lower back, and shoulders, it's too firm. A flimsy or too soft mattress, experts say, can cause back problems.

Does it feel solid? When you pick up one end, you should feel weight; if the opposite side flips up, or the mattress slides across the box spring a bit, pass.

A twin bed mattress of any particular type will feel firmer than the same mattress in a larger size.

Other Options

WATERBEDS

Fifteen percent of your fellow Americans tuck themselves into (onto?) a waterbed, also called a "flotation sleep system." Many people with back problems find waterbeds are the most comfortable, probably because of their "give," which distributes weight evenly and because they're cool in summer and warm (when heated) in winter.

The "hardside" model is a mattress-size vinyl bag filled with water that fits into a supporting frame, with a vinyl liner between the mattress and frame to hold in moisture in case of a leak. A thermostatically controlled UL-approved heater is placed under the liner and on top of the decking. This style has a lot of "slosh." The mattress conforms to your shape, giving you support where you need it, so you think you're floating on the waves. Some hardsides have vinyl or foam inserts that let you limit the amount of motion; a new "wave-less" design further reduces the water motion. Hardsides are less expensive than conventional inner springs but require special sheets.

The "softside" model looks like an innerspring mattress and feels more like one, since it has less give. Instead of coils and padding, it contains a vinyl bag of water, covered in a foam envelope. Softsides cost as much as or more than top-of-the-line innersprings but use standard-size linens and weigh a lot less.

The highest-tech newcomer to the market is the "cylinder" waterbed, which not only reduces the problem of leaks but allows for different firmness on each side of the bed. It looks like a softside, but is constructed of a number of vinyl cylinders that are filled separately. It's easier to fix leaks (just find the cylinder with

the problem), and by adding or reducing the amount of water in the cylinders over which you sleep, you can have a soft mattress while your bedmate has extra-firm. Queen-size models range from $400 to $1,000 for the ride.

These need proper installation and the floor has to be able to support it. Water has to be conditioned regularly with an algicide. Follow the manufacturer's instructions.

FOAM MATTRESSES

Four-inch-thick latex foam mattresses, made in standard sizes, were hot in the 1960s because they were inexpensive and (a shopping consideration if you were a hippie) portable. They were so flexible you could easily roll up a full-size mattress in a wide coil and keep it tied with a ribbon. Placed on any hard surface—a floor or "loft bed" platform—the mattress turned into a bed, until the foam dried up, turned a strange yellow-rust color, and flattened to the height of an oven mitt. With improved technology and marketing, foam has improved in quality so that it is used for padding even in some innerspring mattresses.

Five percent of bed buyers choose a 100% polyurethane foam mattress, primarily because of allergy problems. Foam mattresses are dustless, odor-free, and resistant to mildew and microbes. Because it has no springs or moving parts that may relocate, disconnect, or collapse, a foam bed is also silent and durable. And since foam conforms to individual body shapes, people of different weights can sleep together without rolling toward each other. (To some this is a benefit; to others it is a drawback.)

Although foam mattresses are often sold for platform beds, you can also use a firm foam mattress over a box spring.

Foam mattresses cost about the same as innerspring mattresses, and the better ones have a 15-year warranty. Good quality mattresses are at least six inches thick and have a core of firm, cushiony foam (probably polyurethane) of high density. Density is not related to firmness (though it sounds as if it would be); it's a measure of weight. The higher the density, the better the durability, resilience, and support—so it is a much more reliable indicator of quality than the manufacturer's designation of a foam mattress as "soft," "medium," or "hard."

FUTONS

The chief benefit of a futon, a Japanese invention, is its portability: It looks like a thick comforter than can be rolled up and stored away. The first futon I saw was the one in the film *Sayonara* on which Red Buttons and Miyoshi Umeki came to an unhappy end, so I'm not predisposed toward futons. But they are inexpensive and compact.

Sleeping on the standard futon is a bit like sleeping on a pillow—there's no complicated inner construction to speak of. The futon was once made only with cotton, but now includes foam and polyester combinations for longer wear. The updated futon also comes with an innerspring core.

When you buy a futon at the futon shop, you can also choose from styles of futon frames (basically a supporting board on legs) and standard futon covers, since the major sheet companies don't make futon-size sheets.

CONVERTIBLE SOFAS

While a sofa-sleeper may be more comfortable than a regular sofa (because the springs have been removed and replaced with a sleeper mechanism), it may be less comfortable than a conventional bed because the mattress isn't resting on a box spring. A convertible sofa offers convenience and flexibility, not a great night's rest on a good firm mattress.

Even though the coil spring mattress for convertibles has been improved over the years, it's still a mediocre support system. Aside from lacking a box spring, it has to be flexible enough to fold in half every night and be compressed into the sofa cavity. If you live in a studio apartment and don't have room for a bed and sofa, give your back a break and invest in a bed board, though it's a nuisance to insert on a nightly basis. Slip it under the mattress and on the bouncy springs. Some people find that those foam pads dotted with the small mound shapes give an extra measure of comfort.

Before you buy a convertible sofa, try it out in the shop. Be sure the metal crossbar that extends horizontally across the center of the mattress frame curves downward. Lie down on an open bed; you shouldn't feel the crossbar through the mattress. The bar and collapsible legs that keep the spring and mattress flat should sit firmly on the floor when you open it.

The dimensions of the mattress of a sofa sleeper are not the same as those of a conventional bed. A full-size sofa sleeper mattress is 52" wide by 71" long, which is 2" narrower and 6" shorter than a conventional full-size mattress. A queen-size sofa sleeper mattress is 59" wide by 71" long, or 1" narrower and 9" shorter than a conventional queen-size mattress.

IS THE BED BRASS?

If you're shopping for a brass bed, take a small magnet along. If it's real brass, the magnet won't be attracted to it. If it's brass-coated metal, the magnet will cling.

HEADBOARD AND SIDETABLES

The headboard and (in some cases) footboard of the bed are usually decorative elements, though sometimes the footboard is used to hold the quilt. Headboards can be made of fabric (though these tend to get dirty); or you can use a mirror, or a fan, or whatever you think looks interesting.

For people who read in bed, a headboard may be a more comfortable back support than a wedge or backrest pillow (a thick pillow with arms) made for this purpose. Some headboards are also designed or custom-made to hold tissues, telephone, clock, etc. Or you could use side tables instead.

If you read a lot, get a table that has a bookcase opening, to hold your books and magazines, instead of extra drawers, which tend to collect a lot of junk. Have a glass top cut to protect the table from medicine and other spills.

Wall-mounted swing arm lamps are the best solution for bed lighting. They eliminate clutter on the end table or headboard and can be swung directly over your book for reading or pushed out of the way. If they are used on both sides of a full-size (or larger) bed, each person can decide whether to have the light on or off.

Outfitting the Bed

To make the bed, you need only pillows, sheets, and a blanket (or comforter or quilt), but I would recommend using a mattress pad beneath the sheet and, if you wish, a dust ruffle to cover the box spring and/or a decorative duvet cover or bedspread. Though you may enjoy having a variety of sheets—change the decor by varying the sheets each week—you can make do with two or three sets: one on the bed, one in the wash, and/or one in the closet. Since most people change sheets only once a week, you can probably have the dirty sheets washed by the time you need to remake the bed.

DUST RUFFLES

The dust ruffle covers the box spring. It's a flat piece of sheeting that has ruffles or more tailored-looking pleats sewn around the edges. It's placed flat between the mattress and box spring, and the ruffles or pleats hang over the sides. Dust ruffles generally match or contrast with the quilt or bedspread, and possibly the curtains, too. They come in a variety of fabrics, and unless custom-made, are inexpensive and easy to launder. You don't have to wash them often, but they do tend to get dingy over time. I like them because they make it possible for you to hide things under the bed (storage boxes, golf clubs, your home rowing machine, etc.) without anyone noticing.

MATTRESS PADS

A mattress pad protects the mattress from the inevitable stains (body oils eventually discolor the ticking), provides you with a little extra cushioning under the sheet, and keeps the mattress dust-free. Some pads are waterproof as well. Strictly speaking, I guess you could do without one since a stained mattress is generally covered by a sheet, but it keeps the mattress looking nicer and keeps it fresher.

You can also buy covers for the box springs, but I don't really see the point, other than to keep a slippery mattress from sliding around.

SHEETS

A fitted sheet on the bottom (fitted sheets have elastic at all four corners to make a nice, tight fit) and flat sheet on the top makes bedmaking very easy.

Although there is some variation from manufacturer to manufacturer (makers of 100% cotton sheets, for example, make them a little larger to allow for shrinkage), sheets are usually made to the following dimensions:

Sheet Type	Fitted	Flat
Twin	39 × 75	70 × 96
Full	54 ×75	72 × 108
Queen	60 × 80	90 × 102
King	72 × 80	108 × 120
California King	72 × 84	Use standard king

There are also other odd sizes to fit high-riser or trundle beds (with mattresses as narrow as 30") and bunks in boats. Such sheets are hard to find, but Sears and other large department stores may stock them.

Sheeting fabric is generally 100% cotton or a polyester-cotton combination. If you can afford all-cotton sheets, you had better be able to afford a laundress, too. They are softer and more "breathable," but they need ironing, unlike polyester. Polyester is stronger, too. Cotton sheets may be muslin (which is tougher) but are usually percale (which is smoother). Sheets are also described by thread count—literally, the number of threads in the cloth. Most sheets are in the 180 to 200 range, while expensive sheets can go from 200 to over 300.

There are several alternatives to cotton sheets, including linen and silk, which are fragile and expensive; flannel, which is warm

and soft but may shrink—check that the label says preshrunk, and satin, which adds a touch of glamour (the best quality satin sheeting is polyester satin).

When you hold a top-quality sheet to the light, you won't see any light showing through the weave, and you won't spot any uneven threads or fuzz.

If you are prone to allergies, you can now get unbleached, undyed, untreated cotton, but because of flammability regulations, untreated cotton may be available only by prescription.

You may have heard about pillowcases and sheets being treated with formaldehyde, which is used in printing processes and to lock in easy-care finishes. A single washing dramatically diminishes the amount of chemicals. Afterward, according to the Environmental Protection Agency, there is nothing to worry about.

PILLOWS

TYPE AND SIZE OF PILLOWS AND PILLOWCASES

Type	Size of Pillow	Size of Pillowcase (Approximate; may vary)
Standard	20 × 26	20 × 30
Queen	20 × 30	20 × 34
King	20 × 36	20 × 40
European Square	26 × 26	27 × 27
Boudoir	12 × 16	
Neckroll	6 × 14	

Pillows can be made of down (light and long lasting, the most expensive), feathers (firm, least expensive), or a down and feather combination (which combines the softness of down and the firmness of feathers). Polyester pillows are firm (but not as long lasting) and non-allergenic. Firm is for side sleepers, soft for stomach sleepers, medium for those who lie on their backs and snore.

Pillows slip into the sides of pillowcases or into a pocket in the back side of shams (which have a plain or frilly border).

If the pillow doesn't have a zip-off cover that can be washed, I recommend an inexpensive, zippered pillow cover. Oil from hair (even clean hair) stains the pillow ticking pretty quickly, and it's a lot easier to wash a pillow cover than the pillow itself. (I wash pillowcases weekly and pillow covers every few months, replacing them when they're very stained.)

If pillows and/or pillow covers are not plain white, they may show through the pillow case, especially if it's light-colored and not top quality. I prefer *all* bed linens (and towels) to be white, so I can toss them in the laundry with bleach and keep them sparkling clean.

BLANKETS

The finest quality wool blankets are merino wool, the warmest of all coverings. But synthetic blankets are non-allergenic, less expensive, and easier to wash.

For the summer months, you can get easy-care cotton or thermal blankets. Constructed to let air circulate through them, they're lighter and more comfortable.

If you have a blanket that doesn't match your room or that is soiled, buy a blanket cover for it.

Out of season, wool blankets should be stored with moth crystals.

QUILTS

Quilts come in measurements of 109×90, 90×90, 70×86, 45×65, 45×45, and 36×46. In the old days, quilts were made of feathers or sheep's wool and required dry

cleaning. Today most are down or man-made fiber and machine washable.

BEDSPREADS

Over the blanket may go a bedspread, often of cotton, chenille, or lace, either fitted or non-fitted, custom-made or not. The top can be quilted (with a layer or stuffing) or tufted (with fluffy tufts of yarn). Some bedspreads must be dry-cleaned.

BEDMAKING MADE EASY: COMFORTERS AND DUVETS

To simplify bedmaking, dispense with the bedspreads, the blankets, and so forth and top your bed with a comforter or duvet, made of two pieces of sheeting-type fabric with filling in between, inside its own cover.

Both comforters and duvets come in the following sizes: Twin (60×86), full/queen (86×86), king/California king (102×86). Comforters may be designed with a box stitch (squares), channel stitching (stripes), or karo-step (quilting isn't sewn through to both sides). When the seam is not stitched through, the comforter or duvet is thicker and warmer. The covering fabric should be cotton or cotton/poly, which breathes and wears well.

A duvet or comforter can be filled with down, feathers, or synthetics. A down filling (made of fiber that grows under the feathers of water fowl) has the advantage of adjusting to body temperature, so even in summer it's comfortable—it lets warm air out and cool air in. For maximum life it should be dry-cleaned rather than machine-washed, and aired afterward. A synthetic can be machine-washed.

A duvet cover, a large bag that covers either a comforter or duvet, can be removed and machine-washed weekly, like a sheet. The whole arrangement is very easy to make up and very lightweight—about 3 to $4^1/_2$ pounds compared to the bedspread-blanket-sheet combination that weighs about 15 pounds. If you go for this arrangement, you can also buy any bargain comforter/duvet you find; since it will be covered, it doesn't have to match the room.

Duvet covers, for reasons I could never figure out, are fairly expensive. You can do much better buying a couple of flat sheets in the size you need, sewing or hot-gluing them together on three sides and attaching strips of velcro on the fourth side or sewing on buttons and making buttonholes. Even if you can't sew, I think it would be cheaper to have a tailor make this up from two inexpensive sheets than it would be to buy a duvet cover.

THE RIGHT STUFFING

The greater the loft (or fill power) of down, the lighter and warmer the comforter or duvet. Test it by shaking the comforter firmly, so air can fill it to capacity, then squeeze the center of the comforter and let go. Watch it fill with air. Repeat a few times and you'll see how great the loft is.

KITCHEN EQUIPMENT

Years ago, my stove died and couldn't be replaced immediately. I managed to cook every meal for two entire weeks—including a buffet dinner for twelve—with one electric fry pan. There was a bit of a delay between courses, and sometimes even parts of courses, but that one utensil made the bacon and eggs and oatmeal, heated soup, steamed the vegetables, sauteed the meat, and even boiled the pasta.

For years my electric fry pan had stayed in the original box. When I began to use it, I saw how versatile it was, how easy to clean, how well it regulated the heat. And at the end of those two weeks, I put it back in the box and never touched it again.

The experience taught me two things: that you can manage with very little equipment and that you cook with what you're used to. So, as I thought about this section on stocking your kitchen I tried to keep the list short. And I also realized that trying to tell someone else how to stock the kitchen is a little like trying to tell someone how to pack for vacation. Some people wouldn't leave home without an electric toothbrush and others have a thing about antacid tablets. My basic kitchen list hasn't an electric fry pan on it; maybe yours does.

I've explained why I've put each item on my list. If you have a better reason to leave it off, or add something else, I know you will.

The least you need to know about stocking the kitchen:

- What you need to cook with
- What you need to serve with

Cookware Basics

There are two kinds of cooking—not home and restaurant but *wet* and *dry*. Wet cooking means making a soup or boiling water for pasta. Dry cooking describes browning meat or sautéeing fish. You can use almost any kind of pot for wet cooking, but for dry cooking a heavier pot is better because the food is less likely to burn.

When you put a very cheap pot on the heat, chances are the bottom will ripple like a thigh with cellulite. This means it won't stay level on the heating element and the food won't cook evenly. It will also be harder to clean. So, don't waste money buying crummy pots. On the other hand, you don't need pots so expensive that you have to take out a mortgage to buy them. It's how the pot cooks—not how it looks—that matters.

These are your choices for top-of-the-stove cooking:

Aluminum. Though Alzheimer patients have high levels of aluminum, to date the FDA isn't recommending against aluminum pots other than to say don't store highly acidic foods in them. About 52% of cookware is aluminum; it cooks fast and is fairly easy to clean, but it will lose its glossiness.

Copper and copper-bottomed pots. Famous chefs talk about how copper provides an excellent cooking surface, but famous chefs have someone to clean up after them. As far as I'm concerned, keeping that copper shiny is a big waste of time. Pass.

Glass and ceramic pots are too fragile. If you boil the pot dry, or if it's wet before you put it on the flame, that's the end of it. Corning Ware is one exception to the rule. It's not as fragile as other glass, and it can take temperature extremes from freezer to oven to microwave. Still, Corning Ware for my taste isn't as good as a heavy, cast-iron pot for food that needs a long, low simmer—like a stew. It's also a little heavy and awkward (since it doesn't have long handles) for all-purpose use.

Enamel pots chip and they're heavy, though one large enamel stew-pot, which goes from oven to table, can be useful.

Cast-iron pans are also heavy, require seasoning, and may rust. They also discolor some ingredients. Some of the iron in the pot transfers to the food so they're healthy to cook in.

Heavy-duty stainless steel. Heavy enough so that food doesn't burn quickly but not so heavy that they're hard to lift. Food cooks quickly. Extremely easy to clean. May discolor from high heat but otherwise almost indestructible. My top choice.

In general, avoid a pan that isn't flat on the bottom (lay a ruler across it; you shouldn't see more than a $1/8$" gap) and extra large pans that fit over two surface burners. Pans should be smaller than the burners if possible.

Go around the kitchen every once in a while with a screwdriver and tighten screws on all the handles.

Pasta Cooker

COOKING WITH LESS ELECTRICITY

Although most home appliances operate with 120v of electricity, your home is also specially wired for appliances that need more power, like an air conditioner and an electric stove. (See The Electrical System, p. 206, later in the book.) In the past, heavy power users were wired for 240v, but now some are wired for 208v to keep construction costs and energy usage down.

If you're used to higher-voltage cooking, you may need to change your recipes somewhat. For example, you may need to extend baking time, though preheating the oven and broiler will minimize this need. You also may have to raise the broiler rack higher, but always leave at least 3" between the food and the broiler element. With an oven on top, broiler below, your user's manual may recommend keeping the oven door slightly open when you are broiling.

Use flat and fast-heating pans (aluminum, stainless).

The Minimum You Need in Pots and Pans, Appliances, Gadgets, and Table Service

POTS AND PANS

If you told me to pick the one pot I couldn't do without, I'd choose my **6-quart pasta cooker.** It's a big pot with a lid with two extra pieces. One is the pasta insert, which is a second pot with holes in it that fits inside the big one. You leave it in place when the spaghetti is cooking, then lift it out to drain the pasta.

The other piece is a basket, also with holes, that fits about one-third of the way into the pot and

1-Quart Pot

2-Quart Pot

holds vegetables for steaming.

If you cook the pasta in the bottom, steam the vegetables on top, and toss them all together with a little butter and garlic, you've got a meal. Or boil the chicken in the bottom, steam cauliflower, carrots, and potatoes on top, and you have all the ingredients of a warm chicken and vegetable salad. Because you can also use it for everything from making soup to chili, I think it's essential—along with the short list of items below:

1 1-quart pot. For making rice, vegetables, boiling an egg.

1 2-quart pot. Same purposes as 1-quart but bigger (use for potatoes, vegetables, with a steamer insert). If you're making two vegetables, you'll probably use both these pots.

1 Dutch oven. A Dutch oven is a heavy covered pot for making stews or slow cooking meat on top of the stove or in the oven. Be sure that whatever you buy has ovenproof handles. If it is enameled, you can serve directly from it.

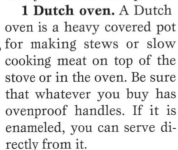

Dutch Oven

2 frying pans. One small one for a couple of eggs (why

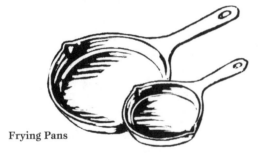

Frying Pans

wash more surface than you have to?), another 12" in diameter or big enough to cook four chicken breasts at the same time. (Even if you rarely fry anything, when you do, it's a real pain to have to do it in shifts.)

1 non-stick 12" skillet. Never use oil or butter on this because it will burn the surface. This skillet can "sautée" vegetables with water only, cook eggs (or egg substitutes), and make pancakes without butter, etc.

Non-Stick Skillet

Corning Ware

Individual Corning Ware bowls. They come in a set of four, with glass covers. For microwave or stove-top, to heat leftovers or make soup for one.

1 2-quart and 1 6-quart casserole dishes. Microwavable and ovenproof, possibly Corning Ware. Use these for everything from baking cakes to making one-dish meals, and take them right to the table.

Casserole Dishes

1 "lasagna dish" 9"×13". Goes in microwave and oven. You may never make lasagna, but you can use this size dish to bake a chicken, make a meat loaf, and cook just about any main course meat; it's also the right size

84

for brownie mix or a rectangular (sheet) cake. If you have a mix for a smaller size cake, make an aluminum foil "pan" of the right size and put it in your lasagna pan.

Lasagna Dish

1 roasting pan 10" × 14". Metal, cover not necessary. Big enough for the Thanksgiving turkey. Buy a small rack that fits inside the roasting pan and set the rack under the roasts or meat loaf, so the fat drains off. I use the rack-and-roast pan combination in my broiler, too, since the fat can drain through the rack into the pan and it's easier to clean these two items than to remove and clean the broiler each time it is used. If a 10" × 14" pan is too large for your broiler, buy a smaller one.

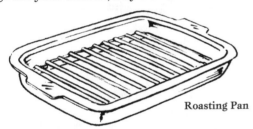

Roasting Pan

1 cookie sheet. (More if you make cookies). To heat the garlic bread or pizza.

Cookie Sheet

Optional:
1 very large skillet. Wonderful if you are sautéeing a lot of food at once.

IS IT SAFE FOR MICROWAVING?

You can't microwave metals (even cartons with metal handles), plates with metal trim, or lightweight plastic refrigerator or freezer food storage containers.

If you cook foods high in sugar or fat in plastic, they get so hot they may crack the dish.

To test if other kinds of dishes are microwavable: Put the dish in the microwave oven next to a glass of water. Turn the oven on high for one minute. If the water is cool and the dish is warm, don't use it in the microwave oven.

Your microwave manual is probably very specific about which dishes are microwavable and which are not.

1 wok for stir frying. Stainless steel is expensive but worth it, since it's durable and easy to clean.

APPLIANCES

When you're stocking your kitchen, don't go appliance-happy, especially if you're limited in space. Otherwise you'll wind up with a bunch of space-eating dust-catchers.

Not everything needs to be electrified. Someone sent me an electric potato peeler that took about twice as long to peel a potato as the old-fashioned, hand-held type. Why do you need an electric can opener if you don't have arthritis? How often do you open cans anyway?

And how often will you use a heavy-duty food mixer, pasta maker, ice-cream machine, rice maker, bread machine, waffle maker, or sandwich grill? (If you want a fast grilled cheese sandwich, just put the cheese between bread, butter the outside pieces, wrap the thing in foil or waxed paper and run a hot iron over it.)

If you're not cooking fancy dishes for a crowd, you may not even need a food processor. (If you do get one, make sure it has a large bowl, so you can process a lot at once, because saving time is the real point.) Most of the time it's quicker and handier to just get out the cutting board and a knife or to use a mini-processor.

Is a toaster oven redundant when you already have an oven, a toaster, and a microwave? Depends. If you bake or broil small amounts very often, it may be more energy-efficient than powering up a full-size oven. If you get one, make sure it can hold one of your larger casserole dishes.

Instead of an electric knife sharpener, have the knives done professionally or do it yourself with a sharpening stone (see box below). When you buy new knives, buy those that don't need to be sharpened.

SHARP THINKING

If you've got a mug that hasn't been glazed on the bottom, you can sharpen a knife on it. Hold the blade at a slight angle. Pull it along the unglazed bottom rim several times (always in the same direction). Then do the same thing on the other side of the blade. Putting a drop of salad oil on the rim as a lubricant will be better for the knife. The same technique can be used with a sharpening stone, which you can buy at the hardware store. Or use fine black emery paper, also from the hardware store.

The few appliances I find myself using regularly are the ones that follow, but if you cook even less than I, you can pare the list even further:

Mini–food processor. Great to cut up a single onion or grate carrots and celery for the meat loaf, process garlic for the salad dressing, or puree some fresh herbs with a little water to add to soups. Takes up little counter space and is easy to wash.

Coffeemaker. Whether you get a drip or percolator is a matter of personal preference, but if you like coffee you'll want one of these.

Mini-mixer. To whip cream and potatoes, mix cake and cookie dough, and blend soup (you can put the beaters right into the pot). Not expensive and indispensable when you need it. I use mine instead of an old-fashioned eggbeater.

Blender. To make drinks, puree soups and too-thick gravies, turn crackers into crumbs, and whip eggs for omelets. Get the glass container; plastic scratches. Easiest to clean: the kind that has blades that unscrew from the bottom.

Toaster. Make sure the openings are wide enough for bagels or other large items.

GADGETS

Pancake turner. To flip eggs or pancakes and stir the pot (the flat bottom edge covers a wider surface at the bottom of the pot than the tip of a spoon).

Slotted spoon. To lift food out of the water in which it's cooked, to separate ground meat from the drippings.

Potato peeler. Peels carrots, potatoes, kiwi fruits, and celery.

Corkscrew. To open wine or champagne.

Beer can opener. Its tip can be inserted under the lid of a jar to release the vacuum and make it a cinch to open, or use it to punch in those boxes that say "Press Here" and don't budge when you do.

Can opener. A heavy, hand-held one lasts the longest and works the best.

Ladle. To serve soup.

Set of stainless steel measuring cups. For dry ingredients and **spoons** for wet or dry ingredients.

Two-cup microwavable plastic or glass measuring cup. You can melt butter in this, microwave sauce to pour over pasta, mix pancake batter in it so it's easier to pour.

Kitchen timer. So the rice, potatoes, or

brownies can be saved by the bell. Even if your microwave has a timer, you may sometimes need a second one. They're handy in other rooms, too—for reminding you to remove a dryer load, for timing the piano practice, etc.

Grater. To grate cheese. Looks like a paddle with holes of various sizes in it. If possible get one that has one sharp side and one dull side so you don't grate your thumb by accident.

Meat thermometer. Even an experienced cook has a hard time figuring out when a roast is done.

Spatula. Rubber, to scrape the edges of bowls.

Knives. A small paring knife, a medium boning knife (great for trimming fat off meat), a carving knife (or electric knife), an all-purpose large knife, and a knife with a serrated edge for cutting tomatoes and bread without squishing them.

2 cake cooling racks. Wire grids or slats on little feet. To use as hot plates, to "sandwich" fish or other items on the grill for easy turning without crumbling (much cheaper than gadgets sold just for this purpose), to cook meat so fat drips below.

GRACIE ALLEN'S RECIPE FOR PERFECT ROAST BEEF

Ingredients:
　　I large roast of beef
　　I small roast of beef

Directions: Put both roasts in the oven. When the small one burns, the large one is cooked.

Mixing bowls. For mixing and storing foods, get a set of stainless steel bowls. They're indestructible and non-porous. Even after you use them for non-food jobs (like doing the hand laundry), they can be washed out and returned

CARRYALL

If you don't have a butler to carry drinks to the table, at least get a tray. You'll save steps carrying the place settings to the table and serving the drinks—and use the tray to carry supplies outdoors, set up the Easter egg dyes, tote foods and medicines to the sickroom, hold a jigsaw puzzle in progress, and more. Covered with doilies, trays can double as big serving platters for a buffet. The most useful trays have handles and sides (in case of spills).

to kitchen use. They usually come as a set of three; if they have rings, you can hang them conveniently. Plastic bowls that have rubber on the bottom (to prevent them from skidding) are a good idea, but you can also put a damp towel under a bowl with the same effect. And since plastic is porous, it may be dangerous to use plastic bowls to hold certain solutions and then return them to kitchen use.

Strainer. One large, one small. (If you use a large one to get stuff into a small container, there will be a lot of spilling.)

Cutting board. Wooden ones split and collect bacteria and dirt. The USDA recommends using plastic for safety's sake. With a small board, there's less area to clean, but chopping is easier on a large board when you're using a large knife. Maybe you need two.

MY FAVORITE KITCHEN TOOL: KITCHEN SHEARS

Use them for cutting pizza, trimming fat off meat or poultry, separating ribs of meat, butchering the chicken into smaller parts, mincing meat for toddlers, trimming the leaves off celery and the stems off spinach. The cheapest ones fall apart, but you can get a good pair for less than $10.

Magnetic knife rack. Very convenient and more efficient than a knife block: it holds more knives (also peelers, shears, beer can opener) and doesn't take up counter space. Also prevents accidents in the knife drawer and keeps your knives in good condition because the cutting surface isn't banged around. You can make a non-magnetic knife rack by gluing empty spools to a board (edges touching) and sliding the knives in between.

DISHES

I know it's traditional to choose a formal china pattern, but if I had to do it all over again, I wouldn't. Most people are a lot more likely to entertain with a buffet meal than a dinner party, which means you need a lot of dinner plates and dessert plates and mugs, not cups and saucers and salad plates and so on. If so, the smartest thing you can do is to buy the dishes you need from a restaurant supply store. They're inexpensive and long lasting and, if broken, easily replaced.

If this is a little too practical for your taste, at least buy dishes that come in "open stock," which means that you can buy individual pieces to replace what's broken or add to the number of place settings.

GLASSWARE

A restaurant supply store is also a good source for glassware.

Two sizes—12 oz. and 6 oz—can serve everything from iced tea to water to juice. When you buy glasses, always buy some extras. For one thing, you'll have breakage. For another, if you have a good supply of glasses (dishes and flatware, too), you won't need to run the dishwasher as often.

You don't need a bunch of different wine glasses, either. A single all-purpose goblet will do. If anyone tells you that's not by the book, tell them it's by this one.

FLATWARE

Did you ever notice that the flatware disappears just like odd socks? Over the years, I have lost a lot of knives and forks and spoons—though never of good silverware. I usually do that by hand and keep track as I wash. And, of course, I have a metal detector at the door.

Buy at least a dozen place settings to allow for loss. Besides, you can always use an extra fork when you're cooking, the extra tablespoons can be used as serving pieces, and you may need one teaspoon for the dessert and another for the coffee. And if your house is like mine, half the flatware is usually in the dishwasher.

Instead of sorting the clean flatware into sections of a silverware drawer, get yourself a caddy. If you can buy an extra dishwasher caddy from the manufacturer, you can remove the one with clean flatware and put it right into your cupboard (then carry it to the table when you set the dishes) and use the alternate in the dishwasher.

> I would like to go down in history as the inventor of the dish that washes itself, then returns to the cupboard.

TABLE LINENS

Straw place mats are easily stained and vinyl needs wiping. The fabric ones made of washable synthetics are the most practical. Just put them in the dishwasher and they come out ready to use. No ironing necessary.

Take the measurements of your table (with and without leaves) when you go shopping for a tablecloth. These come in various standard sizes and shapes, including square, round, oblong (which fits a long rectangular table), and oval, ranging from the smallest (52 × 52) to the largest (60 × 144) for a table seating 12 to 16. The synthetics don't need any ironing, but they do stain. So consider buying cotton or linen if you'll only be using the tablecloth for special occasions. You won't be ironing it often, and you may even send it out for professional laundering.

If you've got a wood table you may want to use a pad under the cloth to protect it from heat. Under a sheer tablecloth, you may also add a decorative table liner. A flat sheet sometimes works for this purpose.

I use cloth napkins every day. I happen to like them, but it also makes environmental sense not to use paper, and washing them couldn't be easier. If everyone has his own napkin ring, you may even be able to use napkins for more than one meal. White napkins, like white towels, are the easiest to maintain. They're easily bleached, while the colored ones, especially if they're polyester, tend to spot and stain.

Large napkins—up to 24" square or bigger, sometimes called "lapkins"—are sometimes used at a buffet. You can get the same effect for much less cost by buying inexpensive bandanas. For outdoor parties, just buy inexpensive washcloths. They're colorful, absorbent, and easy to clean.

KITCHEN LINENS

Appliance covers are just extra things to launder; the appliances you use frequently get wiped frequently. The ones that gather dust should be put away—or given away.

Terry dish towels leave lint all over everything. Cloth diapers or linen napkins from a restaurant supply store do a better job. Put up a hook or "grabber" in a convenient place to encourage everyone to use the dish towel instead of paper towels.

PART 3

CLEANING

DOING IT RIGHT, DOING IT FAST

An interviewer asked me if I thought people cared less about house cleaning these days than they did years ago. Absolutely not, I said. There isn't a house I go into where my hostess doesn't apologize for how the place looks (and most of the time, it looks pretty good).

The big difference is that we have less time to clean house today. Why spend any more than the absolute minimum? Look at it this way: When it comes to cleaning, if you don't get it right the first time, you'll always have another chance.

Besides: You don't need floors clean enough to eat from if you serve your food off plates. With that thought in mind—and before I get into the specifics of how to clean—I've come up with nineteen general suggestions to make cleaning easier and faster.

Some people obsess about housework because it's their only chance to shine.

• •

EIGHTEEN WAYS TO CUT YOUR CLEANING TIME

1. DON'T CLEAN PLACES THAT AREN'T DIRTY. This is not as obvious as it sounds. It means cleaning the handprints off a door without cleaning the whole door, spot-cleaning a rug rather than shampooing it. This not only saves you time and energy but is actually better for many of the things you own. Wash a wall often and you rub away the paint. Shampoo a rug too often and you actually wear it down.

2. STOP CLEANING STUFF YOU DON'T LIKE. Get rid of it. Toss that crocheted toilet paper roll cover and the ceramic toothpick holder and the artificial plant with dusty leaves and the tie with the stubborn stain. If letting go of things is a problem for you, put potential castoffs in a box and seal it. If in six months you haven't looked in the box, deliver it to a charity—sealed. If you look inside, everything will be back on your shelves.

3. MAKE CLEANING CONVENIENT. Put the broom on a nail where you can easily get at it and you're more likely to use it. Leave the cleaners you use most often in the most accessible part of the cupboard. Duplicate tools and cleaning solutions in places where you need them: Keep a sponge under every sink, a can of cleanser in each bathroom. Have vacuums both upstairs and down.

4. SAVE STEPS. Don't walk back and forth across the room. Carry the stuff you need on a tea cart or roll it around in a wagon—whatever works for you. Use a long extension cord so you don't have to keep replugging the vacuum.

5. DO TWO THINGS AT ONCE. Wipe the tub ring while you're waiting for the tub to drain. Clean the perimeter of the sink while you're waiting for it to fill. Use both hands when possible—one sprays, the other wipes.

6. BE PATIENT. Don't rinse until you're done scrubbing a dirty surface; that's just a waste of time. Realize that certain things will come clean with no work if you just let them stand or soak long enough. Baking soda can remove burned-on foods overnight; a soak in ammonia can remove crud from oven racks. See the details in Cleaning the Kitchen, beginning on p. 132.

7. CLEAN FROM TOP TO BOTTOM. On earth, everything—including dirt—is affected by gravity. Unless you're cleaning on another planet, and I can understand that there are days you think you might be, keep this in mind and always clean from the top down because that's the direction the dirt is going.

8. GUARD THE ENTRANCES. If you lay down cement, flagstone, or any surface other than grass near the doors, less dirt will get tracked in. Also put mats at every entrance to the house: A tremendous percentage of the dirt

---

AVOID CLEANING THINGS THAT ARE TALLER THAN YOUR TALLEST FRIEND

What people can't see won't bother them. It shouldn't bother you, either. (Author Quentin Crisp claims that there is no need to clean a house at all. After the first four years, he says, the dirt doesn't get any worse.) Lay down a strip of waxed paper on top of your kitchen cupboards and just change the paper every year. Paint the ceiling a different color than the walls, so no one will know whether the ceiling looks slightly yellow because you planned it that way or because it's coated with dirt.

---

in any house is tracked in from outdoors. Make them as big as will fit; ideally, they should cover four footsteps.

9. VACUUM MORE. Use your vacuum and its attachments to cut down on dusting and avoid ground-in dirt, which is much more difficult to remove. Vacuum upholstery so dust won't attract grease, which stains. Vacuum a windowsill before you clean the windows so you won't have to clean off mud later. Vacuum your bathroom when floors are dry and you won't have to pick hairs off the sponge or mop. Use the reverse blower (or a blow dryer) outdoors to dust lampshades and other items.

10. WASH LESS. The invention of the washing machine seems to have been a signal that everything needs to be washed every time it's worn. This is not true and it wears out clothes more quickly. The reason most people make a habit of throwing things into the machine is frequently not because they're dirty but because it's quicker than hanging up or folding them and putting them away. Once washed, of course, they'll have to be hung or folded anyway.

11. ELIMINATE IRONING. There are many items that do not need to be ironed if they are hung up promptly. See the Washing and Wearing section for more ideas.

12. USE WATERPOWER. Knickknacks are easier to wash in a bowlful of soapy water than individually dusted. Venetian blinds, high chairs, and other bulky items can be washed in the shower, and screens or blinds can be cleaned with the power washer at the car wash. Plants can be misted with a sprayer rather than dusted. Even nooks and crannies in furniture can be washed if coated with urethane or enamel. Your car wash brush attachment can clean patio furniture. And your dishwasher can clean many things other than dishes, as you'll find out in the pages that follow.

13. THINK SMALL. Deal with small jobs before they turn into big ones. Use your hand vacuum on crumbs and spills before the stuff is ground in. And tackle the big jobs a little at a time. Instead of cleaning out the china cupboard twice a year, or polishing all the silver, run a couple of dishes of your good china through the dishwasher for a week or two and the job will be done.

14. BUY A SPEAKER PHONE. The less you concentrate on cleaning, the less it will bother you. This is the same principle the dentist uses when he lets you watch TV or wear a Walkman™ as he's drilling. While talking on the kitchen phone, you can wipe cabinet doors, load and unload the dishwasher, clean the junk drawer, and clean all the old food out of the refrigerator and hardly notice the effort. With a speaker phone, you can clean just about anywhere while you talk.

15. CLEAN WITH FRIENDS. If you've got a big cleaning job that can't be tackled alone (cleaning out a basement or garage, washing down a mildewed wall), get a group of friends to do it with you. Then repay the favor. The work gets done faster and doesn't seem as difficult.

16. KNOW WHEN TO QUIT. When you wipe off the kitchen cabinet, the job shouldn't escalate into cleaning the walls, the lighting fixture, and so forth. Otherwise, you wind up at midnight with half the ceiling done and feeling extremely sorry for yourself. Most cleaning jobs don't have to be done all at once. See # 13.

17. GIVE A PARTY. Most people do not clean for pleasure or even to feel virtuous. They clean to keep up appearances. But when no one's around to notice, they tend to clean less. If you need motivation to do a big cleaning, send out invitations. You have an incentive and a deadline all in one.

18. LET SOMEONE ELSE DO IT.

PROFESSIONAL HOUSE CLEANING

Other than having someone mistake you for an attractive celebrity, I can think of no morale boost as great as having a crew of professionals come in to give your home a really thorough cleaning. This sort of assistance does not come cheap. You can pay up to $1,000 or more to have the job done on a good-size house. My husband once asked me if I'd rather have a Day of Beauty or a Day of Cleaning and I told him that in terms of complete satisfaction, we'd probably both be better off with the cleaning.

A professional service will do the really big jobs—polishing the floors, washing the walls, washing the windows and the blinds. (Of course, you can also call specialists in window washing, rug cleaning, etc., to do one or more of these, but with a service, you're getting the whole thing done at once.)

If you don't have a personal recommendation for a cleaning service, use the Yellow Pages. When you call, ask how long the company has been in business. A firm that's been around at least a couple of years is probably more reliable. (Run the company's name past the local Better Business Bureau.) Make sure you know exactly what the fee covers. And ask who's in charge on cleaning day—the (wonderful and competent-sounding) person you're interviewing or the (unknown) people with whom he's subcontracting.

You should get a contract with the terms and conditions in writing. Ask for proof the company is insured in case of breakage and ask if the crew is bonded in case of theft.

Give yourself a couple of weeks to get ready. This is a good time to unclutter and organize. Make arrangements to have any items you don't need picked up by charity or removed by the Sanitation Department. Pack up the old clothes. And put things away. Their time is your money. You don't want to pay the cleaning crew to pick up checkers from under the sofa cushion or clear the Tupperware from the top of the fridge.

Zsa-Zsa Gabor says she's a great housekeeper; every time she's divorced, she gets to keep the house.

FINDING REGULAR CLEANING HELP

A professional cleaning service, unlike regular household help, brings its own cleaning supplies and will do any heavy work. There's a supervisor in charge and if someone is sick, there are substitutes, so the job always gets done.

An individual worker who cleans for you will use your supplies and may not be willing to do certain chores (like washing walls or windows). But an individual will be more flexible about the duties of the job and may agree to take clothes to the dry cleaner, set the table for dinner, and do some (or all) of the cooking.

Ask your friends for a referral, go through an agency (which may charge you a fee), or the check the bulletin boards or the classifieds. You'll probably make your first contact by telephone. Discuss what days and hours of work are involved and what the fee is, and make sure you're in agreement before you set up a personal interview.

EXPLAINING THE JOB IN DETAIL

People sometimes have trouble interviewing a regular house cleaner because they find it awkward to be explaining to a stranger just how they like their laundry folded and their refrigerator cleaned out. However, it's best to be as detailed and straightforward as possible

Be specific. Don't minimize what you want done or you are certain to be disappointed. Most people do not do more than asked, so if you want something done, say so. In fact, make a written list of chores—better yet, two lists: one for weekly jobs and another for special jobs like polishing the silver or wiping out the cupboards.

Be realistic. The people you hire are unlikely to work faster than you. At best, they work as fast as you, which as a matter of fact is probably a lot slower than you think. If you're paying for four hours of work, list the jobs that you want done in the order you want them done, but don't expect you've hired SuperCleaner who will condense a full day's work into half.

Be clear. If you want sheets folded a certain way, or some item of clothing needs special treatment, you had better write complete instructions or, better yet, spend some time to show exactly how you want it done.

On a routine basis, a house cleaner will probably dust and vacuum, do the laundry, and clean the kitchen and bathroom. If you expect to have the ironing done or have any other particular needs, say so.

Discuss the cleaning materials (and explain where they are). I have found that people you hire often have their own favorite cleaning potions. What's important is not the method but the result, but obviously if you have strong feelings about one product or another, it's your call.

Before the interview is over, make sure you've discussed your policy about sick days, vacation pay, and even overtime. Once someone is hired, you've both made a commitment. The employee is supposed to show up and do the job. On your side, it isn't fair to cance and not pay if you decide the house doesn't need cleaning this week or you have to go out of town.

BEFORE THE FIRST DAY OF WORK

After the interview, check the worker's references. If anything makes you uncomfortable, trust your instincts and don't hire the person. Simply call and say you've changed your mind, but do it promptly. It gets harder the longer you wait.

Contact your insurance agent to see if you need workman's compensation insurance in the event of an accident.

Contact your accountant to find out how to handle the payroll check, deductions, and any taxes that you will owe.

Buy or leave money for any cleaning supplies you don't have on hand. There is nothing sillier than telling someone to clean the oven and not having oven cleaner in the house.

WHAT YOU SHOULD EXPECT

Even though you think it is obvious how to arrange your dining chairs or to fold the napkins all in the same way, it is not necessarily obvious to someone else. People you hire don't do everything exactly the way you would. (In my case, I feel that's often a plus and the very reason why I've hired them.)

I believe it's a waste of time for once-a-week help to make the bed or hang up clothes, though some people enjoy the occasional luxury. That still leaves plenty of jobs to be done: laundry, waxing the floor, cleaning the oven, wiping down and relining the cupboards, or polishing the silver. If you need ideas, check the list of seasonal jobs in this book.

Finally, tidy up. My husband thinks it's funny that I clean up for the maid, but I learned a long time ago that if other people put your stuff away, it's very hard to find it.

CLEANING PRODUCTS AND TOOLS

Some books advise that the best way to eliminate dusting is to acquire little and buy only light color, painted wood furniture, which doesn't show dirt. In that same spirit I would also like to advise that you have a very small house and no children, because that makes cleaning much easier, too.

My hunch is that this advice will be ignored. Once you have your stuff and/or your kids, you're going to have to work around (and sometimes under and above) it/them. That's what this section of the book is about: cleaning what you've got.

It starts with an explanation of what you need to clean. You could skip right along to the shopping lists of products and tools, followed by explanations of how to use them. But if you know something about why each is used, you may be able to solve a cleaning problem that's not specifically covered in this book.

In some cases, I've mentioned the name of a specific product, not as an endorsement but because I thought it might be clearer when I talked about, say, a "sanitizer" to mention Lysol as an example. You may prefer other, similar products, and some of the products I mention may disappear or be reformulated, and new ones will appear, but for purposes of clarity, I decided to include brand names.

The least you need to know about cleaning equipment:
- Cleaning solutions (and when you need them)
- Cleaning tools (and why you need them)

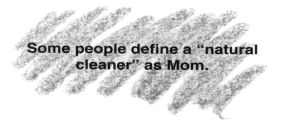

Some people define a "natural cleaner" as Mom.

What Cleaners Are Made Of

As my hairdresser would be the first to tell you, I'm not one of those people whose instinctive reaction to the word "natural" is "I want it." On the other hand, I'm conscious of using products that won't waste and don't hurt the environment. I'm used to this planet, I have no plans to move off it, and I worry about it.

Years ago, I began recommending certain non-polluting cleaners—not because they were earth-friendly (we weren't so aware of that issue back then) but because they were inexpensive and easy to find in the market and, primarily, because they did the job.

There are times, though, when a stronger product is called for, and I will recommend those, too. Let's be practical: When you talk about whether disposable diapers are a good idea, you have to balance the problem of non-biodegradable waste against the environmental problems that cloth diapers create—from the bleach and detergent used to clean them and the energy it takes to heat the water to the wear and tear on the washing machine.

When it comes to cleaning products, you also need to make some compromises. It boils down to this: Use the non-polluting products when you can and the others when you must.

If they help save a rug from being replaced or a piece of clothing from being thrown out, that's beneficial to the environment, too.

WATER AND OTHER EARTH-FRIENDLY CLEANERS

The most earth-friendly cleaner, and a fairly effective one, is plain water. You can use it on most surfaces except wood or in places, like a computer keyboard, where internal moisture might create a problem. If you've got a fresh stain, flush it with water and many times it will just disappear.

MONEY SAVER

One way to save big on cleaning supplies is to buy from a janitorial supply company. You can buy generic cleaning solutions that cost a lot less than supermarket brands. There are also cleaning tools that you'd never see in a supermarket.

If your town doesn't have any such company, a local church, school, or small manufacturer may order from such a place and can piggyback your order with theirs. Or get together a group to buy in bulk.

ALKALIS

Alkali is a generic term for many common cleaning agents.

One of the stronger ones, **trisodium phosphate (TSP),** is an excellent cleaner for jobs that soap and water can't touch, but because of the concern about phosphates (which are thought to harm the environment by promoting the growth of algae in water), it is used much less often today than in the past. A half-tablespoon to a gallon of water will remove most dirt. Used in a heavier concentration, it can cause harm to some surfaces, since it is strong enough to remove paint. But TSP is very effective in cleaning cement, very dirty walls, and other tough jobs. Mex Multi-Purpose Cleaner is a phosphate-free alternative to TSP. Use it with caution and wear goggles. It is extremely caustic.

Washing soda (also called sodium carbonate), found in the laundry section of your supermarket, is a generic heavy-duty cleaner but somewhat toxic. (Read the cautions on the box.) It cuts grease, removes stains, disinfects, softens water, and may even open drains. You usually use about $1/8$ cup to a gallon of water.

Borax is an earth-friendly alkali, but it can be toxic. Though it's not a strong cleaner, it is a good freshener (added to the laundry), deodorizer, and water softener.

Bottled **ammonia** sold as a household cleaner—the kind I am referring to whenever I recommend ammonia—is about 90% water, 10% ammonia. Some brands, which look cloudy, have added detergent. Household ammonia is a good grease cutter, wax stripper, and window cleaner.

Lye is a very strong alkali cleaner, sometimes used to clean pipes. It is extremely powerful and very dangerous and should be handled only with extreme care and at your own risk.

Many all-purpose cleaners contain alkalis along with other chemicals. Although you can find specialized cleaning products for almost every room and every surface, you don't need them all. One good all-purpose cleaner in a spray bottle—a brand like Lestoil or Top Job or a generic product from the janitor supply store—should take care of most concentrated dirt problems including food spills and grease. Unless the instructions tell you otherwise, use the product full strength and rinse it off right away.

ACIDS

Acids are used less frequently than alkalis.

Environment-friendly **lemon juice** and **white vinegar** are both mild acids and effective cleaners, but vinegar is used more often because it's cheaper. You can use it to wash windows, to cut grease, and to freshen the air.

Muriatic acid is sometimes used as a cleaner for badly stained bathrooms or for brick fireplaces.

CAUTION: Muriatic acid is extremely powerful and dangerous. Follow the directions on the product package. Check the warnings on acids under "Recipes for Disaster," p. 99.

ABRASIVES

Abrasives should be used sparingly because they clean a surface by wearing it down. The amount of wear depends on the type of abrasive, how often you apply it, how strong it is, and how strong you are. If the surface can be washed, always try soap and water before you start with an abrasive and always use the gentlest abrasive first.

Non-polluting, inexpensive **baking soda** is a generic, gentle abrasive that you can use on pots, counters, and porcelain fixtures.

Liquid scouring cleaners, like Soft Scrub, are rougher than baking soda. They are not recommended for certain plastic countertops or wood but they can be used almost everywhere else, usually in the kitchen and bathroom.

Scouring powders, like Comet, contain a natural abrasive plus soap or an alkaline salt. Because they are very strong, save them for very resistant stains and where preserving the finish isn't very important.

Rubbing compound, rottenstone, and **pumice,** in order of coarseness (pumice is the strongest) are sometimes used to rub away a spot on furniture. Pumice may also be used to remove very bad stains from inside a toilet bowl.

Metal polishes are primarily abrasives combined with cleaners and/or acids. Claims of one-polish-suits-all are as reliable as most claims of this sort—in other words, not at all. To clean copper and brass you need a much more abrasive cleaner than for silver, which is a softer metal. And if you use the silver cleaner on copper and brass, it takes you twice as long.

Copper and stainless steel **pads** don't rust, but steel wool pads with soap are more convenient for the kitchen and cheaper. To keep steel wool from rusting too quickly, store the pad in a plastic bag in the freezer or keep it in a clay pot, which absorbs moisture. You'll also waste less if you cut the steel wool pads and use only half at a time or buy the junior-sized pads.

Nylon and fiber scrub pads are less abrasive than steel wool, and the ball-type plastic **scrubber** and the sponge enclosed in netting are gentlest of all. You can make home-made scrubbers by wrapping a piece of nylon stocking around a sponge or just scrunching up a mesh onion bag.

DETERGENTS

You think you have it rough? Before they could even get around to cleaning with it, the early settlers first had to make their own soap. They hollowed out a tree log and mixed lye, ash, water, and whatever kind of fat they had available.

Detergents, which are used primarily in kitchen and laundry cleaning, are not the same as soap. They are made from synthetics (which are explained more fully in the Washing and Wearing section). One reason manufacturers use them is that they suds up in some waters much better than soap.

SANITIZERS

Sanitizers, like Lysol, are heavy-duty germicidal cleaners used in the bathroom and kitchen, in a sickroom, to clean doorknobs or telephones or faucets or other surfaces that many people touch. Sanitizers containing phenol are toxic for humans and potentially fatal for cats. Most new-formula sanitizers today contain ammonium chloride instead.

If pine cleaners have 20 % or more pine oil (most don't), they can be considered sanitizers.

BLEACH

Chlorine bleach, which gets your whites whiter (and, if you're careless, gets your colored clothes whiter, too) is often the best choice to remove mold and mildew from everything from shower curtains to aluminum siding. Technically, chlorine is not a cleaning product. To compensate, people often try to mix it with a product that is—a very dangerous idea. Please take a look at the box called "Recipes for Disaster," on p. 99.

POLISHES AND WAXES

It's my sad duty to report that even "no-wax" floors eventually get grimy and need polishing. Other types of floors may need a cleaning with soap and water followed by a coating of water-based polish. Unsealed wood surfaces need stripping with ammonia or another stripping product, followed by a waxing. In the section on cleaning your floor I'll explain in detail which type of product you need for which floor.

Liquid furniture wax cleans most wood furniture, but sometimes paste wax is preferable. See Cleaning Furniture, beginning on p. 126.

ALL DETERGENTS ARE NOT CREATED EQUAL

Automatic dishwashing detergent (for your dishwasher), regular dishwashing detergent (for fine dishes, hand washables, and other cleaning jobs), and laundry detergent are not interchangeable, as you will discover if you pour the wrong kind into the wrong machine. For remedies, see Laundering, beginning p. 170.

CLEANING PRODUCTS: BASIC SHOPPING LIST

You will definitely need:

All-purpose cleaner (such as Top Job, Lestoil, etc.)

Borax

Washing soda

Vinegar

Ammonia

Scouring powder

Liquid abrasive cleaner

Steel wool pads

Medium-rough nylon or fiber scrubbing pad

Light-duty plastic scrubbing pad

Sanitizer (such as Lysol without phenol)

Bleach

Spray furniture polish

Liquid dishwashing detergent

Dry-cleaning solvent stain remover (for carpet)

Solvent- or water-based floor cleaner, plus stripping solution (depending on type of floor you have; see information in Cleaning Floors, beginning p. 118.)

You will probably need:

Automatic dishwasher detergent

Oven cleaner (if oven isn't self-cleaning. Odorless products are weaker but less dangerous. You can also use plain ammonia)

Mineral and lime remover (if you have white scales on tiles, tub, etc.)

Mineral spirits (solvent; often used in stain removal for waxed wood floors)

Naphtha soap (petroleum distillate; great degreaser)

Rust remover

Silver polish

Brass and copper cleaner

Foaming bathroom cleaner (such as Dow), good for a variety of quick cleanups

Wood cleaner (such as Preen), if you have woodwork

Very heavy-duty cleaner (such as TSP or Mex Multi-Purpose Cleaner), for walls, ceilings, brick, concrete

Other items recommended in sections of this book that cover specific cleaning jobs

WATERLESS CLEANERS

You can get waterless cleaners in auto supply stores and supermarkets. They are ideal for cleaning some wood surfaces because they won't cause wood to swell. The cleaners come as a paste that you apply with a sponge or rag, then rub or wipe, using more product as needed until the surface is clean.

HOMEMADE CLEANING FORMULAS

My friend's nine-year-old was thrilled to discover that when you mix a few cents worth of cornstarch with just the right amount of hot water you get a half-liquid, half-solid ooze very much like something that the fanciest toy shop in town sells for $3.50 a tub. While the joy of actually playing with this stuff is a complete mystery to me, I can see where mixing it up might be fun. I myself enjoy concocting a few home-made cleaners that are easy to make and very inexpensive to use. Some have the added advantage of being non-toxic. Here are some of my favorites:

All-purpose cleaner. Pour $1/2$ cup ammonia and 1 cup washing soda into a clean plastic gallon jug. Add 2 cups warm water, cover, and shake. Then add 12 more cups of water. Label the jug so everyone knows it's cleaner, please. Use $1/2$ cup to a bucket of water for large jobs, full strength in a spray bottle for appliances and tile.

All-purpose non-polluting cleaner. Add 2 tablespoons baking soda to 1 quart warm water and you have a wash that will clean plaster, tile, and porcelain. Plain baking soda will substitute for scouring powder all over the kitchen, on appliances, even in the toilet bowl. Or mix 2 teaspoons borax and 1 teaspoon liquid dishwashing soap in 1 quart water for a cleaning spray.

All-purpose pine cleaner. For kitchen floors and ceilings use full strength. For other walls and ceilings use when diluted. Mix 2 quarts of water, 1 cup pine oil, and 2 cups of soap flakes in an empty gallon jug. Toxic. Keep away from kids and cap tightly.

Ceramic tile cleaner. Mix $1/4$ cup ammonia, $1/2$ cup washing soda, and 1 gallon warm water.

Chandelier cleaner. Combine 2 teaspoons rubbing alcohol, 1 pint warm water, and 1 tablespoon dishwasher anti-spot agent (like Jet Dry) in a spray bottle. Make sure lights are off and that fixture is cool, then drench the chandelier and let drip dry. Water will sheet off.

Fixture cleaner. Pour 8 ounces of ammonia and 1 quart of denatured alcohol into a spray bottle. Spray and wipe with tissue and use on small kitchen appliances, chrome faucets, and other greasy surfaces.

Furniture polish, lemon-scented. Mix a teaspoon of lemon oil (from craft or herb shop) with a cup of mineral oil. Pour into a clean spray bottle. Before using, shake well. Use a thin coat and buff well, or the oil will collect more dust!

Furniture polish, earth-friendly. Olive oil works well on stained (but not lacquered or painted) wood. Rub in with a clean cloth until there is no stickiness left.

Polishing cloths. Cut soft cotton or terry cloth into 9" squares. Moisten them with water and put them in a large plastic container. Mix $1/4$ cup water, a cup of mineral oil, and a teaspoon of lemon oil (which you can buy from a craft shop or herb shop), shake well, and pour over the cloths while the oil and water are in solution. Wipe furniture with the cloth, then buff off excess with clean cloth. The cloth can be washed and reused.

Wall cleaner. Combine $1/2$ cup borax, 2 tablespoons soap flakes (like Ivory Flakes), 1 tablespoon ammonia, one gallon warm water. Store in plastic jug. Use full strength in spray bottle or add two cups to a pail of warm water. Or mix $1/2$ cup ammonia, $1/4$ cup white vinegar, and $1/4$ cup washing soda for every gallon of water.

Tools: What's in the Broom Closet?

Having all your cleaner tools handy and in good condition almost automatically helps keep your house clean. Instead of a jumble in the

---

RECIPES FOR DISASTER

I like to remind readers of the danger of mixing chlorine products with baking soda, automatic dishwasher detergent, or other products containing ammonia or acid. When combined, they give off hazardous gases. Some just smell bad and others are actually dangerous.

Read all labels carefully—even on products that you have been using for a long time. Products are often reformulated.

• CHLORINE products include bleach, mildew remover, tile cleaner, powdered cleansers.

• AMMONIA products include glass, floor, and appliance cleaners. Many detergents contain a drop of ammonia. Make sure you're not using one of these.

• ACID products include toilet bowl cleaners.

Also remember to add the cleaning chemical (such as muriatic acid) to the water and not the reverse. If you pour the water into the acid, the splashing can have disastrous results.

broom closet, get one of those wall-mounted organizers that grabs the handles of your mop and broom. Or just screw a little eye screw (a circle with a screw bottom) into the tip of your mop or broom and screw a little cup hook holder into the closet wall to hook it on.

BROOM

To sweep a hard floor, look for one of those broom-dustpan combinations that snap together. Both items have long handles, which is much easier than working with the old-fashioned dustpan that requires stooping. I am willing to stoop only in exercise class, where at least I'm dressed for it.

You'll need a wide "push broom" for outdoor jobs like sweeping the walk or the garage floor. Forget the cheap metal dustpans that don't lie flat. You sweep as much under the pan as in it. Rubber ones are better. Better still, get yourself a child's plastic snow shovel. It can hold more and the longer handle is easier on the back.

IN THE PAN

The dust won't drift right back out of the dustpan if you've dampened it before you sweep debris into it. If you coat it with furniture wax, it'll also be easier to wipe clean.

PAIL

A bucket with two compartments is very convenient. Fill only half with your soapy water. Slosh some around, wring out your mop or sponge into the empty section, and then dip it back into the cleaning solution. Otherwise, you're just moving dirty water around. You'll need to rinse a floor or other surface when you're done anyway or the remaining dirt will attract more dirt faster than a kid dressed for church.

Sponge Mops

Make sure the pail is wide enough for your mop. Trying to dip your mop into a pail it doesn't fit is almost as annoying as trying to zip yourself into jeans that are too small.

MOPS

You'll need a sponge mop with a replaceable head, a feature I wish were available for human beings. Remove the head to clean it or discard it when it's worn. (That sounds good, too.)

You'll need a second mop for applying wax if you're going to be doing a lot of waxing. Yes, you can just change the heads but it's a nuisance and buying a second mop costs only a bit more.

Buy a brand that is widely available so that you can buy replacement heads easily. Also look for a mop with a feature that makes it easy to wring out—rollers that squeeze the water out of the sponge or a doohickey that bends the sponge so it can squeeze itself dry.

Your mops can do more than clean the floor. Use them to clean the shower wall, tub, and, when it's absolutely necessary, the ceiling. You won't need a ladder and you'll be able to go over a large surface with just one swipe.

A string mop is awfully handy for getting up spills quickly, unless you have an industrial vacuum that can soak up liquids. The best mop has a self-wringing feature.

VACUUM CLEANERS

These are all described in the section Equipping.

DUSTING AND POLISHING CLOTHS

The right cloths don't just move dirt around—they pick it up. Nothing is as absorbent as 100% cotton, so if you have a cotton tablecloth with a rip or a worn-out sheet, save it for rags. Don't bother with fabric that is mostly or completely synthetic. It's just not absorbent. Don't use colored fabrics, either. Some cleaning solutions may affect the dye, causing your dustcloth to "bleed" over what it's supposed to be cleaning. Also, there's a psychological factor. When you see dirt coming up on white, you feel you're really accomplishing something.

The cheapest dust cloths are napkins from a restaurant supply store or used linens that a linen supply house may sell you. Cloth diapers are also inexpensive, soft, and (of course) extremely absorbent. Avoid terry cloth. It leaves lint behind.

Real chamois cloth is made of oil-tanned sheepskin. Chamois is good for washing windows or cars because it absorbs water and cleans and polishes at the same time. Chamois should be washed in the machine with detergent after it's used, then stretched out and left to dry flat.

Dust wands with long handles save a lot of bending and stretching, and the head is specially treated to pick up dust.

SCRUB BRUSHES

An old toothbrush is great for cleaning tiny spots (around the nameplate on the refrigerator, in small areas of decorative silver). A nail-brush works well on larger, caked-on spots of dirt. But for some kitchen spills you may need an even larger scrub brush with a handle.

You also might prefer to use brushes rather than sponges to clean inside pots and bowls—whichever feels comfortable to you.

SPRAY BOTTLES

Professional quality spray bottles from a janitor supply store help you work faster, because they do a better job pumping out liquid than the cheap ones from the notions store.

Keep a spray bottle filled with rubbing alcohol in the bathroom or kitchen for spritzing stains and wiping them before they set.

SPONGES

I use cloths for dusting but not for cleaning. Whenever possible, I use cellulose sponges. (Natural sponges, the brown ones, still exist, but cellulose sponges are far more common and available in a wide variety of shapes and sizes.) They can be rinsed as you work and washed in the dishwasher. Put them in the silverware caddy so they don't fly about during the cycle.

I keep humongous rectangles to soak up floor spills (I'd rather throw the sponge onto the spot and let it do the work than get out the mop). And I use thin, clothlike ones, about 8" square, at the kitchen sink and in the bathroom because they cover a larger area than the usual small squares and rectangles. One place I was surprised to find these in quantity and at a low price was at a discount office supply store.

I "color code" sponges. In the kitchen, I use one color at the sink, another to wipe up floor spills. In the bathroom, I use one to wipe out sink and tub, another to clean the floor, a third for toilet seat and tank.

For big cleaning jobs, on walls and ceilings, I'm crazy about a dry sponge. It's made out of rubber and treated with some kind of chemical that picks up dirt the way a magnet attracts metal. It will cut your work time by about two-thirds, and will make the whole job easier. Try a janitorial supply house if your hardware store doesn't carry it.

PAPER TOWELS

Try not to use paper towels for cleaning. It's expensive and a waste of money and trees (and money doesn't grow on trees). One way to cut down your usage is just to cut the roll in half (use your electric knife, if you have to) or select the brand that is perforated to give you smaller sheets.

GLOVES

When you put your hand in most household cleaning solutions, you're not exactly giving them a beauty treatment. A lot of them have warnings that suggest you should be wearing rubber gloves. I have found that the gloves help you do a better job cleaning because you can tolerate water at hotter temperatures when necessary and I think you get into the job better.

WAX APPLICATOR

If you have an unsealed wood floor (without a polyurethane or similar finish), you'll need a wax applicator, a pad on a stick with a flat rectangular bottom, usually made of lamb's wool. Wash the applicator immediately after you use it or the pad gets rock-hard.

WORKING WITH RUBBER GLOVES

• If you have trouble pulling off your rubber gloves, put your hands under cold tap water.

• If you have long nails, protect the inside tip of each finger with a small piece of electrical tape.

• If you rip the right glove on every pair, save the one that's left. Use it turned inside out.

• You can make very strong elastic bands by cutting strips from old rubber gloves.

CLEANING TOOLS: BASIC SHOPPING LIST

You will definitely need:
Brooms—push broom for outdoors, smaller for indoors
Dustpan
Pails (2)
Mops with replaceable heads (2); buy a spare (you'll need it every 3–4 months)
Vacuum cleaner
Hand-held vacuum cleaner
Dust wand and polishing cloths
Scrub brush (with handle, about 6" long)
Sponges
Paper towels
Rubber gloves
Spray bottle
Toilet brush (one per bathroom; get one that comes with its own holder)
Tile brush (to scrub grout in bathroom. More abrasive than a sponge)
Toothbrush (for scrubbing small areas)
Squeegee (to clean windows or tile walls; best are brass or stainless, have a 10"–14" rubber blade)

You will probably need:
Wax applicator
Floor polisher
Dust mop

FLOOR POLISHER

Floor polishers (used on hard floors) often double as rug shampooers. They can be rented or bought. A polisher has two flat pads on the bottom. You may use a fine wool pad to clean a waxed floor or a lamb's wool pad to buff it. See buying information under Floor Machines, on p. 34.

CLEANING FROM THE TOP DOWN

Yet another reason that cleaning often seems unnatural is that the underlying principle is so different. In life, you start at the bottom. In cleaning, you start at the top.

The least you need to know about cleaning ceilings, walls, and windows:

- How to clean ceilings of different textures
- Washing walls and cleaning wallpaper
- Doing the windows

Ceilings

BASIC CLEANING TECHNIQUE

The one time I had to clean my bedroom ceiling was when my son threw a lump of clay that stuck to it. When I climbed down from the ladder after scraping the clay off, I noticed a "stained" spot. Then I realized this was actually the "cleaned" spot and I had no choice other than to clean the rest of the ceiling to match it.

Normally, however, ceilings and walls in the living or bedroom won't need washing. You can reach up with the bare-floor attachment of your vacuum cleaner if you spot a cobweb or two, and if you paint often enough, that's all that will be necessary.

Usually only the kitchen ceiling (possibly the bathroom) will get dirty enough to require cleaning. Sometimes wiping it with a dry sponge will do the job. But if you're going to paint, you'll have to do a more thorough job since the paint won't stick to a grimy, greasy surface.

Use a strong cleaner like TSP or Mex in a very dirty kitchen, ammonia and water (one part ammonia to ten parts water) or an all-purpose cleaner if it's not very dirty. You'll need a sponge, a bucket of cleaning solution and a bucket of clear water, a ladder, and some dropcloths to throw over everything so the dirt won't rain down on top. (Wear a hat, *and if you're using Mex, wear goggles. It is very dangerous to get this stuff in your eyes.* Also, if you don't plan to repaint soon, try some of the cleaner in an inconspicuous spot to make sure it won't damage the current paint.)

Using a dry sponge, which I've described under Sponges in the Tools section, will remove some of the surface dirt and make the job less messy. Then start applying your ammonia or Mex or whatever, using a cellulose sponge (or, if you're doing a huge ceiling, a sponge mop). Work in sections about 3' × 3'. After you wash the area, wipe it with clear water before it's dry to pick up whatever cleaning solution is left and eliminate streaking.

Overlapping a bit on a previously cleaned section will also avoid streaks.

TILED AND TEXTURED CEILINGS

Acoustical tile may be scrubbed if it is vinyl-coated, but to clean non-washable tile just run a dry sponge across it.

You can remove a water stain from an acoustical ceiling, tiled or spray finished, by spraying with a mixture of half water and half bleach. Painting, rather than cleaning, is the best coverup for a tile ceiling, but painting lowers the ability of the tile to reduce sound. Use a paint made for acoustical tile. If the ceiling has a stain, coat the stain with shellac so it won't bleed through, then paint over that. If you don't want to paint, you can investigate having the ceiling sprayed by a professional.

A textured ceiling (spray-on acoustical finish) can be resprayed. It may be less expensive to remove the ceiling texture by scraping a board across the ceiling to remove the "points," and then repaint. Or you can have a professional come in to spray it clean.

Decorative plaster is almost uncleanable. Vacuum it as needed and repaint when it gets really bad.

Walls

CLEANING PAINTED WALLS

In the living room and bedrooms, you can probably get away with spot cleaning the walls. Use all-purpose spray around the light switches and door handles. If the spot is resistant, scour it with baking soda and water, and if that doesn't work, use a liquid abrasive.

The kitchen will need cleaning more often, since the residue from cooking will coat the wall with grease. This is fine—okay, not fine, but you can probably live with it because you don't notice it—until you make the mistake of wiping a single spot and notice that it is about fifty shades lighter than the wall around it. Follow the instructions for washing the ceiling. See also "Back Splash," p. 139.

Clean baseboard and trim with your heavy-duty cleaner.

CLEANING WOODWORK

Painted wood should be dusted or wiped lightly with a dampened sponge. Otherwise the paint may be harmed.

If the trim is made of wood, it probably just needs dusting. If it's absolutely necessary to clean woodwork, use a wood cleaner such as Preen. Be careful that it doesn't stain adjacent surfaces.

CLEANING WALLPAPER

Washable coverings can be cleaned with a sponge dipped in an all-purpose cleanser or $1/8$ cup ammonia mixed in a quart of water. If the paper is scrubbable—it's indicated on the paper care label by a wavy line over a bristle brush—you can use the same cleaning solution but you can apply it with a soft-bristled scrub brush.

If the wallpaper has texture, leave the cleaning solution on it for a minute or two, then rinse thoroughly. Otherwise the residue will attract more dirt. If you leave the dirt on wallpaper for too long, a substance on the vinyl wallpaper called the plasticizer tends to absorb it.

Dry sponges from the janitor supply house can clean non-washable wallcoverings.

REMOVING STAINS ON WALLPAPER

CAUTION: Even water may stain some wall coverings, so always test in an inconspicuous spot.

Crayon. May come out of washable papers with a spritz of prewash spray such as Clorox II or Spray and Wash. Or rub lightly with a dry, soap-filled steel wood pad. Or rub gently with baking soda sprinkled on a damp cloth. On fabric, try dry-cleaning fluid. Call the folks at 1-800-CRAYOLA if all else fails.

Felt-tip marker. If it's alcohol-based, try a shot of non-oily hair spray or rubbing alcohol. Blot up. If it's oil-based apply a little lighter fluid (it's very flammable, so use it in a well-ventilated area and away from flame). If it's

---

OFF THE WALL

• If the handprints on the wall are making you crazy, don't fight them. Instead, get some latex paint, pour it into a shallow bowl or saturate a sponge, and have the kids saturate their hands—then make handprints on the walls. Use different colors; have fun. You can always paint over everything when the children get bigger. Or maybe by then the handprints will make you nostalgic instead of irritable.

• In the kids' room or the kitchen, why not cover one wall (or a part of it) with blackboard paint? When you see the handwriting on the wall, you can stay calm about it.

SPRAY CONTROL

If you're using an aerosol cleaner that may stain an adjacent surface, spray the cleaner onto a cloth, then wipe it on. In fact, this is the best way to use any cleaner.

water-based, use dishwashing liquid mixed with color-safe bleach or prewash spray. Apply just a little, rub gently, blot up.

Grease. Blot it off non-washable wall coverings. Or try a paste of cornstarch and water or baking soda and dry-cleaning fluid (or a commercial paste-like spot remover). Apply to the spot; when the paste dries and becomes powdery, brush off. Repeat if necessary. Try paint thinner on vinyl wallcovers (also painted and brick walls).

Hairspray. To remove it from wallpaper, paneling, and painted areas, use ammonia on a clean rag.

Lipstick. Use a steel wool pad on a wall that can stand abrasion. Or try a dry-cleaning solvent such as Energine. Since grease removes grease, you can try some mineral oil (but only on walls that can tolerate grease).

Miscellaneous spots (non-washable paper). First try a piece of white bread. Otherwise try Absorbene, a kneadable, doughy eraser.

Smudges. Erase light marks (pencil, fingerprints, dirt) with artgum erasers from the stationery store or a piece of white bread, or Absorbene.

To a parent, the handwriting on the wall isn't a sign that something bad will happen. It's a sign that it already has.

CLEANING PANELING

Panels usually need dusting only. If they are waxed or sealed with polyurethane, they can be wiped with a damp sponge.

For heavier cleaning use a commercial product made for waxed finish and oiled wood paneling, or make a cleaner for oiled wood with a half-and-half mixture of turpentine and boiled linseed oil. Shake together, pour onto a cloth, rub with the grain. Though it will appear oily at first, it will be absorbed.

Touch up spots in panels by filling them with a bit of clear wax on a damp cloth or a matching shade of shoe polish or liquid marker.

CLEANING FABRIC AND CORK WALL COVERINGS

Paper-backed, uncoated fabric wall coverings should be dusted with the brush attachment of the vacuum.

Stains are hard to remove from **uncoated burlap and silk.** I'd call in a professional for the silk, but if you but you could take your chances with a sponge and mild detergent or a dry-cleaning fluid, which is better for grease stains. Try either in an inconspicuous area to make sure it doesn't spot the covering. Another remedy for grease is to rub on some talcum, leave it for a while, then brush off.

Felt coverings should be cleaned with a granular rug cleaner to remove grime. Test the cleaner in an inconspicuous corner first. Don't use water, which causes the felt to bleed color and will shrink the surface when it dries.

There are commercial spot removers for **vinyl, cloth, and foils** that may help if you've got a stain problem.

Cork will be a lot easier to clean if you make it washable by sealing it with polyurethane. Use a fine abrasive such as fine sandpaper to clean away small soiled marks.

CLEANING BRICK

If it's sealed, or sealed and painted, it can be sponged off. Otherwise, just vacuum.

If brick is stained, spray on a half-and-half mixture of bleach and water or a foaming bathroom cleaner, then wipe with a damp cloth.

A plain eraser removes some black marks.

See also the instructions for cleaning a fireplace on p. 160.

Windows

Cleaning windows is the metaphor for woman's work. It seems the job is never done. You scrub and polish and spray and rub, then stand back to admire your work, and what do you see? Streaks! Cloudy patches! I've been tempted to leave my drapes drawn twenty-four hours a day, but then my plants would die.

I finally decided to talk to a professional window cleaner, to see if he could help me get the job done better and faster. I figured anyone who had to dangle twenty stories—or more—above the ground would figure out how to get back inside as quickly as possible.

The first thing he told me was to throw away my collection of window-washing solutions. The pros don't use them, because they leave a glaze of oily, waxy film—the very thing that causes streaks and cloudy spots.

COLD TREATMENT

If the weather is freezing but for some reason you need to wash a window, fill your spray bottle with 1 quart rubbing alcohol plus 1 cup water plus 2 tablespoons mild dishwashing liquid. (Or add antifreeze to the windshield-washing solution.)

WINDOW-WASHING EQUIPMENT

A **window squeegee,** preferably brass or stainless steel, with a 10- to 14-inch blade.

A **clean sponge** (for applying the solution).

A **cloth** (for wiping the blade).

A **pail of solution.** In a well-ventilated area, combine $1/2$ cup ammonia and $1/2$ cup white vinegar with a gallon of warm water. Or use car windshield-washing fluid.

WASHING TECHNIQUES

Clean in early morning. I always warned not to wash in bright sunlight, so one woman asked me if it was okay to wash while wearing sunglasses. She missed the point: If you wash in bright sunlight, the window will dry too fast and you'll see a residue.

Apply cleaning solution to the window with the sponge. Don't slop it on. Wetting it lightly is sufficient.

Wipe the blade of the squeegee with the damp cloth. This helps the blade slide easily across the glass.

Holding the squeegee at an angle, pull it across the top of the window. Wipe the squeegee blade again (and every time you take a swipe).

When you're done, you'll notice a few drops of water at the edge of the window. Leave them alone. They'll disappear as they dry, but if you try to wipe them up, they'll just smear. Any drops in the middle of the window you can wipe with your bare hand—having handled the cleaning solution, your hand should be free of oil and will clean the spots without leaving lint.

SPECIAL WINDOW-CLEANING PROBLEMS

Adhesive from masking tape left on a newly painted window can be removed with a little paint thinner or lighter fluid. (Both are flammable; use in a ventilated area away from open flame.) Or use commercial adhesive remover.

Dull and milky windows may require an acid cleaner from the hardware store; if the cause is smoke fumes, 91% isopropyl alcohol will help (but test first, as it may discolor some glass). There is also a possibility that fumes from a factory in your area may have etched glass and they'll need replacing.

Dull glass can be shined with a blackboard eraser. A blackboard eraser is wonderful for giving a little extra shine to glass.

Film from Christmas "snow" can be removed with lighter fluid (which is flammable, so exercise caution), vinegar, silicone spray, or one part ammonia to three parts water. Scrub with a plastic scrubber.

Lime and mineral deposits are sometimes left on a window by a water sprinkler. Spritz some oven-cleaning spray on a cloth, wipe it on, let set briefly, and wipe off; or get a special cleaner for removing water deposits.

Multiple small panes (as on a wood secretary) should be cleaned with a cotton pad soaked in alcohol, one by one. Spraying may damage the wood finish. Larger panes can be cleaned with newspaper, which, after a squeegee, is my second-favorite window cleaning aid. For some reason, newspaper cleans windows better than paper towels or rags.

Outside, screen-covered windows can be cleaned by spraying on foaming bathroom spray (through wire screens only; it will "melt" nylon ones). Hose them off before the foam can dry.

Paint left on the window can be removed with nail polish remover or softened with turpentine and scraped (with a plastic credit card or a special paint scraper). Caution: Nylon pads or steel wool may scratch the glass. If windows are sealed shut, see Painting, beginning on p. 256.

Plastic window film (used to screen out sun) may be peeling. Wet the window with good hot soapy water and wet large black plastic garbage bags. Cover the window with the plastic, smooth it flat against the glass, leave it on about one hour, then remove it. It should be easy to scrape off plastic film with the rubber squeegee or metal scraper. If the problem remains, resoak the windows and plastic and leave another hour.

Scratches on a picture window may be removed by rubbing on some non-gel toothpaste. Or apply automobile heavy-duty rubbing compound with a slightly dampened sponge. Work in the direction of the scratches (deeper ones require more pressure), then wipe with a dry towel and use glass cleaner. (This is also a remedy for windows stained from acid rain.)

CLEANING WINDOW FRAMES AND SILLS

Aluminum windowsills can be wiped with a liquid abrasive. To remove spots, pour a little diluted rubbing alcohol on a soft cloth and rub. Or use a fine steel wool. (Do not use ammonia on aluminum.)

Wooden windowsills should be painted to keep them from deteriorating. If they look very dirty, vacuum them first. If that's not enough, use wood cleaner or a spray-on furniture polish. (Don't use a water-based cleaner. It makes wood swell.)

Waxing the windowsills with car paste will attract dust on either aluminum or wood; however, the smooth surface will be easier to wipe off than a nicked and pitted wood sill. It's your call.

SILL PROTECTOR

If you're having trouble keeping an old, peeling windowsill clean, cover it with tiles. Laying down grout and setting them in place is not difficult, and future cleanups require only a wipe of the sponge.

CLEANING BLINDS AND SHADES

Shades and blinds get dirtier in winter since static electricity (due to low indoor humidity) causes dust to cling.

Metal and plastic blinds that can be easily removed can be brought to a do-it-yourself car wash and hung on the wall. With the pressure hose, shoot streams of hot soapy water.

Or take the blinds outside, lay them flat and sponge them with a heavy-duty detergent ($1/4$ cup to a gallon of water) or wax-free carwashing detergent, hose them off, and let them air dry.

To wash them indoors, let them soak in a tub half-filled with warm water and detergent for half an hour, sponge them, refill the tub with clear water and sponge again. Or let them soak in a wallpaper trough (sold for soaking wallpaper) and rinse them in the shower. Then hang them from their own brackets (put a couple of towels underneath to catch the drips) or from the shower curtain rod. Or, for real convenience, install a couple of cup hooks inside the shower just for the purpose of hanging them.

Washing them in place is awkward but not impossible. Just sponge them from top to bottom with detergent and water solution, then use a fresh sponge with clear water to rinse. Towel dry each slat.

Fabric blinds can be spritzed with spray-on carpet cleaner. Let it dry, then vacuum up the residue. Tape up a plastic dropcloth behind them, or you'll muck up the windows, and try the cleaner in a hidden spot to make sure it doesn't affect the color. An upholstery cleaner applied with a cloth takes longer. Or have the pros clean them.

Vinyl blinds can be sprayed with any heavy- or light-duty detergent.

Wood blinds may warp if you clean them with water. Wipe each individually with furniture cleaner or mineral spirits (a cleaning solvent) and dry right away with a soft, absorbent cloth.

Shades, if unwashable, can be rubbed with wallpaper cleaning dough such as Absorbene or a dry sponge. Washable shades can be laid flat and washed with detergent solution, then left unrolled to dry.

CLEANING SCREENS

Use the same car wash or outdoor cleaning treatment as for metal and plastic blinds. They can also be washed indoors in the tub, but it's a messy job.

Wire screens can also be cleaned with foaming bathroom cleaner: spray it on, leave a few minutes, then rinse off. Don't try this on nylon screens, which may melt.

CLEANING CURTAINS AND DRAPES

Curtains are usually no problem to machine wash. Curtains that have faded from the sun can't be revived, but if they're just dingy, you can use a nylon whitener (which you may find among the dyes in your market or notions store).

If you rehang polyester and nylon while damp, you won't have to iron them. Use a little spray starch to give cotton curtains some body.

If they are noticeably dusty, vacuum **drapes** with the upholstery attachment or toss them in the clothes dryer for 10 to 15 minutes on "Air Only." (However, putting them in the machine means all the removable hooks must be taken off, which can take some time.)

If the drapes are washable, follow the manufacturer's instructions. If the lining is made of a different fabric than the drape, follow the instructions for whichever is the more delicate. Fiberglass must be dry-cleaned. In the washer or dryer, the fibers may break, and if you soak them in the tub, you may get splinters in your hands.

Your local dry cleaner should be able to clean your drapes, but if they're very expensive or the hanging is complicated, take them to a specialist in cleaning window covers who has large-scale machinery and should be able to take down and rehang them. Specialists dry drapes at lower temperatures than regular cleaners in order to avoid shrinking, but if they do shrink, the professional can restretch them.

CAUTION: If you've left the drapes up five to six years without cleaning, sun and heat have deteriorated them. Even if they look okay, they may tear when cleaned.

Dusting: Why and How

The least you need to know about dusting:
• Why bother
• How to do it

There are three reasons to dust:

1. Health. Some people are very allergic to dust. There are, in fact, new vacuum cleaners made specifically to pick up dust mites, and if you have someone with a problem in your family, you ought to investigate this possibility. Furthermore, dust is a pollutant. If I'm going to ruin my lungs, I'd rather smoke.

2. Maintenance. If you do not dust the coils under your refrigerator, eventually the coating becomes so heavy that the heat cannot leave the pipes and the refrigerator doesn't function properly (or breaks down completely). Windowsills may eventually pit.

3. Aesthetics. Most people do not enjoy owning or visiting in a house where it is possible to write your name in the dust.

DUSTING: TOOLS

A vacuum cleaner with a brush attachment and a dust wand are all you need for most dusting jobs.

You may find it easier to use an inexpensive, machine-washable dust mop for floors, ceilings, and walls rather than hauling out the vacuum. Dampen it only lightly, particularly if you're using it on wood.

The dust wand, a big cotton swab with a long handle, is light and easy to handle, can reach high and low and covers a big area with just one pass. Use it for tops of doors, windows, picture frames, cabinets, chair legs, etc.

I'm not a big feather duster fan myself because a feather duster tends to scatter dust instead of collect it, but it's very gentle so you can use it on everything and it's great for an emergency cleanup. (The dust probably won't settle back down until after your guests leave.) Instead of a feather duster, you can use a can of compressed air (from the photo supply store) or a hair dryer to remove dust on delicate items or in hard-to-reach places (lampshades, knick-knacks, artificial flowers). Or remove the bulb end of an old turkey baster and tape the plastic tube to your vacuum nozzle and you can get to hard-to-reach areas.

Though many people use sprays such as Endust or even a shot of furniture polish on their dusting tool in order to keep dust from floating into the air, I believe that water alone can do the job just as effectively. Put the water in a spray bottle to mist the cloth or, if you're doing a floor, your mop.

UNLIKELY DUSTERS

• A small leaf blower can be used inside the house to blow dust from under heavy objects such as beds, sofa, refrigerator, etc., from high places and under car seats. It's easy to vacuum up the dust afterward.

• Throw a clean, slightly damp dustcloth over a helium balloon and float it up to attract the dust from the rafters or unreachable high corners.

SPECIAL DUSTING JOBS

As you have surely noticed, dust falls down. So always dust from top to bottom.

Air Conditioner. Dust inside it with the vacuum while you're washing the filter in lukewarm soapy water—about every month or so.

Baseboards. Wear old socks and use your feet as tools.

Blinds. I prefer washing them to dusting them, but if you're giving the room a quick once-over and notice dust on the blinds, give them a flick with the dusting wand. If your fabric blinds are accordion-pleated (and one solid surface), use the brush attachment of the vacuum cleaner.

Drawers. If you don't want to suck up everything in the drawer but want to remove the dust, remove attachments and cover the nozzle with a piece of cheesecloth or a section of panty hose held in place with a rubber band. This is also a great way to retrieve a light item that's dropped behind an appliance or to find a contact lens lost on the floor.

Heat Grills. Use the upholstery brush or the crevice tool of the vacuum (to either suck up dust or—if your vacuum has a blower feature—to blow through a clogged grill).

Louver Door. A wedge-shaped brush (from the paint store) fits right into louvers for easy dusting.

Narrow Areas. Put a sock or panty hose over an old hanger, wooden spoon, fly swatter, or end of yardstick. Or staple a small sponge to the end of a yardstick. Or slip the cardboard roll from inside gift wrap over a length of your vacuum.

Plants. Give them a flick with the feather duster, but I prefer just to put them under a shower or out in the rain.

Radiators. Use a vacuum brush attachment to dust them regularly or you restrict the flow of steam. Baby bottle brushes can reach into places a vacuum cannot.

> An optimistic housewife thinks the vacuum bag is half-empty, a pessimistic one thinks it's half-full.

CLEANING RUGS AND CARPETS

Obviously, human beings were not meant to clean floors. If we were, we'd have been built with less space between them and our hands. Fortunately, cleaning carpeting and rugs is usually just a matter of vacuuming the paths that get the most wear and an annual shampooing to brighten them up. (And if you don't want to do it yourself, you can hire someone.) The biggest problem is stain removal.

The least you need to know about cleaning the carpets and rugs:

- How to vacuum
- When and how to deep clean
- Dealing with area rugs
- Coping with stains and other problems

Vacuuming

You save yourself a lot of time and trouble if you have the right vacuum—or two. I believe that each floor should have its own vacuum. I also believe each floor should have its own maid, but the vacuum seems more likely. Over the long run, an extra vacuum is not an extravagance (if it is possible to use the word "extravagance" in connection with a vacuum). If the vacuum gets less use, it lasts that much longer.

I always seemed to play bumper car with my vacuum and the furniture. Then I got smart and put foam weather-insulation tape around the side. As I drag it through the rooms, it still hits the furniture, but now it doesn't cause any damage.

See if it is possible to place a couple of ceramic magnets (available from electronics suppliers like Radio Shack) inside the front bumper of your vacuum. They'll snag all paper clips, etc., before they get sucked up into the motor.

If you don't vacuum, tiny particles of dust get ground in and actually cut the fibers, which means the rug wears out a lot faster. The folks from the Carpet and Rug Institute tell you to vacuum twice a week, but I'm assuming you'll do it as often as I do, which works out to be less than twice a week and is still more often than I enjoy.

Actually, routine vacuuming doesn't take that much time, because it has to be done only in high-traffic areas, where people walk. Since no one is grinding down the dirt particles under the chairs or behind the sofa, they can't do any damage. (When you do get around to vacuuming some of the less popular spots,

---

VACUUM STEP-SAVERS

- Add a thirty-foot extension cord to the vacuum so you can drag it from room to room without replugging.
- Instead of bending, attach a magnet to the end of a sawed-off broomstick and take it along to pick up dropped staples, pins, etc.
- If you have to move furniture out of the way (in order to vacuum under it), slip a paper plate under each leg to help it slide.
- Put some dried beans in the disposable bag. When air makes the bean move, they compact the dust and you change the bag less frequently.

---

there is a rarely mentioned bonus—you will excavate many long-lost treasures such as overdue library books and all the cat's toys.)

When you vacuum the entire rug, divide it into sections or quarters, like mowing the lawn—go over it in neat rows. One simple pass isn't enough. I'm told that it takes seven or more strokes backward and forward to get a spot thoroughly clean. Being thorough makes the rug last longer. There's no particular reason to keep going in the same direction other than that the carpet will look neater.

Stairs get a lot of wear and need frequent vacuuming: Work from the top down.

ON THE FRINGE

When you get near the carpet fringe with an upright vacuum, lift the front of the vacuum—just lower the handle and push it off the carpet. Otherwise you may get the fringe caught in the agitator. With a canister vacuum, use the upholstery tool or floor brush to clean the fringe.

If the fringe of your carpet is ever torn, it can be repaired by a carpet specialist.

Shampooing:
Time to Deep Clean

If the carpet doesn't smell fresh, sprinkle around some plain baking soda or borax, let it sit an hour, then vacuum. If it's matted, sweep it (to raise the nap), and then vacuum.

But it's time to deep clean if: the carpet still has an odor and/or looks matted; it feels sticky; there are dark circles around the furniture legs; it no longer bears any resemblance to the remnants left over when it was laid; the kids raise a dust storm when they run across the carpet.

SHOCK TREATMENT

When you cross the room to greet your significant other, what is that tingling you feel? If it's just static from the carpet, mix 1 part liquid fabric softener with 5 parts water, mist the carpet lightly, and let it dry. Repeat every few months. If it's not static from the carpet, lucky you.

DO-IT-YOURSELF CLEANING

I like shampooing a carpet because you can really see the results of your work. On the other hand, you're just shampooing, not performing a miracle. If the rug is in bad shape to begin with, it may look worse after you clean it. Once the surface dirt is gone, worn, badly matted areas will be even more obvious.

There are several ways to approach carpet cleaning. One option is dry rug cleaners (powdered or foam). With some, you use a machine to work in the powder thoroughly so the dirt can be released. This does a very superficial job, but makes sense if the dyes in the rug may run when the rug is wet. However, though I would warn you to try the product in an inconspicuous spot just in case your rug is the exception to the rule, most antique rugs and virtually all modern rugs are unlikely to bleed—even handmade ones, says my carpet expert friend Harold. (They're no longer squeezing bugs to get purple.)

A second option is to shampoo with a sprayed-on aerosol or use a concentrated rug detergent. The detergent can be brushed in with a sponge mop, a hand brush, or a non-electric applicator, but it's easier to use a floor care machine you own or rent. Try the machine first in a hidden area to see if it causes a lot of pilling, which means it's too rough for your carpet.

Water extraction, or "steam cleaning," produces the best results of all. A steam cleaner is larger than a shampooer, but not any harder to use. You can buy one (see the Equipping section), rent one, or call in a professional to do the job. My husband has often done a better job with these machines than professionals I have hired, and I think it's just because he took his time. (Also, he knew the complaint department would be open around the clock.) If a rug is really dirty, you can shampoo it first (I use color-safe bleach, but try this at your own risk), then the extractor.

Before you start, remove all the furniture from the room. If that's impossible, put some plastic wrap, a muffin cup, or aluminum foil under furniture legs until the carpet is dry to prevent staining. And consider the room off-limits until the carpet is dry, which will probably take 12 hours.

The solution should be applied in a well-ventilated area, so open the windows. Read the cleaning product label to see if there are any other safety precautions you should take. Then (as you should always do with any cleaning product, and certainly when you're fooling around with something major like the carpet), test for colorfastness in a hidden area, like a closet, to see whether the product will cause the dye to run or fade. First remove any protective coating, such as Scotchgard, by following the directions in the box "Why Carpet Stain Removal May

WHY CARPET STAIN REMOVAL MAY FAIL

- *If the rug has a protective coating*, the cleaning or stain removal product won't permeate the fibers. Add a squirt of liquid detergent to a very damp cloth, rub in, then blot up. Then use product.
- *If you haven't neutralized the spot* after using another stain remover that didn't work. Mix 1 tablespoon baking soda and 1/4 cup water, rub a small amount of this into the spot, and blot up.

Fail." Next follow colorfastness test directions on product or dip a section of white cloth into a little of the rug cleaner, either diluted or straight (depending on how it's supposed to be used), then rub the cloth against the rug. If the cloth picks up color, don't use that product.

Follow instructions on the machine and use light, single strokes. It'll take some practice before you can figure out how big a section to work with.

When you're done, wipe off any foam that's left on furniture or walls. Brush all the damp pile in one direction with a soft brush or a special plastic or wooden rake finishing tool to raise the nap (so it won't look matted down). Keep off the wet carpet and dry it as quickly as possible with a fan, heat, and/or air conditioner. Otherwise, if the carpet backing is too wet, it may shrink, discolor, or mildew. The odor of a mildewed rug is awful.

PROFESSIONAL CLEANING

If you have a very delicate or expensive rug or can't be bothered, have a professional clean the rug. The range of competence among carpet cleaners I have tried has been about the same range I have found in haircutters—but at least your hair grows back.

Call your carpet dealer or the Better Busi-ness Bureau if you can't get a personal recommendation. Or call the fanciest furnishings place in town and ask who cleans their carpet. (This is also a great way to get a recommendation for a painter or other craftsman.) A lot of companies advertise a very low cost, then try to inflate it when you call them in by offering such services as a carpet restretching. This is baloney; say you want a price for cleaning and applying a protective finish, and that's all. The price should be based on square footage.

Before the worker starts, you should have a chance to explain what your guest spilled in that corner of the room and point out any damage the dog has done. There are so many methods of cleaning that you'll have to rely on the cleaner you choose to make the best choice based on the type of carpeting, color, and kind of soil. Sometimes people discover that they are allergic to a particular kind of carpet cleaner and are forced to change companies—or at least request a different formula—if the carpet is cleaned again.

In addition to spot removal, a cleaner may also do repairs.

Since wall-to-wall carpeting may shrink, it is cleaned in place, but area rugs are removed and taken to the plant. If you are planning to have the walls painted or the floors scraped, do it while the rug is away being cleaned.

There's no such thing as dirt. It's just matter in the wrong place.

Cleaning Area Rugs

Bath Mats. Can be washed in the machine, but be careful to wash the dark ones separately at not more than 90°F and the light ones not above 105°F. Don't iron, but tumble or air dry.

CARPET AND RUG PROBLEMS

Problem	Remedy
Bleached Area	Check the art supply store to find a permanent fabric marker that matches your carpeting, or mix a shade to match with food coloring and sponge it on. Or use Rit Dye, let it dry, then apply a solution of half vinegar and half water to set it. Professionals use a very similar method.
Burns	Remove the singed portion with fine sandpaper. Drip a mild detergent slowly onto the stain and rub with a clean cloth. After five minutes, sponge with a borax-and-water solution (2 table-spoons to two cups). Rinse with clean water and dry well. If the spot is obvious, cut some fibers from an inconspicuous portion of the rug and mix them with white glue and pat into place.
Curling	If the corners of an area rug curl, sew or use a hot-glue gun to attach a small triangular pocket of felt or canvas to the underside, and put inside it a triangle of sheet lead bought from a plumber.
Dents	Leave an ice cube on the spot until it springs back. Or work the carpet pile back into place with the edge of a coin and hold a steam iron at least 4" above the spot until it's warm. Move furniture periodically to avoid dents.
Fluffing	Due to loose bits of fiber left in the carpet during manufacture. Don't worry, your carpet is not disappearing. This is more common with wool than with nylon and other synthetics, but eventually all the bits will have been vacuumed up.
Pilling	Clip with scissors. These are just balls of entangled fibers and lint.
Ripples or Wrinkles	Dampness may cause a temporary problem but if it persists, your dealer may be able to have an installer restretch the carpet with a power stretcher. Your installation warranty should allow for one free stretch.
Slipping	If your rug "travels," you can try a home remedy, such as sewing a rubber jar ring on the bottom or spraying it with hair spray or a commercial solution, such as Afta spray coating. Or buy a special pad for this purpose from a carpet store. Another possibility is to use your hot-glue gun to make zigzags, swirls, etc., on the underside of the rug. Once cool, these will keep it from budging.
Sprouting	A tuft may rise above the surface. Do not pull it out. Just snip it off.
Static	Occurs in cooler weather. Humidifier may help. There are carpets made with antistatic protection. Or you can try the fabric softener solution mentioned in box 'Shock Treatment" on p. 112.

Fur Rugs. Fur itself can usually stand a washing (after all, you can wash an animal). A *sheepskin rug* can be laundered in the machine (cold water) and air dried, but some backings don't hold up to soap and water. An *unbacked fur rug* can be wiped with a cloth dipped in warm soapy water, but don't wet the skin—it may shrink. To clean it dry, rub cornmeal or unscented talc into the pile. Shake it out and repeat until the cornmeal comes out clean. Vacuum away the residue. Otherwise, professional treatment is necessary.

Indoor-Outdoor Carpet. Use a carpet shampoo product, straight or diluted, according to the instructions. If the carpet is outside, you will first have to sweep off surface debris and it will be easier to spread the solution with a garden spray or sprinkling can, then scrub. You can use a hose to clean it off. Like all carpeting, it should be allowed to dry thoroughly to minimize the risk of mildew.

Kilims, Ryas, Tapestry Rugs. After a fresh snowfall, put the rug on the ground, beat it with a rug beater or old tennis racket, then do the other side and shake gently. The rug doesn't get wet, and colors won't run. Lacking snow, hang it on a clothesline to beat it or remove dust from a small rug by putting it in the dryer on "Air Only" for a few minutes.

Rag Rug. May be machine washable. But to protect it from the wear and tear in a machine, put it in a pillowcase that's been knotted closed. Dry cleaning solvent can be used on unwashable rugs.

Sisal, Coconut Rugs. Shake out occasionally, and/or vacuum surface and underside. Rub with a damp cloth to restore moisture. If it's a small welcome mat, beat the dust out (with your kid's baseball bat or an old tennis racket). Sudsy water won't hurt it. Neither will hosing it down.

Carpet and Rug Stains

Stain-resistant carpet has only been around since 1986. Do not think that stain-resistant is the same as stainproof. The fibers in these carpets have simply been treated to make them more resistant to spills containing dyes.

> ### CARPET STAIN REMOVAL BASICS
>
> • Always blot the stain before you start to work on it. Soak up as much as you can, then put down paper towels or a cloth and stand on it for a minute, to get the liquid up from the very bottom of the fibers.
>
> • Remove any protective coating and neutralize any previous stain-removal treatments (see box, p. 113, "Why Carpet Stain Removal May Fail").
>
> • When using any solution on carpeting, always try some in a hidden area first to see if it causes the dye to run or fade.
>
> • Apply the detergent directly to the carpeting, but put the cleaning solvent on a rag. Keep blotting until the spot is removed. Then cover the area with a thick pad of paper towels and weight it down until rug is dry. If all the stain isn't absorbed, the spot will keep returning.
>
> • Rub in a circular motion toward the center of the stain, not outward (or you'll spread it).
>
> • After you've removed a spot, rinse the fibers with warm water to remove any residue from the cleaner.
>
> • You may see a ring around the spot after a stain is removed, because you've cleaned the area. Eventually the area will darken to match the rest.

The phrase "man's best friend" was obviously created before the invention of wall-to-wall carpeting.

REMEDIES FOR CARPET AND RUG STAINS

Stain	First blot, then:
Alcoholic Beverage	Dilute with club soda or baking soda and water. If is non-wool rug, apply mix of one part ammonia and ten parts water, rinse with cold water. (Ammonia sets stains in wool.)
Blood	Work fast. Blot, apply cold water, blot, and repeat. Over and over again. If this stain sets, you can't get it out. Or cover immediately with a corn-starch–cold water paste, rub lightly. It will get so hard you may need to pound it with a mallet. Vacuum powder up. Repeat if necessary. Blood is very difficult to remove, virtually impossible once set.
Butter	Scrape, then apply dry-cleaning fluid; let dry; repeat if necessary. Or try a bar of Lava, wet, and rub into spot. Rinse well.
Candle Wax	Put a plain brown bag over the spot, press with a warm (not hot) iron, and continue to use a fresh piece of paper until all wax is absorbed.
Chewing Gum	Soften with prewash spray (first test on hidden spot for color change). Or use freon freeze from a janitor supply store to make it brittle. Or use a bit of salad oil to make it soft. Pick off the gum, then use dry-cleaning fluid.
Coffee and Tea	Blot, then apply detergent-vinegar water. Rinse, blot, then try dry-cleaning solvent. Dry.
Crayon	Scrape off excess, then see solution for candle wax (above). Or try dry-cleaning fluid. Or call 1-800-Crayola.
Floor Wax	Use commercial dry-cleaning solvent.
Fruit Stains	Dampen spot with water, dump on table salt, rub in lightly. Let set for a few minutes to allow salt to be rubbed into the stain. Brush out and vacuum. Repeat until stain is gone.
Grease, Oil, or Oily Products	If it hasn't dried yet, sprinkle an absorbent such as baking soda or baby powder on the grease, rub it in, let it sit until it dries, vacuum it up, and use a grease-removal product recommended for clothing. Or try solution recommended for Butter (above). For oil on rubber-backed carpet, make a soupy paste of baking soda and warm water, rub into carpet, let dry, vacuum.
Hairball	Blot. Saturate cloth with rubbing alcohol, rub into stain.
Handcream	Apply dry-cleaning fluid. Let dry. Repeat if necessary.
Ink, Ballpoint, or Marker	Use alcohol, paint thinner, or dry-cleaning fluid on a cloth. Be sure to keep using new, clean sections of the cloth as you rub. Let dry. Repeat if necessary.

Stain	First blot, then:
Lipstick	Apply dry-cleaning fluid. When dry, apply detergent solution on p. 116. Let dry. Reapply if necessary. Or scrape up lipstick (or use brown bag treatment, as for candle wax, p. 116), then rub in Lava soap, and rinse with 1/2 cup white vinegar in 1/2 gallon water.
Mildew	Use 1 teaspoon disinfectant to 1 cup of water (making sure that the disinfectant won't remove color; try in an inconspicuous spot). For non-wool rugs, mix 1 part ammonia to 10 parts water; apply, blot, rinse, let dry. Only bleach—which removes color—is 100% effective on mildew.
Miscellaneous Dirt	Make a very sudsy solution of liquid Tide laundry detergent and water. Brush only the suds onto the spot, first vertically, then horizontally. Blot up excess liquid. Place a towel and a couple of heavy books on top of the spot to absorb moisture. I've been able to remove a colored spot from a white carpet with Rit Color Remover. Also, a spritz of foamy shaving cream from the aerosol can makes a good spot remover (but first try in a hidden place to test for colorfastness).
Mud	Let it dry, vacuum loose dirt first, and then work on the stain. Rub on some denatured alcohol, then a teaspoon each of vinegar and dish detergent in a quart of warm water.
Nail Polish	Apply dry-cleaning fluid or (on non-acetate carpets) acetone or nail polish remover.
Paint, Oil-Based	Dab on turpentine. Use cornmeal or cat box filler to absorb the turpentine. Follow with dry-cleaning fluid. Try on hidden spot; turpentine may dissolve fibers.
Pet Accidents	Blot. Pour on club soda. Blot again until almost dry. Or mix 3 tablespoons vinegar and 2 tablespoons Tide in a quart of water. Work solution into the stain, blot dry. Flush with water. Dry. Vacuum. Windex, which contains ammonia and water, also works on fresh stains (not for wool rugs).
Tar	Loosen with non-butane lighter fluid, then use heavy-duty cleaner. If all tar isn't removed, stain will remain.
Vomit	Dilute with club soda or baking soda and water. On non-wool rugs, apply a mixture of 1 part ammonia to 10 parts water. Rinse with cold water, let dry, then vacuum.
Wine	Sprinkle with salt or baking soda, leave until absorbed, then vacuum. Or pour some whiskey on a rag and rub into spot until stain disappears. Or saturate with club soda, then blot. For red wine: Blot, pour on white wine, and blot again. Or test for colorfastness on a hidden area, then try shaving cream from an aerosol can, then sponge with water.

But there are some stains—caused by toilet cleaner, hair dye, herbal teas, liquid plant foods, mildew killers, bleaches, acne medication, and other substances—that redye or bleach the carpeting to the point of no return. Acne medication, for example, causes orange and yellow spots, or pink spots on a blue rug, that appear mysteriously even when there's been no spill but the medicine has simply been brushed off onto the carpet (or upholstery, bed linens, etc.). Green or blue stains may indicate sun bleaching along with a catalyst (like insecticide), red spots on tan or beige may indicate a strong acid.

The best way to solve a carpet situation before it becomes hopeless is by acting fast. Before you try anything, your best bet is to call the 800 number your manufacturer has given you. But if you've got a middle-of-the-night stain, you may be on your own, in which case checking the manual isn't a bad idea. I don't know too many people organized enough to do this. Which is why I've included the list below for your quick reference.

I've been dealing with carpet problems for years, and I eventually worked with a chemist to develop a carpet stain remover that I think outperforms any of the others, but in the absence of Mary Ellen's Wow! Carpet Stain Remover, here's what you should do.

While your first instinct is to rub a stain, that will just make more of a mess. That's why I remind you again to blot it. Or, if there's gunk, such as a piece of crayon, a hunk of non-chocolate candy, etc., scrape it away. A small amount of heat from a blow dryer pointed at the spot can soften up gum and crayon to the point where you can pull it off. Not too much, though, or it'll melt deeper into the fiber.

Detergent Solution. Treat most water-soluble spots by washing them with a mixture of one teaspoon each of vinegar (to remove the odor) and mild dish detergent in a quart of warm water. Let the carpet dry. If the spot remains, try again.

Dry-Cleaning Solvent. In your cleaning closet, keep a dry-cleaning solvent from the supermarket for greasy, oily stains. Don't use it with paddings and backings made of plastic or rubber foam.

If the stain is both greasy and water-soluble (as many food stains, like soup, may be), or if you don't know what the stain comes from, use the detergent solution first, then the dry-cleaning solvent. Otherwise the solvent may remove moisture and set the stain.

● ●
CLEANING FLOORS

Vacuuming the high-traffic areas regularly will protect your floors. They'll also need routine damp-mopping and some cleaning with a heavy-duty cleaner; most will require an occasional waxing.

The least you need to know about cleaning floors:
- Types of wood floor finishes
- Dealing with stains
- Types of non-wood floors
- Specific floor care

Wood Floor Finishes

A wood floor is either given a surface finish (such as polyurethane) or is treated with a penetrating sealer and then waxed.

If you don't know what's on the wood floor in your apartment or house, just rub your finger across it. If you can make a smudge, the floor has been treated with a penetrating seal and then waxed, and if not it was surface finished.

Maintaining Penetrating Sealed Finishes

A penetrating sealer soaks into the wood pores and hardens so the floor is sealed against certain stains and dirt. Wood treated with a penetrating stain shines with a low-gloss finish that will last for a while but eventually wears down. If your penetrating sealed floors are new or recently refinished, you should lay down a wax coating to provide a second level of resistance against wear, dirt, and stains and rewax annually. See section on Waxing and Stripping.

In between annual waxings, there isn't much maintenance involved. Vacuum only, to remove the surface dirt before it gets ground into the floor and to pull the dust from the grooves between the planks. If you can't vacuum the whole floor weekly, at least get to the high-traffic areas as quickly as you can.

If something spills, just wipe it up, then use a clean rag to buff it. But if the area is still dull, use one of the one-step cleaner/polishers such as Preen or Bissell One-Step Wood Floor Care. Spread it, rub to remove grime and old wax, then wipe. After 20 minutes, buff. Repeat if necessary.

If the floor looks grimy, dampen a mop very, very slightly—just enough to pick up the dirt—and rub it lightly over the floor. Sometimes I wrap a damp cloth around my mop, replace it when it's dirty, and repeat until the floor is finished.

Maintaining Surface Sealed Finishes

Surface-sealed floors may have been prefinished at the factory or custom-finished on the site. If you can see V-shaped grooves along the edges where the boards join, the planks were probably prefinished individually by the manufacturer rather than after they were installed. The problem with prefinishing is that the entire surface isn't uniformly covered. Water can get between the cracks and the floor will warp. Follow the guidelines for surface sealed floors and take special care not to use water on it. If you want the floor to last, you should probably have the whole thing refinished.

If your floor boards have no grooves, the floor was probably finished after installation. The builder or floor finisher should tell you what finish was applied. Without more specific information, follow the general guidelines for surface finishes.

The new surface finishes aren't as problematic as the finishes they have almost entirely replaced—lacquer, varnish, and shellac. Shellac is easily stained by spills and needs a lot of waxing to keep it intact. Varnish darkens with age and is hard to touch up; it also may powder and show white scars. And lacquer, though it produces a tough high sheen, is difficult to apply and shows scratch and scuff marks easily. Unless waxed, none of these are moisture-resistant. If you do happen to have a lacquered, varnished, or shellacked floor, always dust with a dry mop. If these floors look dirty, you need to clean and wax them with special cleaners made for these finishes.

Modern surface finishes, which are moisture-resistant, include moisture-cure and water-based urethanes, "Swedish" finishes, and polyurethane. All are blends of ingredients that include synthetic resins and plasticizers and form a film that stands up to splashes and spills even in the kitchen.

They come in a variety of sheens, from high-gloss (very shiny) to semi-gloss, satin, and matte (flat). The exception, moisture-cure urethane, is usually available only in gloss, but is the most durable and non-yellowing. Both water-based and "Swedish" finishes are durable and non-yellowing as well as fast-drying. Polyurethane yellows slightly as it ages.

All surfaces finishes may be used on top of a penetrating seal, but unless the ingredients are compatible, the top coat may peel.

Though floors with surface finishes are sometimes waxed to increase protection in high traffic areas. I don't think this is a good idea. The floor will be very slippery, and since the wax can't penetrate the finish, scuffs and water spots will be more obvious. Also, grit and

STAINS AND FLAWS ON PENETRATING SEALED FLOORS
(Do not use these remedies on urethane or other surface-treated floors)

Stain	Remedy
Alcohol	Rub with paste or solvent-based wax, silver polish, or cloth barely dampened with ammonia.
Chewing Gum	Point hair dryer at spot until warm enough to loosen. Or pour on solvent-based wax, let set until gum can be loosened and wiped away.
Cigarette Burn	Dampen Fine steel wool with solvent-based wax, rub with clean cloth buff to shine.
Crayon or Candle Wax	Point hair dryer at spot until warm enough to blot off. Or put a piece of fabric or brown garbage bag (several layers) over the spot, then iron over that; when fabric or paper has absorbed wax, use a fresh spot until it's all gone. Or pour on solvent-based wax, let set briefly until wax can be loosened and wiped away.
Dark "Mystery" Spot	Dampen Fine steel wool with odorless mineral spirits. Then wash area with household vinegar, let stand for 3–4 minutes, wipe with mineral spirits. Then sand with fine sandpaper, "feathering" out 3–4 inches all around. Stain, rewax, and repolish. If this doesn't do it, mix oxalic acid crystals from hardware store into very hot water, and keep adding crystals until they no longer dissolve. Wear rubber gloves. Pour on stain, leave up to 60 minutes, rinse with water and blot dry. This may lighten wood so much you may need to restain area.
Darkening in Area of Use, such as under rocking chair	Dampen Fine steel wool with mineral spirits and rub. Remove all residue before applying new wax.
Dents	See Floors, Dents and Gouges In, p. 240.
Food, Dried	Rub with damp cloth, dry, rewax.
Hair Dye	Turpentine might remove shampoo-in color (try in a hidden spot first).
Heel Mark	Dampen Fine steel wool with liquid wax or mineral spirits, buff to shine.
Milk	Rub with damp cloth, dry, rewax.
Oil or Grease	Saturate cotton with hydrogen peroxide and place over stain. Then saturate a second layer of cotton with ammonia and place over the first layer. Remove, and repeat process until stain is removed. Wax when dry.
Pet Stain	Dampen rag with white vinegar and rub spot. Then rub with Fine steel wool. Apply buffable wax (in a color to match your floor), rub with a flannel cloth, and repeat as needed.

Stain	Remedy
Scuffs	Rub gently with Fine steel wool, ordinary pencil eraser, or baking soda. Or clean a very small area with a bit of kerosene or turpentine. (Don't cover a large area with either since they are extremely flammable.)
Staple Marks	Sand area, save the sand, and mix it with white glue to make a paste. Fill holes, let dry overnight, re-sand. Stain area to match surrounding wood. Or fill with paste wax, then buff. Or enlarge the hole with a drill, fill with wax stick or colored wood putty, sand and wax.
Touchups	Paste shoe polish in a matching color will both stain and shine. Or, mix oil paints to match. (Best colors to start with are: yellow ocher, burnt sienna, and white). Paint on, wax, and buff.
Water	If water has puddled and left a white spot, rub with Fine steel wool or a paste of ashes and mayonnaise, rewax.

grime will wear and abrade the finish and become embedded in it. Not only will you have the work of waxing and buffing but also you'll be wearing away the finish.

Your best approach is just to be as careful as possible. See the box "Protecting the Surface Finish" on the next page. If there's a spill, wipe it up immediately. Use a damp cloth on sticky spills, a dry cloth on the others.

Vacuum or damp-mop weekly—at least in the high-traffic areas. Damp-mopping is not the same as flooding. Just mist the mop lightly with water or use a quick spritz of dust-remover spray. If you see some grime and want to pick up the dirt and dust together, add $1/4$ cup vinegar to a quart of warm water and dip the mop in the mixture. Before you touch the mop to the floor, wring it nearly dry.

Avoid using ammonia, which will dull the surface, or any product that's diluted with water, since if water seeps into the cracks in the finish, it can destroy the floor.

If a spot is dull, rub it with a piece of waxed paper, or use a touch of one-step or buffable wax (and buff if necessary). If a stain has removed the finish in a particular spot, you can use Fine steel wool or fine sandpaper to remove the finish completely from the entire single board. Re-stain if necessary, let dry, and then apply polyurethane to a single board only. (You may also be able to patch lacquer but not varnish or shellac.) You probably won't get the greatest results from this. A complete refinishing is the only thing that will really help.

When the floor really starts to show wear, you can't avoid refinishing. This is a major job: You have to sand down to the raw wood and apply a new finish. Call in the professionals, be prepared to part with a major chunk of money, and plan to be out of the house for a day or two—this is an expensive and messy job. (See the information on floor finishing in Equipping, pp. 42–43.)

SPECIAL WOOD SURFACES

Bleached floors should be treated like other surface-finished floors but may need cleaning more often because they're so light. During dry or cold weather, when the heat is on, you may notice a very obvious separation between the flooring strips. All wood floors contract when they are dry, but the separation is more obvious when the floors are light. In the summer, the dark lines are less noticeable, but once the heat goes back on, you'll see them again.

Distressed wood floors are brushed with wire to give them a textured look. This traps the dirt, so this type of floor will need to be vacuumed more often. The tough fibers that result once the wood has been brushed don't take stain well so the floor may need a treatment with a colored wax or cleaner/waxer combination.

Cleaning Non-Wood Floors

There are two types of non-wood floors, **resilient** (like vinyl and rubber) and **hard** (marble or stone). On these surfaces, as with carpeting and wood, you should vacuum up the surface dirt as often as possible in high-traffic areas.

Use the right vacuum attachment, the floor nozzle, on a hard-surface floor or you'll damage both the floor and the machine. Go over each section a couple of times. You can clean around the baseboards with the small brush attachment or wear socks and run your foot along the area.

The floor should also be damp mopped about once a week to remove dirt. Just dampen the mop lightly, run it lightly over the floor, rinse it out, then put the mop into a second bucket of clean water and go over it again. Use very little water. If the floor needs some brightening, try the vinegar solution given below in the box or use a one-step cleaner/shiner. A good product should stand up to regular damp mopping without losing its shine. But a dull floor—a very common problem—may have to be stripped, in some cases sealed, and rewaxed.

Waxing and Stripping

Waxing protects the floor against ground-in grime, gives it a smooth surface that's easy to damp-mop, and keeps it looking good.

Wood that hasn't been covered with a surface finish, cork, and certain other floors require **solvent-based waxes.**

For the one big annual wax job, your best choice is **paste wax;** Johnson's is one solvent-based brand. Though it takes more time to apply than liquid wax, paste gives more long-lasting protection. You can apply paste to the brushes of an electric floor care machine (which can shampoo, polish, and—at least in theory—wax), but you'll get a thinner, more even coat if you use a non-electric wax applicator or just spoon some paste wax into an old sock and rub it along the floor. Let wax dry for 5 to 20 minutes. Then use a buffing machine to rub it until it shines. Keep the handle at an angle so it doesn't spin out of control.

One-step cleaner/polishes, also billed as **self-polishing liquids,** like Preen, or Bissell One-Step Wood Floor Care, are easy to use. They're applied with a non-electric applicator. The solvent in liquid wax or oil evaporates and the polish stays behind without any buffing. The catch is that this finish doesn't last very long.

A good compromise is a solvent-based **buffable liquid wax** made especially for wooden floors, such as Bruce Clean & Wax. It can be applied by hand or by machine, though machine application can be a problem: The solvent waxes may clog the machine and it doesn't lay a very even coat. Machine-buff the floor.

Asphalt, brick, ceramic tile, linoleum, rubber tile, slate, terrazzo, and vinyl take **water-based wax,** such as Beacon Floor Wax, Klear Floor Finish, Future Acrylic Floor Finish, and Mop & Glo, which generally do not need buffing.

With either kind of wax, always let the wax dry thoroughly before you put furniture or feet on top of it. An electric fan will speed the process, but it won't be instant. If you're the impatient type, make plans to go out of the house for the evening so you're not tempted to push everything back into place and destroy your efforts.

Solvent-based waxes strip off the old wax as the new wax is being applied. However, water-based waxes have to be stripped periodically, about once a year or when the floor looks bad—either because the "non-yellowing" wax yellowed after all, because you've put down too much wax, or because you laid down a second coat before the first was dry. Buy a **liquid wax stripper/cleaner** such as Mex and Trewax Wax Stripper & Floor Cleaner (follow directions on the can) or make your own. Combine $1/2$ cup Spic and Span, 2 cups ammonia, and 1 gallon clear water. (Wear rubber gloves and work in a ventilated area because fumes are strong, and don't use wherever ammonia is not recommended). Sponge-mop it on, then rinse. Or rent a floor scrubber/polisher to first scrub

on a stripping product and then to wax and buff the floor.

Some floors need to be treated with a commercial **sealer** before they are rewaxed. Check the hardware store for the right one.

WAX FACTS

If you soak the wax applicator in cold water before you use it, it'll absorb less wax and more will end up on the floor. You'll save energy and spend less money on wax.

If your floor polisher pads are coated with wax, put them between several layers of newspaper, then press with a warm iron. The paper will absorb the wax. Repeat if necessary.

Floor Care Specifics

Asphalt. Regularly: Vacuum and damp-mop. Add a cup of fabric softener to half a pail of water. Damp mopping won't dull the shine. Use Mop & Glo or another all-purpose cleaner as needed.

Annually: Strip. Rewax with water-based wax.

CAUTION: Can be pitted by kerosene gasoline, naphtha, turpentine, strong cleansers, or abrasives.

Brick. Regularly: Vacuum and damp-mop. Use vinegar treatment (p. 122) if the floor is dull.

Annually: Strip, reseal, apply a water-based wax.

You can use a solvent-based wax on top of water-based for extra protection (but not the other way around).

CAUTION: Porous. If not well sealed, all stains are potentially permanent. Avoid acids, strong soaps, or abrasives. Requires a lot of care.

Ceramic Tile, glazed. Regularly: Vacuum and damp-mop. Use vinegar treatment if the floor looks dull. Use all-purpose, non-abrasive cleaner as needed.

Annually: Strip, seal, apply a water-based wax.

CAUTION: Easily scratched. Use liquid cleanser or baking powder and soft plastic scrub pad for difficult spots.

Stains: Household bleach removes many stains (leave on for several minutes, then rinse) but may discolor colored grout. Hard water deposits and rust stains may be removed with liquid scouring product or commercial tile cleaner.

Ceramic Tile, unglazed. Regularly: Vacuum and damp-mop. All-purpose, non-abrasive cleaner as needed.

Annually: Strip, seal, apply a water-based wax.

CAUTION: Avoid acids, strong soaps, or abrasives.

Concrete/Cement. Regularly: Sweep and hose or damp-mop and vacuum. A sweeping compound, from the janitor supply store, makes cleaning a very dusty floor (wood or concrete) much easier. It grabs the dust—your broom doesn't just recirculate it.

CAUTION: Stains allowed to stay are easily set. Concrete should be cleaned with an all-purpose cleaner, then sealed because it is very porous.

Cork. Regularly: Vacuum. Do not damp-mop. Annually: Rewax with solvent-based product. Possible, but not easy, to sand down and refinish.

CAUTION: Subject to water stains. Easily scratched. Subject to stains from grease, oil, acid, etc. Seal with urethane or similar product; or use paste wax.

Linoleum. Regularly: Vacuum. Damp-mop only occasionally. (Water makes it brittle.) Use all-purpose cleaner as needed.

Annually: Strip after testing a corner; the wrong stripper can harm flooring. Then apply water-based wax.

CAUTION: Do not use hot water, strong soaps, solvents, grease, or abrasives. If scuffed, use Fine steel wool dipped in liquid wax, rub gently.

Marble. Regularly: Vacuum and damp-mop. Use vinegar treatment (p. 122) if the surface looks dull.

Yearly: Strip, reseal, apply water-based or solvent-based wax.

CAUTION: Easily stained, easily scratched, porous (though polished marble is less porous than unpolished).

Quarry Tile. Regularly: Vacuum and damp-mop. All-purpose cleaner as needed. Do not walk on wet floor.

Annually: Strip, reseal (but test sealer in hidden area because it may darken white stone), then apply a water-based or solvent-based wax. Since paste wax may discolor the floor, test it in an inconspicuous spot.

CAUTION: Very porous, easily stained, easily scratched. Use baking soda or liquid cleanser and a soft nylon pad for stubborn spots.

Stains: Scrub off vegetable oil with washing soda and water solution.

Rubber Tile. Regularly: Vacuum and damp-mop. Add a cup of fabric softener to half a pail of water and the damp mopping won't dull the shine. Use all-purpose cleaner as needed.

Annually: Strip, then rewax with a water-based wax.

CAUTION: May be damaged by strong sunlight. Easily scratched. Avoid strong cleaners or direct sunlight.

REMOVING CEMENT STAINS

Stain	Removal Method
Mold	Wash with one part bleach and four parts water, rinse off thoroughly, wipe dry. (If you use this outdoors, avoid spilling any on grass, as it may be harmful.) Apply with sponge mop, apply rinse water 24 hours later with stiff broom. Or use a mildew killer sold for use around swimming pools.
Oil	Sprinkle with cat box filler or granulated detergent, leave overnight, sweep away. Or use a prewash spray, let stand five minutes, sprinkle on detergent powder, scrub with a broom, and hose off. Or try charcoal lighter fluid. (CAUTION: Extremely flammable.) Or spray on oven spray, let set 15 minutes, hose off, then repeat if necessary. (CAUTION: toxic to surrounding area.)
Miscellaneous (Food, Grease, etc.)	Dishwashing detergent and water worked in with a stiff-bristled brush. Or scrub with mineral spirits.
Rust	Sprinkle on portland cement (a powder used in making concrete), then sprinkle on water and work cement into stain with a stiff push broom. Then rinse. If stain is very bad, mix ten parts water and one part of muriatic acid or slowly add a pound of oxalic acid to a gallon of water. (CAUTION: Splashing is extremely dangerous. Wear goggles, rubber gloves, and boots.) Apply with mop (and discard it afterward), let set 2–3 hours, rinse with stiff-bristled, non-metallic brush. Or hire a professional with a pressure cleaner.

If you have trouble getting **"dimpled" floors** clean, try adding 2 tablespoons of automatic dishwasher detergent to a quart of warm water, mop, leave on for 30 to 45 minutes, wipe clean, then rinse. Since automatic dishwasher detergent has some bleach in it, it may cause color changes so try this on an inconspicuous spot first. Or use very hot water and a heavy-duty cleaner, leave the product on for fifteen minutes, then brush with a stiff-bristled brush to loosen the dirt. Rinse.

Slate. Regularly: Vacuum and damp-mop. Apply vinegar treatment (p. 122) if the shine is dull. Clean with all-purpose cleaner as needed.

Annually: Strip, reseal, then apply a water-based or solvent-based wax.

Terrazzo. Regularly: Vacuum and damp-mop. Use clear water and mild detergent but not ammonia or borax (which will dull it).

Annually: Strip, reseal, and apply a water-based wax or solvent-based paste wax, but first test the paste wax to make sure it won't discolor the floor.

CAUTION: Stains easily. Seal thoroughly.

Vinyl. Regularly: Vacuum and damp-mop. Use an all-purpose cleaner as needed, followed by a self-polishing wax (such as Mop & Glo), if desired.

Annually: Strip, then rewax with a water-based wax.

CAUTION: Strong abrasive cleaners may scratch.

Vinyl, no-wax. Regularly: Vacuum and damp-mop. Use all-purpose cleaner as needed.

As needed: Apply a gloss-renewing product if the no-wax floor loses its shine. Or try one of the remedies that follow.

125

SPECIAL PROBLEMS OF VINYL (NO-WAX) FLOORS

Dingy. May be caused by insufficient rinsing or cleaner residue. Use a self-polishing cleaner and water, and repeat if needed. If it's dull after stripping, you may have left a coat of ammonia. Re-rinse.

Kool-Aid Stain. Apply equal parts vinegar and water, leave on several minutes, then wet with a 5% hydrogen peroxide solution. Neutralize this with a vinegar rinse (1/4 cup to a gallon of water), then rinse again with plain water. Or try liquid abrasive cleaner if all else fails.

Scratches, Burns. Use automobile touchup paint. Work with a fine-haired brush and apply carefully (it's tough to remove). Or sand the burn mark with fine sandpaper, rinse with a solution of 1 cup vinegar in a quart of water, then apply acrylic paint mixed to match with a small brush. After 15 to 20 minutes, seal with acrylic varnish. A buffable water-based wax containing silicone may fill in scratches, too. Apply sparingly from a damp mop head or use a machine, then buff; repeat in high-traffic areas.

Sticky. The problem is due to incomplete removal of old polish, insufficient rinsing, or application of a second coat of polish before the first is dry. Use 1/4 cup Murphy's Oil Soap to one gallon of water. Apply with a sponge mop, then rinse the area with clear, warm water.

Tile, loose. Lay a cloth over the tile, then run a hot iron over the tile to melt the adhesive so that you can lift the tile and spread new glue. Replace the tile, cover with a board and heavy books until the glue is dry. Or seal the tile.

Tile, ruined. Take a scrap piece larger than the damaged spot and tape it on top. Cut through both layers at the same time and you'll have a perfectly sized, tight-fitting patch.

Yellowing. Usually caused by soil caught between layers. Strip with commercial stripper or mix 1/4 cup Spic and Span and 1 cup ammonia in 1/2 gallon of water. Do one 3-foot square at a time. Leave on five minutes, then sponge with clear water to rinse.

● ●

CLEANING FURNITURE

Unless you have very valuable or intricately carved furniture, caring for it won't take much of your time. On a regular basis, you just have to keep the dust off to prevent dirt from being ground in.

The least you need to know about caring for furniture:
• Routine polishing and waxing
• Stain removal
• Specific care for non-wood and upholstered furniture

Basic Wood Furniture Care

Painted wood needs just an occasional dusting and wiping down with a very, very lightly dampened sponge. Cleaning products may harm the finish. If you want a shiny finish, you will have to use paste wax.

Most of your wood furniture is probably **varnished, lacquered, or waxed.** Don't just run a dry cloth across the furniture when you see dust since that just grinds in the dirt. If the cloth is linty, you'll grind in the lint as well. Instead, dampen the cloth with a very light misting of water, dust spray, or (occasionally) furniture polish. All pick up dirt and grime, and the polish leaves behind a thin coating. Don't use polish all the time, as it eventually dulls the finish.

Never apply wax to **oiled wood** furniture, which has a soft glow instead of a high shine. There are some furniture polishes made specifically for oiled wood, but you can get perfectly fine results with a mixture of equal parts turpentine and boiled linseed oil. Don't panic if the wood looks darker at first. The oil will be absorbed. Just rub on a small bit at a time, going with the grain. And let it dry for 24 hours without putting anything down on the surface.

(Incidentally, buy boiled linseed oil at a

hardware or paint store. Don't boil your own. It isn't the same thing.)

CHOOSING AND APPLYING POLISH

Most polishes contain oil, usually mineral oil. Lemon oil polish is mineral oil with a lemon fragrance, and cream (or white) polish is mineral oil emulsified in water.

To make home-made furniture polish, combine 1 cup mineral oil, 1 tablespoon pine oil, $1/4$ cup soap flakes, and $1 1/4$ cups warm water. In a clean one-quart glass jar, mix the mineral and pine oils, then stir in the soap flakes and water. To use, pour a tablespoonful onto a cloth. Polish, then buff with a clean cloth.

If using aerosols or pumps (which give you better control of how much is coming out of the bottle), take care not to spray the polish on upholstery or wall surfaces. You should spray it from a distance of 6", holding the can upright. Any product lasts longer and won't build up if you first wipe, pour, or spray it onto a clean damp cloth, rub it on in a circle, then polish with the grain and buff with a second cloth. No excess will be left behind.

Polish may cover up small imperfections, if it contains some darkening agents. And to a limited degree, it should also prevent smudging. If handprints bother you, and there are lots of hands in your house, you'll be doing a lot of wiping no matter what product you use.

Although the ads for polish may promise extra shine, they can't make a low-gloss finish mirror-shiny. Polishes may add some gloss, and buffing may increase the effect. But if you want furniture you can see your reflection in, buy furniture that's highly polished to begin with.

Nor will ordinary polish provide a protective coating or repel moisture. Polish with silicone adds a glow to the furniture, makes wiping easier and, most important, like wax, makes water bead up, but it isn't suitable for all furniture. Some furniture should be polished and then waxed.

WAXING FURNITURE

Though **refinished antiques** can be cared for like new furniture, liquid and spray products that contain silicone or acrylic resin (read the labels; even some spray waxes contain these ingredients) shouldn't be used on **genuine antiques** or other fine wood because it seals the pores. Instead, use paste wax. Though it's harder to apply, it gives furniture a more durable, longer-lasting finish.

Paste wax will also do a great camouflage job. While liquid or spray polish will seep underneath and may cause flaking, paste wax will fill in hairline cracks. (See Surface Furniture Repairs in the Fixing section, p. 272). If your furniture is badly damaged, though, any product that gives it a high shine will just call attention to the problem. You may need professional refinishing.

Carnauba, which is sometimes used in the highest-quality waxes, is the hardest wax. **Beeswax** and **paraffin** (which is in most commercial waxes) are softer. The softer waxes are easier to work with but leave a duller, less durable finish.

To strip off the old wax before applying a new coat, wipe it dry, then saturate a cloth with odorless mineral spirits or naphtha from the hardware or paint store. Rub it over the furniture in a circular motion, then wipe with a clean dry cloth. Repeat this process until no dirt comes off on the cloth.

To apply a new coat of wax, rub the cloth across the wax, then apply a thin even surface to the furniture, going in the direction of the grain. Use another soft clean cloth to polish it.

Furniture Stain Removal

There are three general solutions for furniture damage. Rubbing and recoloring are the easiest. (See also Surface Furniture Repairs, p. 272.) Refinishing, which is covered beginning on p. 267, is a project. You can do any of these jobs yourself, but proceed at your own risk. If the piece is valuable, your safest move is to take it for professional help.

RUBBING

Use a gentle abrasive in combination with a lubricant and rub the mixture into the damaged area, with the grain, until the spot blends in with the undamaged part. Work very gently with a clean, dry cloth, and treat only the top layer. Polish when you're done. See the box below for three abrasive/lubricant possibilities.

Abrasive/Lubricant	Procedure
Fine grade steel wool dipped in paste wax	Buff.
Rottenstone or pumice (powdered abrasives) mixed with mineral or salad oil	Put a few drops of oil on the spot; shake on powder to make a paste. Rub gently.
Automobile polishing compound (contains abrasive and lubricant together)	Rub gently.

RECOLORING

Choose a color that matches perfectly.

Coloring Agent	Procedure
Wax sticks (like crayon)	Fill in scratches, buff.
Paste shoe polish (too shiny for low-luster furniture)	Apply with cotton swab, buff. If too dark, use mineral spirits to remove.
Wood stains	Apply with artist's brush or cotton swab. Remove excess, buff.
Artist's oil paints	Apply with cotton swab, wipe dry.

SPECIFIC PROBLEMS

Alcohol (Drinks/Perfumes/Medicine). Wipe, then use lemon oil. Or wipe lightly with turpentine or denatured alcohol—a small amount, so you don't destroy the finish. If it still looks bad, use the pumice/oil solution described under rubbing. You may need professional help.

Burn, cigarette. Sand and color with wax stick or some other rub-color remedy. Or dip a cotton swab in nail polish remover and dissolve blackened finish, being very careful not to touch any other part of the surface. Fill in the hollow with a half-and-half mixture of clear nail polish and polish remover applied with the polish brush. Let dry thoroughly. Repeat, drying thoroughly between coats, until it appears repaired. If a cigarette was left burning a while, it may have left a snakelike track that should be filled in with plastic wood.

Or combine two parts isopropyl alcohol (rubbing alcohol) with one part each of glycerin (from the drugstore) and water. Apply to burned area, let set until burned color has disappeared. Rinse with water and dry. If the burned color hasn't been completely removed, use a mild abrasive such as Fine steel wool or extra fine sandpaper. Any depression left in the wood may be filled in with plastic wood (see "Patching Wood," p. 273).

Candle Wax. Soften the wax with a hair

dryer, and remove the residue with furniture polish. If the wax has gotten through the finish, it may have stained the item. This, unfortunately, is permanent.

Darkening or Clouding with Age. Mix up your own furniture restorer: one part each store-bought boiled linseed oil, turpentine, and vinegar. Shake well.

CAUTION: Use in well-ventilated room and wear rubber gloves.

Apply with a soft cloth and wipe completely dry. With a second clean cloth, wipe again.

Gum. Put a rag over the spot, run a warm iron over the rag. The gum should stick to the rag and little by little you can pull it off.

Hairline Cracks. Use a thin coat of paste wax rubbed in a circular motion. Buff immediately with a fresh, dry cloth. Repeat, rubbing with the grain of the wood.

Ink, Milk, Citric Acid Stains. Rub lightly with soap and water. If ink has penetrated the finish through cracks, you may have to strip it and bleach the stain out.

Mildew. See Mold Story on p. 165.

Mystery Stains. Try any of the following: mild soap and water, mineral oil, lemon oil, vinegar and water, or turpentine. Rub gently, wipe dry. Rub with Extra Fine steel wool, repolish.

Paint. Fresh *water-based paint* can be removed with water. For old water-based paint spots, use an expired credit card to scrape off dried spots of any kind, then follow with the rubbing technique. A fresh *oil-based paint* spill can be wiped away with a cloth moistened with furniture polish. If there's a residue of oil-based paint, cover it with linseed oil. Wait a few minutes, until paint is softened, then use a cloth moistened with more linseed oil over the area.

Plant Stains. Acid stain from plants may be irreversible, but I have heard of some success with Formby's Furniture Repair.

Streaking, Smearing. May be due to greasy fumes or incorrect cleaning: using oil and wax-based polishes interchangeably, not using a clean cloth, or using too much polish. Wet the area thoroughly with a generous amount of solvent-based polish, which is self-cleaning. Work on a small section at a time, rubbing in a circle. Wipe immediately with a clean cloth before the polish has dried. Then polish furniture as usual. Or strip the polish just as you would strip wax, explained earlier in this section in the instructions for waxing, or use Murphy's Oil Soap.

Water Rings. The first thing to do is—nothing. The spot may clear up within a day all by itself. If not, use a rub-it method. Or wipe spot lightly with cloth dampened in turpentine or very small amount of denatured alcohol (too much will remove finish). Or try a half-and-half mixture of non-gel toothpaste and baking soda on a damp cloth, buff with dry cotton. Salad oil applied with the finger, or mixed with a little cigarette or cigar ash (which acts like a very mild abrasive) can do the trick, too. Rub it in; leave on briefly; wipe off.

White Rings (heat). Rub in salad oil. Or try cigar or cigarette ashes and/or mayonnaise, a half-and-half mixture of non-gel toothpaste and baking soda, or toothpaste alone on a damp cloth; buff with dry cotton. A stronger remedy is a paste of oil and pumice powder (from the

---

DEFEATING THE ENEMIES OF FURNITURE

- **Sun:** Draw the blinds or rotate furniture.
- **Liquid:** Use coasters, wipe up spills, never leave a damp cleaning rag on the furniture.
- **Heat:** Don't place furniture directly in front of a heater (which can also cause fire).
- **Humidity:** You may need a dehumidifier.
- **Abrasion:** Use coasters under drinks, felt pads under vases.
- **Body Oils:** Wax surfaces that get extra wear, such as a chair arm or headboard.

hardware store), rubbed in gently. Always rub with the grain and follow these treatments with a coat of polish.

Cleaning Upholstered Furniture

Upholstered furniture doesn't need much day-to-day attention. Just dust occasionally with the vacuum upholstery brush.

To deep-clean pillows, put them in a pillowcase. Hold the case tightly around the vacuum hose and turn on the vacuum. It will suck up the dust.

Canvas or sailcloth is washable and sturdy enough to scrub. Use about $1/2$ cup liquid detergent to a gallon of water. Or try naphtha soap rubbed on with a stiff brush, then rinsed. Let it air dry.

The zippered cover from most upholstery pieces, unlike canvas or sailcloth, is not meant to be removed. Cleaning it may cause it to shrink. Even washable **cotton slipcovers** may shrink; launder them in lukewarm water and replace them while still damp to avoid slipcover or piping shrinkage.

Unfortunately, most upholstery cleaners—powders and aerosols—are not, in my opinion, very effective. They also may change the texture and look of the furniture. If you decide to give it a try, follow instructions, work gently so you don't rough up the fabric any more than necessary, and use as little of the cleaning solution as you can. For a very grimy piece of furniture, you definitely need an extraction cleaning, which forces the cleaning compound into the furniture, then suctions it all out. Again, I refer you back to the steam extraction cleaner I mentioned in the Equipping section, which I consider the best cleaning solution for the upholstery problem. Or you can call in the professionals. Still, resign yourself to the fact that furniture—especially when covered with light-colored and/or fragile fabric—isn't very long-lasting.

You can't prevent upholstery from getting dirty, but to some degree you can avoid stains. While nothing makes a fabric absolutely stainproof, a protective coating, like Scotchgard, makes the liquids bead up so they roll off instead of being absorbed. There is no particular expertise involved in putting on the protective finish, and from what I hear, the factories often apply it unevenly. I've applied the stuff in the spray cans myself, but I wouldn't say it's 100% effective.

When you get a stain, your best bet is to clean a spot or stain as soon as possible. If it's dry, vacuum first, then apply one of the solutions below. Although there is a cleanability code (see p. 71 in the Equipping section) don't rely on it completely. To be on the safe side, test any cleaning product in a hidden spot to make sure it won't damage the fabric.

For small, greasy stains, such as lipstick, use a dry-cleaning solvent. Follow directions on the label.

For small non-greasy stains, mix about $1/2$ teaspoon liquid dishwashing detergent in a quart of water, shake it up, and apply suds only. Apply a small amount, and blot between applications. *Don't soak the fabric or you may wind up with both the stain and mildew.*

For small combination stains, greasy and non-greasy (chocolate, coffee with cream, or even general pollution), first use the detergent, then the solvent.

The problem with removing stains from upholstery is that you're working from one side of the fabric only, so no matter what you do, you're driving the stain into the filling.

Badly soiled and stained furniture usually has to be discarded or recovered.

Cleaning Non-Wood Furniture

Acrylic. This scratches easily and attracts dust like a magnet. Use a mild soap and water, rinse, and blot dry. Wiping with a fabric softener sheet will cut down static that attracts dust.

Black lacquer. Attracts a lot of dust and smudges. Polish with car wax. Wipe thoroughly to remove excess wax.

Glass. If the furniture is both wood and glass, take care not to get the glass cleaner (which is probably water-based) on the wood, since it will probably stain. Water rings on a glass table can be removed with dry dishwasher detergent or silver polish.

Leather. Wax won't be absorbed by leather and isn't good for the finish. Neither are detergents. Use real soap products only. Clean with saddle soap, which comes in aerosol or paste form, or mix and shake Ivory Snow and water and apply just the suds with a soft brush.

Condition the leather annually to keep it lubricated and prevent cracking. Buy a leather conditioning product or use a home remedy such as castor oil (for dark leather) or petroleum jelly (for light leather). Buff off the excess and keep everyone off the furniture for a day or so.

Or condition and clean the leather with Amorall or baby oil. Use either to clean leather dashboards and door panels (and also vinyl) in the car—one soft cloth to rub it in, another to remove excess and polish.

Marble. While bathroom and kitchen countertops are usually made of synthetic (cultured) marble, marble used in living room and other furniture is usually the genuine article. Seal it with a stone sealer, because it's very susceptible to stains, and wipe up stains quickly. Dust and/or wipe with a damp cloth as needed. Caked-on spots can be sprinkled with borax or baking powder and rubbed with a damp sponge cloth. Or use special commercial marble polish.

Metal. Follow instructions in the How Do I Clean It…? sections for chrome on p. 159 and in Cleaning the Kitchen, for stainless steel, on pp. 138 and 143.

Suede. Obviously, you are a childless person. Who else has suede furniture? This needs

PROBLEMS WITH MARBLE

Fine Scratches: Use Extra Fine steel wool to apply baking soda and water mixed to a paste. Flush stone with water and let dry; repeat if necessary. Buff with dry cloth (or use a buffing wheel on your electric drill).

Grease Stains: Circular and often dark in center. Wash surface with ammonia; rinse with plenty of water; then repeat. Or cover area with a $1/2$" thick layer of paste made of 20% hydrogen peroxide from the drugstore and powdered whiting from the paint store. Keep it damp by covering it with plastic wrap sealed with masking tape. After 10-15 minutes, rinse with water, avoiding any wood trim. Repeat if necessary. Buff, then polish.

Rust: Colored orange or brown. Rub with rough cloth or make a mix of commercial liquid rust remover and whiting and follow instructions for grease stains. After removing the paste, rub marble with a dry cloth.

Soot and Smoke: Mild dishwashing detergent and a stiff brush, then rinse. If stains remain, cover with a paste of baking soda and chlorine bleach. Cover with a damp cloth, leave in place overnight, wet and scrape with a wooden spatula, plywood, or stiff cardboard.

Tea, Coffee, Ink: Use hydrogen peroxide/whiting method—see grease stains above.

Water: Hydrogen peroxide, applied with a medicine dropper, followed with a drop or two of household ammonia. After 20 minutes, wash area.

Wine: Try straight hydrogen peroxide.

professional cleaning, but the odd spot can sometimes be removed with a pencil eraser.

Vinyl. Use all-purpose cleaner. If the surface is sticky, use a liquid abrasive cleanser. Or mix and rub on 1 part soap flakes, 2 parts baking soda, and 8 parts warm water. A sticky spot can also be removed with saddle soap, alcohol, or nail polish remover applied with a soft rag.

Wicker and Rattan. Scrub with warm soapy water, then rinse with salted water. Air dry. Avoid oil, which makes it "tacky." To keep wicker from turning yellow, scrub with a stiff brush moistened with warm salt water. (The salt does the trick.)

Wrought Iron. Remove rust with a few drops of kerosene or turpentine on a non-soapy steel wool pad. Coat with wax or repaint to seal. You need special paint to keep outdoor wrought iron rust-free.

PATIO FURNITURE

Aluminum, painted. Use hot, soapy water. If dull, rub with baking soda, rinse and air dry. If you need something stronger, use liquid abrasive. Can be waxed with paste wax or car wax for extra protection.

Aluminum, unpainted. Steel wool or aluminum jelly cleaner (from the auto supply store).

Resin (Plastic). Combine $1/4$ cup bleach and 1 quart of water in a spray bottle, spray it on, leave it ten minutes, then wipe dry with a clean cloth or paper towels. Or use a non-abrasive, multi-surface cleaner/polish. Some stains on plastic will fade if you simply leave the item in the sun.

Wood. Clean with an all-purpose cleaner. Redwood can be degreased with 1 cup of powdered detergent and $3/4$ cup of bleach mixed with a gallon of warm water and scrubbed on. While other wood furniture can be hosed down, don't hose painted wood, which needs gentle wiping or it will peel and/or crack.

ROOM SERVICE: KITCHEN, BATH, BEDROOM

The two most important cleaning jobs in the house? The kitchen and the bathroom. These rooms usually have both the greatest number of items and the items that need the greatest attention. They're also a barometer of mental health. When the kitchen and bath start looking seedy, it's a sign that everything's going to pot.

Cleaning the Kitchen

The least you need to know about cleaning the kitchen:
- Weekly cleaning/deep cleaning
- Solutions for specific cleaning problems

WEEKLY KITCHEN CLEANING

If you're not sure where to start (or more important, where to end), here's a weekly cleaning plan for the kitchen.

You'll need: heavy-duty spray, laundry prewash, spray bottle filled with light-duty glass cleaner (1 quart warm water, 1 tablespoon each of ammonia and vinegar), liquid scouring cleaner, a nylon scrubber, gentler plastic scrubber, two sponge cloths, and a couple of dry cloths.

WASH DOWN

To clean patio furniture quickly, use your car wash brush attachment fastened to the hose. Use the detergent solution for aluminum furniture or the bleach/water for resin. The solution gets into all the crevices.

CUSHY JOB

To clean patio cushions and remove mildew and dirt, fill the tub with 8 to 10 inches of water and a cup of heavy-duty detergent and soak them for 10 minutes, scrub with a brush, take them outside in a laundry basket and scrub them clean; or spray outside with $1/4$ cup bleach to a quart of water, scrub and hose. Or take them to the car wash, spray with heavy-duty cleaner, use the hot water power spray and scrub brush.

TO MOVE HEAVY APPLIANCES

If you want to clean behind them (or take them out for repair), soap the floor, put corn pads under the legs, or set the two front legs or weight-bearing spots on a towel, glossy magazine, or anything else that will slide. If possible, slide a skateboard underneath and wheel it away.

First put away anything that's out of place: dishes in the drain, food on the counter.

Toss oven mitts, dishtowels, etc., in the laundry.

Put removable drip pans (also called reflector bowls; the circular or square metal piece under the burner) in the dishwasher.

Next, give a shot of heavy-duty spray to only the surfaces that need it. This means handles only (on fridge, knob, drawer pulls), obvious grease spots on walls, range or oven (front), spills on non-wood countertops. After spraying, use the sponge cloth in one hand to wipe off dirt, cloth in other hand to dry it.

(If you see stubborn food spots, give them a shot of prewash spray, to help loosen them up. Leave them a few minutes while you do something else, then scrape them up with an old credit card or non-metal scrubber and wipe.)

Clean glass, plastic, or chrome surfaces of fingerprints or other smudges with a very light spray of window cleaner. Don't drench appliances like a toaster, where the food will come into contact with the spray. Use the two-handed wipe-up.

Open the refrigerator. Throw out all stale food and leftovers that no one will eat. Use a clean sponge cloth to wipe up obvious spills.

Vacuum or sweep, then damp-mop the floor.

SURFACES

Over the next few pages I've explained in detail how to clean kitchen surfaces and kitchen appliances. My idea was not to overwhelm you with how difficult it was to keep the kitchen clean but to give you a reference source if you weren't sure how to clean a particular surface or a particular gadget. I've also listed options in many cases; use whatever you've got on hand. Frankly, as I'm sure you have already figured out, all-purpose cleaner and water work just fine most of the time.

COUNTERTOPS

Acrylic, ceramic tile (glazed and unglazed), stainless steel, cultured marble, and plastic laminate (such as Formica) can all be cleaned with mild liquid scouring cleaner (unless the manufacturer has specified otherwise), a light-duty cleaner such as the ammonia/vinegar solution on p. 132, or a glass cleaner, or baking soda. Wipe them on with a sponge cloth, rinse, and wipe dry. Read your manufacturer's instructions carefully. You'll be surprised at how many substances can damage countertops!

For stubborn spots, try a shot of laundry prewash spray or a paste of baking soda and water, let it sit a half hour, then rub with a non-metallic scrubber or the edge of a credit card if there is food buildup. Or use a little rubbing alcohol for a greasy stain.

Use appliance or light furniture wax (even car or floor wax) on plastic laminate to help resist stains and scratches. Make sure the undersides of all appliances have pads, or buy felt pads, so they don't add to the scratching.

The grouting on tiled surfaces needs special care. Use a commercial grout cleaner or $1/4$ cup bleach in a quart of water applied with a tooth or nail brush, then cover with a commercial sealant to make your cleaning job last.

Marble should be sealed. Otherwise, both strong cleaners and spills may etch it; so may oil polishes and soft wax, which can also discolor it. Check at the hardware store for a good sealer. You may want to give it a coat of top quality automotive polish. Otherwise, just wash with warm, sudsy water, or a solution of borax, then rinse and buff dry. (For stains on marble, see p. 131.)

Wood (butcher block) is harder to clean than to protect. Since water can damage wood, oil the wood surface frequently. Some prefer mineral oil. I like tung oil. Or use the oil recommended by the manufacturer of the countertop, rubbing it in with a Fine, dry steel wool pad. (Don't use food oils; they get rancid.) Repeat 24 hours later, and blot up extra oil so it won't get sticky. For regular cleaning, mix $1/2$ cup baking soda in a quart of warm water, use a nylon scrubber, rinse with water and blot dry, and follow with an oiling. To remove stains, use $1/4$ cup bleach to a quart of warm water, or rub with a lemon. After treating, wipe area dry. (You will stain a wood counter if you use it for chopping; use a separate chopping board. (For cleaning a wood cutting board, which is exposed to food, see Miscellaneous Kitchen Cleanups on p. 139.)

HOT SEATING

If you can't repair a burned spot on the kitchen counter, glue a glazed tile on top of the area and use it as a permanent hot pad.

FLOORS

See Cleaning Floors, pp. 118–126.

HARDWARE

Wipe hardware frequently.

Faucet heads clogged up by water buildup should be soaked in vinegar and the holes opened with a wire or toothpick. If you can't remove the head, pour vinegar into a small plastic bag, position it so that the head is covered with vinegar, and use a rubber band to keep it in place for a day or so.

If your water doesn't taste right, removing sediments that may have accumulated in the faucet may solve the problem. Unscrew the end of the tap and soak the screen, washer, and end of the tap cap in boiling white vinegar, then see if your water tastes better.

Chrome and stainless can be cleaned with baking soda or rubbing alcohol. (For additional suggestions, see Chrome on p. 159 and "Stainless Steel" on p. 138).

WOODWORK

If painted woodwork has been stained by grease and smoke, paint it with a solution of old-fashioned dry laundry starch in water. If you can't find it, see the box "Starch Substitutes," p. 183, and use the recipe for medium. After it's dried, rub with a soft brush or a clean cloth. This removes stains without harming paint.

Wood cabinets that have a surface finish such as polyurethane need only to be wiped with a damp cloth. But if they're very dirty and greasy, use a wax stripper (such as naphtha, odorless mineral spirits, or a ten-to-one solution of water and ammonia). Or use a heavy-duty cleaner such as Murphy's Oil Soap, which will also strip the wax. Then spray on a polish or rub on a wax.

LARGE APPLIANCES: REFRIGERATOR

If the door is completely covered with PTA notices, shopping lists, and kids' art, you don't need to clean it, but if you notice some grime, just sprinkle some baking soda on a damp sponge cloth and rub caked-on spots with a nylon scrubber.

Some people like to put a coating of car or appliance wax over all the large appliances, but personally I think this is more trouble than it's worth. The new appliances clean up with just a wipe.

For chromium trim, use the glass cleaner mixture I recommended for window washing (p. 106) or a commercial glass cleaner.

THE HUNDRED-CENT SOLUTION

The gasket around the refrigerator door keeps cold air from going out and warm air from going in. To see if it's in good condition, close the door on a dollar bill, leaving a small section sticking out. Then pull on it. If it slides out with no resistance, the seal isn't airtight. The gasket should be replaced or the door hinges adjusted.

To clean the gasket (the white rubber area around the door of the refrigerator that keeps the seal tight), wipe it with baking soda, rubbing alcohol, or whitewall tire cleaner. To keep it from cracking, give it a light coat of mineral oil.

Every once in a while, clean the coils in the refrigerator. They're like the arteries of the fridge; if they're coated with grease, the heat gets trapped inside and the refrigerator won't cool foods properly. If they're in back of the refrigerator, you have to pull it away from the wall. If they're underneath, pull away the louvered base grill or kickplate at the bottom of your fridge and reach inside. This is easier said than done because those coils are unbelievably inconvenient to reach. Use a long-handled barbecue brush or a yardstick covered with a sock. Or use the cardboard insert from a roll of gift wrap slipped over the vacuum wand. (If the coils are clean and the refrigerator still isn't keeping drinks cold and ice cream solid, move the controls up, but only about a half-letter or number a day. If that fails, call for service)

A heavy-duty cleaner will clean the grease on top of the refrigerator.

Refrigerator and Freezer Odor

Leave a cotton ball saturated with vanilla, an open can of coffee grounds, or baking soda in your refrigerator all the time to control odors. Baking soda will deodorize the freezer, too.

If there's a very bad smell in your refrigerator—and you've made sure there's no food spoiling in it or behind it—check the drip pan underneath. If you don't know how to find it and have never cleaned it, it may be the source of your problem. Check your manual or call the manufacturer if you need help locating and removing it. Wash it with baking soda and water or let it soak for a while.

If a terrible odor still persists, it is possible spoiled meat or fish has dripped onto insulation and you need servicing. (Or that there's spoiled meat removed from the freezer and left by mistake on top of the fridge.)

The odor of spoiled meat is horrible. If a power outage causes this in your freezer, give it a rinse with vinegar or even tomato juice (sounds crazy, but this is an old and effective de-skunking remedy for the dog, too!). Or clean everything out, fill the shelves with crumpled newspaper or with large shallow pans spread with ground coffee or activated charcoal, shut the door, and don't open it for 2 to 3 days. Repeat if necessary.

Dishwasher

Takes the same exterior care as the refrigerator.

If it has a butcher block top, clean as you would a butcher block counter.

To clean the interior, fill the cup with Tang (or citric acid from the pharmacy), and run the machine with no dishes inside.

Clean around the door seal, where bits of food get caught.

If you think the holes where water comes out (the ports) are clogged, use a pipe cleaner. In some dishwashers, there is a filter screen (strainer) that can be scrubbed with a stiff brush.

If the coating is wearing off the wire prongs, use white silicone caulking, a product made to repair cracks around the tub. The easiest way to apply it is to slide the caulk tube over the prong and then lift it up; it will leave a coating behind. Or you can buy a dishwasher rack patch product made for this purpose, though it also happens to be excellent for mending rubber gloves.

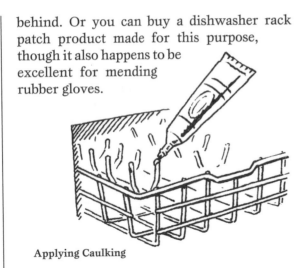

Applying Caulking

FREEZER

Exterior care is the same as for a refrigerator.

Defrosting the freezer or refrigerator freezer should be done when the ice gets to be $1/2$" thick, or about twice a year. Get to it at this stage, since the job is a lot harder when the frost is thick enough to hold the Winter Olympics inside your unit.

Turn off the motor and all controls. Remove the food to an insulated place (a cooler; tub with ice cubes in it; even oven or microwave). Let frost melt naturally or speed up the process with pans of hot water or a hair dryer. Remove chunks or scrape away slush with a wooden or plastic tool (even a dustpan). Resist the urge to hack away at it with a sharp object. In your eagerness to chip away the ice you may damage the whole unit.

Use a sponge or towel (or an industrial wet-dry vacuum) to soak up the drips inside or on the floor. Or put towels on the floor.

Wipe the inside dry of condensation, wipe inside and out with soapy water, dry thoroughly. Plug everything back in and turn the controls on, and wait a half-hour before replacing food. Wait until the controls reach 0°F. before adding anything new.

MICROWAVE OVEN

Wipe the exterior with baking soda or a mild cleanser. When the interior gets dirty, put in a glass of water, turn it to high, and after a few minutes turn the oven off and wipe the inside (the steam will have softened the dirt).

Clean the door with rubbing alcohol or a little liquid detergent on a coffee filter.

RANGE HOOD

Whether it is vented to the outside or unvented (in which case it uses replaceable charcoal filters to clean the air), hood fans have to be cleaned of grease buildup. Use a grease-cleaning dishwasher detergent and hot water (plus ammonia, unless the detergent contains bleach) to wipe the exterior. The filter cover can be washed in hot soapy water, but it should be dried completely before it is put back. Ammonia can clean the blades. Mesh filters need occasional cleaning, but charcoal filters can't be washed and usually need replacing every six to nine months (check your manual).

RANGE

Wipe spills whenever the range is cool enough so that they won't bake on.

Ceramic cooktops, made of glass, are easily

WIPING UP GREASE

Freshly laundered and dried terry cloth towels caught fire for no apparent reason, and investigators determined that the cause was spontaneous combustion. Now washing machines contain a label warning not to use them to wash or dry items soiled with vegetable or cooking oils. These items may contain some oil after laundering that may cause fabric to catch fire. When cleaning up grease stains, use sponge cloths.

OTHER KITCHEN ODOR PROBLEMS

• **Dishwasher:** If there's an unpleasant smell inside the dishwasher, place an open bowl of baking soda inside and leave the dishwasher sealed for 24 hours. If there's a sour odor from dishes that haven't been washed right away, sprinkle $1/4$ cup of baking soda on the dishwasher bottom. As a bonus, it will soften and loosen dried-on foods for easier removal.

• **Hand odors (from fish, garlic, onion):** Borrow this trick from Italians (who know about garlic!): Rub your hands with coffee grounds to get rid of the smell. Works on onions and fish, too. You can also rub on toothpaste, add salt to the soap lather, or wash with vinegar. And here's the oddest remedy of all: Place all five fingers on the handle of a stainless steel spoon and run cold water over them. The smell is gone in seconds.

• **Garbage:** To keep the chicken bones or other leftovers from fouling up the kitchen, stow them in the freezer until the sanitation truck is due.

• **Garbage disposal:** Save citrus rinds in the freezer and every once in a while, toss a few down the garbage disposal. Or sprinkle some baking soda over a few ice cubes and put them into the unit.

• **Ice cubes:** The first few batches to come out of a new ice maker should be discarded. If cubes smell odd after that, they may just be more than two weeks old, food in the freezer may be improperly wrapped, or the freezer (or refrigerator) may need a cleaning. If nothing else helps, the problem may be in the plumbing or the water. Check with your plumber.

• **Microwave:** Your microwave, spice rack, and/or freezer—like your refrigerator—can all be deodorized with baking soda, left inside either in an open box or in a small, perforated container. (Remove the baking soda when the microwave is in use.) If there's an odor, clean the oven and also check the inside vent to make sure food hasn't collected there. If the odor remains, mix a cup of water with 2 tablespoons of lemon juice or baking soda and bring it to boil inside the oven. Leave it boiling for about five minutes in order to give it time to condense inside the wall of the oven, then let it stand about five minutes more. With a soft cloth, wipe dry walls, ceiling, floor, door, and door seals.

• **Oven cleaner fumes:** Bake citrus rinds in the oven at 350°F. (Save and freeze them for this purpose.)

• **Thermos:** If it smells sour, add a half-and-half mixture of baking soda and water. Cover and let soak overnight.

---

damaged or discolored. Don't set a dirty pot down, don't use abrasives, and wipe only when cool. Use a mild liquid scouring cleaner or other mild cleaners.

The easiest way to clean knobs and drip pans is to pull them off, then leave them to soak in a gallon of water and $1/4$ cup of dishwasher detergent. Use a toothbrush for stubborn spots. When you're finished with the stove, you can rinse the other items clean.

If there's a caked-on food spot, use prewash spray or spoon boiling water over it, a bit at a time. That should loosen it to the point where you can remove it with a nylon scrubber.

EXHAUST FAN

Don't soak the blades—just wipe them with a damp cloth or rubbing alcohol—and clean the cover with soapy water ($1/2$ cup of a degreasing dishwashing detergent and a gallon of hot water).

SINK

Porcelain. A sponge cloth saturated with white vinegar will clean mineral stains (hard water deposits) out of a sink. If stains remain, saturate some paper towels with bleach, pat into place, and leave for a couple of hours.

Stainless Steel. You will find that "stainless" stains, just as "no-wax" floors need waxing. Clean it regularly with warm, sudsy water, but if it's spotted, use rubbing alcohol or a commercial stainless steel cleaner. Polish with lemon oil. Spray bad stains with oven cleaner, let stand fifteen minutes, and rinse well. Use only stainless steel wool since ordinary steel wool will scratch. Waxing the surface to keep it glossy adds work and may dull a satin, non-glossy finish.

OVEN

Never use a commercial oven cleaner for a self-clean or continuous cleaning oven.

If you have a **continuous clean oven** that burns away fat as you cook, remove stubborn spots with a soapy steel wool pad and rinse with water. To catch spills, make a disposable foil liner from a roll of heavy-duty aluminum foil just the length of the oven floor. When bake element is cool, lift it just enough to get the feet off the oven floor. Take out the old foil and slide in the new, keeping it unwrinkled. When you lower the bake element make sure all the feet are flat.

In **self-cleaning ovens,** the temperature goes as high as 875°F and the door stays locked for the 3–4-hour cycle plus cool-down. But areas that don't get particularly hot (such as the frame around the oven and the outside of the door) should be cleaned with a steel wool pad and hot water. Clean the gasket with a heavy-duty cleanser before you turn on the oven or the stuff will bake on. (If so, check your manual for instructions on how to remove it.) Do not clean or bend the fiberglass seal.

If you have a **conventional cleaning oven,** you can use the new, fumeless cleaners. The best piece of advice I can give you is to leave the cleaner on as long as is recommended—the longer it stays on, the longer it works and the less you must. After you wipe the oven of the cleaner, wipe it again with vinegar to remove the film.

Less expensive than commercial cleaner—but very potent (use it only in a ventilated area): Leave a bowl of full-strength ammonia in the cool oven, which will loosen grease, then spray on ammonia and wipe. If grease is baked onto a gas oven, you may need an abrasive.

If you prefer something milder, make a paste of baking soda and water, then spread it on the oven walls; leave in place overnight, then clean with a plastic (not steel) scrubber. Rinse clean. Repeat if necessary.

Or try this method passed along to me by an appliance repairman. First warm the oven to 150°F, turn it off, then spray the interior with Fantastik. In fifteen minutes or less, grease will rub off easily.

Put a paper cup over the oven bulb to protect it from your spray cleaner and still keep the oven illuminated as you work.

To clean just the shelves, one easy solution

BACKSPLASH BACKLASH

To cut down on grease splatters:

• Put a colander over the skillet when you cook: It's easier to clean the colander than the wall.

• Keep a spray bottle filled with water or a diluted ammonia-water solution to mist over grease spatters, and wipe them right away. They're much easier to clean fresh than dried.

• Install a window shade on the wall. Pull it down when you're cooking and remove it from the wall for cleaning. Or cover the area with a piece of Plexiglas.

is to put them in your tub on top of a towel. Draw enough hot water to cover and sprinkle a cup of automatic dishwasher detergent over all. They'll soak clean.

Miscellaneous Kitchen Cleanups

Aluminum. To make it shine, combine $1/4$ cup each of cream of tartar and baking soda and add $1/4$ cup of vinegar to make a paste, then stir in 2 tablespoons of powdered laundry detergent. Rub into your pan, and scour with a plastic scrubber (other scrubbers may rust).

CAUTION: Never use bleach on aluminum, metal or silverware. It may cause discoloration. Ammonia may also discolor aluminum.

Back Splash (area of wall behind stove). If the wall has turned brown from the heat, only repainting will help. But if the problem is spatters of grease, make a paste of baking soda and water, leave it for an hour and rinse. Or mix 1 ounce each of milk, bleach, and water. Saturate a paper towel with this mixture and drape it over the stain for a minute, then rinse. Strongest: a paste of powdered cleanser with chlorine bleach. Leave it on five minutes and then rinse off.

Blender. If it can't be taken apart to be washed, pour in a few drops of dishwashing detergent, fill the bowl about halfway with warm water, and run the blender on high for 10 to 15 seconds. Repeat if necessary. Light-duty cleaner will clean the base if a swipe with the sponge isn't enough.

Blinds. If kitchen blinds are greasy, close them, then spray on foaming bathroom cleaner a section at a time. Wipe with a clean cloth dipped into hot water.

Broiler. When you're using the broiler in your oven, remove the top tray (that has the perforated holes) and put about $1/4$" of water in the pan below so it can collect smoke and greasy drips to make cleanup easier. Or put a piece of bread in the bottom pan to absorb grease.

Cast-Iron Pan. Should be "seasoned" to prevent rusting. First scrub with a steel-wool soap pad, rinse, and wipe; then coat the inside with vegetable oil and leave it in a warm oven (about 325°F to 350° F.) for a couple of hours. Wipe off the excess. Wash with hot soapy water and dry thoroughly. Store it without the lid, with a paper towel or coffee filter in the pan to absorb moisture and prevent rusting. If rusting occurs, reseason.

Rust and caked-on food can also be rubbed away with a bit of salt.

Coffee Grinder. Dump out extra grains, wipe out the bowl with a damp sponge. Clean the exterior with warm sudsy water.

Coffeepot, drip style. Use mild detergent and water for all washable parts. Use a percolator brush to clean inside the thin tube, using warm sudsy water or, if you need a little abrasion, some baking soda.

Coffeepot, percolator style. Cool before cleaning. Washable parts can be cleaned in warm water with a little liquid detergent. If abrasion is needed, sprinkle baking soda on a sponge or cloth. Rinse, wipe dry.

Colander. If it's gummy with hardened pasta, soak it in a grease-removing detergent. Next time, wash it in cold water immediately to prevent starch from hardening, or coat it with a non-stick vegetable spray before use.

Copper. A new copper pot usually has protective lacquer on it. Cover it with boiling water, let it stand until it's cool, then peel it off.

Copper is usually lined (with tin or stainless steel) because it may chemically react with food. Protect the lining by stirring only with a wooden spoon or coated utensil made for non-stick pans. Do not scorch the pan.

Clean copper with commercial copper cleaners or use a home remedy—a spray bottle filled with hot white vinegar and three tablespoons of salt (spray liberally, let sit briefly, then rub clean) or one part each salt and vinegar (rub on, rinse off, wash with hot soapy water, and dry as usual).

Cork Coasters, Trivets, or Mats. Wash in cold water, rub with a smooth pumice stone, and rinse with more cold water. Dry thoroughly in a cool dry place.

Crock Pot. Put a soapy solution inside and "cook" on high for an hour or so.

Cutting Board, wooden. Will absorb lard, oil, or soap, and steel wool may splinter into it. Instead, cover it with bleach and salt, scrub with a stiff brush, then rinse with very hot water and wipe with a clean cloth. Or use a mixture of 3 tablespoons bleach to a gallon of water. Reapply to keep surface wet for two minutes, rinse, and dry. (Safe for surfaces where food is handled because when it dries it leaves no active residue.)

Remove gummy dough by sprinkling salt on a wet sponge and start rubbing. Or use a plastic windshield scraper. It won't mark the wood.

Dishrag or Sponge. Clean in the dishwasher after anchoring it so it won't fly around. (I usually put mine under a glass.)

Drainboard, rubber. Soak in warm sudsy water with $1/2$ cup of bleach to a gallon of water. Rinse after a half-hour. To remove a hard water stain, tilt the low end of the board slightly and pour one cup of white vinegar over it. Let it set overnight and rub off with a sponge in the morning.

Use an old rack as a lid holder inside your cabinets. The grooves work perfectly.

Rack as Lid Holder

Electric Can Opener. Remove the section with the cutting wheel and lid holder if you can and soak them in hot sudsy water. Otherwise, use an old toothbrush and a little powdered cleanser to remove packed-in dirt. Rinse thoroughly.

Enameled Pots. If food is baked on, sprinkle on some baking soda and a little water; let it soak overnight. Or combine a quart of water with 3 tablespoons baking soda, boil 15 minutes then let mixture stand to cool. Use a plastic scrubber; steel wool will scratch. If it's stained from cooking food such as prunes, fill with warm water and $1/3$ cup bleach, and soak for a couple of hours. If stain remains, repeat.

Food Processor. Washable parts can be put in hot soapy water. The base can be washed with light-duty cleaner. A little non-stick spray on the center shaft will keep gooey foods, like dough, from sticking.

Food Grinder. Spray with non-stick vegetable spray and foods won't stick. Grind a piece of bread through after you've used the grinder for meats or other sticky processing.

Garbage Disposal. Always run cold water when you pour down greasy foods or liquids; warm water makes the grease more likely to stick to the disposal interior than be flushed away.

Glass Cookware. Use a sponge saturated with vinegar.

Kitchen magnets. Put them in a panty hose leg, knot it and run it through the dishwasher. If glue loosens you can always reapply it.

Non-Stick Coated Pans. If you never put

oil or butter in these pans they will remain extremely easy to clean—at least on the inside. Use warm sudsy water and a nylon scrubber to get off stubborn spots. If it's sticky, boil two tablespoons of baking soda, $1/2$ cup vinegar, and 1 cup water in the pan for 10 minutes. Reseason with salad oil. The underside is almost impossible to get clean. If the black stains bother you a lot, give it a shot of oven spray, leave it ten minutes, and rinse. Scotchbrite scrubbers do a decent job, too, if you've got elbow grease to spare.

Plasticware (such as Tupperware food storage containers). Use baking soda and water. But if it's stained, just put it outside in the sun. Even tomato stains disappear.

Pots, easy cleaning. Put an inch of water in the pot and put it on a high burner for two minutes. Empty the water, spray with oven cleaner, let stand a few minutes, then rinse.

CAUTION: Be careful not to inhale fumes.

Reflector Bowls, porcelain. Hand or machine wash; or place upside down on oven racks in oven during self-cleaning cycle.

Reflector Bowls, chrome. Hand or machine wash. Do not place in self-cleaning oven, but use oven spray if badly stained. (For blue/gold stains, see stain problems that follow.) Or pour some ammonia in a plastic bag, slip reflectors in, and leave it sealed overnight. Turn your face away when you open the bag since the fumes will be strong. The best place to do this is outside, where you can just hose them down. Otherwise, just rinse them thoroughly and use a nylon scrubber on any stubborn spots.

Toaster Oven. Empty out the crumb tray occasionally; it's a fire hazard. Before you clean the oven, cool it down, then use a nylon scrubber to clean the racks. The outside can be cleaned with a gentle abrasive or baking soda on a sponge. Plastic sides can be cleaned with dishwashing detergent or baking soda and water.

Toaster. Remove the crumb tray or (if it doesn't have one) hold the toaster upside down over the sink or garbage pail and "burp" it gently, like a baby. Use a pipe cleaner or thin brush—called a percolator brush—to clean out stubborn crumbs.

To clean the exterior, rub with baking soda on a sponge cloth or spray some glass cleaner on a sponge cloth, not into the toaster, and rub gently. Or see Chrome, p. 159. Plastic-sided toasters can be cleaned with mild dishwasher detergent or baking soda and water. Never immerse the whole toaster in water.

Waffle Iron. If the waffles are sticking, wash the grids in warm sudsy water, rub away the burned-on spots with a nylon scrubber, and season it by rubbing on a little vegetable oil, then wiping off the excess. Dishwashing detergent can clean an enamel exterior. Baking soda cleans an exterior made of metal.

Wok. In non-stainless woks, rust spots can be removed with a cork sprinkled with scouring powder. Then season the pan properly. Wash with warm soapy water, dry, then cover with a thin coat of mineral oil. Repeat after each use to prevent rusting.

KITCHEN STAIN REMOVAL

Black Stains, on aluminum. Tomato (or other acids) cooked in aluminum may discolor or pit the pot. Fill the pot with water, add three tablespoons of cream of tartar per quart of water. Simmer until the discoloration has disappeared. Steel wool will clean the outside.

Black Marks, on dishes. Black or gray marks are caused by dishes rubbing against metal utensils in the dishwasher. Use a mild abrasive. In the future, load aluminum items carefully and don't stack them next to white or light-colored dishes.

Black Stains, on non-aluminum pans. Spray them with oven cleaner, let set a few minutes, then wash.

Blue/Gold or Brown Stains, on drip pans or reflector bowls. The cause is probably overheating. Overheating happens when you use pans that are larger than the cooking unit or that don't have a flat bottom (such as woks and teakettles, or pans that are damaged). Since I've tried everything and concluded that these stains can't be removed, replace the pans from time to time if you can't live with them.

Brown Spots, on toaster. Use a nylon scrub pad and heavy-duty cleaning spray, then (if you're not chicken) gently scrape with a single-edged razor or (if you are) use a plastic credit card or dry, not damp, Extra Fine steel wool.

Burns, on pots. Leave it to soak. Sprinkle on baking soda (or vinegar if it's aluminum), add a little water, and bring the solution to a boil. Let it cool, then wash the pot as usual. The burned spot should be eliminated. Or make a paste of baking soda and water and let it sit overnight. Rub stubborn spots with a nylon scrub pad. For very bad stains, see box "Super Stain Remover," above.

Coffee, on a countertop. Scrub with a paste of baking soda and water. Let set for a half-hour, then wipe paste with wet sponge.

Coffee, in a coffeepot. Boil a half-and-half mixture of white vinegar and water in your coffee maker, followed by a carafe full of plain water. Use a clean filter (or cover a permanent filter with paper toweling that you can discard afterwards). Rinse with clean water.

Copper, discoloration on. May be due to salt water air, excessive heat, or hanging over stove. See instructions for cleaning copper.

Ink, on counter (laminate or stainless). Give it a spritz of hair spray. Baking soda and water or a weak solution of bleach may also remove these and other dye stains.

Lime Deposit, in teakettle. Mix half-and-half vinegar and water, bring to a boil, simmer until the problem disappears. Rinse well, and repeat if necessary.

Plastic, melted. To remove it from an electric burner, hold a hair dryer 6" to 8" away.

As the plastic softens, scrape with a putty knife. If it's on a toaster, reheat until warm, then unplug. Use a plastic scrubber or paper towel soaked in vinegar to remove the plastic, then clean item with rubbing alcohol, lighter fluid, or nail polish remover.

CAUTION: Area should be well-ventilated; don't use near open flame.

Rust, on metal. Sprinkle scouring cleanser powder on a cork, then rub it on the stain.

Stainless Steel, discoloration on. Cooking dried fruit containing sulphur dioxide or foods with a high starch content may discolor stainless. Leave utensil uncovered for first few minutes of cooking to prevent this problem, and don't use too high a flame. You may need a commercial stainless steel cleaner if the spot is stubborn.

Water Stains, inside teakettle. To remove white deposits, simmer 1 tablespoon white vinegar in a cup of water in the pot for half an hour. Using an agate marble to collect water deposits works, too. Finish cleaning process with steel wool if necessary. To clean a Corning Ware glass kettle, boil two parts vinegar to one part water for 15 minutes.

> **If you want to be alone, announce you're going to wash the dishes.**

HAND-WASHING DISHES AND FLATWARE

I probably can't tell you much that's new about washing dishes unless you've led a very sheltered life—but I can make some suggestions about how to do a better and faster job.

Wear rubber gloves. Your hands will take hotter water and the dishes will get cleaner faster.

NO-EFFORT WAYS TO KEEP YOUR POTS LOOKING BETTER

The same thing is true of pots as of people: it's not the outside that counts. Having pots you can use as makeup mirrors is time-consuming, but there are some ways to keep them in better shape that take no work at all.

- Keep the gas flame low, not crawling up the side. You'll reduce the number of carbon deposits.
- Don't subject the pots to sudden temperature changes (off the heat and into a sinkful of cool water or from freezer to stovetop). That makes the surface warp.
- Storing or cooking salty or very acid foods or soaking pots in chlorine bleach will cause pitting, which can't be corrected; it may also be a result of hard water.

If you've misplaced the cleaning instructions for your pots, write to the manufacturer.

If you have a two-part sink, dunk dishes in soapy water and sponge clean in one section, rinse in a second. To keep the water as clean as possible, wash the least greasy items first and progress to the greasiest and dirtiest—such as pots—last.

Wooden salad bowls shouldn't be soaked. Sponge clean and relubricate with mineral oil when necessary.

One capful of a low-quality dishwashing detergent is a lot less effective than a capful of

GARBAGE DRAIN

If you don't have a garbage disposal, one of the handiest things you can do is put a colander in the bottom of the sink. Scrape the food into it before you use the dishwasher, and the liquid goes down the drain. No soggy mess at the bottom of the garbage pail.

a good-quality brand. Gauge quality by comparing how long the suds last.

USING THE DISHWASHER

You can find out how particular people are by the way they load the dishwasher. The most compulsive woman I know puts on her rubber gloves and washes the dishes before she puts them in the dishwasher, then sponges the door if any liquid spilled during loading. This is totally unnecessary.

Scrape off the large pieces of food (particularly those your manual cautions you about), and put the dish right in the machine. Since a dishwasher is designed to remove small food particles, there is no point wasting time and energy (not to mention water) prewashing the dishes. Only if the dish is crusted with dried food, extremely dirty, or covered with rice should you give it a quick rinse or extra scrape.

Place dishes in the dishwasher so they face the water spray.

Loading the dishwasher in a systematic way—glasses of a like type together, spoons and forks in one compartment, knives and soup spoons in another—saves you unloading time.

Whichever brand of dishwashing detergent you use, I have found and read reports confirming that you will probably get better results from the powdered version than from the liquid (or gel) formulas.

Don't use lumpy detergent. It has picked up

ARE THE DISHES DIRTY OR CLEAN?

Place an uncapped spice bottle upright in a front corner of the top rack. During the washing process, it will fill with water, so if you see the filled bottle, you know the dishes are clean. When you get around to unloading them, empty the bottle and replace it in the dishwasher. When it has no water in it you'll know the dishes are dirty. Just make sure some well-meaning person doesn't remove the spice bottle and upset your system.

---

moisture and may not dissolve properly. Grit or film is a sign of stale detergent (or that the water temperature isn't hot enough).

If the dishwasher utensil caddy is damaged at the bottom (or the slots are too big) cut some plastic needlepoint canvas to fit each compartment.

Your machine may have a special dispenser for an automatic rinse agent (or you may have to add it separately). This type of product, such as Jet Dry, helps to eliminate spotting by letting water "sheet off" dishes instead of drying in

---

SUDS CONTROL

Using liquid dishwashing soap that is not meant for the automatic dishwasher may create oversudsing that causes the machine to stop up. Pour in a capful of liquid laundry softener and run the machine for about 10 seconds. This neutralizes the bubbles so the machine will drain freely.

HOW MUCH DISHWASHER DETERGENT TO USE

• Read your manual; you may be surprised to discover exactly how much is recommended.

• Stepped ridges in the cup of your machine may help you measure the amount of detergent to use. With soft water, you use the least, with hard water the most.

• Too little detergent leaves heavy soil spotting, odor problems.

• Too much detergent causes etching, lumps of detergent on dishes, fading and a strong chemical odor.

WHAT NOT TO PUT IN THE DISHWASHER

Fine crystal. Wash it by hand, and put a towel in the bottom of the sink to cushion it.

Gold-rimmed dishes or glasses

Antique dinnerware, hand-painted china

Lacquered metal

Gold-plated flatware (one very good reason not to buy gold-plated flatware). If it needs polishing, rub on a paste of baking soda, rinse, and buff dry.

Anything with a bone, ivory, or wood handle

Woodenware (it will swell and crack)

Glasses—if you have soft water. Soft water and automatic dishwashing detergent together cause etching. My solution to this would be to buy the cheapest possible glassware, continue to use the dishwasher, and replace glasses as needed.

Sharp knives. They will rub up against other knives and get dull.

Silverware and stainless—touching one another. See explanation in the section on washing silver.

WHAT TO PUT IN THE DISH-WASHER IN ADDITION TO DISHES

Since the manufacturers do not advise cleaning anything but dishes in a dishwasher, do this at your own risk. Items that are light (small pieces of plastic dinnerware, for example) should be put in mesh onion bags and sealed at both ends with a strong twist tie. Some other items for a dishwasher:

Baseball caps

Combs and brushes

Rubber dish drainboard

Toys (put small pieces in mesh bag)

Plastic picnic flatware

Hub caps

Toothbrushes (To sanitize, if you've had a cold or dropped one on the floor.)

LET IT SOAK

If the water won't stay in the sink, put a piece of plastic wrap under the drain stopper and you'll have a tight seal. Great if you're soaking something overnight.

drops—very helpful in hard water areas.

If the dishwasher works better in summer than winter, there may be a chill on the hot water line. Turn the machine on during the middle of the day, when it's warmest, or run sink water until it's hot before you switch the dishwasher on. Otherwise, you may have to insulate pipes or install a hot-water booster. (Ask your plumber.)

When you empty the dishwasher, wrap a flatware place setting in a napkin for each family member instead of returning the pieces to the drawer. Children are able to help set the table, and the job gets done faster.

STERLING SILVER AND SILVER PLATE

Eggs or salt will stain silver so rinse them off right away. If the egg has caked on, rub it off with a little salt, then wash.

A rubber band will leave a stain around sterling, and newspaper ink will remove silver plating.

You can avoid cleaning decorative silver by having it lacquered, but that is in the same category as covering your upholstery with plastic—just a little too practical.

Though you can't prevent tarnishing, there are several ways to reduce it:

• Store your silver in specially treated cloth bags or chests lined with special fabrics sold in jewelry shops, the silver department of a department store, and sometimes even in hardware stores. Or use it every day. That keeps it from tarnishing as well.

• Fabric stores also sell specially treated cloth with which to line your silverware drawer.

• Buy anti-tarnish strips or camphor squares that should be put away with—but not touching—the silver. (Some people wrap silver in plastic wrap, but over time this may trap moisture that spots the silver.)

• Don't wear rubber gloves when you polish. They create tarnish.

Silver polish is an abrasive, so ask the hardware store (or a silverware dealer) to recommend the gentlest one and use it infrequently. Avoid harsh products that contain silica, ammonia, or a tarnish inhibitor—such as dips. Make your own with calcium carbonate (hardware store item) and equal parts denatured alcohol and distilled water—just enough to make a paste. If you have just a piece or two to polish, you can make do with a paste of baking soda and water or a bit of non-gel, white toothpaste. Rub on with a soft cloth, rinse, and buff. Always remove the cleaner after you polish by washing the silver with mild dishwashing detergent.

There is a quick way to clean sterling silver (but not plate) called the electrolytic method. It does such a good job it removes shading in figured pieces and your silver looks like stainless. On the other hand—it's easy! Boil up a quart of water in a non-aluminum pot, add a tablespoon or two of baking soda and a tablespoon of ordinary salt and put a 4" piece of aluminum or a crumpled ball into the pot. Put each piece of silver in separately—don't stack. The tarnish collects on the foil (and on any silver that's sticking out of the water.) Remove pieces with tongs after about 5 minutes.

CAUTION: Don't mix stainless and sterling in the dishwasher. If they touch, it will create a chemical reaction that will leave black spots on the silver.

FINE CRYSTAL

Slide it into the water bottom first to prevent breaks. Line the sink with a towel to cushion the glassware. Add a little ammonia to the dishwater, but not with chlorine products, to cut grease.

Cleaning the Bathroom

I owe my education to the bathroom—not because of all the reading I did in there but because my mom, Pearl, supported our family selling whirlpool tubs. She started her own manufacturing company, Pearl Baths, when she was in her fifties and is still going strong today. When interviewers ask me how I got so smart, I tell them that obviously it's genetic.

And I never mind cleaning the bathroom.

The least you need to know about cleaning the bathroom:
• Weekly maintenance/deep cleaning
• Bathroom cleanup timesavers
• Specific cleaning problems

TWO ITEMS YOUR BATHROOM SHOULD NEVER BE WITHOUT

A plumber's helper in case the toilet backs up.

Extra rolls of toilet paper in a place where a guest can find them.

WEEKLY CLEANING

You need liquid scouring cleaner, heavy- and light-duty cleaners, a sponge cloth, sponge mop, broom or vacuum, and toilet brush and cleaner.

Remove bath mat so you can later shake it out and toss it in the wash.

Squirt liquid scouring cleaner on the floor of the shower, inside of the tub, bowl, sink, and soap dish. Wipe with one sponge cloth, use a second to rinse.

Spray heavy-duty cleaner around the base of the toilet and under the sink. Use a sponge reserved for toilet cleaning to wipe, another sponge to rinse clean.

Spray the underside of the toilet seat with heavy-duty spray. (For this job I use toilet tissue and throw the paper away.) Then clean the top of the seat the same way.

Spray toilet cleaner in the toilet, wipe with a toilet brush. Or, if you don't like that method use the disposable pads (Johnny Mops).

Spray glass/light-duty cleaner on the mirrors and front of the vanity, on counters, and sides of the tub. To do it twice as fast, use one sponge cloth to clean, the other to rinse.

Sweep the floor of hairs and give it a sponge mopping, using a cleaner recommended in Cleaning Floors, beginning on p. 118.

CLEAN AS NEEDED

If they are dirty, the shower curtain, shower liner, and vinyl bath mat can be washed in the machine. (Instructions on next page.)

Use a descaler (a cleaner that removes mineral and lime deposits) to remove hard water spots on the shower wall, shower door, and tub.

If the tile grouting is mildewed, use a mildew cleaner or $1/4$ cup bleach to a quart of water. Spray it on, leave briefly, then rinse. Use a grout sealer afterward and you won't have to do the job soon again.

The entire shower wall may need an occasional spray with heavy-duty cleaner; use one sponge cloth to rub, a second to rinse.

SEVEN ITEMS THAT SPEED UP BATHROOM CLEANING

Some, if not all, should work for you:

1. Bubble Bath. Not only is it one of the last guilt-free indulgences (what else is left once you've given up alcohol, cigarettes, coffee, sugar, fat, and driving when you should walk?) but also it eliminates ring around the tub. Experiment until you find one that works; generic kids' hair shampoo is my choice.

MIRROR DEFOGGER

Spray a thin coat of shaving cream onto a dry mirror, rub with a lint-free cloth until the cream disappears, and the mirror won't fog up when you're taking a steamy shower. An ex-Marine told me he learned this trick in the service. He didn't know why it worked (and neither do I), but it does. Repeat the process from time to time. Or keep candles lit while you take your bath or shower. Or run an inch of cold water before adding hot water to the tub. Or wave a hairdryer at the mirror.

---

2. Sponges. Wipe the tub before you get out of it; sponge the sink immediately after brushing your teeth. The job gets done without your having to think about it. Everyone in the house should do the same; compliance is likelier if you put sponges and liquid abrasive within easy reach. Put a small sponge under the soap and you'll almost never have to clean out the soap dish.

3. Squeegee. Hang it near the shower. If the shower is squeegeed after each use, you won't get mildew and accumulated deposits.

4. Child's Mop. Reach out and clean the tub or shower walls without stooping, kneeling, or stretching.

5. Furniture or Car Wax. To reduce the problem of soap scum and lime and mineral deposits, wax and buff everything from ceramic tile to shower door (but not the tub bottom; it will be too slippery). Soap film won't accumulate, and lime and minerals will be repelled.

6. Vacuum. Vacuum the floor when the surfaces are dry to pick up hair.

7. Roller or Paintbrush. If you're using a strong cleaning product or bleach to clean tiles, skip the rubber gloves and speed up the job by "painting" the product on, then rinsing it off.

COUNTERTOPS

Bathroom countertops are usually tile (with grouting), cultured marble, or plastic laminate. All of these are vulnerable to scratching, but cultured marble, since it is solid rather than a veneer, can be most easily repaired if burned or otherwise damaged. Use a liquid abrasive cleaner.

If tile grouting needs cleaning, use $1/4$ cup bleach to a quart of water or a commercial or mildew grouting cleaner.

HARDWARE

To clean stainless steel, see p. 138; to clean chrome, p. 159.

Use regular furniture polish on wooden towel racks, toilet seats, and other wooden accessories. Apply and buff.

For brass, use a commercial brass cleaner, a lemon dipped in salt, or a paste of equal parts vinegar, flour, and salt. Buff with mineral oil.

CAUTION: Harsh but effective cleaners may leave a film on many kinds of plated (gold- or brass-) hardware. Read labels and try the cleaner in a hidden area.

MEDICINE CABINET

Metal medicine cabinet shelves become rusted. Line them with contact paper to make wiping easy.

MIRROR

Clean with homemade window cleaner (see Windows, p. 106) or plain vinegar rubbed on with a sponge cloth and wiped off with newspaper. Or spray on a mixture of ammonia and water (1 tablespoon ammonia to a quart of water) and wipe with a clean dusting cloth.

Remove hair spray with rubbing alcohol. Or apply paint thinner (diluted) in a well-ventilated room.

SHOWER CURTAIN, PLASTIC OR VINYL

Fill the washing machine with warm water, add $1/2$ cup each of detergent and baking soda. Put the curtain in with two bath towels, run through the entire wash cycle, and add 1 cup of vinegar to the rinse water. Do not wash out the vinegar, do not spin dry, and hang the curtain immediately.

To avoid or eliminate mold from the bottom of the shower curtain or liner, cut an inch or two from the bottom. Continue to give the liner a trim whenever it's necessary. If curtain gets very short, add another set of curtain rings below the first set.

SHOWER DOORS

Clean glass doors with lemon oil, window washing solution, or (if they're scummy) descaler or laundry prewash spray. Then give it a coat of wax.

To clean the track itself, remove the doors by lifting them up. The best tool for cleaning the track is one of those foam rubber "brushes" sold in the paint department.

TUB AND BASIN

Most tubs are porcelain on steel, which resist stains better than the old porcelain-on-cast-iron tubs and the new fiberglass tubs. Porcelain can be cleaned with liquid scouring cleaner. For fiberglass, there are special cleaners available at the supermarket or from boat dealers.

HOLE THAT LINE

To reinforce the holes in a shower curtain (or repair it once it's torn) get some clear, waterproof tape, run it along the top of the curtain, and use a hole puncher to repunch the holes.

TOILET BOWL AND TANK

Pour a little liquid cleanser into the bowl and slosh it around with the toilet brush or a disposable Johnny Mop.

In-tank cleaners (which should never be mixed with in-bowl cleaners) help prevent buildup of stains in the toilet bowl but don't really clean. If the toilet isn't flushed once daily, the accumulated chemicals can damage the tank. I don't think these serve much purpose unless you enjoy having blue water in your toilet bowl.

The tank itself can be cleaned with Iron Out,™ a job I wouldn't bother about.

TUB MAT, RUBBER

Throw it in the machine. If it's mildewed, toss it in with any load to which you're adding chlorine bleach. Air dry, preferably in the sun.

WASTEBASKETS

Wicker can be scrubbed with warm sudsy water, then rinsed with salt water, then air dried.

Plastic can be washed with a liquid cleanser when it's looking grimy.

BATHROOM STAINS AND OTHER PROBLEMS

Brown Stains, in toilet. First pour a bucket of water into the toilet so it will empty out. Squirt in a bowl cleaner, let it set 2 to 3 hours. If the toilet is badly stained, you may have to resort to a chemical cleaner containing sulphuric or hydrochloric acid. Handle with extreme caution.

If that doesn't do the job, rub the area with a pumice stone made for cleaning porcelain. Or talk to the local swimming pool supply house or building supplier about a water test and two-stage treatment system to remove iron and soften water.

Clogging, in drains. If you have a lot of hairs caught in the drain, that fondue fork you never use makes a good tool for digging them out. Then put a small ball of net deep into the drain to catch the hairs; replace the net with a new piece every once in a while. I'm against chemical drainers except in a desperate situation. Since chemicals may damage porcelain, never leave the solution standing in the bowl. See ideas for drain repair on p. 216.

Mineral Deposits, on fixtures. White vinegar will remove hard water stains on your shower head. If you can't unscrew the shower head and soak it in a bowl, pour vinegar in a bag, fasten the bag over the shower head neck with a rubber band, and leave it in place for several hours. Remove the bag and scrub off the residue with a nylon scrub pad. Open any clogged holes with a toothpick.

If stains remain, try a commercial product that removes lime and minerals.

Mineral Deposits, on marble. Soak a few white paper towels with a solution of hydrogen peroxide and leave covered with a piece of plastic for fifteen minutes, then rinse. If the problem is severe, you may need a commercial tub and tile cleaner or descaler that contains phosphoric and other acids.

Rust, on fixtures and sink. Try lemon juice and salt. Or use a commercial rust cleaner. Or once a month sprinkle a layer of Tang or lemon Kool-Aid on the sides and in water, leave for an hour, brush and flush. Repeat if necessary. (The citric acid oxidizes the rust.) Or use bleach-soaked papers on side of a white sink, leaving them in place for an hour.

Tub Stains. To clean a badly stained tub of

any type, spray from the bottom up with oven cleaner, leave for 15 to 20 minutes, then wash down. If it's scratched, sand with sandpaper made for using with water, then use car wax to buff out fine scratches, rubbing in a circular motion.

White stains (on tile). Efflorescence is the technical name for a whitish powder that appears at time of installation or periodically at later dates. Since it's just a layer of water-soluble salts, brush it off dry. Or allow it to disappear in time. An acid wash should be used only as a last resort, particularly since you may wind up with an off-white deposit that is much more difficult to remove than the original.

Cleaning the Bedroom

The least you need to know about cleaning the bedroom:

- Weekly cleaning/deep cleaning
- Bed-making shortcuts

Wouldn't it be efficient if you could just make the bottom of the closet into a compost pile?

WEEKLY CLEANING

You need: vacuum, glass/light-duty cleaner, heavy-duty cleaner, furniture polish, dust cloths.

Put all the clothes away.

Open windows to air the room out.

Spot-polish mirrors and windows with light-duty cleaner; spot-clean furniture smudges with furniture polish and marks on walls with heavy-duty cleaner.

Change sheets.

Use dusting wand on windows, blinds, furniture.

Vacuum high-traffic areas.

CLEAN AS NEEDED

Reorganize drawers or shelves.

Vacuum closet shelves and floors.

Vacuum drawers. (If you don't want to empty them out, pull a panty hose leg over the vacuum hose so you don't suck up any jewelry or other small items.)

Vacuum carpet or rug entirely or polish/clean wood floors.

Vacuum window ledges, walls, ceilings, upholstered furniture.

Vacuum mattress (every few months).

Polish furniture.

Wash mattress pad, pillow covers, pillows, curtains.

Dust lamp shades, photographs.

Wash or dry-clean bedspread and drapes.

Turn mattress.

Put pillows into dryer on no-heat cycle. This removes dust.

HOW TO TURN A MATTRESS

Put a strip of masking tape marked 1 at the spot where you now put the pillows, and a second strip, marked 2, at the foot. Turn the mattress and mark one end 3, the other 4. Every six months or so, move the next number to the pillow position. This chore never seemed important to me until I saw a baby's crib mattress that had split open after only two years of (non-rotated) use. Imagine the difference between the wear an infant gives a mattress and the wear you give one.

Foam mattresses need turning less often.

HOW TO MAKE A BED

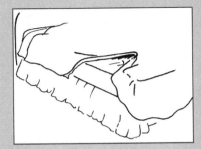

If you like a bed with the traditional bed and sheet setup, and you didn't learn how to make a bed in camp or the army, here's how:

1. Straighten the mattress pad.

2. Put on bottom sheet. If fitted, it will slip into place easily. (Otherwise, see instructions for hospital corners).

3. Center top sheet on bed. Wide hem goes at the top, about one foot from headboard. If sheet is patterned, lay sheet wrong side up, so when you pull top hem over blanket, it will be right-side up.

4. Lay blanket on top of sheet, about $1\frac{1}{2}'$ from headboard. (If you use a laundry marker to mark a small X at the top center of the blanket, you can line it up easily.)

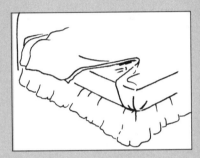

5. Go around the bed just once, the way the hotel maids do, tucking in the sheet and blanket together. To make a "hospital corner," pick up the edge of the sheet (and blanket, if you're going to make them together) about 15" from the foot of the bed. Lift it up so it makes a diagonal fold. Lay the fold on the mattress.

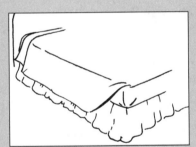

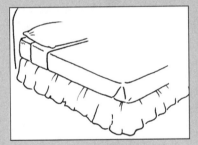

Take the part of the sheet and blanket that is hanging and tuck it underneath the mattress. Drop the fold, pull it smooth, and tuck it under the mattress, too.

6. Turn top of sheet over top of blanket near headboard. Replace pillows. Cover with bedspread if desired.

BED-MAKING MADE EASY

I assume you're already using fitted sheets on the bottom. My suggestion is that you also use a comforter or duvet with a cover as a combination top sheet/blanket/bedspread (see the section Outfitting the Bed, beginning p. 79).

By eliminating the bedspread and combining top sheet and comforter, you can have a neat-looking bed in a few seconds. And you'll save at least 5 minutes a day, which works out to 30 hours, or almost a work-week, per year.

This arrangement is not for people who like that big pile of pillows and quilts—I'm one of them—but there are timesavers for us, too.

Fold the sheets lengthwise when you put them in the closet (and always fold two sheets together with the pillowcase in one easy-to-find package). When you put them on the bed, there will be a nice long straight crease in the center so you can center the sheet perfectly right away. The center of your headboard may even have a design right in the middle that you can use as a marker.

If you need a place to hang the bedspread at night, fasten a towel rack on the back of the bedroom door.

FOLDING A FITTED SHEET

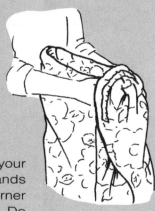

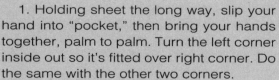

2. Then repeat, turning the doubled pockets on the left inside out so they fit over the other two. They're all nested.

3. Lay sheet flat, smooth down, and fold until you've got a neat package that fits onto your linen shelf.

1. Holding sheet the long way, slip your hand into "pocket," then bring your hands together, palm to palm. Turn the left corner inside out so it's fitted over right corner. Do the same with the other two corners.

OTHER BEDROOM CLEANING

Most modern beds just need an occasional dusting around the bed frame.

Head/Foot Boards. Both varnished and brass beds can be dusted, then rubbed with a mop or rag dampened lightly with lemon oil. Wood headboards can be cleaned with furniture polish, laminates with all-purpose cleaner or liquid abrasive, enamel with soap and water.

Mattress. If the mattress is musty, use a commercial foam upholstery cleaner. Or mix $1/2$ teaspoon liquid dishwashing detergent in a quart of warm water. Whip it with an egg beater to get a froth, and apply the suds with a sponge or soft brush without soaking the mattress. Work on a small area at a time, overlapping areas to avoid spotting. Change the rinse water frequently to keep it clean. Let one side dry thoroughly before you do the other. (A fan may help.)

I have heard of using a hypodermic needle to inject a musty mattress in various spots with commercial odor-remover, but that's not a solution for everyone. For the most effective home cleaning, you need an extraction cleaner. (See Vacuum Cleaners in the Equipping section on p. 34.)

Pillows. Except for kapok, a seed covering, most pillows can be washed.

Polyester, foam, feather, and down can be hand washed with a liquid detergent in cool water or machine washed, preferably two at a time on a short, delicate cycle in a tumble-type machine. (If they're really big, take them to a large commercial machine.) They should be thoroughly rinsed.

Pillows other than foam can usually be machine dried on low heat. If they're feather or down, put a couple of tennis balls in the machine to fluff them up. Or hang them on the line to dry.

From time to time, a non-foam pillow can also be tossed into the dryer briefly on low heat—you needn't wash it first—to kill mold and prevent new growth. A spin on no-heat will fluff it up, remove dust.

Wash pillow covers occasionally (and zip them before putting them in the machine).

Blankets. Except for older wool blankets, most blankets are machine washable—including the new wools. Make sure the machine is big enough for the blankets to move freely. To avoid pilling, let them soak for about ten minutes and then wash them on a short cycle.

Electric blankets should not be washed or dry cleaned with solvents or mothproofing solutions that may damage the wiring.

Comforters and Quilts. New comforters are machine washable but older comforters and quilts may run or fall apart (especially if you don't mend small rips or tears before washing and definitely if they have a cotton batting).

When machine washing, soak them for ten minutes in detergent and water solution and wash them on a short, gentle cycle.

If you want to hand-wash them, first test for colorfastness (see box, p. 178), rinse out all detergent after washing, and dry them thoroughly, especially if you plan to store them.

Sheets. See Washing Towels, Sheets, and Pillowcases, p. 195.

> **Housework would probably attract more people if designers made special outfits to do it in.**

Cleaning the Living Room and Family Room

WEEKLY CLEANING

Clear all surfaces of items that belong elsewhere, discard all magazines, news-Scheduling the Cleaningpapers.
Heavy-duty cleaner to remove smudges on walls, around light switches.
Dust surfaces.
Light-duty cleaner to wipe windows and TV screens and glass tabletops.
Vacuum high-traffic areas.

CLEAN AS NEEDED

Vacuum entire rug; shampoo or deep clean.
Furniture polishing and/or waxing.
Dust pictures, lamp shades, vacuum behind or inside piano.

• •

SCHEDULING THE CLEANING

DO YOU NEED AN ANNUAL CLEANING?

Whether to have an annual cleaning depends on your metabolism. Some organized folks like to spread work out and others like the pressure and immediate gratification of a blitz.

The simultaneous arrival of spring fever and spring cleaning always seemed to me to be a classic example of bad timing. The custom is a leftover from the days coal-burning days, when the house was coated with soot by spring, but some people like to clean in spring so, like Mother Nature, they can renew and refresh.

But other people have an easier time doing the chores in the fall. If you live in the North and will be spending a lot of the winter inside, you'll enjoy a clean house more; and since the windows will stay closed much of the time, it'll stay clean longer. And if you'd be cleaning for the holidays anyway, a major fall cleaning makes very good sense.

YOUR PERSONAL CLEANING LIST

No matter how casual you are about cleaning, there are some jobs you have to get to. These are not necessarily the jobs that make the house look nice but the ones that keep away the germs and insects and keep the things you own in reasonably good shape. If you don't clean the air conditioner filter, the thing may get clogged up and break down. If you never turn a mattress, it may quite literally split down the middle. On the list of routine jobs below, I've marked these essential jobs with a star: on a scale of 1 to 10, they are the 10s.

As for the other jobs on the list, they're there in case you'd like some guidelines or you have some spare time and don't know how to fill it. I personally hate lists because they remind me too much of school, and I can't point out too strongly that cleaning is largely a matter of taste and lifestyle.

If you put the spread on the bed on the morning, go off to work, and then carefully fold it at night, you probably don't need to clean it more than once a year. But if the kids and the dog are rolling around on it regularly, I'm sure you'll want to clean it more often than that.

In my house, the pictures and photos get dusted and cleaned about once every two weeks. On the other hand, I never have the drapes cleaned since I think they will never look or hang the same again. I just vacuum them periodically to get rid of the dust and when they start looking worn and dingy, I replace them.

To make you feel better about what you're doing (or not doing), I would like to remind you that despite the rumors, nowhere in the Bible does it say "Cleanliness is next to Godliness." Being a little deficient in the dusting and wiping departments may displease your mother, but it won't get you into trouble in the afterlife.

WEEKLY

★ Vacuum high-traffic areas of hard surface floors and carpets
Dust, polish furniture
Empty wastepaper baskets
★ Change bed linens
★ Kitchen cleanup (described earlier)
★ Bathroom cleanup (described earlier)
Living room cleanup (described earlier)

EVERY TWO WEEKS

★ Clean or replace the air conditioner filter (summer only)

MONTHLY OR AS NEEDED

Wash bathroom rugs
Clean TV screen, mirrors, pictures, knick-knacks
Clean oven
Vacuum

EVERY TWO OR THREE MONTHS OR AS NEEDED

Polish silver
Wipe windowsills
Dust knickknacks

SEMIANNUALLY OR AS NEEDED

★ Defrost refrigerator/freezer (or when ice is more than 1/4" thick)
★ Vacuum refrigerator coils
Clean lamp shades
Wipe out kitchen cabinets
Polish furniture
Dust outlets, picture frames, tall things, books, pictures, lamps
Clean windows and screens
Clean light fixtures
Wash walls and woodwork
Wash mattress pad and pillow covers, air pillows
★ Turn the mattress
Wash shower curtain
Clean out floor of closet; organize closet
Vacuum drapes and upholstery

ANNUALLY OR AS NEEDED

★ Shampoo carpets and rugs; turn rugs (for even wear)
Vacuum rug pads
★ Strip and reseal hard surface floors
Wash curtains, blinds
Clean drapes or toss them into dryer on "Air Only"
Wash bathroom walls
Wash bedspreads, blankets, slipcovers
Clean out and organize workshop

Move heavy furniture and clean behind it

Wipe pictures, frames, and walls behind

EMERGENCY TEN-MINUTE CLEANUP

If you don't have cleaning help (and even if you do), your house is probably not always ready for visitors. So the basic nightmare is friends calling from the road to say they're in the neighborhood. You do the nice thing and invite them over, but the place is a wreck and you've got ten minutes to clean up.

Here's what to do, in the order you should do it.

1. Comb your hair and check your makeup. They'll notice how you look before they notice the house.

2. Close doors to whatever rooms will not be in use.

3 Get a carton. Clear floors and table surfaces of anything that doesn't belong in both entry hall and living room. Hide the carton where it won't be seen.

4. Take a light-duty cleaner and furniture spray into the room where you'll be sitting, and wipe visible dirt off all surfaces such as glass-topped coffee table or end table.

5. Fluff up all pillows.

6. Check the bathroom. A toothpaste-stained or hairy sink makes a very negative impression. Put all clutter, including dirty towels, in hamper or behind pulled shower curtain. Wipe out sink with sponge or toilet tissue. Put up clean towel and make sure there is toilet tissue. Little things mean a lot.

7. Go back and vacuum living room if you have time.

8. Go into kitchen and stow unwashed dishes in the dishwasher or oven. Clear off counters. You may have a few minutes grace here to do extra work when, after greeting your guests, you go back to the kitchen to fix them a drink, but there is always the chance that the guest will follow you.

9. Spray a pine cleaner all around. It creates the impression that everything has been thoroughly scrubbed.

It seems unfair that to get anything clean you have to get something else dirty.

HOW DO I CLEAN THE. . . ?

Though the major cleaning jobs that I've already described represent most of the cleaning problems in the house, the chances are you also own a number of things that will require special attention. When do you clean them? When they look dirty. How? The answers are here.

AIR CONDITIONING FILTER (WINDOW AIR CONDITIONERS)

Clean it regularly to keep it working right, following instructions in your manual. It will probably tell you to vacuum coils and remove as much dirt and dust as you can. If they're not accessible to you without removing the entire unit, you may need to call for professional help.

A washable filter is usually dipped into detergent and warm water, sometimes with a few drops of sanitizer. Rinse and dry it thoroughly before putting it back in place. If it's a real mess, replace it. The cost of a replacement filter is minor compared to the cost of replacing the whole unit because the filter isn't doing the job.

ALABASTER

Use a damp cloth to apply lukewarm water with a few drops of dishwashing detergent. Rinse well or you'll leave scum behind.

Alabaster knickknacks sprayed with a ceramic glaze will attract less dust.

ARTIFICIAL FLOWERS, DRIED OR SILK

If the flowers aren't crumbling, put them in a bag with salt and shake. Although you won't see a huge difference, check the color of the salt and you'll see how much dirt was removed. You can also clean silk flowers without water by placing them in a clean pillowcase, tying a knot, and putting the case into the clothes dryer with a damp washcloth. Set dryer to "Air Only" for 20 minutes.

FLORAL DESIGN

If you have a specially designed artificial flower arrangement and want to keep it intact, before you remove the individual flowers for cleaning, mark the places where stems are removed with knitting needles, shish kebab skewers, or chop sticks.

ARTIFICIAL FLOWERS, POLYESTER

Give them a good coating of acrylic spray (from the craft shop) and they'll resist dirt and soil. If they're very dusty, run them through warm soapy water or clean them with window cleaner or $1/4$ cup ammonia plus enough water to fill a one-quart spray bottle. Spray generously, rinse with clear water, shake, and then drip them or pat them dry on a towel. You can also saturate a cloth sponge with a dust remover, furniture polish, or a light misting of water and wipe off leaves and flowers.

AWNINGS, CANVAS

Hose clean. If they're very dirty, rub a stiff brush over a bar of naphtha soap and scrub—going in the direction of the seams. Sprinkle with dry washing soda, then hose well to rinse. Don't roll awnings until dry.

Worn-looking canvas can be covered with special canvas paint.

AWNINGS, METAL

Buy one of the gadgets for spraying insecticides. Fill the bottle with water and a few drops of detergent. Spray, scrub with a long-handled brush. Hose down.

BARBECUE KETTLE AND GRILL

Use an all-purpose cleaner or washing soda on a cool kettle, but if it's very dirty, use paint thinner.

CAUTION: Very flammable. Wear rubber gloves.

Dip a clean cloth into the thinner and rub. Grill can be cleaned with paint thinner applied with a wire brush (unless surface is non-stick). Rinse thoroughly afterward.

The inside of the grill can be cleaned with oven spray.

Permanent briquettes can be cleaned by removing the grill, closing the lid, opening the vent, and turning the heat to high for about 20 minutes. Brush afterward if necessary.

BOOKS

A cloth, feather duster, or dust wand along the spine does a fast job. If books haven't been cleaned in years, take out each one separately and go over it with the brush attachment of your vacuum, a dry paint brush, or cloth misted with water. If you have leather-bound volumes, you could use a fine leather polish—or have the butler do it.

BRASS

If the brass is lacquered (as it might be on a lamp base), clean it with soapy water or ten parts water and one part ammonia. Anything stronger may ruin the finish.

Finish that's cracked or peeling should be stripped with lacquer thinner or acetone. Or soak item in a gallon of boiling water mixed with $1/2$ cup of baking soda. When it's cool, peel off the lacquer. The brass can be left unfinished or recoated with clear lacquer. If it's large or valuable, have it relacquered professionally.

To clean unlacquered brass, mix equal parts of salt and flour and add enough vinegar to make a paste. Spread a thick layer on the brass and let it dry, then rinse to remove. Or dip the cut side of half a lemon in salt (or salt dissolved in some white vinegar) and rub it on, then rinse with cold water. Buff with a soft cloth—dry or dipped in some mineral oil. Coat with silicone car wax to keep it shiny.

Or use a commercial copper or brass cleaner.

Some all-purpose bathroom cleaners will discolor brass. Read instructions before you use them, and always rinse off cleaner residue.

BRONZE

If it's not an antique and it's lacquered, mild detergent and water should clean it. If it's peeling, it needs professional relacquering.

Unlacquered bronze can be cleaned with the salt-flour-vinegar mix that cleans brass or with a commercial brass or copper cleaner.

For a badly stained antique, get professional help.

To clean bronze baby shoes, use Extra Fine steel wool dipped into copper or brass polish. (First test on an inconspicuous area.) Rub lightly and wipe with a dry cloth.

CALCULATORS

Use baby wipes or a soft cloth and rubbing alcohol.

CAMEOS (MADE FROM SHELLS)

Wash with warm soapy water, scrub with a soft toothbrush, then rinse.

CANDLE HOLDERS

Put glass (but not lead crystal) holders on folded paper towels in the microwave, heat on low for 3 minutes, and the wax will just drip out.

Putting a teaspoon of water or some petroleum jelly in the bottom of candle holders will make the stubs easier to remove.

Weighted or hollow candlesticks can't be washed or they may fall apart. Lacquered ones should be wiped only with a damp cloth.

CANDLES

When decorative candles get a coating of dust, clean them with a cotton ball dipped in rubbing alcohol.

CANVAS TOTE

If you can't machine wash canvas because of the design, briskly rub on cornstarch with a nail brush, then brush off excess. If you're willing to take the risk, rub on some Lava soap with a very small amount of water. I can't guarantee the design won't run.

CAT LITTER BOX

Don't use bleach! Residual ammonia from the cat's urine can mix with it to create hazardous fumes. Just wash out box with soapy water and more ammonia if you want something stronger. (Don't use a sanitizer with phenol, either—highly toxic to cats.)

CD

Wipe the disc with a clean cloth, rinse it under running cool water, and blot dry with a lint-free towel. Always wipe in a straight line from the center to the edge. If it has a smudge, blemish, or large scratch, and conventional

CAR TRICKS

The auto supply store sells all kinds of cleaners for cars, tires, and windshields, and I'm sure you have your favorites. But I've got a few shortcuts you might prefer:

- **Blackwalls:** Rub on a thin coat of brake fluid and wipe dry. They'll look like they just came from the tire store.
- **Carpeting:** Remove tar by scrubbing with a prewash spray.
- **Exterior:** Use a child's mop as a car-washing tool.

Or use the lawn sprayer that attaches to the garden hose, and put liquid detergent in the container. This lets you control water pressure with your thumb. Water, then wash and rinse.

If you use household detergent to wash the car on a hot day, be sure to rinse each section immediately. Heat dries detergents fast and may leave a permanent streak in your paint. Add a teaspoon of rinsing agent made for dishwashers, such as Jet Dry, to the pail of rinse water. Sponge it on, let the car air dry.

Remove fly spots with ammonia and water, and tar with WD 40. Remove salt with a bucket of soapy water and cup of kerosene (CAUTION: flammable) or mild dish soap and a scrubber.

- **Odors:** See Odors, p. 166.
- **Wheel cover:** A spoked wheel cover can be cleaned in the dishwasher on the pot-scrubber cycle.
- **Wheel:** Foaming aerosol bathroom cleaner sprayed on, left for 30 seconds, then washed off will remove street dirt and road oils.
- **Whitewalls:** Foaming bathroom cleaner sprayed on, then hosed off after 15 seconds, is an inexpensive cleaner for tires, dirty rims, and hub caps.

Or wash tires with detergent, waterless hand cleaner (use on a dry tire, then scrub with brush and soapy water), or Shout laundry stain remover (no scrubbing).

Or wet the tire; spray with any oven cleaner; swish around the whitewall with a brush; spray with hose after half a minute.

Or spray each tire with a prewash spray before going to the car wash. When the hot sudsy water hits, they shine.

To remove tar, apply paste wax, then polish. Tar is removed; and you have a nice shine.

- **Windows:** Cola gets grease and film off car windows. Pour some on the windshields and let the wipers cut the grease. In winter, save a lot of scraping by filling an empty spray bottle with alcohol, then spray it on the windows. You can wipe frost off easily since alcohol doesn't freeze.
- **Windshield:** A quart of water with $1/2$ cup baking soda is a great solution to wash insects off the windshield and radiator or to clean the wipers. Apply with a piece of mesh onion bag wrapped around a large sponge.

cleaners won't clean it, use a dab of non-gel toothpaste. Rub gently, then remove with a moist tissue or rag. You may get a few surface hairlike scratches, but they won't affect play.

CEILING FAN

Wooden blades will be easier to clean if you cover them with a coat of furniture polish. Wipe off excess.

CHALKBOARD

Wipe with baking soda sprinkled on a damp rag.

CHANDELIER

See p. 98 for a homemade cleaning formula or mix two teaspoons of rubbing alcohol in a pint of warm water. Hang an umbrella upside down and open it, with the handle attached to the

Chandelier
Cleaning

center of the chandelier. Spray on the cleaner and let the umbrella catch the drips.

CHROME

Rub it with dry baking soda or flour.

Or use rubbing alcohol on a soft cloth to clean up drips and grease. Dry the item thoroughly.

Aluminum foil crumpled in a ball will also clean chrome like magic.

Mild phosphoric acid will remove stubborn water deposits.

Murphy's Oil Soap (2 tablespoons in a gallon of water) is also effective on dirty chrome.

COMPUTER KEYBOARD

Vacuum regularly with a soft brush attachment. If dust needs to be dislodged, turn the keyboard upside down and hit with the flat of your hand several times. Or buy a can of compressed air.

To remove built-up grime, unplug the computer and use a Q-tip dipped in rubbing alcohol on the keys. Or use a baby wipe for a quick cleanup.

COPPER

See instructions for treating brass. Lacquered and unlacquered finishes must be treated differently.

CORK

Vacuum loose dirt. A dry sponge provides just enough abrasion to pick up dirt without damaging the surface.

CURLING IRON

The most common cleanup problem on a curling iron is accumulated hair spray! When curling iron is cool, apply rubbing alcohol or nail polish remover with a clean dry cloth. If stubborn spots remain, rub gently with the fine side of an emery board or fine sandpaper.

DECKING

Use a mild household detergent applied with a stiff brush or special deck-cleaning products. A bleach-water solution (one part bleach to three parts water) should take care of any mildew problem, and mineral spirits will remove sap from unfinished wood.

DOLL

Crisco removes dirt from a plastic doll face. Hair spray removes ink, or rub it with butter and leave it in the sun for several days.

For cleaning soft dolls, refer to Stuffed Toys, p. 164.

DOOR, ALUMINUM

Clean with whitewall tire cleaner or aluminum jelly. Rub in with soft damp rag, rinse rag, and wipe again.

DRYER, AUTOMATIC

Remove lint from the lint tray regularly. You can just "rub" it off; don't bother to get out the vacuum. (If you're a pack rat, save the lint for stuffing toys, put it out for the birds to collect for nests, or try your hand at "lint art"—collages made from a variety of different colored lints.)

To clean the dryer thoroughly, unplug it, attach the vacuum hose to the blower end and move the nozzle around the spinner inside the basket, moving from the top down the sides. This will blow lint into the air-intake opening.

Then, reverse the vacuum cleaner hose, and put it in at the suction end. Remove any lint still inside the dryer.

FABRIC-COVERED ALBUMS, PICTURES, LINED BASKETS

Use a soft-bristle baby's brush. Wash the brush with soap and water.

FIREPLACE, BRICK

The best way to keep the bricks or stones in the façade of a fireplace clean is to seal them. Otherwise, since they are so porous, any cleaning solution you use may just drive the dirt farther in. The brick or stone will look clean—then the spot will reappear within the next few days.

Bricks or stones that have been sealed can be cleaned with diluted ammonia.

If you need a stronger cleaner, shave 4 ounces of naphtha soap into 1 quart of hot water. Heat until the soap dissolves. Cool, then stir in $1/2$ pound of powdered pumice and $1/2$ cup of household ammonia. Mix thoroughly. Remove as much of the smoky deposit as you can with plain household detergent in water, then apply a coat of the naphtha mixture with a paintbrush. Allow it to remain on for 30 minutes. Scrub with a scrub brush and warm water. Rinse thoroughly by sponging with a lot of water. Or use Mex Multi-Purpose Cleaner or other commercial product.

Dirty grouting can be cleaned with smoker's toothpaste. (Don't rinse, just wipe off excess with a damp rag.) Or spray on whitewall cleaner, rub off with newspaper, and finish with window cleaner.

FIREPLACE, GLASS DOORS ON

Spray cool glass with a mixture of $1/2$ cup vinegar, 1 tablespoon ammonia, and 1 gallon clear water. Rinse, and repeat if necessary.

Or use foaming bathroom cleaner or white-wall cleaner, wipe with newspapers, then shine with window cleaner.

FIREPLACE, INTERIOR (ALSO CALLED FIREBOX; MADE OF METAL OR FIRE BRICK)

Keep a pan or bucket in the fireplace and shovel ashes into the bucket rather than sweeping them to avoid sooty dust flying around. (Dump ashes in an outside garbage pail, or if you have an ash pit, remove the grate.)

FUR, SHEEPSKIN

A sheepskin throw can be washed by machine with detergent or by hand with Murphy's Oil Soap (which will take out stains like cola, coffee, grease, and oil without drying the leather). Add some hair conditioner to the rinse water to make it fluffy. Machine dry on "Low," remove while damp and air dry to avoid shrinkage or discoloration.

Yellowed fur can be dyed. (It's hair, after all).

GARDEN TOOLS

Store garden tools in a bucket of sand (to keep them dry and free of rust). In humid areas, both the working part and the handle should be treated with oil or sprayed with silicone lubricant.

GLASS-TOP TABLES

Use commercial or home-mixed window cleaner (see the information on cleaning windows, p. 106).

Prevent lint buildup on glass by adding a capful of any fabric softener to a bucket of warm water and using this as a rinse.

GOLF BALLS

Soak balls in a cup of water and $1/4$ cup of ammonia.

GOLF CLUBS

Rub shaft and club heads lightly with dry, Fine steel wool. Rinse off residue; dry thoroughly.

HOT TUB

Use a water-testing kit to check the acid/base balance (pH) and mineral and chlorine levels. You'll avoid maintenance problems. Follow instructions in the manual for cleaning the filter, skimmer basket, and pump strainer. The manual should recommend a cleaner that will dissolve scum. When the tub is empty, clean it with a liquid cleaner as suggested in the manual, and then use a silicone sealer.

HUMIDIFIER

Clean a cool, empty humidifier by swishing around a solution of one cup of bleach in a gallon of water, then rinse.

If there are mineral deposits on the removable plastic rotor tube and locking ring, bring hot vinegar to a boil, remove it from the heat, immerse the tube and ring, leave for a few minutes only, rinse and dry.

In cool mist or ultrasonic humidifiers use only distilled water. Otherwise, dustlike mineral particles that should not be inhaled will be deposited everywhere.

CAUTION: If you have allergies, you must pay special attention to cleaning these units. Read the manual very carefully and/or check with your allergist.

HURRICANE LAMPS

Wash them in a plastic bucket to prevent chips or cracks. Add a tablespoon of rubbing alcohol to a quart of the rinse water and they will sparkle.

JEWELRY

If stones are glued in place, don't immerse the jewelry in water. **Jewelry that is glued, along with turquoise, opals, ivory, and porous cameos,** should simply be wiped with a damp cloth.

Plastic jewelry and **real or cultured pearls** (but not simulated pearls or mother of pearl) can be washed in warm water mixed with soap suds (like Ivory Snow; no detergents) and dried.

Gold and diamonds can be wiped clean and immersed in 1 cup warm sudsy water plus one tablespoon of ammonia. Let chains or rings sit in the solution for ten to fifteen minutes. Scrub jewelry with soft brush and rinse under warm water—with the sink drain closed. This will remove grime but not oxides.

Rubbing alcohol removes oil from diamonds and gold.

To remove tarnish on **silver,** see Sterling Silver and Silver Plate, p. 145.

KNICKKNACKS

Dust with a blow dryer, put them all on a tray, and submerge into a solution of soapy water or put under a fine spray shower.

If the items in the china or curio cabinet get very dusty, seal the doors tighter with self-adhesive polyfoam weather stripping.

LAMP BASES

Porcelain bases can be wiped with sudsy water. For metal bases, refer to cleaning instructions for the particular metal.

LAMP SHADE

Determine, if you can, whether the shade is washable. Shades that are sewn can be washed, but shades that are glued or stapled may fall apart. If the lining of the shade is made of paper or plastic, water may also destroy it. If an unwashable shade is in bad shape, get professional help or replace it. Before you toss it out, you can always try a damp sponge on it and if it holds up, proceed to soap and water.

Unwashable shades should be taken outside and dusted with a leaf blower or dusted inside with a hairdryer or man's shaving brush. Prevent a shade from attracting too much dust by rubbing it gently with a fabric softening sheet to remove static electricity.

Silk or parchment shades that are sewn, or plastic shades, should be vacuumed or brushed, then washed briefly in cool or lukewarm water with mild detergent. A kneadable wallpaper cleaner like Absorbene can clean spots off parchment shades.

LIGHT BULBS

There is no need to go around checking to see if your light bulbs are dusty, but occasionally one may come to your attention. Make sure the power is off and the bulb is cool, then dust with a cloth or dampened sponge cloth.

If you're discarding burned-out fluorescent bulbs, wrap them first in several layers of newspaper, then step on them. Otherwise, they can explode and create a lot of problems.

LIGHT FIXTURE

Window cleaner solution works on glass light fixtures.

LOOFAH SPONGE

If it's growing brown spots, soak it in a solution of one cup vinegar and one quart water, then rinse it thoroughly.

MACRAME

To dry-clean it, rub on cornmeal with a nailbrush or other small brush, then brush off the excess. But if you're sure it's washable, use a gentle detergent or baby shampoo in cold water, scrub gently with a nail brush.

MENORAH

Spray it with a non-stick cooking spray and it'll be easier to clean after the holiday. Or point your blow dryer at it and let the wax melt off.

MIRROR

Use regular window cleaner or two tablespoons vinegar, ammonia, or denatured alcohol per quart of water.

Remove nicotine mist with rubbing alcohol on a cloth.

When cleaning **mirrored tiles,** avoid getting water or cleaner between the cracks. (If that happens over time, cover the spaces with wood molding strips. The wall will have a clean and different look.)

MODELS, PLASTIC

Since a dust cloth or a brush might ruin models, use a blow dryer held 6 to 8 inches away to gently blow off dust. Or put them outside, turn hose to "fine spray," and briefly hose them down.

NEEDLEWORK

If it's colorfast, wash with baby shampoo or a gentle detergent.

Dust it regularly, but don't rub the brush hard across the work or you'll damage the fibers.

Don't frame needlework under glass with glass touching the needlework; use a thick mat to separate them.

PAINTINGS, OIL

Give them an occasional light dusting, preferably with a clean, lint-free silk cloth or soft brush. Spot clean if necessary with a barely damp rag or a piece of white bread.

However, if the painting is worth a lot of money or simply valuable to you, take it to a professional. Even a soft dust cloth can snag on a piece of raised paint and cause a chip.

PEWTER

Never use a strong abrasive or leave acidic or salty foods sitting in pewter. And don't wash it in the dishwasher.

If dusting and washing with mild soap and water doesn't clean it, wipe it with leaves of cabbage. Or dampen cheesecloth, dip it into cigarette ashes; it will turn black as you rub but when rinsed will shine. Or use Extra Fine steel wool dipped in olive oil. Or mix whiting (a chalk) from the hardware or paint store and rubbing (denatured) alcohol to make a paste. Apply, let it dry, polish. After any of these treatments, wash, rinse, and dry.

Or use a commercial silver cleaner.

PIANO KEYS

Use white (non-gel) toothpaste and baking soda in equal parts or plain milk on ivory.

If keys are plastic, use an all-purpose cleaner. Pull gloves or old socks on your hands both to

PICTURE PERFECT

If you have a picture that's stuck to the glass, immerse the glass and photo in a pan of room-temperature water and keep testing until the photo pulls free. (Don't rush it!) Then let it air dry. Since most photo prints get a water bath during processing, there shouldn't be any damage, though this is not 100% guaranteed. Next time, use a cardboard mat around the photo to keep it away from the frame.

apply the cleaner and to wipe keys clean and dry.

PICTURE FRAME, WOOD

Pour a few drops of oil on a cloth and rub gently. Don't spray: Sprays may seep behind the glass and affect the painting or photograph.

PICTURE FRAME, GILT

Remove stains by rubbing gently with a cloth moistened with milk.

PICTURES AND PRINTS

Wipe on window cleaner gently. Sprayed cleaner may seep behind the glass to the painting or portrait below.

PLAYING CARDS

If sticky and soft, plastic-coated cards may be wiped with a baby wipe, then dried with a clean dust cloth. Or wipe them with fabric softener sheets. (Cards that are bent may straighten out after a very brief zap in the microwave.)

PLAYPEN, MESH

Mix 1 tablespoon mild dishwashing detergent, $3/4$ cup bleach, and 1 gallon hot water. Work outdoors if possible. Wear rubber gloves and slip a sock over them. Dip your hand in the cleaning solution and rub, then hose (or rinse) it clean. Or shake up upholstery shampoo, dip a sponge into the foam, wring it out and wipe the playpen.

PLEXIGLAS

Never clean it with a dry cloth. The cloth just rubs in the grit.

Liquid automatic dishwasher detergent in solution with water cleans without scratching the surface. Or try a pet store for a cleaner for Plexiglas fish tanks. Or find a Plexiglas windshield cleaner in a motorcycle shop.

Clear nail polish can fill in tiny nicks, but eventually Plexiglas scratches and must be replaced.

Sconce

If dripping wax has hardened in the narrow part of a sconce, melt it with a hair dryer and blot drippings away.

Shells

To clean and disinfect shells for your collection, soak overnight in 1 part bleach and two parts water.

Or boil for ten minutes with bleach added to the water.

Stuffed Toys

If the tag says "all new materials," a toy can be machine washed. Use regular or gentle detergent, fabric softener if desired. Select cold/gentle cycle, put the toy in the dryer on "Air Only" briefly, leave it out overnight if further drying is necessary.

If you will be machine-washing the toy, cover the toy "hair" with net, cheesecloth, a stocking, or a mesh bag tied closed. Put non-washable toys in the dryer on "Fluff" or "Air Only" to remove dust. Or rub in cornmeal, then brush it out.

For a stubborn stain, beat 1 quart warm water with 2 tablespoons or more dish soap until it foams. Then beat the foam only (without dipping beaters below foam level) until it's the consistency of meringue. Dip a dry brush into the foam and spot clean the item, a small spot at a time. Blot off excess moisture with a clean, dry towel. Air dry for 1 to 2 days, then "fluff" with a dry hairbrush, brushing first in one direction, then the other.

Don't use harsh cleaners or foam rug or upholstery cleaner on stuffed toys if the children are still at the age when they put items in their mouths.

Telephone

Isopropyl (rubbing) alcohol does the job. Put it in a spray bottle for easier application, but don't spray right into the holes.

TV

Never put a liquid (including a plant that needs watering) on the television set. And don't spray the screen clean, or the oil or water will go into parts where it shouldn't. (If you spill a liquid on the TV, keep the thing unplugged for a few days until it dries thoroughly.)

Wipe the screen with rubbing alcohol with a fabric softener sheet, which will help repel dust.

Dip a cloth or sponge into mild soap and water to wipe down plastic casings, or into Murphy's Oil Soap to clean wood casings.

Vase

If the vase is stained on the bottom or the inside, soak tea leaves in warm water, pour them into the vase, shake them around, pour them out, and rinse. Or let cold tea or vinegar stand in the vase overnight.

A cloudy glass vase should clear up if you pour in some automatic dishwasher detergent and fill it with water. Or fill it with water and drop in a denture tablet or two or a few teaspoons of ammonia (shake it around). Uncooked rice, beans, or sand in the vase along with the cleaning solution will help clean the surfaces. If these solutions don't work, try a commercial mineral and lime remover.

If other glassware has been etched in your dishwasher, wash your vases by hand or they may be etched, too.

VIDEO GAMES

Dust with a dry anti-static cloth or anti-static fabric softener sheets. If static electricity is building up, touch the game module to any metal object.

WASHING MACHINE

Clean the outside baked enamel surface with baking soda or liquid scouring cleaner on a damp sponge or cloth. If you apply car wax or appliance wax from time to time, it will be especially resistant to handprints.

To clean the inside and remove soap scum, run the machine through a rinse cycle with 2 cups of vinegar.

If clothes show rust marks, check the washing machine (or dryer) drum to see if it needs a coat of paint. (Paint store specialists can tell you which type to buy.)

• •

MOLD STORY: REMOVING MILDEW

For mildew on clothing, see Washing and Wearing.

In a perfect world, it would be easy to grow flowers and hard to grow mildew, but in our world the opposite is true.

Mold grows in damp, uninsulated attics, crawl spaces, drain systems, tubs, refrigerator drip pans, inside humidifiers and air conditioners, in ductwork—forced–air heating systems in particular—and foam rubber furnishings. And if there is any water damage in the house, mold spores are probably present.

While mildew loves dampness, it can also thrive in an airtight and underventilated building—particularly when there is a lot of cooking, a lot of toilets, and a lot of people.

If clothes dryers are properly vented and bathrooms have exhaust fans, mildew prob-

HOME-RELATED ALLERGENS

If you're one of the 30% of people who have an allergy to **mold** and **mildew,** you may have symptoms such as rashes, eye and nose irritation, nausea, and wheezing that is worse in spring and autumn.

Asthma, allergic pneumonia, allergic eczema (an itchy rash), contact dermatitis (itchy blisters), allergic rhinitis (sneezing, stuffy nose; watery, itching eyes), and sinusitis are all linked to mold and/or three other major groups of allergens:

Dust (including cotton lint, furniture fabrics, feathers, pillow stuffing), which causes rashes and rhinitis. New super vacuums are available that are specially designed to pick up dust mites.

Pets (mostly cats, also dogs, and even birds).

Miscellaneous (including paint fumes, chemical solutions, down, feathers, fiberglass curtains, kapok, and wool).

To reduce allergens in a room, seal it with weather-stripping around the door and clean it with a damp mop (to avoid spreading dust), and don't use wax (since it attracts dust). Avoid dust-catchers such as rugs, curtains, and venetian blinds, as well as mildew-breeders, such as wallpaper, and items that are both, such as wall hangings.

lems are reduced. It also helps to keep your furnace clean. If the problem is chronic, or you have an allergy problem, consult an expert, who can advise you about buying a dehumidifier and may recommend installing vapor barrier insulation in the basement.

Since mildew is especially common in **closets,** leave a low-wattage bulb burning and/or buy a desiccant (moisture remover) such as activated charcoal or similar product from your hardware dealer. Some disinfectants also prevent mold.

To remove the smell of mildew slowly but effectively, buy charcoal filter rocks used in fish tanks and pack them around the item, then leave in a sealed bag or box for a month—or until the odor is gone.

All of the following mixtures remove mildew but may harm some surfaces or cause colors to bleed, so always test on an inconspicuous surface first.

- Rubbing alcohol: mix half alcohol and half water
- Hydrogen peroxide: use 2 tablespoons per gallon
- Tri-sodium phosphate: use 4 to 6 tablespoons per gallon
- Chlorine bleach: use $1/2$ to 1 cup per gallon of water

If **books** are mildewed, vacuum or dust off loose mold. If books are damp, sprinkle cornstarch or talcum powder on the pages, leave it for several hours and brush off. Place a box of silica gel or some activated charcoal in the bookcase to prevent future mildew.

If **furniture** is mildewed, wipe off spores carefully so they don't fly elsewhere in the house. Mix a small amount of dishwashing detergent in water, apply sparingly (since water isn't good for wood), and wipe dry. If mildew remains, wipe with rubbing alcohol (testing first in an inconspicuous spot to make sure it will not harm the finish), then wash and dry again.

If **plastic shower curtain** or **other plastic item** (such as outdoor furniture cushion) is mildewed, scrub with a brush in warm water and soap or detergent or, if the item is bleachable, in the chlorine solution above. Rinse and dry. To prevent mildewing, pull the curtain along the rod after showering. Don't stack outdoor furniture cushions when they are damp.

If **upholstery, rugs,** or **mattresses** are mildewed, vacuum. Then sponge them with upholstery or rug shampoo or the alcohol solution above, first checking the label and testing in a hidden area to make sure the color will not run and the fabric will be unaffected. Wipe with a damp towel and spray with disinfectant, also testing before you apply it. Dry with a hair dryer, electric heater, or fan.

If you see white furry deposits or black spots on (bleach-tolerant) **wallpaper, outdoor siding, tile roof, brick, stucco,** or **patio,** wear a face mask and goggles and brush it off with a stiff brush. Mix $3/4$ cup liquid bleach with a gallon of water. Wet the surface with the bleach-water for 5 to 15 minutes but avoid applying in direct sun or the solution will evaporate too quickly. Rinse thoroughly, particularly aluminum window frames or unpainted gutters, which may corrode. *Do not use this mixture on unfinished wood.* If the problem persists you may need a commercial fungicide; follow the manufacturer's instructions. (Do not confuse mold with wet and dry rot. See p. 9.)

• •

ODORS: WHAT'S THAT SMELL?

I've mentioned that spraying pine oil around the house gives the impression you've been cleaning all day. It's also true that no amount of cleaning will impress anyone if the house smells bad. Nose news is bad news.

If you're lucky, removing an odor is no more complicated than removing its source. I once eliminated a horrible smell the minute I found a potato that had fallen behind the refrigerator and rotted. If the problem is more complicated, you can choose from a zillion different commercial odor removers—or get excellent results with some home remedies.

The least you need to know about odor removal:
- Everyday items that remove odor
- Solving common odor problems

Home Remedies

There are eight common household items that have excellent odor-removing properties. These include activated charcoal (from the hardware store), baking soda, cat box filler, crushed newspapers, coffee grounds (new or used, then dried), fabric softener sheets or liquid fabric softener, tomato juice, and vanilla extract. I've recommended different ones in different situations on the pages that follow, but in some cases one of the alternatives will work just as well. Try them before you go to a commercial remedy from the hardware store or supermarket.

Listerine or douching solution will remove the smell of urine (also other unpleasant strong odors), but since it may harm some finishes, test some in a hidden corner first. You can also make a potent odor-removing mixture by combining two tablespoons of citronella oil (from drug store) plus $1/2$ cup rubbing alcohol in a gallon of mop water.

Solving Common Odor Problems

ASHTRAYS

Cat box filler extinguishes the cigarette and absorbs the odor.

BEDDING

Sprinkle bedding, futon, or mattress with baking soda, borax, or a mixture of spices; leave overnight, then vacuum. Deep cleaning with an extraction machine (see Vacuum Cleaners on p. 32) may be necessary.

BABY BOTTLES

Eliminate sour milk smells from plastic bottles by filling the bottle with warm water and adding one teaspoon of baking soda. Shake well and let set overnight, then wash thoroughly.

CANISTER, WOODEN

Fill with crumpled newspaper or coffee grounds, seal for a couple of days. If odor isn't gone, repeat.

CAR

Place some activated charcoal, containers of coffee, or cat box filler in the trunk; fill ashtrays with baking soda or cat box filler. (Both will extinguish cigarettes and also deodorize.)

Carpet freshener, sprinkled on and vacuumed off as normal, is a good car freshener, especially in fall and winter. Or use a small cellophane pack of potpourri. Poke pinholes in it and the heat in the car will release the fragrance naturally.

If the car hits a skunk, saturate a cloth with vanilla extract and leave it in an open container in the back seat. Or de-skunk with a cup of dry mustard dissolved in a bucket of water. Use a mop to wipe the wheels and underbody, repeating if necessary.

CARPETING

Sprinkle on borax (in a pet-free household) or baking soda, leave for an hour, then vacuum.

CAUTION: Since baking soda works when slightly damp, it may get onto the lead ends of wiring and corrode your vacuum cleaner motor. Use the treatment only occasionally.

For bad odors, you may need to use an extraction machine (see Vacuum Cleaners).

TO MAKE THE AIR FRAGRANT

- Simmer a potful of stick cinnamon, orange peel, and whole cloves, add water as needed; place small bowls of vinegar around room.
- Put your favorite spice blend into a length of panty hose tied at both ends, then place it inside a heating vent.
- Add some spices (even kitchen spices that are too tired to use in food) to the vacuum cleaner bag.
- Add a couple of tablespoons of potpourri to a can of water and place it (or an adhesive air freshener) inside your heat register to spread moisture as well as scent throughout the house.
- My favorite way to make a house smell good is with a trick I call "faking baking." Sprinkle some cinnamon on a pan and warm it on the stove. But you'd better make sure you have some food on hand. This tends to make everyone hungry.

CIGARETTE SMOKE

If the odor is all around the room, dampen a dish towel with vinegar and wave it around the room. Small bowls of vinegar around the room will keep it deodorized, and filling the ashtrays with cat box filler will not only put out cigarettes but also will get rid of the odor.

If a small item (such as a book) is full of the odor of cigarette smoke, put it in a bag with a couple of fabric softener sheets. Seal and leave for several days.

A piece of clothing that smells smoky can be put in the dryer for 5 to 10 minutes with a couple of fabric softener sheets. The controls should be set to "Air Only" or "Cool."

CLOSET

Make sachets of cat box filler, or hang activated charcoal in mesh bags or old panty hose.

DOG

If he's run into a skunk, wash him with tomato juice or vinegar.

DRESSER DRAWER

Make sachets of cat box filler or line with fabric softener sheet.

GARBAGE PAIL

Pour a layer of cat box filler at the bottom.

KITCHEN

See general information beginning p. 132.

LAUNDRY

Pour some baking soda into the hamper if you're not going to get to the wash for a day or so.

MATTRESS

Sprinkle baking soda between the mattress and box springs and leave. Vacuum occasionally. If it's an old, musty mattress, sprinkle cat box filler on top, leave for a week, or wipe with a sponge dampened with vinegar. Or see p. 166.

MISCELLANEOUS SMALL ITEMS (SUCH AS A BOOK, A NEW LEATHER WALLET)

Place it in a plastic bag with one of the dry household deodorizers; seal and leave it for a week. If the odor is not gone, repeat the process.

PAINT

A couple of drops of vanilla extract in the can will make the paint odor go away.

THERMOS

See Canister, Wooden p. 167.

CAUSES OF "MYSTERY" ODORS

Anywhere. Roof leak may be wetting the insulation; check if roof needs repair.

Basement. If activated charcoal doesn't remove all odor, there's probably mildew growing. When you find it, use a half-and-half mixture of water and bleach to sponge it away. After a flood, you need professional help. Until it arrives, your best bet is to dry water-damaged items as quickly as possible.

Bathroom. Caulking around the tub may be cracked and need patching. Or the wall covering around the tub and shower may have pulled loose enough to allow moisture to seep in behind it.

After a Fire

To remove sooty odor from your clothes, make a mixture of half water and half Formula 409 (an all-purpose cleaner), then briefly spray light items, such as clothing, or soak heavy ones, such as towels. Then launder as usual.

Or add 1 cup washing soda, $1/4$ cup ammonia, and $1/2$ cup vinegar to the washload—and DON'T add bleach.

A pet who has been exposed to smoke should have his fur clipped close. Then, when he's exercised, he'll sweat it out. You can also wash him down with a paste of baking soda and water, vinegar water, or plain tomato juice (wait fifteen minutes before rinsing).

PART 4
$\mathcal{W}$ASHING AND WEARING
SO CLOTHES LOOK GOOD

I discovered the quickest solution to the laundry issue once my first book hit the best-seller list. The minute I had extra cash, I started dry-cleaning everything. Fortunately for everyone except the dry cleaner, that phase didn't last very long. Not only is it expensive, it's hard on clothes.

Once you've found the "On" switch and figured out where to put the detergent, you've mastered the basics of machine washing. It's a lot easier than driving a car. If you're happy with the way your wash has been turning out, stick with your system.

But if you've got stain problems; or if the wash is a little dingy; or if you'd like to know exactly when to add the bleach or whether to use fabric softener, the answers are all here, along with information about drying, ironing, and mending and caring for special possessions like shoes, bags, and coats.

• •

LAUNDERING

The least you need to know about laundering:
• What needs special care
• Sorting the wash
• Setting the right controls
• Selecting the cleaning agents
• Spot and stain removal

Getting Organized
WHEN TO DRY-CLEAN

Despite the name, dry cleaning involves liquid. There is a precedent for something being dry and liquid at the same time—think of a martini. In this case, the process is called "dry" because the liquid involved is waterless, usually a solvent called perchlorethylene ("perk") plus detergent. During the dry cleaning, the perk-detergent combination passes continuously through the clothes, dissolving dirt and stains, which are left behind in a filter.

Unlike water, perk won't cause dyes to bleed or run, is unlikely to cause shrinkage, and won't wash out details like pleats, so you should probably dry-clean clothes when the dye is questionable, if you are concerned about shrinking, or if the detailing is delicate or special (like beading).

On the other hand, dry cleaning creates

some problems. The chemicals can scratch and bruise fibers. Though the heat of dry cleaning doesn't cause fabrics to shrink, shrinkage may occur if there is moisture in the machine. And being tossed around the drum of the dry cleaner can stress fabrics, especially old clothes already weakened by age, to the point where they fall apart. With very fragile clothes, you may be willing to go to the expense of having your clothes professionally dry-cleaned by hand rather than machine.

Always dry-clean both parts of a two-piece outfit together, even if only either the pants or the jacket needs cleaning. Since subtle color changes can occur during the process, what started as a black suit may wind up as a black suit jacket and a grayish-black pair of pants.

As a rule of thumb, clothes should be dry-cleaned as little as possible. Clothing that is only wrinkled may not need cleaning at all. If you don't want to iron it yourself, you can pay to have the job done. Many cleaners are willing to press a garment without cleaning it, which may be easier on your budget and is certainly easier on the clothing. On the other hand, don't have something pressed that is soiled, because the heat may turn invisible stains brown or "set" the stain into the fabric—probably permanently.

If the smell of solvent is noticeable the minute you go into the shop, you may be dealing with a second-rate operation. There should be no solvent odor remaining in any clothes that are properly dry-cleaned. On the other hand, a lot of fancy dresses hanging in the window is one sign of a good dry cleaner. Anybody should be able to clean a blazer; a beaded, pleated gown is a challenge.

You can also expect a good cleaner to press a fabric without leaving dents from the buttons, repair small tears and rips, and remove and resew any fancy trim (or shoulder pads) that might be damaged during cleaning.

The problem is that too many people don't know what to expect from the cleaner. If your clothes come back with a button missing or a shoulder pad ruined, that isn't normal, and you should complain about it. I've had more clothes ruined by cleaners than by my own carelessness, and believe me, that took some doing on the part of the cleaners!

Now services are springing up that pick up clothes from the workplace, and I'm all for this. It's not only convenient, but you've got might in numbers; if you're not getting good services, you and your co-workers can threaten to take all your business elsewhere.

Of course, it's not always the cleaner's fault. Sometimes the manufacturer is to blame if the garment falls apart right away. When this happens, bring the thing back to the store. They don't want to lose your business, so generally they'll take it back. If enough stuff starts going back to the manufacturers, maybe they'll wise up. You will, however, run into salespeople looking at you as if you're nuts when you complain that your $200 sweater fell apart during the first cleaning. Sometimes I'm ready to bag the whole wardrobe thing and just start wearing combat clothing—low-maintenance and very durable.

WOMEN WHO WASH TOO MUCH

A friend of mine showed me a survey of her twentieth reunion class. "What about your life has most surprised you?" inspired one answer that stood out in my mind. "I never expected to spend so much time doing laundry." The reason laundry takes more time than any other household job is not because it's so hard to do, but because we do so much of it.

I believe that we all spend more time at the washing machine than necessary. Many things wind up in the machine because it was easier to crumple them up and drop them in the hamper than to put them away properly. They'll have to be folded or hung up eventually; the washing is an unnecessary step. Not only that, it's hard on the clothes. But I can't imagine that we'll break the washing habit unless water-metering becomes universal and water costs a lot.

SETTING UP THE LAUNDRY ROOM

If you're having a house built or remodeled, consider putting the washer and dryer on the main level, or upstairs, rather than in the basement. It took architects all these years to discover that the ideal spot for the laundry room is on the same floor as the bedrooms. That's where your clothes, your bedding, and your towels—the bulk of the wash—comes from and must go back to. Now they're putting laundries in places that used to be used as dressing rooms.

Even if you're living in an apartment, or space is tight, you can usually fit a stackable washer/dryer setup into a closet. (See the Equipping section for more information.) Create a mini-laundry center by adding a compact ironing board that folds into its own small "closet" (surface-hung or set into the wall) or hangs over the back of a bedroom door. Some door-hung ironing board holders also have a compartment that holds the iron.

In a closet laundry room, you probably won't have a spot to let clothes drip dry, and the bathroom is the obvious solution. But clothes hanging on the shower rod may leave puddles on the floor. Adding a second rod over the middle of the tub (either hung from the ceiling or running from wall to wall) adds extra space and keeps drips in the tub.

If the laundry room can't be placed on the second floor, see if you can figure out a way to put in a laundry chute. The idea is to toss the dirty clothes into a hamper on the second floor so they fall directly into a laundry basket in the basement. I would imagine some people would find this chute idea appealing even if they never saw the clothes again.

One consolation for working out of a basement laundry room—rather than one on the main floor—is that you will probably have a lot of working space. Build shelves to hold your laundry supplies and put up hooks or a rod to hold clothes that are drip drying or freshly ironed. Hang a bulletin board to post the care tag from any garment that needs special attention or tack up buttons that come with new clothes. Poke in a couple of threaded needles, stick up a couple of packs of iron-on patches, and attach a few shirt buttons with a couple of straight pins so you can make quick repairs before the clothing goes into the wash or back into the closet.

In a basement, you may have room for racks that hold large, open laundry hampers (like those you see at a professional cleaning operation). Ideally, the family can bring down their soiled clothes and sort them into darks and lights. If you're in a one-story house, rolling carts like the ones you see in commercial Laundromats are great to collect dirty clothes and deliver clean ones.

IF YOU USE COIN-OPERATED MACHINES

Using a Laundromat in a shopping center or the machines in your apartment house basement differs from using a home laundry primarily because the machines may not offer the wide variety of features and can't be used for a long presoaking. (Of course, you also meet more interesting people in a Laundromat.)

The care information is generally the same. If you sort your clothes at home and take a small container of the detergent (rather than lugging a giant-sized box, or buying the detergent in small boxes at high prices at the Laundromat), you'll save time and money. Keep the detergent container in a small bag along with the prewash spotters, enzyme spot removers, and other items you normally use—along with a stash of coins—so you can grab them quickly on the way.

So as not to use several dryers, you may

combine clothing of various weights. This means paying close attention to the timing and stopping the machine once or twice during the cycle to remove lightweight items when they're ready. Overdrying can set in wrinkles and damage the fibers.

Don't forget to take hangers for shirts and other items that should be hung rather than folded. Also, rather than crushing folded items back into a laundry bag, bring along a lightweight carton or two, or large basket, to transport the fresh laundry back to your house.

Also carry along a small sewing kit (needles, thread, extra shirt buttons). If you spot something that needs a repair while you're sorting through your clothes, you can mend it while you're waiting for your laundry to wash and dry.

Care Labels

Most clothes (and other fabric items, like pillows and stuffed toys) made and sold in the U.S. have permanent care labels attached. They tell you the fiber content of the material and how to wash it.

When the label says *"Use a mild detergent,"* buy a gentle detergent meant for cold-water washing of delicates. A regular (all-purpose) detergent may cause light spotting, especially on pastel cottons. (If this happens, soak the item in a solution of four parts water and one part regular detergent. That should lighten the whole garment and even out the color.)

On the next page is the American Apparel Manufacturers Association's interpretation of the care labels. Even though some of this information seems self-evident, I think it's worth noting since a lot of us (me included) don't seem to follow instructions correctly. I'm sure it would help if we actually read them, but it would also help if they were better written. I've added my two cents' worth where I thought it counted.

Even when you carefully follow instructions *your wash may not turn out perfectly because the labels do not tell you everything you need to know.* For example, you will not always be warned that:

• The garment may shrink if washed.

• You cannot use chlorine bleach on colored items.

• When it says "Hand wash," you should use lukewarm water.

On the other hand, I have found that some of the "rules" can be broken without causing any problems. Sometimes manufacturers advise you to dry-clean or hand launder an item rather than machine wash it so that you don't run into any problems that might cause you to complain to them. Whether the dry cleaning or hand laundering costs you time or money is not really the manufacturer's concern.

Sometimes when you wash clothing contrary to instructions you'll just lose some "body," or stiffness in the fabric. The bigger danger is that the color will run. Knowing that people washed silk for centuries before dry cleaning was invented, I didn't understand why so many silks were marked "Dry-Clean Only." Then I learned that many of them are dipped in vegetable dyes, which are safe in dry cleaning solvents but may bleed or fade during washing. Always do a colorfastness test as described in the box on p. 178. If the garment fails the test, follow the washing instructions for silk on p. 176.

If it appears to be colorfast, sometimes I machine wash an item that says "Dry-Clean" or "Hand Wash," using a delicate cycle and cool water. I wash it inside out and let it dry flat so the color won't run or streak. (If it does, and the garment was supposed to be washable, I return it to the store.) If it's not very expensive, I figure the washing risk is worth taking. Since I never intended to spend a lot of money keeping the garment dry-cleaned and wearable, I don't fall apart even if it does. If, on the other hand, it stands up to machine washing, then I'm ahead of the game.

TRANSLATIONS FROM THE CARE LABELS

MACHINE-WASHABLE CLOTHES

When label reads: | **It means:**

Machine wash | Wash, bleach, dry, and press by any customary method including commercial laundering or dry cleaning (but solvents used in dry cleaning may cause some dyes to bleed, and soil may be redeposited, especially on white cottons).

Home launder only | Same as above but don't use commercial laundering.

No chlorine bleach | Do not use chlorine bleach. Oxygen bleach is okay.

No bleach | Do not use any type of bleach.

Bleach when needed | Oxygen or chlorine bleach okay.

Cold wash/ Cold rinse | Use cold water for hand laundry or cold washing machine settings.

Warm wash/ Warm rinse | Use warm water for hand laundering or warm washing machine settings.

Hot wash | Use hot water for hand laundering or hot washing machine settings. Any rinse temperature okay.

No spin | Remove wash load before final spin cycle.

Delicate cycle/ Gentle cycle | Use appropriate machine setting or wash by hand.

Durable press cycle/Permanent press cycle | Use appropriate machine setting or use warm wash, cold rinse, and short spin cycle.

Wash separately | Wash alone or with similar colors.

NON-MACHINE-WASHABLE CLOTHES

When label reads: | **It means:**

Hand wash, Lukewarm water. | Launder only by hand in (hand-comfortable) May be bleached. May be dry-cleaned.

Hand wash only | Same as above, but do not dry-clean.

Hand wash separately | Hand wash alone or with similar colors.

No bleach | Do not use any kind of bleach.

Damp wipe | Surface clean with damp cloth or sponge.

DRYING

When label reads: | **It means:**

Tumble dry | Dry in tumble dryer at specified setting— "High," "Medium," "Low, or "No Heat."

Tumble dry/ Remove promptly | Same as above, but if you have no cool-down cycle, remove item at once when tumbling stops.

Drip dry | Hang wet and allow to dry with hand shaping only. (Do not wring.)

Line dry | Hang damp and allow to dry.

No wring | Hang dry, drip dry, or dry flat only.

No twist | Handle gently to prevent wrinkles.

Dry flat | Lay garment on flat surface.

DECODING THE INTERNATIONAL FABRIC CARE SYMBOLS

Colors

Red	Do not perform this action.
Amber	Exercise caution.
Green	Go ahead.
Blue or black	No significance.

Washing symbol

Green	95	Machine wash, hot water.
Green	60	Machine wash, warm water.
Amber	40	Machine wash, gentle.
Amber		Hand wash, lukewarm water.
Red		Do not wash.

Bleaching symbol

Amber	Cl	Chlorine bleach okay.
Red		Do not chlorine bleach.

Drying symbol

Green		Tumble dry, "Medium" to "High"
Amber		Tumble dry, "Low."
Green		Line dry.
Amber		Hang wet to drip dry.
Amber		Dry on flat surface.

Ironing or pressing symbol

Green		Maximum setting of "Cotton and Linen."
Amber		Maximum setting of "Medium."
Amber		Maximum setting of "Low."
Red		Do not press or iron.

Dry Cleaning symbol

Green		Okay to dry-clean.
Amber		Okay to dry-clean, but tumble dry "Low."
Red		Do not dry-clean.
Green or Amber	P	Use any solvent except tri-chloropethylene. If the circle is underlined, meaning "sensitive," reduce cycle and/or heat.
Green or Amber	A	Use any solvent.
Green or Amber	F	Use petroleum or fluorocarbon only. If the circle is underlined, meaning "sensitive," reduce cycle and/or heat.

SOURCE: ADAPTED FROM A CHART PROVIDED BY THE NEIGHBORHOOD CLEANING ASSOCIATION.

Fabric Content

In addition to labeling garments with washing instructions, manufacturers also must list the fabric content. Many fabrics today are blends (such as cotton/polyester, wool/acrylic). There are two rules of thumb about blends.

Clean a blend just the way you would treat the predominating fiber. If a shirt is 60% cotton and 40% polyester, treat it as 100% cotton. If it's 70% acrylic, 30% wool, treat it as 100% acrylic.

175

For stain removal, the opposite is true. Spot-treat a blend as you would handle the most delicate fiber. Even if only 10 % of the garment is rayon, use the procedure recommended for rayon.

NATURAL FABRICS

There are only four "natural" fabrics: cotton, linen, silk, and wool.

Someone who was allergic to some synthetics asked me how to tell if a bolt of cloth she had was natural or not. I told her to take a tiny swatch of the fabric and hold a match to it. Natural fibers char; synthetics bead up. I don't recommend holding a flame to clothing, obviously, but a home sewer might be interested in this little trick.

Cotton fabrics include denim, corduroy, and percale (as in sheets). Cotton is durable and absorbent, but it wrinkles, so it is often combined with other fabrics. It can be machine washed and dried. Use all-purpose detergent and follow temperature instructions on fabric. Fabric softeners will improve the texture and reduce wrinkling but affect absorbency, so don't use them when you're washing towels or diapers, and don't use them often on other items. Frequent bleaching may eventually damage fibers. Use a hot iron and spray starch or spray sizing. Cotton should be prewashed and preshrunk before home sewing.

Linen, which (like cotton) wrinkles, is often combined with other fabrics or given a special wrinkle-resistant finish. It can be dry-cleaned or machine washed and dried. Chlorine bleach can be used on white linen—if manufacturer's instructions say so. Press with a hot iron while still slightly damp.

Silk of a stiffer quality, which has more threads, has a better chance of being laundered than silk that feels flimsy and wrinkles easily. I never launder the latter. It's impossible to iron, and there's often a problem with the dyes. Certain dyes will bleed or fade during washing (and will even be degraded by perspiration, perfume, and deodorants). Test for colorfastness before attempting to machine or hand launder silk. If the label doesn't say to machine launder, use a protein hair shampoo and don't twist or pull. Handle the silk gently and hang it to dry. To spot-treat washable white or light-colored silk, use oxygen bleach or a mix of one part hydrogen peroxide and eight parts water.

Wool shrinks and mats at high temperatures. Dry-clean all wool unless it's specifically marked "Washable"; then wash it by hand unless the label specifically says "Machine Washable."

MANMADE FABRICS

The opposite of natural fabrics is not unnatural fabrics, it is manmade fabrics. The early versions of some of these synthetics did in fact feel unnatural, like wet suits disguised as streetwear. They wore like iron, which was nice, but they retained heat like iron, too, which is a useful quality for cooking a pot roast but not in summer clothing. Fortunately, synthetics have become more attractive without losing any of their hardiness.

While there seem to be an endless number of synthetic fabrics, there are actually only several generic types commonly used in clothing. Here's some information on each one as well as a short list of common brand names:

Acetate. Brand names include Chromspun and Estron. Acetate is often combined with satin and taffeta. It resists moths, mildew, and shrinkage.

Dry-clean acetate unless the label says "Hand Washable"; if so, use warm water and gentle detergent. Dry it on a line away from heat or direct sun.

Iron acetate while damp, on the coolest setting, either on the wrong side or with a pressing cloth on the right side.

Acrylic. Brand names include Acrilan and Orlon. Acrylic is often blended with wool. It is soft, bulky, and wool-like.

Hand or machine wash and dry-clean acrylic. It tends to pill. Do not wash acrylics with towels, corduroy, or other rough-textured material. Turn the garment inside out before washing. Dry it in the machine on "Low."

Iron an acrylic garment on the moderate setting. Use steam.

Pretreat oil-based stains with a prewash spot and stain remover (such as Shout or Spray 'n Wash). Other stains will be removed by your regular detergent.

Modacrylic. Soft and bulky. Modacrylic is used in stuffed toys, fake fur, etc.

Machine wash it in warm water, on the gentle cycle; use regular detergent. Tumble dry this fabric on "Low."

Iron it on the cool setting.

Nylon. Brand names include Antron and Cantrece. Nylon is strong, but lightweight. It is often combined with spandex. Whites are very likely to yellow. Avoid buying them.

Machine wash sturdy items made of nylon and hand wash delicate items or put them in the machine in a mesh bag. Follow the manufacturer's instructions. Use warm water and regular detergent. Don't combine white nylon items with colored clothes. Dry nylon in the dryer on "Low," or hang it to dry.

Iron nylon garments on the cool setting.

Olefin. Used primarily as filling.

Machine wash Olefin in warm water; use regular detergent. Tumble dry on the lowest setting.

Ironing is not recommended since Olefin may melt.

Polyester. Brand names include Dacron, Fortrel, and Trevira. Polyester is used for clothes and sheets. It resists wrinkles and abrasion.

Dry-clean or machine wash polyester on the warm setting. Use regular detergent. Due to pilling, use the same precautions as with acrylic. Oil-based stains can be treated with a prewash spot and stain remover (such as Shout, Spray 'n Wash), or you can rub an all-purpose detergent or dishwashing liquid into the spot. Dry polyester items in the machine on the lowest setting, or air dry them. Overdrying will cause shrinkage over time.

Iron polyester on the moderate setting or use steam.

Rayon. Brand names include Zantrel. Rayon is strong but gets flimsy when wet. It is soft, easy to dye, and drapes well.

Dry-clean or wash rayon garments by hand. If you wash, use lukewarm water and gentle detergent. If the item is labeled "Machine Washable," use warm water, the gentle cycle, and a gentle detergent. Drip dry.

Iron rayon on the medium setting while the fabric is damp.

CAUTION: Rayon often needs sizing (a stiffener) because the fabric doesn't have much "body." When a sized-rayon item is stained by a water-based substance, the water may interact with the sizing to cause spots that are difficult to remove.

Spandex. Brand name is Lycra. Spandex can be stretched 500% without breaking— *who couldn't love a product like this?*—and it's more durable than rubber. It is always used in a blend.

Hand or machine wash spandex. Use warm water and regular detergent. Do not wash white spandex with any colored garments. Do not use chlorine bleach on any spandex. Drip dry or machine dry at the lowest temperature.

Iron spandex at the lowest setting while damp.

Newer, less common generic synthetics are **aramid, PBI, sulfar,** and **vinyon.**

Loading the Machine
How To Sort

The old books told you to sort first by color, then by fabric, then by amount of soiling (in order to avoid bleeding), then by water temperature, and finally by the proper strength of detergent. It seems to me that by doing this most people would wind up with six different piles of wash, each with one item in it.

As you've probably discovered, if you put a mixed load in the wash, use all-purpose detergent and a cold water setting, then tumble it all dry at a low temperature, the clothes will come out clean. But you may wind up with socks, underwear, and towels dyed to match and/or dingy clothes. Both dark dyes and soil may dull either white or colored clothes. In some cases, sorting is necessary.

Don't mix these combinations:

• **Light and white clothes with dark ones.** Why? Because all light colors, and particularly colored and white synthetics, will pick up dark dyes.

• **Chlorine-bleachable light and white clothes with non-bleachables.** Why? Because if you add chlorine bleach to the wash, the other items may fade or streak.

• **Very dirty (oil-stained, muddy) clothes with lightly soiled ones.** Why? Dirty ones should be presoaked and washed in hot water if the fabric can take it.

• **Clothing marked "Wash Separately" with whites or differently colored clothes.** Why? Because the color will probably run. Wash it with similar colors.

• **Sweat shirts, chenilles, and new towels with permanent press and corduroys.** Why? Because the former are lint depositors, and the latter pick up lint.

A BUTTONED-UP WASH

Button buttons, zip zippers, and hook hooks so they don't get ripped off or snag onto anything

WHAT'S COLORFAST AND WHAT'S NOT

Colorfast is a word that's been around since 1954, and the only word I can think of that has caused more problems than this one is the word *relationship* (as in, "Are we having a relationship?") Colorfast dyes do not fade or bleed when chlorine bleach is added. Jeans, for example, are *not* colorfast. Read this before you ruin a wash:

• Testing for colorfastness (bleachability): Mix 1 tablespoon chlorine bleach and $1/4$ cup warm water and dab on a drop with a cotton swab in an inconspicuous area. Wait for one minute, blot dry. If there is no color change, chlorine bleaching is safe. Otherwise wash item separately. Test all colors and any trim.

• Silks are a special case, since vegetable dyes in some foreign-made silks are very unstable. They won't stand up to bleach, and even plain water may cause them to run. Wet an inside seam with water and rub a white handkerchief against the spot, or dunk a hidden corner in cool water, and if it runs—or if you don't even want to take this risk—take the garment to the dry cleaner. Otherwise follow washing instructions for silk, p. 176.

• Wash questionable items separately the first time. If color shows up in the wash or rinse water, continue to wash item separately until it doesn't.

• To set color: You can make a colored fabric colorfast by soaking it for an hour in a mix of $1/2$ cup vinegar, $1/2$ tablespoon of salt, and $1/2$ gallon of water. If the rinse water shows color, repeat the process. Use this only on a single-colored fabric or madras. Other multicolored items should be dry-cleaned.

else. Tie belts so they don't get all tangled up or sucked into the land of lost socks.

Repairmen tell me that those odd socks often turn up in the outlet valve. To avoid this, pack small items at the bottom of the tub, heavy items on top. In the notions section of a department store, you can find circular plastic gizmos that hold socks by pairs. Saves them from disappearing and saves time matching socks. Alternatively, wash socks in individual drawstring mesh bags, a separate bag (or two, for light and dark socks) for each person in the house.

Sock Gizmo

Mesh bags also save panty hose and lingerie from being ripped during machine agitation.

Sweaters, sweatsuits, corduroy, and other clothing that might pill should be washed inside out.

Check pockets for stray crayons, pens, or tissues.

Repair little rips and replace loose buttons before you do the wash. The rip will get worse and the button will be swept away.

Size of Load

Never cram the wash into the machine. It needs room to be agitated—just like humans.

Overloading the machine interferes with proper circulation. Clothing near the central agitator gets beaten up, but what's on the edges doesn't move at all. There should be enough water moving around to carry the dirt away.

Washing Temperatures

These are the usual guidelines, but always check the care label:

Hot water (130°–150° F.) is appropriate for very soiled or greasy clothes, diapers, whites that are being bleached, other whites and light cottons.

MARKED FOR TREATMENT

Put a basketful of colored clothespins near the hamper and make it a habit to snap one onto any wash item that's badly spotted or needs some kind of special care so it can be treated before it goes into the machine. Otherwise, the stain may set in.

Warm water (100°–110° F.) is recommended for wash and wear, light and moderately soiled permanent press, dark colors, moderately soiled wash, some washable wools, some woven or knit synthetics.

But you can use cold water (80°–100° F.) for any lightly soiled wash, bright colors, fragile items, and colors that might bleed. The water shouldn't be ice cold, however. Washing isn't effective if the water is below 80° F.

Use cold rinse water routinely. It saves energy, prevents permanent press clothing from wrinkling, and makes ironing easier.

Length and Strength of Cycle

Dirtiest clothes may need the longest cycle, 10 to 12 minutes. A normal cycle is 6 to 8 minutes, and lightly soiled clothes may need only 4 to 6. Your machine can probably be set for "Normal" for virtually all washes, but it may have cycles for "Gentle" (for delicate fabrics and knits) and/or "Permanent Press."

Laundry Products

Soaps and Detergents

Though you may use the words interchangeably, soap and detergent aren't the same thing. Soap is made from fat and alkali. In soft water, soap will do a good job of washing away soil. But in hard water, it will react with the minerals and leave a residue.

How do you know what kind of water you

have? You probably have hard water if you have rings around the tub, soaps and shampoos don't lather easily, there's white residue around faucets, and fabrics feel stiff after laundering (though this can be due to other problems; see Stiffness, Scratchiness, p. 193). See the box below for a simple test.

Detergents work in either kind of water. By surrounding and holding the dirt, they also keep it from being redeposited on your load. That's why you will find only a few soaps—and many detergents—on the supermarket shelves.

TEST FOR WATER SOFTNESS

To a pint of hot water add a teaspoon of laundry detergent and shake the mixture. If you get a lot of sudsing, and the suds remain for a few minutes, the water is soft. If there are few or no suds, and if the bubbles break up quickly, you've got hard water. A professional tester—call the Department of Health to find out how to locate one—will give you the results in terms of grains per gallon (a measure of calcium carbonate): soft or slightly hard water has $3^1/_2$ grains, moderately hard from $3^1/_2$ to $10^1/_2$, and very hard water $10^1/_2$ grains or more.

Detergents have two key ingredients, surfactants and builders. Surfactants dissolve dirt and come in hundreds of types. Builders, such as phosphate, soften the water to make surfactants work better. The most effective detergents for stain removal purposes contain phosphates, but many states ban them for environmental reasons since phosphates encourage the growth of algae and make water unsuitable for swimming, boating, fishing, and drinking.

Some brands of powdered detergents come with and without phosphates, but there is none in liquid detergents. To compensate for the lack, some powders use washing soda and other ingredients. Some liquids use alternative

DETERGENTS

Type	Comments
Super Concentrates	Newest. You use smaller amount of the product but product costs more. Still, I find the small box convenient.
Powders	Fine for general wash. Good for ground-in dirt and clay.
Liquids	Also all-purpose. Good for laundering and for pre-treating spots (just rub a little into the problem area; keep a plastic mustard dispenser filled with detergent for easy application). Particularly good on foods, grease, and oils.
Combinations	Detergent plus fabric softener or detergent plus color-safe bleach (I think separate products do a better job).
Light Duty Liquids and Powders	For hand or machine washable, delicates, baby clothes, lightly soiled clothing.
Dishwashing Liquid	For dishes and also for hand washables. *Not for machine use.*

water softeners such as sodium citrate. These detergents perform less well in hard water, so you may want to add a water softener to get more sudsing (refer to p. 183). Some health store brands of detergents claim to contain surfactants that are better ecologically than others.

Detergents may also contain non-chlorine bleach; fabric softeners; enzymes for stain removal and perfumes for fragrance, either of which can cause allergies; and optical brighteners. Brighteners convert part of the invisible light that comes from the sun or fluorescent bulbs into visible light, so fabrics glow a little, though in incandescent light you won't notice. (Too bad—such a harmless way to get a little glow on.)

Most of us choose the detergent we're used to or whichever one is on sale. From the charts above and on p. 180, you can see that you have a variety of acceptable options.

How Much Cleaning Product to Use

Manufacturers tell you how much detergent to use based on a 5- to 7-pound load, moderate soil, moderately hard water, and an average water volume of about 17 gallons for a top loader and 8 gallons for a front loader.

Read the instructions. Products are concentrated differently, so even though products may appear similar, you may need different

amounts. You may also need more product if you have a heavily soiled or large load or less for a lightly soiled or small load. Since manufacturers change the formulas for their products occasionally, the instructions may change even on a familiar product.

Cutting down on the amount of detergent a manufacturer calls for may decrease its effectiveness. However, adding extra detergent doesn't mean your wash will get cleaner and may in fact cause a problem in your machine.

Laundry Helpers

The greatest laundry helper is a person who comes in and does it for you. But here I mean solutions you can add to the detergent.

Bleaches. Bleaches brighten and whiten fabrics and lighten stains by converting soil into colorless, soluble particles that can be easily removed by detergents and carried away in the wash water. There are two types of bleach: chlorine bleach and oxygen (or color-safe) bleach. See the chart on p. 182 for bleaching options.

CAUTION: Never mix chlorine bleach with ammonia. A deadly gas is created.

Fabric Softeners. Detergents rinse out of fibers so thoroughly that they can leave clothes feeling scratchy, and dryers cause a static charge to build up, especially in synthetics and permanent press. To eliminate both those problems—to soften fabrics and remove the charge—you need a fabric softener.

Softeners are waxy materials related to soap that coat laundry with chemicals that lubricate and humidify. Lubricated fibers slide past each

CHLORINE BLEACH

What it does:	Deodorizes, sanitizes, cleans. Boosts cleaning power of detergents.
Use for:	Whites and colorfast clothing only.
How much to use:	Add it full strength or diluted, whichever the label recommends. Extra-large capacity machine: $1\frac{1}{2}$ cups. Normal machine: 1 cup. Add an additional $\frac{1}{4}$ cup per load for heavily soiled wash. Hand wash: $\frac{1}{8}$ cup to 2 gallons sudsy water.
When to add it:	As machine fills with water, pour it in with detergent, then add clothes after agitation begins. To get brighter results: add detergent, then clothes, then add bleach (diluted in I quart water) once clothes have begun agitation. Never pour bleach directly onto fabric.
Why:	Adding bleach early may destroy enzymes and fluorescent whiteners in the detergent. But if you add it after the wash cycle, it may not be completely removed during the rinse.
Which brand to choose:	Not all bleaches are the same. Some disintegrate faster than others; better bleaches have a filtering system that removes impurities that cause this problem. The quality of generic brands varies.
Not for:	Colored clothes, silk, wool, mohair, spandex, leather.
Important:	Bleach works almost immediately and the effects don't last long. Leaving a garment to soak in bleach overnight won't make it whiter than if you left it only 15 minutes, but it may damage fibers. I have a unique product, Bleach Booster, that doubles the effect of bleach and helps it work into fibers even faster so it does less damage.

OXYGEN (COLOR-SAFE) BLEACH

What it does:	Brightens colors. Keeps whites white. Only occasionally restores whiteness to dingy clothes; try putting garment in lukewarm water and oxygen bleach for 24 hours; and then rinse with vinegar and water (one tablespoon to one quart).
Use for:	Any colored fabric, unbleachable whites.
When to add:	Before clothes are put in machine. *Don't pour it on wet clothes.*
Water temperature:	Most effective in warm to hot water.

other, so they don't wrinkle, and won't mat down, so they feel fluffy. Humidified fibers don't retain a charge.

You buy fabric softeners in one of several forms. As **liquids**, they're usually diluted and added during the rinse cycle. **Sheets** of fiber or foam impregnated with softener can be tossed into the dryer, where heat will release it. You can also buy **detergent-softener combina-tions**. Liquid softeners are most effective, combinations the least. Follow instructions carefully.

CAUTION: If a small load with a softener sheet or liquid softener is dried at a high temperature, or if fabric softener is poured directly on clothes, it may cause staining. Instructions for removing these stains is in the section on stain removal that follows.

What used to be a common problem—fabrics became less absorbent over time—has been almost eliminated with the new formulas. But over time, the waxy coating of the softeners may make laundry dingy, and despite the claims, I don't think they're great protection against stains.

Some fabric softeners may reduce the effectiveness of flame retardants on certain fabrics, such as children's sleepwear. Also, they may leave greasy-type stains on fabrics. Remove the spots by rubbing them with a bar of soap, then putting the item back through the laundry.

My recommendation is that you use fabric softeners only occasionally, not with every washload.

Starches, Finishes, and Sizings. If you want your garment to have more "body" and soil resistance and be easier to iron, use a starch, finish, or sizing in powder, liquid, or spray form. Starches are good on cottons and cotton blends, while fabric finishes and sizings are preferable for synthetics.

Bluing. Blue coloring added to wash or rinse. May be an ingredient in other laundry products. Countereffects yellowing of white fabrics.

Water Softeners. "Hard water" that contains calcium and magnesium interferes with the effectiveness of detergent, destroys the effectiveness of flame retardant, and may leave a residue called washing film on the wash load. Remove it by soaking clothes or towels in a

---

MAYBE YOUR WASH NEEDS AN EXTRA FEEDING

• Black cottons or lingerie faded? Add bluing, strong coffee, or tea (2 cups) to the rinse water. They'll turn from brownish black to black. (And in the future, be gentler to black cottons by washing them with Ivory Flakes plus only a small amount of detergent).

• Permanent press items are limp? Add 1 cup of powdered milk to the final rinse water (one-half cup liquid starch or 1 cup Epsom salts). Then turn last rinse to wash and wear cycle.

• Polished cotton lost sheen and body? Add a packet of plain gelatin to the final rinse of polished cottons.

---

plastic container with a mixture of water (one gallon) and vinegar (one cup).

Some detergents have added water softeners that may be listed on the box as sodium carbonate (washing soda, sal soda, or soda ash).

You can add a water conditioning product, generally a powder, along with the detergent to the rinse water. Or just use a cup of borax. It will soften the water and freshen the wash as well.

Or you may decide to add a water softener to your water tank to deactivate the minerals or remove them completely. (Information about testing for water softness is on p. 180 and about buying water softeners is in the Equipping section, p. 31.)

● ●

STAIN REMOVAL
Marking Clothes for Pretreating

Since heat sets some stains, it is best if you deal with them before the soiled item is laundered and machine dried. If you can't treat the stain immediately, tie a loose knot in clothing that

---

STARCH SUBSTITUTES

• If you can't find powdered starch, stir 1/2 cup cornstarch into a cup of cold water. Add 2 quarts of boiling water for heavy starch, 4 for medium, 6 for light. Dip clothes into starch, dry, sprinkle with warm water and fold lightly. Let stand 1–2 hours before ironing.

• Want to "starch" crocheted doilies fast? Coat them with white glue. (It'll come out in the machine when you wash the doily.)

(SHE WAS RIGHT.)

A REFRESHER COURSE IN THINGS YOUR MOTHER TOLD YOU ABOUT STAIN REMOVAL BUT YOU'VE FORGOTTEN. (SHE WAS RIGHT.)

- Blot up the spill immediately if possible.
- Act quickly.
- Test any solution in a hidden area to make sure it doesn't create yet another stain.
- Apply water or stain-removal solution to the stained spot only, using an eyedropper or a bottle with a small pouring spout. Otherwise you'll spread the stain.
- A heavy glass pie plate, turned upside down, makes a good working surface for removing stains. When you sponge off a stain, use an absorbent cloth beneath.

needs attention before you toss it into the hamper or use a clothespin to mark the spot.

Another helpful technique is to use a disappearing fabric marker to circle all stains as you toss the item into the hamper.

Then go through everything before you load it into the machine.

Principles of Stain Removal

Spot cleaning clothes isn't a high-stress situation, but close enough. I would say it comes somewhere in between flipping an omelet with one hand and going through a day wearing panty hose that are too short.

The cause of the stain is often complex. Protein stains (from food) and grease stains (from oils) need different treatments, but some stains are a combination of both. On top of that there are many fabrics and fabric combinations, all of which react differently to different stains.

On the other hand, this is not, as they say, rocket science. For non-washable clothes, sometimes a dry-cleaning fluid such as Carbona or Energine will do the trick, though it may leave a white ring on dark garments.

On washable clothes, detergents—particularly the new formulas—are surprisingly effective. You can make your own detergent into a prewash stain remover by combining a little powder with some water until it forms a paste. Rub it on the stains with an old toothbrush. If that doesn't solve the problem, try a home remedy. Or turn to a commercial stain remover. Be sure to read instructions carefully and make sure that the product is recommended for the particular fabric and stain that you are dealing with.

Stain Remover Arsenal

Absorbents for removing grease. Cornstarch, cornmeal, or talcum powder can be shaken on, left to stand, then brushed off. This treatment is safe for fur, leather, suede.

Acetone dissolves nail polish and airplane model glue. Buy it at the drugstore. But don't use on acetate or triacetate.

Bleach (chlorine and oxygen), see p. 182.

Color remover (such as Rit; sold with dyes). For one color that has bled onto another or whites that have yellowed.

Dishwashing detergent, both for automatic dishwasher and for hand dishwashing. The former is very powerful and contains bleach, so use with care.

Dry-cleaning fluid (such as Energine or Carbona; petroleum distallate products) for non-washable clothes.

Enzyme presoak or liquid (such as Biz or Axion). Boosts cleaning power of detergent and removes protein stains such as foods, milk, tea, coffee, baby formula, and fruit juice, blood, other body fluids, and grass. The enzymes digest the stain as your body digests food. Not effective on wax, rust, ink, crayon, or oil. Biz and Axion come in powdered form. My own Wow! Formula 1 (for whites and bleachables) and Formula 2 (for colored clothes) are unique: They're in liquid form, work instantly, and I don't think anything comes close in terms of effectiveness.

Glycerine from the drugstore.

Hydrogen peroxide, 3 %, the kind sold as an antiseptic, not as a bleach.

Oven cleaner (such as Easy-Off) removes paint from fabric as well as stains on bathtubs and glass. Oven cleaner is not recommended by the manufacturer for these purposes, so I tell you to use it at your own risk, but it's amazingly effective. I have never used anything but original Easy-Off in these cases, so I can't guarantee that other formulas will work.

Petroleum jelly softens hardened paint, tar, and rubber cement. (Then launder.)

Prewash soil and stain remover (such as Shout, Spray 'n Wash) for heavily soiled load, cooking oils, motor oils (very effective on synthetics). Liquid and sprays are applied just before laundering the garment and reapplied if the stain doesn't go away. The product in stick form should be used on the fresh stain, but laundering can be postponed for up to a week. Use the hottest water the fabric can stand.

CAUTION: These may make neon and fluorescent colors fade and run.

Rubbing alcohol for colored candle wax, also some ballpoint inks, and fresh alcoholic beverages.

Soap bars are great for removing fabric softener. Fels Naphtha can remove perspiration and tobacco stains.

White vinegar, an odor neutralizer, helps with pet stains and with perspiration stains after ammonia has been used.

Window cleaner (specifically Windex), a good spot remover for fabrics and rugs. Use at your own risk since the manufacturer doesn't recommend it for these purposes.

HOME AND OTHER REMEDIES

Every so often another magic formula comes out—the one stain remover that's going to take out every stain. There is no such possibility: There are too many different kinds of stains, and each needs to be removed with different kinds of chemicals.

When you see those amazing demonstrations on TV, you're being tricked. What you see are people removing fresh stains, many of which can be removed by water or dishwashing detergent. The key to a good product (or home remedy) is whether it can remove a set-in stain.

With all the effective commercial solutions around, it seems to me the only reason to try a home treatment is if it's quicker, cheaper, or more effective, which are the ones I've included below. (Still, I'd like to point out that a little patience comes in handy. If a stain doesn't come out the first time, try it again. Stain removal is a lot like learning to ride a bike: The more you do it, the better you get.)

I've called for some products that are not on the basic list of stain removers—because I didn't think you would be using them on a regular basis—but are likely to be in the house; or I include them because I have had a unique success with that product.

Sometimes the only solution is a commercial one. I know people aren't always certain which category of stain remover to turn to, so I've mentioned certain products by name—because they are good and widely available (other, equally effective possibilities may exist) or because they are unique.

These remedies have all been tested and they work. Though I am always concerned that you may be dealing with an unknown factor (some fiber in a blend, some ingredient in a spill or stain) that will change the situation. I've decided to go out on a limb and mention all of them—on the assumption that you may have the ingredients for one solution but not another—but want to remind you to *exercise caution and be aware of the risks.* If an item is especially valuable to you, you may want to take the safe course and dry-clean it.

ALL-PURPOSE HOMEMADE STAIN REMOVERS

• For non-oily stains on washable fabrics (except washable wool, silk, spandex, acrylic, acetate): Mix equal parts ammonia, water, and liquid dishwashing soap in a squeeze bottle, shake before using, and work into the spot. Let stand a few minutes and flush with water. Good on milk, blood, perspiration, and urine. *For beverages, fruit, and grass, substitute vinegar for ammonia.*

• For oily stains on washable fabrics (except acetate, triacetate, or rayon): Mix 1 tablespoon of glycerin, 1 tablespoon liquid dishwashing soap, and 8 tablespoons water. Same procedure as above. This works on the principle that grease removes grease.

Stains and Solutions

ALCOHOLIC BEVERAGE

• Soak (fresh!) stains in cold water with a few tablespoons of glycerine (a drugstore item). Then rinse in a sinkful of water to which you've added half a cup of vinegar. Act fast. Stains turn brown as they age.

BABY FORMULA

• On whites: After the miracle of birth comes the miracle of laundry. How do such tiny clothes make such a gigantic washload? For fresh stains, moisten a cloth with water and dip it into baking soda and dab at the dribbled spot. Rub stubborn stains with paste of automatic dishwasher detergent. Let set overnight, then wash as usual. My Bye Bye Baby Stains Formula was designed to solve just this problem.

• For colored clothes: Rinse and then apply an enzyme paste. Let it stand an hour and then launder.

BATTERY ACID

• Rub a paste of baking soda and water into the spot right away, leave for two hours, then launder.

COLOR BLEEDING

• If dye transfers from colored clothes to bleachable whites or colors, rewash right away with chlorine bleach, and if problem persists, use a commercial color remover.

BLUE DETERGENT SPOTS

• Blue spots on laundered towels may be "bleeding" or simply the result of undiluted fabric softener or detergent. Rub them with a bar of soap and wash again, or soak in undiluted white vinegar until spots disappear, at least 15 minutes but no more than 30.

BLOOD

• Fresh bloodstains can be removed with salt, which breaks down red blood cells, or 3 % hydrogen peroxide solution. Or cover the area with meat tenderizer. Apply cool water to make a paste. Wait 15 to 30 minutes, then sponge with cool water.

• For a set-in stain, use a commercial enzyme remover like Biz, or my product, For Those Days.

BURN

• The old-time remedy for scorched clothing used to be a paste of vinegar, fuller's earth, soap, onion juice, and chicken manure, spread in a paste. Let it dry, then wash the item twice. I think the Mary Ellen of 1692 must have come up with this one and they probably hanged her as a witch, though I suppose if you managed to get the rest of this stuff out you probably wouldn't notice the scorch mark. Modern solution: Sponge it with 3 % hydrogen peroxide.

CRAYON

• If you haven't done a pocket check, you may wind up with crayons all over the wash. Sometimes dipping the clothes in hot water alone will cause the wax to run out. Or apply prewash stain remover and launder with soap flakes (not detergent) and 1 cup baking soda.

• If stains remain, presoak bleachable colors or whites in bleach according to package directions or overnight in a plastic basin filled with $1/2$ cup of liquid dishwashing detergent and $1/2$ cup of water. Then launder as usual.

• For fresh or heat-set stains on colored clothing, put item stained side down on paper towels, spray with WD-40, the lubricant and adhesive remover, let set a few minutes, turn fabric over, and spray the other side. Apply liquid dishwashing detergent and work it into the stained area, using new paper towel as stain is soaked up. Wash in hottest water fabric can stand with laundry detergent and oxygen bleach (heavy soil setting, or 12-minute wash). Tumble dry. **Clean drum of dryer to remove any wax residue** by spraying it with WD-40, wiping with soft cloth, and running a load of dry rags through a dry cycle.

• For crayon, tempera, and other stains, you can also get help by dialing 1-800-CRAYOLA.

FABRIC SOFTENER

• To remove "grease stains" caused on manmade fabric by fabric softener sheets, wet fabric and rub area with soap or a liquid dish detergent made to remove grease.

FRUIT STAINS

• I know a woman who lets her kids drink orange juice only when they're wearing orange or red, grape juice when they're in purple, and so on. If you're not that organized, you may have to deal with these stains. Rinse a fresh stain with water or try this crazy but effective solution: Stretch the stained area over a bowl, pour boiling water from a height of several feet through the stain. Or try the all-purpose homemade stain remover with vinegar (on p. 186). Commercial solution: enzyme stain remover.

> The person who said
> "It will all come out in the wash"
> obviously never did one.

GLUE

• Scrape soft glue with dull knife. Then wash item in soapy water.

• Soften hard glue with dampened paper towel left on spot for 30 minutes. Rub with towel to remove the rest. Repeat if necessary.

• Or use hot white vinegar or dry-cleaning solvent or non-oily nail polish. Place cloth on stain, then pour on more of the stain remover, repeat until the glue is softened, then wash.

• On suede, wet a cotton swab with lighter fluid and rub lightly over glue until it's loosened. When dry, brush suede with rubber sponge to raise nap.

GRASS

• I know it's spring when I see the first grass stain on my son Andrew's clothes. After checking for colorfastness, rub in some rubbing alcohol, then flush with clear cold water. If the stain isn't gone, try a few drops of vinegar. Or try the all-purpose homemade stain remover with vinegar.

• Commercial solution: enzyme stain remover.

GREASE

• See homemade solution in box on p. 186.

• Or rub Crisco into grease-stained clothes, then launder.

• Or sprinkle baby powder or talcum on the fresh stain, let dry, brush off, then wash. This is especially good for workclothes.

• Or rub dishwashing liquid or waterless mechanic's soap (from auto parts store) on the spot right away, then launder as usual.

• On manmade fabrics, freshly laundered, see Fabric Softener on the preceding page.

• On suede, rub with a clean cloth dipped in glycerine.

GUM

• Freeze article and chip off as much as you can with a dull knife. Let it come to room temperature, dampen a cloth with dry-cleaning solution or lighter fluid. Rub, then launder.

• Or saturate with salad oil or peanut butter, remove as much as you can, then launder.

HAIR DYE

• If you use a water-soluble (shampoo-out) product and the stain is very fresh, use a few drops of the shampoo that comes with the haircoloring kit.

• If color has dried, hairdressers have told me they have removed hair dye with hairspray, a skin astringent called Sea Breeze, or Tilex, the bathroom spray cleaner. (Test in an out-of-the-way spot first; these may cause color to bleed, fade, or spot.)

HEMLINES

• On jeans: Get a blue crayon or blue magic marker the same color as the jeans and rub it on the line. Then iron the fabric under a pressing cloth, using a medium setting. The white line should disappear.

• For a wool skirt, dip a pressing cloth into a solution of one part vinegar and two parts water, wring it out, lay it over the clothing and press. (This will eliminate creases in "permanent press" garments, too.)

INK, BALLPOINT

• Squirt on a generous amount of aerosol, not pump, hairspray (the cheap kind; expensive brands contain oils that may stain), then rub with a clean dry cloth. This is most effective on polyester.

• If some still remains, try a full-strength dose of rubbing alcohol.

• A large spot (bigger than a dime) can be soaked in wood (methyl) alcohol for 15 to 30 minutes. (Exceptions: rayon and acetate should be dry-cleaned.)

OFFICE HELPER

Keep a box of individually packed alcohol wipes on hand for neat, quick first aid on a ballpoint pen stain. Bring a couple home, too.

INK, MARKER PEN

• Rinse stain with cold water until it runs clear, place fabric on paper towel, and saturate with alcohol (using a cottonball as a blotter). Change paper towel as it absorbs the color. Wash in hot water with laundry detergent and powdered bleach (for colored clothing) and rinse in warm water.

• Or call 1-800-CRAYOLA.

INK, PRINTER'S

• Lava Soap rubbed into dampened material, then rinsed, will do the trick.

JAM, ON FABRIC

• Use distilled white vinegar as a spot cleaner.
• Commercial solution: enzyme stain remover.

KOOL-AID

CAUTION: Use this remedy only on non-elastic white or colored clothes that can stand up to chlorine bleach. If you're not sure, do a colorfastness test. See p. 178.

• Run hot water in the tub about 2" deep. Stir in 1 cup bleach, and one cup each ammonia-free powdered laundry detergent and automatic dishwashing powder until dissolved. Add 4 or more gallons of hot water. Soak clothes 20 minutes, drain tub, rinse clothes very well, and wash as usual. (I think they ought to outlaw this stuff. I'm sure there's a whole landfill consisting just of clothes, carpeting, and upholstery that it ruined. I came up with a Kool-Aid remover and the company made me take it off the market because I'd used their name.)

LIPSTICK

• Rub the stain with a slice of white bread.
• Or try non-oily makeup remover.
• Or use a non-gel toothpaste.
• Or use dry-cleaning solvent. (Put the item down on an old towel, apply solvent, and use an edge of the towel to soak up solvent and stain.) Launder as usual. If color remains, try ammonia and water.

MAKEUP

• Rub in dish detergent (one that is especially good on grease) or shampoo, or spray with hairspray, then launder as usual.
• Or use non-oily makeup remover.

MILDEW

See p. 192.

MUD

• Let the mud dry, brush it off, use a bar soap.
• Or rub on a solution of 1 tablespoon borax in a cup of water, and launder as usual.
• Or rub on Murphy's Oil soap, leave 15 minutes, and rinse with cold water.

• If the spot persists, use an enzyme presoak or soak the item in a gallon of water to which you've added a cup of ammonia (or, with whites, a cup of bleach).

MUSTARD

• Treat the item before you launder it and the stain sets. You can rinse it, then spot clean with a bar soap or soak it overnight in a hot detergent solution.
• Or immediately sponge on a little glycerine you've warmed by standing the bottle in hot water (away from flame!), then launder.
• For non-washable fabrics, try sponging with one part alcohol and two parts water.
• This is a tricky stain. A commercial enzyme remover may help.

OINTMENT, DESITIN OR ZINC OXIDE

• Use hot water and detergent, and rub fabric against itself to remove the oil. Then soak garment in white vinegar 15 minutes to remove the zinc oxide.

PAINT, LATEX

• Treat immediately with soap and water.
• If stain persists, check for colorfastness. If it doesn't run, rub with automatic dishwashing detergent or liquid dishwashing detergent, let stand briefly, then wash.
• Or spray with Easy-Off oven cleaner, let set about 30 minutes, then launder. (I've found this safe for polyester fabrics and cotton fabrics, but try at your own risk.)

PAINT, OIL-BASED

• Use thinner recommended on the label. Or try thinner for typewriter correction fluid.
• If that doesn't work, pour on full-strength Lestoil, let it set overnight, then wash.
• Or use equal parts turpentine and sudsy ammonia.

PERSPIRATION STAINS, ON FABRIC

• Dry cleaning does not remove perspiration stains. They must be dissolved with water. I've heard 800 ways to remove these stains and most of them are incredibly complicated and don't work. The problem is that the perspiration may have damaged the fibers (or in the case of silk, made them yellow or faded) so that the problem is not that you have a stain, but that you have fabric which has been ruined. However, white sudsy ammonia or vinegar is sometimes very effective in removing stains and/or odor.

• On collar and wrists: Use talcum powder to absorb ring, then launder. Or remove ring with an old toothbrush and generic shampoo (the fancier "designer" shampoos sometimes compound the problem), then wash item promptly. If you have a perpetual problem, splash witch hazel on your neck before you put the clothing on.

RUST

• On white fabric: Apply lemon juice, rub with salt, let item bleach in the sun.

• Or cover the stain with cream of tartar, gather up the edges of the item (to keep the powder on the spot), then dip the spot into hot water. Let stand 5 minutes, then wash as usual.

• Zud, Whink, and my own Wow! Rust Stain Remover (the only one safe for most colors) are among the few commercial remedies.

PURPLE TINGE, ON SYNTHETICS

• Happens from repeated washings. Soak in Rit Color Remover and launder as usual.

RING

• If a ring remains around a stain after you've washed a pretreated item, you probably needed to use more stain remover or detergent.

There must be enough to hold the loosened dirt suspended until it can be washed away. Otherwise the dirt moves to the edge of the area and leaves the ring. Solution: Treat again, wash again.

SAUCE

• The owner of a barbecue restaurant removes sauce stains on bar rags, aprons, slacks, and jackets by dumping a cup of dishwashing detergent in cold water in the washing machine, letting items soak a couple of hours, then laundering as usual, and rinsing items in cold water. Try this to whiten old or dull polyester, too.

CAUTION: May discolor or fade fabrics that can't take chlorine bleach.

• Or add one-half cup white vinegar to the rinse water. If you use this with nylon or synthetics, allow water to cool a bit, as hot water sets wrinkles.

SHOE POLISH

• On colored fabrics, try a little rubbing alcohol mixed with two parts water. On white fabrics, use alcohol straight. If that doesn't work, try paint thinner.

SILK, SPOTS ON

• Dry-cleaning solvent may spot clean silk but often creates a ring in the process. (And rubbing removes color in some silks.) Eliminate the ring by steaming the item over a tea kettle (*but hold it at some distance; do not get the stain wet*), then rub fabric briskly against itself. This works on wool, too.

• Energine removes grease stains from silk.

SILLY PUTTY

• Turn the item upside down over a bowl and wait for gravity to remove it.

SOOT

• Mix Formula 409 with an equal amount of water, then soak or spray items, and launder as usual.

TAR

• The best remedies are prewash sprays, mineral spirits, or turpentine. (Baby oil may leave a stain and others may remove color, so test first.) Scrub with a soft brush. Rub the spot until it's out, then wash with detergent and water.

TEMPERA PAINT

• Sponge with rubbing alcohol, putting clean cloth underneath to blot up color as it comes out. Use liquid abrasive cleaner on any remaining stain, then launder. (*Not for silk: alcohol will remove dye.*)

• Or call 1-800-CRAYOLA.

TYPEWRITER CORRECTION FLUID

• On fabrics, use correction fluid thinner, paint thinner, or isopropyl (rubbing) alcohol. Works on rugs and furniture, too.

URINE, DIAPER STAINS

• Presoak in ammonia ($1/4$ cup to a gallon of water) for five minutes, then launder as usual with hottest water recommended.

WINE

• Saturate fresh stains with club soda, then wash.

• Or try a mixture of dishwashing liquid and vinegar. Safe even on silk, if it is washable.

• Or put shrinkproof cotton item into a pot containing enough milk to cover the stained area, bring to a boil, remove from stove, then let sit until stain has disappeared.

• Or stretch the soiled spot across the sink and pour boiling water through the fabric from a height of two to three feet.

YELLOW STAINS

These maddening yellow spots appear when whites stored in dark areas are brought into the light or when they are covered with plastic. They may be caused by tannin (the substance that makes a cut apple turn brown); by brighteners in the fabric that turn yellow in the sun; by body oil buildup (in which case try color remover, available where dyes are sold); by bleach the fabric retained in the mill; or by iron and manganese in the water (in which case you need a rust remover; or, in the case of delicate fabrics, 1 tablespoon oxalic acid in a cup of hot water). If you don't know the source of the problem, there are many remedies to try:

• Soak items with warm water and a few denture tablets overnight.

• Or combine a tablespoon each of white vinegar, salt, and water softener with one pint of water, dip area up and down in solution, rinse well, and launder.

• Or rub white toothpaste into spot, wash in cold water.

• Or, for whites and colorfast, put dishwashing powder (make sure it contains no ammonia) in a gallon pail, add boiling water until half-full, then add $1/4$ cup bleach, and fill pail with cold water. Add this to wash water.

• Or combine a tablespoon each of white vinegar, salt, and water softener with a pint of water; dip spotted area up and down in solution, rinse well, and launder.

And in the future, don't leave white clothes covered in plastic. Protect them from dust with a piece of sheeting instead.

SPECIAL HANDLING

Laundry Problems

LINTING

To avoid lint, separate clothes that are linters from those that are lintees. See Sorting earlier in this section. Always check pockets for tissues, which will shred all over everything. Lint is also caused when:

Washer is overloaded;

You haven't used enough detergent to hold the lint in suspension;

You haven't used enough water to rinse the lint away;

Lint filter isn't clean;

Too much bleach has caused lint shedding;

Or cycle went on too long, causing abrasion.

Using fabric softener will reduce the static attraction of lint. So will adding a cup of plain vinegar to the rinse cycle. You can rewash the items with either of these solutions.

If despite all this you still have lint, lay the item flat and shave it with double-edged disposable razors, or rub it with medium or lightweight sandpaper, a nylon scrubbing pad, a stiff, short-bristled nylon hairbrush, or a grooming block (from a shop that sells supplies to horsemen).

MILDEW

To treat mildew on fabrics—clothing, outdoor fabrics, cushions, and umbrellas—work quickly once it's discovered. Brush off the item in the tub or outdoors, and avoid scattering the mold spores.

If garment is bleachable, use chlorine bleach. Otherwise soak clothing in warm soapy water and borax. If that doesn't work, combine $1/4$ teaspoon of oxygen bleach and $1/4$ cup of 3 % hydrogen peroxide. Make sure the hydrogen peroxide is relatively fresh, since it loses its strength over time. (Liquids that tend to decompose are sold in brown bottles.) With a clean cloth, gently rub the stain until it's gone. Launder the garment and air dry—in the sun, if possible.

An old-fashioned remedy that works, but isn't what I'd consider extremely practical, is to dip item in sour buttermilk—it sours about 3 to 6 weeks after the expiration date on the carton—and let it dry in the sun, then rinse with cold water.

If a musty odor remains, sprinkle the item with baking soda, leave for a couple of hours, then soak in water or launder. Dry-clean unwashable mildewed clothes.

To reduce the chance of mildew, store clothes so air can circulate around them, eliminate dampness by hanging silica gel in cloth bags and/or keep a low-wattage bulb burning in the closet. Never store clothing that is dirty or wet. Mold feeds on dirt and grease as well as dampness.

OVERDRIED CLOTHES

Overdried clothes are permanent-press clothes left so long in the dryer that they've become wrinkled to the point where pressing doesn't help. To solve the problem—or remove wrinkles from any permanent press item, for that matter—return clothes to the dryer, throw a damp towel into the machine, and run them through one cycle on "Warm." Or press the item with a pressing cloth dampened with white distilled vinegar, either straight or diluted with water. Vinegar may affect the color so make sure you test it first.

PILLING

To cut down on pilling of sweaters, sheets, and quilts, wash manmade fabrics separately from towels, which tend to rub. Also, line dry items that tend to pill. If item has already pilled, shave it—as I've recommended for years, and as professionals do. But my preferred solution is rubbing it with a pumice stone or using a product called Sweater Stone made for this purpose. It's time-consuming but effective.

STIFFNESS, SCRATCHINESS

If your clothes don't need ironing because they stand by themselves, you're doing something wrong. If you've got hard water, increase the amount of detergent, install a water softener, or use a water conditioner.

Usually the problem is that too much detergent is left in the clothing. Use less detergent (if you're using more than recommended), add a commercial rinse agent or white vinegar to the first rinse, or add a rinse cycle.

WEAR, EXCESSIVE

If the washing machine is putting more wear on your clothes than your kids are doing on the playing field, you may be adding too much bleach. Chlorine is tough on fibers. Be sure to add it at the proper time in the cycle and/or dilute it before you add it to the machine.

Hand Washing and Other Special Situations

If you want to wash lingerie or stockings by hand, dissolve gentle detergent or baby shampoo in a basin of water, put the washables in the basin, and leave them for five minutes. Squeeze detergent through, but don't rub or wring the clothes. A clean plumber's helper (a.k.a. toilet plunger), reserved specifically for this purpose, is a useful tool for hand washing if you need a little agitation. Rinse until water runs clear, then hang the items to drip dry. Towel dry knits before hanging them up if the water they've absorbed will pull them out of shape. See "Blocking," next page.

ZAPPING ZIPPER PROBLEMS

If a zipper continually unzips: Spray on a shot of hair spray, put a button at the top of the zipper and fasten an elastic loop to the zipper to hook it onto, or sew on Velcro dots.

If it sticks too much: Apply soap to teeth or spritz with spray-on silicone lubricant, but put masking tape along the sides of the zipper before you apply it to avoid spotting.

SWEATER CARE

Washing. Spot clean with a prewash spot and stain remover, then launder sweater in machine if label allows, using a gentle detergent on a low temperature setting.

Acrylic and certain other sweaters can be machine washed (check the label), but turn them inside out and use cold or warm water and a short cycle.

To hand wash, use cool to lukewarm water and mild detergent. Squeeze out suds gently. Don't wring or rub. Rinse thoroughly, then lay flat on a light-colored towel. Roll up the towel, jelly roll fashion to absorb excess moisture. If the sweater is very wet, repeat the process with a second towel.

If the care label says tumble dry, do it. The heat is meant to allow the fabric to return to its correct heat-set shape. But use very little heat and don't leave the sweater in the dryer any

---

CAR WASH

If you're on an extended car trip, put your clothes in a plastic pail with some warm soapy water, snap on a lid, and put the pail in the trunk. The agitation of the ride will get them clean without any effort on your part! Rinse and proceed as directed under hand washing.

longer than necessary or it may shrink. You can hang machine-washed cotton ramie sweaters to drip dry, then tumble on "Medium" to pull them back into shape.

Blocking. Some clothes say "Dry Flat," which is also called blocking. Ideally this involves making a pattern by tracing the sweater before it's washed on a brown paper bag, but I just calculate by eye. After washing, remove it from the machine (before it spins dry) or from the sink, and roll up in a towel jelly roll fashion to absorb moisture.

Lay a second towel on a window screen, a webbed chair, oven rack, or other surface that lets air circulate from beneath, and put the sweater on top. When the sweater is partly dry, put the paper outline on a table and lay the sweater on it, gently pushing it into shape. When it's completely dry, if you want to raise the nap put it in the dryer on a no-heat setting for about five minutes.

Let it dry thoroughly before you put it away or it will wrinkle all over again. If you need to iron it, use a damp cloth between the sweater and iron.

Unshrinking a Sweater. I can't guarantee you success with this project, but it sometimes works.

Soak the sweater in a hair conditioner and water solution, and pull gently to reshape.

Or dissolve one ounce of borax in a couple of tablespoons of hot water, add the mixture to a gallon of lukewarm water, immerse the garment, pull gently into shape, and rinse in a gallon of warm water to which you have added 2 tablespoons of vinegar.

Or dissolve one or two cups non-iodized salt in enough hot water to cover the garment. Let cool, and leave the sweater to soak for three hours. Wash it in mild suds, rinse three times, spin or roll the sweater in towels. Reshape and let dry.

Or add 2 tablespoons detergent shampoo (containing no soap) to a gallon of lukewarm water. Dip the garment until wet; squeeze,

IF THE LABEL'S A PAIN IN THE NECK

Some children and delicate adults complain that clothing labels irritate the back of their necks. But if you cut the labels off, the short remaining piece may be equally (or more) irritating. Besides, the label's handy on kids' clothing to check the size for hand-me-downs. Cut a patch of iron-on interfacing and iron it down over the label. You will still be able to read it, but it won't be causing a problem.

If the reverse side of embroidery inside a T-shirt is irritating, iron-on interfacing works equally well.

don't rinse. Reshape on a flat surface, let dry.

Shrinking a Sweater. I have been able to shrink sweaters, but never on purpose. I have been asked if it's possible and the answer is yes, theoretically. Wash it in very hot water and block it on a pattern you've made from a sweater in the smaller size.

Yellowing. If a white sweater is yellowing, add 2 ounces hydrogen peroxide to a gallon of warm water, soak it for 3 to 4 hours, then wash and dry it. Or use a hair lightener. The foam type works great; pick a white platinum shade.

FIXING A SHEET

If you rip a sheet, don't throw it away. Don't ignore it, either, or the rip will get bigger. Buy adhesive-backed, lightweight sheeting fabric patches in a sewing store or the notions section of a large department store. Follow the simple instructions on the package. (Cut the patch to size, lay it adhesive side down on the wrong side of the sheet or inside the pillowcase, and iron it on, with a dry iron.)

WASHING TOWELS, SHEETS, AND PILLOWCASES

Wash new towels before you use them. Washing tightens the weave of the foundation that holds the loops in place and makes them more absorbent. Launder dark towels separately the first half-dozen times, since they may bleed.

Also separate dark sheets and pillowcases from any light clothing for the first few washes, but keep them with each other so that if they fade, at least they'll fade to match.

White, 100% cotton sheets can take extremely hot water (up to 200° F.) and colored 100% cotton sheets can be washed in very hot water (up to 140° F.) but there's no reason to wash them at such high temperatures after normal use. Cotton/polyester or nylon sheets should be washed in warm, not hot, water.

• •

DRYING
Machine Drying

To get the best results, read the manufacturer's instructions.

Keep the lint screen cleaned.

Don't dry clothes on too high a temperature (it's better to remove them when they're almost dry, which is less hard on the fabric than spinning them until they're bone dry).

Take clothes out promptly to avoid overdrying, which is explained on p. 192.

Sometimes giving clothes an extra spin in the washing machine—to remove excess moisture—makes more sense than running the dryer (at higher cost) for a longer period.

Line Drying

What really gets my goat is that line drying is prohibited by law in some communities. Liquor stores are fine and triple-X video stores

Line Drying

Clothesline Extension

are okay, but the sight of someone's shorts flapping in the wind is an eyesore.

Nothing smells as fresh as line-dried clothes, but the sun may fade some clothing. Don't hang clothes outdoors to dry unless you know they are colorfast.

To prevent a shirt or other item from blowing away, slip it over two hangers, one hanger hook facing the other, then slip both over the line. Button the shirt and the hanger won't fall down nor will the shirt blow away.

Using a piece of chain as a clothesline in the laundry room (or to extend your regular line) is doubly helpful. You get more hanging room and the hangers won't slide together.

IRONING

When I was growing up, it wasn't chic to wear natural fabrics. They were just the only kind of clothes we had. Naturally, we did a lot of ironing. The easiest way to iron natural fibers is to sprinkle them with water, roll them up in plastic bags, and put them in the fridge overnight. But since I never got around to ironing them, I'd freeze them to prevent mildew. While most frozen clothes iron up nicely, colored things may run and the fibers may be damaged if you don't let them thaw first.

I tried to make wearing wrinkled clothing fashionable when I was a teenager, but I was ahead of my time. By the time it got to be all the rage, I had enough natural wrinkles so that I didn't want them in my clothes, too.

Unless you're willing to pay the cleaner to do it, or to wear nothing but synthetics, you have to know something about ironing. The most important thing, of course, is to have a good iron. If you don't, check out the buying information in the Equipping section.

THE DIFFERENCE BETWEEN PRESSING AND IRONING

- In **pressing,** you lift the iron and lower it onto the fabric, then repeat.
- In **ironing,** you glide the iron over the fabric.

Knits, wools, and very fragile clothes should be pressed rather than ironed, but I'd been ironing for years before I discovered this (and fortunately, had been sending my knits and fragile clothes to the dry cleaner). You may discover that you naturally begin to press rather than iron when you are working on a knitted cotton because otherwise it feels as if you are stretching the material.

To Keep Ironing to a Minimum

Hang clothes as soon as you take them from the dryer.

Use a plant mister on wrinkled clothes or hang them in a steamy bathroom until wrinkles fall out. (About 10 minutes of a hot shower does the job; especially good for knits.)

Dry clothes outdoors or in front of a fan indoors.

Use your fingers to "press" the item while damp and it'll wrinkle less. Or take damp clothes out of the wash, snap them against a hard surface, and hang them to dry.

When you're packing for a trip, roll clothes instead of folding them.

Spray collar and cuffs with spray starch when you hang a shirt to drip dry and you may need to do no more. Or iron just the collars and cuffs, if you'll be wearing a shirt under a sweater.

Use a steamer or a steam iron to point a jet of steam at the garment. (Careful: This sets stains).

Don't iron a pleated curtain: Use a trouser hanger to "press" it into place while it's still damp from the machine.

How to Iron

PRESSING CLOTH

To avoid scorching a fragile fabric or making a dark one shine, use a pressing cloth—a piece of cloth laid between the iron and the garment. Any old piece of lightweight cotton will do.

For thick clothes, use a piece of white or neutral toweling; and for wool, a heavy, lint-free napkin or another piece of wool.

For light clothes, use a dry cloth with a steam iron.

For medium-weight clothes, use a wet but not soaking sponge to dampen the cloth, then lay it on the fabric. The iron should not be on a steam setting. Don't keep it long in any one

PRESSING CONCERNS

Test iron first and if it sticks, jerks, or produces a glaze, stop. The plate needs to be cleaned. (See p. 198, Cleaning the Iron.)

Don't iron dirty or sweaty clothes. You'll set the stain and damage the fibers.

Don't iron over zippers, buttons, or other lumps, including that forgotten item in the pocket that may melt.

Don't iron rubber, Ultrasuede, or stretch clothing. Use only a cool iron on synthetics.

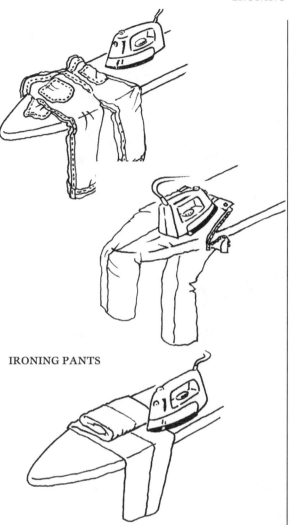

IRONING PANTS

spot. Lift from time to time so steam can escape, and don't press wool while steam is rising from the garment.

For heavy clothes, make a pressing cloth "sandwich" with the item in between.

Be careful to avoid getting water spots on silk and other non-washable clothing.

Since sizing or starch may come off the garment, wash the pressing cloth after you've used it.

Radio comics Bob and Ray used to talk about Dry Cleaning School: Monday: Ironing pants. Tuesday: Ironing jackets. Wednesday: Graduation.

Embroidery. Place the embroidery face down on a folded towel or blanket, then iron it on the wrong side, under a pressing cloth.

Leather. Hang it in a steamy shower; if it's really bad, place a heavy piece of cloth between the leather and iron and turn the iron to low.

Natural Fiber Clothes. If very wrinkled, you may have to press seams and pockets separately. Press seams open (make the iron flatten them out) and iron the pocket flat on the board by itself.

Pants. Turn pants inside out, iron pockets first. Turn pants right side out. For dark pants, use a pressing cloth. Lay pants flat and iron hip portion. Then lay the pants on the board with the creases aligned. Flip back the top leg and iron the inside of the bottom, then turn the pants over and iron the opposite side. Then iron the outsides.

Shirts. Even if you usually have shirts done at the laundry, one day you may need to iron one by yourself. If the shirt isn't damp, dampen it slightly with water from a spray bottle. Some people tell you to start with the collars and cuffs, and others tell you to iron the parts that are least visible first (like the back and tails), and the parts that are most visible (cuffs, collars, front), last. Obviously this is a matter of preference. My way: Do the collars and cuffs on the wrong side first, starting from the outside tip and ironing into the center. Then do the yoke, moving toward the sleeves and going toward the cuff. Then I do the body, front panels last.

Silk Tie. Wrap the steam iron with a damp cloth (which creates gentle steam). Hold the wrapped iron near the tie but don't let the iron touch it.

RIGHT SIDE OR WRONG

Which side do you iron?
- Cotton, net, or silky rayon is ironed right side up.
- Polyester may be ironed either way.
- All other garments should preferably be ironed inside out.

IRON DANGER

If the steam iron is filled and on and not steaming, turn it off immediately, pull the plug, and stand it on its heel. The vents are clogged and the thing could explode.

Cleaning the Iron

The bottom of an iron picks up dirt that it may leave on another piece of clothing. Even if you can't see any dirt, play it safe and rub the hot iron over an old piece of towel before you start working on a fresh garment.

An iron with a non-stick finish can be wiped clean. If it's dirty, put a dab of prewash solution on a cloth and wipe. A plastic scrubber will clean it without damaging the finish.

An iron without a non-stick finish can be cleaned on a hot, non-steam setting: Run it over table salt sprinkled on a brown paper grocery bag. Or let it cool, clean it with prewash solution sprayed on a rag, or use oven cleaner sprayed on directly, then sponged off. Or use a de-liming solution (sold usually for the bathroom).

To clean steam parts annually, pour white vinegar into a cold iron with steam button in up or on position, leave for two hours, then drain.

● ●

SEWING FOR NON-SEWERS

Even if you haven't handled a needle and thread since kindergarten, you can probably figure out how to use one to sew on a button and mend a tear in a seam. A very basic "sewing" kit will help you out of a lot of emergencies (see box on facing page).

GETTING THE THREAD OF IT

If you have trouble getting the thread through the needle, pull the thread over a bar of soap (that keeps it from tangling, too).

Or use a needle threader, a thin wire loop; you pass the thread through the threader loop, then squeeze the loops through the eye of the needle.

Needle Threader

Self-Threading Needle

Better still: a self-threading needle. It has a tiny slot on the top and you pull the thread down through it.

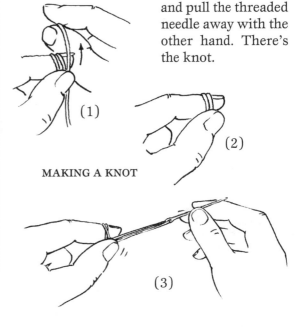

and pull the threaded needle away with the other hand. There's the knot.

MAKING A KNOT

Sewing On a Button

The reason buttons come loose so often is that the labor unions have managed to get a contract that spells out the maximum number of stitches in a button—and it's not enough! If a button is coming loose, try to find the end of the thread on the loose button and pull gently. Most of the time you'll find enough thread to use to replace the button. To cut the button off without nicking the fabric, slide a comb underneath it, then cut the thread with a razor blade.

Removing Button

After threading the needle, the hardest part of sewing on a button is making the knot at the end of the thread. Thread the needle, pull about 12" of thread through the hole, and leave a second length of 12" hanging on the other side. Make the knot by winding both ends of the strands around your index finger, then use your thumb to push the circle of thread up to the top of your finger. Hold the circle lightly in place with your thumb

Push the needle up from the inside part of the garment and the knot will hold the threads in place when you start to sew. Bring the needle up through one hole and down through the other. Choose two holes to work with. (*Do the other two holes separately; that way if one thread breaks, the button is still held on partway.*)

If you sew the button tightly to the fabric, it can't stretch enough to fit through the hole. You need to leave what's called a shank—a short length of thread—under the button. The easiest way to do this is to slip a match (from a book of paper matches) under the button, and then sew around it. After you've gone in and out of the two holes six times, bring the needle up to the right side of the garment. Slip out the match, wind the thread around the spot a few times and bring the

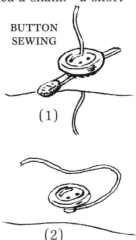

BUTTON SEWING

199

needle back into the inside of the garment, sew a few times through the thread under the buttonhole, then cut the thread.

If your old clothes are so raggedy you're going to trash them rather than give them away, first remove the buttons and save them for some future use.

When you're using black or white thread, thread the needle, cut the thread, then tie the knot at the cut. For colored thread, cut the appropriate length from the spool, thread the cut-off end through the needle and tie the knot in the other end. (In the manufacture of all threads, black and white cord is twisted one way while colored is twisted another. I can almost guarantee you will be the only person who knows this in almost every crowd.)

BUTTONED UP

One way to avoid having to sew on buttons entirely is to make sure they don't fall off. Put a dab of superglue in the middle of the button, over the thread, before you ever wear the garment. That should keep most of them from ever falling off.

Velcro

Do you know about Velcro-jumping, a barroom sport? The wall is covered with Velcro and "athletes" wearing shirts with Velcro strips throw themselves at it and—if they do it right—hang there. Which gives you some idea of how powerful Velcro is.

For more routine use, it comes in several colors, by the yard in fabric stores and in packages of strips, dots, and squares. I use it all the time, both for sewing and non-sewing jobs. It's self-sticking, but if you use it on fabric, you have to sew it on to make sure it doesn't loosen in the wash.

Use Velcro to keep a wrap-around skirt from unwrapping, close a gap in a blouse, and to hold

Iron-On Patches: How and When to Use Them

The iron-on patches I recommended for your home sewing kit should be used if you get a hole in a shirt or a rip in a sheet. If you mend it while the rip is small, you can save the item. Packages of several patches in assorted colors, either lightweight (like sheet or shirting fabric) or heavy (cotton knits, jeans), are sold in fabric stores or in the notions section of department stores. You can also buy elbow patches to put on the sleeves of sweaters. A package may contain several smaller patches or one large one.

There are instructions on the package, but the idea is to cut a patch, round the edges (it's less likely to peel), and place it sticky side down on the underside of the rip. You use the heat of an iron to "solder" it in place.

More advanced sewers can use a patch if a torn button leaves a hole. Sew the button securely to a bit of matching fabric, push the button up through the hole. Sew the loose ends of the fabric onto the underside of the garment.

VELCRO FOR NON-SEWING PURPOSES

- Put one strip on the remote control and the other on the arm of your TV chair.
- Put a Velcro dot on a pencil and another on the telephone.
- Use Velcro strips to seal sections of a briefcase or paper file.

a tab waistband flat. Instead of buttons and buttonholes, use Velcro dots and sew on a decorative button if you wish.

Hemming

I like being able to do my own hems on simple clothes because I save a lot of money. For the very simplest hems, if you have a piece of clothing that already has a straight hem, cut the fabric at a point about $2\frac{1}{2}$ inches below where you want the hem to be. Turn the garment inside out. Turn the bottom of the garment up about $\frac{1}{2}$ inch all around, pinning it in place, then iron it, so you have a good strong crease. Remove the pins. Now turn it up again, this time about an inch, repinning and re-ironing.

To hem, the idea is to make big stitches in the inside of the material, and just pass your

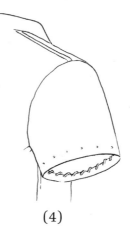

(4)

needle through a single strand of fiber on the part that will show (on the right side of the garment, you'll see just a dot of thread). Like all craft instructions, this sounds far more complicated than it is. Take a look at a hem and you'll see what I mean, though a machine-made hem stitch is more complicated than the one you'll have to do. You can also use iron-on double-sided fabric tape made for hemming purposes; check the notions section of a department store.

If you use a piece of checked or striped fabric as an ironing board cover, you can use the squares or lines as markers when you're working on the hem.

Don't use very long strands of thread to sew a hem. Use several short lengths. Otherwise, if you rip it, the whole thing will come down.

If you've got no help marking the hem when you're trying to shorten your own jeans or casual pants, stand sideways in front of the mirror and hitch up your pantleg at the thigh until the pants bottom is at the level you desire. Pin the extra material ("tuck") formed at the thigh, measure material taken up by the tuck, and take this amount off the pants bottom. This saves trial and error measuring—and the cost of a tailor visit.

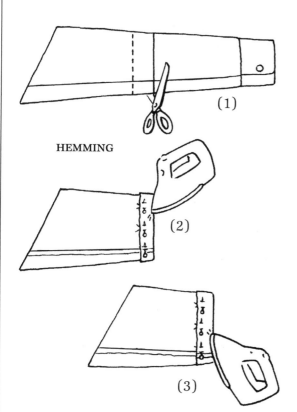

HEMMING

(1)

(2)

(3)

ALTERNATE THREADS

Use elastic thread on a waistband button. If you grow a little, the waistband stretches, too. This is helpful for children's buttons, too.

Fishing line (or dental floss) makes really strong thread for sewing buttons on jeans.

Sewing On a Badge

To hold the badge in place while you're sewing it on, staple it or fasten it with white glue. The glue comes out in the wash.

When the Drawstring Comes Out

The first thing you should do before you wear new clothing with a drawstring is to thread a needle and sew the drawstring in place in the middle of the back. If the drawstring comes out and is lost, put a safety pin through a piece of $1/4$" or $1/2$" ribbon and guide it through the waistband.

Getting Professional Help

If you want nothing to do with sewing or repairing your own clothes, you've no doubt found a tailor to sew on buttons and take up hems. There are other services a tailor can perform that you may not know about.

The tailor can replace collar and cuffs of leather and other jackets, replace zippers, add buttonholes, and turn (reverse) collars and cuffs on shirts that are frayed. If the lining of a coat is discolored or torn, it can be replaced for a lot less than the cost of a new coat, and a new white collar or cuffs can make an old dress wearable again.

Alterations you might not have thought of can be suggested by a good tailor, so ask advice about any garment that's a problem. For example, a skirt can be taken up from the waistband if it's too long but the hem is finished in some special way.

Shoemakers can replace entire heels and even cut down too-high heels as well as resole. They can repair zippers, briefcases, pocketbooks, jackets, and other leather items—including baseball gloves.

ACCESSORIES

Shoes

SHOE BUSINESS

Boots, waterproofing. Wipe leather boots with cloth sprayed with Endust and rain will roll off. Or treat new boots with silicone or with mink oil, which softens as well as waterproofs. Rub it in, then buff. Boots will hold their shape and last longer if you use boot trees. If you don't have the real thing, you can make do with a rolled-up newspaper.

Canvas Shoes, waterproofing. Use a thin strip of glue along the seams, and spray fabric protector over them.

Gold or Silver, scuffed. Dry toothbrush and white toothpaste will remove scuff marks.

Leather, dull. Rub shoes with cloth that's been sprayed with furniture polish. Or saturate a clean, unused powder puff with motor oil, then let dry over night. Will give a beautiful shine. Or use soapless hand cleaner: Lanolin will leave a soft shine and a protective coating, too. In a hurry? Use baby wipes.

Leather, mildewed. Wipe with a half-and-half mixture of water and alcohol or laundry detergent. Air dry. Use wax polish.

Leather, white, dirty. Clean with white-wall cleaner or ice skate cleaner from sporting goods shops.

Loose Insole. Pull off, then use rubber cement to reapply.

Patent Leather. Rub petroleum jelly into leather to prevent cracking. To cover a spot on

KNOT AN ISSUE

• To loosen a difficult knot in shoelaces, sprinkle it with talcum.

• To keep a knot in place all day, dampen the lace before you tie it.

HOW TO POLISH SHOES

When you've cleaned superficial dirt off shoes, use a dab of good quality cream or wax, polish, rub in a circle. With a cloth, buff until the finish is glossy. Apply a second coat and buff with a second clean cloth. If you're going all out—and want a dazzling shine—reapply paste wax from a wet cloth. Let shoes dry, buff a final time.

white patent, use typewriter correction fluid topped with colorless nail polish.

Rope Soles, waterproofing. Protect the fabric near the rope with masking tape, then apply silicone spray. After the first coat dries, apply a second.

Scuffs and Tears. If there's just a black mark, try a dab of nail polish remover or rubbing alcohol or lighter fluid on a clean cloth. On a heel, use a razor blade to trim away a flapping piece, smooth the edges with your palm, then polish. The shoemaker can repair a large tear.

Scuffs, on white leather. Rub with non-gel toothpaste, rinse, wipe, let dry.

Sneakers, deodorizing. Put shoes in freezer for a night or two and bacteria that cause the odor will die. Or put wood chips in them and leave in sealed plastic bag for a week. Rotating wear among several different pairs will cut down on odor, too.

Sole Worn, on rubber. Cut a new surface texture for a better grip with a soldering iron. Run the point of the iron over the surface to get a groove $1/2$" deep, which will raise beads along both sides of the line. Use parallel lines $1/2$" apart to make a diamond pattern.

Sole, squeaking. On leather shoes only (and using shoe trees to keep shape), scrub the outside of the shoe until dull with hot water and liquid dish soap and a scrub brush. Rinse thoroughly, dry overnight, then apply Neat's Foot oil (from the hardware store) with a small paintbrush to both shoes and soles. Let dry overnight again. When all signs of oil have disappeared, apply shoe polish.

Stiff, after water-soaking. Rub a damp cloth on saddle soap. Rub the lather on the leather. Stuff inside with black-and-white newspaper. Let air dry and leave soap on at least 24 hours. Dry them away from heat to prevent stiffness. Polish as directed in the box, left.

Suede, dirty. Clean with rug cleaner, let stand 10 minutes, brush with wet toothbrush and air dry. Or rub oatmeal into the stain with a clean cloth and a circular motion. Brush out powder with a suede brush; repeat if necessary. If suede is spotted, remove spots with fine grade sandpaper or spray-on carpet cleaner, let set a few minutes and brush. If they're in really bad shape, consider redyeing.

Tennis Shoe, rubber torn off. Buy glue sold to mend rubber.

Tennis Shoes, cleaning. Remove grime with Absorbene, the kneadable wallpaper cleaner. Or use upholstery cleaner. Easiest of all: Take them to the car wash and blast them with the pressure hose. Don't wear them when wet or they'll stretch. And don't dry them in a hot place or they'll shrink.

Sole, slippery. Rub it with sandpaper.

Tennis Shoes, white. Spray starch or Scotchgard will keep them clean.

Vinyl or Plastic, scuff marks on. Use lighter fluid.

White Marks, from winter salt. Sponge on a half-and-half solution of vinegar and warm water, then wipe dry.

White Shoes, polish rubbing off. Dust with baby powder after applying polish.

Coats, Gloves, and Bags

General. Air your coat before you put it in the closet so wrinkles will fall out (and leave it in a steamy bathroom if they haven't). If you're caught in the rain, dry the coat away from heat.

(Fur or suede may need professional attention.)

Leather/Leatherlike. You can do a spot cleaning with a sudsy sponge, but don't use solvents or shoe cleaners. Real leather needs professional cleaning by a specialist. Imitation leather can be cleaned by your local dry cleaner.

Leather- or Suede-Trimmed. Loss or transfer of dye is very common, and after dry cleaning the garment will rarely look or feel the same. Pigskin and cowhide are the most delicate, lambskin the least.

Suede/Suedelike. Brisk rubbing with a dry sponge or terry towel can perk it up, but it needs professional cleaning by a suede specialist. Ultrasuede is machine washable, but if there is a lining involved you might need dry cleaning.

Buckskin. Don't use detergents, gasoline,

or harsh petroleum on it. To clean unlined gloves, or smooth-grained deerskin garments and bags that have a soil-resistant finish, wash with a damp cloth and mild dishwashing soap, using gentle strokes. Rinse thoroughly, air dry away from heat or direct sunlight. If you need a little abrasion to clean grime, scrub the garment with damp sand or salt, very fine sandpaper, or commercial buckskin cleaner. Rinse with warm distilled water. Don't twist or wring. Line dry or lay flat and let water drip out.

Fur, fake. Brush and shake to fluff up. Generally moth- and mildew-proof so no special care needed. Can probably be dry-cleaned (check label), but if it has long pile may need to be cleaned by a furrier.

Fur, various. Rub in cornmeal, then brush it out, to get rid of superficial grime. Unless you wear it daily, you don't need a fur coat cleaned more often than once every two years, because the process is hard on furs. First it gets tossed around with cleaning fluids and absorbents, then it gets dematted and glazed (to restore the shine). If it's an old coat, don't clean it too much. See Furs, in Storing and Saving, p. 306.

Gloves, leather. Slip leather gloves on your hand, wash with cold water and mild soap, air dry flat. Saddle soap or Murphy's Oil Soap will clean up dirty leather. Leather conditioner such as Lexol will make it pliable, prevent cracking.

Pocketbooks. A damp cloth cleans up imitation leather and a spritz of non-oily hairspray removes ballpoint pen stains. Real leather can be cleaned with saddle soap or Murphy's Oil Soap and conditioned with Lexol.

A leather bag, like leather shoes, can be restored by a good shoemaker or bag repair shop. If it's expensive to begin with, it's probably worth the cost of polishing and replacing fittings, lining, and strap if needed.

Raincoats. After being dry-cleaned, a raincoat may absorb water instead of shedding it. Ask for a water-repellency treatment each time.

PART 5
$\mathcal{M}$AINTAINING
KEEPING THE SYSTEMS GOING

There are people who enjoy an intimate relationship with the heating, plumbing, and electrical systems of their homes, and then there are people like me, who are to home mechanics what Albert Einstein was to steer wrestling.

But so far as I know, he never faced a steer. I, on the other hand, have found that the things I half-learned and quickly forgot in general science class have turned out to be—just as the teachers warned—not only handy but necessary. Even if your eyes tend to glaze over at the mention of words like *volts* and *valve*, it's very helpful to have some elementary understanding of what they are and what they do, if only to describe a potential problem or an actual emergency to someone who's coming to help.

And help is not only expensive, but it is not always available. In fact, the only way to guarantee that you can have an overflowing toilet fixed in the middle of the night or the lights back on before dinner gets cold is to live with someone who possesses knowledge and a toolbox, which is what I did.

Or you can live in an apartment, in which case someone else is generally responsible for all this stuff. Even then, there will be a Sunday when you are on your own to cope with an electrical or plumbing emergency. You might not be willing to venture down into the basement of an apartment building if the lights go out in the middle of your party and the super is nowhere to be found, but someone else might. Knowing the location of the main panel may come in handy. You could certainly attempt to tackle a problem of an overflowing toilet.

If you live in a private home, it is even more likely that you will have to deal with an emergency of this sort. For your safety and convenience, you shouldn't be completely helpless.

What follows is the least you need to know. I'm assuming at one point or another, professional help will come in. I strongly advise that when it arrives—or whenever the fuel service person or the plumber or electrician is on call—you should make a point of asking how to maintain equipment or anything else you're wondering about. You'll make better use of the opportunity if you keep a notebook to jot down questions that come up from time to time about your appliances, your air conditioner, and your heating system.

My experience has been that a lot of people who are experts in their fields actually enjoy showing other people how things work; I've gotten some of my best ideas from them. Do not worry that asking questions makes you look dumb. Not asking keeps you that way.

• •

THE ELECTRICAL SYSTEM

The least you need to know about your electrical system:
- What to do when the lights go out
- What grounding means and how to ground appliances

Once you turn off the power, I'm told, working with the electrical system is very safe. On the other hand, the same person who told me this also persuaded me I should go to the top of the mountain the first time I tried skiing, so I tend to be a little skeptical of his advice.

There is one electrical emergency that you should be able to cope with, though, and that is an overloaded circuit. Pun intended, there is no reason to be in the dark about this one when solving it is so easy.

How the Electrical System Works

In most houses built after World War II, electric service comes into the home over three wires, only two of which are live. It passes through the meter and goes into the service panel, also called the control panel, breaker box, or fuse box.

The control panel is near the electric meter and close to where the power lines come into the house, usually in the basement but possibly in the kitchen.

The control panel is the central command system for the circuits—electrical paths—that are in most homes.

If you have a new home you probably have **circuit breakers,** either switches or buttons. One is the main cut-off breaker, which can shut off all the power in the house at once. There are other switches or buttons, clearly marked "On" and "Off," that control the individual circuits that serve different rooms or (in some cases) individual appliances. To turn off all the power in the house, you flip the main switch to "Off."

Older systems use **fuses,** and the fuse box may be in the kitchen or the basement. At the top of the box may be one or two panels with handles. The electric range may have a separate panel.

Circuit Panel

In still older systems, next to the fuse box is a "knife switch" inside a metal box. To shut off the house power, you pull the lever down.

In an apartment building, the circuit breaker panel or fuse box that controls the circuits in your apartment is most likely in the kitchen.

Most of the individual fuses or breakers control regular 120 volt circuits that each supply up to ten power or lighting out-

Fuse Box

lets. But some circuits supply up to 240 volts to equipment that draws a lot of power, such as the electric range, water heater, electric dryer, and air conditioner. There can also be a low-voltage circuit that has a special transformer especially for the doorbell.

You should know how to turn off the power if, for example, you're wallpapering a room and you want to paper around or behind the light switches, and you should know how to restore it if lights and appliances go out when the circuit that controls that set of lights flips off ("trips") or a fuse burns out ("blows").

Obviously it's important to know which circuit breaker or fuse controls the circuit that you want to turn off or on. If the panel is not already labeled, take the time to work with someone to label it before the emergency arises.

When working at a fuse box always wear rubber soled shoes and stand on dry ground. (If the floor is wet, stand on a dry board).

Some fuses can simply be pulled out. Old-fashioned cartridge fuses must be removed with a special tool called a fuse puller. They usually govern electric ranges and large appliances and are mounted in fuse blocks that have wire handles. Most likely you will be dealing with screw-in (plug) fuses. To remove them, stand on a dry surface, touch only the glass portion, use only one hand to remove them and don't touch anything with the other hand. It can be very shocking to complete a circuit with your body.

To figure out which circuit breaker or fuse controls which area of your home: First turn on all the lights, then one at a time turn off each circuit breaker (by flipping the switch down) or remove each fuse. As you turn off circuit breakers or remote fuses, see which appliance and/or light switches are affected. Most rooms have one or perhaps two circuits, and a kitchen may have four or more.

Label the panel with tied-on tags or sticky labels. Or put a well-marked chart inside the control panel door.

Also, make sure to have a flashlight near the control panel. If there is no other convenient place to put it, attach it to the wall with Velcro.

Finally, if you have a fuse system, have some spares on hand. The sizes in any system vary depending on the size of the appliance and the capacity of the house wiring, from 15 to 20 amps. The replacement fuses must be exactly the same as the old ones. There are tricks to extend the life of a blown fuse, but I won't tell you about them (and don't let anyone else, either): Tricks are dangerous. (Always check why a fuse has blown before you replace it.)

If you are still uncertain how to go about this, contact your utility supplier and ask for help.

Troubleshooting

TO AVOID A CURRENT OVERLOAD

If there is no electrical storm or other unusual occurrence that might have caused a problem in the main power lines and all appliances were working just before the outage, the cause of power failure in just one part of the house is probably an overload.

The overload is just what it sounds like: There is too much electrical power being used on that circuit. Appliances that require heavy-duty wiring, like clothes dryers and ranges, should be put on a separate circuit, as their instruction manuals explain. Since this is usually done, it's more likely that a home overload problem comes from plugging two hair dryers or a couple of other high-wattage appliances such as a toaster and waffle iron into a two-opening (duplex) outlet or into different outlets on the same circuit.

The Underwriters Laboratories, Inc. (UL), a not-for-profit organization that tests thousands of consumer and industrial products for safety standards—manufacturers submit their products voluntarily, pay for the tests, and are subject to random, unannounced factory inspections in order to get the UL mark on their products—recommends that you never plug any combination of appliances into the same circuit if the total combined wattage exceeds 1,500 watts. If you don't know the exact wattage of any item, check it on the manufacturer's nameplate that is attached to the housing of the fixture.

BALANCING THE LOAD

Never plug in two appliances from the high wattage group below into a single outlet or into separate outlets on the same circuit. Two medium-wattage appliances (or one high-wattage with one medium) can be used on the same circuit only if their combined wattage isn't more than 1,500 watts.

High wattage (1,000–1,500). Air conditioner (window), air heater, portable broiler, car block heater, deep fat fryer, dishwasher, frying pan, portable hair dryer, hot plate, iron, kettle, lawn mower, oven, microwave, roaster, sandwich grill, sun lamp, toaster, waffle iron.

Medium wattage (300–800). Attic fan, blender, bottle sterilizer, clothes washer, coffee maker*, computer printer, corn popper, deep freezer (15 cubic foot), dehumidifier, egg cooker, floor polisher, freezer, heated glass tray, hedge trimmer, projector, record player, refrigerator/freezer (14 cubic feet or over), frostless refrigerator (12 cubic feet), TV (color, tube), vacuum cleaner, vaporizer, washing machine (does not include water heating), waste disposer.

Low wattage (up to 200). Air cleaner, electric blanket, can opener, carving knife (electric), electric clock, clock-radio, dehumidifier, electric fan, window fan, infrared heat lamp, heating pad, humidifier, knife sharpener, massager, food mixer, PC, radio, refrigerator (12 cubic foot), sewing machine, shaver, tape recorder, toothbrush, black-and-white TV or solid state color TV, typewriter, vibrator.

Other

Musical instruments	200–800 watts
Power tools	250–1,200 watts
Christmas tree lights	Varies; check label

*Check label; new ones sometimes have very high wattages.

SOURCE: REPRINTED WITH PERMISSION OF UNDERWRITERS LABORATORIES, INC. COPYRIGHT © 1992.

IF AN OVERLOAD OCCURS

If the lights dim when an appliance is plugged in or the appliance doesn't heat up properly, that's a warning to reduce the overload immediately. Otherwise, the breaker will trip or the fuse will blow so the lights will go out and/or the appliance will stop working.

If so, go to your control panel. If you have a **circuit breaker** setup, the switch will have flipped off automatically or moved into the tripped position. If the overload has been eliminated and the problem has been corrected, you can simply flip it back on; or you may have to push the switch to "Off" or "Reset" and then to "On."

If you have a **fuse** panel and there was an overload, the window of a plug fuse will be clear, but you'll see a broken strip, and you have to replace the fuse. (If the fuse is blackened, you may have a short circuit, in which case see below.) First shut off the main power supply, which may involve pulling out the fuse block (or blocks) labeled "Main." (Before you have an emergency, find out how to do this if you aren't exactly sure.) To replace the fuse, stand on dry ground or a dry board and with one hand, grab the outer ring of glass on the fuse and unscrew it. Then replace the fuse with one that is the correct size.

SHORT CIRCUITS

If you flip the switch or replace the fuse and the power goes back off again, or if the power has failed just when the appliance was plugged in or a switch was turned, the problem may be a short circuit in the appliance or lamp. Unplug the questionable item and restore power as instructed on the preceding page.

If lamps or appliances do not appear to be faulty, the trouble may be in the switch outlet or in the wiring between the service panel and outlet, in which case you need an electrician.

If you receive an electric shock when you touch a switch, chain, or appliance, turn the power off and disconnect equipment. Again, if the problem doesn't seem to be the appliance, you need an electrician.

OTHER POTENTIAL EMERGENCIES

If your outlet or appliance makes a crackling noise, feels or smells hot (not just a bit warm after use), emits a spark, smoke or flame, or delivers a shock when you touch it (or the chain), do not unplug it or touch the outlet; you must first go to the panel and turn off the breaker or unscrew the fuse controlling that circuit, following the safety precautions described on the preceding page. Then, with dry hands, cover the appliance plug with a thick, dry towel and pull it out. If the problem is in the switch, turn it to "Off" using a clean, dry stick or wooden spoon, not your hands. Have a repairman look at the appliance or call an electrician to check the outlet.

If your appliance has fallen into the sink or toilet or is lying in a puddle, do not touch it or the water or the plumbing fixture. Follow the instructions in the preceding paragraph, starting by turning off the power to the circuit.

A balky outlet, which works sometimes and other times does not, should be plugged up. Call an electrician or, if you live in an apartment building, advise the super and/or management agent, and do it in writing and keep a copy. If ever a fire results from neglect, you should at least have a record that you reported it.

GROUNDING

To prevent electricity leaks that can cause a shock or create a spark that could start a fire, appliances and tools are insulated. In addition, everything that can leak electricity is

---

MAY THE POWER BE WITH YOU

If you don't have enough electrical outlets, or they're in the wrong place, you may consider using an extension cord. Often, however, the size of the wiring in the cord is not appropriate for your purposes. (See box "Is the Extension Cord on Overload?," p. 212.)

While installing new wiring inside the walls is expensive, an electrician can install a metal conduit on the wall more reasonably. Another possibility is adding plastic "raceways" for appliances that don't draw much power, such as lights, radios, and clocks. You plug one end of the raceway into a power source and snap together plastic links to route wires across baseboards and up walls.

Metal Conduit

Electrical Raceway

"grounded" to prevent shocks. If there is an electricity problem, the extra charge will flow, literally, into the ground, where it is made harmless.

That third, rounded prong you see on the plugs of certain appliances and extension cords is there to ground it properly. If your outlets are properly grounded, but they aren't set up to receive the third (round) prong, you can use an

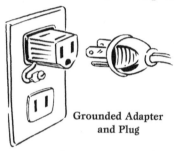

Grounded Adapter and Plug

adapter—sometimes called a "cheater"—that can receive all three prongs. Hanging from the adapter is a little green "ear" that should be connected to a screw on the cover plate so that it is permanently grounded.

To do this, turn off the power to the circuit at the control panel, loosen the metal screw that fastens the cover plate to the outlet, slip the ear underneath the screw, and retighten it. Then restore power. *Although people often use a cheater without screwing it in place, this is not safe.* By doing so, you are exposing yourself to a significant amount of danger.

Circuit Analyzer

There is a home tester—called a three-pronged circuit analyzer—that you can use to see whether each of your outlets is grounded. It comes with instructions and is easy to use. In an old house, even one that you know is grounded, the electrician may have made an error. This tester will tell you what the story is on each and every outlet. Even in a new house, grounding is not always done as a matter of routine.

(Some appliances are permanently connected to a grounded, metal, permanent wiring system. Ask your serviceperson about doing this).

In addition to having proper grounding, have the electrician install a ground-fault circuit interrupter (GFCI) in circuits to the bathroom and kitchen or anywhere else where you're mixing electricity with water. As a general rule, unplug all appliances near water, because even if a plugged-in appliance is off, it can shock you—sometimes fatally—in certain situations: if it falls into water, is cleaned with a damp rag, or if you touch a live part and a ground such as a faucet at the same time. Making contact with an electric current while you are standing on a damp floor can be deadly. A GFCI will beep in the event of such a situation. If an appliance is receiving more electricity than it is giving back—if a hazardous amount of current is seeking ground by way of anything other than the circuit (and this includes your body)—the GFCI cuts off the current immediately, quicker than a heartbeat. It may not prevent a shock, but it will prevent a fatality.

A GFCI will also provide electrical safety throughout your house. Without it, if there is a short circuit and the motor of an appliance continues to run without blowing the fuse or tripping the breaker, the appliance becomes "live." Touching it would give you an electric shock.

A GFCI can be installed in a circuit, a circuit breaker box, or an outlet; there are also portable ones.

THE CHARGE FOR YOUR CHARGES

The current that comes into your home is measured in amperes (amps), and the voltage measures the pressure at which the amperes are delivered. Most appliances need 120 volts; the oven, air conditioner, and heaters may need twice that. Multiplying the amperes times the volts gives you the watts, the measure of the rate you use electricity. Your bill is calculated

in kilowatt (1000-watt) units. How many of them you use depends on how long you keep the appliances and lights on.

The meter usually consists of three or four dials, with numbers from 1 to 9. Read them from left to right to see how many kilowatts you've used. When the pointer is between two digits, read the lower number.

Cord Management

To avoid shorts, don't use appliance or extension cords that are cut, damaged, repaired, hot, or even just warm. Don't leave the cords of new appliances coiled when you're using them. Don't let any cord run under rugs (because the cord can fray or the heat from the cord can start a fire); through standing water or over a wet flooring; or near toasters, ovens, or any other high heat source.

Use the right cord for the job. If the wire is too thin, the current can overheat and damage the cord and may start a fire. Tell the hardware store clerk what you're going to use the cord for to make sure it's the right length and wire size. Never use an extension cord thinner than the appliance cord it attaches to; it's almost sure to overheat.

Keep cords out of the way so that people won't trip over them. You can buy stick-on wire clips to attach cords behind furniture; one clip will hold and guide up to four cords. Cable ties are available to bundle wires or cords together. Insulated staples can tack down individual or bundled wires to keep them running straight along the ground.

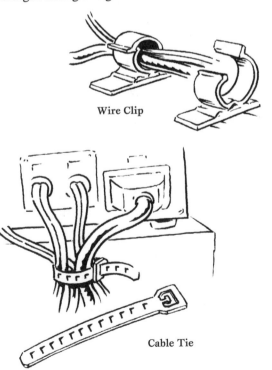

Wire Clip

Cable Tie

You can also make or buy a cord shortener. Use a small piece of cardboard or plastic, make a notch in it to guide the cord through, wind the excess cord around the piece of cardboard or plastic and make a notch to guide it back out. But don't wrap them tightly because they can heat, dry out, or crack—and cause a fire. Cord guards are sold to cover both cords hanging down from a wall lamp and cords running across the floor.

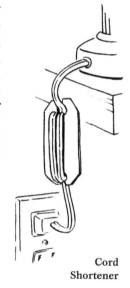

Cord Shortener

If you have a lot of computer wires running across your desk, drill a hole in the desktop to pass them through and edge the hole with a bronze grommet. You see them in most home/office furniture today. The grommets are only around $5 a piece, but you

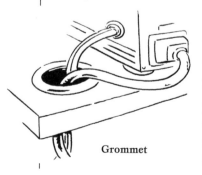

Grommet

may need a special bit for your electric drill to make the hole that will accommodate one.

Check the Securing section regarding fire hazards.

• •

PLUMBING

The least you need to know about plumbing:
• How the water comes in
• How the water goes out
• Dealing with minor plumbing problems

How the Plumbing Works

The idea behind the plumbing system is pretty basic: One part brings fresh water in, the other carries used water out. A pressure system forces hot and cold water into sinks, tubs, and showers for washing and drinking. Gravity carries the waste away through a separate set of pipes into the drainage system.

The one thing you absolutely should know is how to shut the water off in case there is a leak. This is just a matter of turning the handle of the main shutoff valve. The valve may be in the basement or the crawl space under your house or even under the kitchen sink. In an apartment, it may even be in a closet.

If you have a water meter in your home, there's a shutoff valve before the meter and one afterwards; use the one that precedes the meter to avoid damaging it.

Once you have located this valve, or you have had the plumber locate it for you, put a big tag on it so you will have no trouble finding it again. Periodically, check to see that it is not "frozen"—stuck so that it cannot be turned. If it is, call in a plumber. Fiddling around with it, you might break it off, and then you'll have a real problem. If it's just stiff, apply silicone spray.

Connecting to the main shutoff valve are branch lines, several of which carry cold water and one of which goes right to the hot water

TESTING THE METER

You may have a meter that looks like a car odometer, or one that's a series of dials, which should be read clockwise. (The digit on the first measures hundreds of thousands of gallons, the next tens of thousands, and so on.) If it seems as if you're being billed for much more water than you use, turn off everything that uses water in the house and watch the meter for about half an hour. If the dials move, there's a leak someplace.

heater. More branch lines from the hot water heater will carry hot water to various fixtures. At each joint where a riser (a pipe going up) separates from the main pipe, there should ideally be a valve and a drain.

It is a good idea to take the time to figure out which valve works for which fixture, since you always have to close the shutoff valve when doing any work to prevent a flood. Do this by closing the valves one at a time, then testing which faucets you can turn on without a flow of water. Then tag them. While tagging your pipes, like tagging your electrical circuits, might not be your idea of a weekend's entertainment, think of it as no-cost flood insurance.

There should be also be a shutoff valve and drains right at the hot water tank, boiler, toilet, kitchen sink, and bathroom sink. (Tubs and showers don't always have their own shutoff valves.) Test these from time to time to make

OPENING AND CLOSING A VALVE

Face the valve. To close it, or turn it off, turn it clockwise or to the right. (To remember, I think of the word *write-off*, like a tax write-off.) To open it, turn it counterclockwise, or to the left.

sure that they aren't frozen—if they are, call the plumber—and also check to see if they actually work and hold back the water. A washer, which is a rubber or metal ring that helps make a seal, is the key part of these valves, and if the washers are worn, they won't work. If there are leaks, the packing should be replaced.

Purity of Water

If your water is supplied by a well rather than by the town, you should have it tested for bacteriological impurities once a year by your local health department. If your well water needs purification, you may have to call in a professional to install a purification system to treat all the house water.

The Hot Water System

Water comes into the house at a temperature of about 55° F., cooler in winter. To make it hot enough for laundering, dishwashing, and bathing it must be heated in a coil that passes through a boiler or, more commonly, a gas, oil, or electric hot water heater.

The rule of thumb is that gas and oil heaters last about ten years, electric heaters somewhat longer, but in my experience they have all lasted much longer than that, and they rarely give you any problems. Which you choose is a matter of balancing costs and other concerns—electric is more expensive than gas, but gas causes indoor pollution.

The amount of draining your new water heater requires may vary; check your owner's manual for instructions. Draining "blows off" the sediment that might make the machine operate less efficiently. Turn off the hot water supply using the shutoff valve (at the top of the heater) and don't use the hot water for an hour or so, to give sediment time to settle. Put a bucket below the drain valve at the bottom of the tank, and open the valve. Let the water run until it's clear, then reverse the process. Turn off the drain and turn on the water supply.

You should also check the pressure-relief valve at the top of the heater. Just turn the handle. If it's working, there will be some hot water released.

In a gas heating system, the flue should be checked semiannually to see if there's any gas escaping. See the box in this section, p. 224, on checking your gas heating system for safety.

PROBLEMS WITH WATER HEATERS

If water won't heat in an electric system, first see if the fuse has blown or the switch has tripped. If you have a gas system, the pilot light, located at the bottom of the heater, may be off. The restarting instructions may be marked on the heater. Usually, you hold the restart button for five seconds. If you close the gas shutoff valve and clean the ports (the little holes in the ring that surrounds the flame), you can relight it yourself (see information p. 224 on relighting pilot lights). If you've never done this before, get professional help but ask how you can do it yourself in the future.

To save energy, wrap the water heater tank with an insulation blanket sold for this purpose (inexpensive and easy to do), install a thermal trap (ask your plumber), and keep the thermostat on the heater at 140° F. or lower. In fact, the only appliance that needs water at 140° F. is the dishwasher; if the machine has its own temperature booster, which is available in some models, you can keep the house water temperature set to 115° F.

If the water is too hot, first check to see if the thermostat is set too high, but if turning it down doesn't help, call for service right away. A faulty thermostat can cause scalding.

THE PIPE SYSTEM

The best pipes are made of copper. They last a minimum of 20 years and may last 50 years or

PREVENTING HOT WATER BURNS

• House hot water temperature is often set to 140° F., but water scalds human skin at 137° F. (At least one gas company warns that any setting above 125° F. may cause severe burns). For a comfortable shower you need water between 100–115° F. As a safety measure and energy saver, you can have a plumber install a mixing valve in the hot water line to the bathroom (or to the tub or shower) to make sure this temperature is not exceeded. Larger boilers may already have mixing valves.

• Always turn the cold water on first and off last. (If you've got a single-lever faucet, a self-sticking colored dot—from an office supply store—can be pressed right onto the bathtub tile to mark the correct faucet position for the perfect bath temperature.)

more. Brass piping, which is less common, is also sturdy; it lasts 20 to 25 years. Older houses may have galvanized steel piping. You can tell at a glance if pipes are copper because of the distinctive reddish color, but to tell whether pipes are brass or galvanized metal, put a magnet to them. Brass pipes won't hold a magnet, but galvanized steel will.

Unfortunately, galvanized steel pipes will last only about five years because the inside of the pipe corrodes. Rusted steel expands to sixteen times its original size, so the rust eventually clogs the pipes like cholesterol in an artery. The clogging starts on the top floors. If the water pressure is beginning to fail on the top floor, it's a sign that the galvanized steel needs replacing. If there has never been sufficient pressure anywhere, it's a sign that the pipes are sized incorrectly or the main supply line is too small.

Occasionally, pipes may leak or corrode, usually at a joint. Use an epoxy made for repairing leaks. It comes in a package of two tubes. You mix what is inside them together and get a product the consistency of children's clay. Patted around the outside of the joint, it hardens and makes the joint waterproof.

Though hot and cold water pipes usually run side by side, there should be at least 6" of space between them, and both should be insulated. You insulate hot water pipes to keep the heat from going out and heating the room rather than staying in the water. You insulate the cold water pipes to prevent them from dripping and sweating as a result of condensation. Since cold surfaces don't hold moisture, when moisture from the air remains on an uninsulated pipe, it condenses.

How Water Leaves the House

The pipes in the drainage system ("soil stacks") are usually made of cast iron or—most likely—plastic, specifically PVC (polyvinyl chloride), which is the cheapest and easiest to install. They lead from all plumbing fixtures to one main line. They're generally larger than the risers that carry water up, and they work on gravity and pitch. Waste leaves the house through the drain line and goes either to a municipal system or your own septic tank.

Body waste and deteriorating food both contain bacteria, which produce gas. To allow the gas to escape and to equalize the pressure on the water leaving the system and prevent the formation of a partial vacuum, which would block the flow of waste, pipes in the walls above the soil stacks, called vent stacks, lead from the drain line upward to a vent opening in the roof. As you can imagine, this opening must never be covered or clogged. To keep leaves and debris out, place chicken wire over the vent.

Every drain also has a trap, a water seal that prevents gases from coming back up. The internal shape of a toilet bowl makes it a self-trapping fixture. The water that stays in it prevents gases (and odors) from coming back into the house. Under the kitchen and bathroom sink there is an S- or P-shaped pipe that is a trap. The tub or shower trap may be set in the floor under the unit.

Septic Tanks

If you aren't connected to city sewers you will have your own steel or concrete underground septic tank. It must be inspected every couple of years and pumped out if necessary. Otherwise, the tank will fill up, and your drainage system will back up. The results will be every bit as horrible as you might imagine and will probably occur when you have a house full of company, a situation that stinks in every sense of the word. Regular maintenance and bacterial additives also prevent the pipes from clogging to the point where they have to be snaked (unclogged) or replaced.

If you're thinking of installing a garbage disposal, make sure your septic tank has the capacity to handle it.

Repairing Plumbing Problems

Even if you haven't been able to figure out how to program the VCR you might still be able to handle simple plumbing repairs. Before you start, keep two things in mind.

First, always shut off the nearest shutoff valve to any appliance so you don't have a flood and create an ever bigger problem. Second, be careful about protecting the appliance. This

WHAT NOT TO PUT IN YOUR PIPES

WHAT NOT TO PUT IN YOUR PIPES

• Chemical solutions such as paint thinner, cleaning fluids, or any chemical drain cleaners. Toxic substances (even the ones sold specifically to clean out your pipes) not only may eat away the pipes but also kill the good bacteria in your septic system that work to break down and liquefy the solid wastes.

• Grease, because it will harden and clog the line. If grease is mistakenly poured down the drain, follow it with a kettle of boiling water.

• Tea leaves or rice, because either will swell and clog the line.

includes covering any decorative fitting with cloth or tape before you use a wrench, lining a tub with paper or towels so if you drop a tool you won't crack the surface, putting the stopper in the tub so the parts you've dismantled don't go down the drain, and not using an electric snake or other inappropriate tool on porcelain.

Dishwasher (or Washing Machine) Overflowing

A portable machine (that empties into a sink), may just need to be unplugged. But if you have an automatic machine, turn the dial to the end of the cycle and the machine will begin to empty. Use a wet vacuum or home extraction machine to suck up the water, or use towels. If the problem was just using the wrong detergent, put the clothes or dishes through a couple of rinse cycles. Otherwise, drain it, turn it off, unplug it, and call a plumber. See also p. 250.

Drain, Clogged

The usual causes of clogged drains are hair and bits of soap in the bathroom, grease and other foods in the kitchen. Do not wait until the drain is completely clogged. Deal with it once it starts running slowly. There are several solutions:

1. Try one of the home remedies in the box on p. 217.

2. Put a heat lamp or hair dryer (turned to hot) directly under the sink trap until the grease has melted. *Do not do this if you have plastic pipes.* Flush the drain by running hot water for a few minutes.

3. Use a plunger (also known as a plumber's friend), an inverted rubber cup with a wood handle. Close the overflow (probably in the front lip; it's where the water goes when your kid leaves water running in the sink) by plugging it with a cloth. Otherwise, when you plunge, water will go down one hole and come back up the overflow. Fill the sink with about 4 to 5 inches of water. Put the cup of the plunger over the drain, and press down hard. Then pull the handle up, push down again, and repeat ten or twelve times. The work is done as the plunger is pulled up. Adding a little petroleum jelly around the rim gives it better suction.

4. If that doesn't work, you need a drain auger (sometimes called a snake)—a long, flexible cable with an auger hook at one end and a handle at the other. You have to insert the auger into the trap. Either open up the plug in the trap with a wrench or, if there is none, use the wrench to remove the trap itself. Put a pail beneath it to catch the water. The idea is to push the auger in little by little, 18" at a time, or it will tangle. When that much is completed, put in another 18". When you reach the obstruction, either break it up or snag it with the hook and pull it toward you. If you don't have an auger, you can simply use a coat hanger and make a little hook at the end.

5. If you can run a garden hose into the house, you can use it to give you extra power. Wrap a towel around the hose to fully close the drain opening and push the nozzle as far into

NON-TOXIC, HOMEMADE DRAIN OPENER

Pouring caustics down the drain is bad for your pipes but this home remedy isn't. Pour in a cup of salt and a cup of baking soda, followed by a kettle of boiling water. If the problem is just coagulated grease, it will usually dissolve immediately. For best results, though, don't use the drain for several hours. If you need something stronger, but not as strong as lye, dissolve 2 tablespoons of washing soda in a quart of hot water and pour it slowly down the drain. After 10 minutes flush with hot water.

CAUTION: Washing soda may irritate skin and mucous membranes so wear rubber gloves.

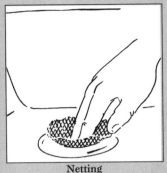
Netting

SAFETY NET

Prevent most clogs in the bathroom by using a strainer cup. Or push a piece of netting (the kind of netting you've seen in prom dresses or ballet costumes) into the drain. Pull it out, discard it, and replace it with a new piece from time to time.

Strainer Cup

the drain as possible. Hold on tightly while someone else turns on the outdoor faucet. Whatever is clogged should be forced out by the water pressure.

Only in desperate circumstances should you use a chemical drain opener. These come in three forms: granular, which contains lye; liquid, which contains lye and other chemicals; or pressurized. If you use granular drain cleaner, don't allow any standing water to remain in the sink or tub. If the chemical remains in place, it may damage porcelain. Read the instructions carefully.

Never mix chemicals. If you've used one and are about to use another, flush or rinse away the first completely. Never use a plunger or pressurized drain opener after you've used chemicals. The chemicals may splash on you. If you wind up getting professional help, be sure to tell the plumber what you've already poured down the drain even if you're embarrassed to say it.

FAUCET LEAKING FROM BASE

Drips from the faucet or leaks at the base of the faucet handle are usually caused by a worn washer or deterioration of the packing or the valve seat. If reading these terms convinces you that you're already in over your head, bear with me for another paragraph or two while I try to convince you that fixing a faucet is much easier than helping your kid play with an Erector Set, and saves you money besides.

You need a crescent wrench or pliers, screwdriver, and new packing or new O-rings from the hardware store. Turn off the shutoff valve under the sink. Then remove the decorative cap on the faucet. Cover it with a piece of cloth so that when you grab it with pliers or a wrench you don't scratch the chrome. Keep loosening whatever pieces you find until you come to the packing nut. You may have thought a packing nut was someone who took too many suitcases on vacation. Here, it refers to a six-sided, dough-

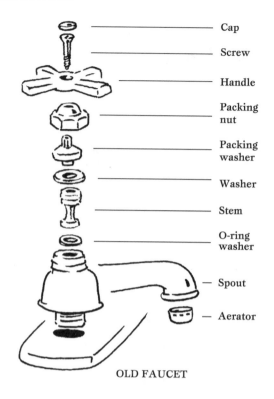

Cap

Screw

Handle

Packing
nut

Packing
washer

Washer

Stem

O-ring
washer

Spout

Aerator

OLD FAUCET

nut-shaped piece. Tighten it with your pliers or wrench (right is tight; left is loose). Then replace everything.

But if the leak persists, or if you have to turn the nut so tight you can't operate the faucet, you have to replace the graphite packing (in an old faucet) or the narrow O-ring washers that are at the base of the stem. Disassemble the faucet once again, loosen the packing nut, turn the handle as if you're opening the faucet, and pull out the stem with an adjustable crescent wrench. Dig out the old packing and replace it. Or remove the washer by unscrewing the small (bib) screw at the base of the stem that holds it in place. Replace the O-rings. Reinsert the stem, put the washer back on, and replace the packing nut and the faucet handle.

In a new single lever faucet the cartridge will probably need to be replaced. Ask your hardware clerk or plumbing supply dealer to help you select the right one.

FAUCET DRIPPING

If a drip starts to bother you in the middle of the night, just stick a piece of rag or a piece of string into the faucet to carry the water into the sink silently, go back to sleep and deal with it in the morning.

Fixing the problem is really not very hard. If you have a two-faucet, single spout setup, follow instructions above to take the faucet apart. (If you have another kind of faucet, check a good how-to book.) While leaks are probably due to a packing or O-ring problem, drips are more likely to be caused by a deteriorating washer. As it gets old, a washer gets crushed, frayed, pitted, and grooved to the point where it's hard to tell what the new one should look like. So take the stem to the hardware store to fit a replacement washer that's exactly the right size. Replace the washer (and if the bib screw has deteriorated, replace it, too), reinsert the stem, and continue to reverse your previous steps.

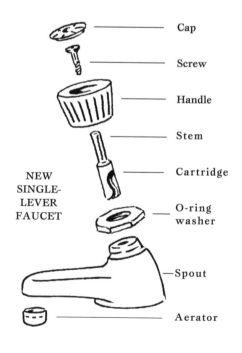

Cap

Screw

Handle

Stem

Cartridge

O-ring
washer

Spout

Aerator

NEW
SINGLE-
LEVER
FAUCET

If the washer is really ripped up or it needs replacing every couple of days, the thing it rests on, called the valve seat, needs to be replaced or smoothed down with something called a dressing tool. Check the how-to books for further advice (it's not hard to do this job if you have the right tool), or call a plumber.

PIPES FROZEN

Thaw them right away to prevent bursting. Shut off the water at the main valve and open the faucet nearest the frozen pipes so water can drain out as it thaws. You can cover them with hot towels or wrap a heating pad around the pipes or direct a hair dryer at them if they're not plastic; the thawing should be gradual to prevent cracking. If the pipes are hidden behind walls, ceilings, or floors or are near gas lines, call a plumber for help.

To prevent this problem, install pipe insulation. Try not to have your pipes run on exterior walls. And in an emergency—if your heating system goes down and it's very cold—try the country trick of leaving one faucet running with a slow drip.

PIPES SWEATING

Wrap them with adhesive-backed insulating tape or with pre-slit, sleeve-type insulation. (If you want to know why pipes sweat, see Toilet Sweating, p. 221.)

PRESSURE INADEQUATE/EXCESSIVE

Sometimes solving the pressure problem in pipes is only a matter of cleaning or replacing the aerator, the little mesh screen at the end of the faucet that easily screws off. A de-liming solution, or a half-and-half vinegar and water solution, should do the job. Otherwise, you or the plumber can make sure the shutoff valves are all properly opened. In the worst possible case, the pipes are clogged due to too much lime and must be replaced. If you have the opposite problem, too much pressure, you can have pressure-reducing valves installed.

TOILET FLUSHING CONTINUOUSLY

My friend's building superintendent told her that the reason her toilet flushed continuously was that she wasn't flushing hard enough. I told her I was sure her flushing technique was flawless. The problem was in the toilet. Making repairs to your toilet is actually not very hard. Often the solution is simply to repair a single worn part (which is easily done; all hardware stores sell replacements and they often come with instructions). Better still, you can completely replace the inside of some units with more modern flush retrofits that are quieter, save water, and need less maintenance.

Before you start, turn off the shutoff valve under the tank or the valve that supplies cold water to the bathroom.

Then look inside the tank and push the lever to flush. You will see two things happen. First, upper and lower lift wires pull up a rubber stopper (tank ball) from the bottom of the tank

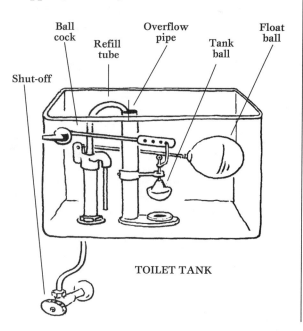

TOILET TANK

so water flows out and into the bowl. Second, as the tank is emptying, the float drops, and opens a supply valve (ball cock) that lets more water into the tank.

You may get continuous flushing if the wires are misaligned going into the tank ball so that the seal between it and the part it rests on isn't tight. Or the seal may be incomplete because the tank ball developed tiny holes over time (or from tank treatments) and/or the part it rests on is slimy.

First, make sure the guide arm that lifts the stopper is perfectly vertical. Loosen the thumbscrew that holds it in place, straighten out the arm, then retighten the screw. Second, remove the worn stopper (it just unscrews) and clean the slimy area underneath with steel wool, then screw on a replacement.

Another possibility is that there is a problem with the float. After the shutoff valve has been turned off and the toilet has been flushed once, unscrew the float. Shake it out. If it contains water, replace it. Otherwise, screw it back on, and open the shutoff valve so that water is running normally into the tank.

There is yet another thing you can try. Lift the float with your hand. If the water continues to run, you must replace the washer in the ball cock, the supply valve in the pipe on the left-hand side of the tank. This is not at all complicated, but describing it makes it sound as if it is. The part costs pennies; see if the hardware store clerk can help you or ask if you should replace this whole system. You will need to buy a toilet repair kit. When you buy it, you will find instructions on the package.

TOILET LEAKING AT BOTTOM

Simple. If the tank is sitting on the bowl, tighten the nuts at bottom of the tank. Drain the tank, reach down inside, use a screwdriver inside the tank and a wrench outside. Use penetrating oil to loosen the bolts before you retighten them. *Whenever you tighten nuts on a toilet, be careful not to overdo it as the tank can crack.* If that doesn't do the job, replace the washers.

If the leak is at the water supply pipe, tighten the nut that holds the fitting in place. If the leak persists, shut off the water supply and replace the washers.

A leak at the toilet base can sometimes be fixed by tightening the hold-down bolts. Otherwise, you may need to replace the entire toilet and install a new seal.

TOILET OVERFLOWING

The next time the toilet threatens to overflow, remove the top of the tank and pull up the float (so-called because it's that big ball floating in the tank). If this stops the flow of water, unscrew the float from its rod. If there's water inside, it's got a leak and needs replacing. If there is no leak in the faucet, bend the rod down about $1/2$ inch.

Otherwise, the problem is in the ball cock, which is the supply valve that should close off once the float is at the proper height. The washers inside the ball cock probably need replacing. Remove the screws on the side of the ball cock and you'll see the washers attached to the plunger that fits inside it.

NO TANKS

This talk of toilet tanks may be confusing to you if there is no tank on your toilet, just a small metal part rising slightly above the toilet handle. This is called a pressure flush valve and is used most commonly in apartment buildings because they require larger pipes than in most single homes; you do see them in new homes, condos, and co-ops. You can buy parts to repair leaks, and instructions are available in any good do-it-yourself book.

CONSERVING WATER IN THE TOILET

The amount of water flushed is regulated by the height and pressure of the water over the stopper. You could have a taller, narrower tank (with less water) that would work just as well. Since you can't redesign the water tank, fill up some of the space with plastic bottles containing water.

Or just bend the guide wire on the float slightly so it's lower in the tank. If flushing isn't complete, you've overdone it: Bend the bar back slightly.

There are now products available that will retrofit large toilet tanks so they use less water.

It is also possible that the refill tube between the ball cock and the overflow pipe doesn't fit properly (or needs replacing).

TOILET STOPPED UP

Something's down there. Something big. Like a roll of toilet paper, your hairbrush, or your kid's rubber ducky. Faced with this problem, your real inclination is probably just to leave and move somewhere else. However, the more repulsive but economic solution is to bail out the water, slip on your rubber gloves, and reach in. If you can't get the item out, try a plunger. Put the cup of the plunger over the drain and press down hard. Then pull the handle up, push down again, and repeat ten or twelve times until the toilet empties. If that doesn't work, either call a plumber or borrow or rent a closet auger (like a drain auger, but designed so it won't hurt porcelain).

Plastic items are especially difficult to remove since they slip past the auger. If you have shelves above the toilet, be careful about what you keep there.

TOILET SWEATING

Cooled by the water inside the tank (usually at 55° F.), the surface of the tank is cooler than the air around it (usually 68° F.), and cool surfaces don't hold moisture. So the moisture in the air condenses on the tank and drips. Reducing the overall humidity in the house would help, but that's a big job. One inexpensive but complicated solution is to have your plumber glue a thin foam liner inside the tank after removing the whole inside mechanism; an alternative is running in a hot-water line and connecting it to an "anti-sweat" valve to warm the tank during warm weather. The easiest solution is buying a tank cover in a bath shop. Wash it regularly or it gets mildewy.

TUB OR SHOWER LEAK

Shower body stems are basically the same design as faucet stems, except they are longer and set deep into the wall. You can get to the nut and loosen the stem and fix it as you would a sink faucet. You'll need a special tool, a deep-set socket wrench, in order to change the washer.

If there is plumber's putty or grout that doesn't allow you to get the tool around the stem, you may need to chip it away with a screwdriver and replace it afterward.

WATER PIPES BANGING

You hear what's called "water hammer" when flowing water is forced to stop suddenly—for example, when the faucet is closed or a washing machine changes cycles. Just close the faucet more slowly.

You (or a handy friend) can install girdle-like supports around horizontal pipes so they don't vibrate as much. Or you may need a plumber to put in an extra length of vertical pipe, called an air chamber, that acts as a shock absorber.

• •

HEATING AND COOLING

The least you need to know about your heating/cooling system:

- Fuels: oil vs. gas
- The three heating systems
- Maintenance required for your system
- How to correct minor problems

Gas and Oil Heating Systems

Your house may be heated by burning oil or by gas. Even if you use oil for heating, though, gas probably fuels the stove and dryer. Gas-fueled air conditioning systems exist but are rare.

If you burn oil fuel, you will have several deliveries during the cold season. Check the oil readings before and after delivery, and watch the gauge periodically. If the amount of oil in the tank goes below 10% of its capacity, impurities are sucked out of the bottom of the tank into the oil burner, and then both the burner and filter will need cleaning. By-products of oil burning are sulphur and water vapor, which makes a mild sulphuric acid. This tends to corrode the chimney.

Gas is a more efficient fuel, so you burn less of it; it's relatively non-polluting and readily

---

MAINTENANCE REQUIRED FOR BURNERS

For oil burner: The fuel company should inspect and service annually. Make arrangements.

Gas furnaces should be inspected annually also, but gas burns cleaner than oil. See p. 225.

---

available, but you have to pay more to equip your house for gas heating. Which you choose depends on what is most economical for you.

IF YOU SWITCH FROM OIL TO GAS HEAT

Clean the chimney completely at time of conversion and for the first year or two, check the chimney twice a year: once during the heating season and once during summer. The problem is that burning oil leaves a carbon residue that can't be completely eliminated. Since gas burns drier than oil, it dries out the carbon, which then loses its adhesion to the walls of the chimney and tends to create a blockage. After a couple of years, you can cut back to an annual cleaning, after the middle of the heating season. Do that for the first three years or so, and after that it's a judgment call. However, the chimney should be inspected annually to prevent carbon monoxide poisoning.

When making the change, you may have to decide among the various gas heating systems. Call in a gas heating contractor to help you estimate the needs of your home and choose among the conventional warm air furnace, high-efficiency furnace, pulse combustion boiler, heat pipe high-efficiency furnace, condensing furnace, heat transfer module, and a combination space-water heater. Why you would choose one of these over another is a matter of economy. The measure of the differences among furnaces is the AFUE, the Annual Fuel Utilization Efficiency. That's the total heating output divided by the total fuel input. Furnaces can have AFUEs ranging from 57% to 97%. The higher the better, of course, but also the more expensive to purchase. Over the long run, you have a savings in your fuel costs.

HOW GAS WORKS

You don't need delivery of gas; it's always available to you. The gas company main line is connected to a service line into your house. When gas comes into the house, it flows into a chamber, fills it up, then flows into the next of three additional compartments. As gas is used, the pressure drops in one of the chambers, and gas flows into it from another chamber that has higher pressure. Your gas meter has four parts, each of which measures the amount of gas in each chamber. The total gas you use is measured in cubic feet, which is then converted into your monthly bill.

IS THE GAS ON OR OFF?

Whether the shutoff valve has a handle or a key, it is open when the handle or key is parallel with the pipe and off when it's perpendicular to it.

Shutoff valves at the meter and each unit let you turn off gas in the entire system or at any appliance. Some are manually operated and others need a special key.

What's brought to your home through gas company pipes is usually 95% to 98% methane gas. Methane won't burn except in the presence of both oxygen and heat in just the right amounts. If there is too much or too little oxygen in the air, the gas won't burn. (The reason it is safe to weld near a gas line is because inside the line, there is no air at all—and when there's no oxygen, there's no burning.) You also need quite a bit of heat. The ignition point of methane is 1100° F. (Even so, a gas leak is highly flammable because an open flame or even a match can momentarily produce temperatures up to 1200° F.).

THE DANGER OF LEAKING GAS

The major problem with a gas leak is not that you will be poisoned (methane is not toxic) or even because of the risk of fire, but because

methane replaces all the breathable air. If the windows are open, this is not a big problem. Methane is lighter than air and will find a way out. But if the room is sealed, the methane will fill it and there is a danger of suffocation.

You can't see methane, and you can't smell it—it's odorless. So to warn people of a leak, the gas companies odorize it with an unpleasant, distinctive, sulphurlike smell. If ever you smell a gas leak, refer to If Gas Is Leaking, pp. 274–275.

DETECTING CARBON MONOXIDE

The ideal air/fuel ratio for burning is 15 parts oxygen to 1 part gas. If the ratio is 10 to 1, combustion is incomplete and you get carbon monoxide. Carbon monoxide displaces oxygen in your red blood cells, a life-threatening emergency.

Incomplete combustion is obviously harder to detect than a gas leak unless you are actually looking for it, in which case it's not hard at all. Just check the flame in your gas burner. A normal flame is bright blue, with a yellow tip. In the case of incomplete combustion, the flame becomes more and more yellow. The cause is either an excess of fuel or a lack of available air. If any flame (from the dryer or the range) is burning only yellow and/or if anyone in the family is showing the symptoms of carbon monoxide poisoning, leave the building. Call the gas company immediately.

One of the problems with carbon monoxide is that it can build up over time and without warning; it has no odor. If you are exposed to it for a while, carbon monoxide poisoning can cause headaches, nausea, dizziness, coughing, ringing in the ears, and spots before the eyes. If anyone in your household is chronically complaining about these symptoms, get medical attention. Check out the possibility of carbon monoxide accumulation. If it's not taken care of, it can be fatal. (See p. 275 for more information about gas leaks.)

CHECKING YOUR GAS HEATING SYSTEM FOR SAFETY

Chances are your utility company performs free annual inspection. You can perform your own venting check twice a year. Operate the furnace or boiler for at least ten minutes, then hold a lit match to the edge of the draft hood or access panel (a rectangular opening at the top of the casing around the furnace), and move it across the opening. If the flame is going up, the flue pipe and chimney are clear. If the flame is blown downward or extinguished, turn the furnace off and call your fuel company.

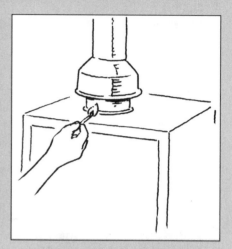

Other things to look for:

• Soot or carbon deposits or yellow flames. These are signs of incomplete burning and dangerous, so call your fuel company. These may be caused by inadequate air supply or the failure of the venting system (probably due to blockage).

• Rust or holes in the flue pipe. If you see any, the pipe needs replacing.

• Excessive smoking. When first turned on, the boiler should smoke for only a minute. Otherwise you are wasting fuel, converting it to soot instead of heat. Check with the serviceperson.

IF THE PILOT LIGHT GOES OFF

New stoves don't have pilot lights, the eternal flame that ignites stovetop burner. But if yours does and it goes out (or the pilot light in your hot water heater does the same), you will need to relight it. Allow time for any gas accumulation to escape before you strike a match. On the stovetop, you can usually light your match and hold it to the pilot light head (you may have to lift the stovetop first), then turn on the gas. The procedures for a gas heater and an oven may be a little more complicated but should be on an instruction plate on the appliance.

If the pilot doesn't light immediately after you've followed the instructions, turn off the gas at the main shutoff valve and call the fuel company.

A gas heater may shut down automatically if there is a problem with the pilot light on the boiler. In this case, you won't be able to reset it and must call the gas company.

If there is any kind of problem with leaking gas due to a defective appliance, the gas company will cut off your gas until the appliance is replaced.

If you turn off a pilot light for the heating system in the summer months, the fuel company will restart it as a regular service.

WHEN A GAS STOVE BURNER DOESN'T LIGHT

Sometimes you may simply have some clogging in the burner ring. Turn off the gas and use a needle or pin to poke at the little holes. There could also be dirt in the pipe that faces the burner ring. Clean it with a pipe cleaner. If that's not sufficient, you may need to adjust the flame, which is pretty simple and should be described in your user's manual. Otherwise, you may need professional help.

CENTRAL HEATING SYSTEMS

They say that English women traditionally had wonderful complexions because there was no central heating, which so far as I can figure, is the only really substantial argument against it. Though some American homes have direct heat—from a stove, for example, or electric baseboard heat (which is a very clean, but expensive system)—central heating is typical in most American homes.

The system has three parts: the heat **source,** the heat **plant,** and the heat **distribution system.**

The heat **source** is usually a gas or oil furnace, an electric heater, or a heat pump. It is hooked up to a heat **plant**—a furnace that heats air or a boiler that heats water or makes steam. If flames are involved, they are separated from the air or water and the waste products from the heat are expelled through a flue—a single metal pipe or an opening through the chimney. One chimney can have several flues. They carry away heat from burning oil or gas. (Wood-burning fireplaces have their own flues that run up through the chimney.) New heating systems have a "spill switch," or a vent system safety switch that automatically shuts off your heating system if your flue pipe or chimney becomes blocked. If you don't have this already, call your plumber or fuel company to have it installed.

Warm air, hot water, or steam may be the **distribution system** that carries the heat from the plant to the various rooms in the house. It travels through ducts or pipes and is controlled by a thermostat.

MAINTAINING THE HEATING PLANT

The maintenance for a **gas furnace** includes checking for flue leaks, relighting the pilot if necessary, replacing the filters, and servicing the blowers. Consult your manual and schedule annual servicing. (To check for a flue leak and relight the pilot see page 224).

If an **oil burner** goes off, check the thermostat. Or see if the emergency switch has been flipped off by mistake. (Look for a switch on a red plate, usually located some distance from the burner.) Or see if the recycle switch is on (it's on a metal box attached to the pipe that runs from heater to chimney). Flick it on and the burner should start; give it a little hit if it doesn't start right away. Finally, make sure you have oil in the tank; check gauges or stick a rod down into the underground tank after removing the cap on the fill line. Schedule annual servicing.

Heat pumps, which are usually used in areas where the temperature doesn't go below 15° F., draw the heat from outside air (which, even at low temperatures, has a surprising amount of heat) to heat the inside. If the pump's not working properly, your electric bill will go way up. At low temperatures, there may be a heavy accumulation of ice or no ice whatsoever; both indicate a problem. Check the outside coil to make sure it's not obstructed by snow or leaves; it should work properly within an hour once you clear them away. If ice remains, call your heating contractor.

Boilers are like giant kettles, but the amount of water within them must be regulated by various controls. For example, there is a low-water cutoff valve on the boiler so that the burner won't go on if the water level is too low. Otherwise, if the water runs out in the boiler, the boiler will crack. (Old-timers who run boilers in big apartment buildings put a little oatmeal in a cracked boiler because that seals it right up. I don't think I'd try this at home.) There is also a pressure control regulator on the boiler so the pressure doesn't get too high. You have to check to make sure these valves are working and manually open the "blow-off" valve to drain out water monthly and remove any rust or other sediment. Sometimes water has to be treated to prevent rust. Check with your serviceperson.

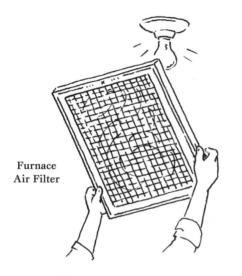

Furnace
Air Filter

Heating Distribution and Problems

WARM AIR HEATING CIRCULATION

After the air is heated in the furnace, it's forced through supply ducts to registers around the house. Cooled air is pulled back through return ducts and blowers force it back into the furnace, and the cycle begins again. (Old systems work similarly but rely on gravity instead of blowers.)

Before leaving the furnace, the air passes through a filter that removes dust and dirt. You have to clean the filter periodically. If it is not clean, the furnace uses extra energy (which costs you money), and over a period of time, it may overheat to the point where it burns out. Some filters may be cleaned and reused, generally by vacuuming, and others are disposable. This is an easy job. You hold the filter up to the light and if you can't see light through it, it should be replaced. I've suggested you do it at least semiannually, but you could check it as often as once a month.

The forced air system obviously creates a lot of dust and dirt as it moves the air around, but on the plus side, it doesn't depend on water (so you have no pipe problems).

If you're putting in a system, make sure the vents are all on the walls. If they're on the floor, they send dirt up along the walls and they're likely to catch anything that spills.

COMMON PROBLEMS WITH FORCED WARM AIR

If the house is not warm enough, and you've checked the power switch, you may be having a problem with the burner or thermostats. You can also check to see if the air filter or warm air register is dirty, or if any return-air grill (which is larger, and there are fewer of them, maybe only one per floor) is blocked.

If you're hearing a lot of noise, the blower belt may be worn-out or the blower may be running too fast. Call in a service person.

HOT WATER CIRCULATION

Water in this setup is heated to between 180° F. and 240° F. in a boiler, then pumped through pipes that lead to radiators, baseboard units, or coils set in a concrete slab floor. Pressure-reducing valves in the water supply line add water to the system when needed, and valves on radiators, etc., allow air to escape to allow in more water. The boiler heats water in a separate system for the house hot water supply.

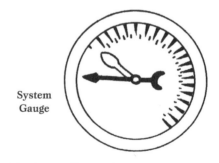

System
Gauge

A black needle on the gauge shows the height the water should be at, and a white needle indicates the actual height. If everything is working correctly, the white needle should be directly over the black one.

COMMON PROBLEMS WITH CIRCULATING HOT WATER SYSTEM

If the heat goes off or is turned off, the water can freeze. If you're planning to leave a house on a trip, you can call the plumber and either have your pipes drained or add antifreeze.

If you hear a lot of noise in this system, there may be something wrong with the circulating pump. Call your serviceperson.

If the radiators are cold, they may need to have air released. If this isn't done automatically by the system, look at the top of the radiator for the air release vent, which may have a slot in the top for a screwdriver (or a special key). When you turn the screwdriver to open it, you'll hear a hissing as the air goes out of the tiny spout. After the air is released and water begins to spurt out (have a cup ready to catch it), close the vent immediately.

If the system has shut off, it may not have enough water and the low-water cutoff has turned it off automatically. Call your serviceperson to see how to fix this.

Air Valve

Inlet Valve

STEAM HEATING CIRCULATION

Older homes and apartments use steam systems that work on a simple principle that water heated to 212° F. will turn to steam and rise. Since it costs more to heat water to 212° F. than just enough to run through a hotwater system, steam heat is not used in newer buildings.

Pipes carry the steam to radiators throughout the house. As the steam cools, it condenses and runs back down to be reheated and then is sent back upstairs as heat again; it's a sealed system.

COMMON PROBLEMS WITH STEAM HEATING

If heating isn't satisfactory, the air valves may be clogged or worn-out, so steam is not able to enter the radiator on the side. The air valve is high on the radiator. The air vent could be painted and the opening closed. It should be upright or it won't work. Try opening the vent wider by using a screwdriver to turn the dial to a lower number. (The screwdriver fits right into a slot at the vent.) Or buy a new one at the hardware store (no equipment needed to install it).

If you hear a lot of knocking, check to see if the radiator inlet valve is fully opened or closed. A lot of people think that you can open a valve partway, to let in just a bit of heat, but that's not so. When the on/off valve is opened partway it creates a puddle of trapped, condensed water. The passageway isn't fully opened or closed, it's blocked. Steam traveling out of the boiler at 350 mph (the rate of warm air under pressure) hits the puddle of water and makes that familiar knocking sound. It's particularly loud in the morning, as a building heats up. If closing the valve doesn't work, you may need a new valve.

Or if the knocking continues or the radiator warms evenly but not enough, it's possible that water has been trapped in the radiator rather than drained back into the boiler. To correct this, you can put a $3/4$" block of wood under the legs of the radiator at the end opposite where the pipe is connected. This is called changing the pitch. Be careful you don't loosen the radiator from the pipe by lifting it too high.

If the system has shut off automatically,

there may not be enough water in the boiler and the low-water shutoff shut the boiler down. Contact your serviceperson.

If you lose a lot of heat during the heating season, there may be a leak in the steam line. If you lose a lot of heat in your hot water system (during the summer) there's probably a leak in the return line, which is underground.

RADIANT SYSTEMS

Radiant heating warms the floor, ceiling, or baseboard units with electric cables or circulating hot water (which requires a boiler). This system is expensive but requires little maintenance, except for the boiler.

HEAT PUMPS

Heat pumps use electricity to take heat from air inside the house in summer and push it out and do the reverse in winter, so they're often used where central air conditioning is a necessity. They work fine in mild climates, but if the outside temperatures go down very low, the system uses a supplementary heater that runs the operating cost very high. The distribution method is the same as in a forced warm-air system. Blowers, ducts, and filters need periodic cleaning. Ask your serviceman to show you what you need to do. If the weather is very cold and the coils are iced over, contact the serviceperson for repairs.

SOLAR HEATING

A solar heating system has three parts: the solar collector, an underground storage tank, and a distribution system.

The collector is usually placed on the roof. It's a series of panels of glass, metal, and insulating material that traps the rays of the sun and turns them into heat. Then water, oil, or water and antifreeze, which travels through coils in the collector, carries the heat to an underground storage tank. Heat-exchanging pipes then remove the heat and send it through the house.

A secondary system heats water, and a backup heating system is used if the solar heat collected is not enough—either because the temperatures are very low and the house needs a lot of heat or because the storage system isn't big enough. The backup system may be a heat pump (which can also air-condition the house in summer) or an oversize hot water heater.

A solar system can be used even in cold areas since it's based on collecting heat from the rays of the sun and not on the outside temperature.

Though it costs a lot to install, it's inexpensive to operate. You just need enough electricity to run the motors that circulate the fluid plus energy for a standby system. The system can last up to 15 years or more, and, in milder areas where there is not a lot of cloud cover, it can be very effective.

It may pay to use solar power just to heat your hot water, since this is a much smaller task.

CHECKING THE THERMOSTAT

The thermostat is the brain of your heating system. It's the device that calculates whether the temperature is low enough to demand heating. If the thermostat is old, or in the wrong place—such as outdoors, in the sun—it won't be accurate. The northwest side of the house is usually the coldest part. If you're having problems keeping the house at the right temperature, the thermostat is the first thing to check.

If you have an old thermostat, which is vertical rather than circular, it has be cleaned at the start of the heating system (or, even better, completely replaced). Take the cover off and clean the contacts by slipping a piece of paper between them.

Sometimes a speck of dust prevents the thermostat from working correctly. Just wiggle it back and forth a few times or rely on that old fix-it standby: Hit it lightly. If there's heat from any other source (even a candle!), the thermostat may not be registering your heat needs correctly. To check its operation, tape a thermometer next to it and see if the figures match. Otherwise it may need to be recalibrated.

Finally, if it's a horizontal thermostat, it must be level or it will be inaccurate. If it's not level, remove the cover and reset the screws in the mounting plate behind it.

Cooling the House

Air conditioning cools the air and dehumidifies the room. A unit that's too small for the room doesn't cool fast enough. One that's too big makes the air cold too quickly to remove the moisture (and also costs a lot to operate). That's why you should always buy the right size for the room. (See information about buying an air conditioner, p. 32.)

You can use a forced warm-air system to cool the house by just turning the fan switch from "Auto" to "On" so the cooler basement air goes upstairs. Or you can add a special cooling unit to the warm-air furnace. Nearly all furnaces are constructed so that units are easily added, but the problem is the ducts. They must be in the right place and big enough to handle the large amount of both hot and cold air being moved out and in. The blower that moves the air has to be very powerful, too.

Most residential central air conditioners and heat pumps are split systems, with both indoor and outdoor heat exchangers (or coils). The inside evaporator coil cools the house, and the outdoor condenser coil removes the heat. If you are purchasing a new, high-efficiency central air conditioner, you have to replace the indoor coil as well as the outdoor unit. If the two aren't matched, you won't get any better cooling or any energy savings. Ask the installer if you will be getting a higher-efficiency indoor coil and whether the new one matches the manufacturer's specification for the installation of the unit. The SEER (Seasonal Energy Efficiency Ratio)—ask to see it—should be 10.0 or higher.

FANS

You can install a large attic exhaust fan to pull cool air in from open windows and force hot air out of the attic louvers; or you can install a fan right on the roof that pulls fresh air through vents in the eaves and blows hot attic air out.

OTHER HEATING AND COOLING OPTIONS

A power humidifier can add moisture to a home that's too dry.

An electronic air cleaner removes pollutants in the air. You can buy a portable unit or have a professional hook one up to some heating and cooling systems.

If you need other heating, there are small multi-fuel furnaces, wood burning heaters, electric heaters (require wall installation), and gas or oil wall furnaces that must be installed and vented.

An open fireplace sends more heat out the chimney than goes into the room. It is considered a net energy loser. Have it lined with a cast-iron insert and you lose less heat.

SCHEDULING THE MAINTENANCE

On the next couple of pages is a list of regular maintenance jobs that are essential to keeping your home in good shape. As you acquire possessions and make changes, you no doubt will have other items to add to the list.

When a serviceperson calls or you buy new equipment, use the occasion to ask what maintenance you should perform.

As you'll see, many of the jobs require nothing more than a visual inspection. Others require some hands-on work and/or a little know-how.

If you live in an apartment building where a staff takes care of the heating and plumbing, of all these items the only job that may apply is checking the fire extinguisher.

Whenever you feel you're in over your head (and certainly the first time you attempt any of these chores), don't hesitate to call in an expert—a plumber, gardener or yardman, roofer or chimney sweep, or fuel company serviceperson. *At the end of this list is an explanation of how to do the jobs that are starred or who to call to do them for you.*

Service people may also say I've been a little conservative. Maybe some of these jobs can be done less often. But rather than ignore it entirely, ask.

WINTERIZING A ROOM AIR CONDITIONER

After disconnecting electric power, remove foreign matter (such as leaves) from air conditioner and clean it according to the care manual. Cover any part of a through-the-wall unit that's exposed to the outside. Inside the house, insert a plastic sheet behind the front panel to keep out drafts, but leave a small opening at the bottom so moisture doesn't build up.

If you're removing a window unit, follow instructions from the manufacturer and be careful to keep the unit upright. Never put it down on the end, back, or sides. You can use a dust cover, but leave some room for air to circulate.

When to Do It

MONTHLY

★ Check fire extinguisher
★ Check GCFIs (consult manual)
★ Clean filter in stove exhaust fan
★ Drain electric heater

★ Steam boiler system: check valves, blow off rust
★ Check central air conditioner

SEMIANNUALLY

Roof check:
Replace torn or loose shingles
Check blacktop to see if patching is necessary
If flashing has pulled away, secure and add roof cement
Look for signs of water leaks in attic
Check mountings and fittings of TV antenna
Clean out clogged gutters
★ Reinforce gutter if necessary
See if attic louvers are open to allow moist air to escape

Exterior wall check:
Nail any loose boards or shingles on siding
Touch up any areas where paint is worn, remove old, flaking paint with wire brush
★ Patch hairline cracks in masonry
Have brick remortared (pointed) where necessary
Caulk joints between siding and window and door frames
Check for wood decay (see box "Wet Rot/Dry Rot," p. 9)

Yard check:
Clear away all dead leaves and plants
Trim back shrubs and plants
Look for physical evidence of termites (see Termites, p. 315)
Spring only:
Check for any loose joints in water line to outside faucets
Turn water on by slowly opening shutoff valve
Oil snow-removal equipment before storing
Clean and repair play equipment and patio furniture

Fall only:

Call power company to trim any dead branches along power lines; they'll do it for free

Reinforce or protect trees and shrubs

★ Drain outdoor faucets and cut off water

★ Drain gas from power mower

Oil power tools before storing them

Cover patio furniture, rust-proof if necessary

Window and door check:

Paint wood frames if necessary

Spackle cracks

Replace loose putty in wood frames (and don't repaint for a week, so it has time to cure)

Check that doors close properly

Spring only:

Remove storm windows

Patch screens

Fall only:

Replace storm windows

Plumbing/drainage and heating/cooling check:

★ Check sump pump

★ Test water valves to see if they're frozen

★ Inspect your heating system

Spring only:

Clean or replace filters in room air conditioners

Vacuum and reinstall units

Schedule tuneup for central air conditioner

Fall only:

Clean contacts in vertical type thermostat

Clean and lubricate ventilating fans and exhaust fans

★ Check house trap plug

Store air conditioners, cover and seal window units; cover central air unit and schedule cleaning every few years

Clean filters and reservoirs of humidifiers

Inspect weather-stripping at door to unheated garage

Drain room radiators and boiler

★ Clean gutters, placing a leaf catcher in vertical drainspouts

ANNUALLY

★ Inspect boiler of gas or oil furnace in late spring or early fall

★ Check fireplace

★ Have chimney cleaned and flue pipe inspected

If you have changed from oil to gas heat, see special instructions in Heating and Cooling, p. 222.)

★ Check water quality if you have well water

★ Check septic tank (clean every 2–3 years)

How to Do It (Or Whom to Call)

Many of these jobs sound more complicated than they really are. Personally, I'd rather have someone who's experienced show me how to handle these important maintenance jobs than to read how to do them in a book—and I'm assuming you would, too. You should have a service visit from your fuel supplier annually at least, so asking for help will involve no additional charge.

BOILER INSPECTION

A professional should do it. The inspection should start with a CO_2 test to check that the barometric damper is balanced, and it should include a draft test (to make sure you aren't losing too much heat up the chimney) and a smoke test (to see if the fuel is being cleanly burned).

CENTRAL AIR CONDITIONER MAINTENANCE

Remove debris. Have the serviceman check if condensate drain is carrying off moisture and show you how to clean filter.

ELECTRIC HEATER, DRAINING OF

Shut off power to the heater at the fuse box. Ask the plumber how to drain the heater completely to flush out scale, rust, and sediment.

FILTER CLEANING, IN STOVE EXHAUST FAN

Check the manufacturer's instructions.

FIRE EXTINGUISHER, INSPECTION OF

See that the pressure gauge is high, the lock pin is in place, and the nozzle is not clogged. Don't partially discharge an extinguisher; if you have done so, have it refilled. Refill it every six years in any case. If you are not sure it's working right, check with the manufacturer.

FIREPLACE, CLEANING OF, AND CHIMNEY INSPECTION

The chimney should be professionally inspected for ashes, corrosion, or birds nests. (Even the chimney liner ages. If it's more than 60 years old, accumulated soot and sulfuric acid may cause problems.)

Open the damper (lid that seals off the chimney; it's above the fireplace opening). Look up the flue (the opening that goes through the chimney) and see if there's blockage. The damper itself must seal tightly or you'll lose air. If bits of mortar are caught, brush them away. The bricks in the firebox (sides and wall of the fireplace) should be intact. If the ashes in the ash pit are soggy, the pit may need sealing.

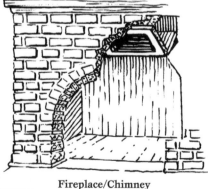

Fireplace/Chimney

FORCED AIR HEATING SYSTEM

Ask the serviceperson to demonstrate how to clean the filters, perform needed lubrication, and open the temperature pressure relief valve.

GAS FURNACE/BOILER CLEANUP

Shut off and check the vent openings for dirt. Wipe off dust and dirt on the unit. Ask the serviceperson about any additional maintenance.

GUTTERS, REINFORCEMENT OF

Check with your roofer about any or all of the following: Do the gutters need supports? Should you install screening or a leaf catcher? To prevent galvanized gutters from rusting and wood ones from rotting, should you line them with gutter cement? Discuss ways to construct ice dams if necessary.

HAIRLINE CRACKS, REPATCHING OF

Check the chimney, siding, basement, walks, and driveway. Have your hardware store recommend the compound and tools needed.

HOUSE TRAP PLUG, CHECKING OF

This is usually located in the basement just before the sewer pipe goes through the building wall. It may be located under a wooden or metal cover. If the plug is missing, gases, pests, or odors can enter your house. Make sure the plug is tightly closed or replace it. Grease the threads for easy opening.

OIL SYSTEM MAINTENANCE

A professional should check the filter, strainer, gasket, and fan blades. Have this person lubricate the burner motor. Ask for tests of draft readings, flue temperature, smoke, and carbon dioxide. Ask what maintenance you should perform regularly and ask how to look inside the flue pipe yourself. (Heavy soot deposits show that the equipment isn't running efficiently or being maintained properly.) Have an efficiency rating done during the heating season to see if your burner needs a tuneup.

IS YOUR OIL BILL FUELISH?

Get your supplier to give you the bills for your house for the past five years plus the annual "degree day" total, that is, total days when the temperature dipped below a certain number. The gallon/degree day ratio should stay constant. If you add insulation, storm windows, etc., it should go down. If that's not the case, you're burning excess fuel.

OUTDOOR FAUCETS, DRAINING OF

Close the shutoff valve, open the faucet, and turn the knob on the side of the shutoff valve to drain the valve and pipe. Check with the plumber if you need heating cable for exposed pipes or pipes next to outside walls.

POWER LAWN MOWER, DRAINING OF

Turn off the gasoline supply and let the motor run until it stops. Scrape dirt off the blades and body of the mower, and if it has a battery, remove it. Put a bit of lubricant such as WD-40 in each cylinder and store the mower covered in plastic and, if the floor is damp, on blocks.

RADIATORS, DRAINING OF

With a screwdriver turn the bleeder (air) valve at the top; have a can ready to collect the water.

STEAM BOILER SYSTEM MAINTENANCE

Check that the valves open regularly; blow off rust by opening the valve and letting water

drain until it's clear. Have your serviceperson show you how.

SUMP PUMP, CHECKING

Pour water into the pit and see if the pump operates electrically.

TERMITES, CHECKING FOR PHYSICAL EVIDENCE OF

Look for piles of discarded wings or $1/4$"-wide mud tunnels along foundation walls, posts set into ground, and water pipes. Have a professional inspection done periodically; check with your exterminator to see how often he recommends this be done, which may be as infrequently as every five to ten years unless you see signs of problems. (See also Termites, p. 315.)

TRIMMING SHRUBS AND PLANTS

Trim back any that are closer to the house than 18". Trim evergreens in winter and other plants and shrubs when they're not in bloom.

WATER QUALITY, CHECKING OF

Take a well water sample in a sterilized bottle to the local public health office.

WATER VALVES, CHECKING

If they are stiff, apply silicone lubricant or Liquid Plumber. If they're leaking, replace the graphite packing. If frozen, see p. 212.

WOOD DECAY, CHECKING FOR

Where untreated wood is near the ground or exposed to other moisture, prod it with an ice pick to see if there's softness. Remove any rot and use a plastic filler. See box "Wet Rot/Dry Rot," p. 9.

233

PART 6

FIXING

HANDYWORK AND APPLIANCE TROUBLESHOOTING (YES, YOU CAN DO IT)

Nothing is forever, including your house and its contents. Even the things you thought were inert, like walls and floors and pipes, can change. Pipes can lengthen and shorten, to a degree and at a rate depending on what they're made of. Rust growing inside can make them narrow. Wood can swell or shrink. Every change is a potential problem: When the pipes are clogged, the water backs up. When the wood warps, the door sticks.

It is possible that someone capable of home repairs is living in your very own house. It is even possible this person has agreed to do the job "pretty soon." In such a case, "pretty soon" is often meant geologically—in other words, within the next half million years.

You can hire someone, at least in theory. But labor is expensive. A minimum charge for a service call for an appliance repair is a lot of money and particularly aggravating when you find out the "problem" is that you haven't flipped the switch on. And while there is no shortage of people thrilled and delighted to give you an estimate for a major renovation, trying to hire someone to come over just to patch some plaster or put up a picture hook is like trying to find a babysitter for New Year's Eve.

That's why I'm all for knowing how to do it yourself. You won't have to pay for it and you won't have to wait for it. And, since you'll have to live with the results of your work, chances are you'll also do it more thoughtfully than someone you hire. In my house, a carpenter installed bi-fold doors on a track that gave me problems from the minute the job was done. Years later, I learned the problem was the cheap track the carpenter had chosen (without my knowledge) to save me money. Grand total of the savings? Five dollars.

Ideally, of course, I'd have installed the track myself, but I can't. In my twenty-five years as a homeowner, I have tackled only the simplest jobs, and those are the ones I am going to tell you about because they're the ones that come up most often.

If you want something more advanced, you have your choice of dozens of terrific how-to books. Which one should you buy? Whichever has the illustrations that seem clearest to you.

Whether you're inclined toward fix-it or among the mechanically challenged, I suggest you browse in the hardware store. You'd be surprised at how you can find gadgets, solutions, tools, and/or compounds that will solve

234

problems you have now or will have some day. A lot of them (like new glues) require no technical abilities whatsoever.

Certainly whenever you're starting a specific home repair job you should take a few extra minutes to ask the hardware store manager or owner for expert advice or suggestions about materials that could make the job easier, better, or faster.

● ●

HOME REPAIRS

The least do-it-yourself information you need:
- Basic tools and equipment
- How to make minor repairs
- Gluing and ungluing
- Appliance troubleshooting

Stocking a Tool Kit

If your present tool of choice is tape, I would recommend that you scale up. Even if you don't expect to use tools yourself, the unpaid help you recruit to lend you a hand will certainly need them—and particularly for emergency repairs.

Also, buy a toolbox or a fishing tackle box to hold your tools rather than trust them to the jumble of a kitchen junk drawer. Since you usually need more than one at a time, the box is a caddy. Get one that's sturdy and big—your collection will expand quicker than you'd expect. The main thing is to keep your tools hidden from friends and family: If someone else touches your tools, they're screwed up, and if you lend them, they're gone. The ideal, but unlikely, solution would be to keep them with you at all times.

DRILL

A drill is the one electric tool that is worth owning, even if you never do anything more than hang things with it. The drill will make the hole and (with a screwdriver attachment) drive in the screw. You can use a nail to hang certain lightweight things, but a properly installed screw fits into the wall much more securely. Besides, with a drill, you'll do a better, faster, neater, and maybe a safer job. You're less likely to damage a surface than with a manual drill, which is awkward to handle. If you're hanging anything heavy, like a mirror, it's a must.

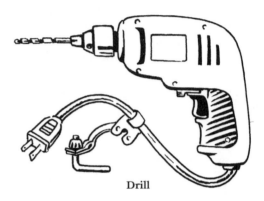

Drill

The drill is also a versatile tool. In addition to the drilling and screwdriving bits (or tips), there are other accessories available to stir paint, remove paint and rust, buff, and sand. If the drill is reversible, the screwdriver bit can also unscrew things, which is handy if you're trying to take down shelves.

Drills come in $1/4$", $3/8$", and $1/2$" sizes. The measurement refers to the largest bit it can take. The $1/2$" is the strongest, but $3/8$" is adequate for home use. Get a reversible, variable speed drill so you can use it for virtually every purpose.

You need different sizes and types of bits to drill different size holes or holes in different materials. Basic drill kit sets cover your needs for most small drilling jobs on both metal and wood.

When drilling through wood you use a high speed; for metal, you use a lower speed.

GLUE GUN

A hot glue gun is an inexpensive new tool that has a huge range of applications—from crafts to home repair. One of the best uses is to skid-proof a surface, such as the underside of a chair that slides along a hardwood floor, a pet's water dish, and so on. Just make zigzags and swirls along the base.

HAMMER

Buy a 16-ounce, flat-faced hammer, with a wide striking surface. It should have a good rubber grip that absorbs the shock when you drive it or a shock-resistant graphite handle. The longer the handle, the better the balance. Test the balance on any hammer by gripping it. Whatever feels comfortable is the best tool for you.

A curved claw hammer has a claw-shape end that is used to pull out nails that are driven at the wrong angle or into the wrong place.

Tack hammers, with magnetic heads—so they can hold tacks in place when you drive them—are one of several specialty hammers.

PLIERS

A slip-joint plier, a pincer-like tool that comes in a variety of sizes, is used to hold and turn. It also comes in handy for loosening bolts, pulling out staples, or using as a vise if you're gluing something small. (Put the item between the tips of the pliers, then secure the grip with a rubber band.) A lineman's pliers, which can cut metal, bend wire, and pull nails, is another versatile tool.

PLUNGER

Also known as a plumber's helper. An ordinary plumber's helper has a flat bottom (like an overturned cup) and is used for clogged-up sinks. A special plunger—with an extra lip—can be used for toilets. This is a wonderful housewarming gift, as far as I am concerned. One size fits all, and chances are your gift will be unique.

SCREWDRIVER

You will need several of these to fit different sizes and type of screws. A cheapo special will slide out of the slot on the screw while you're working, which is maddening and also dangerous.

There are two basic types of screwdrivers (three if you get thirsty).

Flat-head (or slotted) screwdrivers come in a variety of sizes to fit slots in different size screws. If the tip of the screwdriver you're using is too narrow, it will slip and damage the screw. If it's too wide, it will scar the area around it. You can buy a set of 3 or 4 flat-head screwdrivers in a variety of sizes.

Phillips screwdrivers, which fit the screws that have a small "star" in the head, come in various sizes, too. Ask the clerk to help you choose one small and one large.

With a ratchet-handle screwdriver, pressure from your hand creates a corkscrewing action that helps drive the screw into place.

You can also buy a cordless electric screwdriver, but I think an electric drill with a screwdriver bit makes more sense.

WRENCHES

If you have a plumbing emergency, you'll probably need an adjustable crescent wrench, which opens and closes valves, and you will also need a pipe wrench to hold the pipe. A 14" pipe wrench will cover most situations. Don't buy the cheapest. If the jaws don't meet at the correct angles, they won't do the job.

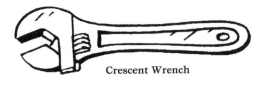

Crescent Wrench

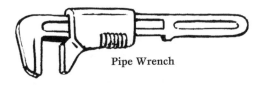

Pipe Wrench

HANDLE WITH CARE

If you are working on any finished material (such as a chrome fixture), do not use a tool with teeth. Wrap the item with a rag before you apply pressure. If you are having problems with a stiff valve increasing the pressure may damage the piece. Use Liquid Wrench or silicone. If it's *really* stuck, don't risk breaking it by forcing it. Call a plumber.

Such items as saws, files, chisels, etc., are often recommended for the home tool kit. If you need them for a special project, just buy or rent them as needed.

OTHER BASIC DO-IT-YOURSELF SUPPLIES

Ladder. A wood ladder is the cheapest, but it's hard to lug around. Aluminum ladders weigh less, are quite steady, and won't loosen up over time. For do-it-yourself work, you can pick a ladder with a Type II or Type III "working load" rating—meaning that it can safely support, respectively, a 200- or 225-pound working load but has been tested to support a load four times its rating. However, it's safest

LADDER SAFETY

Don't leave anything on the top step of a ladder.

Never put the bottom of a ladder at a distance farther from the wall than one-quarter of its length. (If the ladder is 16 feet high, don't place the bottom more than 4 feet from the wall.)

if the ladder is carrying only your weight plus the weight of the materials.

CAUTION: Anyone working with electric tools or power lines should use a wood or fiberglass/aluminum ladder, not an aluminum one.

When you carry a ladder horizontally, unless you pick it up in the exact center, part of it will drag on the ground. Once you find the balance point, mark it, and always lift it there.

Lubricants. There are three generic types of lubricants. Silicone spray (like WD-40) is an all-purpose product. Powdered graphite should be used in locks since it contains no oil that will attract dirt. Penetrating oil (like Liquid Wrench) loosens rusted plumbing connections, screws, and nuts.

Nails and Screws. Buy a small kit of assorted nails and screws to start with, even though you may wind up buying the specific nails and/or screws you need for a particular job.

Common nails have flat broad heads. (Coated ones hold better than uncoated ones.) *Finishing* and *casing nails* have smaller heads. *Brads,* used on thin molding or picture frames, have the smallest heads of all. When they're driven into place, the heads barely show.

Roof nails, or any nail used outdoors, should have a rustproof galvanized coating. It is important to remember this if you decide to make window boxes or other garden pieces.

Masonry nails, which have vertical grooves in them, are used for driving into brick walls, usually into the mortar, and also used for hanging pictures. However, picture-hanging kits, which include nails and a slotted guide that helps you drive them in straight, work for most picture-hanging jobs. The kits are marked according to the weight of the picture they can carry.

Screws grip better than nails. Most screws are slotted (with a notch across the top) or are the Phillips type (with a small star in the head) that are driven flush with a surface. Round and oval head screws, are decorative and meant to stay on top of the surface.

Retractable Tape Measure. (My favorite tool!) Inexpensive retractable tape measures are sometimes intractable tape measures—they come out and won't roll back. Buy a good one, about 16' or 25' long by 1" wide, and keep it in the toolbox, so you'll at least know where it is. I often take one along when I go shopping for furniture or curtains or in any other situation where measurements are important.

The new rolling tape measures are excellent. You don't pull out the tape, you just roll the tool along the place to be measured and a number appears in a window.

Safety Equipment. For working with power tools, working above your head, and/or working with caustic chemicals, you should wear goggles with plastic lenses.

When you sand, you need a dust mask; and when working with certain toxic fumes, use a cartridge respirator. Some sanders come with vacuum cloth bags.

You also need rubber gloves when working with many solvents. Warnings on the label will advise you. *Always read labels carefully.*

Tape. You need electrical tape and masking tape in your tool kit as well as that great emergency tool, duct tape (often, but incorrectly, called duck tape). I have even used it to keep a hem in place when I was really desperate. The good news is that it has a deadly grip.

The bad news is that it has a deadly grip. It's incredibly strong, so be careful about using it on painted or wallpapered walls. If it leaves residue when you remove it, use a commercial adhesive remover or alcohol, salad oil, nail polish remover, or lighter fluid.

CAUTION: Nail polish remover, alcohol, and lighter fluid are very flammable.

Along with the tape, I also include a pair of **scissors.**

TAPE A BREAK AND OTHER USES FOR TAPE	
Temporary leak stopper	Electrical tape
Plastic repairs	Duct tape
Sealing joints in ducts	Duct tape
Sealing, clamping	Masking tape
Metal patching	Aluminum tape
Shower curtain repair	Transparent weather stripping
Sealing doors, windows	Transparent weather stripping
Package sealing	Strapping tape

Problems and Solutions

BLINDS, LOPSIDED OPERATION

Look at the loop on the cord that lifts the blinds and find the "buckle," which goes around the cord near the bottom, where it loops. Make sure the lengths of cord above it are equal.

BLINDS, CORDS BROKEN

Repair kits for broken tilt and lift cords are available at the hardware store.

BLINDS, CORDS ARE JAMMED

Remove the blind and untangle the cords inside the upper part of the blind, called the headbox.

BLINDS, SLAT STRINGS OR TAPES NEED REPLACING

There are kits at the hardware store.

CAULKING, WORN

Don't caulk any area that is not dry, clean, and, if necessary, scraped.

Buy caulking that is appropriate to the area—whether it is interior or exterior, whether it will be exposed to the sun, and whether you are going to paint it. You will need to read labels and/or get suggestions at the hardware store.

To patch around a tub, use silicone tub caulking that comes in a tube with a nozzle. First, remove all loose pieces of old caulking and wash the area with a detergent to remove soap and grease. (Also remove mildew if necessary). Rinse, wipe down, and let dry. Then force the caulking into the cracks with the tip of the caulk gun.

Caulking may not stay in place if the gap between the wall and the tub widens when the tub is weighted down with water. If so, fill the tub with water before you do the caulking and repair the gap when it's at its widest.

CERAMIC, CHIPPED

White glue can be built up in layers in an especially deep chip in ceramics. Apply a layer, let it dry, then repeat, and so on. After the hollow has been filled, cover it with model paint or marker, then coat it with clear nail polish.

CHAIR, SAGGING SEAT ON

If springs sag, turn the chair upside down and make a pattern of the seat frame. Transfer the pattern to a piece of scrap masonite or $1/4$" plywood. Cut out and nail this piece over the frame to push the springs back into the chair and eliminate the sags.

CHAIR OR TABLE, LOOSE JOINT IN

Since new glue over old doesn't make the strongest bond, to make a strong repair pull the loose joints apart. If that's impossible, spread them as wide as possible and use some dental floss to work the glue into place. Or drill a hole into the joint and use a hypodermic needle or glue injector from the hardware store.

Disassemble a shaky piece completely. Remove the old glue by boiling half vinegar and half water and pouring it over the surface or by using a commercial adhesive remover. Wipe off loosened glue or rub it away with steel wool. Don't chip the glue off or you may remove wood plus glue. Sand the surfaces, wipe them with turpentine, then use a wood glue. To make an extra-tight fit, coat the glued surfaces with a bit of steel wool, stick a couple of toothpicks into the hole, or wrap the part to be inserted with a bit of cloth. Clamp with rubber bands.

CHAIR OR TABLE, SHORT LEG ON

Put a dab of wood putty or plastic wood on waxed paper, set the short leg on top, allow to dry. Then trim off the paper with a sharp knife and smooth with sandpaper. Or hot glue a button to the chair leg bottom.

CHIPS, IN PAINT

Use typewriter correction fluid on appliances, plastic lawn chairs, etc. It comes in several colors.

Car enamel touch-up kits or nail enamel (which, depending on the fads of the year, may come in many colors other than red) are perfect to cover a small chip because the little brush makes the paint easy to apply.

Always store leftover paint in small bottles for touch-ups.

Use a paper match rather than a brush for a small touch-up: no brush strokes or excess paint. An old car dealer's trick!

COMPUTER KEYBOARD, JAMMING

If it jumps or is acting strange, before you run to the computer store, tilt the keyboard on its side and, with a flat hand, hit the back. You'll dislodge dust and other particles, clearing the board.

CRACK, IN WOOD OBJECT

Spread the crack as wide as possible. Use a piece of string or dental floss to work in the glue, then clamp the object closed. Wipe off excess glue, use rubber bands as clamps, and let the object set overnight before removing the rubber bands.

DOOR, STUCK

The door may be sticking just because the screw hinges have become loose. If you can't tighten the screws because the holes are too large, try using a wider flat-head screw, or put a wooden match in the hole to give the screw something to "bite" into. Or follow instructions under Screw, Loose, p. 242.

If the problem is a sagging frame, apply a silicone lubricant. Or hammer a finishing nail into the frame at the point where it's rubbing in order to force it back into position.

If humidity is causing the door to swell, wait until it is dry to seal all edges with a wood preservative, paint, or candle wax (just rub the candle around it). If you sand the door heavily, when it shrinks back to size, a gap will remain. But you can sand it very gently by attaching some sandpaper to the sill at points where it sticks. As the door is opened and closed, it will rub against the paper.

If the door is sticking because it's been hung wrong, insert one or two pieces of cardboard, or "shims," under the hinge that's connected to the doorjamb. Slip a book or couple of magazines under the door to keep it upright: If the door sticks at the bottom, shim at the bottom and tighten the top hinge screws; if it sticks at the top, vice versa.

If it's sticking on the carpet, install rising butt hinges. They are installed like normal hinges but lift the door clear of the carpet. Remove the bottom hinge first so door doesn't fall on you.

DRAWER, STUCK

Open it with a suction cup or plumber's rubber plunger, which will grip it without damaging the surface.

If you can't remove it, remove the drawers that are near it and aim a blow-dryer (set no hotter than medium) several inches from the wood. This heat removes the moisture that's caused the drawer to expand. Move the dryer back and forth for several minutes along the length of the drawer. Try to open the drawer once it's cool.

Once it's open spray the metal runners with a lubricant, such as WD-40, or rub wooden ones with a candle or soap.

FLOORS, DENTS AND GOUGES IN

Before you mend any dents or gouges, strip the floor of wax, polish, dirt, and anything else that would interfere with the adhesion of any compound.

For a shallow dent in wood, just lay a damp cloth or several layers of brown paper garbage bag over the spot and run a warm iron over it. The wood fibers will swell and rise up. If the dent is still there, put a gallon jug filled with very hot water on the spot for half an hour, remove, and re-iron.

For shallow nicks or holes, use wood-patching compounds such as wax stick or patch with some sawdust (taken from the same kind of wood) mixed to a paste with white glue. (Same technique goes for linoleum floors: pulverize a bit of the linoleum in a blender, then mix with white glue).

For a hole big enough to use for putting practice, use plastic wood or wood putty. Be sure to overfill the spot, since these compounds shrink when they dry, sand it flat with a piece of wood larger than the hole, and cover with a stain. You can also cut a patch from another piece of wood, using plastic wood to fill any cracks, and then stain everything to match.

A variety of compounds are available, all with instructions, and are quite easy to apply. See Choosing Patching Compound, p. 273, for a chart, but also go to the hardware store and check to see what the clerk recommends or just poke around yourself and read some labels. There are often improved products on the market that will solve your problem perfectly.

FLOORS, SQUEAKING

In an old house, you may be able to solve the problem of a squeaky floor with talcum powder or powdered graphite (use a powder puff to get it into the cracks) or a few squirts of heated liquid soap between the boards. Or dip a knife blade in liquid glue and work the blade in and out of the trouble spot. If those solutions don't solve the problem, write to the National Oak Flooring Manufacturers Association, P.O. Box 3009, Memphis, TN 38173, for their very helpful booklet of additional suggestions.

LIGHT BULB, BROKEN

If a bulb has cracked off in the socket, press a dry soap bar into the jagged edges, then turn the soap bar counterclockwise to loosen the base of the bulb and remove it.

MOLDINGS, CHIPPED

Rough up the gouged area with coarse sandpaper. Drive several nails into the wood, leaving the heads above the surface of the gouge so the filler can have something to hang on to. Overfill the gouge with auto body filler. Sand, then paint.

NAIL, DRIVING

Just like in the cartoons, people hit their thumbs with hammers when driving in a nail. It won't happen if you hold the nail in place by sticking it between the teeth of a comb. Or poke it through a couple of pieces of paper or cardboard, hold that in place, and when the nail is secure, pull the paper or cardboard away.

To hold the nail in place in a tight spot, thread a bolt partway onto a nut, leaving just enough room for the nailhead. The nut holds the bolt in place, and you can hammer on the bolt to drive in the nail. If you are afraid you're going to damage the surface by pounding it with a hammer, ask for a nail set and instructions at your hardware store.

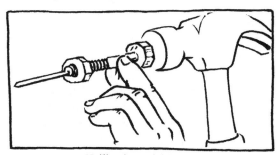

Nailing in a Tight Spot

PLASTER, CRACKED

To repair a small crack in a plaster wall, clean out the hole, remove all loose plaster, wet the sides of the crack, and fill it with spackle, using your finger or a putty knife. Or smooth it with a damp sponge and scrape it with a stick that's longer than the hole is wide, so that the patch area is level with the wall. You won't need to sand.

PLUMBING PROBLEMS

See in Maintaining section, pp. 215–221.

IF TURNING THE SCREW IS A PROBLEM

If a screw won't go in easily, coat with a bit of soap, salad oil, or silicone spray.

If your fingers are too large hold the screw in a tight place, slide a bit of plastic tubing over screwdriver blade so it can grip screw head.

If you can't keep a drill level to make a straight hole, tape a small level to the side of drill and keep your eye on the bubble.

If you don't want to drill too deep a hole, slip a piece of masking tape on the bit to mark point where you want it to stop. The tape will also collect some of the sawdust. It may move around on the bit, so check its position against a ruler regularly.

SCREW, LOOSE

If the hole has become so large that you can just pull out the screw, push a wooden match, plastic wood, or one or two toothpicks into the hole or wrap the screw itself in a bit of plastic wrap. Then replace and tighten the screw.

If that doesn't solve the problem, slip an anchor (which fits the screw like a sheath fits a sword) into the hole to fill it up, then put in a new screw. If the hole is too small for the anchor, you may have to enlarge it slightly; if it is too big for the anchor, add some spackle (in a plaster wall) or wood putty (for a wood wall) and let it dry around the anchor before you insert the screw. Or fill the hole completely with spackle or putty and start all over again.

SCREW, TIGHT

If you're having trouble loosening a screw, heat the edge of the screwdriver before you insert it or cut out or clean out the slot with a small piece of a hacksaw blade. Or use penetrating oil, white vinegar, or a carbonated cola drink to loosen it up.

WINDOW SHADE, WORN OR STAINED HEM ON

Remove the material from the roller and reattach it upside down. To do this, first unroll the shade, remove it from the window, and pry off the staples that fasten the material to the roller. Remove the narrow slat, pull the ring from the hem and open the hem so the material lies flat.

Sew or hot-glue a new hem in the upper edge of the material. Insert the slat and reattach the old pull ring or use a new one. Refasten the material using staples or carpet tacks. Work carefully. The roller won't operate smoothly unless the long edges of the shade are exactly perpendicular to the roller.

SHADE, TOO MUCH/TOO LITTLE ROLL

If the shade goes up too fast, take it down, unroll it a few turns, then rehang it. (Repeat if necessary.) If it's not going up fast enough, take it down and roll the shade several turns the other way.

SHADE, WON'T UNROLL

Take it down. There is a flat-sided pin on one side of the roller. Use pliers to twist it slightly clockwise. Then give the shade roller a couple of turns. If further adjustments are necessary, see above.

SPACKLING

Spackle is a paste-like compound the texture of cream cheese. It hardens as it dries. As a spackle substitute in a small hole, you can use white toothpaste, kids' clay, or a mixture of white glue and baking soda or talcum powder mixed with boiled linseed oil until you get the right consistency. Apply with your fingers. You won't need to plaster for a while.

For recurring cracks—between woodwork and sheetrock, for example—use silicone tub caulking. Unlike spackle, it contracts and expands.

While spackle is generally used for plaster cracks, wood putty is used for cracks in wood and plumber's putty is used for sealing pipes.

STEM, GOBLET, BROKEN

Turn the glass upside down and fasten the stem with epoxy glue. If it won't stay in place without support, roll two lengths of modeling clay and use them vertically along both sides of the stem as a "collar." Make sure that the clay is pushed away slightly from the joint itself so it won't interfere with the repair. Leave in place overnight. Since epoxy is very water-resistant, the repair should hold up in the dishwasher.

TILE, LOOSE

Scrape off the loose adhesive, apply tile cement from a hardware or home supply store, and push the tile into place. After it's thoroughly dry (read directions to see how much time is necessary), apply paste grout (the filler around the tiles) with your finger. Sponge off excess paste grout.

WALL, HOLE IN

The basic framework of a house consists of pieces of lumber called 2 × 4s that are actually $1^1/_2$" × $3^1/_2$". (All lumber is at least $1/_2$" less than the nominal measurement.) When vertical, they're called studs, and positioned 16" or 24" from center to center. In hollow wall construction, they're covered with siding on the exterior of the house and with sheetrock or wallboard on the interior. There is usually 3" to 4" of insulation in between.

A hole can be made or punched in any of the $14^1/_2$" areas of sheetrock in between studs. To make a repair, you'll need some sheetrock for patching, a cutting tool, spackle (or an adhesive the hardware store recommends) to position the new patch, tape to hold it in place, and paint to cover it all.

Turn the sheetrock onto the back. (To tell the back from the front: The front is smoother and the front edges of sheetrock are beveled, or slightly trimmed, to allow neat taping of the seam.) Trim the hole neatly to the nearest inch or half-inch. Then cut a patch that is as big as your hole with a one-inch border all around. In other words, if your hole is 4×6, cut a 6×8 patch of sheetrock. On the backside of the patch, carefully score the lines that are the correct size of the hole, then apply a little pressure to the border. The excess sheetrock will break off. Peel off what remains of the material on the paper: You'll have a sheetrock patch with a one-inch sticky paper border, or flange.

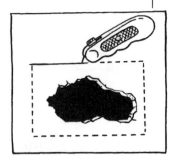

Cover the edges of the hole with spackle or other recommended adhesive compound, press the patch into the hole, and smooth the flange flush with the wall. Swipe off excess spackle with a putty knife, first moving straight sideways, then straight down, then make a swipe diagonally at each corner. Repeat the spackling process for two successive days. On the fourth day, you can paint the repair.

REPAIRING SHEET ROCK

Window, Stuck

If the windows are painted shut, see p. 261.

If summer moisture has caused swelling, you may not be able to do anything until the air is drier. At that time, spray some lubrication on the tracks.

If a metal casement window sticks, tighten the hinge screws. Then clean and oil the working parts. Remove old paint. Keep the track clean and lubricate the windows regularly.

CLAMPING DOWN

Tape, rubber bands, a clothespin, or a bit of florist's clay can be used as a clamp when mending a small item. A hemostat, a surgical clamp (from the drugstore) is handy for many small jobs. Or use your pliers and hold them with a rubber band.

Coming Glued and Unglued

Types of Glues

If the glues you use never seem to work as well as they're supposed to, maybe you're using the wrong kind. One of these four will do most home repair jobs. Check the label for the generic ingredient and also follow instructions. For a special job such as laying tile, cementing veneer, etc., the supplier of the goods can also recommend the right adhesive.

Carpenter's glue or yellow glue. (Aliphatic Resin Glue) Excellent holding power. Fair water resistance. For wood or porous surfaces such as leather, felt, and cork.

Requires clamping. Cures (comes to full strength) in 24 hours. Will not fill gaps. Remove excess with water. Dries a light cream color and can be sanded and painted.

Super glue. (Cyanoacrylate) Excellent holding power. Fair water resistance.

Liquid for non-porous surfaces like glass.

Gel on porous surfaces like china.

No clamping required. Cures in 24 hours. For small repairs only. Will not fill gaps. Dries clear. Remove with acetone, nail polish remover, or special product to remove super glue.

Household cement is similar to cyanoacrylate and less expensive but weaker, slower to dry, and needs clamping. Solvent-based kind is harmful to breathe but gets sticky in one minute; silicone-based is safer, but takes 10 minutes to get sticky.

Epoxy. Excellent holding power. Excellent water resistance. (Perfect for outdoor jobs.)

Epoxy usually comes in two tubes, one resin and one hardener. Mix as directed. Too much resin slows drying, and too much hardener weakens glue.

Clamping is required, but the quick-setting type needs pressure for only about five minutes. It cures (depending on type) in 30 minutes to 3 days.

It dries to a cream color. It may be painted (but is hard to sand).

Caution: Flammable. Skin irritant. Use in well-ventilated area.

White Glue. (Polyvinyl Acetate, or PVA) Good holding power. Poor water resistance.

Similar to carpenter's glue.

REMOVING LABELS FOR COUPONING

To remove a label intact, soak container in hot water for 30 minutes or so, pat it dry, then apply clear cellophane tape to the label leaving a strip at both ends in order to lift it off. Then place label on a card or piece of paper.

Or cover the label on a glass or plastic bottle or jar with a wet paper towel, dish towel, or hand towel. Remove metal lid, then microwave container on high for two minutes.

Use for lightweight, porous material such as paper, cardboard, cloth, leather.

Dries clear.

If it dries out, mix it with some white vinegar. Or put it in the microwave and zap it for 15 seconds. Repeat if necessary.

"Make-Do" Glue. Clear nail polish and raw egg white (on paper, jewelry, china).

To repair a crack in china, simmer item in milk for 30 to 40 minutes.

Sticky Problems

Bathtub Decals. The new decals, mercifully, are easy to remove, but the old ones hang on the way I wish most glues would! Rubbermaid recommends that you pry the things up with a sharp-edged plastic scraper, then remove adhesive with a prewash spray like Shout or Spray 'n Wash; if you can't pry the things up, then try to work the prewash spray underneath the decals. Saturating with baby oil or WD-40 and leaving for a couple of hours seems to work, too, and a lot of people tell me that they sprayed on oven cleaner, let it set briefly, then rinsed, with great success. You may need to use a commercial adhesive remover, salad oil, or lighter fluid to remove the residue.

Epoxy. If you want to know when the epoxy has "set," save the palette on which you mixed the glue. When it's hard, your glue job is set as well.

Gum. Each new generation of moms discovers that when gum gets in hair, you can reach for the peanut butter (or salad oil; or prewash spray) rather than the scissors. Peanut butter also gets gum off clothes, furniture, and the rug. After working in a bit of it to soften and loosen the gum, wipe carpet or couch, then rinse with a rag.

Price Stickers, Labels, Decals, Bumper Stickers. Most sticky labels can be removed if you saturate them with hot vinegar, salad oil, nail polish remover (caution: this may harm

---

CONTACT PAPER: APPLYING IT, REMOVING IT

• To keep contact paper from sticking while you're positioning it correctly, put a little soap on a damp sponge, then rub the sponge very lightly on the sticky side of the contact paper. The paper will slide until you get it in the right position and then will stick without any problem.

• To position contact paper so it can be removed easily later on, don't remove all the backing paper. Strip only the edges before putting it in place.

• Remove contact paper by pointing the hot end of the hair dryer on it briefly. Or lift up a corner and mist with hot water. This dissolves the adhesive. Pull and continue to spray, a little at a time. If there's any glue left behind, use a commercial adhesive remover, salad oil, or lighter fluid.

---

some surfaces so try it in an inconspicuous area), or Energine. Lighter fluid is effective, too, but since it's flammable, use it with caution. Some residue may remain, which you can remove with a lubricant such as WD-40, lacquer thinner, or rubber cement thinner (test in an inconspicuous spot first), and/or a single-edged razor (held at a right angle to prevent gouging), nylon netting, or a stiff brush.

On wood, use rubbing alcohol. Or heat decals with a hair dryer, then peel them off.

Hanging It All

Basic Hanging

On a non-wood wall of plaster or masonry, if you hang anything heavier than a poster, the nail will probably come right out of the wall along with whatever you tried to hang. Even screws that come with some of these items (such as shelf brackets) may not hold them in

PUTTING UP SHELVES

Ready-made shelves come in various colors and standard lengths and both 8" and 12" widths. You install vertical strips with screws, slip brackets on the strips, and rest the shelves on top of the brackets. For longer shelves, you may need a center strip for support in addition to strips at both ends.

You can also buy cut-to-order shelves of vinyl sprayed on wire. Because they're not solid, they don't require dusting. Also, they come in longer lengths than the solid shelves. (If you prefer a solid shelf, you can always cover it with a piece of flooring cut to size; this is easy to remove and clean.)

The really tricky part in the whole operation is to make sure that the holes in the shelf supports are straight and that the supports are lined up with one another. If one support is $1/2$" or even less higher than another, the shelf won't lie properly.

HOW DO YOU FIND A STUD?

This is of course a kind of question that cries out for a joke answer, but I'll rise above that and remind you that I'm talking about wall studs. Studs are vertical boards in the wall, usually placed 16" apart, though in newer houses they may be 24" apart. The best place to look for them is not around door or window openings or at the ends of a wall but in the center. Without a magnetic stud finder, which locates the nails in the studs, try knocking on the wall (distinguish the sound of a hollow wall from the solid thunk of a stud), check the baseboard (nailheads are usually driven into a stud center) or remove the faceplate of an outlet. The box behind it is usually nailed to a stud.

place. You can't hang anything that weighs more than 35 pounds or is too heavy for a picture hanger kit without using an electric drill with the proper bit. Which bit you need will depend on the composition of the wall—one type is appropriate for wood, another for plaster.

If a nail driven into the wall goes in easily, the wall is hollow. If it starts going in easily, and then you have to pound, the wall is hollow but you've hit one of the studs. (See an explanation under Wall, Hole In, p. 243.) Use a drill.

HANGING LIGHTWEIGHT THINGS

For pictures or mirrors under 35 pounds, use a picture-hanging kit (a nail and a slotted guide to help you drive it in at the right angle). It makes only a small hole in the wall and the nails can even be easily removed if you wish.

Most lightweight items can be attached to walls with a sewing machine needle or hot glue gun. A few seconds with your blow dryer will reheat the glue, and the item can usually be removed without leaving any traces. This method avoids nail holes that may mar the surface.

HANGING MEDIUM-WEIGHT THINGS

Don't drive the screw right into the wall. Make a starter hole with a drill. Prevent wall damage by first making an X with two strips of masking tape and driving the nail into its center. (If you don't have a drill, a hammer and nail will do). The starter hole mustn't be too big or the screw will slide in instead of screwing in.

To keep an item firmly in place (a shelf, say, or a wall-mounted medicine cabinet or mirror), drill a hole slightly bigger than the screw. Then push in an anchor, which is a sheath for the screw, or tap it in with the hammer. Then insert the screw. As you tighten it, the anchor spreads slightly in the hole, making the grip more secure. The anchor should be the right size to fit the hole that you drill and the screw should be the right size to fit the anchor. You can buy anchors and screws packaged together. On the package is information about what size hole to drill.

If you're having problems with the screw, see the information about screws on p. 242.

HANGING HEAVY THINGS

If you've got a heavy object, you need a toggle bolt or a molly instead of an anchor.

The toggle bolt is a bolt with two "wings" that fold down; you drill a hole big enough to fit the bolt plus folded wings, push the screw through the item to be hung, then replace the folded wings and push them through the wall. Pull the screw toward you and tighten so that the wings spread. How many people do you need to screw in a

Toggle Bolt

toggle bolt? Two: one to hold the item with the screw in it, the other to do the screwing.

A better choice is a molly, which is a screw in a metal casing. You also drill a hole and slip the molly through, then insert and tighten the screw. As you do, the casing flattens against the wall from the other side. (You know it's in place when it's hard to turn and when the little metal collar behind the screw starts turning along with the screw.) This is easy to understand when you take a look at the molly. The casing remains permanently in place but you can remove the screw, which gives you the flexibility to change whatever it is you are hanging.

Molly

HANGING VERY HEAVY THINGS

A very heavy object such as a mirror or a moosehead or a bookshelf may come down and take a piece of the wall with it. Such items should always be nailed to a stud. If the stud is not in the right place, put up one or more **furring strips,** a horizontal, 2-to-3-inch strip fastened to the wall studding with 3"-long wood screws or lag bolts. How do you find the studs? The easiest way in this case is just to

HANGING THINGS ON BRICK OR OTHER MASONRY

You'll need a masonry bit for your drill and a masonry nail, which is vertically grooved. To provide even more gripping power, you can first install a lead anchor, then drive in the masonry nail.

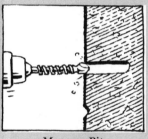

Masonry Bit

Masonry Nail

drill a series of small holes in a line behind where you're putting the furring strip, and when you get sawdust, you've hit a stud. Measure 16" and you'll get to the next one. (See also p. 246.)

The most popular labor-saving device is a good excuse.

● ●

APPLIANCE TROUBLE-SHOOTING FOR THE MECHANICALLY CHALLENGED

BEFORE YOU CALL IN THE EXPERTS

I have taken my computer printer in for repair because paper wasn't feeding automatically, only to discover the machine was set to "hand feed." I have called the heating man in because the house was too cold and then found the thermostat was set low. Apparently, this kind of dumb move is not at all uncommon. An unplugged appliance is the number one cause of all the problems repairmen are required to investigate, and an estimated 49% of all service calls are unnecessary.

If the "obvious" places to check aren't obvious to you, get out your manual and look for a troubleshooting section that tells you how to solve some of the more common problems.

If that's fruitless, call the hotline number on your warranty. Even if the warranty is no longer in effect, the technicians at the company may be able to help you diagnose and possibly even correct the problem over the phone. Make sure you have the serial and model number before you call. You should have recorded it in the owner's manual or on a copy of the warranty registration that you photocopied for your files.

Most of the following has been adapted from the excellent material provided by the Appliance Information Service of the Whirlpool Corporation.

Generic Troubleshooting: What to Check First

PLUGS AND CORDS

Are they pushed in firmly? Do prongs fit tightly? (If not, bend ends with pliers.) Are prongs clean? Is cord worn or broken? If so, replace it.

FUSES AND CIRCUIT BREAKERS

Are fuses blown? Has circuit breaker tripped? If so replace fuse or reset circuit breaker. If it blows again, call the serviceman. If there is no power anywhere in your house, call the power company.

SWITCH

Is it on? Is the start button pressed? Perhaps the machine appears to be on but contact isn't made, so switch it off, then on. Or perhaps it was accidentally shut off.

DOOR OR LID

Is it shut? Many appliances won't begin until the door or lid is secured.

OUTLET

Try an appliance you know is working to see if the outlet is faulty. If so, call an electrician.

OVERLOAD SWITCH

Some appliances, such as washing machines and garbage disposals, have a fail-safe system: If the appliance is overloaded or the motor is overheated, the overload switch (often a little red button) cuts off the power. Remove overload or cool down machine and reset the switch by pressing it down.

LOCAL POWER FAILURE

The problem may not be in your appliance but a local power failure. You may not notice it in the daytime other than to realize that your TV picture is fuzzy. Call your cable company or power company to see if the entire area is affected.

Specific Troubleshooting

If you've gone through the list and none of the above generic problems is affecting your machine, check whichever of the following applies:

AIR CONDITIONERS (WINDOW STYLE) AND DEHUMIDIFIERS

If it won't run:
- Check if dehumidifier humidistat control is set to "Off" rather than "Dryest."
- If your machine has a water pan, is it full?

If it blows fuses/trips breakers:
- Is correct outlet, wire size, circuit breaker, or time-delay fuse being used?
- Is unit plugged into extension cord? *This is unsafe!*
- Is a separate circuit used for air conditioner? Needed for all models except 115 volt models rated less than 7.6 amperes (check serial plate).
- Was it turned off and then on immediately? Wait at least two minutes.

Air conditioner not cooling/turns on and off:
- May be incorrectly sized. Too small runs all the time, cools poorly, ices up. Too large feels cold, clammy, doesn't remove enough moisture.
- Filter may need cleaning. Panels and seals may not be in place.
- Are inside (evaporator) and outside (condensor) coils clean?
- Is room very moist from cooking, showers, or laundry?
- Are controls high enough? (Fan on correct speed, thermostat cold enough.)
- Is unit set for "Energy Saving"?
- Is front of air conditioner blocked (by curtains, something out of place)?
- Are doors open to other, hotter areas?

Unfamiliar sounds/noises:
- Ignore normal sounds (pings or clicks as drops of water hit condensor; fan is loud at high-speed setting; thermostat cycles cause clicks) if unit is cooling properly.
- If it vibrates or rattles, check installation, window design, and house construction.
- Set control to Continuous Fan to reduce frequent stopping/starting.

Dehumidifier ices up:
- Is room humidity too low or control set below 65° F.?
- Is room temperature below 65° F.?

Dehumidifier leaks:
- Is unit level?
- Is pan properly positioned on rails?
- Is pan overflowing? Empty it often when humidity is high.

DISHWASHER

Will not start/timer does not advance:
- Check generic possibilities.
- Is power cord on portable model plugged in and water turned on?
- Is control at the beginning of cycle?

- Is a high-temperature washing cycle on? Timer delays cycle until water is heated.
- If motor hums but nothing starts, there may be a jam in the spray arm. Turn off the power and remove the object.

Dish load not clean:

- Is water hot enough (140° F.)?
- Are racks loaded so that spray arm can turn freely and large items don't block water to door dispensers and baskets?
- Have you used enough detergent? Fresh detergent? Sandlike particles on glasses and upper rack items means old detergent.
- Does your unit have a filter screen and removable filter guard that need cleaning? Check your manual or call manufacturer.
- Water pressure may be too low if water is being used elsewhere in the house. If the problem persists, call the water company.

Load not dry:

- Is water at least 140° F.?
- If set to "Air Dry," may take overnight.
- Is water left in dishwasher after cycle? Drain hose may be kinked.
- Use rinse aid, such as Jet Dry, to promote better water draining and faster drying.

Leaking:

- Don't use any detergent other than automatic dishwasher detergent.
- Foamy food soils (eggs and milk) should be discarded before loading.
- If item was added during cycle, water may have splashed on floor.
- Is rack in backwards (with bumper in back) or was it removed?
- Is large item jammed against water inlet?
- Overflowing: see p. 216.

FREEZER

Frost buildup on inside lid (manual defrost):

- Is freezer door sealing properly? Gasket may need repair or replacing. Or door hinges may need adjustment.
- Is humidity high?
- Is frost localized? Usually forms first on top shelves, heaviest there.
- If frost is over $1/2$" thick, defrost unit.

Top of chest freezer feels warm:

- Normal when freezer is first started. Warm walls indicate normal cooling

DRYER

Won't start:

- Check generic solutions/ also are controls set to a drying position?

Runs but won't heat:

- There are two fuses to an electric dryer. Are both working?
- Is gas turned on at both main gas line in home and gas valve behind dryer?
- Is dryer control set on "Air Only" rather than heat?

Loads not drying properly:

- Clean lint screen.
- Check instructions for automatic dryness control.
- "Time Dry" should be set for at least 15 minutes or dryer may be in cool-down with only a short heat cycle.
- If load is very small, use time dry cycle and add dry, lint-free towels.
- Is exhaust duct clean and unblocked?
- Is dryer overloaded or drying mixed weight loads at the same time?

Drying time seems long:

- A load rinsed in cold water is wetter and colder.
- Synthetics need more time at lower heat

settings (plus 10 minute cool-down).

- Low speed in washer spin cycle (which wrinkle-proofs synthetics) leaves more water in load.
- Load may be too large.
- Dryers in unheated areas have longer drying cycles.
- Low voltage dryers are slower than 220/240 volt dryers.
- Is installation and ducting of dryer correct?

Timer starts and stops:

- On automatic custom dry setting, control doesn't move until load is partially dry.

GARBAGE DISPOSAL

Motor stops running:

- Wait 3–5 minutes for cool-down, then press overload protector. If disposal has jammed on something, turn off power and check your manual. Wait for a cool-down (3–5 minutes), then press the overload protector.

MICROWAVE OVEN

Does not operate:

- Check generic possibilities.
- Are controls set, is door latched, start button pushed?
- Is on/off switch set to "On"?
- Is oven on "Hold" after defrost—or set for delayed cooking?

Oven cooks too fast/slow/uneven:

- Is power setting correct?
- Are food quantity and temperature just as listed in cookbook?
- Have you left standing time for food as called for?
- Is vent on top of oven covered or blocked?
- Was food turned or stirred as directed?

Arcing (lightning-like flashes and sizzling sound):

- Was metal tie or "twistee" left on package?
- Was dish metal? Did it have metal trim, pattern, or circular band? Was it made of leaded glass?
- Did you use foil? Did it touch side wall of oven? Foil is prohibited in some ovens and in others, safe only in small amounts. Check your manual.

Temperature probe does not work properly:

- Is it plugged in securely?
- Is sensing end (first half of probe) in center of food or beverage?
- Have you left standing time to finish cooking?
- Is probe in center of largest meat muscle (not touching bone or fat)?
- Are controls properly set?

Television interference when oven is on:

- Should be on separate circuit, but some interference is normal (as with CB radios, garage door openers, electric razors).
- In weak reception areas, interference is most noticeable.

RANGE

Doesn't operate:

- Check generic possibilities.
- Is oven selector knob turned to a setting ("Bake" or "Broil'), which operates immediately?
- Is oven temperature control knob at a temperature setting?
- Are surface units plugged in all the way?
- Do control knobs turn? Push in and turn knobs.

Surface unit control knobs won't turn:

- Did you push control knob in before you turned it?
- Was knob removed for cleaning and spring not replaced?

Food boils at low surface unit setting:
- Turn knob past the lowest marked setting (toward "Off") to lower heat to simmer.

Self-cleaning oven won't operate:
- Are oven selector and oven temperature control both set to "Clean"?
- Does "Start Time" knob show correct time?
- Is "Stop Time" knob set ahead (2 to 4 hours) for cleaning cycle to stop?
- Is door locked ("Clean" light will glow)? Check oven selector setting (or door latch for complete locking).
- Has window shield been raised before setting controls?

Continuous cleaning oven looks soiled:
- Baking temperatures around 400° F. must be alternated with broiling. Oven cleans only in baking mode.
- Door may require some hand cleaning (but don't use commercial oven cleaner or you may damage the finish or create fumes.)
- Without foil liner on bottom, spillovers may be difficult to remove.

Range doesn't cook as expected:
- Oven: Check that range is level. Allow 2 inches on all sides of pans for air circulation. Place food in center of oven not too near top or bottom. Select oven for "Bake," not "Pre-Heat" or "Broil." Make sure oven vent is not blocked.
- Surface units: Pans and pots should have smooth flat bottoms and be correct size, or do not use.

REFRIGERATOR

Not operating:
- Check generic possibilities.

Not cold enough (ice cream soft):
- Are controls properly set (allow 24 hours for new setting to stabilize).

- Are coils clean? Can be clogged by dust, lint, pet hair, and cooking grease.
- Is proper air space allowed for back condenser models?
- Are doors tightly closed with good gasket seal? (If light stays on, seal is poor.)

Water in defrost pan or crisper:
- Pan is normally less than half-full; in hot weather may be half-full.
- Some water in crisper is normal; too much means you should wash and dry food before storing. Old, decayed foods may cause moisture.

Moisture/sweating on outside of cabinet/lid:
- If humidity is high, turn unit to Power Saving control (it activates a low-wattage heater in front of cabinet).
- Move unit away from hot, humid area: near heater, dryer, range, or in sun.
- Is cabinet level? Is door/lid gasket sealing properly?

Rattling sounds:
- Anything on top, behind, underneath, or inside to vibrate when compressor runs?
- Is cabinet level and floor supported to hold weight of unit?
- Do water lines or condenser coils touch wall or cabinet?

(See Noises That Usually Needn't Be Corrected, on p. 254.)

Icemaker isn't working:
- Check generic possibilities.
- New installation needs overnight cooling.
- Is water supply hooked up, lever turned to "On," water valve turned on?

Uses too much energy, runs too often:
- Firmness of ice cream and coldness of milk is guide for temperature setting; try one lower.
- Adequate air circulation around unit?

- Doors held open often?
- Is unit level, sealing properly?
- Does freezer need defrosting?
- Is room hot? If near 100° F. may run continuously.
- Is fan inside freezer running all the time? (It should, unless it is defrosting.)

Ice cubes disappear or shrink:
- If they have been around a while, evaporation is normal.

Washing Machine

Vibrates in spin/noisy operation:
- Are styrofoam shipping blocks under tub removed?
- Is machine level and installed on a sturdy floor?
- Is load properly balanced? Stop washer and rearrange load.
- Are pins or nails caught in holes of basket, causing a whistling sound?

Won't run or won't spin:
- Check generic possibilities.
- Is cycle in cool-down or pause position? May restart in 2 minutes or so.
- Is lid closed? Won't spin with open lid.

Won't fill/buzzes/fills then drains:
- Are both hot and cold water faucets turned on?
- Is control set for a wash time (14 mins., 8 mins., etc.)?
- Are inlet hose filter screens clean?
- Does washer have single hose? Connect to upper inlet port and set water temperature selector to "Cold Wash/Cold Rinse."
- Are fill hoses kinked?
- Is drain hose jammed into a standpipe, leaving no air space, causing water to siphon from the washer?
- Has drain hose fallen or is it installed lower than washer top?

No hot water:
- Is washer set for cycle that will accept a "Hot" selection?
- Is hot water supply exhausted or water heater setting too low?
- Have hot and cold fill hoses been reversed?

Load too wet after spin:
- Cold rinse leaves loads colder and wetter than warm.
- Have you used proper cycle? "Normal/Regular/Heavy" must be used for heavy cottons such as towels and jeans.
- Is washer overloaded?
- Is load properly balanced? May need rearranging.
- Is water remaining in washer at cycle's end? Kinked drain knots may cause slow spinning.
- Is lid closed? Washer won't spin if it isn't.
- For linting see p. 192. For detergent problems, see in section Washing and Wearing pp. 179–183.

Trash Compactor

Won't operate/stops/drawer won't open:
- Check generic possibilities.
- Is drawer wedged open or restart light on? Push drawer in firmly while turning key knob to start.
- Has loose material fallen behind drawer, wedging it open?
- Are rigid items (cans, bottles) at front of drawer? Rearrange load.

No compaction/poor compaction:
- Is drawer at least one-third full to start compaction?
- Is compactor run each time trash is added?
- Is house voltage low or an extension cord being used?
- Have large sturdy bottles been added to a paper-base trash load? Bottles won't break because the paper has cushioned them.

LOW-TECH FIXITS FOR HI-TECH EQUIPMENT

• **Radio:** If you get static when it's turned off or being tuned, spray lubricant around the knobs or the sliding selectors, using the small, tubelike attachment that comes with the lubricant can. Problem may simply be dust.

• **CD:** If it goes off for no reason when you touch it, you may just have generated a spark when you crossed a carpeted floor. Turn the player off for 30 seconds, then restart it.

• **Camera:** If it won't click and the shutter seems jammed, it may need new batteries. Camera batteries need replacing so infrequently you may not even realize they're there.

Noises That Usually Needn't Be Corrected

Like a first-time parent, the new owner of an appliance has a jittery breaking-in period until he or she learns what certain sounds mean, which are normal and which require action. Does that dull thump in the kitchen mean (a) the refrigerator is on the fritz; (b) the cat has knocked groceries off the counter; or (c) someone is breaking in via the window? Actually, the answer is none of the above. The thump means the icemaker is producing cubes.

Generally, a beep indicates that the selection has been programmed or that there is something wrong (power is off, door is open), and a buzz is either a warning (load unbalanced) or the signal for the end of a cycle.

For other diagnoses, consult the following information adapted from material prepared by the Whirlpool Appliance Information Service.

AIR CONDITIONER (WINDOW TYPE)

NOTE: High velocity of air movement may be surprising to you in a new machine.

Thump, Hiss. Compressor may be turning cycles on or off.

"Boiling." Refrigerant moving through tubes right after compressor stops.

Ring, Drip. Water droplets hit blades of cooling fan or drip from coils into bottom of appliance.

Tick, Click. Controls turning compressor on and off or metals contracting and expanding.

DEHUMIDIFIER

NOTE: High velocity of air movement in a new machine may be surprising to you.

Thump, Hiss. Compressor may be turning cycles on or off.

"Boiling." Refrigerant moving through tubes right after compressor stops.

Dripping, Ringing. Water dripping from coils into water collection pan.

Ticking, Clicking. Humidistat control, compressor, and fan tick when turning off and on; metal may be expanding or contracting.

DISHWASHER

Spray, Hiss. Water rushing through hoses and pipes; sprayer splashing dishes.

Tick, Click. Detergent dispenser clicks as it opens; heating element expands and contracts as it heats and cools.

Thump, Crunch. Grinding of food particles; movement of items not loaded properly (with possible damage).

DRYER

Click, Thump. May be related to ignition (and may happen several times during cycle);

metal buttons or buckles may strike drum; small load may not tumble freely and you will hear sound of items dropping (so add dry lint-free towels to improve action).

Tick. Timer is moving through cycle.

MICROWAVE

Whir. From cooling fans or stirrer blades.

Pop, Sputter. May occur while cooking certain foods. Make sure you are following manual directions for preparing food.

Change in Pitch of Sound. Depending on power setting, magnetron tubes turn on and off during cycles.

RANGE

Pop, Creak. During baking or with high-heat self-cleaning, result of expansion and contraction.

Hum, Hiss. Self-cleaning oven door latches may buzz or hum when locking or unlocking during the cleaning cycle; grease may pop or hiss; fan may be operating.

Click, Snap, Whoosh. Electronic ignitions (on gas ranges) may click, and ignition of oven and surface burners may cause the sounds.

REFRIGERATOR, FREEZER, ICEMAKER

Hum, Hiss. From fans and compressor motors, air circulating through cabinet. Or refrigerant is "boiling" in the evaporator right after compressor stops.

Buzz, Trickle, Thump. Water valves from icemaker or water dispenser opening and closing; water pouring into icemaker; ice falling from mold to storage bin.

Click, Snap, Rattle. Defrost timer may click when starting and stopping defrost cycle; or something in or on top of appliance may cause rattle.

Compressor Motor. Runs half-time in a cool dry room, continuously in a hot, humid room.

Gurgle. Water flying in tube or dripping into exhaust pan.

TRASH COMPACTORS

Whir, Whine. During a cycle, chain drive of the power ram (part that crunches) normally sounds whiny. Pitch gets higher as load is being compacted.

Crack, Pop, Bang. Cracking of bottles. Large items placed against sides rather than in center may bang as ram descends. Sounds increase toward end of cycle.

Pause, No Sound. Typical when ram reaches the lower point and is about to reverse. Or item may be jammed so drawer won't close, machine won't start.

WASHING MACHINE

Spray, Hiss. Washer filling with water or rinsing spray beginning.

Buzz. Valve opening to release bleach or fabric softener from dispensers or for cycles such as wash, rinse.

Click, Gurgle, Thump. Timer clicks as cycle goes on; washer gurgles as water is pumped in, air sucked out; washer pauses and may thump as motor changes speed.

Noises That Can Be Corrected

Bathroom Sounds Are Transmitted. Add a veneer to door. Carpeting on floor as well as curtains and vinyl wall coverings all absorb sounds. If there are big openings around heating and water pipes, fill them in with caulking or insulation.

Ceiling Noises. If they are bothersome, carpeting is the easiest solution. Lowered ceiling and other solutions require expert help.

Doors Don't Shut out Noise. You may need weather stripping around edges and an adjustable threshold gasket under the door. Adding a veneer of $1/4$" plywood will help make hollow-core and panel doors more soundproof.

Doors Slam. Install rubber-cushioned doorstops on wall or floor, rubber stops on door itself, or automatic closing device from hardware store that lets door shut gently.

Heating System. If you hear a drum sound when forced air heat comes on, the ducts may need to be reinforced. A strange sound when gas furnace (or oven or water heater) or oil burner goes on means burner is dirty or needs adjustment. If you hear knocking in the radiator, see Common Problems with Steam Heating, pp. 227–228.

Pipes Are Noisy. Check heating and plumbing sections of this book.

Walls Are "Thin." A solid-backed bookcase, filled with books and not touching the wall, will help soundproof a room. Unfortunately, acoustical tiles won't help. You may need to install gypsum board.

Water Heater. A rumble or gurgle may be sediment; flush tank.

● ●

PAINTING

The least you need to know about painting:
- Equipment and paint to buy
- Preparing the surface
- Which paints for special jobs
- Basic techniques
- Cleaning up

Though paint is used to decorate your home, it's also important in home maintenance, usually to seal and protect but for other purposes as well. You paint wooden window sills to keep them from deteriorating, use paint with mildew preventors to keep mold from growing in damp rooms, and use paint with grit in it to increase traction on stairs.

A major interior or exterior painting generally calls for professional help, which I discussed briefly on pp. 47–51, but you may decide to tackle some of the smaller jobs yourself. Some people believe that making this decision is your initial painting mistake.

In fact, the most common mistake is rushing—not preparing the surface correctly. The second is economizing: buying poor quality materials. The third is not reading the paint label and therefore buying the wrong paint for the job or applying it incorrectly. And the fourth is using the wrong tools. These are all completely avoidable.

Getting Ready

PREPARING THE SURFACE

Painting is like everything else in life. You can't just make a surface improvement and assume all the problems underneath will be covered up.

Holes must be plastered. For big plastering jobs you'll need a professional, but if you're just dealing with a few holes here and there, use spackle (for plaster) or colored putty (for wood) and sand them smooth. Read the label to see how long you should leave the spackle to cure, or come to full strength. If you're covering raw wood, you should cover the knotholes with shellac. If you have no spackle, a little toothpaste or Play-Doh will fill a small hole.

Both **rough areas** and certain **glossy surfaces** need sanding, in the former case to make the wall look uniform and in both cases to make the paint adhere. On a glossy surface such as a cabinet, use a medium-grade sandpaper or a liquid sanding preparation from the paint store.

If you use a **water-repellent coating** (around windows, for example), buy one that can be painted, and check the label to see how long to wait before the paint is applied. Generally, two days is suggested.

Paint that is **peeling** should be removed with a paint stripper.

CAUTION: If you have any suspicion that there is lead paint on the walls (which is the case in three-quarters of all housing built before 1980, according to the Federal Department of Housing and Urban Development, more often in private houses than apartments), you should have an inspection made and bring in a painter who specializes in lead abatement to scrape the walls.

For more information on lead, see Securing, p. 283.

Wallpaper that is peeling or that contains **dyes that may bleed through** should also be stripped. (If you're not sure about the dye, cover a small patch of paper with your paint and see what happens.) Follow the instructions for wallpaper removal later in this chapter. Any **adhesive** that remains should be removed with a commercial adhesive remover.

Rust should be removed with a commercial rust remover or a wire brush and coarse sandpaper.

Grease spots should be covered with shellac so they won't bleed through a new layer of paint.

Remove **mildew,** but don't use a household spray cleaner. Most of them contain oil. Even a fine residue can prevent paint from adhering well. Get a commercial mildew killer or use a solution of one part bleach, two parts water (or stronger, if necessary).

Clean any superficial **dust or grime** or the paint won't hold. Vacuuming and dusting, or a swipe with a dry sponge may do the job. But if the wall is greasy or dirty or covered with crayon marks, it will have to be washed with a strong ammonia-water solution. Try to paint within 24 hours so the surface will still be clean.

MATCHING THE PAINT OR STAIN TO THE SURFACE

You probably need a primer or undercoat in most cases and definitely if you are making a drastic color change or painting on a surface that's in bad shape or never previously painted. Don't wait more than 14 days to paint over the primer coat.

Different surfaces require different sorts of priming. A metal wall may need a rust-resistant primer, garden furniture an oil-stain preservative, and an exterior wall may need masonry paint. Interior walls may use a polyurethane seal or seal and stain, interior floorboards a yacht varnish. As I mentioned before, ask the paint store manager for recommendations for your particular job.

Be careful about "bargains." Cheap paint may go on easier and it will also come off easier: It may wash away when you scrub it. Read the section on selecting paint and suggestions for quantities to buy in the Equipping section, from pp. 48–51.

SPECIAL PAINTS FOR SPECIAL JOBS

Acoustical Tile Ceilings. Latex may interfere with sound absorption. Use a thin coat of casein or oil-based paint.

Aluminum (furniture, trash container, etc.). Wipe clean, then cover with a zinc-chromate metal primer, and finish with two coats of enamel. Or simply clean up the aluminum. Use a phosphoric acid-based cleaner (following caution instructions), rinse, polish with fine-grade steel wool, clean with a paint thinner, and then coat with a clear non-yellowing acrylic.

Bathroom Fixtures (porcelain and ceramic tile). Use epoxy paint for a hard, durable pigment. You need one ingredient for color, the other for hardening, and once you mix them, use them right away. Read directions for cautions and instructions for preparing the surface. Usually this involves washing, rinsing, scrubbing with powdered pumice stone, and a second rinse. Let surface dry and then paint.

This will not give you a high-quality result—you need professional reglazing for that—but it may be satisfactory for a country cabin.

Basement. You'll need a rented spray gun to cover exposed ceiling joints and underside of floor above. (This is not a simple job.) Use latex masonry paint for walls (if covering latex blocks, use a coating of latex block filler first). **Water or Damp-Proofing Paints** are available. How well they work depends on how moist the area is and how well the paint is applied. Use special **porch and floor paint** for floor.

Blackboard Paint. Can be written on with chalk. Good for a section of the kitchen or kid's room.

Canvas. First hold material to light. Paint will adhere only if you can see through it. Otherwise, it was treated with paint-resistant waterproofing compound that resists paint. If it can be painted, buy **awning paint** (for both awnings and directors' chairs). Before you paint, scrub canvas with water and detergent, hose off and let dry.

Closets and Other Damp Areas. Ask for paint that resists mildew and mold.

Concrete Floor. Concrete should be left to cure for three months before painting.

Your paint dealer may recommend application of a muriatic acid solution before painting. The acid "etches" the floor and helps paint adhere. Straight vinegar, which is a mild acid, does the same thing more safely but less effectively. If using the acid, follow instructions and work carefully: Always add acid to water and not the other way (or you risk splatters).

If you have put down a concrete sealer, tell the paint dealer.

Floors and Decks. Floor paint is tough. Added rubber may make it more durable. In a high-traffic area, you may need a finishing coat of polyurethane or varnish, but this coating may yellow.

Kitchen Cabinet Interior. Don't use toxic paints. Ventilation will be a problem.

Metal (fences, bicycles, outdoor furniture). Use steel wool or stiff wire brush or commercial paint remover to remove old paint, medium steel wool and/or medium grade sandpaper or commercial rust remover to remove rust (you may have to chip it off with a chisel), follow with a phosphoric metal conditioner, then wash and dry. You may have to etch the surface with vinegar or light acid. (See "Concrete Floor" above.) Then use a metal primer and enamel paint.

Pipes. Copper pipes don't need painting. That green stuff you see is oxidation; to remove it, use a steel wool pad.

Use metal primer on cast-iron drainpipes, galvanized iron pipes, and heating ducts. Galvanized steel resists paint when new but once worn can be primed and painted with two coats of enamel. Buy special primer and paint for this purpose.

Since cold-water pipes sweat when it's humid, you'll get the best results if you paint them in dry weather or when the heat is on. For hot water pipes, there are heat-resistant enamels, sometimes called engine paint. Your paint dealer can help you figure out what degree of resistance you need.

Radiator. Dust it well and don't paint it until it's at room temperature. The most practical color to paint it is black, which absorbs heat, but you won't win any decorating awards, so hide it behind a radiator cover. Use a rust-protecting primer and a top coat.

Steps. Add sand or sandlike material. Buy it premixed with the paint, or blend a mixture of one-third sand, two-thirds paint. This can also be used to take the slickness out of **high-sheen floors.**

Textures. Sand is only one type of texturizer that can be used to cover up problem walls. You can buy or make them yourself. A friend matched the texture of her wall by mixing cat box filler with the paint.

Using different applicators such as a sponge can make a flat wall look textured. Decorating books are full of such ideas.

Wicker and Rattan. Use spray paint. Prepare the surface by scraping with a stiff-bristled brush to remove old, loose paint, then wash with warm water and detergent, hose down, and let dry.

Wood. See the section that follows on furniture finishing and information on stains.

BUYING BRUSHES

Cheap brushes fall apart. Long after the paint has dried, you may spot a loose hair in the middle of your wall or ceiling. The quick solution in such a case is to give the hair a quick wipe with sandpaper, but you're better off buying a quality brush in the first place. Here's what to check:

The **ferrule,** the band wrapped around the bristles, should be tight. If it's loose, bristles can be pulled out. Unfortunately, this problem may not be obvious until you're actually doing the painting.

Tapered Paintbrush

Also check the **shape** of the brush. You get a better stroke and coverage when the bristles of a brush are cut so they look like a wedge or chisel from the side. The tip of the bristles should taper to a fine, narrow, almost invisible edge. A cheap brush has a blunt edge.

Bend the **bristles** against a hard surface to check the spring. They should be firm without being stiff, flexible without being floppy. When you press down on a cheap brush, it will form a lot of gaps between the bristles. This means it will shed.

Use synthetic brushes for water-based paints, since natural bristles absorb too much of the moisture. They should be used for enamels or alkyds only.

For walls, the standard brush is four inches wide, but there are also various specialty brushes for special jobs. Ask your dealer for recommendations for your particular job.

OTHER SUPPLIES

Drop Cloths. Big sheets of plastic. Remove as much furniture as you can, then push the rest into the middle and cover it.

Ladder. You'll need a tall ladder with a shelf to hold the paint tray. (See information under Ladders, p. 237.) If you're painting a long wall, use two ladders or sturdy stepstools, with a plank extended between them. Walk along the plank to reach a high portion of the wall instead of climbing up and down.

You can buy a strong hook that slips over a rung of the ladder to hold the paint can.

String. Tape a piece of string or wire across the top center of the can to wipe your brush against; if you brush it against the rim, the paint will collect there and the lid may wind up sticking.

Paper Plates and Sponges. If you're painting overhead, slip the roller brush through a paper plate or the brush handle through a sponge to pick up the drips. And glue a paper plate under the can rather than setting it down on newspaper sheets, which wind up trailing behind you.

Gloves. Lightweight handyman's cotton gloves will keep your hands clean. Your hands will sweat too much in cotton-lined rubber gloves.

Rollers. For a big surface like a ceiling or wall, it's easier to work with rollers and to use brushes only to finish the corners. Rollers come in various widths and naps (height of the roller surface). A short nap makes a smooth surface, a longer one gives you some texture. Foam rollers give a smooth finish to high-gloss paint. See if electric rollers suit your purposes.

Paint Bucket or Roller Paint Trays. To pour paint out in small quantities. A "mesh roller grid" lets you dip the roller in paint, then press excess through the mesh. It looks like a mini Ping Pong net. The mesh is tacked to thin strips of wood and placed vertically in a five-gallon bucket.

It's easy to wash latex paint out of a roller tray, but if you're using oil-based paint, cover it with a plastic grocery bag. Once you spill any paint into it, the bag will conform to the shape of the tray. When you're done, turn the bag inside out and dispose of the whole thing.

Extension Pole. To screw into roller handle for painting ceiling.

Vanilla Extract. Put a couple of drops into the paint and it'll cut the fumes.

Rags and a Bucket of Water. Or solvent if you're using alkyds, for cleanup.

Skateboard. If you're painting down low, you can use this as a movable seat.

Safety Equipment. A mask if you're plastering. Clear goggles to protect eyes from fumes, dust, paint splatters, etc. Cartridge respirator to protect you from breathing in paint fumes if you're going to be working in a place that isn't perfectly ventilated.

PROTECTION FROM DRIPS

Although it is a lot of work to prepare thoroughly for painting, it is even more of a task to remove dried paint afterward. Besides, if you've covered areas that shouldn't be painted, the painting process will go much more quickly.

If possible, remove ceiling fixtures or wall sconces or cover them with plastic garbage bags. Remove switchplates and outlet plates or make a protective border with masking tape. Remove or cover door handles with a plastic bag or tape. Put the telephone handpiece in a plastic bag so you'll be able to grab it if it rings without leaving drips.

You can apply masking tape around the edges of each window pane, then remove the residue with commercial adhesive remover, salad oil, or lighter fluid (CAUTION: Extremely flammable). However, I prefer to cut newspaper to size, dampen it, and press it on. When wet, it will stick, and when dry, it will be easy to remove. If you have trouble sticking it into place, add a little detergent to the water you dip it into. Or paint the window with a detergent-water solution.

How to Paint

START FROM THE TOP

Before you start, figure out where you'll end. Start from the top down and paint in this order: ceiling, walls, windows, woodwork, and doors.

If you have a ceiling that's a different color from the wall, or if you are painting around a door or window frame, the hardest part is

---

NO FLIES IN THE PIGMENT

If you're painting the exterior of the house, or just doing a painting job out of doors, add a couple of drops of citronella to the paint and insects won't fly into it.

getting a nice straight line ("cutting the edges") where the two colors meet. Start your job by using a small slant-edge brush where ceiling joins walls and walls join baseboard.

Slap (don't scrape) the brush against the side of a bucket or tray to get the right amount of paint.

Paint a wide W shape about 3 × 3 without lifting the roller and first pushing away from you. Then redip for more paint and fill it in, working horizontally across the W, a small area at a time. Y a W? you may ask. The idea is always to be working from a wet edge, and if you walk the length of the room making stripes, you may wind up with a striped pattern in the paint.

You're more likely to get splattered with paint when you go too fast with a too-wet roller. Work across the shorter end of the room.

To paint a wall, make a big M or similar zigzag shape about three feet high and three or four feet across, with the top points touching the top of the wall and the bottom going to the baseboard or floor.

If you're using a brush, fill in the M starting from the ceiling, going horizontally and making short stripes adjacent to each other. If you're using rollers, roll horizontally back and forth to fill in the M.

FINAL TOUCHES

Moldings. Use a smaller brush to get a smooth finish; don't soak brush; watch for drips and smooth immediately.

Windows. Make sure the glass is masked as described in Protection from Drips above. Use a tapered sash brush loaded but not dripping with paint. First paint the verticals around the panes, then the horizontals, then the inside of the frame. Do the sill fourth and the outside of the frame last.

Avoid painting the glass or just let the brush overlap slightly, then wipe off the excess imme-

---

IF YOU'VE PAINTED THE WINDOWS SHUT

Use a pizza knife to "slice" through the paint. Or put a small block of wood or putty knife at the sealed edge, and tap with a hammer. (Don't use a chisel; it may chip paint.) Repeat at various points around the wooden part of the window. Once you've got it started, use your car jack to nudge it further, but be careful. Too much pressure may cause the window or frame to crack. Use a silicone spray around the tracks afterward and slide the window up and down a few times.

---

diately. Remove masking tape while the paint is slightly wet so the paint on the work won't bond to the paint on the tape. If you live in a warm climate or are painting on a sunny day, don't leave tape on the windows since it bonds to the glass in the sun.

Doors. Fold newspapers over the tops, then close the doors before you paint.

Do the frame first, edges next, front and back last. (If the door is new, paint the top and bottom edges so they will be sealed against moisture.) Paint small recessed panels first, starting at the top, then any horizontal portions, finally the verticals.

Baseboards. They'll be neater if you use an "edge guide," which is basically a strip of plastic (a bit wider than a ruler) with a handle on one side. Buy one at the store or improvise your

---

WHICH PAINT FOR THE DOOR?

If you're painting a door between two different-colored rooms, match the hinge end to the room it opens away from and paint the lock or latch end to match the room it opens into.

own. Press the edger between floor and base-board (it goes flush to the edge or fits in a fraction of an inch), hold it with one hand, and paint the baseboard, trailing some paint on the top of the edger.

RENTING A SPRAYER

Spray painting is a more complicated how-to job than I want to go into here, but I think if you're painting an outside surface that's textured, like stucco, or has multiple surfaces, such as shutters, this is the way to go. It's a messy job, and a lot of paint gets flung around, so you need to be very careful to cover and mask areas that shouldn't be painted. Use goggles and wear gloves when holding the sprayer. The pressure from the paint nozzle can squeeze paint under your skin, which is a health hazard.

CAUSES OF PAINT FAILURE

If paint is peeling or cracking soon after you've painted, the problem is probably moisture from one cause or another: leaking from the roof or around window frames, backup in the gutters or downspouts, not enough venting from a very moist house.

The problem can also be traced to too many layers of paint, incorrect preparation of the surface, or painting over a type of paint that's incompatible with the top coat. For example, you can't use a mid-quality latex over alkyd.

IN THE BAG

To protect the windows from paint when you're doing the exterior of the house, slip the screens into plastic leaf bags, then put them back in place. Tape up the bag if the fit isn't perfect. There's no scraping afterward, and the bags can be used again.

You should also check that windows are properly caulked and that there are no leaks in the roof, flashing, and gutters.

If the house paint is peeling outside your bathroom, kitchen, or laundry room, you probably need to add vents for washers and dryers and install exhaust fans in the bath and/or kitchen.

Very General Guidelines for Painting the House Exterior

For a masonry exterior, you may use cement paint (comes dry), exterior latex (like interior but with weatherproofing and mildew-resisting additives), reinforced latex with added fine sandlike material that is very weatherproof, solvent-based masonry paint, or textured coatings. Check the manufacturer's instructions to find out what primer is correct.

For a wood exterior you can use latex or alkyd paint. If you're using alkyds, work in the afternoon when you're painting the side of the house that gets full sun. Paint will blister on a surface that will be in the direct line of the sun a few hours after it has been applied.

Spray painting goes a lot faster than painting with a brush.

You get better results if you paint in fair, dry weather. Don't paint if the weather is too humid or in the early morning when surfaces are still covered with dew. Stop at least an hour before evening damp sets in. Paint doesn't adhere well to damp surfaces and may buckle or streak.

Leave the overhangs and details (eaves or windows) for last.

PREPARING THE EXTERIOR

To clean mildew off siding, scrub the area with a mixture of three quarts warm water, one quart chlorine bleach, and one tablespoon of dry powdered laundry detergent. (Wear protective glasses and rubber gloves.)

Check with your paint store for exactly how to prepare the surface if you have cracking, peeling, blistering paint. You'll probably have to remove loose paint with a paint scraper, wire brush, or small orbital power sander. (Wear goggles to protect your eyes from dust and chips.) If the paint is too thick, you may have to take it down a few layers or straight to the bare wood.

A heated pad-type paint stripper is an interesting gadget to help remove paint from siding. Small, safe, and easy to use, it looks like a shingle with a handle and heating element. Another alternative is a water-pressure spray gun that removes dirt, peeling paint, chalk, salt crystals, and mildew.

Use galvanized nails on exterior repairs since they won't rust and bleed through the paint.

Use caulking to seal gaps and cracks between eaves and walls where moisture can enter. Check the label to be sure the caulk can withstand paint.

CHOOSING OUTDOOR PAINT COLOR

Some colors will turn out to be better investments than others.

Red and yellows fade the fastest, and you may need three coats to get an even cover. Blue and green are better at hiding the colors underneath, and many blacks and whites can cover with just one coat, though black alkyd may fade to gray.

White paint that "chalks" off is usually a disadvantage but good in a sooty, dirty city because as it erodes, it takes soot and grime with it.

Light or warm colors will make your house stand out or seem closer to the curb.

A house looks smaller if the contrast between the color and intensity of the shutters and the house is very great (extreme example:

CLEAN-UP TIPS FOR THE HOME PAINTER

Don't bother to wash the brushes every day. If you will be using them again the next day or relatively soon, wrap them in foil and leave them in the freezer. Allow thawing time when you're ready to use them again. You can also save a small foam brush loaded with paint in a plastic bag in the freezer at the end of the job for future touchups. Thaw and refreeze as needed.

Before you put the paint can away, paint a line around the outside of the can to indicate the level of the paint and let you know what color is inside.

---

white house, black shutters) and bigger if they're closer in tone.

CLEANING UP

Clean brushes in the solvent recommended on the paint can or ask the paint dealer which to use, then wash them in soap and water. Wrap them in paper and lay them flat or clamp the bristles with a pants hanger. Or drill a hole in the handle of each brush so that you can pass a wire through it (snip a wire hanger—the kind Joan Crawford didn't like—at one side, slip the brushes onto the hanger, and twist the cut sides together). Just make sure the bristles don't touch any surface.

To clean rollers easily, fill an empty quart milk carton or tennis ball can with solvent, put the roller inside, crimp the ends shut. Give the carton a few shakes, then let it sit for a couple of hours.

When you scrape the windows, first scrape a clear path along the window near the frame. That will help keep you from scraping the paint off the frame itself as you work.

● ●

WALLPAPERING

The least you need to know about putting up wallpaper:
- What you'll need
- How to do it
- Correcting minor problems

What You Need to Put Up Prepasted Paper

I'm giving you the instructions for prepasted paper because it's the easiest. If you're using paper that requires pasting—or you would like more detailed instructions for wallpapering—your dealer can supply you with literature or get a publication from the National Decorating Products Association.

For choosing a wallpaper and calculating the amount you will need, see information on pp. 51–54. Before you start, let me warn you not to attempt to hang the most expensive (and difficult) papers yourself and caution that you and your partner may wind up not speaking to one another by the time the job is done. Even my mother and I have had some close calls. The job is always more complicated than you expect. If you're determined, though, here's what you need:

Table on which to lay out the wallpaper and apply the paste with a roller. If it's not a worktable, protect the top by covering tightly with clear plastic and brown Kraft paper that comes in a roll. Don't use newspapers to cover the pasting table since the newsprint will bleed through onto the wall coverings.

Dropcloths. (Inexpensive; plastic; buy them at the paint store.) If you can, remove all furniture from the room, but if you must, push it in the center and cover it (and the floor) with dropcloths.

Ladder. See "Ladder," p. 259.

Painter's pad to moisten prepasted paper.

Yardstick for measuring and cutting.

Level to mark a perfectly straight line.

Razor knife with a package of new sharp blades to cut the wallpaper. Cut the length of wall covering at least 4" longer than the wall, then trim to size with the knife when it's pasted to the wall.

Wide putty knife. Used with the knife for trimming the paper at baseboards and ceilings. Putty knife holds paper in place, razor does the cutting.

Twelve-inch smoothing brush with slightly firm bristles: to remove the air bubbles and wrinkles when you get the paper up.

Seam roller sets smooth, tight joints between the edges of the wallpaper. Or use a window squeegee.

CURLING PAPERS

Rolling the paper the opposite way a couple of days before you're going to hang it will straighten it and make it much easier to work with.

Preparing the Walls

Strip. Remove nails, hooks, etc., and put toothpicks in nail or hook holes you want to find again. (When you put the paper up, just press carefully so the toothpick punctures the paper.)

You can paper or paint directly over old paper if it's in excellent condition. (Ask your dealer whether you should use a primer.) But it it's peeling, you'll have to remove it.

Strippable wallpaper can just be pulled away. Some leave a paper backing behind, which may be an ideal lining for new paper, but the dealer may suggest removing it completely.

If there are plaster walls underneath paper, you can use a dry scraper (buy it from the paint store). Make sure the floors are protected with plastic or rolls of brown Kraft paper, because this is a messy job. The dry scraper strips several layers of paper at a time, and then you remove the residue with an adhesive remover from the paint store or steel wool and warm water. If you use the steel wool, make sure to rinse thoroughly so no particles are left behind. Cover with a primer.

Paper that is resistant to water should be scored with a scraper or scraped with a putty knife. Or you may have to sand all or a portion, to get the surface closer to the backing. After sanding, sponge the wall with cold water mixed with wallpaper remover additive. Follow instructions for soaking time, and use a scraper. Or make a solution of equal parts of vinegar and hot water. Wet the paper thoroughly with a big sponge or roller or spray it on. Paper should then peel away from the wall.

Peeling paint must be scraped off, too, and sanded flat. If there are more than three layers of paint, you should strip the whole surface.

CAUTION: *If the house was built prior to 1980, there may be lead paint underneath. Please see p. 283 before you strip paint.*

Patch. Cracks and holes have to be filled with spackle or wood putty. Then sand smooth. Leave sufficient time for spackle to cure according to the instructions on the package. Drywall surfaces should be smooth—taped at the seams, with no nail heads showing.

Clean. The cleaner the surface, the better the new paper will look. Wash down all greasy and sooty spots and rinse. If you have a stubborn greasy spot, cover it with a coat of shellac and let the shellac dry. Otherwise it will stain through a paper.

Paint. If you're papering over a bright color, it may show through if you're not 100% accurate about aligning the top of the paper with the top of the wall. So paint a strip of color that matches the ceiling (or plain white paint). *If you plan to paint the ceiling or woodwork around the wall covering, do all painting before you paper.*

Prime. Unless there was a high-quality oil-based paint underneath, you may need a primer/sealer under the paper to prevent the wall from absorbing moisture. Otherwise, paste won't adhere. Primer also prevents the underlying paint from showing through the wall covering. Check with your store to find out whether to use an oil or acrylic-based, water-soluble primer and allow 2 to 4 hours drying time. New primer/sealers have almost eliminated the need for sizing, a wall-prepping product used in the past.

You may need to "etch" a too-shiny surface so it will hold a wall covering. This means sanding or washing with soap and ammonia or using a special primer/sealer for this purpose.

Never put wall covering up on a new drywall or freshly plastered walls. The paste won't adhere properly.

To Cut the Lengths

Make sure you have the right number of rolls of the correct pattern and that the dye lots are the same.

Before you cut, check the entire roll, or at least a few feet, in the event of a defect. You can't return a cut roll. If one roll has to go back, unless you can match the dye lot number you will have to send the whole lot back and start over again.

You have to plan carefully if you have a pattern. Hold up the first strip along the wall to gauge how the pattern should fall. Leave about 3" extra for the top and bottom. Once that's in place satisfactorily, cut the next strip long enough for the wall plus one pattern repeat. You'll waste a little paper, but you'll get the correct match.

Hanging the Paper

Turn power off to outlets and remove covers. (You will paper right over the opening, then press your fingers to get an indentation to use as a cutting guide, then use the razor to trim away excess.)

Use a pencil and level to make a perfectly straight plumb line on the wall to guide you. Calculate the number of strips you need and adjust your starting point. (Position the first strip no less than 4" from the corner of the wall.)

Dampen the cut strip with a pad, then fold the wet surfaces together. This is called "booking" the strip and instructions on the paper will indicate booking time (anywhere from one to five minutes). Don't crease the folds, just gently bend the paper. This process activates the paste, helps the strip relax, and keeps it from drying out.

Booking the Strip

Put the strip in place, using your marked guide.

Brush with smoothing brush. (Work up and down, not sideways.)

Use the seam roller to get the paper tight into the corner. Use the putty knife to push the paper against the ceiling. Place the blade in front of the putty knife and trim away the

PAPERING A CORNER

Because corners are not always even, placing the corner strip is a little tricky. When you're about to put up a strip that will reach the corner of the room, measure the distance between the corner of the room and the last strip that's been pasted in place. Measure in several places and allow the widest measurement, then add another 1/2" to go around the corner. Measure and cut the corner strip before you dampen it.

Butt the finished edge against the previous strip and let the cut side be the one that goes around the corner. Use the seam roller to press the paper firmly into place. Trim off the excess at the ceiling.

Draw another plumb line to start the next panel to make sure it hangs perfectly straight.

excess. Same technique trims away excess at baseboard.

Sponge down the strip to remove excess paste and to press down the strip again. Clean any excess paste from baseboard or molding.

When you've cut the second strip (so as allow for the pattern repeat), place it so it matches the pattern and place the edges so they touch, not overlap.

Wallpaper paste dries slowly, so you have a few minutes to adjust any mistakes.

To paste down paper behind a radiator, smooth paper down as far as you can with a squeegee, then wrap a hand towel around a stick and poke it down behind the radiator, smoothing as you go. Turn off heating for 24 hours or paper will dry too fast.

Put paper around a door or window, trim carefully. Tiny diagonal cuts at the corners will help make the fit tighter.

In rooms that get hot or steamy (kitchen, bathroom, laundry room, basement), your dealer may advise painting seams with a light coating of clear varnish to prevent buckling or peeling.

Troubleshooting Wallpapering Problems

BLISTER

Normally, air bubbles that you see while you put up wallpaper collapse and disappear when it's dry. If there are a lot, you probably rolled down the surface too many times. Use a razor knife and slit an X in the center of the bubble. If your paper is patterned, cut to follow the lines as best you can to insure invisibility of the repair. Gently lift each corner and brush the adhesive on the underside of the paper and the wall. Press into place, sponge off any excess paste and roll seam edges.

CURLY EDGES

When the strip was put up, the seams were rolled down too many times—or too vigorously. If you're still working on the room, wait briefly (fill your time by hanging a few panels), then roll on the seams just once firmly with even pressure.

If you've finished papering the room and see curly edges the next morning, go back and dab paste on the back of the covering and on the wall, then press. Roll with a seam roller. Wipe away excess paste.

THE WALLPAPERING NIGHTMARE

It's right out of an "I Love Lucy" episode: The paper that looked perfect last night seems to have shrunk. The seams are pulling away from one another with large gaps in between. Cause: cheap wallpaper. It actually does shrink. You could, of course, reprep the walls and start again, this time letting the seams overlap about 1/8" instead of making them meet. If you have the patience for this, I would like to offer you a job...working for me.

DAMAGED SPOT

To patch, tear, rather than cut, a piece of wallcovering larger than the damaged area, and paste it on top, matching the pattern if the paper is patterned. After an hour, use a razor knife to cut through both layers and lift off both pieces. You're down to the wall surface now. Sponge the spot clean, separate the layers of wallcovering, and paste the new top piece on. After another fifteen minutes, use a small roller (a seam roller) to smooth down the edges.

● ●

FURNITURE REFINISHING

The least you need to know about refinishing:
- Alternatives to stripping
- Tools and equipment
- How to strip

The techniques for refinishing any wood surface—floor, wall, or furniture—are the same, but I'd recommend that you call in the pros if you're dealing with a floor or wall.

Is Stripping Necessary?

Plain water and a mild detergent can do a surprisingly good job cleaning up just about any wood finish except lacquer or shellac, on which it will cause white spots, rings, or film. (Test with a bit of nail polish remover on a cottonball in an inconspicuous place; if the cotton softens or sticks to the finish, don't use water on it.) After the cleaning, you can give wood a coating of mineral oil to give it a bit of a shine. I happen to like furniture and other wood surfaces that look a little lived-in, so I'd quit at this point.

But if you don't like the way it looks after it's been cleaned, and if it isn't peeling, you can repaint it. First reglue any loose parts, then remove the glue film—or the paint won't stick to the surface—using a commercial adhesive remover or a half-and-half solution of boiling vinegar and water. Sandpaper to remove any glossy finish that remains. Then paint with enamel, following manufacturer's instructions.

Some problems can't be solved by cleaning or painting. For example:

If the wood is badly discolored—the clear finish has blackened, the wood grain is hidden.

If there are fine cracks, called "alligatoring" or "checking," all over the finish.

If the finish is peeling or flaking.

If there are worn spots all over the surface.

If the finish is soft and sticky.

In such cases, you have three choices: Live with the furniture, discard it, or refinish it. Refinishing is a two-step process. First you strip off the old paint and get down to the bare wood, and then you apply the new finish.

How to Strip with Your Clothes On

Work in a mid-range temperature and in a well-ventilated area unless you're using one of the newer solvents with which ventilation isn't a problem. To avoid dust, handprints, and other foreign matter on your work while it's drying, it's helpful if there's a way to seal off your work area. A fly trapped in the finish has a certain value as a conversation starter but is really only suitable to country decor.

If the wood isn't especially attractive or if you intend to use an opaque or semi-opaque finish, you can remove the old finish with a mechanical sander. But if you want to preserve the look of the wood, the process is slightly more complicated. Fortunately, new solvents have made the job easier and less dangerous.

Here's what you'll need:

Newspapers or plastic mat to work on.

Old clothes to work in. If you plan to wear them again, turn them inside out. If they get stained, at least the stain won't show.

Good supply of lint-free cloths. You can buy tack rags, which are usually made of cheesecloth, from the paint or hardware store. Or use fabric diapers and other types of cloths I've mentioned as acceptable dust cloths.

Solvent to remove the old finish. Different solvents work on different finishes. On a clear finish, try the nail polish remover/cottonball test described above; if the cottonball sticks to or softens the finish, it's lacquer or shellac; buy a solvent that will remove those. If it's a clear finish but not lacquer or shellac, it may be varnish. Mineral spirits or turpentine remove oil-base varnish and enamel; lacquer thinner removes lacquer; paint thinner removes oil-base paint; and water removes latex paint. In the past most solvents were made with irritating volatile solvents such as methanol and acetone, whose vapors caused headaches and nerve damage, or with metylene chloride, which caused heart attacks. You had to wear rubber gloves and masks and work in good ventilation.

New, less toxic and less irritating strippers may have no odor, ventilation isn't a problem, and rubber gloves aren't required. If you get these on your hands, they don't eat through to the bone. The catch: They may be much more expensive and they take longer to work. Ask the clerk and read the label to see if the solvent is right for your job and what, if any, cautions are advised.

Solvent applicator—usually a natural bristle brush or pad of coarse steel. See instructions on the solvent label.

Lifters to clean off the sludge that the solvent has softened. See what the label suggests. Lifters include hardwood scrapers; putty knives, which may gouge wood; steel brushes, which may scratch; nylon scrubbers (use only with non-toxic solvents); a toothbrush; or an old credit card.

Non-plastic container to drop the old, dissolving finish into.

Sanding tools may be needed, but with some solvents you don't need to sand. If you do, you can use steel wool. It's flexible, can be used wet, won't scratch, and produces a finer surface, but it sheds fine metal particles that are hard to remove. The alternative to steel wool is sandpaper and a sanding block—a block of wood, piece of rubber, or felt pad with sandpaper attached that gives you a better grip and control. If the surface is large, you may want to rent an electric sander.

For sanding special surfaces, you may need one or more special tools. These include a cabinet scraper for coarse sanding, when you can't get old material off easily; a hand scraper, which makes the surface even finer; and a spoke shaver that smoothes curved surfaces, such as legs. Or make your own spoke shaver by stapling several thicknesses of sandpaper to a length of nylon webbing from a home store or upholstery supplier. The webbing is flexible, and you can rip off each layer of sandpaper as it becomes worn.

Stains or paints, brushes, jars for mixing.

REFINISHING TOUCH

While you're refinishing the furniture, put the furniture hardware in a jar of liquid jewelry cleaner. Removes tarnish, adds shine.

Prepare the piece by removing the hardware and covering the floor. Tap a nail partway into the bottoms of the legs of chairs or tables to raise them slightly. When the finish runs down them, they won't stick to the newspaper or plastic mat.

Apply the solvent. In a few minutes, the surface will start to wrinkle. (Less toxic solvents are slower; check label instructions.) Then gently use a lifter to remove the gook that comes off. If a lot of finish remains, repeat.

STRIPPING WITH A HEAT GUN

Heat guns are sometimes used to strip paint from large surfaces because they're fast, but they're not recommended for painted metal, on surfaces that have a thin coat of paint, or to remove clear finishes such as varnish. They're also not recommended if you're removing paint containing lead, since it may spread lead-containing dust throughout the house. (Check the Securing section for information on lead paint, p. 283.)

Since the nozzle can singe your skin and the heat can cause burns or even a fire, don't use a heat gun unless an experienced person can show you how, and get one that has a rapid cool-down.

(One of the reasons the non-toxic solvent is slow is that it dries out. If you cover the container of the stripper with plastic wrap, you'll keep it sticky longer and it will work better.)

For heavily carved or vertical surfaces you may need to use an aerosol paint remover.

Once most of the old finish is gone, rub rounded surfaces with Fine steel wool. I feel that leaving a little of the old finish in the niches and crevices gives the piece some character. Most solvents today can be washed away with plain water. Wipe dry and allow to dry further according to the label instructions before you sand.

Preparing Wood for a New Finish

If the solvent you used doesn't require sanding or comes with a wash that removes every bit of pigment, you can skip this section.

The point of sanding is to remove every last bit of finish and surface imperfections and to make the wood uniformly smooth. For flat surfaces, you can use a sanding block, as I have said, or sandpaper. If you use the paper, begin with a medium-coarse grit (which one you use depends on the softness of the wood) and proceed to a finer grade. Always rub with the grain.

If there are dents in the surface, cover them with a few layers of cloth and press down with an iron, set to its lowest steam setting, for 30 seconds or a minute. Repeat until wood fibers swell. Work cautiously; the heat and moisture could cause white spots. Dents and holes that remain should be filled in with wood putty, plastic wood, or wax sticks in a matching color.

Vacuum off the sawdust and wipe everything with a dry, lint-free cloth.

The next step is to raise the grain of the wood and make sure that whatever comes up uneven is sanded down. Just sponge the wood surface with cold water until it's soaked, then wipe away the excess. When the furniture is dry, sand the area clean.

BLEACHING WOOD

Bleaching is a process that has intrigued me for years, primarily in relation to hair. I learned that bleaching furniture is similar, in that you can either make colors lighter or remove them completely. You can use undiluted household bleach—flood the surface and let it dry without wiping—but the commercial bleach solutions, which usually require a two-step process, are the most effective.

Bleaches, like strippers, should be used in a well-ventilated area. Wear rubber gloves and protective goggles to reduce the chances of eye and skin irritation.

DARKENING WOOD

You darken wood with a stain, then cover it with a protective finishing coat; some products combine the two processes.

Prepare the wood properly. If it needs patching, use the right filler (explained later in this section). Read and follow the instructions on the can of stain, and let the furniture dry thoroughly between coats to avoid swelling or shrinking.

Exposed end grains are very porous, so they absorb more stain and come out darker than other areas. Cover them in a sealer one or two shades lighter than you use for the rest of the piece.

To be on the safe side, choose a stain that's slightly lighter than the color you like most. You can always make the furniture darker by adding more stain. It is also possible to lighten furniture when you've used a stain that's too dark, but it's slightly more trouble; see the section on Refinishing Problems, pp. 271–272.

Don't mix and match colors from different manufacturers. If you're going to need more than one canful and you have an assortment, mix everything together before you start so you have a uniform color. Work on a horizontal surface when possible to avoid running.

Paint with the grain if possible.

Overlap only wet surfaces to keep the color uniform. View the piece at an angle to check for missed spots, which will look dull. Touch them up immediately.

Stain the largest exposed area last.

Read all the cautions on the label.

Choosing the Finish

Whether or not you bleach or stain the wood, you will have to finish it to protect it from damage and moisture. In deciding on a finish, the major consideration is the amount of hard use the furniture will get. A bookcase gets less use than the front of a dresser. Anything in a kid's room gets very hard use. (An all-steel room would no doubt be the most sensible choice, but it lacks warmth.)

Some finishes are harder to work with, some are more durable, and some cost more. But I imagine that your biggest concern will be how the furniture will look. Check out the possibilities at the paint or hardware store. Finishes come in various colors and degrees of transparency—from clear to translucent to opaque. There are also special kits and techniques for antiquing, marbleizing, and other customized looks.

OPAQUE FINISHES

Opaque finishes include enamel, paint, and pigmented lacquer. Lacquer finishes are difficult to apply on large areas because they have to be sprayed on. Working with a professional spray gun and compressor takes a certain amount of skill. But spray paints work well on a small area or a small piece of furniture.

WORKING WITH SPRAY PAINT

- Label may advise wearing mask.
- Shake the can well. Before you start to work, test spray a piece of paper. If the paint looks thin, it needs more shaking.
- If you spray from too close, the paint will run; if you spray from too far away, you'll get dust clouds and a gritty finish.
- Spray all surfaces, including corners, straight on; don't move your hands in an arc.
- Spray from left to right, then from right to left, moving down a row at a time and overlapping the previous row by half.

Any kind of paint can be brushed on. Though latex paint raises the grain of wood because it is water-based, just sand once it is dry and apply a second coat.

SEMI-OPAQUE FINISHES

A semi-opaque finish looks transparent but in fact works like makeup: The surface of the wood is either partially or completely obscured.

This is often used to make an inexpensive wood look like one that is costlier. Use either a clear finish that has been mixed with a coloring agent or a colored stain.

Of the oil and wax finishes, the best are penetrating finishes, which have a resin-oil or wax-resin base with a sealer stain added. Since they soak into the pores of the wood and form a solid layer inside it, they don't work well on bleached wood, whose pores are already clogged by previous finishes. Otherwise, they have several advantages. It's easy to apply a penetrating finish over bare wood or a stain since you just rub it on, there's no need to sand between coats, and the finish is durable, waterproof, and easy to repair. (To fix a scratch, just rub it with a bit of steel wool and apply another coat.) The disadvantage, of course, is that they're very difficult to remove.

CLEAR FINISHES

If the wood is beautiful and you want to show the grain, or if you have already stained the color that you like, you'll just want a protective but clear finish. This can be a seal such as polyurethane, an oil-based stain such as linseed oil or teak oil, or varnish and lacquer. To stain and seal all in one, you can use an oil-stain preservative that combines transparency with the protective power of paint or a stain-and-seal combination.

Refinishing Problems

Bleeding. After an oil finish has been applied, some woods "bleed" extra finish. Just rewipe occasionally until this stops. If spots are left to dry, buff gently with Fine steel wool.

Blotching. Some woods (pine, fir, birch, maple) may stain unevenly because their pores are variable. Put some finishing oil on a cloth and wipe the blotches lightly, but test this on an inconspicuous spot first.

Color Too Dark. If it looks too dark in the can, add a lighter stain of the same brand from the same manufacturer. If you notice it's too dark only after it's painted on, wipe part of it off. If it's already dried, wash wood down with mineral spirits. Let it dry. Then sand lightly, wipe clean, and apply a natural finish to keep the wood light or a darker color if desired.

Sticky, Tacky. The finish wasn't wiped dry, the wood is too moist, or the color is "bleeding" out of the wood. Rewet wood with more finish, then wipe with dry cloth. If this continues, buff with Fine steel wool and mineral spirits.

Water Spots. If finish is uncured, water may spot. Buff with more finish and Fine steel wool.

SURFACE FURNITURE REPAIRS

(See also Furniture Stain Removal, p. 128–129.)

Cracks, Scratches. Many fine scratches can be covered with furniture polish. Or you can use a simple home remedy as a cover-up: mercurochrome, and iodine for mahogany, cherry, or maple; liquid shoe polish for walnut and oak. Apply with cotton swab, buff with a cloth after it dries. Or rub a scratch in walnut with a broken piece of meat from a walnut or pecan. Sounds like voodoo, but it works.

Fill a deep scratch by filling the spot with crayon or a wax stick. (Melt the crayon or wax and guide liquid by heating the tip of an ice-pick over a candle, placing the tip in the scratch, and holding the crayon or wax stick against it). Fill to overflowing, and after it's cooled for an hour, use a plastic credit card to carve away the excess.

A group of hairline scratches can be eliminated if you dissolve the surface very slightly and the liquid sort of flows together in a process called reamalgamating. (I wish they could figure out a way to do this with aging skin.) First use a wax stripper to clean off the accumulated wax. Then you'll need to find the solvent that dissolves this particular finish. If

---

WHEN CARVING CAN'T BE REPAIRED

A lot of "carving" in inexpensive furniture is really plastic. If it's nicked or burned, it can't be repaired by any of the wood repairing methods. If it is damaged, check the furniture label—I hope you saved it—or contact the manufacturer to find out what kind of wood the furniture is made of, whether it is solid or veneer, and what manmade components, if any, were used to look like carving.

---

you don't know what it is, you've got to do a trial and error test on an inconspicuous part of the item. Try a bit of solvent and if the surface liquefies, you've hit the right stuff.

Start with denatured alcohol (it dissolves shellac). If that works only partially, you've probably got a shellac/lacquer finish, so combine three parts denatured alcohol with one part lacquer thinner. If the finish is varnish, you can mix half-and-half turpentine and boiled linseed oil. If it's lacquer-based enamel, you need lacquer thinner. You need a very gentle touch to make this work correctly. If you're not up to it, or if there are a lot of scratches, stripping and refinishing may make more sense.

However, this problem might be a result of too much moisture in the wood because the environment is too humid. Even if you refinish, the problem may reoccur.

Dents. You're working with heat and moisture here, so be careful or you'll get white marks that are worse than the dents themselves. Place a few layers of cloth on the dented area, then set a steam iron to low and hold over the pad for 30 to 60 seconds, and repeat. A wax stick can also fill in a shallow dent. Otherwise, get professional help.

Dry Rot. As I explained earlier (see "Wet Rot/Dry Rot" on p. 9), moisture may cause mold to grow on wooden and other walls. It can also affect furniture and may eventually cause it to powder. If you see mold, scrape it off and ask at the hardware store for a mildew killer and a dry rot retardant. If you have had to scrape away a lot of the disintegrating wood, you may need to patch.

Patching Wood. Read the package label to make sure you have the right kind of filler for your job. Apply it properly and let it dry thoroughly before you cover it with any finish or it may swell or shrink or develop tiny pinholes.

A small patch may be smoothed with a rubber spatula and sanded with an emery board. Cover it with clear nail polish or eggshell varnish if you want a shiny finish.

Peeling or Blistering. When a finish is applied incorrectly, or when you've mixed it with another finish with which it's chemically incompatible, paint will lift off the wood and it will have to be stripped. Lots of tiny blisters confined to one small area could be reamalgamated (see "Cracks, Scratches," p. 272), but if the problem is an environment that's too humid, you can treat it but it may reoccur.

HEAT TREATMENT FOR BLISTERS

You may repair a small blister in a veneered surface by covering it with cardboard and running a warm iron over the top until the spot is flat. Leave cardboard, weighted down by books or other heavy items, on the area for a day or so.

Warping. Warping occurs on a table when the underside, which is generally left unfinished (for reasons of cost) absorbs moisture, but the top (which has been waterproofed by the finish) does not. As a result the table becomes slightly rounded and you may find the place setting and the salt shaker in your lap. To correct the problem requires both moisture and pressure. Lay the table top unfinished side down on some wet grass and put some weights on the top. After it has dried, finish both sides. Or take the whole thing to a cabinet shop.

CHOOSING PATCHING COMPOUND

Compound	Good News	Bad News
Plastic wood	Strong; quick drying; premixed. Comes in colors to match different woods	Ungrained, opaque, very obvious patch
Wood putty	Quick drying; less shrinkage than plastic wood	Ungrained, opaque; makes an obvious patch; (for easy coloring, mix with liquid shoe polish)
Putty stick	Easy to use; rub in, wipe off excess	Not so durable
Wax stick	Comes in colors; rub, easy to apply and redo	Doesn't wear well; may bleed into other finishes
Latex wood compound	Durable; may be painted and stained	

PART 7
SECURING

AVOIDING AND HANDLING EMERGENCIES

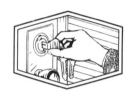

The least you need to know about home safety:

- Dealing with gas leaks
- Fire prevention
- Safety checkpoints
- Preparing for a power outage
- Handling environmental hazards
- Guarding against intruders
- Childproofing
- Safe food handling
- Medicine cabinet checklist

The problem with a lot of safety information is that it's not *where* you need it *when* you need it. If there's a kitchen fire, I doubt that you'll have the presence of mind—or the time—to pull this book out and look through the index. So photocopy and post information where it's needed—the information about kitchen fires, for example, inside a kitchen cabinet.

• •

IF GAS IS LEAKING

Go over this information with all members of your household.

Never use a match to check for a gas leak.

If you *think* you smell a leak, brush a soapy solution over the pipe in the area you think it's coming from. If there's a leak, you'll see bubbles form at the site.

If there's an unmistakable strong odor of gas, don't check anything. Act immediately:

Extinguish all open flames—cigarettes, stove, etc. But if you can see a flame burning at the source of a leak, leave it alone. It is burning off gas and reducing the possibility of an explosion. It also marks the source of the leak. Generally a flame won't travel through pipes if the valves are shut.

In a private house, you can close the main shutoff valve that brings gas into the house by turning it clockwise or to the right. (Remember: Right is off.) Don't touch the switches. Once you've turned it off, only the gas company can turn gas back on.

Open the windows.

If the odor is very strong, evacuate the building.

Do NOT light matches or operate any switch with a motor.

Do NOT turn any electrical appliance either on or off. The spark created in switching may be enough to ignite leaking gas. Because of the danger of sparking, do NOT use the telephone inside the house. If you live in a multiple dwelling, knock on doors to warn other residents of the need to evacuate but do NOT ring doorbells. The small switch inside the bell may create enough of a spark to be dangerous. Instead, pound on doors to alert your neighbors.

Call the gas company from a phone outside the building.

BEWARE OF CARBON MONOXIDE POISONING

Incomplete burning in your gas burner can cause carbon monoxide to accumulate. Over time, this may be toxic. If you or others in the household chronically complain of headaches, dizziness, coughing, and ringing in the ears and/or seeing spots in front of the eyes, you may be suffering from carbon monoxide poisoning. Get immediate medical attention and alert the gas company.

In more advanced cases victims become nauseated, vomit, lose muscle control, and eventually become unconscious and die.

If any gas flame in the house is burning yellow instead of blue, the situation is critical. Call the gas company.

OTHER SAFETY PRECAUTIONS

• Do not store bleach (or any other chloride product) anywhere near your gas heater. The mixture of gas and chlorine fumes causes hydrogen chloride, which rots pipes and chimney.

• Keep paint thinners and cleaning fluids stored away from gas.

• If you have an appliance that is lit by a match, hold match at the burner BEFORE you add the gas.

• Before you dig in the yard, call the gas company to make sure where lines are. If any gas lines are ever disturbed, even slightly, call the gas company to rebury or repair them.

• Your burner man should do an annual inspection.

ANTICIPATING FIRE EMERGENCIES

Fire Prevention

I imagine you already know the usual cautions, but I'll repeat them for the record: Don't smoke in bed; don't accumulate flammable trash or oil-soaked rags (see p. 136, "Wiping Up Grease"); have the chimneys cleaned regularly; and correct or eliminate any of the problems below.

FIRE HAZARDS INVENTORY

(See also Potential Emergencies, p. 209.)

Faulty Outlet. If it is not working properly (for example, an appliance plugged into it may work sometimes but not others), it should be investigated and corrected or sealed up.

Space Heater. Should be away from combustible materials. Keep it clean.

Loose Connections. May occur if appliances vibrate. Wiring should be tight. Switches or plugs should be secure.

Frequent Tripping. Talk to an electrician to get at the root of the problem.

Excessive Extension Cords or Multiple-Plug Adapters. You may need an extra circuit.

Baseboard Heater. Drapes that cover it can catch fire.

Heat Lamps in Ceiling. If a door swings directly under a bathroom heat lamp, a towel draped on top of the door could cause a fire. Warn family and guests.

Faulty Electrical Equipment or Appliance. If it's not working correctly, has a damaged wire, a loose plug, or is connected to a damaged extension cord, or if the control panel isn't properly in place, a problem or fire can occur.

Warning Systems

Smoke Detectors

In our house when the smoke detector goes off, we know the bacon is done. False alarms can be incredibly annoying but are worth putting up with, since smoke detectors and heat detectors are life-savers. I know a woman who puts a shower cap on her smoke detector when she's cooking and other people who disconnect them, but these practices are potentially dangerous. You may not remember to remove the shower cap or reconnect the alarm.

BEST WAY TO TAME A WILD SMOKE ALARM

If the thing is clanging and there's no fire, mist the air underneath with a plant watering bottle. This quiets the alarm without your moving it from its place.

Install smoke detectors over doorways throughout your home, at least one on each level and one to serve each sleeping area. (If bedrooms are clustered together, one may be enough. If individual bedrooms are placed far apart, you may need one for each.) On a floor without bedrooms, put the smoke detector near the living area. There should also be a smoke detector at the head of the basement stairs. Install them following the manufacturer's instructions, or ask the Fire Department for help.

There are two kinds of detectors. In a **photoelectric smoke detector,** a photoelectric cell "sees" smoke molecules and responds to smoke and smoldering fire—the kind a smoker is most likely to cause—rather than to fumes. Experts usually recommend photoelectric detectors. Nearly all house fires produce dense smoke rather than fumes before bursting into flames, and photoelectric detectors give you an earlier warning.

Most homes, however—about 85%—have an **ionization smoke detector.** This kind senses ionized particles and responds quickly to hot fires with little smoke. It is also more likely to set off false alarms.

A few companies have combined the technologies—using photoelectric sensors that also have heat sensors.

Some smoke detectors have a built-in light, which helps illuminate an escape route when the detector sounds. Others come with computer-synthesized voices that give fire exit instructions. And though most are battery-run, there are also hard-wired detectors connected into the electrical systems. (They should be wired so that they all sound simultaneously.) The problem with this system is that in case of a power outage, it's useless.

Check the sound level of the detector. Some go up to 95 decibels. The minimum should be 85, and the sound should carry through a few rooms. At least make sure that everyone in the family is familiar with the sound of the smoke alarm so that if it goes off, they don't mistake it for the car alarm down the street.

A friend once remarked of birth control pills that it's amazing how they lose their effectiveness if you leave them in the drawer. Similarly, smoke detectors have no value if they're broken or the battery has run down. Some of them buzz when the batteries need replacing. I think it makes sense to use marker dates like your birthday or the first day of a new season to remind you to take care of periodic tasks like changing the smoke alarm batteries (and scheduling your annual physical).

When you change the battery, clean it also. An all-purpose cleaner or some rubbing alcohol should do the job (but read the labels in case there are specific instructions). Dirt on the surface is one of the reasons for false alarms, or—worse yet—no alarm.

The Underwriters Laboratories, Inc., recommends testing and cleaning alarms *once weekly* to make sure they're in working order.

OTHER WARNING SYSTEMS

Heat detectors are particularly useful when placed in the basement near the furnace or water heater. They can detect a change in temperature caused by a sudden hot fire that may not create smoke until it's well under way.

There is also **"smart" wallpaper,** which works in combination with an ionization-type smoke detector. Early Warning Effect©, found in Koroseal vinyl wallcoverings, can "sense" fire before it ignites and even before a smoke alarm detects smoke. If one square foot of it is heated to about 300° F. (well below the ignition point of most common objects in a room, even paper, which ignites at 445° F.) it gives off an odorless, colorless vapor that sets off an ionization-type smoke detector. The Early Warning Effect© can give you a few more seconds of time in the event of a rapidly moving fire or as much as a half-hour when the heat of an impending fire is just building.

An Emergency Fire Plan

Everyone in the household should know where to find the closest fire alarm if there is a fire and calling from inside the house may cause a dangerous delay. Children should know how to call the fire department and use the fire alarm.

Designate an escape route for every room and discuss it with the family members. Tell them that if they hear the alarm, they should close the door to the room they're in. If it feels warm, the door shouldn't be used as an exit. Plan an alternative escape route if the obvious exit is not available. A window over a roof that shortens the jump to the ground is a good choice. Avoid windows located right over other windows, since flames may be coming out of the lower one.

For safety's sake, store a collapsible escape ladder near any window that might be used as an escape route. If a room has only narrow, high windows, or a basement has only one flight of stairs that offer an escape, think about installing a larger window or even a second flight of stairs.

If you live in a high-risk area where fires are common, you may want to put important papers in a strongbox that you can easily grab on the way out. Pet carriers and leashes should also be where you can get them in a hurry.

Decide where you will congregate outside if there is a fire. If there is an agreed-upon spot, you can do a head count right away and figure out if everyone has escaped.

If there is a child or invalid in the house who will need special help in the event of fire, contact the local fire department to see if they have special stickers with this warning that can be posted on the house.

Have a fire drill. Companies and schools have fire drills but families rarely do. Until you have a practice run, you won't know where the potential problems are.

Buying and Using Fire Extinguishers

A multi-purpose dry chemical fire extinguisher with the highest rating (ABC) is effective against any small, contained fire caused by an electrical appliance, flammable liquid, or other everyday situation. Look for the stamp that says UL (Underwriters Laboratories, Inc.) or CSA (Canadian Standards Association).

The amount of pressurized material is related to the length of time it is effective. A typical extinguisher contains from $2^1/_2$ to 7 pounds that last from 8 to 20 seconds. Select one that contains at least 4 to 5 pounds.

Check the pressure gauge of the extinguisher

monthly. If you've discharged it for a fire, or if the arrow points to "recharge," have it done professionally or get a new one. Mount one away from an open flame at least 5 feet from the floor in every room with potential fire hazards (kitchen, workroom, utility room, garage).

House extinguishers smother the fire, either with dry chemicals or carbon dioxide. It is very dangerous to pour water on an electrical fire because if liquids are flammable, water can cause the fire to spread. And if there are any exposed wires, you can get a terrible shock.

TRYING A FIRE EXTINGUISHER

Try it out on a windless day on a small fire. To operate, remember the PASSword. P: Pull the pin. A: Aim. S: Squeeze the handle. S: Sweep from side to side at the base of the fire. Don't hold the fire extinguisher too close to the fire. Afterward, it should be recharged.

Kitchen Fire Procedures

Copy these cautions and put them where you can find them in a hurry.

NO WATER ON AN ELECTRICAL FIRE.
Water may spread flames or cause shock.
Use a fire extinguisher.

NO WATER, FLOUR, OR CORN-STARCH ON A GREASE FIRE.
Use a fire extinguisher. Or toss on baking soda or salt.
(The baking soda releases carbon dioxide. Salt smothers the fire.)

IF THE STEAK'S ON FIRE.
Turn off the flame, pull out the tray, and throw a damp cloth on it.
If you don't tell the family, you may be able to get away with serving the steak as usual.

FIRE IN A POT.
Put a lid, another pot, or even a plate on top.
That smothers it.

FIRE IN A WASTEBASKET.
Water is okay.
It's probably from a match.

IF THE FIRE IS ESCALATING, CALL THE FIRE DEPARTMENT.

• •

OTHER POTENTIAL HAZARDS

Appliances

The key issue in appliance safety is installation. All should be properly installed by a licensed electrician who knows how to comply with the codes, how to ground equipment, and how to make the right connections to water, gas, drain, and vents.

Don't use extension cords or modify the power cord or plug.

All major appliances should be connected directly into a separate, grounded electric circuit.

Unplug appliances before cleaning and servicing, and unplug small heated appliances after use.

Freestanding kitchen range oven doors should never be used as a seat or a stepstool.

The temperature conditions should be correct for operating all appliances.

Check the manual to make sure you're operating all equipment safely.

CAUTION: There is some concern about the carcinogenic effect of low-level electromagnetic waves, particularly when they affect your head and shoulder area. Some sources advise against the use of hair dryers and recommend that you don't sleep with your head closer than three feet from an electric clock.

DISHWASHERS

Use only chemicals recommended by the manufacturer.

Don't let kids climb or sit on the door.

Load sharp items point side down.

If something has dropped below the bottom shelf, don't reach in to retrieve it until the machine has cooled (at least 20 minutes after a cycle).

WASHING MACHINE/DRYER

Don't combine chlorine with ammonia or chlorine with vinegar, rust remover, or other acids. Hazardous fumes may result. (See "Recipes for Disaster," p. 99.)

Keep flammable liquids such as dry-cleaning solvents, gasoline, and kerosene away from a washer and dryer.

Hand wash and air dry any fabric that has been treated with a flammable liquid before you machine wash it. Some oil-soaked rags have also been known to burst into flame in washing machines and dryers (see box, p. 136).

Safety in the Bathroom

To prevent scalding, see the box "Preventing Hot Water Burns," p. 214, in the Maintaining section.

If your tub isn't safety-textured, install **no-skid stickers.** Remove and replace old ones that are peeling off.

Grab bars installed next to the tub are helpful not only for older people but also for children.

Replace glass shower doors with tempered glass or Plexiglas.

Hair dryers, electric toothbrush, and other appliances should be positioned far from the bathtub. If someone is sitting in a tub and drops the appliance while the power is on, the results can be fatal. (Some new appliances have an automatic cutoff feature designed to prevent this from happening.)

Water Supply

Lead (from municipal supplies) may accumulate in pipes and be passed into your drinking water. Use only cold tap water, and let it run for two minutes in the morning before using it for drinking. (Save the runoff to water plants, for laundering, or for bathing.) Boiling the water won't help and may even concentrate the lead, which is very dangerous if you are using the water for a baby's bottle. New studies show that no level of lead is safe for children.

Car Safety

A fluorescent strip around the car door or trunk lets other drivers see if your door is open or your car is stopped with an open trunk.

I bought a large vinyl sign that could be folded into the glove compartment and said HELP! CALL POLICE. You put it in the rear window in case you have to pull over. I think it's a great safety measure. If you can't buy such a sign, then make one on a large piece of plastic using a contrasting-color fluorescent marker.

In the winter keep your trunk equipped with a shovel and cat box filler or sand (for getting traction).

Swimming Pools

Pools are what is legally considered an "attractive nuisance" and if there's an accident, you're the one they blame—not the kid who falls in. There are probably local regulations that require you to fence a pool, but if not, do so anyway. The fence should have a locked gate and warning alarm system. Be sure the lock is childproof.

A life preserver, lifeline, and rescue hook

should be instantly available. Post emergency life-saving techniques where adults and older kids can see them.

Remove all inflatables floating in the pool when you leave the area so a child isn't tempted to go back and retrieve them.

If you have tile around the edge of the pool, put down bathtub appliques, especially if there are small children. They don't make the area absolutely skidproof, but they help.

Many public pools forbid children to use inflatable arm supporters because they make a non-swimmer overconfident. If your child uses them, warn him or her that these cannot be removed unless you are present.

After parties, clean up so that small children won't be tempted to investigate leftovers. Immediately remove drinking glasses, bottles/pitchers, and alcoholic beverages.

Stair Safety

Strip lights are great for stair treads, especially for basement stairs or steep, narrow back staircases. Fluorescent tape or paint can be used on treads that aren't well lighted.

If you're designing the steps from scratch, make the treads deep enough to ensure a good foothold.

Mixing sand into stair paint gives it more traction.

You can also use V-shaped metal or vinyl "nosing" guards. They fit over the edge of the steps, on the tread and the riser, about an inch and a half. The top, where you step, is ridged. Buy them by the yard at a home building supply center. Metal guards are screwed on, vinyl ones pasted with strong contact cement.

Or use carpet runners. To calculate yardage, measure the treads and risers and add 10 inches. Choose a flat, dense weave. Secure the runner with a tack every 2 inches (brush the carpet pile back and forth a few times to hide the head). Or use a metal rod on each step, hooked

into place with screw eyes. Treads that are worn are very dangerous; shifting the carpet periodically (see box "Taking Steps," p. 40) helps reduce wear.

If your staircase has no handrail, install one along the outside of the steps or attach a "floating" handrail along the wall. You can buy handrails at a lumber yard or building supply center with the proper mounting brackets. Add a second handrail at child height if there are young children in the house.

Staircases must be lighted from the top and bottom, so be sure you can switch on a light at the top before going down and can turn the light on at the bottom of the stairs before going up.

Paint the top and bottom tread of a basement staircase in either white or yellow gloss paint—or neon. Helps people spot top and bottom steps at a glance.

Preventing Outdoor Safety Problems

Path and driveways should be unobstructed and clear.

Keep **garden hoses** coiled and hung or shelved, not snaking through the lawn where they can be tripped over. On a very hot day, water left in a garden hose can actually heat up to near scalding temperature.

If you have an **outdoor electrical outlet,** close it with a weatherproof snap-in cover.

Install low-voltage **ground level illumination** for walkway, driveway, patio, or pool that turns on or off with a switch (from inside the house) or automatically on a timer or light, sound, or motion sensor.

Mount an **automatic overhead light** for the house entrance about eight feet above ground level.

Stand on wooden plank or rubber mat when working on damp ground and **turn power off before replacing an outdoor bulb.**

Other Safety Checkpoints

Carpeting. Increase traction on area rugs with a carpet liner or carpet tape. Carpet liners or padding are sold by the yard at a carpet shop. Buy a piece that's about a half-inch smaller all around than your area rug. Place the liner down, then cover it with the rug. If you're using double-sided tape, buy enough to fit the perimeter of your rug, excluding fringes. Cut strips to measure and lay down one at a time. Peel off only about a foot of the top protective paper to start, then put your rug in place and press firmly. Continue along all four sides.

Fireplace. Creosote, a tarlike, flammable substance, accumulates in the chimney and flue. One way to avoid this is to burn only seasoned, well-dried wood—not paper products and raw wood. Let the hearth cool for 12 hours after a fire, then clean away dust and soot that can carry sparks. The chimney should have a periodic professional cleaning. (See Fireplace, Cleaning Of, p. 232.)

Sliding Doors. Put decals at eye level on sliding doors. Even sober people have an unfortunate tendency to attempt to walk right through them.

Telephone. To minimize risks from shock and fire:

• Do not use any kind of telephone in a bathtub, shower, or swimming pool.

• Don't use a phone anywhere near a gas leak. Sparking may cause a fire.

• Don't use a phone during a storm, since lighting may strike lines.

• •

PREPARING FOR POWER FAILURES

If you live in an area where electrical storms are common, make the following preparations:

Emergency Supplies. a transistor radio, waterproof flashlights, batteries, a high-power lantern, hurricane lamps and candles, plus a couple of oil lamps in a place where you can find them. (Don't leave fuel in the lamps but make sure it's easy to locate.)

Food and Water. If freezer isn't full, store clean empty milk cartons filled with water in it. If the freezer goes off, the ice will keep the temperature low. Keep a gallon or two of bottled water and a supply of canned and dry foods, and replace them every year or two with fresh supplies.

Cooking Equipment. If the power goes off, so will your stove—even the new gas ones, which have electric ignition—so buy some kind of hibachi-type grill.

Heat. If there is a way to operate your gas or oil heater manually, you should know how to do it. If you depend on electric heat, you could investigate a non-electric gas heater, but these are dangerous and outlawed in some communities, such as New York City.

If you have advance warning:

Buy food, water, batteries, candles, or fuel for hurricane lamps.

Gas up your car.

Fill the tub with water, since service may be interrupted.

Take out the candles and oil lamps.

If time permits, move ice that is already frozen into the refrigerator and prepare more in water-filled cartons.

Turn off all electrical equipment so that if power is suddenly lost and then suddenly restored, there isn't a sudden surge that will create damage.

When the Freezer Fails

If it's full, it will keep food frozen for two days. If half-full, it's good for about a day. Keep the door closed and try to find out how long the power will be out.

If the freezer can't be restarted and power will be out for more than two days, see if friends (or the local school, church, or store) can keep your food in their freezers. You may even rent space in a commercial freezer or cold storage plant, but wrap the food in newspapers to insulate it while you carry it there.

Or purchase dry ice, about $2^1/_2$ pounds per cubic foot for a freezer compartment, about 25 pounds to keep a half-full, 10-cubic-foot freezer cold for two days. Have it cut into slabs, carry it in a container and don't touch it. It freezes everything it comes into contact with, including your skin. Ventilate the area you're working in because dry ice removes oxygen from the area as it evaporates. Place the dry ice on empty shelves around the frozen items but not directly touching them—or put cardboard on top of the food and put the dry ice on top. Twenty-five pounds of dry ice will hold a 10-cubic-foot freezer below freezing for 3 to 4 days, a half-full freezer for 2 to 3 days.

If you have a freezer full of dry ice, don't put your head down into it because it draws oxygen from the air and you may have a breathing problem. Let the air mix into the freezer for a few minutes before you look at it.

Any food that seems strange—color or odor—should be thrown out. When in doubt, get rid of it.

To refreeze food, don't jam it together. Spread it apart so cold air can circulate around it. The food will be safe if you stay within the guidelines, but the quality may be affected.

Thawed meat, poultry, and vegetables can be refrozen after they have been cooked. If you have a batch of thawed food, cook up a big batch of Mustgo Stew ("Everything in the kitchen *must go*") and freeze it for another day. For more about frozen food, see pp. 291–292.

When the Refrigerator Fails

Food will last up to 4 to 6 hours, less time if the kitchen is very warm. You can add block ice to the fridge to keep it going a while. Here are some specific guidelines.

The following foods should not be kept at temperatures above 40° for more than 2 hours: Casseroles, cottage cheese, cream, custards, eggs, hams, hot dogs, lunch meats, meat, milk, pasta salads, poultry, puddings, seafood, soft cheese, sour cream, stews, and yogurt.

WHAT TO DISCARD IF THE FREEZER FAILS

Type of Food	What to Do
Poultry,* meat casseroles,* meat* pizzas, eggs, ice cream, soft cheese, cheesecake	Refreeze if it still contains ice crystals and feels as if it's been refrigerated. Toss out if it's been thawed and has been above 40° F. for more than 2 hours. (Check by putting a thermometer between the wrapping and the food.)
Hard cheese (cheddar, Swiss, Parmesan)	Can still be refrozen even if it's thawed and has been above 40° F. for more than 2 hours but quality is unchanged.
Seafood	Do not refreeze.
Vegetable juices and vegetables	Refreeze if still contains ice crystals and feels as if it's been refrigerated. Throw away items that have thawed and been above 40° F. for 6 hours.

*Call USDA Meat and Poultry Hotline with any questions: 1-800-835-3455

ENVIRONMENTAL HAZARDS
Testing for Problems

Now there are more things to worry about than ever—environmental hazards that, a decade ago, we had never even heard of. Certainly you'll want to run tests on a house that you're thinking of buying, but the one you're already in should probably be tested also. An on-site safety inspection of your home, with standard testing, costs about $250. If problems show up, and more elaborate inspection is necessary, the laboratory tests may jack up the tab to $500 or more. You should call in a professional (look in the Yellow Pages under Environmental and Ecological Services or call the Department of Health for a recommendation), but you can start with an inventory of your own.

Asbestos. Asbestos is an effective insulator, but as it deteriorates, carcinogenic fibers get into the air. What may be surprising to you is how many sites contain asbestos—including sheetrock, tile floors, roofing, heating, and duct work, insulation, acoustic ceilings, and even decorative plaster. Before you do any renovating, have your contractor arrange for an inspection. A friend of mine was about to rip up a section of old vinyl flooring until she had it tested and discovered it was 45% asbestos. Instead of ripping it up, she took the safer route and covered it with another flooring. This would have been required by law in some states.

For example, in Connecticut, it's illegal to rip out a section of asbestos flooring larger than 3×3 feet. If asbestos is found in the walls or floor, your solution is to seal it over and leave it untouched during remodeling.

Fumigants. A highly toxic termite killer called chlordane was used until 1987. Its effects last for years and cause such concern that some people will not buy a house that reveals any traces of chlordane.

Lead Paint. Though the lead content of paint has been limited by law since 1978, it is still very common in housing constructed before 1980. Single-family houses usually have more lead-based paint than apartments, typically on metal surfaces (radiators and railings), and often on windows, doors, stairs, columns, and trim. Since it causes neurological damage (especially in children), it's a great cause for concern.

Test kits aren't as reliable as an inspection by an expert to determine if you have lead, but old, chipping paint almost inevitably contains some. If you sand it, the dust goes all over the house; if you chip at it, the chips go into carpeting or soil. The best solution is to cover it with fresh paint or wallpaper.

If a chipping, peeling wall has to be scraped and repainted, hire a painter who is a lead abatement specialist; this is not a job to attempt yourself. Workers should wear masks with "high-efficiency" air filters. To limit dust, hang plastic sheeting and ask that cleanups be done daily. Don't vacuum the stuff up yourself because some particles will cling to the vacuum bag and be spread around the house. Stay away from the house while lead paint is being removed. The dust is a real problem for everyone, particularly pregnant women.

Water dripping off the eaves of the house and over lead exterior paint can eventually cause lead contamination in the soil—so this is not a good place to grow vegetables.

Free booklets on preventing lead poisoning are available from the State of Maryland. Phone (401) 631-3859 or write Maryland Department of the Environment, 2500 Broening Highway, Baltimore, MD 21224.

Radon. More common in the eastern United States, underground radon gas is a leading cause of lung cancer. You can get a kit for home testing and send the completed test for laboratory testing. If radon is present, arrange for radon abatement, which involves installing a venting system that contains the radon gas and sends it up and out of your roof.

PREVENTING INTRUDERS
Burglar Control

I have read a lot of articles about burglarproofing your home and they give advice like, "Don't show off what you own." In other words, if you've got it, don't flaunt it, which is advice I think some people are temperamentally unsuited to follow. If you fall into this category, then you should pay particular attention to the advice about burglarproofing your house.

A lot of this advice just boils down to common sense. Leave lights on when you're out of the house so someone thinks you are home. Everybody knows this, including burglars, but I still think it's worth doing. Most burglars take advantage of dumb luck. The typical burglary occurs on a warm summer day, and one in four burglars enters through an unlocked window or door. They usually leave TVs, computers, and other heavy stuff behind and take portable items such as radios, VCRs, cameras, and jewelry.

You can buy expensive devices that turn lights on when you're not there—they work through your electrical system and involve wiring—but there are many inexpensive alternatives that plug into wall outlets:

• Small automatic night lights have a "daylight sensor" that turns on light when it's dark and off when it's light again.

• Automatic light switches can be equipped with a sound sensor that turns on a lamp when it "hears" a sound, then turns off the lamp when the sound goes; it's useful in an empty house. A lamp timer can be programmed to turn the lights on and off, either at the same time every day or at varying times.

Obviously, you should set timers so that lights go on (and off) in various rooms at the appropriate times—dining room and kitchen at dinner, bedrooms later, hall lights or outdoor lights last of all. To be a little extra cautious, you can hook radios or TVs to the timers, so there's the sound of someone talking.

Shades that are pulled down advertise the fact that you are not home. Garage doors that are up—with no car inside—send the same message. A friend who lives alone keeps a dilapidated, undriveable second car in the garage to make the place look occupied when she's away.

Keep the perimeter of the house and the entrance to your house well-lighted and visible from the street. Cut back shrubs and trees that may be too close to the windows and doors.

Install window guards in a high-risk area.

In an apartment building, you may have a special fire-resistant front door, but if your house or apartment has softwood or hollow core front doors, replace them with ones that are solid hardwood or metal. Or reinforce a hollow one so it can't be pushed in so easily. You can do this yourself by nailing a sheet of $1/2$" plywood or sheet metal inside. (You'll need to drill a hole for the doorknob and reinstall deadbolt locks.)

To test if the door is secure on its hinges. hold a piece of $3/8$" thick wood against the metal strikeplate of the lock and try to close the door. If the door closes over the wood scrap, the hinges are loose and need repair.

Security Check

Security Devices

Alarm Systems. Since homes without alarms are six times as likely to be burglarized, it makes good sense to have one installed. As of 1992, 17 million homes had done so. As alarms have become more popular and more companies have begun to manufacture them, the prices have gone down. In addition, home insurers discount policies from 2% to 15% when the homeowner has an alarm system.

See if local police will recommend the most useful system. Some are audible, and some sound an inaudible alarm. To be well protected, you need an alarm system with sensors that monitor boundaries, such as the front yard or gate, windows, or doors.

Motion/heat sensors alone, like inexpensive stand-alone alarms (battery-operated or plugged in), are prone to false alarms. And since they don't go off until the intruder is already inside, they aren't much help if you're home alone.

As an additional safety measure, you should have an external siren or automatic dialer to alert someone outside the house that it has been broken into.

Wireless systems use sensors to send radio transmissions to a central control. Hard-wired, low-voltage systems are usually armed or disarmed by a keypad at the front door. Usually, the basic package for a system includes installation; a control panel with a battery backup (4, 6, or 12 hours); a keypad with a panic button; a digital dialer for the phone line that automatically contacts local police or a central security monitoring service; a motion and/or smoke/heat detector; three door/window contacts; and an interior siren (or other noise, bright lights, or both).

Extras might include an additional keypad, more window contacts, and sliding glass-door sensors with a glass-break detector. Some companies sell you a system and installation package. Others let you install it yourself or hire a contractor to do the job. Installation for a central system costs $2,000 and up; doing it yourself can run as low as $300.

Installers should be certified by the National Burglar and Fire Alarm Association. Get bids from two or three, and before you sign a contract make sure it includes a complete plan that spells out the following:

Equipment installation (including control panel).

Location of every sensor.

Wiring if any, and if installation requires cutting into walls.

Name and rates for monitoring service. If the alarm is tripped by the automatic dialer, the service calls your home. If someone gives the prearranged password, the call is considered a false alarm. Otherwise, the service contacts the police or fire department. Often police departments don't want systems connected directly because false alarms are so frequent.

Terms of warranty—usually between 90 days and 18 months.

Door Viewer. This is a peephole that gives you a wide-angle view of any callers while the door is closed. If your kids rush to answer the door, consider installing a second one at their level.

Locks. For complete security you need a deadbolt lock, mounted on the surface or installed in a cylinder through the door. In either case, you turn a key or press your thumb to release a bolt that falls horizontally or vertically. I don't like deadbolts that require an inside key, and in some places they are illegal. Though you may plan to leave the key permanently in place, things don't always work according to plan. If there's a fire or gas emergency and the door is locked from the inside with no key in sight, you could have a disaster. And if it is left in place near a glass opening, a thief could break the glass and turn the key from inside.

Check the screws in the strike plate, the metal "frame" through which the deadbolt passes. If they're less than 3" long, replace them.

Metal Guard Plates. These provide excellent protection. They are bolted in place through the door to cover lock cylinders. They're hard for burglars to drill and remove, since only the key slot is exposed.

Outdoor Lights. A switch by your bed that can turn out outside lights is not only a good deterrent but a great comfort. If you hear a suspicious noise outside, you can floodlight the area.

Sliding Doors. Can be secured with a special wedge lock. Or just buy 3/4" wooden dowel cut the right length to fit into the bottom track with the door closed. No one can open the door this way, even if the lock is opened. (Similarly, if you edge a dowel into the runner vertically

just above the lower window sash, the window can't be opened.)

Window Locks. Simply latching the window lock often discourages a would-be intruder. Use the dowel system, or secure a double-hung window by drilling a 5/16" hole into both sashes where they

Nail Lock

Securing with a Dowel

overlap. (Don't drill through the exterior sash.) Slip in a 3-inch-long bolt or nail, then slip it out if you want to open the window from the inside.

• •

CHILDPROOFING

In the last decade, manufacturers have come out with an amazing array of childproofing gadgets (locks, grids, knobs, etc.), but no gadget can guarantee absolute safety. I know of a child who managed to find and swallow an asthma pill that was inside a sealed container in a closed purse in a closed cupboard in a closed room. Houdini couldn't have done better.

Nothing takes the place of personal policing, but you should also take every mechanical precaution possible. Most of the new parents I know make a point of going to the store where they buy their bottles, diapers, and other infant supplies to investigate the various devices designed to childproof a house. I am assuming you will, too. A lot of the following information, then, you may be aware of, but I tried to include some problems you might not have already anticipated. Some people feel that training a child to obey a loud "No" is an adequate substitute for babyproofing, but obviously they were the parents of unusually docile children.

Inside the House

Appliances. Small appliances with rotary blades or choppers, like blenders and food processors, should be stored out of reach. Never let a cord dangle over the countertop or the child can grab it and pull the appliance down. Unplug the toaster—and other appliances—whenever they are not in use.

Baby Pillows. If they are filled loosely with plastic pellets, beads, or foam, they can cause suffocation.

Bath. A child can drown in as little as an inch of water in a tub and children have even toppled over and drowned in the toilet bowl. There is a hinged toilet lid lock that clamps to the lip of the bowl.

Cabinets and Drawers. Very little ones can be kept out of cabinets if you simply stretch a rubber band over two parallel knobs, but you will need something more sophisticated as your child grows. A variety of locks is available, from a U-shaped contraption that slips over two cabinet doors at once to catches that prevent a child (but not an adult) from being able to open a door or slide open a drawer.

Crib. New cribs must have slats less than $2^3/_8$" apart. A hand-me-down crib may have slats so wide the child can slip his head through them and get caught. Make sure no slats are loose, that all the parts work (the side that drops doesn't drop simply from the pressure of a child leaning against it) and that there are no sharp edges or loose hardware. If the crib is old, see the cautions about lead paint, p. 283.

Doorknobs. Special covers prevent the child from turning the knob and going into the wrong room or being locked in or out. There's even a lock for childproofing a folding door.

One great safety tip is to throw a towel over the door whenever a child's in the bathroom: There's no way the door can close or snap shut. (But if there's a heating unit in the ceiling, this may be a fire danger.)

Doors. If there's a pet or a toddler in the house, you may not want him/her to wander in the room when the baby's asleep. Installing a screen door to the room keeps unwanted guests out but lets you keep an eye on what's going on. Or install a Dutch door (closed bottom, open top).

Hiding Places. Get rid of empty or nearly empty storage chests or broken freezer or dryers. Remove doors. Call to see if your local sanitation department or utility company has a program to pick these up.

High Chairs and Strollers. These must have safety straps. Putting a rubber drainboard or rubber appliques on the seat helps make it less slippery.

House Plants. Aside from the potential problem of dirt and pot shards when a child knocks the plant over, there's also the chance of inadvertent poisoning. Get rid of small potted plants or put them where they're completely inaccessible.

Outlets. My son was able to take out the plastic plugs from outlets very easily. I finally stumped him with a double-outlet cover that screws into the plate; each cover must be turned 90 degrees to expose the slot. You can also find tiny padlocks that fit the holes in the prongs of electrical appliances. When they're in place, the item can't be plugged in. When you do remove the padlock to use the appliance, store it temporarily around the cord so you can find it.

Patio Door. There's a safety lock with a suction cup device that prevents the child from opening the sliding doors and a slam-guard that prevents the child's fingers from getting caught as the door closes.

Poisons. Almost every household chemical can be toxic to children. Stock ipecac, which induces vomiting, if there are little children and check the expiration date periodically. However, if you believe your child has swallowed anything other than food, do not administer ipecac or any anti-poison remedy without calling the Poison Control Center in your area. (Post the number where you can find it quickly. In some cases, you should induce vomiting and in others it is very dangerous, so find out what's correct before you act.)

Playpens. If made of mesh may form pockets between the side and bottom that can trap kids. Weave should be no more than $1/4$ inch.

Refrigerator. Some have locks built in, but you can also buy one that locks over the bar handle attached to the door.

Sharp Edges. Get rid of your glass coffee tables and put a throw over chairs with sharp edges.

Space Heaters. Need special attention. Install a three-sided mesh screen around the heater (attach the sides to the wall with wall brackets) so the child cannot touch it or tip it over.

Stairways. New-style safety gates (with vertical slats across top and bottom of staircase) are better than the accordion-style models in which kids can get their heads caught.

POISONOUS SUBSTANCES

Common household items that are potentially poisonous include:

- Bleaches
- Cleaning solvents
- Cleansers
- Dishwashing detergent
- Drain cleaners
- Hard-water (mineral and lime deposit) removers
- Laundry detergents
- Oil furniture polishes
- Oven cleaners
- Prewash stain removers
- Rust removers
- Toilet bowl cleaners

Stove. If range dials are on the side of the stove, remove them. It's a nuisance to pop them back on when you want to turn the burner on, but unattended they're a great danger. Turn pot handles toward the rear of the stove when you're cooking. (If you won't remember, post a reminder.)

Throw Rugs. The fabric equivalent of a banana peel. Hazardous.

Windows. Make sure furniture or objects aren't placed so a child is able or attracted to climb on a window or ledge, and install window guards (which may be required by law where there are young children).

SAFE TOYS

There's a tremendous amount of self-regulation in this industry and you often hear reports of recalls. But no one can anticipate what a toddler considers a "toy," an edible toy at that. Scrabble tiles, popped balloons, and even tiny Lego pieces may qualify. Still, there are some safety features you can be on the lookout for:

Hand-me-down toys from prior to 1976 may be painted with lead paint. Discard them.

Rattles should have no sharp edges and be sturdy enough not to come apart if the baby knocks it around, since pieces may wind up in the baby's mouth.

Pull toy strings should be 12 to 14 inches and no longer, in order to guard against accidental strangulation.

Soft toys should be labeled "fire retardant." Seams should be strong so the child can't pull the toy apart. The safest toy faces are embroidered on, because features such as doll nose, eyes, mouth, eyes, ears, and tongues may be pulled off and swallowed.

Squeeze toys are safest when the squeaking device is molded into the toy, rather than either flimsily suspended in the toy cavity or partially sticking out (like a bellybutton). Kids who pull apart the toy can swallow the squeaker.

Stacking ring toys are okay but beware of

one with a fixed wood center pole. Kids can trip and tumble onto the pole. Choose one with a rocking base or no base.

Toy chests should either have a lightweight removable top or include a contraption that keeps the lid securely open. Kids are bound to climb in, even if it's filled, so be sure the chest has proper holes for ventilation and smoothly finished edges that can't scrape or puncture skin.

Supervise every game where young kids want to play with older kids. My friend's six-year-old nephew was feeding corn chips to his two-year-old cousin—but he had checked to see that the baby had teeth. Not all kids are so thoughtful of what a little one can—and will—chew on.

Outside the House

Though this topic is slightly outside the concerns of this book, I'd like to point out that how careful you are about making and communicating rules may make a life or death difference.

Still, *don't tempt fate.* A small child alone in a backyard or open area will ignore your warnings to wander or crawl toward anything interesting and may consider "fast food" anything that crawls.

A cordless phone and/or a long extension cord is a good investment in safety: With them, you can be outside and on guard even if the phone rings.

One of the most useful guidelines for children is to tell them that if they're separated from their parents, ask for help from *someone who is working* rather than appealing to just anyone. With just a little bit of practice, even very young children can identify who's working—a shopkeeper, a person in uniform, a ticketseller—in most situations.

Animals. Teach children not to touch, run after, or feed any animals they don't know by name.

Child-Proofing Balcony

Balconies. Chair webbing can be woven through balcony railings whose openings are dangerously wide. Or cover railing with garden netting (sold to keep birds away).

Cars. When you're looking for a car seat, select one that's labeled "dynamically tested." This means it's gone through crash tests in the factory. Follow the manufacturer's directions to the letter when installing the seat. If the child is active, be sure he/she can't fiddle with door locks or somehow pull him/herself out of the car seat and dangle out the window. Be sure windows are rolled up, leaving about an inch open. Tell children the car won't start unless everyone is belted in.

Fences. Should have vertical slats (tougher to get a foothold and climb over) and the gate should have a tamperproof lock or catch.

Poisons. All fertilizers or pesticides should be locked away.

Swings. Make sure your swing set is at least six feet from a wall or fence so kids don't hit any solid objects when they swing. Check the mooring, especially after the winter, when the snow and frost may have done some damage. See that all the parts are working properly—seats still attached on all corners, no ropes or chains in need of replacement and all bolts on tight. Badly rusted chains should be replaced, but slightly rusted ones can be covered with PVC (plastic) piping, and a split length of garden hose can cushion the front of a swing seat.

Tools. A power mower and sharp garden tools are tempting toys, especially if kids have seen them in use. Lock them up.

Wading Pools. Bathtub appliques on the bottom help keep them skidproof.

• •

SAFE FOOD HANDLING AND STORAGE

To Avoid Food Poisoning

For me the most dangerous things in the kitchen are the cookies. But food illness is no joke. Older people, people with weakened immune systems, and kids are the most vulnerable, but a lot of so-called "flu" cases and upset stomachs are actually cases of food poisoning.

Make sure your refrigerator is at 40° F. and the freezer is at 0° F. or colder.

Canned goods should be in a cool dry place, not above the stove, under the sink, or in a garage or damp basement.

Don't thaw food at room temperature.

Don't spread bacteria from raw food to other food. Wash your hands, use a plastic cutting board, and don't put the cooked hamburgers or steak on the unwashed platter in which you

HOW DO YOU KNOW WHEN FOOD IS DONE?

Buy a meat thermometer. The bacteria isn't killed until you've cooked meat long enough for it to reach an internal temperature of 160° F. for red meat, 170° F. for poultry breasts, and 180° F. for whole birds. You can do a visual check, too. The USDA says poultry is done when the juice runs clear, fish when it flakes with a fork, and red meat is done when it's brown or gray inside. Bad news for those who like pink, rare meat (about 140° F.) and feel guilty enough about eating meat anyway—the USDA says some food poisoning organisms may survive at that temperature. Some risks a person's just gotta take.

marinated the meat or carried it out to the barbecue.

Don't leave meat at room temperature more than two hours. If you can't keep all the buffet items on ice, then just put out a little at a time. Same goes for the hot foods.

Don't partially cook food, then cook it later. Bacteria can grow, and they aren't destroyed by the final cooking.

If you have a lot of hot food to refrigerate, pour it into smaller, shallow containers for quick cooling.

IN CASE OF FOOD POISONING

If the food came from a source where others might eat it (at a restaurant, catering hall, large party; or from a sidewalk vendor; or if it's sold commercially), call the local health authorities. They'll want to know the source of the food and any information on the label.

Is It Still Okay?

People have very strange ideas about how long food lasts. I know some people who won't eat

THAWING THE THANKSGIVING TURKEY

If you thaw it in the refrigerator, allow from 1–2 days (for 12–19 pounds) to 4–5 days (for 20–24 pounds). To rush-thaw that turkey, put it in the sink or cooler in the unopened plastic bag it's packed in, and cover with cold water. Drain and add fresh cold water every quarter hour. Thawing this way takes anywhere from 4–6 hours for an 8–12 pound turkey to 11–12 hours for a 20–24 pound bird.

any leftovers, including a slice of American cheese from a package opened yesterday. And I know others who eat anything that isn't actually furry.

With some foods, the only difference is that the quality deteriorates. But with others, like meat, you're taking a big health risk. Luckily, the meat questions can be answered easily. The U.S. Department of Agriculture has a Meat and Poultry Hotline 1-800-535-3455 (in Washington, D.C., 447-3333) that can give you just about any information you need.

If you're very concerned about this topic, you can also order The Food Keeper, a large chart showing storage times for many foods, from the Food Marketing Institute, 1750 K Street N.W., Washington, D.C. 20006; (202) 452-8444. Enclose 50 cents and an oversize stamped and self-addressed envelope.

In the box below are some typical foods and how long they last, according to the manufacturers.

FROZEN FOOD

In your **freezer,** these are clues that the food is old and should be used as quickly as possible (if the food smells bad, discard it, of course, but otherwise this food is not dangerous to eat, just not top quality):

Ice. Ice crystals mean the food has been thawed and refrozen. This happens a lot with frozen vegetables—sometimes they're frozen into one solid block.

WRAPPING FOOD FOR FREEZER

Okay: Plastic wrap, heavy-duty plastic wrap, glass freezer jars with straight sides, polyethylene containers with tight lids, wax-coated freezer boxes with plastic liner, freezer-weight plastic bags.

Not okay: Bread wrappers, waxed paper, wax-coated freezer wrap, thin non-polyethylene plastic wrap, non-polyethylene plastic containers.

EXPIRATION DATES

Food	Lasts for:
★ Applesauce, once opened	2 weeks
★ Baby food, once opened	2 days
★ Catsup, once opened	2 months in plastic, 3 in glass (caps on glass bottles fit tighter)
Coffee, freeze-dried	2 months
★ Coffee, opened, ground	2 months
Coffee, unopened, in can	2 years
Flour	6–8 months, in a tightly lidded canister
★ Hams, canned	9 months
★ Meat, fresh	3–5 days, in refrigerator
★ Meats, vacuum packed	2 weeks unopened, 5–7 days opened
★ Pet food, opened can	3 days
★ Pickles, open jar	2 months
★ Poultry, fresh	1–2 days, in refrigerator
★ Spaghetti sauce, open jar	5–7 days unless you've added your own meat, in which case 2–3 days
Sugar	2 years, in a tightly lidded canister
Teabags	18 months, in a tightly lidded canister

Starred items should be refrigerated and, where applicable, tightly capped.

MOLD STORY

You can't tell if moldy food is edible by smelling it. Some moldy foods should be tossed. Others can be saved if you cut around the spot (leave an inch of clean food, and don't contaminate the knife as you cut). Then rewrap and use as soon as possible.

Can be saved: Hard cheese, salami, hard fruits, vegetables, and jams.

Toss: Dairy foods, baked goods, flour, whole grains, nuts, dried peas and beans, peanut butter, corn

COLD STORY

What freezes:

bacon, crumbled
bread crumbs
brown sugar
coconut
dried fruit
eggs, raw (freeze in ice cube trays, whole or separated; transfer cubes to plastic bags)
ham, chopped
hard cheese
herbs (except cilantro and dill)
milk (shake well after thawing)
nuts
onions, raw, chopped
peppers, raw, chopped

What doesn't (and why):

buttermilk (loses texture)
cottage cheese (separates)
custards (get watery)
egg whites, cooked (toughen)
greens (wilt)
light cream (loses texture)
mayonnaise (separates)
potatoes, cooked (soften)
yogurt (loses texture)

Freezer Burn. Those dry, grayish spots show the food has lost moisture and may not be tender.

Odd Texture. Limp vegetables, tough meats, sauces that seem odd.

Faded Color. It's too old or exposed.

PLAYING "CHICKEN"

Can you freeze "fresh" chicken that looks frozen at the market, but is thawed when you get it home? Yes, because it was never really frozen. Although it appears frozen, the processor has just kept it very well refrigerated. Though the surface tissues may have frozen, it is still safe for you to freeze.

CANNED FOOD

When you buy canned goods, push the older cans to the front and use them first.

Cans or jars with botulism-contaminated food will usually be leaky, bulging, dented, or cracked; or lids may be loose or bulging; or food may smell bad; or can may spurt liquid when you open it. Use no cans or glass jars with dents, cracks, or bulging lids. And if you think food is problematical, don't taste it—toss it out.

Low-acid foods such as meat, poultry, stew, and vegetables are safe to use for 2 to 5 years. High-acid products such as tomato-based foods, fruits, juices, vinegar-based salad dressing, and sauerkraut should be used within 18 months. Home-canned food should be used within one year.

If a can is accidentally frozen, move it to a refrigerator and thaw it immediately, then cook and use the food, or cook and refreeze it. If the food in the can thawed while not under refrigeration, or if the seams have rusted and burst, or it's been frozen and thawed more than once, toss it.

Storing food in an opened can isn't dangerous, but the food may not taste as good.

DELI FOOD

Safe storage for deli-sliced bologna and salami is 3 to 5 days; for sliced turkey, chicken, and roast beef 2 to 4 days. Vacuum-packed cold cuts and hot dogs are okay for two weeks unopened and refrigerated, one week opened. Eat foods marked with a "Sell by" date within five days of purchase and foods marked "Use by" as indicated. But if any of these foods are slimy or sticky, smell bad, or are discolored toss them. Also discard hot dogs if the liquid around them is cloudy.

However, that shiny green color on the corned beef may be another story. This might be a result of the light hitting the fat and iron in

WHAT NOT TO PUT IN A MICROWAVE

- Eggs in the shell, eggs that don't have the yolk broken
- Popcorn except in microwave bag or container
- Paraffin
- Twist ties
- Leaded glass
- Any dish that's not microwavable. To test, see p. 85.
- Brown paper bags, synthetic fibers, non-microwavable paper towels (they may have metal particles)
- Anything metal (though some can take small quantities of foil. See Arcing, p. 251.)
- A stuffed bird—should be cooked in regular oven only
- Fatty foods covered with plastic—carcinogens from certain chemicals can "migrate" out of plastic wrap and into the food. Saran and Glad Wrap contain fewer of these than some brands.
- Baby bottles—contents may get too hot and liners may explode over the nursing child

FREEZER STORAGE
(HOW LONG ITEM WILL KEEP AT 0° F.)

Meat, Poultry, and Eggs	Months It Will Keep
Bacon and sausage	1–2
Egg whites, egg substitute	1–2
Gravy, meat or poultry	2–3
Ham, hot dogs, lunchmeat	1–2
Meat, roasts uncooked	9
Meat, chops or steaks	4–12
Meat, ground	3–4
Meat, cooked	2–3
Poultry, whole raw	12
Poultry, parts raw	9
Poultry, ground, raw	3–4
Poultry, cooked	5–6
Soups and stews	2–3

Dairy Products	
Milk	1
Cheese, hard	4
Butter	9

Side Dishes	
Cranberries, fresh	12
Pasta, cooked	1–2
Rice, cooked	1–2
Stuffing or dressing	1–2
Vegetables	8

Desserts and Breads	
Cake	3
Cookies	8
Bread and rolls, baked	3
Bread dough, unbaked	1
Ice cream or sherbet	2
Pies, baked	2
Pies, fruit unbaked	8

SOURCE: USDA

293

the meat, or a result of the heat and processing. If it's spoiled, the meat would also be slimy and sticky and have an off odor.

Prestuffed whole poultry is not a good idea, but smaller stuffed products (like pork chops or chicken breast) are okay. Use on date of purchase.

• •

MEDICINE CABINET CHECKLIST

I'm assuming you have a favorite pain reliever and upset stomach-medicine, cold and cough or allergy remedies on hand. You should also have the items listed in the box below.

WHEN DRUGS GET OLD

Get rid of drugs that have changed color, smell like vinegar, crumble easily, or are past their expiration date. Although some medicines past expiration just lose their strength, others may cause side effects or serious problems.

When liquid evaporates from codeine cough syrup, for example, it becomes more potent and you may become dizzy. Even more seriously, outdated tetracycline can cause kidney damage.

WHAT'S IN THE CABINET

Item	Use
Adhesive bandages	For minor cuts; some are made just for joints or knuckles
Adhesive tape	To secure gauze; comes in a roll
Adhesive medical tape	Holds the dressing and bandage
Anti-itch lotion or spray	Calamine or hydrocortisone; for poison ivy, bites
Antibiotic ointment	For localized infection
Antidiarrheal medicine	Ask the pharmacist for a recommendation
Antihistamine	Reduce cold, allergy symptoms
Aspirin or substitute	To reduce fever, inflammation, pain
Boric acid/eye cup	On doctor's advice, for eye irritation
Burn ointment	For minor burns
Burrows solution	For soaking sprains
Epsom salts	Add to bath to relieve foot or body aches due to tired muscles
Eye drops	For eye irritation
Gauze bandage	To keep dressing in place, comes by the yard
Gauze dressing	Square, sterile pads to cover larger cuts
Hydrogen peroxide	Like alcohol, cleans wounds that aren't deep
Ipecac	To induce vomiting of poison (call doctor first!)
Medicine dosage cup	Or spoon; measures out dosages for kids
Nasal spray	To clear nasal passage
Reusable ice pack	"When in doubt, apply cold"—to most injuries
Rubbing alcohol	Sterilizes thermometers, tweezers, cleans wounds
Sterile cotton balls	Applies alcohol or calamine
Thermometer	Digital or old-fashioned glass model
Triangular bandage	Fold as sling or tourniquet or head bandage

PART 8

STORING AND SAVING

A (SAFE) PLACE FOR EVERYTHING

When Freud asked what women really wanted, I could have told him: More storage.

I suppose men need more storage, too. Where men and women differ is in what they think is worth storing. Women store unfinished crafts projects, old shoes to wear in the rain, and clothing in sizes they've outgrown. Men store magazines, extension cords, and broken parts that may come in handy for repair someday. Experts say couples fight mostly about money, sex, and relatives, but I believe that storage issues are right up there.

The problem gets worse once you start a family. Not only does each child save things, but having children adds a purpose to your saving. You become even more likely to hang on to loose photographs of unidentified relatives and completely useless items that may turn into valuable collectibles just for the children's sake.

Choosing what to store, and finding room for it, are only two major storage concerns. The third is making sure that whatever you store is safe against dust, dampness, and insects—no matter how unlikely you will ever use it again.

The least you have to know about storing and saving:

- Using all available space
- Safekeeping important papers
- Storing Christmas decorations
- Protecting your clothes
- Pest control

• •

MAKING EVERY CORNER COUNT

One way to make your storage space larger and more convenient may be simply to rearrange what you already have.

Are your storage boxes too big for what's inside?

Are storage units the wrong shape? (Square storage units, when available, use space more efficiently than round ones.)

If you have a bulky item—such as a TV—that doesn't quite fit into a cabinet, does it make any sense to cut out the back of the cabinet so that the item is flush with the front?

Is there a lot of wasted air space? Do you have two shelves in a place where you could fit three?

Can wall space below a window be used for low bookcases or a window seat?

ORDER, ORDER EVERYWHERE

Your storage will look better—and work better for you—if you just use some common sense.

Things should be where they are most convenient instead of where they are most conventional. If the only time you have to put on makeup is while the kids are having breakfast, shouldn't makeup and mirror be in your kitchen cabinet? Wouldn't it make more sense to keep chandelier bulb replacements in a drawer in the dining room, where they're needed, than in a drawer in the workshop? Wouldn't it be better to store flatware, china, and glasses in cupboards and drawers near the table to make place setting faster and have extras handy during a meal?

Things you use often should be easy to reach. If there's a pot you cook with regularly, don't put it in the back of the cupboard so you have to move a million other pots to get at it. This seems obvious, but I find even myself breaking this rule. Don't store pans in the oven or cleaning products in your cleaning bucket so that everything has to be rearranged if you need to turn the oven on or use the bucket for mop water. Find another place for those pots—hang them from the ceiling—and put up a shelf for the cleaning supplies. Reserve inaccessible places for things you probably don't need but can't bear to discard, such as out-of-date tax returns and old love letters.

Things that are needed at the same time should be in the same place. Keep sewing equipment for minor repairs near the washing machine, stationery supplies near the mailing labels and stamps.

Give everything a place of its own whenever possible. If each attachment for the vacuum belongs in a particular place, and if your tools aren't jumbled together with picture hooks and loose screws and washers, they'll be easier to find and use, and they'll probably stay that way. Put pegs near the back door, since everyone is more likely to hang coats on pegs than on hangers. If there are children, put up a second set of pegs at their height. Hang a shoe bag or attach snap clothespins to a board to hold mittens and gloves.

Label everything. You shouldn't have to open a carton to know what's inside. If you have an opaque hanging bag for clothes, identify the contents somewhere on the outside. Tape inventory lists to the fronts of the cartons or put them in a convenient folder.

Keep things covered (so they won't get dirty) and in containers that give the impression of order. Office supply stores and moving companies sell good-size filing cartons with tops for as little as a dollar. If you don't want to pay for the cartons, gather what you can from the grocery or liquor store and make them look uniform by covering the fronts with contact paper. (Don't bother to cover the sides and tops unless they'll be visible.)

Maximizing Bedroom Storage

Dressers need polishing, dresser tops collect junk, and clothes deep in dresser drawers are less accessible than clothes stacked on shelves. Consider putting up a wall of 12"-deep shelves behind louver doors instead of buying a dresser. Lower shelves can hold shoe boxes; middle ones, underwear, socks and stockings, sweaters, and T-shirts (in vinyl-covered wire bins that need no cleaning); high ones, out-of-season items. Instead of folding nightgowns and pajamas, hang them in the closet. They'll wrinkle less.

Drawers built into bed platforms can hold extra bedding, an extra mattress for a guest, or even a model railroad setup.

Decorative pillows can be used as bolsters against the wall. The cases can hold extra blankets or ordinary pillows, both to be used to make a guest's bed.

Used gym lockers can be bought, repainted, then put in a kid's room to store mitts, bats, helmets, skateboards, and toys.

Night tables can hold out-of-season clothing or extra linens. Buy a large garbage pail, have a round plywood top made, and cover the plywood with a circular cloth. Order a round glass top to put over the cloth to keep it looking fresh.

Drawers from a discarded dresser can be used for under-bed storage. Fasten casters to the bottom and the drawer will be easy to roll in and out.

Blankets can be stowed between the mattress and box spring.

INCREASING YOUR CLOSET SPACE

Can your closet accommodate one or two rods running from front to rear instead of one pole hung horizontally? You may wind up with more hanging room. You will have to change the top shelf as well. If you're using a two-pole arrangement, with a corridor between, make the top shelf into a U-shape that's accessible all the way around.

A conventional closet can be made into a closet and a half if you reserve part of it for long clothing, such as dresses and coats, and convert the rest into two-tiered storage, with blouses or shirts on top, skirts or pants on the bottom. Making the switch is easy and inexpensive.

The first step is to raise brackets that hold the main rod to a height of six feet from the ground. Then get a piece of 1×4 lumber about 40" long, and drill a $1^1/_2$" hole in each end. Slide the old rod through the top hole, and replace the rod in its bracket.

Now slide the 1×4 to the middle of the top rod. Slip a $1/_4$" diameter rod through the bottom

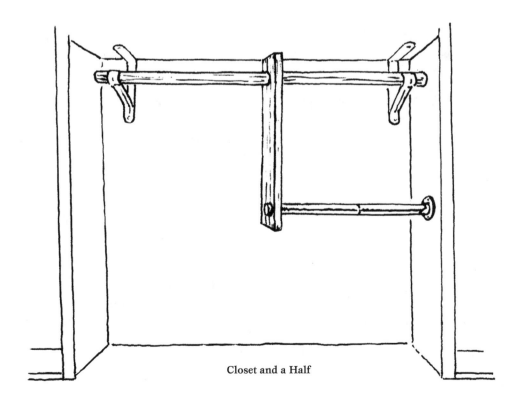

Closet and a Half

hole of the 1×4 and push it until it touches one wall. Mark that spot to install a bracket. Once it's in place, slip the second rod through the bottom of the 1×4 and rest it into the bracket.

If you want to keep things really neat, file notches into the wooden rod about 1" apart and hangers won't slide together.

THE SIZE OF YOUR HANGUPS

Most closets are designed to allow 39" hanging room for blouses, skirts, and pants, but when you make a two-tier closet, you won't have quite that much room. You may raise the top rod higher than six feet if you have room; or change the position of the holes in the 1×4 to allow extra hanging space on the top or bottom tier.

These figures give you the guidelines for hanging space, but my best advice is to measure what's in your wardrobe to see how much hanging room you need. (Women should remember that hemlines that go up may also go down. Don't assume you'll be wearing 21-inch miniskirts forever. Or even next year.)

Garment	Inches of hanging room needed
Long dresses	69
Robes, coats	50–52
Skirts	31–34
Blouses, shirts	28–32
Garment bags	57
Dress bags	48
Suit bags	41
Jackets	38
Cuff hung pants	41–44
Double hung pants	20

Closet poles should be hung 12"–14" from the wall. You could manage with 10", but it would be tight.

Space between shelves should be 7" for shoes, 8"–10" for hats.

REPLACING THE CLOSET ROD

When the rod in your closet is bending under all the weight, get rid of some clothes or replace the wooden rod. Order a length of 1/2" galvanized pipe and a length of 3/4" thin-wall PVC (plastic, polyvinyl chloride) piping, both the same length as your rod. Slip one inside the other. If the manufacturer's name on the PVC pipe bothers you, remove it with lacquer thinner.

CLOTHES CLOSET SPACE-STRETCHERS

Belts. Screw cup hooks onto a wooden clothes hanger. Or pull off the spine of a three-ring binder, nail it up on its side, and use it to hold belts.

Boots. Attach an elastic pony tail loop through a small hole punched into the top of a rubber boot and the boot can be hung instead of tossed on the ground.

Costume Jewelry. Brooches can be stuck into a padded hanger.

Delicates. Extra shoulder pads can be fastened to the edges of your hangers to make padded holders for knits and other delicate clothing.

Kids' Clothing. Sew a big loop at the neck

WHAT'S UP THERE?

Put a square mirror tile on the closet ceiling to check the contents of the top shelf without a ladder.

KEEPING THE CLOSET DRY

You can buy commercial dehumidifiers for a closet that tends to be damp, or just put charcoal briquettes in an empty coffee can and punch holes in the lid. One can will do for a 3×5 closet.

of all jackets. This ups the odds that the jacket may be hung up, instead of landing on the floor, banister, or living room couch.

Spaghetti Straps. If you put a strip of Velcro at the end of the hanger, the grip will keep thin straps from sliding off it.

Expanding Bathroom Storage

Add a cabinet under the sink, one that rests on the lid of the toilet tank and/or a set of those new tall, ultra-slim bookcases (as little as 12" square) to hold towels and other items.

Be careful about what you store in shelves over the toilet. Small plastic items that fall into the toilet are a real problem to retrieve.

An extra wall-mounted medicine cabinet is an inexpensive and very helpful way to add space.

Inside the medicine cabinet, glue small magnets to the door to hold files and cuticle scissors.

Hang caddies over the shower. Over the curtain rod, slip new double hangers—one hook faces the shower wall, the other hook faces out. They can hold both bath sheets and/or robes conveniently and compactly. Install wall dispensers of shampoo and hair conditioner inside the shower.

Shoe bags on the back of the door or three-tier kitchen baskets suspended from the shower rod can hold soaps, disposable razors, shampoo, cottonballs, etc.

Take an undershelf basket—the kind made of vinyl sprayed on wire—and bend hooks in the opposite direction so it'll hang over the side of the tub. Use it to hold shampoo, tub toys, whatever.

Install a second shower curtain rod level with the first, over the tub and far enough back to clear a moving shower curtain. It's great to drip dry clothes, to hang laundry, or to hold the rubber bath mat while it drips dry.

The worst thing in the world—okay, *one* of the worst things—is to find yourself in a bath-

---

WHERE TO PUT THE TOWELS

Roll them: Keep them in a basket or rattan wine rack.

Rod them: Increase hanging space by installing a long closet rod the length of the tub wall.

Rack them: Use hotel-type racks that stow towels horizontally.

Hook them: Install pegs instead of bars (which your family probably never uses anyway) and you'll have room for many extra towels. Put name tags above the pegs to help family and guests know which towel is whose.

Bar them: Install a rod behind each bedroom door and have family members hang big towels in their bedrooms to dry. This eliminates clutter, reduces bathroom moisture, and humidifies the bedroom.

Sack them: Do away with them entirely! Give everyone in the family a terry robe which they can hang on hooks in their own rooms. You won't be washing a lot of bath towels, just the terry robe once a week.

---

room where there's no toilet paper. Keep a roll handy under one of the plastic covers made to fit a tall, square tissue box. Or stow two rolls on their sides in one of the rectangular tissue holders. Or put up a long dowel, meant to hold paper towels, instead of a conventional toilet tissue dowel: It'll hold two rolls.

PAPER TRAIL

My favorite trick for making sure we don't run out of paper goods like toilet tissue and paper towels: Buy one roll in a color I don't ordinarily use and put it at the back of the storage cabinet. If that roll shows up in the bathroom or kitchen—I know it's time to stock up!

Basement or Attic Spacemakers

Metal utility towel racks can be used as brackets to keep long lengths of poles, pipes, rods, and lumber. Attach them vertically to the wall in the basement or garage and rest poles and pipes between them.

Storage shelves can be easily installed with lengths of chain and eight S-hooks, four fastened to shelf corners and four fastened to the ceiling or beam above. They're easy to remove, relocate, adjust. (See also "Putting up Shelves" p. 246.) Make a clothes rod in the attic with a length of pipe. Use pipe clamps to attach it to the rafters.

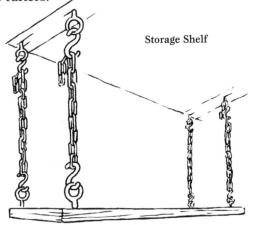

Storage Shelf

The doorway to your basement can make a temporary coat "closet" when you entertain. Install brackets and buy a clothes pole to fit (or buy a chinning bar with brackets). Put the pole up when it's needed and dismantle it when it's not.

Keeping Work Supplies Organized

Silhouetting kitchen or workshop tools on a peg board helps keep them neat and lets you know at a glance where something belongs and what is missing.

Anything that's off the ground is neater than anything that's on the ground. If you don't have special hooks or clamps that hold mops, brooms, etc., put a cup hook in the tip of each and fasten another hook to the wall to hang them on.

Save small jars and their lids. Screw lids to the underside of a shelf and use the jars to hold nails, picture hangers, screws, etc.; screw the jars onto their lids.

To keep the plastic containers and the lids organized in the kitchen, stack lids in one place, containers in another. Very organized people tell me they number-code tops and bottoms so they can put them together in a hurry. I just put lids in a small plastic basket and pull the whole thing out to find just what I need.

TOOL SHEDS AND TOOL CHESTS

You can buy plans for easy-to-build outside storage buildings or outside tool chests. My friend Dick has even built one on his Manhattan terrace to keep extra flower pots and barbecue tools out of the way.

Wherever you keep tools, always keep things separate from one another: tools separate from extension cords, screws separate from picture hangers. If everything is in a jumble, you won't want to use it.

Other Storage Possibilities

UNDER AND BEHIND SEATS

If you have a platform-type couch built to order, you can have storage behind the back cushions, in bins below the seat cushions, or in drawers below. (This type of couch can be constructed relatively inexpensively, with cushions made to order. You can refurbish it when it's worn just by recovering or replacing the cushions, so it's a good investment.) Store seasonal items, old files, other things you won't need regularly.

Build a coffee table that's a hinged-top bin or that contains drawers.

ON BACKS OF DOORS

Pegs, hooks, rods, and shallow shelves can be hung on backs of doors. So can fold-away ironing boards.

IN SUITCASES OR DUFFEL BAGS

Store quilts, blankets, Christmas presents in November, out-of-season sports equipment, and smaller bags.

THROUGHOUT THE KITCHEN

Install a drop-leaf table.

If you have a small space between refrigerator and wall, it may be wide enough to hold a narrow cart on casters.

Inside doors of the kitchen cabinets can all be put to use. Attach a lid rack holder, a caddy for aluminum foil and plastic wrap, pegs to hold dish towels, spice racks, garbage bag holders, corkboards to hold PTA notices, cards from repairmen, and grocery lists.

Canisters that are square rather than round don't waste space.

Flatware can be hung in slings beneath a cupboard. Stem glassware can be hung upside down so that the bottoms slip into tracks (as in many bars).

A square flat tray placed over an open drawer gives you extra counter space in a pinch.

Small cabinets fastened together can make a base for a kitchen table.

If there is a lot of air space over top cabinet shelves, build in an extra shelf or skip the installation problem and just buy the vinyl-coated wire shelves with legs in the housewares section of a department store. You get a second level of storage for groceries or dishes.

If you don't have enough wall space to hang all your utensils, put them in a large pitcher

GET A HANDLE ON IT

Odd flatware pieces collected at yard sales make interesting drawer and cabinet pulls. Lacquer or polyurethane them so they don't require polishing.

rather than jumbled in the drawer. But if the pitcher isn't heavy, it will tip over every time you remove an item.

My friend Karen bought a bunch of letters and numbers from old printing presses—they're in antique shops everywhere—and put them at random on the cupboards. When anyone asks where to find a plate or a soda glass she points them toward cupboard A or cabinet 7.

Use the entire front of the refrigerator as a message center (with a waterproof marking pen) or use a piece of black contact paper as a blackboard. You can even write the snack menu on the door. If you let the family know what's okay to eat, they'll spend less time rooting around in the fridge with the door open, won't waste electricity, and may not eat the leftovers—tonight's dinner—by mistake.

INSIDE CLOTHES HAMPERS

Store blankets and pillows.

ALONG A HALLWAY

Install narrow bookshelves. Paperbacks need hardly any room.

IN THE DINING ROOM

Use brackets to fasten extra leaves under the table itself. (Or hang them on a basement or utility room wall to use as shelves. If you don't like the look of the pegs sticking out, drill holes to accommodate them in a small strip of molding, then slip it over the pegs when the leaf is being stored.)

Or stow a folding table pad under the table. Find hooks or angle irons and install them so pads can rest on them.

Build a narrow ledge all the way around the room and use it to store dishes as they did in old taverns. (A groove in the ledge, or molding around the edge of it, will hold the dishes in place). Serving carts on casters can store serving dishes, napkins, fancy flatware, etc. But if you live in a place that is sooty or dirty, or you don't circulate all your dishes and flatware often (as you would with a large family) open storage of these items is not for you.

BEHIND A CURTAIN ROD

Attach one to a wall as a lid holder (knobs will keep lids from slipping through). Or attach two on a closet door as a shoeholder. For a decorative touch, slipcover the rod (by making a casing three times its length, which gives it the correct amount of fullness) and use S-hooks to hang flower baskets from it.

ON A WINDOWSILL

If you install a curtain rod as a guard rail about an inch above a narrow windowsill, you can use it to hold plants. Though the bottom of the plants will hang slightly over the edge, the rod will hold them in place. Paint it to blend with the sill.

AT CEILING LEVEL

You can build a strip of bookshelves high up on the wall, just below the ceiling.

Slightly below the ceiling of a garage, you can make a loft platform.

UNDER THE STAIRS

Store cleaning equipment, and out-of-season items. If there's a plumbing line, install a small shower or sink. Or make a small telephone booth for privacy if several teenagers in the house each want their own phone.

Install drawer runners under open stairs and slide in drawers. They can hold linens, clothes, and more.

ON LANDINGS

Use the space for shelving to hold books, sports equipment (even a bicycle hung on its side), and outer clothing. If it's deep enough, the landing may hold a wardrobe containing out-of-season clothes or be converted into a mini home-office area.

HANGING DOWN

A three-tier basket, which I recommended for the bath, can also be used at baby's changing table to hold small toys, pacifiers, etc., and in the kitchen to hold small tools.

• •

HOLIDAY UNDECORATING

Although there is no end of suggestions for decorating your house for the holidays, I think where most people need help is in the less glamorous part of the job—taking everything down and packing it away so it will remain clean and unbroken.

Leftovers

Don't toss gift wrap in the fireplace. It can ignite and cause a flash fire. Crumple it around ornaments.

When artificial trees no longer look good, save the branches. They can be attached to a bendable wire like a coat hanger with floral wire or bag ties to shape wreathes.

Lights

To store lights, wind them into loops and place them in coffee cans. Or wind light string around a small cardboard tube, then slip a larger one (a cylindrical oatmeal box, for example) over it for protection. Seal ends with masking tape.

Or see if your friendly local electrician will give you some of the 6-inch spools from wholesale electrical wire. Wind the light strings around those.

Miscellaneous

When putting out your decorations at Christmas (and other special times), put the everyday items that you are temporarily replacing in the box in which the decorations are stored. Instead of being stuffed in cabinets and drawers, they'll be neatly out of the way until it's time to put them back in place.

Along with holiday towels, linens, fabric decorations, and wreaths, pack away the records, tapes, and aprons.

Add a few small bags filled with cinnamon sticks and whole cloves to storage boxes. Make pinholes in the bags and tightly seal the boxes. Everything will be pleasantly scented when you open it next year.

Wrap the storage boxes in gift wrap so they will be easy to spot on the shelf.

Make (and mark) one box to be opened in November that contains items you will need early in the holiday season: Christmas cards, lists of supplies purchased at post-holiday sales and supplies still to be bought, Advent calendars, etc. The box may also include the video of last Christmas, a holiday photo album including the family card, and diary notes about how the holiday was spent—things to look through to get into the holiday mood. The remaining boxes may be opened closer to decorating and tree-trimming time.

Save boxes from appliances, toys, etc., to store some ornaments and other holidays supplies, so if something goes wrong, you have the original carton to mail the item for servicing to the manufacturer. The warranties usually last a year.

ORNAMENTS

Holiday balls that are unraveling can be sprayed with hair spray and ends pressed into place.

Glass ornaments that are peeling can be stripped with ammonia and water. When the old paint is gone, spray them with glossy enamel and reuse them.

For storage, slip ornaments into odd socks (inside the toe; roll top over it) or into small, zip-top plastic bags (blow in air with a straw, remove straw, seal bag; the air cushion gives it lots of protection). Or pack them in fruit boxes, liquor boxes, toilet paper cylinders, and lightbulb cartons.

If you put ornaments into a box with shredded newspaper (covering them well on both top and sides), you don't have to wrap them separately. But print may rub off on certain ornaments. Shredded computer paper or used gift wrap would work just as well.

RIBBONS

Store lengths of ribbon on an empty rolls of plastic wrapping and place them back in the dispenser boxes, or hang them on a heavy-duty curtain rod installed in a closet, using a small piece of tape to keep the loose ends from rewinding.

Or use a cardboard tube left over from the wrapping paper. Slit the tube lengthwise, squeeze the sides together, and slip ribbons on. The tube will expand when you release it and hold ribbons firmly; a 36" tube will hold up to 32 one-inch ribbons. Stand it on end or hang it for easy accessibility.

TREE

An artificial tree can be stored fully decorated. Cover with a sheet or plastic bag.

WREATHS AND BOWS

To avoid crushing the wreath, tie it to a hanger (with floral tie or a long bag tie). Cut a hole in the bottom of a drawstring garbage bag and pull the hanger through, then slip the bag over the wreath, pulling the string closed at the bottom. Hang the wreath on a nail in the attic or garage.

Stuff tissue or crumpled holiday wrap inside bows before you pack them away to preserve their shape. A hair dryer or curling iron can get them back into shape.

WRAPPING PAPER

Put gift wrap in a garment bag, golf club box, or florist's box. Or roll paper tightly and slip it inside the cardboard tube, to keep it from becoming dog-eared. Put a swatch on the outside to identify it.

Or slip a leg cut from old panty hose over each roll to protect it.

● ●

PROTECTING YOUR VALUABLES
Documents

When my friend's mother became widowed, my friend made up a file folder system to help her get organized. She labeled one file for medical expenses, one for household expenses, one for insurance, and so forth. Several months later my friend checked to see how the system was working. All the folders were empty, except for the one marked "Miscellaneous." At least all the papers were in one place.

Set up a file drawer, or buy cardboard files from an office supply shop, to keep all your papers in order. In a file labeled "Important Papers," put photocopies of the documents you may need to refer to (stock certificates, for the number of shares; passports; etc.) and a list of where all originals can be found (see box).

Leave a set of instructions in the "Important Papers" file that tells your executor what to do in case you become ill or die. This should include, for example, names of your lawyer, insurance agent, and accountant, a document explaining what life-supporting medical treatment you do or do not want if you are seriously ill (the original of which your lawyer should hold), information about your house mortgage, pension plans, safe deposit box, and so forth.

My friend was widowed several years ago and was grateful to have such a list. Along with the other important information, her husband had included an item labeled "Smithfield Ham," along with a name and phone number. "If I am very ill," the document said, "I would like to have this dish one final time. This person has the recipe."

WHERE TO KEEP IMPORTANT DOCUMENTS

Bank safe deposit box: Stocks and bonds, marriage license, birth and other certificates, legal documents (mortgage, deed, and copy of will; lawyer should have the original will), military papers, pension plan, passport, inventory of household goods, and record of household costs (as described under Selling, in the section Changing, p. 326.)

Since the safe deposit box is sealed in the event of death, you may want to keep copies of some or all papers in a home file.

Fireproof strongbox: Insurance policies, bankbook.

File drawer: Bank statements, tax returns, photocopy of all IDs (credit cards, driver's license, social security card), warranties, list of instructions to be followed upon your death, record of household costs.

Make a second file labeled "Credit Cards." Photocopy every card in your wallet—a lifesaver if your wallet is lost. A copy is the surest way to be certain you have the correct number when you call the toll-free number to report the loss.

Photos

You may have heard that some photo albums may damage your photographs. The cardboard backing in a magnetic album can stain the white portion of the prints, and the adhesive may make the print bond to the page. The black backing paper in older albums and the plastic covers in newer ones give off gases that attack the photos, as will rubber cement and animal glues.

Safe plastics for use in an album are nonpolyvinyl chlorides such as polyester (Mylar™), polyethylene, polypropylene, triacetate, and Tyvek™. You can also buy special archival albums from some photo dealers.

Another alternative is to store the pictures loose in 3 × 5 or 4 × 6 card files, which keeps them neat with very little work. Use the cardboard dividers to indicate the dates. Use metal files. Wood, particle board, pressboard, and cardboard give off fumes that attack the photos.

Negatives and slides should be stored in steel, stainless steel, or aluminum cases or archival albums with non-polyvinyl plastic covers or acid-free sheets of treated paper (not brown paper and not glassine).

To preserve a photo in a frame, use an acid-free paper mat so that the covering glass doesn't touch it directly. Put it in a non-wood frame, and leave the backing unsealed to give the photo some ventilation.

Clothes

Never store clothes without having them cleaned. Over time, some stains become more difficult to remove.

Take special care when laundering clothes that will be stored. Rinse well to remove any traces of detergent, which may cause chemical changes. Wash everything in soft water to avoid eventual yellowing and rust spots. Don't starch stored items, since starch is also corrosive.

Clothes should be covered to keep out water, dust, mold, bacteria, and smoke. You can buy storage bags made of "barrier materials" like Gore-Tex™ (they let air in and won't cause chemical changes because they are acid-free), use muslin bags, or throw a sheet over the hanger. Just make sure the clothes are covered completely.

Never store fine fabrics, leather, or suede in plastic. Plastic cuts off air, so leather and suede will dry out and fabrics will break down and disintegrate. (You'll get some of those mysterious yellow stains.) As the threads rot, buttons,

LIFE EXPECTANCY OF CLOTHING AND DRAPES

How long should a dress last? What's the value if the cleaner damages it when it's two years old? Clothes depreciate just as cars do, and the following Fair Claims guide should give you an idea of what to expect if a problem occurs—or whether you got your money's worth out of that expensive suit.

Garment	Life Expectancy in Years
COATS	
Cloth or Pile	3
Leather	4
SHIRTS	
Cotton and Blends	3
Other Fibers	2
SWEATERS	4
RAINWEAR	2
DRESSES	
Daytime	2
Fancy or Evening	3
SUITS, JACKETS, SLACKS	
Wool and Blends	3
Other Fibers	2
Lightweight	2

SOURCE: NEIGHBORHOOD DRY CLEANING ASSOCIATION

beads, and sequins fall off and may also discolor and disintegrate. (Clothing with beads, sequins, or rhinestones should be stored inside out so they won't catch or snag.)

To avoid stretching or ripping, don't stress clothing. For example, don't leave knits on hangers for long periods of time.

Wedding gowns can be "heirloomed" for you, or you can store them on a wooden hanger padded with unbleached, clean cotton sheeting. So that shoulders aren't stressed from the weight of the dress, sew a loop of cotton tape at the waist and hang it over the shoulders. Stuff sleeves with acid-free tissue paper (a museum or good dry cleaner can recommend a source), and cover with a bag made of an old sheet.

Christening gowns should be covered and stuffed with acid-free tissue, then stored flat in a box lined with acid-free tissue. Make as few folds as possible.

For storing cottons or linens, some experts recommend slightly alkaline paper; and for wools and silks and any other fabrics that are slightly acidic, tissue with a neutral pH.

Metallic fabrics should be stored flat or rolled because they may stretch on hangers.

The oils from sachets can eat away at fabrics. Use them only in drawers with clothing that is rotated.

To keep fabrics pest-free, see p. 308.

Linens

If you've got room, hang linens (on a skirt hanger, a padded hanger, or a hanger with the cardboard roll that you get from the cleaner). Or roll them over the cardboard insert from gift wrap and tie ribbons around them to hold them in place when you put them on the shelf. Ironed, rolled holiday tablecloths and napkins that are used only once a year can be wrapped with tissue or put in a golfclub box.

If you fold linens to leave them on the shelf, refold them from time to time, since they tend to disintegrate or yellow along crease or fold lines. To wrap them, use acid-free paper.

Furs

Cold storage prevents furs from drying out and also avoids gradual discoloration and fading, but the most important reason to store furs is to protect them from moths. If you have forgotten to send the fur coat away and it's already moth season (call your County Extension Office to find out for sure), put your coat in the freezer for two or three days to kill moth larvae. Then put a sheet over the coat and hang it in a cool, dry place or send it to storage.

• •

PEST CONTROL
Making Pests Unwelcome

The two best means of pest control are exclusion and sanitation. First try to keep them out, but if they get in, make it hard for them to settle down.

They crawl through any opening they can find. Never underestimate the ability of pests to get into your house. If you can stand a nickel on edge in the space under any outside door, it's a possible entry point for mice. Smaller insects get into tighter spots. Seal holes or cracks in wall with silicone caulking, screening, or weather-stripping. Even toothpaste or baking soda pressed into tiny holes in a kitchen can do the job.

Or drill holes into spaces that need filling and fill them with a do-it-yourself foam insulating kit. It comes with double tanks, one filled with liquid and the other with oxygen under pressure. When activated and mixed, they bubble into a foam that turns solid as it dries.

Pests also ride into the house on pets, a situation which is not always within your control, and in packages from the grocery store, which is. (To prevent them and deal with them, see Kitchen Invaders, p. 309.)

Insects may also travel in the pages of used books. If you suspect that any books are contaminated, put them in a sealed bag in the freezer for several days before you put them in your library.

Don't provide food and shelter for pests looking to settle down either outside the house or in. Pick up all fruit that drops from trees. Keep your garbage to a minimum. (You may want to freeze chicken bones or other particularly pungent garbage, then discard it on the morning of a pickup.) Be careful about kitchen sanitation. Put food into the refrigerator or into sealed containers and keep storage and counter areas clean. Scrape out cracks where food is trapped. Wipe up spills. Clean out garbage pans. Throw out the vase water when the roses have wilted. (Insects can breed in stagnant water.) Clean under the stove and refrigerator and between the cushions on the couch where the family snacks (and drops crumbs) in front of the TV. Dust and vacuum often and thoroughly—in corners, under things, behind things—to keep pests from nesting.

Avoid using contact paper if you have insect problems in the kitchen. It makes a nice, cozy, sealed home for insects. To remove paper that is in place, heat a corner with a blow dryer and pry up an edge. You should be able to remove the rest easily. Adhesive remover or salad oil will take off the residue. Clean thoroughly and reline the shelves with strips of vinyl flooring. It's reusable, easy to cut to size, and easy to take out for cleaning.

AN INEXPENSIVE, ALL-PURPOSE CHEMICAL PEST DETERRENT

If you are having a problem with an unwelcome animal visitor, mothballs are an inexpensive, widely available deterrent. Mice, raccoons, visiting dogs and cats, and many insects are put off by the smell. However, they are potentially very dangerous to both children and pets, so they should be avoided completely or used with extreme caution in households with either. Don't just scatter them around loose. Put them in a closed container with holes punched in the lid to let out the aroma. Place them behind stoves, refrigerators, and beds and around the foundation of the house and near the doors.

THE MOST EFFECTIVE ROACH KILLER

Cockroaches are probably the most common household annoyance. Other than sanitation and traps, the most effective, least expensive, most easily applied pesticide for cockroaches is boric acid dust at a 99 percent concentration—get one registered for pesticidal use—injected with a "dust bulb" into cracks and crevices.

CAUTION: Do not use this concentration in any area accessible to children or pets.

To kill a crawling roach, use bug spray. If you're allergic to that, try a shot of rubbing alcohol from a spray bottle.

Even ordinary boric acid from the pharmacy, applied without special applicators, can work wonders. If you are moving into a new home or apartment where there may be roaches (and they are common in many older buildings in big cities) empty the cupboards, use roach spray or traps, and leave the place undisturbed for a week. Then clean the cupboards thoroughly (making sure not to leave any water in the corners, or mold may start to grow). Leave a trail of boric acid in all the corners and possible points of entry. My friend did this in an old New York apartment where many neighbors complain of problems, yet thirteen years after moving in she claims that she has never seen a single roach.

Boric acid works well as a barrier for ants, as well.

Keeping Clothes Pest-Free

MOTH-PROOFING

Don't carpet closets. The darkness makes an ideal breeding spot (you know how romantic dark places can be), and once the carpet starts to collect dirt, you've created an ideal environment for moths and carpet beetles, which eat hair, lint, dust, and also your clothing. Even an uncarpeted closet should be thoroughly vacuumed before you use it for storage to remove insects and anything else they can feed on.

Since soiled material is much more likely to attract bugs, store only clothes that have been washed or dry-cleaned—or aired in the sun and then brushed—and keep them in a tightly sealed area or container.

Cedar closets usually aren't tight enough or kept closed long enough to retain the cedar oil, which many people consider a very effective moth repellent and others do not. It certainly can't hurt. Still, while cedar may deter moths, it won't kill larvae, so if clothing is dirty and has been infested, the moths will still be a problem. (Incidentally, if the cedar scent is fading, rub the walls with fine sandpaper.)

Either DDVP (comes in strips) or PDB (mothballs and flakes) will kill moths. Both are more effective than a third common moth deterrent, naphthalene, because they also kill crickets, carpet beetles, water bugs, silverfish, cockroaches, etc. They must be used in a sealed area. They should be hung high in the closet or in the storage bag (in a perforated container, if necessary), since the vapors travel downward, and must be used in a sealed area. *Both are very toxic.*

Some people prefer camphor, which is also poisonous, has the same noxious odor, and is used like the other products but is reported not to build up in body tissues as they do.

Although many people believe that certain herbal treatments keep clothes mothproofed, I have read numerous reports that indicate this is just not true. I wish it were.

Keep mothballs and flakes away from plastic dry-cleaning garment bags, coat buttons, and metallic fabrics. The chemicals can make plastic become sticky and damage your clothes.

Moth repellents may cause leather to fade and are unnecessary for leather and imitation fur, both of which are mothproof.

IF YOUR CLOTHES HAVE BEEN ATTACKED

If you spot holes with jagged edges or white larvae, you've got moths; if you see round holes, you've got carpet beetles. Examine everything in the closet. Either throw away or dry-clean anything that looks suspicious. Use a damp cloth to wipe off all the accessories that were in the area, then discard it.

One check may not be enough. Larvae may remain alive for a while.

REMOVING THE ODOR OF MOTH-PROOFERS

Once you remove the items from storage, the odor of moth and carpet beetle repellents tends to linger, though less with camphor cakes than with the other products.

To remove the smell from clothing, put three or four fabric softener sheets in a garbage bag or suitcase along with the clothes, then close it tightly. In three days to a week, most of the odor will be gone. After clothes are aired for a couple of days longer, all the odor should disappear.

If you want to wear a garment right away, put it in the dryer with a couple of sheets of fabric softener and turn the machine to "Air Dry" or "Cold" for 15 to 20 minutes. If odor lingers, repeat.

Home Remedies for Pest Control

Aside from the remedies I have just mentioned, there are many commercial brand-name insecticides, some for one kind of insect or animal pest, some for a whole variety. Most of these are as toxic as they are effective.

I decided to include here the best of home remedies, virtually all of which won't harm pets, children, or the environment. Try them first. If your problem persists, you can always ask your local hardware store or garden supply center to recommend a stronger commercial product.

KITCHEN INVADERS

The crawlers in your cabinet include the Indian meal moth, a variety of worms, and beetles, including weevils. They infect some foods right

---

GIVING PESTS THE COLD SHOULDER OR THE HOT FOOT

Put small packages of dry food that may contain pests in a freezer for three days and large ones in the freezer for a week before you put them inside your kitchen cabinets or pantry. Or spread flour, beans, nuts, and whole grains in shallow pans and heat in a very low oven, 150° F., for 15 to 20 minutes. Dried fruit can be put in a cheese-cloth bag and dipped into boiling water for 6 seconds.

---

in the fields and are carried into your house in food, pet food, and seed. (A threadlike web in the box is a sure sign of beetles.) Prevention and treatment for all of these pests is the same.

Always check for infestation before you put grains, flours, and other suspect items in the cupboard. This may mean opening cardboard packages, which I would advise anyway, since they're so vulnerable to penetration. If you suspect any kind of infestation—or just want to be on the safe side—give them a hot or cold treatment (see box above), then store the food, seed, or kibble in tightly sealed glass or plastic containers so other pests won't be attracted to them.

If you actually see infestation, seal the affected food in a plastic bag and toss it out. Check the cupboard for old stores of food that may have been infected and get rid of them also. Clean out the food containers.

Then clean the shelves with a vacuum or cloth. If you use water, make sure you wipe the shelves completely dry so mold won't grow.

You may have some success preventing insect contamination without any chemicals—or at least preventing its reoccurrence once you've disposed of the infested foods and cleaned the cabinets—by leaving a few bay leaves or cloves, a thin line of cayenne or black pepper, or a few pieces of mint gum, wrapped or unwrapped, at the point of infestation.

If you have to resort to a commercial pesticide, use a surface spray that crawlers will pick up as they move. (Airborne sprays kill flying insects but work only on direct contact.) The spray is usually applied on the outsides of emptied drawers and along runners but not inside drawers or on food containers, since it is toxic. When all surfaces feel dry, cover the shelves with paper and restock your cabinets.

Ants. Place cucumber on kitchen shelves, sprinkle shelves or windowsills with cinnamon, or leave out sticks of gum. Or grow mint around the house.

Or wash counters with vinegar and water; or sprinkle on baking soda (and press some into crevices with a cotton swab). After the initial application has succeeded in killing the ants that were already present, a bit in each corner will keep them from returning.

To keep ants from invading the playpen, fill paper cups or jar lids with water and place one under each playpen leg. And put the pet's food bowl into a shallow bowl of water.

Wrapping the hummingbird feeder pole with a sticky tape such as Tanglefood or rubbing it with baby oil or petroleum jelly discourages ants and doesn't bother the birds. (Re-oil once every two weeks or so, depending on the amount of rain that hits the feeder.). Rubbing oil or petroleum over possible points of entry is also a good way of keeping ants out of your home.

If you can, go right to the source of the nest, usually at the bottom of a wall, in the lawn, under a flat stone or under a path, about twenty feet from the house. Pour boiling water into the entrances (though be careful; this may damage plants). Or pour ammonia into the nest and then into a circle around it. This is most effective on a cool, sunny day, when ants will move up close to the surface.

To kill ants already on the premises, zap them with a little liquid dishwashing detergent, a spoonful or so, in a spray bottle filled with water.

Fruit Flies. Since fruit flies grow in decaying fruit, refrigerating fruit tends to eliminate the problem.

Fresh basil in the fruit bowl will also repel fruit flies. So will basil that is grown in pots outside the door.

Trap them with a little bit of cut-up ripe fruit, liqueur, or beer in a jar. If you put a funnel over the top, they get in and can't escape. If they don't drown, pour boiling water over them to kill them.

BARNACLES

If they're attracted to the hull of your boat, add a good dose of cayenne pepper to the paint the next time you spruce up the hull. The barnacles will attach elsewhere.

BEES

Avoid wearing bright colors and perfumes that attract bees.

Keep the picnic bee-free by hanging a sausage on a string at a distance from the picnickers.

You can get one bee out of the house by darkening the room—he'll fly toward the light of an open window—but if your bee doesn't get the message, vacuum him up. Or give him a shot of hair spray. However, if you see a lot of bees going in and out of the house, exiting quickly but weaving around as they enter, chances are you have a swarm somewhere inside the house. If you see a swarm or suspect there is one inside the house or out, call a beekeeper.

Should you be stung, *scrape* the stinger out. If you try to pull or squeeze it out, you may squirt more poison into the wound. A paste of baking soda and water absorbs and draws out the poison.

BEETLES

To discourage Japanese beetles, plant regular spring onions or garlic. Dust rose bushes with self-rising flour and you'll smother the beetles.

Carpet beetles, which look like black lady-bugs, are a big indoor problem because they thrive on the same "food" as moths—particularly wool and fur and also most kinds of fabrics and rugs. Careful vacuuming—under, behind, and in back of everything—is the best way to keep them under control. Moth repellents work on carpet beetles, too.

Wood-boring beetles that grow inside wood walls and furniture can also do a lot of damage. Tiny holes where the adults chew their way out are a sign of infestation. Call in the pros.

BIRDS

It's very sad when birds build their nests around the air conditioning units because the heat prevents the babies from surviving. Try placing a big-eyed stuffed animal at the window: It acts like a scarecrow.

Any kind of noisemaker, particularly a bright one, also discourages birds. Make one from tin can lids or foil-covered styrofoam cups hung from strings like wind chimes. Or try kids' toy pinwheels stuck in a window box or Christmas tinsel garlands attached to a porch column or a TV antenna.

Keep them off a fence by attaching little screw eyes to the fence posts and running fishing line through them. The birds can't perch on the fishing line.

BOOK LICE

Put books in plastic freezer bags or wrap them in newspaper and store them in the deep freeze 3 to 4 days.

Or cultivate a hardy perennial herb called Costmary or Alacost. Its large fragrant leaves do such a great job of repelling insects when used as a bookmark that early settlers named the plant Bible Leaf.

Book lice may also get into bed linens and clothing. Try washing them out.

BOX ELDER BUGS

Mix water and dishwashing detergent (about 8 parts water to 1 part detergent). Spray this on bushes, shrubs, trees, etc. The mixture won't hurt shrubbery.

Or deter them by leaving onion tops around.

CATS

I don't mean to offend cat lovers by listing cats under pests, but even their greatest fans must admit that at times they make themselves pestlike—by digging into your houseplants or scratching the furniture.

To keep cats away from the house plants, add white vinegar to the misting bottle or put pine cones or horticultural charcoal around the plant. Or cover the plants to protect them. Put a plastic saucer over the plant (cut a hole for the stem, and use that spot to water it). Or make a doughnut-shaped cheesecloth cover with a hole big enough for the stem (stitch up the inside circle, and use elastic thread for the outer circle so it fits over the pot).

Keep cats off the couch by covering a pillow with aluminum foil. Or rub on a small amount of tabasco or chili sauce (on dark wood) or linament (on light wood). You can't smell it, but the cat can and may stay away.

Some people find that planting rue in the garden discourages cats from digging. Rue is a perennial that grows two feet tall and stays green year-round in mild climates.

CRICKETS

The noise of one cricket inside the house can be wildly irritating. Worse, crickets eat woolens, silks, paper, and food.

Keep window screens and screen doors secured. Find the area where crickets enter and put a length of tape on it, sticky side up. Turn ends under to keep tape in place. When the crickets get stuck on the tape as they try to enter, you can remove them.

DEER

Deer-repellent cocktails: Mix 1 cup milk, 2 eggs, 2 tablespoons liquid detergent, and 2 tablespoons cooking oil into 2 gallons of water, and spray your plants with it. Or mix 18 raw eggs with 5 gallons of water (enough for one acre). The scent offends deer, but is too faint to bother humans. After a while, the rain washes it away, and like all organic treatments, it will have to be reapplied.

Or use dried blood from the garden store.

Or spread human hair clippings. (See if your barber will save some for you.)

Or hang bars of soap on trees and bushes.

Or tie a cord around the garden about three feet high and tie a piece of white cloth along it at two-foot intervals. The flash of white at tail height is a sign of danger.

DOGS, VISITING

Spray the garbage pails with pine-scented cleaner or ammonia. That often keeps the dogs away.

Another home remedy that works, though I don't know why, is placing around the border of your property glass or plastic gallon-sized containers filled two-thirds full with water. If this fails to work when you first try it, put out more bottles placed closer together.

FLEAS

Not sure if your pet has fleas? Comb his hair over slightly dampened white paper. The flea excrement, which looks like tiny black dots, will turn red (from the blood they've ingested). If you comb on a regular basis, you can remove fleas as necessary and drown them in soapy water.

Although there is some dispute about whether these remedies work, there are many people that swear by them. Check to get your vet's okay first: Add garlic to the dog's food or mix brewer's yeast into the food or rub it into the coat. Or make a "tea" of lemon peels and water left to steep overnight, or a bathing liquid of 3 orange skins and 3 cups of boiling water in the blender. Sponge the lemon or (cool) orange water over the dog's coat.

Experts say that mixing $1^1/2$ ounces of Avon's Skin-So-Soft with a gallon of the dog's rinse water (and using this mixture along with a flea dip) is very effective, too.

If you have no pets at all but have moved into a house where the previous owner left fleas behind, sprinkle the floors with borax and leave for 48 hours, then vacuum.

CAUTION: Don't use this remedy around children or pets since it is poisonous.

USE YOUR HANDS AS A SWAT TEAM

If you approach the fly with not only the hand holding the flyswatter but *both* hands extended and each moving to and fro, you have a better chance of hitting your target before it flies away. The fly can't calculate the best angle for takeoff fast enough to avoid the blow.

FLIES

As you should to discourage all pests and flies in particular, cover all points of entrance and clean away potential breeding grounds such as wet garbage and dirty diapers.

Basil, bay leaves, cloves, or mint planted near the house or hung in homemade sachets all help repel flies.

Or trap them with one of the many fly traps on the market or with old-fashioned flypaper. If you want to make a sport of it, zap them with hair spray or rubbing alcohol in a spray bottle and watch them drop. This is an outdoor activity that will amuse the children (but make sure they're old enough to avoid zapping one another with the stuff).

If a swarm of flies has invaded your house, suck them into the vacuum, then suck in some insecticidal powder. Wait a couple of hours before you empty the bag.

GARDEN PESTS, GENERAL

Boil one gallon of water with about four large onions and lots of garlic for about 45 minutes. When the solution is cool, spray the plants with it. It does not smell and won't hurt the vegetables.

Or get a turtle. Turtles live on insects.

GNATS

Rub a little vanilla extract on your skin. Or mix half Avon's Skin-so-Soft and half water, and spray it on.

GOPHERS

Place a patio stone at least 12" in diameter in the middle of the lawn. Take a shovel with a straight wooden handle and pound it on the stone for 2 to 3 minutes twice a day for 2 to 3 days. The vibration drives them away.

If you're using a gopher trap, bait it with peanut butter.

HOUSEPLANT PESTS, GENERAL

Wiping flat leaves with a wet cloth removes many common insects from houseplants, or wash them with a mild solution of dishwashing detergent and water ($1/2$ teaspoon to 1 quart). Or give the plant a shower to shake the pests off.

Or mix $1/2$ cup cigarette or cigar butts in 1 quart water, let it come to a boil, cool and strain the mixture, and pour it into a spray bottle; then spray the plants.

Or put a strip of flea collar in the dirt of the houseplant.

Since African violets don't like baths, slip a plastic bag over the tip, zap in some non-aerosol hair spray and quickly seal with a twist-tie. Leave overnight and remove the bag.

MICE

If you aren't sure whether you have mice or rats, sprinkle baking soda or powder around the infested area and check the footprints— $1/2$" for mice, 3" for rats. You can also track the prints back to the nest. If the problem is rats, call in a professional. They are dangerous.

Mice are easier to deal with, but since they reproduce very quickly you may have a major infestation that will require an exterminator. If you live in a building with many stories— and lots of walls to hide behind—the problem may be major before you're aware of it.

Seal up mouse holes wherever you see them. Steel wool makes good packing.

Everyone seems to have a favorite mouse bait. Ours is peanut butter. Some people claim that string that can be used as nesting material is effective bait and I suppose this makes more sense if you're buying peanut butter just to feed the mice.

Whether you use glue traps or conventional mousetraps is a matter of personal aesthetics. If you put traps in an open paper bag with the sides turned back, so it will be more rigid, when the mouse is caught you can just seal and discard the bag.

If you're an animal rights person, or you're trying to retrieve your child's pet (mouse, gerbil, or hamster), you may want to use one of the Havahart traps that catches rodents alive. A big glass or steel bowl, well greased, with a bit of bait in the middle also is a kinder, gentler alternative. If you provide a way for the mouse to climb in (a stack of books, a magazine "ramp"), he'll dive for the bait, then find the sides of the bowl too slippery to get back out.

Moles

Pinwheels placed at intervals in the lawn scare away moles. Flooding their tunnels will also work but may take a while, especially if they have dug extensively. (Flooding works with **chipmunks**, too)

Mosquitoes

Clean away breeding grounds. Drain all water sources including clogged gutters and down-spouts, even saucers under potted plants or vases filled with stagnant water. If you have a shed with flat roofing, drop oil in any puddles that may collect to make them less inviting.

Chamomile rubbed on the skin is a Native American remedy to repel mosquitoes. You can try drinking chamomile tea as well. Also, don't wear fragrance, and eat less sugar (mosquitoes attack people who eat a lot of sugar).

Or rub yourself with vinegar or a cucumber ice cube. (To make a cucumber ice cube, peel and strain cucumbers and freeze the liquid in ice cube trays. Rub the cubes on your face and hands.)

Pennyroyal and citronella, which both come as oils, are considered good mosquito repellents. Just open a bottle and let the vapors fill the room. Citronella candles are available in garden and camping stores.

Outdoors, hang Christmas tree lights for illumination. Amber won't attract mosquitoes as white lights will.

Rabbits

If the rabbits are getting more salad from your garden than you are, scatter human hair cuttings around or hang them in bags made of old panty hose. Or sprinkle red pepper powder or dried blood meal from the garden store.

Plant horseradish (or strongly scented herbs) to keep rabbits from nibbling vegetables.

Raccoons

If they're raiding the garbage pail, sprinkle cayenne pepper around the cans. Or spray the cans with ammonia or hot sauce.

Keep raccoons from attacking your corn by planting it in the middle of squash, which they don't like.

Silverfish

These breed in high humidity (so you may see them in the bathroom) and also get into books. Vacuum and dehumidify, but if they're still around, sprinkle the area with cloves or Epsom salts, or use boric acid (not near kids or pets). The good news: They eat baby ants in the nest.

Skunks

Sprinkle dried blood from the garden store, and they'll stay clear.

Slugs

Fill an old margarine tub half-full of beer and put it on the ground near the plants the slugs prey on. They'll be attracted by the yeast smell, fall in, and drown. What a way to go.

If you don't feel like treating the slugs to a keg party, mix a couple of tablespoons of flour with a teaspoon each of sugar and yeast and add a couple of cups of warm water. It's cheaper.

Snails

Spread ginger around the plants. This also works on slugs.

Or distribute pieces of eggshells around the newly planted garden to keep them away.

Spiders

Leave hedge apples on the windowsill.

Soap scraps and perfumed deodorant blocks also deter spiders.

Dust high corners to get rid of cobwebs. A damp cloth tossed over a helium balloon can also remove a web in a very high place.

Or spray cotton with pennyroyal (a variety of mint, from the herb store), rubbing alcohol, or insect spray, and tack or place it where spiders enter, also rub the inside and outside of the windowsills. If you are trying to clean spiders from under trash, etc., wear gloves, since they may bite.

Or let them be. They eat flies.

SQUIRRELS

To keep squirrels out of a tree or off a pole, snap stove pipe around the base—there's not enough traction for the squirrel to crawl on it—or coat tree with petroleum jelly.

Squirrels will probably clear out of attics and fireplaces if you put out moth crystals or ammonia in pie tins. Then cover the louvers and chimney top with a screening such as hardware cloth (ask at hardware store).

TERMITES

Of the three types of termites—subterranean, damp-wood, and dry-wood—the first do the most damage. They avoid light and air and burrow deep into the ground, so they're hard to detect. In spring or early summer, they swarm—perhaps only for a few hours—to find a new colony, then drop their wings and settle underground.

Since termites can't live in the absence of moisture, keep masonry patched and don't allow any wood to come in contact with soil. If you have a woodpile, stack it on concrete, so it will be dry.

Damp-wood termites, native to the West Coast, don't need wet soil, just wet wood. Dry-wood termites, along some coastlines, need very little moisture and have a pattern of going into above-ground wood (such as furniture) and plugging holes behind them.

Shelter tubes, which look like dribbled sand, are signs of termites. Soft spots in wood that give way when you tap with a screwdriver—or, in worst cases, when you touch them with your hand—are another.

Winged carpenter ants look like termites and create a similar type of damage, though not as severe. Ants have a waist and two pairs of wings of unequal width, while the termite has a straight body and all its wings are the same length. Termites leave a sawdustlike deposit in their tunnels, but carpenter ants don't.

To eliminate either carpenter ants or termites, you need commercial pesticides or a professional exterminator. Though you can get rid of termites in small wooden items by placing them in the freezer for a few days, if you even suspect you have a structural termite problem, get professional help. By weakening the foundation, termites can actually destroy your house. There are new methods of non-toxic control, including heat, cold, electricity, and certain kinds of parasites.

WASPS

Make a sugar-water solution in a small, covered margarine tub, make a small hole, and hang the tub in a tree where the wasps will crawl in and won't get out; or put fruit juice in a plastic jug with a small opening (again, they won't make it back out). Put the trap downwind of the area you're trying to keep clear, since they come from that direction.

Although there are several ways to get rid of a nest (the easiest of which is to put a glass bowl over the opening to a ground nest; or you can ask at the garden store about a smoke generator), you must be completely covered. Wasps are pretty ferocious, and if you don't know exactly what you're doing, I'd recommend calling in a professional.

An antihistamine treats a wasp sting. A cold compress gives some relief.

PART 9
CHANGING

RENOVATING, SELLING, AND MOVING

After having gone through it twice, I've discovered that renovating is always more complicated and expensive than you anticipate. What started out as a simple wing turns into a whole air force.

If you're not refinishing a basement or adding to your space (and if you're in an apartment or town house, it's unlikely, unless you annex whatever is next door), the biggest and most expensive changes you make will probably involve the kitchen and bath.

Or you may choose the completely foolproof way to get your house in really good shape—move to another one.

• •

RENOVATING

The least you need to know about renovating:
- Finding a contractor
- Details of the contract
- Cost cutting possibilities

Is Renovating Worth It?

If you're renovating your home because you think you'll get back your investment dollar for

dollar when it's time to sell, cancel your plans immediately. Making a $15,000 renovation will not automatically add $15,000 to the selling price of your house or apartment. If you're going through the time, cost, and trouble of making a renovation, do it for your own pleasure, not for the resale value.

I'm told that you shouldn't spend more than 30% of the total market value of your home in renovating it, but this piece of information is coming to you from a woman who has done that very thing—not once but twice. If you love the neighborhood you live in, you'll probably thumb your nose at the rules of thumb.

CREATIVE RENOVATING

Even in an apartment, you can expand—by buying the apartment next door or the one on top or below and breaking through walls. Or you can buy a portion of the hallway to add to a foyer. When you add a second apartment, you can transform it entirely or just build a common entry hall; the latter is called a mother-in-law apartment, but is also a nice place to house a child who's graduated from college and returning to your formerly empty nest. A good architect can help you look at your space—even small apartment space—in new ways: A linen closet may become a laundry room if it backs up to the necessary plumbing; a second kitchen in an annexed apartment may become an expanded master bath. A terrace can be enclosed or roof rights can be purchased and decking laid to make an outdoor garden one flight up.

In a house, your possibilities are even greater, since it can be expanded upward, sideways, downward, or in two ways at once. Friends and neighbors who visit your home frequently may have creative suggestions if you're planning to expand, so ask their advice. And when the time comes to consult a professional about construction, make a list of all your goals—dressing room space, more privacy for each child, a home office—even if you're focusing on just one. There may be a solution that gives you more than you had originally hoped for.

BEFORE YOU START

The zoning laws in your neighborhood may affect what you build, even when your plans involve only the interior of the house. Finishing a portion of the basement, for example, may require permits and compliance with the local building code because once you have the basement remodeled you've changed the basic amount of living space in your house from storage space to "livable" space. (It's considered "livable" even after a teenager moves the drums in.)

If you own your apartment, the board of directors may have to approve your plans. If you plan to break down a wall and change the configuration of the interior space or take over a part of the hallway, the local department of buildings may also get into the act.

If your job is complicated—which it may be even in the case of a kitchen or bath refurbishing—you may want to call in an architect. Get recommendations and find out at every step of the process just what fees are involved. When an architect offers to draw up some plans, there may be a charge.

However, there is no point in having architectural plans drawn up if you will not be permitted to go ahead with your project, so before you spend any money on it, make a preliminary inquiry to your board or put in a call to the local Buildings Department or Town Hall to investigate what if any prohibitions you may run up against.

FINDING THE CONTRACTOR

The architect may recommend a contractor or you may find your own. Most people who have been involved with construction find it a grueling and expensive process. Maybe you'll be lucky.

There seems to be a general feeling that a contractor's estimate is based more on his needs than yours: not, for example, on the cost of labor and raw materials for the stone fireplace you want to install, but on how much he'll need for a nice two-week vacation in the Bahamas and a new station wagon. This attitude doesn't tend to create a general atmosphere of friendliness and goodwill. So that you won't feel ripped off, check around to get references and invite competing bids.

Your best bet is to get references from people you know personally, but you may want to go further. Check with the National Association of the Remodeling Industry. Not every contractor may be a member, but one who is can be assumed to have met certain professional standards.

Get in touch with your local and/or state government to see if local contractors must be licensed or registered. If so, ask to see the license and bonding papers. Also check with state, county, or local consumer protection agencies (such as the Better Business Bureau) to see how long the company has been in business and whether the mention of your prospective contractor's name sets off any kind of alarm.

Hiring someone experienced rather than an amateur gives you a better chance of having everything done right and according to the law. An experienced contractor can help you avoid major pitfalls. He should be prepared to inspect for asbestos—which can be in sheet rock, flooring, and insulation (dislodging it is a major health hazard)—and anticipate any problem in removing old paint contaminated with lead. (Check the information on asbestos and lead paint on p. 283 in the Securing section.)

Get two or three written bids based on identical specs—materials, design, and time. (A bid, by the way, is a written legal document; an estimate is just a guess.) If one bid seems extremely out of line with the others, question it carefully. What seems to be a bargain may simply be an incomplete or incompetent bid.

If you want some kind of yardstick to compare your job to, I can tell you that the 1992 national average for the cost of a new kitchen (including 20 linear feet of counter space) was over $9,000; for remodeling a 5 ×7 bathroom about $7,250. Those costs can vary tremendously, of course, depending on where the job is being done and what is being done (and perhaps what the contractor thinks the market will bear).

The Contractor's Arrangement

Ideally, you should have a written contract that includes the following:

Contractor Information. Name, address, phone number, and professional license number. There should be no blank spaces on this (or any other) contract.

Materials List. Should be detailed (specific as to size, color, weight, model, brand name, quantity) and list exact prices.

Escrow Obligation. Obligation to keep your money in an escrow account if there are many subcontractors and/or a release-of-lien clause to prevent liens against your home in case of nonpayment to subcontractors.

Cost Overrun Limit. Provision limiting the maximum of your cost overrun. This should probably be no more than 10%, since the contractor should have estimated accurately in the first place.

Payment Schedule. (May be determined by local law.) You shouldn't pay more than 30% down and you should try to pay as the work goes along. Ideally, there should never be more than a 10% discrepancy between the amount of work that has been completed and the amount paid for as the job goes along. Always try to hold back 10% until the final inspection is done.

Guarantees. That appliances will be installed and materials applied as the manufacturer directs so that the warranty will remain in effect; that work not done to code will be brought to code following an inspection, at no extra charge; and that you are protected against damage to your household goods.

Daily Cleanup Provision. For which there may be some extra charge.

Cancellation Provision(s). If you signed for the renovation work with a salesman, you have a three-day "cooling off" period, but if you signed directly with the contractor, there's no turning back—unless you have a written cancellation provision. For example, if you need a loan to get the work done, it should be noted that the contract isn't valid unless you can get the financing. Find out if there is a cancellation penalty and what it is.

Insurance. Ask to see a copy of the contractor's insurance certificate for your job. It should have your name on it. The certificate of insurance should cover workman's compensation, property damage, and personal liability to protect you in case of an accident.

Permit. Make sure application has been made. If the contractor applies for it in his name, he's the one who is financially responsible for corrections if it doesn't measure up.

Warranties. Get them in writing. (See What Warranties Warrant, p. 18.)

Before you sign a completion certificate and make the final payment, make an inspection.

GET IT ON TAPE

Videotaping the progress of your construction may help you keep track of things like the placement of the water pipes, vacuum cleaning ducts, electrical wires, and so forth when you're planning to do more work. (Also, if people insist on showing you the video of their child's birth, you can retaliate with a twenty-minute documentary of your kitchen in progress.)

COST CONTROLS

Do some of the contracting yourself. Professional contractors put a 30% markup on both labor and materials. For this, they buy the materials, organize the job, and stay on top of the crew. If you have a full-time job this may be too time-consuming. Even if you don't, it may be more than you can handle. Finding sources for everything from tiles to sinks involves a lot of legwork, but the bigger problem is dealing with the help. If the electricians, carpenters, and plumbers have to decide between doing your job or finishing work from a professional contractor who may rehire them in the future, which do you imagine they'll do first? Similarly, a professional will probably get greater discounts or service from the suppliers than you will. Still, doing it yourself can save you a lot.

Refurbish rather than replace. Instead of ripping out the kitchen cabinets, you can paint or put on new doors and hardware and make the room look completely different. There are only so many ways you can stack cans and boxes, after all—one cabinet interior (unless you go for some extremely high-priced, custom-made stuff) will look pretty much like another. For another example, instead of putting in a new tub, you can have the old one reglazed for about a fifth (or less) as much because the labor charges for the installation are the major part of the cost.

Use standard-size items in your plan. Find out the conventional sizes for windows, cabinets, etc., so you can buy from stock. Cabinets represent about one-third the cost of redoing your kitchen, and cabinets from the kitchen department of a lumberyard or home center may cost one-fourth to one-eighth (or less) the price of those custom-made. If you have an opening of 54" and the cabinet comes in a 48" width only, it still may be worthwhile to buy the standard-size piece (with shelves and/or drawers included) and have a less complicated piece made to fill in the gap. Sometimes little odds and ends of space can be used constructively; for example, a narrow vertical cabinet in a kitchen can hold trays, cutting boards, cookie sheets, etc.

Avoid structural changes. Partition walls separate one room from another. But load-bearing walls hold the weight of the roof. If you change one, you need an alternate means of support. That airy, open space you pictured mentally might wind up with a large beam in the middle of it—a large, *expensive* beam. Moving appliances like the refrigerator and stove or the toilet to a different wall may mean that a water and/or gas line has to be changed. Is the cost worth it?

Don't change your mind. Naturally, people do, and the contractor may be surprisingly pleasant when you tell him that you've changed your mind. The reason for his pleasant response will be clearer to you once he presents you with the work order and you see how much money he'll make in accommodating you. The dreaded work order, a supplement to your contract, covers whatever changes are made from the original fixed-price bid. Work orders are a double-whammy: They jack up the prices and also delay the project. And of course, paying more money and waiting longer for the job to be done are always helpful in times of stress…

LET THERE BE INSPECTED LIGHT

Before making any electrical improvements, check your home insurance policy. It may require a professional inspection of a new installation before you turn on a single light.

I would really trust an architect who included a junk drawer in the kitchen plans.

Redoing the Kitchen

If you're buying or living in a home with an out-of-date kitchen, you'll probably want to redo it in part or completely. The location of the pipes will dictate where you put the new equipment, but the goal is to have a "triangle" setup linking sink to stove to refrigerator, the arms of the triangle measuring in total no less than 12 feet and no more than 22 feet. The idea is to have unobstructed movement along a relatively short distance.

The recommended distance from range to sink (the busiest area) is 4 to 6 feet; sink to refrigerator 4 to 7; and refrigerator to range (least busy) 4 to 9. Design the basic triangle before you lay out the rest of the kitchen.

If you will have a dining area in the kitchen, try very carefully to envision the final result. Friends of mine built a kitchen that's terrific in every respect except for the table where they eat. It is crammed into a corner and none of the

seats has a view—even though the kitchen overlooks the garden. Architects should think of these things for you, but sometimes they don't.

Work out the storage space for all your equipment. Make it neat but also convenient. A too-cluttered kitchen looks sloppy and is hard to clean, but a certain amount of "clutter" makes sense. I've found that the minute I decide to store an appliance in a cupboard, it's as if it's gone into a black hole. I hardly ever use it again.

Built-ins reduce clutter—everything from corner shelves to pull-out trash cans and recy-cling bins to a drop-down cookbook rack or a pull-out cutting board. A friend who bakes included a section of marble countertop that is perfect for rolling out dough. But some of these options aren't really worth the money. Lazy Susans, for example, are costly to install, and though they increase accessibility, they reduce storage room. If you still want them, you can always buy inexpensive plastic models in the housewares section of a department store.

COUNTERTOPS

A great luxury, if you're shorter or taller than average, is having countertops tailor-made for your needs. The gauge to determine the most comfortable measurement is usually the dis-tance from your bent elbow to the floor. The next owners of the house may not be the same height you are but are unlikely to notice the countertop problem until after they move in.

You can rationalize this by reminding your-self that the countertop height should vary depending on the chore, anyway. Mixing and chopping should be done 6 to 7 inches below the usual counter height, and the sink should be two inches higher than usual.

If the person who lived in the house before you installed counters that are uncomfortably high, use the solution often used in profes-sional kitchens. Build and stand on a skid—

two vertical lengths of wood, with slats placed horizontally across it (food dropped in between can easily be cleaned up). If the countertop is too low, raise the work area with a couple of cutting boards.

Counters deeper than the usual 25" are convenient for storing appliances at the rear. Allow 24" to 36" of width on both sides of the sink, or at least a minimum of 18" for a drainboard. Always allow a 24"-wide space near the sink for a dishwasher to be installed—if not now, then at some future date.

Here are the major pluses and minuses of each kind of countertop surface (but before you decide read the manufacturer's information carefully—you'll be surprised to see how prone to staining most surfaces are):

Acrylic is very durable.

Marble is unaffected by heat but is easily stained so it should be sealed and resealed regularly. **Cultured marble,** an acrylic that looks like marble, doesn't have to be sealed.

Ceramic tile, glazed or unglazed, can take a lot of heat and the tiles are fairly durable. But it's expensive. Besides, the grouting traps food and is a pain to clean.

Plastic laminate (Formica is one brand) may burn, stain, or scratch. It consists of thin layers of plastic or Kraft paper that are laid over particle board or plywood. Only the top layer is colored and finished, so if there's a scratch or gouge, it's hard to correct the damage. Newer laminates like Colorcore™ are colored throughout. If you go with laminates, pick a glossy finish rather than matte or textured. It's easiest to keep clean.

Corian™ (from DuPont) and **other solid plastic countertops** are expensive but practically indestructible—even scratches can be removed with fine sandpaper.

Granite is also expensive but durable, though I have heard of problems with water stains.

Stainless steel wears well, but you can't use it as a cutting surface. It also needs a lot of wiping up, especially if the finish is shiny. Go for a brushed look but not for the cheapest grade, which scratches easily.

Real **butcher block** looks terrific until you actually prepare food on it. One small section that looks beat-up gives the impression that you cook often. An entire counter that looks beat-up gives the impression that you rarely clean. Heat and water will stain and discolor wood, especially around the sink area. But a polyurethane finish contains toxic materials.

One of the best investments you can make is putting a heat-resistant section next to the stove on which to set down hot pans. Use stainless steel, tiles, or butcher block, though butcher block may scorch. If you inadvertently burn one part of the counter, make the best of it and replace that section with a couple of tiles to use as hot pads.

THE BEST KITCHEN GARBAGE SOLUTIONS

My friends Jerry and Elaine cut a square hole in the butcher block counter and stowed a huge garbage pail in the cabinet beneath. A chopping block covers the hole most of the time. They slide it aside to dump in any kind of debris, and when working with the chopping block, they just push peelings into the hole.

If space permits, you can stow a rolling cart next to the can and build in shelves or slide in boxes to hold newspapers and bottles and cans. (If you box paper, put the strings in first, draping them over the edges. When the pile is complete, draw up the ends of the strings and tie.)

If you want to use the can for composting, it should be flush against the opening. You need a deodorizer (such as cat box filler) and pest repellent (such as mothballs), and the compartment should probably be insulated. Contact your state conservation department to get specific suggestions.

Don't cover the backsplash area behind the counter with enamel or wall covering. For durability and easy cleaning, use the same laminate or stainless as your countertop.

KITCHEN CABINETS

American-style cabinets have the doors mounted in front of the frame, while European cabinet doors are flush (and so easier to clean).

Unless you have a lot of spare time and cleaning is your hobby, don't pick those attractive but high-upkeep glass door cabinets. Glass itself is easy to clean, but glass divided into a bunch of tiny panes is not. Besides, everything, including the occasional or chronic clutter, is always on view.

I wouldn't have open shelves in the kitchen. Cooking always creates some grease and carbon residue, and it's a lot easier to wipe the stuff off the front of a cabinet than off a bunch of bowls and plates. But if you must have open shelves, reserve them for dishes and glassware that you use—and clean—frequently.

Refurbishing cabinets, as I have pointed out, is much less expensive and may be as satisfactory as buying new ones. If you do buy new ones, minimize cleaning by choosing recessed hardware that won't collect dirt around the handles, or cabinets that you pull open from underneath and have no hardware at all. Wood covered with moisture-proof paint or varnish is more durable than lacquer, which chips, or automotive lacquer, which is toxic. Cherry and oak cabinets with hardwood fronts and plywood frames wear very well. Laminates and metals both scratch and chip, but metal won't stain.

Build cabinets all the way up to the ceiling. You'll get extra space and won't have to bother cleaning dirt off the cabinet tops.

Plexiglas shelving is an excellent idea. It's unbreakable and you can see through it to shelves above. But it does tend to attract grease, so I wouldn't use it on open shelves.

Dark-colored cabinets show handprints more than light ones. My left-handed friend Jill installed cabinets that open to the left.

Plan for the least amount of unnecessary movement. If you install the dishwasher higher than usual, you'll bend and reach less and have easier access.

For the same reasons, you're better off with drawers instead of shelves under the counter. There's no reason that drawers can't hold glasses and mugs.

KITCHEN FLOORS

Read about buying wood, resilient, and hard flooring on pp. 42 to 47.

There are some considerations that apply specifically to a kitchen. You'll be cleaning it more than most floors, so avoid carpeting and textured surfaces. Keep in mind that sealed wood will need refinishing fairly often. And resilient flooring is more comfortable to stand on and dropped items are less likely to break.

KITCHEN SINKS

Replace a single sink with a double: Use one to wash and one to soak, one for soapy water and the other for rinsing, etc.

Colored sinks don't hold up as well as white porcelain, which can be cleaned with abrasives for years without showing wear.

Stainless needs a lot of wiping up but is even sturdier than porcelain. Though a "brushed" finish doesn't sparkle, water spots and marks don't show as they do on regular stainless.

Wire baskets and/or cutting boards that fit the sink opening are convenient options that come with some sinks.

To modernize a sink, you can replace double faucets with one lever, add a spray attachment, a soap dispenser, and/or a tap that produces boiling hot water. Moen makes a "rising faucet" that can be raised 6" higher than normal:

You can put a large pot beneath it for easy washing.

Allow a 20" loading area when the dishwasher door is open. Don't install the dishwasher at right angles to the sink or next to a sink that's angled in a corner or directly across from the oven or refrigerator.

LIGHTING

For an average-size kitchen (between 7' × 10' and 10' × 12') you need about 150 to 200 watts of incandescent light and 60 to 80 watts of fluorescent.

COMPUTER

While a computer isn't yet a kitchen accessory, I imagine one of these days it will be—as a source of quick nutritional information on fats and calorie counts, to keep recipes handy (and to search through the files for a particular ingredient, in case you have a leftover), to inventory (so you know what's in the back of the freezer), and to help you entertain (so you can keep track of how much soda and beer you used the last time that you had 20 guests). If you're planning for the future, make room for it now. It could be part of a kitchen home office center that would also contain a file drawer to hold your paid and unpaid bill files as well as records of house costs, warranties, decorating information such as the color numbers of the paint you used throughout the house, and so on.

Redoing the Bathroom

When my mother started out in the Whirlpool bath business, long before she founded Pearl Baths, outfitting a bathroom was easier because your choices were fewer. The toilet, for example, was pretty standard (one of the few "one-size-fits-all" situations that actually did). Now you have many decisions to make if you're doing a total or partial bath overhaul. Not only does major equipment come in an incredible number of models, colors, and types, but also all the fittings—like faucets and pop-up drains—are sold separately.

Investing money in a bathroom seems to add greatly to the resale value of a home. Apparently everyone has makeup-mirror or other bathroom fantasies.

COUNTERTOPS

Cultured marble is the most durable, plastic laminate the least. General comments about kitchen counters apply here.

TUB

Tubs come in porcelain, fiberglass, and marble or cultured marble. Cast iron covered with porcelain is less likely to chip than steel covered by porcelain. Solid vitreous china is durable and long-lasting but can break. At the low end of the durability and cost scales is fiberglass, which scratches and stains easily; at the high end of both is marble. Cultured marble—since it is solid and not a veneer—is especially practical. It's very resistant to damage and can be easily repaired if necessary.

In addition to the standard tubs, you can get a soaking tub (it's short, but deeper than average) or that great luxury, a whirlpool. (Because of its weight, your apartment building management may not approve.) Most of these are made of molded plastic, which is no more durable than fiberglass. Because faucets and showers come out of the wall, the tub itself has no fittings except a drain, so it can be a freestanding unit or placed in any number of different positions.

Prefabricated tub-and-shower combos are watertight and don't require tiling or grouting; this makes cleaning easier.

Very dark and very light colors are more of a cleaning problem than mid-range colors.

SHOWER

Corian and cultured marble are expensive but easy to maintain; so are laminates, vinyl, and ceramic tiles. Fiberglass may stain.

Water stains (from hard water) will really stand out on dark-colored walls.

Prefab, seamless shell showers are easy to clean. You can also get an "enclosure" that covers the back and side walls of the tub.

TELEPHONE SHOWER

A European "telephone" shower has a flexible hose connected at one end to the shower plumbing and at the other to a small shower head that fits into a separately mounted hook. You hold the head like a microphone, or a telephone, and direct it where you want. A telephone shower can be added to a conventional shower head setup; you just flip a switch to divert the water to the telephone shower.

This item is a great convenience for washing and shampooing small children (who may find the regular overhead shower frightening), for directing a flow of water when you're cleaning the tub, and for anyone who finds it physically difficult to get into a tub or stand in the shower, as you can use the telephone shower while sitting on a bath stool.

SHOWER DOORS OR CURTAIN?

If you hang a mildewproof translucent shower curtain or a vinyl curtain, you've only one item to clean, but you may prefer a fabric curtain and liner combination. Sheer fabrics are often backed by solid color vinyl liners, and transparent vinyl is often used behind a solid color fabric. You'll need rings or hooks to slide over the rod. The rings that snap into place grip the curtain better than hooks do.

Shower rod covers—molded lengths of plastic slit on one side that simply slip over the rod—are available at the hardware store in various colors. Not only are they decorative, but they also help the rings slide more easily if the rod is old and slightly rusted.

I had a lot of fun making a fabric shower curtain to match a friend's patterned tiles. To custom-make your own, use washable fabric such as cotton duck or sailcloth and sew or use iron-on two-sided tape or hot glue to fasten elements onto the background fabric. Then sew, iron tape, or hot-glue a bottom hem. At the top, you need twelve holes (grommets) into which you put the shower hooks. You can buy a grommet-making kit from the hardware store.

Shower curtains can be tossed into the washing machine (p. 148), while shower doors—especially the tracks—are harder to clean. On the plus side, doors keep the water inside the shower better and you'll rarely have post-shower mopping up to do.

If you go for the doors, buy translucent glass. It gives you privacy and is easier to keep clean than clear or textured glass.

For easier cleaning, specify top roller tracks instead of bottom. And don't stint on quality because it is very annoying to have a door that jerks along the track or jumps off it.

SINK

The bigger and deeper the sink, the less water will be splashed out of it.

If the sink is wall-mounted, you don't have to clean the pedestal.

If a sink is molded into the vanity rather than placed into it, you won't have to clean around the fittings.

White or very dark sinks both require a lot of cleaning.

Chrome hardware needs the most attention. Brushed brass plating looks fine almost all the time and is hardly any trouble.

One faucet is obviously less trouble to wash

than two. Get the one with the best valve you can buy to minimize leak problems.

TOILET

In toilets, the hot news is low-flush, a type of toilet that uses only 1.6 gallons per flush. This is an advance over the water-conserving 3.5 gallon flushers introduced 20 years ago and a giant step beyond the standard American toilets (many of which are still in use) that use 5 gallons. Since a toilet has a 20-year life expectancy, if your water rates are high, it's almost always an economical move to change to a low-flush toilet.

For cleaning purposes, a wall-mounted toilet—the kind they use in most public places—is ideal. If you can't find one, go for one that has the smallest tank (and smallest surface area to clean) that you can find.

A cheap, painted toilet seat will start chipping immediately (or maybe the hardware will go first); the soft vinyl ones crack; oak and other fancy varieties are trouble to clean. Look for a sturdy model in the mid-price range.

If you've had a condensation problem (water collection around the sides of the toilet) consider buying a toilet tank that comes with a liner. Or install a tempering valve (which allows hot water into the tank). See also Toilet, Sweating, p. 221.

VANITY AND MEDICINE CABINET

Avoid cluttering the top of all bathroom surfaces by hanging items such as a hairdryer in a wall caddy, buying wall-mounted appliances when you can, and installing a second medicine cabinet.

Bottles, brushes, etc., on top of the toilet tank or vanity attract dirt and slow you down when you surface clean. And if you have a problem inside the tank and have to get the lid off in a hurry, you don't want to waste time clearing things away.

FLOORS AND WALLS

Any water-resistant wall covering (ceramic tile, vinyl, wallpaper, enamel) is fine. Avoid black tiles, however, which show every spot, or very tiny tiles, which mean extra grout to clean.

Water can seep below vinyl and into bathroom carpeting and create a major mildew problem. Water-resistant, easy-to-clean tiles are better. Try to use a grout other than bright white, which is hard to keep sparkling.

REPLACING YOUR BATH ACCESSORIES

When you redo the bathroom, you may want to start all over with new accessories.

A **bath mat** that can be taken up regularly is a lot more sanitary than carpeting. Pure cotton mats are the most absorbent. Rubber-backed mats skid less, but eventually the rubber wears away, especially if you put them in the dryer. Replace them or fix them. (See Slipping, in the box on p. 114.)

Now's the time to replace those bath **towels** with terry robes. The average bath towel is only 27" × 52". Bath sheets, which are much bigger (44" × 72") are bulky to store.

Hand towels (12" × 16") are only slightly

JUDGING TOWEL QUALITY

Good towels have thickly packed loops of cotton and a strong selvage (the woven side edge). Check the "underweave," which is the heart of the towel, by separating the loops (or looking at the plain part of the towel near the hem). A good quality towel has a tight underweave.

Loops that are sheared produce a velour towel, which feels like velvet (but is not as absorbent as terry).

On some towels, the design is printed on, but in jacquards it's woven in.

bigger than washcloths. Buy the better quality ones for drying your hair, less absorbent ones in a contrasting color to set out as guest towels.

If you are buying bath sheets for a summer cottage or beach house get them in a variety of different colors. If guests can keep track of which one is theirs, they won't continually use fresh ones.

A **toilet tank cover** is helpful if you have a problem with your toilet "sweating," but is otherwise just one more thing to be laundered. However, a **toilet seat cover** is nicer and warmer to sit down on than a cold toilet seat lid. A cover may pose a problem for the gentlemen in the family if it prevents the lid from staying up while they are using the facility. Solve this problem by sewing or hot-glueing one Velcro dot on the tank and a matching one on the lid cover.

If you can't find a lid cover for an elongated bowl, make your own from a towel. Hem it and run elastic through the hem, or have someone do it for you.

When you buy a trash can or scale for the bathroom, try to find one with small legs or a non-metal (or non-wicker) bottom. Or glue buttons underneath so the trash can rests above occasional water on the bathroom floor.

• •

SELLING

The least you need to know about selling your home:
- Minimizing the tax consequences
- Using a broker—or not
- Sprucing up

Financial Calculations

When you are selling your home, it's useful to have a complete record of all the money you've put into it, since that will lower your capital gains tax. It's also helpful to have these costs calculated if you ever plan to apply for an equity loan, since it will help determine the actual worth of the house.

Keep a record of the original purchase price and all expenses connected with the purchase. You will also need contracts, estimates, bills, receipts, and canceled checks covering labor, materials, and other costs for renovations, plus any building permits or certificates of occupancy connected with a major alteration or improvement. (Take photographs—before and after—to document the difference between major changes and routine maintenance.)

If you have a home office, keep records of when the office was opened plus costs to maintain it. These, too, can affect the taxes after sale and will certainly affect yearly income taxes. Don't bother to keep records of routine maintenance, like repainting, since that doesn't affect your capital costs.

On the other hand, painting and repairs as well as capital improvements started no more than 90 days before you sign the sale contract can also be deducted. So, of course, can title insurance premiums, mortgage origination fees, attorneys' fees, survey and appraisal fees, and closing costs. Buying another, more expensive home within 24 months also lets you postpone any capital gains tax. Or at least your accountant may be able to work out an installment payment plan schedule that spreads your taxes over two or more years.

There is also a one-time $125,000 deduction available if you're over 55 when you sell, provided you have lived in the home for three out of the five years prior to the sale. Contact the IRS for information about this and other tax consequences of selling.

Who Handles the Sale?

There are four ways to be listed with a broker:

The **open listing** allows you to contract with other brokers or make the sale yourself, and for obvious reasons, most brokers aren't interested in this arrangement. A broker who agrees to it may not be making his or her best efforts on your behalf.

Most brokers aren't too crazy about a **net listing**, either, which allows you to set a firm base price to which the broker adds his or her commission.

The exclusive right to sell gives the broker a commission even if you sell it yourself (although it may exclude a commission if you manage to sell immediately before being listed). That is different from an **exclusive listing,** which gives a particular broker unique rights to sell your house for a specified period of time or until the home is sold.

Multiple listings allow brokers to represent the properties of other brokers, all of whom share the commission. Its major drawback is a possible breakdown in communications. Since the selling broker and the buyer and seller may not have all met, some of the specifics of the deal, such as what appliances are included, may be misunderstood. Make sure you get any offers through the listing broker.

SELLING YOUR HOME YOURSELF

Basically, you have to do the same things involved in buying—only in reverse. Selling it yourself, without a broker, can save you a lot of money, but think twice if the market is weak and you're not a good deal maker. To have a realistic idea of what your house is worth, get a professional appraisal.

Talk to your lawyer and accountant before you do anything.

INEXPENSIVE WAYS TO SPRUCE UP FOR A SALE

• Repaint front door, garage walls.
• Replace medicine cabinet, shower curtain, towel bars, kitchen cabinet hardware.
• Buy new bathroom rug and towels, kitchen linens.
• Install new lighting fixtures at front door, in kitchen.
• Add flowers and a hammock to the yard.
• Recoat the wood floors, re-stain the wood deck.

GET IT ON PAPER

• Help people remember your home by preparing a "takeaway" that you can have duplicated at the quick copy shop. Include a simple floor plan, list of vital information, and major selling points. Use it to clarify what is—and what is not—included with the house or apartment.

• To answer questions most buyers will ask, gather the following information about your home:

Co-op or condo: annual financial report, year building was co-oped.

House: pictures of the house in different seasons; oil company costs; service and maintenance records for the heating and septic systems and pool.

Apartment: how many units in the building, the amount of service help, information about the board, name of the management company.

Any home: when it was built, annual taxes or apartment maintenance costs, heating and cooling costs, information about community summer/sports facilities; list of neighboring children and their ages.

• When you've actually sold, the new owner will be grateful if you provide any special history of the house; map of neighborhood with names, numbers of neighbors; school bus schedule; renewal form for newspaper delivery; information about appliances, fabrics, paint, or carpeting you will leave behind; list of service people (everyone from the newspaper boy to the window cleaner, in an apartment; or gutter cleaner, in a house).

Your lawyer should draw up a purchase agreement to be signed by a prospective buyer. It should include a down payment or binder large enough to justify taking your home off the market and a clause that allows you to look for other prospects if the prospective buyer can't get financing or meet your deadlines in time.

Preparing for an Open House

Clean. If you can't face doing a major cleaning by yourself, hire a professional.

Clear. Maybe some people will see the potential in a dirty, overcrowded home. But they won't offer to pay as much as if it were clean and airy.

Fix. An obvious repair that isn't made, even if it's very minor, gives the impression that the whole place hasn't been properly maintained.

Groom. Mow, weed, and sweep. The outside should look good.

Freshen. Open the windows. Put pets away. Refer to Odors, pp. 166–169, for suggestions and remedies.

Gild the Lily. Add an extra touch—flowers, a platter of cookies, something baking in the oven, a fire in the fireplace, whatever will make the place seem more like "home"—or at least, the way home's supposed to be.

• •

MOVING
Choosing the Mover

If you're making a major move, I assume you'll be working with one of the major moving companies. Most of them supply literature that includes suggestions to help you with your packing and planning.

The rates for interstate moves are competitive, but the vast majority of states have regulated prices for intrastate moves. Get a written estimate and, if you can, a guarantee that the mover will show up. Some have been known to abandon a job that they decided was too small.

For local moves with items that aren't especially valuable, you can take a chance with a local, unlicensed mover. For moves from state to state, use one of the big names. For one thing, it's easier to settle problems with a bigger company.

Since rates are based primarily on weight and distance, now's the time to get rid of big or heavy furniture of dubious value. Do you really want to move that soiled couch from Seattle to Jacksonville? Old furniture looks particularly dirty in a new home, and replacing it may be almost as cheap as moving it.

Check if your homeowner's property insurance covers items while they are being moved. It probably does not, so take the mover's coverage. The best value is probably the coverage that pays the cost of replacing a damaged or lost item after a one-time deductible of at least $250.

Preparing for the Move

• Fill out one post office change of address card, then bring a package of 4 × 6 blank, unlined index cards or postcards to the local quick copy shop and have them make duplicates. The small charge is made up for by savings in time and energy. Don't forget to send one to all the magazines to which you have subscriptions and to let your insurance company(ies) know about your move.

• Once the move is planned, get both the White and Yellow Pages from your new community because you'll be working with suppliers from that area. It's also helpful to have an advance subscription to the local newspaper. And if you can get in touch with the new school, see if you can make arrangements for a pen pal for your children in their new community.

• Make a list of items in your refrigerator a

few weeks before you leave and use that as a master list for restocking in your new home. Put the master grocery list, a list of emergency phone numbers, and any other special lists on a clipboard that's hard to lose.

• One odd piece of information: It's illegal for professional movers to transport plants without an inspection sticker from the Department of Agriculture. Call your county agricultural extension agent beforehand and arrange for an inspection a day before you move.

• Movers probably won't take perishable foods or combustibles such as cleaning fluids, paints, or firewood. Personally carry valuable or irreplaceable items—stamp collections, photos—or ship them insured by UPS or by registered mail.

• If you live in an apartment building, make sure that the personnel know that you will be moving so that they can reserve a service elevator and hang padding.

• Refrigerators, washing machines, and other major appliances should be serviced for protection during shipping.

• Don't have the water and lights turned off until the day after you've moved. At the same time, make sure to notify new utility companies to turn water and lights on in your new home.

• If you have assembled any arrangement of photos or pictures on the walls that you're especially fond of, photograph it so you won't have to go through the bother of working it out all over again.

PACKING

• If you're packing yourself, do it a little at a time. Start weeks ahead. Several big cartons are easier to move than many small ones, but (depending how quickly you'll be unpacking) for certain rooms—like kitchen and bath— you may want smaller cartons, each containing items you may want immediate access to.

STRIP-EASE

Before you tape a box shut, run a piece of string along the path where you'll be laying the tape. Press the tape into place over the string, and leave a bit hanging loose. When it's time to undo the boxes, you can pull on the string and rip the tape open.

• Dressers will be moved with drawers intact, so leave soft items inside and tape the drawers shut.

• Make sure each box is labeled for the room where you want it placed. Color coding is the most obvious and probably the best solution, and/or also assign each room a number and write that number on the box. Give the mover a plan of the new house along with room numbers.

• When you label the boxes, be detailed— Kitchen/Pots, Kitchen/Dry Goods, Kitchen/Flatware, and dishtowels—so you don't have to unpack everything looking for the kettle.

• Also, number each box for your own inventory list. Have someone in the family check each item as it is loaded onto the truck and again when it is unloaded.

• If you're using professional movers they'll pack up everything, including the cigarette butts. Reserve a small supply of soap, toilet paper, paper towels, and whatever else you may need until the last minute. (It's also nice for a new tenant to find these items where they're needed.)

• The local discount office supply store can sell you inexpensive boxes, bubble wrap, and other moving supplies. But if you use the boxes from the grocery store, make them easier to move by cutting slots in the sides to use as handles. Reinforce their seams with strapping tape, too. They're more fragile than you may think.

• Make one box for the bedroom (with bed

linens, favorite stuffed toys), one for the bathroom (soap and toilet paper, along with medicine cabinet items), one for the kitchen (including detergent for that load you may want to do right away, paper plates, coffeepot), and one with tools. Boxes from the liquor store with dividers are ideal for this purpose since you can pack kitchen tools, workshop tools, and medicine cabinet items, etc., in separate compartments where everything is within easy reach. You can use the divider boxes as temporary storage units for days if necessary.

• Bring a supply of lightbulbs.

• If you've not having the mover pack the breakables, do it yourself, using linens—sheets, towels, napkins, and tablecloths. If you use newspaper, the print may rub off, so see if the local newspaper will sell you the stub end of a roll of unprinted newsprint paper.

• Don't bother to pack your hanging clothes. Just put a twist tie around hangers of like items and slip a garbage bag over the top. You can just carry them inside and hang them right in the closet. Or lay clothes on a sheet, and tie the corners at each end to make a loop for carrying. To keep the clothes from getting dusty, you may want to use pins along the length of the sheet. Working together, two people can carry even a heavy load.

• If you're removing shelves, photos, etc., from a wall, use duct or masking tape to tape all the screws (and small bits of hardware) to the item to which they belong.

• Finally, if you move often, it helps to have certain things always in the same place. For example, bills are always put in a particular secretary, the drawer next to the silverware drawer is always the "junk drawer," etc.

PART 10

ENJOYING

ENTERTAINING, OUTDOOR PLEASURES, AND GETTING AWAY FROM IT ALL

GIVING A PARTY

The least you need to know about entertaining:

- The easiest way to do it
- Quantities
- Checklists

No-Strain Entertaining

Unless you're a terrific cook and you love high-stress situations, never have a sit-down dinner party. The only way to entertain, as far as I'm concerned, is to have a buffet.

A buffet is a flexible format—you can have a brunch buffet (fruits and cheeses, a variety of breads, quiches, and/or salads); a tea buffet (tomato and cucumber sandwiches, a big selection of your favorite cookies, scones, and jam); a barbecue buffet; a cocktail party buffet (cheeses, raw vegetables, hot meatballs); a dessert buffet; a hot buffet (chili, casseroles, and so on); or a cold buffet (cold meats and salads). You can prepare things yourself, have friends help, buy dishes ready-made, have it catered, or any combination, and if you plan carefully, just about everything can be done in advance.

If you live in an apartment with a dining area, you probably don't have room for a dinner party, but even the smallest apartment seems to be able to accommodate a lot of people for a buffet, which eliminates all the problems you encounter with a dinner party. For example:

- **If you have to leave the room.** When you go to check the roast, the table conversation may grind to a halt. At a buffet, you're not responsible for keeping the whole room buzzing.

- **If your guests don't get along.** When your guests start arguing about politics or someone hogs the floor, a dinner party can be a disaster. At a buffet, people drift around.

- **If people cancel at the last minute or an extra guest shows up.** One or two more or less makes no difference if you're prepared for a crowd.

- **If the entree burns or one or more guests are vegetarians or on a low-cholesterol diet or are allergic.** Finicky eaters can usually find something on the buffet table. If they can't, at least their empty plate isn't making everyone else uncomfortable.

• **If you're not a great cook.** The food for a dinner party is the main event, but no one expects fancy food at a buffet. People give you a lot of credit just for having had the courage to give a big party in the first place.

I always make the list as large as possible—once you have to clean the house and make the preparations for guests, it's hardly more trouble to prepare for forty than it is for fourteen, and not everyone will show up anyway. How many people you invite is, of course, up to you, but my rule of thumb is always be sure to invite a few more people than there are chairs and you'll get small groups of people chatting together rather than a panel discussion.

A good hostess makes everyone feel at home even if she wishes they were.

PARTY PLANNING

When you send out the invitations, state the hours of the party (from 4 until 7) so that people won't arrive or leave too late. I don't know who started the custom of coming to a party fashionably late, but it's really caught on. The only people who arrive on time are the host and hostess, and sometimes even they aren't ready, as you will discover if you ever make the faux pas of arriving at the time specified.

If you have a really large crowd, you can stagger the arrivals by inviting half from 4 until 7 and the rest from 5 until 8.

Put out extra soap, toilet tissue, and hand towels in the bathroom, and have lightbulbs on hand in case you need an emergency replacement.

When you're doing the cleaning, don't bother to wash the rug. If there are enough people in the room, no one will notice it. And you'll probably have to clean it afterward anyway.

Setting Up for a Crowd

Rent a coatrack or see the suggestion in Storage, p. 300, for installing one in the doorway to your basement.

If you need extra equipment, call a rental company. Items such as a big punch bowl, extra chairs, and a coatrack may also be rentable from a local hotel, country club, church, or fraternal organization.

Party soda and ice can be stashed in the washing machine. It's insulated and easy to clean. At the end of the party, remove the cans, let the ice melt completely, and set the machine on "Spin" to remove the water.

Put the bar in one place, the food in another. And, if you have the room, serve the dessert and coffee in a third place. This prevents congestion, keeps people circulating, and gives you room to clear and rearrange the serving table.

Use a pair of ladders with a plank between them to create an impromptu bar.

Make a list of what you're serving and put it on the refrigerator door so you'll remember to put everything on the table.

Put flatware in ordinary highball glasses, use tongs for serving implements (easier than fork and spoon in a salad), and serve in slow cookers or crock pots.

Try to make as few things as possible that require last-minute preparation. Serve meatballs from chafing dishes, or a hot crab dip, but avoid hors d'oeuvres that have to be warmed in the oven. You don't want to run your party with an oven mitt in your hand.

Hire help if you can. You could use help for the setup, help at the bar, and—most important—help to clear up. If you want to keep the costs of help as low as possible, hire someone to come in just toward the end of the party to clear dirty dishes, set out coffee and dessert, and wash up.

Stocking the Bar

My drinking days are over and I'm not much interested in this aspect of entertaining, but a caterer whose savvy I trust told me to assume that with a crowd of moderate drinkers, half the guests will drink wine and the other half will drink liquor and mixers.

If you have a party of 50, that means 25 people will be drinking wine. Count on one bottle for every three of them, and order eight bottles (the small 750 ml bottles, not the jugs) of wine. Choose a dry white wine. Most people like it, and in case of a spill, your rug won't be damaged.

Figure one bottle of liquor for every six or seven of the liquor-drinkers. To serve the 25 in this example, a good shopping list would include half a bottle each of sweet and dry vermouth, a fifth of gin, a fifth of vodka, and a quart of scotch. (In summer reverse the proportions of vodka and scotch.)

You'll also need one quart of mixer for every three of the liquor/mixer drinkers. In this case, you'd be buying eight quarts in the following proportions: 1 each of tonic, cola, and orange juice; 2 of diet soda; and 3 of club soda or seltzer.

Figure half a pound of ice per person.

Planning the Menu

It's impossible for anyone to tell you how much food to prepare because the amounts will vary according to the season and the number of your guests who are on diets. When you have a party, keep a record of everything you've served and the quantities you've used. If you repeat the party the following year, you can repeat the whole menu and you'll know exactly what

CHECKLIST FOR THE BAR

Wineglasses
Old Fashioned glasses (10 or 12-ounce)
Highball glasses (6 ounce)
Napkins
Coasters
Liquor
Wine
Mixers
Lemons
Limes
Small cutting board and knife
Olives
Ice bucket
Ice
Bottle opener and corkscrew
Swizzle sticks

and how much to buy. If you're very organized, you may even keep a record of what dish you used to serve it in.

No matter what other entree dish I plan, I always serve turkey. It's inexpensive; it's easy to prepare; most people didn't have it for dinner the night before; and no matter what diet they're on, most people can eat it. You can serve a variety of condiments (corn relish, cranberry sauce, mayonnaise dressings), depending on the season.

Serve a couple of starchy dishes—beans, potatoes, pasta—because they're easy to make, inexpensive, and everyone likes them. If you make dishes that freeze easily, it doesn't matter if you make too much because the leftovers can serve as future family meals.

If you're serving food that must be heated, prepare it in several smaller dishes and put them out one by one. A hot dish left out for several hours starts to look unappetizing after an hour or two of being picked over, not to mention the fact that you may poison your guests because it's begun to spoil.

A platter of raw vegetables is easier to pre-

333

pare and serve for a crowd than tossed salad. Also, you can reuse the leftovers or freeze celery and carrots to use in cooking (to toss into soup or stew, or to process as ingredients for meat loaf). A dressed salad wilts.

A big coffee urn is a wonderful help at a party. I borrow a second urn these days because I find that some of my guests won't drink coffee with caffeine and the others won't drink coffee without it.

CHECKLIST FOR THE BUFFET

Plates
Napkins
Tablecloth
Flowers
Flatware (and highball glasses to hold flatware)
Hot pads or trivets
Crock pots or Sterno setups to keep food hot (insulated ice buckets work, too)
Salt and pepper
Condiments
Coffeepot and cups
Miscellanea for coffee: sugar, sugar substitute, creamer, spoons, bowl to hold used spoons
Bread basket
Butter dish
Serving dishes and serving pieces

• •

DESIGNING THE BACKYARD

The least you need to know about your yard:
• How to choose fences, patios, plants
• Simple garden maintenance

If you live in a city apartment or in a garden apartment or town house community where the management deals with the landscaping,

your planting is probably confined to pots and window boxes, but if you're a homeowner with a yard of your own, taking care of it can take over your life.

A few years ago, I took the advice about smelling the roses and started gardening as a hobby. Once you get into this in a big way you're so busy pruning, fertilizing, and spraying the roses that you hardly have any time to smell them. But I still think gardening is one of life's greatest pleasures.

Gardening and landscaping are enormous subjects, and there are dozens of wonderful books on every aspect. I'd like only to pass on a few practical suggestions and observations.

Fences

Good fences make good neighbors, according to Robert Frost, but you will not have a wonderful relationship with the people next door if you violate the unwritten law that the structural side of posts and rails should face your property rather than outward. Things may get especially tense if you build your fence on a neighbor's lawn or destroy a fence that isn't yours to tear down. Make sure you know your boundaries before you start any such work.

Also check the zoning restrictions. You usually can build fences up to 6 feet high without a variance, but if you're adjacent to a highway different rules may apply.

BASIC TYPES OF FENCES

Metal. Chain-link fences are good for boundary markers and can support lightweight plants. Though not very durable, they're inexpensive and, when they're made of galvanized metal, which is rustproof, low-maintenance as well. Wrought iron, however, must be primed and repainted.

Wood. Wood fences come in various styles, including closeboard (overlapping strips of vertical planks, usually made of cedar or treated pine; expensive but durable), trellis, and blockade or ranch style (which should be familiar to you from cowboy movies). Some of these are made of prefabricated panels that are pressure-treated to resist decay. Others are constructed to order, in which case all the rails and especially the posts (the pieces stuck in the ground) should be treated with preservative for several days before installation. Though usually anchored in concrete, they can sometimes be anchored by being snapped into the socket of a metal spike. Only galvanized or aluminum nails, nuts, and bolts should be used in any outdoor construction or they'll rust, disintegrate, and stain the wood.

Preservative may need to be reapplied to wood fencing and gates. Some preservatives are colored and some are clear so you stain over them. In my opinion, you shouldn't even consider painting a fence because you'll constantly be redoing it.

Plastic. Picket fences, blockade fences, and trellises are now prefabricated in plastic. I'm a big fan of these. They look good. And though they're a little more expensive, in the long run they save you a tremendous amount of maintenance time and, since they're durable, money as well.

Masonry. Brick and stone fences are expensive but extremely durable and need no maintenance unless the mortar needs to be replaced or the fence has been attacked by dry rot. Because bricks are heavy to ship, you usually build a fence of bricks that are made in the area, but generally there will be many varieties available. Bricks come in yellow, blue, and gray, in addition to red, and in different surface textures. Concrete blocks also come in a range of variety, quality, and type. Structural blocks are used only for interiors, but facing blocks have one decorative side, and screen blocks are purely decorative. Fences are also constructed of stones, either dressed (cut and squared) or undressed (natural).

HANDLING TREATED WOOD

Pressure-treated lumber stamped LP-22 is for use in soil, LP-2 is for aboveground wood. Wood for fencing that has been pressure-treated with preservative may be harmful to plants. Never burn scraps of this wood or saw it without wearing a protective mask since it can be very toxic.

Fencing wood that is not pressure-treated must be treated with preservatives, which are flammable and whose fumes are dangerous. You should use them only in places where there is good ventilation, and always wear protective gloves and a face mask.

Hedges. These look nice but may be attacked by insects and need constant clipping. Local laws may also restrict their height.

GATES

Cedar or **oak** cost more than other woods but last longer.

Wrought iron must be primed and galvanized. Posts should be set in concrete.

Metal gates include hinges and latch, but you need separate fittings for wooden fences. Choose strong hinges and rustproof metal. After being cleaned of rust, hinges need regular painting.

Threads of screws should be dipped in grease first to be given additional protection.

PATHS AND STEPS

Make sure that stones on paths are well spaced (a comfortable stride apart) and below ground level so they don't interfere with the lawnmower.

The risers for all steps should be uniform, 4" to 6" high, with treads ideally at least 1' deep and 2" wide.

Patios and Decks

After you've made a plan for your garden and patio, mark it out with stakes. Use a garden hose or bricks to mark a curved line. Walk through it to see if you've made the paths wide enough, if your furniture will fit on the patio, if the barbecue and table will be too far from the kitchen.

You don't always need a concrete base for a patio. You may be able to use compacted broken brick or stone chips or the new plastic trays that make a pattern on which you lay the brick.

Since grouting will crack at temperatures below 32° F., you may prefer to use sand brushed across the surface to fill the gap between bricks or stones. This wears away and must be occasionally replaced but is still less of a problem than grouting. Though sand may work for a path, you may not like it for a patio.

If you're concerned about keeping a patio clean, raise it off the ground.

On wooden decking, as on wooden fences, I would recommend stains rather than paints. You need a stain made especially for exterior use. Penetrating oil stains generally give wood the best protection. Clear finishes don't wear well.

Driveways

Allow about a 10-foot width for a driveway—it should be wide enough to accommodate not only your car but also a delivery truck—and make sure there's room to open the car door without scraping it along a wall.

If your driveway is on a hill and the grading isn't correct, you may hit the muffler whenever you come in or out, especially if the car is loaded down.

Concrete, consolidated gravel, and asphalt driveways all need a sub-base. Consolidated gravel requires occasional rolling and maintenance. Asphalt is the most expensive.

Why do people have to go out to exercise when there's plenty of yard work to do?

Plantings

If you've never been to a nursery, here's the least you need to know:

Annuals (flowers) last one year only and many are suitable for container gardening, like window boxes.

Perennials (flowers) come back over and over again but usually have a shorter growing season, so plan a garden with several types, each of which will bloom at a different time.

Broad-leaved evergreens (typically shrubs such as azaleas and rhododendrons) and **conifers** (means cone-bearing; taller trees) are both permanent.

Fruit trees blossom in spring; they may need ideal growing conditions.

Consult with a gardener or landscaper about the kind of plants, shrubs and trees to buy for your garden. You'll be limited by a few general factors:

Climatic Conditions. What's the minimum (and hottest) temperature in the area, how much rain do you get, what's the exposure? (For plants, western and southern exposures are best.)

Elevation. Cold air comes down to rest in low areas. Plants that like warmth should be planted at tops or sides of hills and plants that can resist frost pockets, at the bottom.

Shadows. Does the area get full sun, part sun, no sun?

Soil Conditions. Some plants like sandy soils, some don't. You can adjust the soil to some degree.

The local extension service or agricultural

college can give you a climate map, and garden catalogues contain a lot of useful recommendations concerning what grows where. Also, your neighbors can be helpful in telling you what works in your area and what doesn't.

PLACING TREES AND SHRUBS

The biggest mistake in buying shrubs is overbuying. Most plants grow faster and need more room than you expect.

Trees and shrubs should be planted far enough from the house so that you can get behind them to do exterior work such as paint, clean windows, and remove mold.

The rule of thumb is to plant a tree at a distance from the house equal to two-thirds its mature height in order to avoid problems with the roots. If roots draw a lot of moisture away from the house, the dried-out earth beneath the foundation may sink and cause structural damage. On the other hand, if you cut down a tree close to the house, the earth may become so moist that it swells and causes foundation cracks or other damage.

When planting a tree, put a large piece of plastic sheeting or an old flannel-backed tablecloth next to the hole and pile the dirt on that. Once the hole is dug and the tree positioned, you may be able to slide at least some of the dirt back in.

Don't plant where there's no drainage. To test this, fill the planting hole with water. If the water's still there 12 hours later, you have a drainage problem. And don't plant trees too near a vegetable or flower garden. They will soak up nutrients and may block out sun.

Before you cut a tree, get the advice of your gardener. You may have to contact the local building department to find out if the tree is preserved. You can be fined for cutting a preserved tree. Furthermore, in some parts of the country, it's not always clear who is responsible for cutting back branches on the trees lining the street in front of your house.

LOW-MAINTENANCE YARD PLANNING

When people speak of the pleasures of gardening, I don't think any of them are talking about mowing the lawn or cleaning away broken branches. You can't eliminate these chores, but you can speed them up.

For example, if you put cement edging around all the flower beds, and have a concrete "lip" that extends a couple of inches from the foundation of the house, you can run the lawn mower right up to the edge of the building or around the beds and won't need to use an edger.

Use rock rather than wood edging around the flower gardens and you won't have any problem with the wood rotting or becoming infested with termites.

Certain types of lawns are slower-growing and need less frequent mowing. Your local garden supply store can advise which might be suitable for your area.

Watering lightly and frequently develops shallow roots. Instead, give the lawn a deep watering once a week to encourage the roots to grow longer and seek moisture from the earth below. The lawn will become accustomed to less frequent watering and can survive a dry spell. Most lawns need about an inch of water, spread out over a week. Clay soil needs less watering than loam (a mixture of dirt, sand, and clay) or dry soil because it doesn't absorb water as readily. To see if a lawn needs watering, pull out a sample 2-inch plug. If the dirt feels moist, you don't need to water.

Ground covers such as wood chips, gravel (not too fine or it will erode), or ivy need practically no maintenance. They are especially practical around shrubs because they hold in moisture and the plants don't need as much watering.

Shrubs and trees that don't shed a lot of pods and cones, or an excessive amount of leaves (as weeping willows do), etc., need less work to maintain.

EASY WEED CONTROL

Wait until after a heavy rain has soaked the ground, then use a sharp knife to scoop out the weeds between sidewalk cracks. The job will be much easier.

A quick way to remove grass growing between cement is to boil water in a kettle and pour it on. Or pour salt on the grass, let it stand all day, then pour hot tap water over it.

To clean away poison ivy, spray the area with a solution of two gallons soapy water to three pounds of salt. A few dousings will kill it.

GARDENING SHORTCUTS

Drill a hole for a pull cord in a large sheet of masonite and you can pull heavy loads over grass and pavement easily. Or use the children's sled.

Pull out tiny seedlings with a pair of pliers.

If flying insects bother you as you work, pin a fabric softener sheet around your neck and/ or hair.

Put your seeds into the ground at the proper depth by marking inches on the trowel with red nail polish.

HOSE HANDLING

If you coil your garden hose while the water's still running through it, it won't kink up. And turn the water on before pulling the hose to the garden area.

Yard Equipment

HAND TOOLS

Use a little liquid car wax on the lawn mower and other tools—also metal lawn furniture and swings—to keep them clean and rust-free. Apply once a year, more if items are heavily used.

To clean tools, fill a metal bucket with dry sand, then pour a quart of lubricating oil on top. Push your tools up and down in the bucket to get them clean. Tools can be stored in a bucket of sand or with a stick of chalk to prevent rusting.

LAWN MOWERS

Choosing a lawn mower is very confusing. I counted over twenty models in one large store. The best choice is easy to maneuver, covers a large area, isn't too big or expensive for your purposes, and needs servicing rarely. Because there were a lot of mower injuries in the past, all machines now must have a device that stops the blade when you let go of the handle.

If you're not mowing with a grass-catcher, you want the mower to scatter the clippings evenly and widely so you don't have to rake.

A large riding mower is great if you have much acreage but not if you have many flower beds and trees. For a small backyard, you might not need a power mower at all. See the box, next page.

Buy the mower from your local hardware store rather than from a discount store. The hardware store people will help you select the best machine for your purposes and be responsive to maintenance and service problems.

LEAF GATHERING

Since you can't burn leaves, I recommend getting a chipper or a mulching mower to condense all the fall yard debris.

Use a sheet as a tarp and rake all the bits of leaves and twigs onto that, then just pull up the corners and lug it to the trash can.

Or use an old TV tray stand with folding legs as a portable trash holder for bagging leaves (and for picnic trash, too). Set the tray aside, then insert a large plastic garbage bag between the legs, folding the top of the bag over the top of the legs. The bag will stay open until it is full and ready for discarding.

MORE MOWER OR LESS?

Lawn Size	Type Mower	Maintenance
$1/8$ acre or less	3–5 blade reel	Sharpen blades
$1/8$ acre or less	Electric	Recharge battery
$1/2$ acre or less	3–5 hp gas-powered rotary	Annual change of filter, oil, spark plug
1 acre	8–12 hp riding mower	Annual check on tire, belt, more

Leaves can be used as the basis for a composting heap. Compost, a soil substitute, can be made of any combination of tree and shrub leaves and other organic substances such as weeds, grass clippings (unless the lawn has been treated with hormone weed killer), potato peelings, tea leaves, crushed eggshells, torn-up newspapers (but not glossy magazines), soft hedge clippings, dead flowerheads, pea pods, vegetable leaves, and stems. You gather the items in a bin, then process it. I was a little uncertain about doing this myself, but then I got in touch with the county extension office and got the information. Doing it is no big deal, and it's great for the environment and for your garden.

If you don't want to hose down driveways, patios, and walks to remove leaves and find raking too fatiguing or are concerned the rake may scratch your decking, you can use a small electric broom, a hand-held blower (which though lightweight is easier to use if you wear a shoulder strap), or a heavier-duty blower whose power unit straps on like a backpack while you use a hose and tube to move the leaves out of the way. If you have a lot of trees—or if you're interested in using the machine to clear your gutters and deck overhangs—a backpack blower may be worth investing in. (They're noisy, though; wear ear protection.)

SNOW REMOVAL

Power shovels, which are usually electric, are for small jobs like porches, steps, decks, and tight spots. They can clear a 12- to 20-inch path and throw upward of 200 pounds of snow a minute.

Snow throwers are for heavy work like driveways and other large areas. When you're choosing among the various models, remember that electric starters are more reliable than recoil systems. Also, the chutes should rotate so that you can get close to foundation walls and garage doors. And the throwers should have variable speeds to avoid jamming in heavy or wet snow.

• •

POTS AND FLOWERS
Container Gardening

When you're putting up your window boxes, attach them to the house with pinned door hinges. They're easy to remove if you want to work with the flowers on a table or bring them inside at the end of the season. Also, you can flip them up when it's time to paint the house.

Use a painted broomstick or mop handle to make a rod for hanging plants. Use lengths of chain to suspend the rod from S-hooks screwed into the porch or patio roof, then hang the plants.

To make a lightweight cement-type planter, combine three parts vermiculite to one part cement, add enough water to moisten, and shape it into the form you wish. If you want a bowl-shaped form, make a hollow in your child's sandbox or another pile of sand and use it as your mold.

339

Watering small potted plants is easier and neater if you put a coffee filter or fabric softener sheet next to the drain hole so dirt won't flow out.

If you stick a funnel into the plant to water it, dirt won't run over the side. Extra vermiculite in the potting soil keeps it moist; the plant needs less frequent watering.

Put a plastic bowl cover underneath hanging plants to catch drips when you water. Better still, transfer the plants to the shower or tub or over the sink; you can hang the plants

TO PRESERVE FLOWERS

Leave stem or remove it below base of calyx (green leafy part of the flower). Place flower in box containing mixture of 1 part borax and 2 parts cornmeal, and gently (without crushing) cover flower with additional mixture. (For many-petaled flowers, like roses, sprinkle mixture directly into blossom before placing them in box.)

Leave no air space around the flower and don't let flowers touch one another. Seal box with tape and store at room temperature in a dry place for 7–10 days. Gently pour off mixture until you can grasp flower with two fingers, then pour off rest.

Clean off any mixture that clings to petals with a soft artist's brush since borax residue may cause burn spots. (Broken-off petals may be reglued.) Strain mixture to remove debris, then store in cool, dry place for future reuse.

If mixture becomes moist, bake it in a low oven—about 200 degrees—for an hour.

NOTE: This may not work on cut flowers that have been put in water to which preservative has been added by a florist or by you. Best suited for asters, chrysanthemums, daisies, forsythias, lilacs, marigolds, peonies, and zinnias.

TO KEEP HOUSE PLANTS MOIST WHEN YOU'RE AWAY

Water them thoroughly (but don't add plant food, which may encourage the growth of mold). Seal them in clear plastic dry-cleaning bags, closed at both top and bottom. For large plants, tape a couple of bags along the seams. They should last several days without additional watering.

Or run 1 to 2 inches of water in your tub. Use upside-down strawberry baskets as stands. (Plants shouldn't sit right in the water.) Cover plants loosely with dry-cleaning bags. They'll last up to two weeks since water will condense on the inside of the bags and "rain" on the plants to give them moisture.

from hooks fastened in the ceiling or a swag hook attached to the wall just for this purpose.

Hanging wires are not attractive and may be too short, and macrame hangers may cause broken-off stems and blooms. Instead, remove the original wire hanger, place small drapery hooks in the holes and attach pretty cording in colors that complement the flowers.

Arranging Cut Flowers

To carry flowers as a gift, keep them fresh by sticking the stems in a balloon filled with water and secured with rubber bands.

Poke stems through a coffee filter or doily to hold the flowers in place.

If the vase is the wrong size for your bouquet, put an olive jar inside the larger container and put the flowers in the jar. The jar won't show, even through a transparent vase. Or crumple plastic wrap in the bottom of the vase.

Cut stems at an angle with a very sharp scissors or a knife and split the ends of thick stems before putting flowers in water so they can absorb moisture better. Remove leaves below the waterline since the decaying vegetable matter is toxic to the cut flowers.

I've heard all the tips about what to add to the vase to keep the flowers fresh, and I like putting a penny in with tulips, but I think a couple of tablespoons each of vinegar and white sugar added to the vase water is the best all-purpose solution. The vinegar is an anti-bacterial; the sugar feeds the flowers. Adding 2 ounces Listerine per gallon of vase water works in a similar fashion: Listerine provides sucrose (food) and bacteria killer, and its acidity promotes quicker intake of water by the flower stems.

Putting the flowers in the refrigerator nightly will also keep them fresh.

• •

OUTDOOR PLEASURES

Pool Maintenance

Here are some general guidelines, but *be sure to follow your pool manufacturer's recommendations.*

OPENING THE POOL

Before refilling the pool, check the threads of the water pressure relief plug and pipe for a tight fit. Clean out clogs. Replace and tighten the plugs.

Check pH level, the acid-alkaline balance, with a test kit. If it is high, lower it with pH minus (ordinary baking soda). Throw a couple of handfuls into the pool and wait 24 hours to take another reading. If you put in too much, you'll see milky or green water. If pH is too low, the water will burn your eyes. Raise the level with a bit of soda ash and take a reading after 24 hours.

Add chlorine stabilizer to previously untreated water.

Use clarifier (liquid clarifier for most filters,

alum for a sand filter). This clears the water and neutralizes minerals to prevent the pool from staining.

Run the filter 24 hours a day at beginning of the season until water is perfect.

IN SEASON

Add chlorine every two days, in liquid rather than granular form and at night so it won't dissipate. Check the level weekly (should be 1 to 2 parts per million).

Run the filter 4 to 5 hours a day.

WINTERIZING

Use an algaecide.

Check the pH and use the winterization chemicals your pool service recommends.

In an undrained pool, lower the water level to where the service recommends. Do not put any objects in the pool to prevent freezing.

Drain water from the piping and skimmers.

Winterize the pump and heater.

Wash the filter elements and rinse the tank with fresh water.

Cover the pool before leaves fall or remove any leaves before covering it. If water accumulates on the cover, you may need to remove it with a pump; ask at the swimming pool store.

KIDDIE POOLS

Bathtub decals at the bottom of a kiddie pool make it safer.

Make a skimmer of a wire hanger covered with the top of an old pair of panty hose (cut it off at the legs and tie). It's not classy, but it works.

A simple, flannel-backed vinyl tablecloth, laid in the pool flannel side down, can extend the life of your pool liner.

It'll be the buffer between the original liner and the children's toys, pebbles, sand, etc.

Barbecue table covers fit perfectly over some children's molded plastic swimming pools. (Cover the umbrella hole with duct tape.) Fill the pool early in the day and cover it. This keeps out dirt and insects while the water warms up.

To empty the plastic pool easily, purchase a small rubber sink plug and cut a small hole close to the bottom of the pool. Children can handle the job themselves.

Cooking Outdoors

Buy metal S-hooks at the hardware store and slip them over the edge of the grill to hold the long-handled fork and tongs.

Lettuce leaves can be used as disposable basters and on top of the fire to keep the flames under control.

Rub the bottom of a pan with soap before you put it over the fire and it'll be easier to wipe clean. And rub a little petroleum jelly over your fingers and nails before you do messy work with the barbecue and they'll be easier to clean.

If the fire's died down before you've toasted the marshmallows, revive it by sprinkling a few teaspoons of cooking oil on top.

The grill can clean itself if, when coals are hottest, you wrap it tightly in a huge sheet of heavy-duty aluminum foil, shiny side in. Place it on the coals for ten minutes, and when you unwrap it, charred food will fall off.

If your grill has a lid, you can also cut down cleaning by steaming off the crud. Put newspapers in a tub of water when you start the charcoal. As soon as you remove the meat from the grill, put several layers of wet newspaper on top, close the lid, and let the hot coals steam-clean the grill for you. When grill is completely cool, remove the newspaper.

For cleaning a cold grill, see the section on Cleaning, p. 156.

PICNIC TIME

Slabs of polyfoam from the fabric store can be used to line a picnic basket. Glue them in place, and pack only items that have been thoroughly chilled. In the shade, contents will stay cool for 2 to 3 hours or more.

Chill watermelon thoroughly in fridge, then wrap it in several layers of dry newspaper to take along on the picnic. It will stay cool for several hours. So will wine and other foods.

FIRE STARTERS

• **A three-pound coffee can with charcoal briquettes:** Add enough charcoal starter to cover them. When you want to barbecue, just put 5 or 6 "marinated" briquettes on the bottom of the grill, adding dry ones as needed from the bag. Both your charcoal and starter will last longer and you'll never have trouble keeping your fire going even in bad weather.

• **Bits of burned-down candles:** Cut old candles into small pieces. Sprinkle on top of the charcoal before you add and light the starter fluid.

• **Dryer lint:** Break it up and put it into the cups of an empty egg carton. Melt paraffin and pour it over the entire carton, being sure to fill all the cups. When wax is dry and hard, break the carton into two-part sections and put them on top of the charcoal or wood to start the fire.

• **Paper towels:** Twist the ends into knots. Dip each knotted end in cooking oil or whatever cooking grease is available. Place oiled end under kindling and ignite dry end.

• **Half-gallon milk cartons:** Fill with crumpled newspaper.

NO-STRAIN DRAIN

To make a quick and easy drain plug for styrofoam ice chests, take the top of a squeeze bottle of dish soap (the kind you have to pull up in order to open), measure it, and drill a hole near the bottom of the chest exactly that size. Push the top from the squeeze bottle into the hole and glue it in place with waterproof carpenter's glue. Whenever you need to drain the ice chest, tip it and pull the top into the open position.

Newspaper wrappings are cheaper, cost less than foil, and work better—and you can still recycle the paper afterward. (Incidentally, it keeps hot foods hot, too.)

Serve hot foods (like baked beans) or cool ones (like cole slaw) in an ice bucket. The insulation will keep them warm or cold.

A hole in a large foam cooler can be plugged with melted paraffin. (*Handle carefully; it's very flammable.*) A small hole can be sealed with a bit of clear nail polish.

Soap in a mesh bag can be hung near an outside faucet for quick cleanups.

Play Equipment

Spray some WD-40 on a new **baseball glove** to help break it in.

To avoid having to clean rust off your **bike,** wipe a light coat of corn oil (or non-stick vegetable spray) on the metal wheel around the spokes to prevent rust from forming. Or polish with Lemon Pledge.

Revive dented (but uncracked) **Ping Pong balls** by dropping them into a pan of boiling water with a pinch of salt. Keep turning the balls for a few minutes and the dents will pop out.

If a children's **slide** loses its zip, spray on a generous coating of spray starch, then wipe it off with paper toweling. Or rub it with waxed paper.

If chains on **swings** are rusty and dangerous and the seat itself is splintery, buy a stair tread to cover the seat. And cover the chains with rubber crashpads (bicycle handlebar covers) or plastic shower rod covers. If the seat is too slippery, coat it with an outdoor polyurethane enamel and sprinkle some sand on top before the enamel dries to give some grip to the seat.

Revitalize **tennis balls** by putting the can (with lid off) in a closed oven overnight. The heat from the pilot light will get them back into shape.

GOING AWAY

The least you need to know about leaving your home:
• Closing up a vacation home
• Pre-vacation planning

At Week(end)'s End

Closing down a vacation home for between weekend visits or for several weeks only isn't very complicated.

ICE CHECK

If you are leaving a freezer/refrigerator for a short period of time and have left it plugged in, you may wonder if there was a power shortage during your absence. Always keep a bowl of ice cubes in the freezer section, or put a penny on one section of the ice tray. If the cubes are intact, or the penny is still on top, the fridge/freezer was operating properly. If you have one frozen block of ice, or have a penny in the middle or bottom of the cube, the system was down.

343

Mildew may be a problem in humid climates, so never leave without making sure everything is clean and dry.

Don't leave any food decomposing in the refrigerator and disconnect all small appliances. Neither the dryer nor the dishwasher—or any other appliance—should be running after you leave.

Lock windows and doors.

Winterizing a Vacation House

If you are leaving a home or condo for several months, in addition to normal cleaning, you may want to use dust covers on small appliances or throw sheets over furniture—though this is always a tipoff to a would-be intruder that no one will be around.

If you will be leaving a home unused for several months in temperatures that may drop below freezing, disconnect electric power on all appliances, clean the interiors, and check the use and care guides for all your appliances to find out what routine maintenance you should perform and to see what should be de-installed (and how to reinstall it when you return). You may need to call in a plumber.

Specific instructions follow.

Circulating Hot Water System. Pipes may burst if the temperature of a building is colder inside than out. In a building that is left unheated for a brief period, pipes should be insulated. The alternative is to leave the faucet on just enough so that water is steadily dripping (running water freezes at a lower temperature), but this doesn't make much sense over a long period of disuse. Pipes should be drained and the system should be freeze-proofed.

Doing this yourself means turning off the water at the supply source (or calling the Water Department), opening every faucet, indoors and out, then adding antifreeze to the drainage system. If you are uncertain how to do it, call the plumber.

Turn off the gas valve, but leave the flexible gas line attached.

Washing Machine. When you leave: Turn off the water supply hose and disconnect the fill hose only. Pour 1 quart of automobile antifreeze into the washer tub. Set the washer for drain and spin and run it for at least 30 seconds to mix the antifreeze with the water left in the washer. Then disconnect the electric power and the drain hose. Put a note on the washing machine to remind yourself that the machine contains antifreeze and must be conditioned and flushed before next use.

When you return: Reconnect the power and hoses. Set the washer for the normal cycle and low, hot water fill. Add 1 cup detergent. Run the washing machine through a complete cycle without loading it. Check for leaks.

Automatic Dishwasher. When you leave: Disconnect the electric power. Disconnect the water supply lines attached to either side of the water inlet valve (following operating or installation instructions in the manual) and drain the lines into a bucket. Disconnect the drain hose from the side of the pump and motor assembly. Use a bucket to catch the water that will drain out, about $1/2$ quart. Put a note on the dishwasher to remind yourself that hoses have been disconnected.

To restart: Reconnect drain and inlet lines. Turn on the water supply. Connect the electric power. Add 1 quart of water to the inside of the tub and look under the dishwasher for leaks. Add detergent and run the empty dishwasher through a short cycle to clean it and make sure it's working.

Refrigerator, Freezer, Icemaker. When you leave: Disconnect the refrigerator water supply at the appliance. Drain all water tubing. Clean the drain pan. For freestanding icemakers, refer to the use and care guide. Remove the grill, disconnect the water supply at the appliance, and drain it. Remove the water pan drain plug (located beneath water pump pan), drain, and dry the pan thoroughly.

To restart: Clean and sanitize before reusing. Reconnect water supply.

Dehumidifier. After disconnecting the power, clean the dehumidifier, remove any water, and dry the cabinet interior. Store the appliance upright and not on its top, side, or back.

Trash Compactor. Disconnect the compactor, lock the control to "Off," and remove the key and store it in a safe, convenient place.

PROTECTION FROM WEATHER AND PESTS

Metal can't be penetrated by mice and other pests, so if possible install metal storage cabinets in the kitchen and use metal camper trunks to store bedding. Wood cabinets can be lined with aluminum sheeting.

Holes behind plumbing and any cracks should be plugged up. Chimneys should be covered with mesh to protect them from squirrels and birds.

You're less likely to get up on the wrong side of the bed if you know someone else will be making it.

Leaving on a Trip

There are people I know who would not only like to take the kitchen sink but also the whole house along on vacation because they are so concerned that it won't be intact when they

---

PREPARING YOUR HOUSE FOR YOUR VACATION

Week or more in advance:

- Have the newspapers hold the paper
- Have post office hold mail
- Leave the keys with neighbors and instructions for watering plants
- Make arrangements with dog or cat walker/sitter or vet
- Prepare itinerary/vacation contact for whoever is watching your home
- Store valuables (visit safe deposit box)

Day of departure:

- Lock and secure all windows and doors
- Set timers for lights
- Unplug appliances
- Empty refrigerator
- Empty garbage
- Turn off faucets and flush toilets
- Adjust thermostat, turn off burner or hot water heater

---

return. In the Securing section, you will find information about guarding against intruders. You also have to prevent damage from leaks, electrical fires, and animal pests. Ask a trusted neighbor to keep an eye on the house in the event of a possible fire and make a checklist of pre-vacation chores.

Home. There's no place like it.

On the other hand, there's nothing wrong with checking into a five-star hotel once in a while.

ACKNOWLEDGMENTS

WHILE MY COLLABORATOR, Dale Burg, and I would like to believe we know everything, we don't. So we are grateful to the people and organizations who helped us gather—and in some cases, interpret and correct—the information contained in this book.

We found information from the following organizations and manufacturers extremely valuable: The American Gas Association; American Fiber Manufacturers Association; Association of Home Appliance Manufacturers; The Carpet and Rug Institute; Gerber Products Company; National Decorating Projects Association; National Home Furnishings Association; National Oak Flooring Institute; Soap and Detergent Association; S. C. Johnson; and the Wallcovering Information Bureau. *The Retailer's Guide to Home Textiles*, published by the National Bath, Bed and Linen Association was especially useful.

We are particularly indebted to the Whirlpool Appliance Information Service for permission to reprint information from some of its outstanding brochures and to Underwriters Laboratories for its assistance and reprint permission.

For personally reviewing sections of this book and providing reassurance and encouragement, thanks to Randy Amengual, a lawyer who understands fuse boxes; Jack Rosmarin of Alwyn Hand Laundry & Curtis Cleaners; Lt. Drew Kelly of the New York City Firefighters' Association; Brad Burg; and Harold Koch, President of International Carpet Importers.

For advice and expertise, thanks also to Susan Treanor of Susan Treanor Associates; Nadia Henry, publisher of the *Safe Home Digest*; Michael Lennon of Home Pro Systems, Inc.; and caterer Nicholas Baxter.

For permission to attend the outstanding Building Maintenance Training Program sponsored by the City of New York Department of Housing Preservation and Development, our appreciation to Solomon Schwartz, director of the Management Alternatives Training Program, and very special thanks to LaVerne Lum, deputy director. Their professionalism and devotion to their work are an inspiration.

Thanks also to our pal Connie de Swaan for her superb research assistance and to the folks at Crown Publishing who helped get this book in shape, notably our excellent production editor, Pamela Stinson, and Art Director Ken Sansone.

Our gratitude to our good buddies Dick Marek and Joyce Engelson for believing in us and in this project. Every writer should have an editor as supportive as Joyce.

Finally, thanks to our families, to Tom and Andrew and Dick and Alden, for being in our respective (and usually dust-free) corners.

ℐNDEX